W9-AMB-337

HANDBOOK OF FAMILY DIVERSITY

highlights
or
water damage 1-07 9B

Damage:

Date:

PROPERTY OF TEXTBOOK SERVICES
UNIVERSITY OF WISCONSIN-RIVER FALLS 410 S 3rd ST, 54022
LOANED SUBJECT TO PURCHASE IN CASE OF LOSS OR DAMAGE
DUE BY CLOSING TIME ON THE LAST DAY OF FINALS
DUE IMMEDIATELY IF CLASS IS DROPPED OR UPON WITHDRAWAL
NO HIGHLIGHTING, UNDERLINING, OR WRITING IN TEXTS
FINES WILL BE LEVIED FOR INFRACTIONS

Handbook of
Family Diversity

Edited by
David H. Demo
Katherine R. Allen
Mark A. Fine

New York   Oxford
OXFORD UNIVERSITY PRESS
2000

Oxford University Press

Oxford   New York
Athens   Auckland   Bangkok   Bogotá   Buenos Aires   Calcutta
Cape Town   Chennai   Dar es Salaam   Delhi   Florence   Hong Kong   Istanbul
Karachi   Kuala Lumpur   Madrid   Melbourne   Mexico City
Mumbai   Nairobi   Paris   São Paulo   Singapore
Taipei   Tokyo   Toronto   Warsaw

and associated companies in
Berlin   Ibadan

Copyright © 2000 by Oxford University Press, Inc.

Published by Oxford University Press, Inc.,
198 Madison Avenue, New York, New York, 10016
http://www.oup-usa.org

All rights reserved. No part of this publication may be reproduced,
stored in a retrieval system, or transmitted, in any form or by any
means, electronic, mechanical, photocopying, recording, or otherwise,
without the prior permission of Oxford University Press.

Library of Congress Cataloging-in-Publication Data
Handbook of family diversity / edited by David H. Demo, Katherine R.
Allen, Mark A. Fine.
p.   cm.
Includes index.
ISBN 0-19-512038-8 (hbd. : alk. paper). — ISBN 0-19-512039-6
(pbk. : alk. paper)
1. Family.   2. Marriage.   3. Interpersonal relations.
4. Ethnicity.   I. Demo. David H.   II. Allen, Katherine R.
III. Fine, Mark A.
HQ518.H1538   1999
306.85—dc21   99-15341
CIP

Printing (last digit): 9 8 7 6 5 4 3 2
Printed in the United States of America
on acid-free paper

To our children

Michael, Brian, Matthew, Zachary, Aubrey, and Julia

CONTENTS

Foreword

As a new century arrives, it is clear that a varied and changing array of family arrangements has replaced the breadwinner-homemaker household that once predominated as both a lived reality and an American ideal. Even the concept of "the family," with its implication of a unitary, archetypal standard, has become a contested idea. The rise of diverse and increasingly fluid family forms has prompted analysts from varying disciplines and political persuasions to posit vastly different—and largely opposing—visions of what a family is and ought to be.

It should come as no surprise that a period of such widespread, rapid, and generally unanticipated change has spawned intense controversy. Political conflict and scholarly debate are, in fact, an integral part of the process of change. Yet this context makes it difficult and perhaps undesirable to formulate an overarching framework for defining and analyzing family life. One paradoxical consequence of the diversification of family forms and family meanings is that it has become both more urgent and more problematic to identify the central questions that need to be asked or the range of answers that may be found.

Amid this intellectual ferment, *The Handbook of Family Diversity* provides a welcome and much needed guide. Demo, Allen, and Fine offer an up-to-date compendium on diversity among and within families. As important, they show how these pivotal social changes have become a contested arena for theorists and policy makers. They thus extend the analysis of family diversity beyond a mere cataloguing of the various forms families are, assuming to include a consideration of diversity in the theoretical frameworks, ideological commitments, personal experiences, and methodological approaches that can be used to examine family life.

For those attempting to understand or help families living through these tumultuous times, several features make this volume invaluable. First, rather than simply reviewing the current state of family diversity, they provide an overview of the central pedagogical dilemmas and controversies that family analysts and practitioners now confront. Perhaps the most important of these controversies centers around the distinction between family structures and family processes. While theoretical and political debate has more often focused on the growing diversity in family structure, the *Handbook* makes it clear that the interpersonal dynamics and interactions within households are as, and perhaps more, consequential. As they state, "the differences in family functioning and well-being *across* family types tend to be small, while the differences *within* family types (including "benchmark" families) tend to be large" (Chapter 1, pp. 3–4). By highlighting the importance of family processes, they draw attention to the fundamental questions we should be asking. Rather than engaging in irresolvable debates about what constitutes the "best" family form, researchers and practitioners need to gain a deeper understanding of how different types of families can best meet the needs of their members.

In a similar way, the *Handbook* confronts the difficult issue of how to assess and evaluate family welfare. Here, too, they clarify the issues that matter. Acknowledging the tension between the absolutist belief in one unwavering standard and the relativist implication that no standard should be imposed from without, they propose an intermediate position that recognizes the importance of making contextually grounded evaluations. Instead of holding families to an ideal and largely unreachable "benchmark," whatever form it may take, the focus should be on investigating the processes within families and the contexts outside of families that promote (or inhibit) the social, emotional, and material well-being of its members. This framework provides a middle path between the Scylla of rigid absolutism and the Charybdis of valueless relativism. Most important, it places the welfare of families and individuals, rather than ideological agendas, center stage.

The *Handbook* also considers the ways that systems of social stratification form the context in which families must cope with varying options and constraints. Diversity is not simply a matter of family form or process but involves intersecting inequalities of race, class, gender, and sexual orientation. Not only is family diversity broader than typically presented, but it is inextricably linked to larger institutional structures that shape the dilemmas families confront and the resources available to respond successfully. Only by recognizing these differences can we move beyond an implied standard based on a presumed white, middle-class, heterosexual ideal.

Demo, Allen, and Fine thus provide a collection that focuses on the experiences of families which diverge in some way from this traditional model, incorporating two-parent, "European American" families as a comparison group rather than a norm. This approach makes clear just how perilous it has become to draw generalizations about family life. It reminds us that, although it may be tempting simply to describe the typical characteristics of different "categories" of families, it is better to reject stereotypical images in favor of considering family differences *and* similarities along a range of dimensions. Again, the case is made for tolerance and pluralism. Families facing different contingencies may meet their emotional and material needs in contrasting, but equally beneficial (or disadvantageous), ways.

Finally, the *Handbook* extends the perspective of tolerance and inclusiveness to include methodological pluralism as well. The editors argue forcefully and convincingly that debates pitting methodologies against each other set up false dichotomies that can only hinder a full understanding of contemporary family life. Methodological diversity is, indeed, our best hope for grappling with the complex and multilayered changes now underway. We need quantitative studies to map the parameters and contours of family arrangements and qualitative studies to discover how family life is experienced and enacted in different circumstances. We need "insider" accounts that provide a "subjective" perspective on family life and "outsider" accounts that offer more "objective" measures. Moreover, methodological pluralism is inextricably linked to theoretical expansion. Once dominant "positivist" (and functionalist) explanatory frameworks now vie with a range of "post-positivist" approaches offered by feminists, life course analysts, interactionists, and others. We need to incorporate the theoretical insights from all of these perspectives to avoid limited and misleading conclusions.

While many vantage points are needed, some are nevertheless irreconcilable. In a world where "family values" have become as contested as research findings, it simply may not be possible to establish consensus on many fundamental issues. Those who uphold a vision of family life that embodies such values as gender equality and the expansion of personal choice will inevitably clash with those who believe that two-parent, male-breadwinner families are inherently superior. This unavoidable conflict makes it important that we all clarify how our own personal experiences provide a backdrop for our intellectual perspectives. We are all born into and grow up in families, and we must all confront profound family choices over the course of our lives. No one can thus claim to approach the subject of family diversity with pure neutrality. Our obligation, then, is to be honest and clear about our ideological standpoints, while also recognizing and respecting the paths that have led others to different conclusions.

To make this point in as compelling a way as possible, Demo, Allen, and Fine offer their own biographies and have their authors reflect upon the link between personal experience and scholarship. They conclude that, "diversity is a strength (that is) best reflected in attitudes—an openness and acceptance of difference and a critical stance toward social mores of what is 'normal' family life" (Chapter 22, p. 443). By taking this ecumenical and reflective approach, *The Handbook of Family Diversity* offers more than a guide to the changing ways that Americans organize their personal lives. By its own example, it provides a model for other family scholars and practitioners to follow.

KATHLEEN GERSON
New York University

ACKNOWLEDGMENTS

Planning, writing, and editing this book has been a challenging collaboration and a labor of love. As co-editors, we've had numerous conversations with each other in a variety of forms—planning meetings at conferences, telephone calls and teleconferences, E-mail exchanges, and extended visits to each others' homes. We began the project four years ago with a desire to work with and learn from each other, and we've accomplished that and much more. Throughout the years, our bonds of friendship and our interactions have been strengthened by association with each other and with the friends, colleagues, and students who share an interest in creating knowledge that makes a difference in the world.

We gratefully acknowledge the assistance and support provided by our departments: the Department of Human Development and Family Studies at The University of North Carolina at Greensboro, the Department of Human Development at Virginia Tech, and the Department of Human Development and Family Studies at The University of Missouri-Columbia. The staff at Oxford University Press has also been helpful in shepherding the manuscript through the editorial process, and they have provided technical assistance that has greatly improved the readability of the volume. In particular, we thank Jeffrey Broesche, our editor; Christine D'Antonio, production editor; and Wendy Almeleh, copyeditor.

Finally, we owe a special debt of gratitude to our contributors, each of whom stuck with us through multiple revisions. Indeed, without exception, our contributors responded with intelligence, care, and good humor to three sets of editorial comments. We thank all of them for their scrupulous and timely investment in this work.

CONTRIBUTORS

Karl L. Alexander
Department of Sociology
Johns Hopkins University

Paul R. Amato
Department of Sociology
Pennsylvania State University

Maxine Baca Zinn
Department of Sociology
Michigan State University

Victoria Hilkevitch Bedford
Department of Psychology
University of Indianapolis

Rosemary Blieszner
Department of Human Development
Virginia Tech

Denise Ann Bodman
Department of Family Resources and
Human Development
Arizona State University

Kevin R. Bush
Department of Family Resources and
Human Development
Arizona State University

Stephanie Coontz
The Evergreen State College

Debra Madden-Derdich
Department of Family Resources and
Human Development
Arizona State University

Doris R. Entwisle
Department of Sociology
Johns Hopkins University

Kristin G. Esterberg
Department of Sociology
University of Massachusetts-Lowell

E. Mavis Hetherington
Department of Psychology
University of Virginia

Masako Ishii-Kuntz
University of California Tokyo Study Center

Colleen L. Johnson
Department of Medical Anthropology
University of California-San Francisco

Joan Laird
School of Social Work
Smith College

Richard M. Lerner
Center for Child, Family, and
Community Partnerships
Boston College

Leigh A. Leslie
Department of Family Studies
University of Maryland

Laurie D. McCubbin
Center for Child, Family, and
Community Partnerships
Boston College

Stephen R. Marks
Department of Sociology
University of Maine

Judith A. Myers-Walls
Department of Child Development and
Family Studies
Purdue University

Gary W. Peterson
Department of Sociology
Arizona State University

Mark R. Rank
George Warren Brown School of Social Work
Washington University

Virginia Rutter
Department of Sociology
University of Washington

Ritch C. Savin-Williams
Department of Human Development
Cornell University

Pepper Schwartz
Department of Sociology
University of Washington

Ellen Slaten
Population Research Center
University of Texas at Austin

Elizabeth E. Sparks
School of Education
Boston College

Judith Stacey
Department of Sociology
University of Southern California

Margaret Stanley-Hagan
Department of Psychology
University of North Carolina at Charlotte

Ronald L. Taylor
Department of Sociology and Institute for
African American Studies
University of Connecticut

Jay D. Teachman
Department of Sociology
Western Washington University

Debra Umberson
Department of Sociology
University of Texas at Austin

Barbara Wells
Department of Sociology
Maryville College

CHAPTER **1**

An Overview of Family Diversity: Controversies, Questions, and Values

KATHERINE R. ALLEN, MARK A. FINE, AND DAVID H. DEMO

This Handbook offers a way to expand how family structures, processes, and experiences are represented in scholarship about families. For many years, a discourse on "The Family" has dominated the information we teach students, the methods we use to generate empirical data, and the theories we use to guide practice and public policy. A positivist ideology, espousing ideas of appropriate family structures and functions, with the implication that what is optimal for family development over time is certain, is increasingly being challenged by pluralist views about families (Cheal, 1991; Thomas & Wilcox, 1987). Scholars on the family are not unified in claiming what a family is and how a family should function. At the crossroads of the unitary standard that has defined family studies in the past and the endless possibilities that threaten our security about what we know, we face the difficult but exciting challenge of defining, describing, and evaluating knowledge about *families*. In this chapter, we offer an inclusive definition of families without imposing a new orthodoxy. We also examine some of the tensions surrounding contemporary family scholarship and consider strategies that are useful for balancing the issues created by being inclusive of diversity.

DEFINING FAMILY DIVERSITY

In our view, a family is characterized by two or more persons related by birth, marriage, adoption, or choice. Families are further defined by socioemotional ties and enduring responsibilities, particularly in terms of one or more members' dependence on others for support and nurturance. By adding *diversity* to *family,* we recognize that there are different types of families who use a multitude of ways to meet their needs for reproduction, cohabitation, nurturance, economic cooperation, affection, protection, and meaning. These strategies are, in some ways, shared across families, but in other ways, all families have their idiosyncrasies. Furthermore, some families have protected legal ties, particularly those in which heterosexual adults are married, whereas others do not have protected legal ties (e.g., families headed by gay or lesbian partners; certain immigrant families). Even within families, individuals and relationships have different levels of protections, rights, privileges, and responsibilities, and being male typically has more privilege than being female (Ferree, 1990). There are many different types of families, with many different needs, and many different ways of meeting those needs. Family diversity is a way of characterizing the variability within and among families.

As we describe in more detail later, by emphasizing diversity, we do not mean that it is impossible to identify some similarities and generalizations across families. Although we are critical of the view that there is one inherent family form or process that is superior to others, we do not wish to generate an alternative myth by merely noting the potentially infinite dimensions of family diversity. The tension between diversity in family structure and process is a familiar one in our society, captured most recently in the highly politicized and polarized "family values" debate (Stacey, 1996). Our consideration of family variation and plurality is enriched by our recognition that families are embedded in societal contexts in which power and privilege are distributed unequally. Inequality is maintained through institutionalized and internalized systems of oppression, including racism, classism, sexism, heterosexism, ageism, ethnocentrism, and nationalism, in which particular groups are perceived as inherently superior to all others, thereby allowing them to claim "the right to dominance" (Lorde, 1984, p. 115). In this Handbook, we emphasize that families share a contextual background of tremendous economic and social stress at the beginning of the 21st century, and we argue that all families can benefit from an increased focus on strengthening the supports that ensure the well-being of all members in all families.

CONTROVERSIAL QUESTIONS

In our discussions on family diversity and our deliberations about how to structure this volume, we struggled with several important issues. We regard these issues as controversies because they stir debate and engender various perspectives in the literature, many of which are presented in this book. In the following sections, we describe what we consider the most important of these controversial questions and how we chose to address each here. In discussing controversies, sometimes we frame the issue in the language of "either-or" (e.g., similarities and differences, insiders and outsiders), not to reinforce a dichotomous view of an issue, but

to dramatize the extremities in the ways some topics are characterized in the literature. It is important to keep in mind, however, that most of these issues are best viewed along a continuum and that there is no easy way to resolve the tensions each issue presents.

Should We Focus on Similarities or Differences?

Scholarship on family diversity tends to emphasize *differences* in the family experiences of variously defined groups. When we ask if and how African American parents differ in their parenting behaviors from European American parents or how stepfamilies differ from single-parent families, we are asking questions that are concerned with difference. Taken to its extreme, the emphasis on difference leads to the conclusion that each family is unique. Although there is some veracity to this conclusion, it is limited from a scientific standpoint. A comprehensive view of families requires that we also address the *similarities* among different types of families. In trying to determine the commonalities in parenting across different socioeconomic groups, we are seeking to understand similarities in family experiences. It is just as dissatisfying, however, to take the similarity position to its extreme by suggesting that all families function the same and are equally beneficial for their members. We have tried to reach a dynamic balance between these two perspectives, and the variety of contributions in this volume illustrate various ways that scholars have approached the similarity-difference dimension of family diversity.

Important commonalities and meaningful differences exist in the experiences of all types of families. In this book, we strive to maintain a balance in which commonalities and differences can be recognized by identifying major subgroups of families on the basis of important dimensions of social stratification (e.g., race, class, gender, and family structure), thereby addressing a difference perspective. But we also asked the authors to attend to similarities in family experiences across diverse types of families, thereby addressing a similarity perspective. Of course, in a volume on family *diversity,* more emphasis is placed on differences than commonalities, but we have tried to achieve a reasonable balance without privileging one over the other.

What Is the Best Way to Characterize Family Diversity?

The next challenge we faced was to identify the most desirable way to characterize family diversity. We considered which dimensions to use to depict the diversity of families. How many dimensions are enough? Should we emphasize structural characteristics, such as race and socioeconomic status, or should we emphasize processes, such as intergenerational relationships, marital commitment, and parenting behaviors?

Because we believe that the literature on structural characteristics is more bountiful and illustrative than that on processes, we chose to be sensitive to the three major dimensions of social stratification that have been identified in the literature—race, socioeconomic status, and gender. Because families are the primary unit of analysis examined in this volume, we added a fourth dimension, family structure, commonly found in the literature. Family structure is broadly defined to include marital status, sexual orientation, and age. Consequently, readers will see chapters on African American families, gay and lesbian families, and stepfamilies, to give just a few examples.

We also asked the authors to devote some attention to processes that are integral to four types of relationships: marital-partner, parent-child (which we defined as involving minor children), intergenerational (which we defined as involving older children and their aging or elderly parents), and kinship relationships. Thus, we emphasize structure, the changing forms that families take over the life course, as the majority of previous authors have done, but extend our coverage to include family processes. By family processes, we mean the dynamics of interpersonal relationships (e.g., love, nurturance, acceptance, conflict, violence, disclosure, and trust) among people tied to one another by blood, marriage, adoption, or choice. In doing so, we tried to provide a familiar base for readers, but also one that challenges current thinking beyond the traditional ways of stratifying families as either normative or deviant.

Can and Should Families Be Compared Against a Benchmark?

Like other authors who are familiar with the polarized, politicized, and ideologically laden standard against which families are judged (the two-parent, dependent child, heterosexually married, white, middle-income family), we wondered if there is an *empirical* standard against which all families should be compared? Are some family forms inherently better for their members than others? Is there an optimal environment for rearing children, maintaining equality or sexual intimacy between adult partners, or caring for elderly parents? At one extreme, these questions can be answered in the affirmative: Some types of families function more effectively and achieve better outcomes for their members than do others. For example, women are less likely to be abused in relationships characterized by equality than in those in which they have greater or lesser status and power than their husbands (Thompson & Walker, 1989). At the other extreme, one might answer in the negative: No type of family or way of functioning is inherently better than any other. For example, children raised by lesbian or gay parents have similar outcomes to children raised by heterosexual parents (Patterson, 1992). According to this view, all types of families and ways that families achieve their goals and adjust to their environments are equally adaptive.

There is also an intermediate position on this controversy. Yes, some types of family relationships are closer, more supportive, and healthier for family members than are others, but no, positive and nurturing relationships are not found only in "benchmark" families. For example, the findings of large-scale survey research suggest that parents and children enjoy slightly more supportive family relationships and higher levels of well-being in first-married, two-biological-parent families than in single-parent families or stepfamilies. But the differences in family functioning and well-being *across* family types tend to be small, whereas the differences *within* family types (including benchmark families) tend to be large (Acock & Demo, 1994; Amato & Keith, 1991). Furthermore, not all family structures are represented systematically in large-scale surveys of family structures and relationships. Indeed, gay and lesbian individuals and their families are systematically excluded from the major surveys that constitute the bulk of family research (Allen & Demo, 1995).

The "optimal environment" controversy appears in a number of ways in the literature. For example, there have been numerous debates about whether two-parent, biological families are inherently better for children than are single-parent families or stepfamilies, whether lesbian and gay parents are as effective as heterosexual parents, whether authoritative parenting is the ideal way to socialize children, and whether policies should encourage the two-parent, nuclear family form. We, as editors, share the view that there is no universally applicable standard type of family or way for families to function. Rather, what is best or most desirable for a particular family or group of families depends on a number of contextual conditions that render generalization difficult. Readers of this volume will see various stances taken on this important issue, often with compelling empirical data to support divergent positions. The issues associated with family diversity are complex and difficult to summarize. Although many authors agree that poverty and economic well-being are embedded in social and historical structures (see Chapters 3, 15, and 19), the particular ways in which economic inequities and opportunities are manifested in racial-ethnic groups (see Chapters 12, 13, and 14), between genders, and across sexual orientations and ages create unique challenges and strengths for individuals and families.

Can Research on White, Middle-Class, Heterosexual Families Be Generalized to Other Families?

One of the driving forces that led us to edit this book is that most of the research on families has been on European American, middle-class, heterosexual families, and we wanted to redirect attention in new and integrative ways to other types of families. Thus, although a thorough and broad coverage

of family diversity suggests that we review literature pertaining to more mainstream families, we chose not to include these families but to use our limited space to focus attention on families that are not as frequently represented in the literature. Consequently, European American, middle-class, heterosexual families are often used as a comparison group in many chapters, but specific chapters are not devoted to them.

We take the position that we cannot assume unreflectively that knowledge gained from studies of certain groups of families applies to other groups of families. As social scientists, we believe that more information is needed before we can infer that different types of families share common characteristics, purposes, and processes. In the chapters that follow, the authors generally take the view that knowledge is contextualized and empirical confirmation is needed before findings can be generalized to other types of families. In some chapters, authors make it clear that there are sufficient data to warrant comparisons among diverse structural types. For examples, in Chapter 4, Rutter and Schwartz build on earlier research that compared heterosexual and gay or lesbian couples to assess the dynamics of couples in general.

Can Outsiders Understand Insiders?

Related to the controversy about the extent to which data about European American, middle-class, heterosexual families are applicable to other types of families is the controversy about whether it is possible for individuals to understand some aspect of family diversity if they have not experienced it. In what ways can outsiders understand insiders' experiences (Merton, 1972)? For example, must I be European American to understand what it means to be white? Can I also use my experience as a member of one minority group, say, as an Asian American, as a bridge to understanding other minority experiences, such as living in a single-parent family (assuming I live in a two-parent family)? This controversy is reflected in the literature on ethnic-minority families. On the one hand, some researchers (e.g., Cannon, Higginbotham, & Leung, 1991; Dilworth-Anderson, Burton, & Johnson, 1993) argue that a research team investigating the experiences of people of color must include a member who shares the same minority experience. On the other hand, Henderson (1994) described his success in studying aging ethnic-minority members in spite of his privileged status as a white man.

An important lesson from this dilemma is to be sensitive not to objectify others as we conduct research about them. Feminists have long argued for research *for* women, not solely about or on them (Smith, 1987). This strategy seems to be an important one for studies of family diversity, in which many researchers, by virtue of their educational and employment opportunities, share few characteristics with the people whose lives they study. There is a dire need to correct the lack of knowledge about minority populations, that is, those who differ from the benchmark in terms of race, class, gender, or family structure. In Chapter 5, on gender and parent-child relationships, Peterson, Bodman, Bush, and Madden-Derdich pinpoint one of the major impediments to generating knowledge about family diversity. Not only does the overreliance on static models of gender-role socialization exclude the active role of children in the socialization process, but these static models make gender difference the major distinguishing feature in how children are reared.

Are Existing Family Theories Relevant for Inquiries About Family Diversity?

Increasingly, postpositivist ideas are competing for prominence with positivist views. Some of the foundations of family theory are crumbling in the face of challenges from scholarship that deconstructs and reconstructs ideas about how families are and should be studied and treated in society (Cheal, 1991; Coontz, 1997; Stacey, 1990; Thomas & Wilcox, 1987). Rather than frame our understanding of family diversity from either a positivist or postpositivist position, we drew from ideas that are useful in defining families and characterizing their differences. Old and new ideas about families and their potentially infinite variations appear in the chapters in this book because they coexist in the discourse about families. For example, in Chapter 3, Teachman points out that most research on economic changes affecting families is embedded in a social exchange framework. At the other end of the spectrum, in Chapter 21, Stacey uses a poststructuralist account to speculate about the transformation in kin relationships at the end of the 20th century. The search for a single theory of family structure and process has been undermined by the challenge of diversity, but we share the view that inquiries into family diversity should be grounded in a theoretical framework (Doherty, Boss, LaRossa, Schumm, & Steinmetz, 1993). As Myers-Walls describes in Chapter 18, on family life education, our value positions undergird what we teach and communicate about families. It is important to assess the embedded meanings about families that we all bring to practice on behalf of families and to the data we analyze and interpret.

In this volume, we draw assumptions from several family theories to justify the need to examine family diversity. From the life-course perspective, we recognize that multiple temporal dimensions shape individual and family lives across changing sociohistorical contexts. From an ecological framework, we assume that families are nested within micro, meso, macro, and chrono systems. From a feminist perspective, we assume that power and privilege are systematically distributed inequitably by gender and generation and that families are further divided by variations in race and class. From a symbolic interactionist framework, we recognize that reality is socially constructed. Families are microsystems in which selves are formed through interactions with significant others and meanings are generated through interactional processes. All these assumptions, sometimes competing and sometimes overlapping, offer insights into diversity.

What Criteria Should We Use to Evaluate Families?

A key issue in the literature is the ways in which we judge how successful or effective families are in meeting their needs. There are numerous dimensions on which families can be evaluated. One simplistic way that this issue is manifested is whether economic and materialistic dimensions (e.g., educational achievement, income, and occupation) are valued as desirable outcomes relative to socioemotional outcomes (e.g., life satisfaction, satisfaction with relationships, and extent of emotional problems). Of course, the success and effectiveness of families are based on a range of outcomes, but authors often focus on one or another set of outcomes in isolation from each other. For example, as Chapters 8, 9, and 16, by Amato, Hetherington and Stanley-Hagan, and Entwisle and Alexander, respectively, discuss, there is an extensive literature on the degree to which divorce affects later socioeconomic outcomes for children and young adults and a largely separate literature on the socioemotional sequelae of divorce. Despite the interrelationships between and among various outcomes, researchers often tend to focus on one set of outcomes to the exclusion of others.

Why is it important to be sensitive to the various ways that families can be evaluated? Views of healthy family functioning reflect underlying values of desirable goals for individuals, relationships, and families. An emphasis on socioeconomic status, to some extent, reflects the belief that conformity to the status quo is a desirable outcome and that successes can be measured by criteria that reflect cultural values (e.g., number of years of education completed). In contrast, a focus on socioemotional status partially reflects the belief that individuals can subjectively evaluate their own well-being (e.g., life satisfaction, extent of depression) and that individuals and families can function well regardless of their socioeconomic position. In this volume, different evaluative dimensions are emphasized. Consider the issue of diverse sexual orientations among parents and partners. In Chapters 4, 10, and 21, by Rutter and Schwartz, Savin-Williams and Esterberg, and Stacey, respectively, rather than take a stance in which heterosexuality is the standard used to evaluate gay and lesbian experiences, the authors present evidence about the unique and shared aspects of the strengths of gay and lesbian families that are applicable to heterosexual families as well.

Should Oppression and Privilege Be Described Subjectively or Objectively?

A major issue in studying family diversity is the comparison of the *objective* material conditions of people's lives—their socioeconomic statuses;

educational opportunities; living conditions; life chances; and restrictions based on racism, classism, sexism, ageism, and heterosexism—with their own *subjective* perceptions of those conditions. For example, is a woman who "stays at home" and does not work for wages disadvantaged if she does not consider herself to be oppressed? Although feminist analyses have objectively documented the exploitation of women's caring labor in families, it is dismissive to label women who prefer homemaking as having a false consciousness (Billson, 1995; Lather, 1991). The study of family diversity must include individuals' subjective perceptions about oppression and privilege, such as their right to define and describe their own experiences in the world. Rather than an either-or stance, we see value in emphasizing both subjective and objective perspectives on the life circumstances of diverse families.

Why Do Different Methodological Approaches Often Generate Different Findings?

Many strategies are used to generate knowledge about family diversity, yet different methods often generate different types of data. Survey data capture broad trends that help us to understand similarities and differences among family types, but qualitative data often provide deeper insights into how different families share basic human qualities. We emphasize the importance of methodological diversity in understanding family diversity. Greater variation in the ways in which data are collected and analyzed should deepen and extend our understanding of the complexity of families.

For example, several large national surveys of household labor across diverse family structures have yielded quantitative evidence that wives perform two to three times as much housework as their husbands, that both husbands and children perform more domestic labor when wives-mothers are employed, and that husbands' and children's family labor increase as women's earnings increase (Acock & Demo, 1994; Goldscheider & Waite, 1991). Complementing and elaborating on these findings, qualitative investigations using in-depth interviews and ethnographic methods illustrate the "invisible" nature of much family labor. DeVault's (1991) open-ended interviews with a racially, ethnically, and socioeconomically diverse sample of women and men depicted the creative and relentless ways that women construct, maintain, care for, and cater to their families through the gendered labor of feeding them. DeVault documented, for example, how women bring families together by arranging mealtimes that are responsive to different family members' work and school schedules, downplay their own needs and prioritize their husbands' needs, personalize meals by attending to idiosyncratic tastes, and cook extra meals for those who arrive late, need to leave early, or want different foods.

In short, different research methods provide different vantage points on family labor and family diversity. Because each method has its strengths and limitations, a fuller understanding of family diversity requires that we evaluate the merit of studies that have used a diverse array of methodological approaches. In this volume, methodological approaches include Coontz's historical analyses (Chapter 2), Laird's use of narrative and metaphor (Chapter 17), Rank's combination of qualitative and quantitative data (Chapter 15), and Marks and Leslie's application of feminist and queer theories to earlier empirical findings pertaining to multiple family and work roles (Chapter 20).

Should We Make Our Values About Family Diversity Explicit?

As a result of our extensive discussions in collaborating on this Handbook, we came to understand that we, as editors, share certain values, which we tried to reflect in this volume. We asked the authors to be explicit about their values, as well. Consequently, multiple perspectives and voices are represented. We asked the authors to write comprehensive, but highly readable, chapters, reflecting the value that knowledge is not worth much if it is not accessible to and read by others (Bertaux, 1981; Mills, 1959). We asked the authors to define their use of *family* in their work, to attend to diversity within and across the family structures and processes they described, and to situate their own attraction to studying diversity in brief personal reflections. The authors' unique approaches to these

requests are evident in how they chose to comment upon their personal and intellectual interests in studying diversity. In Chapters 6 and 11, respectively, Umberson and Slaten, and Bedford and Blieszner, for example, connect their experiences with gender and intergenerational relationships and describe how their research careers have been shaped by issues reflected in their family histories. In Chapter 7, Johnson links her interest in diversity to the changing research currents in the applied fields in which she has worked—anthropology, family studies, and gerontology. In Chapter 12, Taylor puts a human face on racial segregation in the South in which he grew up and accounts for his lifelong interest in research on African American families. And in Chapter 14, Ishii-Kuntz uses stories from her childhood to illustrate gender, race, and national tensions in studying Asian American experiences.

As editors and colleagues, we share several core values. First, we emphasize the importance of developing an informed reflexive consciousness to deal with family diversity personally and intellectually, taking a critical stance on how knowledge is produced and recognizing the intersection of private and public experience (Thompson & Tyagi, 1996). Second, we believe that knowledge does not exist for its own sake: It must be applied to matters of social justice. As feminists, we believe it is important to use knowledge toward ends that improve the condition of people's lives. Many of the authors in this volume reflect this view as well, in their decisions to include particular value stances, from Savin-Williams and Esterberg's arguments about gay marriage (Chapter 10) to Rank's commentary on welfare reform (Chapter 15), to Bedford and Blieszner's criticism of ageism (Chapter 11) to Laird's presentation of strategies to deepen practitioners' understanding of clients' cultures (Chapter 17). Third, we believe it is important to use interdisciplinary perspectives to describe families and analyze diversity. Together, we represent various disciplines, including family studies, gerontology, women's studies, psychology, and sociology. Fourth, we share the belief in the importance of integrating theory, research, and practice with our value claims and in so doing, try to make the unsystematic systematic. All knowledge is guided by some theoretical framework, and we believe it should be made explicit.

PERSONAL REFLECTIONS ON FAMILY DIVERSITY

As social scientists, we are interested in family variations and social change. We share an understanding that our private concerns and experiences with gender, race, class, and family structure have shaped our interest in diversity. Each of us has a complex history of relative privileges and disadvantages that shaped our experiences in the world. Our academic interests are informed by our private experience, as well. Because we asked the authors to reflect on their interest in family diversity, we, too, spent some time reflecting on how the public and private intersect in our lives. We each wrote initial narratives in which we disclosed content related to childhood recollections of gender, race, and class, as well as the educational experiences, mentors, and texts that have been the most influential for our academic interests in family diversity. All three of us were born in the 1950s, and as members of the post–World War II baby-boom generation, we share certain realities, such as middle-class upbringings, to various degrees, in suburban, primarily white neighborhoods.

As we discussed the definitions and controversies we present in this chapter, we noticed how the very goals of this volume were also reflected in our conversations. How do we represent a variety of perspectives on family diversity, some of which are irreconcilable? In addition to our shared experiences, we also noticed many differences in our current family structures, as well as in our views about what counts as private information. For example, what does it mean to disclose that one of us is in a first marriage to a partner of 20 years? What does it mean to disclose that one of us is divorced and that the experience of parenting with another partner, not the child's biological father, has shaped a new understanding of diversity? Our narratives are patterned around some common themes, such as childhood and educational influences on our desire to study family diversity, but also on some differences,

such as how public we wish to make our private family experiences.

We now describe ways in which our personal and academic interests in family diversity have led us to edit this Handbook. We want to make transparent our own understanding of how our knowledge of diversity has shaped our perspectives and values. We want to demystify how we came to understand family diversity through complex processes associated with our individual biographies, professional collaborations in interdisciplinary family studies programs, and commitment to knowledge that makes a difference in the world—beyond our private experiences.

Katherine's Reflections on Diversity

Long before I learned to name my intellectual interest as "an interdisciplinary approach to family studies," my frame of reference was structured by my birth as the second child of young parents struggling for financial independence in the postwar years of the 1950s. Until I was 15, I lived in a row house with my parents and four siblings in suburban Baltimore. My mother was 26 and my father was 27 by the time they had five children. My father went to night school and finished his B.S. degree in engineering in 10 years. For the next several decades, he had a successful career. My mother was a homemaker, active in community and church groups. Her creative outlets included singing in a choral group, sewing dresses for herself and her two daughters, and entertaining family members and friends. Before my mother married at 18, she had been enrolled at a state teachers' college, but early marriage, the demands of raising five children, and several cross-country moves precluded the fulfillment of her dream for advanced education.

My parents were the first generation in my family to move outside the city, following the typical urbanization pattern characteristic of eastern cities. My grandparents bought their row house on the edge of Baltimore in 1932, raising six children there. Like the generation before them, they held on to their home despite the alleged redlining they attributed to Jewish businessmen buying up homes for a fraction of their value and reselling them to black families. I heard snippets of this complaint, but it was more inuendo and fear than substantiated fact.

On April 4, 1968, I was ironing in our basement, in charge of my three younger brothers while my mother was at a PTA meeting and my father was away on a business trip. The television program we were watching was interrupted with the news that Martin Luther King, Jr., had been shot in Memphis. I recall my mother coming home from the meeting and calling her parents because the threat of riots near my grandparents' home was escalating. I can still see my mother dropping to her knees, crying, and saying the Lord's Prayer, after talking to my grandparents and learning that their neighbor, a black man, was standing on their front porch with a shotgun, protecting them from potential rioters. We drove down to get my grandparents the next day, and our car was pummeled with rocks. Things settled down, and my grandparents decided that when we moved to California, they would leave their home in the city and move into ours.

In 1969, we moved to the Irvine Ranch and watched a large city emerge in the next few years out of scrubby orange groves. We were active in the United Methodist Church, and I sharpened my concern about social issues in this spiritual context. The church I attended was deeply committed to social change. We spent spring break and summer holidays in Arizona at an Indian reservation. I sang in a folk group with other youths, and protest music, particularly against the Vietnam War, was welcomed in my church. The evangelical movement was making a comeback, and I was baptized in the Pacific Ocean. After high school, I toured California with other youths and adult sponsors from my church, visiting diverse locations, from the United Methodist and Episcopal African Church in Watts to the barrios of East Los Angeles, to Cesar Chavetz's picket lines to Glide Memorial Church, a ministry for primarily gay people in San Francisco. Despite my white, middle-class upbringing, the communities in which I lived provided an openness to question and challenge the status quo.

I was introduced to feminism in my first year at San Diego State University. I recall feeling intrigued and frightened by some assertive women on a panel who talked about oppression without covering their feelings or acting nice. The excitement of coming of age comingled that year with a more despairing experience of sexual assault. The women's movement provided the words for events that had already occurred in my life. That year in San Diego launched my interest in feminism; the first women's discussion group I attended was the kind of defining event Erikson (1975) described in *Life History and the Historical Moment*—I heard language that expressed the deep confusion I felt as a young, intelligent, and idealistic woman.

Education provided words and theories to help me understand my marginalization as a female in a male-dominated society. In 1973, I transferred to the University of Connecticut and began to take women's studies courses. I worked as a bank teller and contemplated a career in accounting. After I was fired from my job for trying to organize the tellers, I knew that the conformity required by the pink-collar business world was not for me. I taught third-grade Sunday school at my parents' church, but on Sunday mornings, I often had a hangover from staying out late the night before. I kept this "good girl-bad girl" ambivalence to myself because there was little support to work out the confusing messages of the sexual revolution that permeated my coming of age.

In my junior year, my courses in child development, family studies, and sociology turned me on to learning about families. After I graduated from college, I worked for a year as a VISTA volunteer in impoverished communities in northeastern Connecticut. My clientele were older immigrants, which led to a career focus in gerontology. During graduate school at Syracuse University, I deepened my involvement in the women's movement and campaigned for passage of the Equal Rights Amendment, which was finally defeated in 1982.

I have written about these fragments of my life in other publications. I recount some of the events now to recover strands that affected my interest in diversity. My fascination with marginalization was the impetus for my dissertation research on older single women (Allen, 1989). I have traced the linkage to my Irish heritage and the Western European marital pattern of women relinquishing marriage and motherhood to maintain their families of origin (Allen, 1994). As a white woman and a feminist, gender has been the primary stratification I have struggled with in life, but postmodern ideas have raised my consciousness about the impossibility of separating race, class, sexual orientation, and age from gender. I am motivated to study diversity as well as to help ameliorate oppressive conditions in our society. After contemplating many career choices, I settled on family studies, given the opportunities to write, teach, study, and affect change as a professor. An adage from my youth, "If you're not part of the solution, you're part of the problem," is a touchstone for me and has guided my career ever since.

My personal experiences have often provided the motivation for my academic pursuits, and my academic knowledge has often been the impetus for personal change. At 35, my husband and I divorced, and I began to live as a lesbian. This life became a possibility for me only after I read many books and studies about the *logic* of a woman-identified life. Living openly as a lesbian was a rational choice. Reading about others' experiences, teaching a variety of students, working with women who were lesbians, going through my own aging process, and having intense feelings for another woman broke down the rigid belief of this society that only heterosexuality is normal. For me, this change has been an important step in developing an informed consciousness about family diversity. One of the benefits of pursuing a chosen life is the possibility of integrating the personal and the intellectual.

Mark's Reflections on Diversity

I have had a long-standing interest in individuals whom I refer to as "underdogs." These are people who, for reasons generally outside their control, face challenges, barriers, and difficulties that those of us who are privileged do not. I am not sure why I have this interest, but it may be related to my perception as a child that I was somewhat of an underdog. I also felt alienated from my popular peers because I am Jewish. Despite having the privilege that comes with being male, white, middle-class, and educated, I was not fully aware of these advantages as a youth. In addition, my parents and some of my friends strongly stressed that oppression and discrimination were evils that needed to be eliminated from our society.

One memory from when I was about 11 stands out as an illustration of my early identification with underdogs. I was attending a weeklong program on Nigeria, offered during the Christmas break at the Jewish community center in my hometown of Toledo, Ohio. We were taken by our parents to one of several possible shopping centers and then a bus took us downtown to the center and, at the end of the day, we were told which stop to get off the bus. I recall being upset because the daughter of a friend of our family was hearing impaired, and I knew that she could not hear the directions about which stop to get off the bus to meet her parents. For some reason, on the bus ride home the first day of this program, I recall being distressed. I do not remember the details now, but I believe that I asked her to get off at the stop where I was going to get picked up, and my mother took her either to her home or to her stop. Even after she was told which stop she should get off on subsequent days that week, I recall feeling upset about the disability I perceived that she had.

My interest in diversity and underdogs was given an academic underpinning in my last two years as an undergraduate at Cornell University. I happened upon a course on the helping relationship in the College of Human Ecology, in which the professor, Donald Barr, exposed us, in an experiential and empowering way, to issues of power, oppression, sexism, racism, and other forms of discrimination. Taking this course was one of the most exciting events of my life to that point and literally changed the course of my professional career. In my last two years, I took advantage of every experience I could from this professor, served as a teaching assistant for the course that had been so influential to me, changed my major from economics to psychology, and decided to apply for graduate school in clinical/community psychology. These experiences showed me the passion I feel for understanding and trying to address discrimination and oppression. The memories I have of the many discussions, meetings, struggles, debates, and protests we attended are among the most vibrant and exciting of my career.

In graduate school in clinical and community psychology at The Ohio State University, I joined a research group studying the effects of divorce on families because of my adviser's interest in this area. I felt comfortable with this topic, which has been a major research focus of mine since then. I viewed studying divorce and single parenthood as extensions of my interest in discrimination and oppression, although we approached it in a way that was somewhat removed from the social-change position that I had become accustomed to and comfortable with at Cornell. In other words, rather than attempt to change social conditions that might lead to divorce or that might stigmatize those who were divorced (as my colleagues and I might have done at Cornell), my counterparts at Ohio State focused on understanding and providing assistance to those who had experienced divorce. This was part of a gradual intrapersonal process in which I shifted from emphasizing social-community change to focusing more on families. I have retained my commitment to social change, but I focus most of my professional energy on families—in research, teaching, and outreach activities.

Also while at Ohio State, I studied African American families and, in both writing and discussions, explored how a white psychologist could help advance the understanding of the experiences and plights of these families. I was (and am) concerned about the negative images that are often used to portray African American families, and I thought that being white might give me the opportunity to provide alternative images. I think that I was successful to some extent, but, as one might expect, in searching for answers to the appropriate role for a white professional in the African American community, I reached no definitive conclusions.

While serving as a professor of psychology at the University of Dayton, I retained my interest in diversity, although it was difficult to do so because much of my time was spent in fairly mainstream clinical activities—teaching courses on psychological assessment and psychopathology, maintaining a small private practice, and conducting research on personality disorders. I consciously made a choice to extend my research into the area of remarriage and stepfamilies, feeling that this decision was jus-

tified because most divorced parents eventually remarry and form stepfamilies. Nevertheless, I realized, somewhat slowly over time, that my interests were moving away from mainstream psychology, particularly clinical psychology, toward family studies. In 1994, when I moved to the University of Missouri, I also moved out of a psychology department into a human development and family studies department. Since then, because I view human development and family studies departments as generally being more sensitive to diversity issues and to the cultural and social contexts in which individuals and families function, I have felt much more at home professionally.

Before I arrived, our department had identified its unique niche as family diversity and multiculturalism, which is a focus that is consistent with my interests. My interest in diversity remains strong and now revolves primarily around family transitions (e.g., the effects of divorce and remarriage) and family processes. I feel particularly passionate about the dimensions of race, sexual orientation, and family structure.

Dave's Reflections on Diversity

My interests in family diversity are both personal and professional. As a child growing up in a relatively affluent family in Newburgh, New York, in the richest country in the world, I did not have the language or the sophistication I have now to understand the prejudice, discrimination, and oppression I saw around me. But several early experiences and events stimulated in different ways my interests in social inequality and its consequences for individuals. My mother was a caring and sensitive person who often alerted me to the plight of poor people. Part of her sensitivity toward poor people stemmed from her early life course, growing up during the Great Depression. Like most people at the time, she and her family did not have much money and lived on a meager income. During her childhood and adolescence, my mother lived with her mother and grandmother, and most of the family's income came from renting out rooms in the building where they lived and which my great-grandmother owned. As an adult, my mother often told me stories about the less fortunate, not only to make me appreciate what our family had, but to teach me that wealth is unequally distributed and does not define whether one is a good person.

A lasting image I have of my father, who was a highly successful hospital administrator, is that several times a year he would ask me if I wanted to go with him to work. In addition to the thrill of getting to spend time with my father, who was absorbed in his career, I always enjoyed watching him walk through the halls of the hospital greeting all the employees. Many members of the housekeeping and laundry staffs were minorities, and I can remember to this day how my father knew each one by name, greeted them with a big smile, and shook their hands. What I saw and appreciated in his behavior was warmheartedness, friendliness, sincerity, and a disregard for skin color or social position. What I did not understand at the time was that it was also in my father's political interests (and thus in our family's interests) to develop and maintain a strong rapport with the employees because each one had a vote in elections to unionize the hospital, which my father was trying to prevent.

As I entered early adolescence in the mid-1960s, the race riots went through my hometown, and I can remember watching scenes from the local riots on the national news. My parents were generally quiet about such matters, but they taught me the importance of treating all people with respect and dignity, regardless of their race or social background. For many years, we had a maid who was African American, a gentle and hardworking woman who was probably the only minority person I really got to know during my youth. Everyone in our extended family, including an exchange student from Spain who lived with us for a year, enjoyed talking with and loving this person who served (at modest wages) as our domestic servant. Yet there were reasons, which I did not understand until many years later, why I did not have many African American friends or neighbors. Segregation and racism take many forms, of course, and one way my parents had structured my environment and ensured that I had "the best education" (and only white classmates) was to enroll me in a private, Catholic elementary school.

In these and other ways, a conflicting and highly contradictory set of messages resonated through our family environment. Both my parents espoused strongly anti-Semitic sentiments, which confused and at times angered me. I had a number of Jewish friends in the public junior high school and high school I attended, and as I got older, I questioned and challenged my parents about their beliefs and how those beliefs cast shadows over my friends and their families. We did not resolve any of these ideological and political differences, and when I entered my first semester at the University of Richmond in 1973, the first elective I enrolled in was a course in the Religious Studies department entitled, The History and Culture of the Hebrew Man. At the time, I did not realize the sexist aspect of the title (and content) of the course, but the course taught me a great deal about the narrow worldview I had developed during my childhood and adolescence and introduced me to critical concepts, such as ethnocentrism.

As an undergraduate student at the University of Richmond, I double-majored in sociology and psychology, largely because I wanted to understand both the societal forces that impinge on individuals and families and the psychological processes involved in personality development. I took several courses on sociology of the family and became interested in adolescents and their relations with their parents, in part to understand better my own close relationships and periodic (sometimes intense) conflicts with my parents. A couple of professors encouraged me to consider graduate school, and I had to make the difficult decision whether to pursue sociology or psychology. I chose sociology because, at least at the time, I thought it explained more, but I did not allow myself to wander too far from psychology. I studied and read widely in social psychology and examined socioeconomic correlates of adolescents' self-esteem for my master's thesis, and I have seen the world through a social psychological lens ever since.

During my doctoral studies at Cornell University, I benefitted from a unique and truly multidisciplinary program in sociology, social psychology, and human development and family studies. This training gave me the theoretical and methodological tools I needed to study issues that I remain interested in to this day: the influence of macrostructural arrangements (such as race, class, and gender) on family relations and personality over the life course and the mechanisms through which parent-child and parent-adolescent relationships affect child and adolescent development and well-being. My primary interest in studying family diversity, and in editing this book, is to identify ways that family processes (parent-child relations, partner relations, sibling relations, and relations with extended and chosen kin) are similar and different across diverse family forms.

ORGANIZATION OF THE HANDBOOK

In the chapters that follow, experts on specific dimensions of family diversity review, discuss, critique, and reflect on the latest research and theoretical developments in their areas of interest. The remainder of the book is structured in seven parts, each devoted to a central theme in the literature on family diversity.

In Part II, "Reflections on Family Diversity: Past and Present," Coontz and Teachman examine the historical, demographic, social, and economic forces that are shaping contemporary and future family living arrangements.

In Part III, "Gender Dynamics in Families," Rutter and Schwartz address how gender influences close relationships, including marital and committed partnerships. Peterson, Bodman, Bush, and Madden-Derdich explore the intersections of gender and parent-child relationships. Umberson and Slaten discuss intergenerational relationships, particularly that of aging parents and adult children. Johnson examines how gender and kinship are mutually influential.

In Part IV, "Family Structure and Family Diversity," the four chapters examine different types of family structural variations: Amato's chapter on single-parent families, Hetherington and Stanley-Hagan's chapter on stepfamilies, Savin-Williams and Esterberg's chapter on sexual orientation, and Bedford and Blieszner's chapter on aging families.

In Part V, "Racial, Ethnic, and Cultural Diversities in Families," Taylor discusses diversity in African American families, Baca Zinn and Wells consider Latino families, and Ishii-Kuntz addresses Asian American families. We regret that a commissioned chapter on indigenous families could not be included, and we look forward to subsequent publications in which Native American families are incorporated into the discourse on family diversity. The research base on indigenous families must be strengthened so that a greater number of voices can be heard in volumes covering a wide range of family experiences.

In Part VI, "Class Diversities in Families" are addressed in two chapters: Rank's chapter on poverty and economic hardship and Entwisle and Alexander's chapter on the effects of family diversity on schooling.

In Part VII, "Applications for Working With Families," three practical contexts for family change are considered in light of family diversity. Laird addresses clinical practice; Myers-Walls examines family life education; and Lerner, Sparks, and McCubbin consider family policies.

Part VIII concludes the volume with three contributions. Marks and Leslie provide a complex commentary on family diversity and intersecting categories of race, class, gender, and sexual orientation. Stacey reviews the concept of family diversity in relation to projections made about the future of the family nearly two decades ago. As editors, we conclude the Handbook by reflecting on what we have learned about family diversity from the authors in this volume and by suggesting implications for future research on family diversity.

REFERENCES

Acock, A. C., & Demo, D. H. (1994). *Family diversity and well-being*. Thousand Oaks, CA: Sage.

Allen, K. R. (1989). *Single women/Family ties: Life histories of older women*. Newbury Park, CA: Sage.

Allen, K. R. (1994). Feminist reflections on lifelong single women. In D. L. Sollie & L. A. Leslie (Eds.), *Gender, families, and close relationships: Feminist research journeys* (pp. 97–119). Thousand Oaks, CA: Sage.

Allen, K. R., & Demo, D. H. (1995). The families of lesbians and gay men: A new frontier in family research. *Journal of Marriage and the Family, 57,* 111–127.

Amato, P. R., & Keith, B. (1991). Parental divorce and the well-being of children: A meta-analysis. *Psychological Bulletin, 110,* 26–46.

Bertaux, D. (Ed.). (1981). *Biography and society: The life history approach in the social sciences.* Beverly Hills, CA: Sage.

Billson, J. M. (1995). *Keepers of the culture: The power of tradition in women's lives.* New York: Lexington Books.

Cannon, L. W., Higginbotham, E., & Leung, M. L. A. (1991). Race and class bias in qualitative research on women. In M. M. Fonow & J. A. Cook (Eds.), *Beyond methodology: Feminist scholarship as lived research* (pp. 107–118). Bloomington: Indiana University Press.

Cheal, D. (1991). *Family and the state of theory.* Toronto: University of Toronto Press.

Coontz, S. (1997). *The way we really are.* New York: Basic Books.

DeVault, M. L. (1991). *Feeding the family.* Chicago: University of Chicago Press.

Dilworth-Anderson, P., Burton, L., & Johnson, L. B. (1993). Reframing theories for understanding race, ethnicity, and families. In P. G. Boss, W. J. Doherty, R. LaRossa, W. R. Schumm, & S. K. Steinmetz (Eds.), *Sourcebook of family theories and methods* (pp. 627–646). New York: Plenum.

Doherty, W. J., Boss, P. G., LaRossa, R., Schumm, W. R., & Steinmetz, S. K. (1993). Family theories and methods: A contextual approach. In P. G. Boss, W. J. Doherty, R. LaRossa, W. R. Schumm, & S. K. Steinmetz (Eds.), *Sourcebook of family theories and methods* (pp. 3–30). New York: Plenum.

Erikson, E. H. (1975). *Life history and the historical moment: Diverse presentations.* New York: W. W. Norton.

Ferree, M. M. (1990). Feminism and family research. *Journal of Marriage and the Family, 52,* 866–884.

Goldscheider, F. K., & Waite, L. J. (1991). *New families, no families? The transformation of the American home.* Berkeley: University of California Press.

Henderson, J. N. (1994). Ethnic and racial issues. In J. F. Gubrium & A. Sankar (Eds.), *Qualitative methods in aging research* (pp. 33–50). Thousand Oaks, CA: Sage.

Lather, P. (1991). *Getting smart: Feminist research and pedagogy with/in the postmodern.* New York: Routledge.

Lorde, A. (1984). *Sister outsider.* Freedom, CA: Crossing Press.

Merton, R. K. (1972). Insiders and outsiders: A chapter in the sociology of knowledge. *American Journal of Sociology, 78,* 9–47.

Mills, C. W. (1959). *The sociological imagination.* Oxford, England: Oxford University Press.

Patterson, C. J. (1992). Children of lesbian and gay parents. *Child Development, 63,* 1025–1042.

Smith, D. E. (1987). *The everyday world as problematic: A feminist sociology.* Boston: Northeastern University Press.

Stacey, J. (1990). *Brave new families: Stories of domestic upheaval in late twentieth century America.* New York: Basic Books.

Stacey, J. (1996). *In the name of the family.* Boston: Beacon Press.

Thomas, D. L., & Wilcox, J. E. (1987). The rise of family theory: A historical and critical analysis. In M. B. Sussman & S. K. Steinmetz (Eds.), *Handbook of marriage and the family* (pp. 81–102). New York: Plenum.

Thompson, B., & Tyagi, S. (Eds.). (1996). *Names we call home: Autobiography on racial identity.* New York: Routledge.

Thompson, L., & Walker, A. J. (1989) Gender in families: Women and men in marriage, work, and parenthood. *Journal of Marriage and the Family, 51,* 845–871.

PART II

Reflections on Family Diversity: Past and Present

CHAPTER **2**

Historical Perspectives on Family Diversity

STEPHANIE COONTZ

As a freshman at the University of California, torn between history and literature, I took a poetry class in which we read an anonymous 11th-century poem called "The Wanderer." The poem was about a warrior whose liege-lord had been defeated and who was now in exile, far from his comrades; kin; and patron, the "goldgiver." My professor and most of my classmates were extremely moved by the way this poem spoke across the centuries to universal themes of loss, grief, and loneliness.

To me, however, the fascination lay in how foreign the emotional focus of the poem was to my own experience. None of the young men in my circle, would-be warriors all, would ever have said, as did the man in the poem, that he missed laying his head against the knee of another man or being a dependent in his halls. No homemaker of my acquaintance would have admitted that her husband's status as "goldgiver" had anything to do with the services and gratitude she extended her husband. Taking my teacher's word that poets are interested mainly in the universal human concerns beneath the superficial differences, I decided I must be a historian.

The exploration of differences, contrasts, and transformations in history immediately fascinated me. Over the years, I became convinced that most seeming universals exist only at an abstract and general level—that beneath what we share with cultures of the past lie profound, qualitative differences in social dynamics and outlooks, differences that can be examined to interrogate our own institutions and values more closely. Yet it was many years later, while team-teaching with an anthropologist at The Evergreen State College, where I now work, that I realized I had never been trained to view family life, love, child rearing, and sexual relationships as historical phenomena. Rather, my readings and university classes had treated these as natural, universal, and comparatively static arrangements or relationships that might be modified or "disrupted" by social change but otherwise tended to operate in pretty predictable ways. My exposure to anthropological studies of kinship rules, gender roles, and family life made short shrift of these assumptions.

FAMILY DIVERSITY IN CROSS-CULTURAL PERSPECTIVE

Not only do family structures, norms, and values vary tremendously, I found, but even the biological building blocks of families are less solid than my training had led me to believe. In kinship societies that trace descent through the maternal or paternal line, children are considered part of the family of only one spouse. When a woman of the Toda of southern India gets married, she marries all her husband's brothers, even those not yet born. Each child she bears is assigned an individual father, but the assignment is based on social, rather than biological, criteria. In many African and early Native American societies, a woman could become a female husband and be counted the social parent of any children her wife brought to the marriage or afterward bore by various anonymous lovers. Among the Lakher of Southeast Asia, a child is viewed as linked to the mother only by virtue of the mother's marriage to the father. If the parents divorce, the mother is considered to have no relationship to her children. She could, theoretically, even marry her son because the group's incest taboos would not be considered applicable (Coontz, 1988; Ingoldsby & Smith, 1995; Leibowitz, 1978).

Although prohibitions against incest are nearly universal, the definition of what constitutes incest may vary considerably. In traditional Islamic societies, marriage between the children of two sisters is considered a form of incest, but marriage between the children of two brothers is a favored pattern. Brother-sister marriages, complete with romantic sexual attraction, were accepted among the aristocracy in ancient Egypt. The medieval church of Europe, in contrast, prohibited marriage between cousins up to the seventh degree removed. Yet despite ecclesiastical sanctions against incest, sexual relations between even closely related family members did not become a criminal offense in England until the first decade of the 20th century (Hawkes, 1973; Ingoldsby & Smith, 1995; Morris, 1993).

Following G. P. Murdock, many anthropologists have defined the family as a social unit that shares common residence, economic cooperation, and reproduction. But among the Yoruba of Africa, the family is often not a unit of either production or consumption because husbands and wives do not even share a common budget. In some tribal societies, husbands and wives live apart, while in oth-

ers, the basic unit of economic cooperation may be the band, age group, or foraging team, rather than the family. Among many 18th-century Austrian peasants, the legally and religiously sanctioned family, which determined the child's social status, did not share the same household, engage in child rearing, or cooperate economically in either production or consumption (Coontz, 1988).

VARIABILITY IN THE EUROPEAN AND AMERICAN HISTORICAL RECORD

In the ancient Mediterranean world, households and kin groupings were so disparate that no single unit of measurement or definition could encompass them. By the late 14th century, however, the English word *family,* derived from the Latin word for a household including servants or slaves, had emerged to designate all those who lived under the authority of a household head. The family might include a joint patrilocal family, with several brothers and their wives residing together under the authority of the eldest, as was common in parts of Italy and France before 1550, as well as in many Eastern European communities into the 19th century. Or it might be a stem family, in which the eldest son brought his bride into his parents' home upon marriage, and they lived as an extended family until the parents' deaths. The son's family then became nuclear in form, until the eldest son reached the age of marriage. Owing to late marriages and early mortality, most such families would be nuclear at any particular census, but most of them would pass through an extended stage at some point in their life cycle (Berkner, 1972; Coontz, 1988; Hareven, 1987).

Until the early 19th century, most middle-class Europeans and North Americans defined *family* on the basis of a common residence under the authority of a household head, rather than on blood relatedness. This definition thus frequently included boarders or servants. Samuel Pepys began his famous 17th-century English diary with the words: "I lived in Axe Yard, having my wife, and servant Jane, and no more in family than us three." In 1820, the publisher Everard Peck and his wife, of Rochester, New York, childless newlyweds, wrote home: "We collected our family together which consists of seven persons and we think ourselves pleasantly situated" (Coontz, 1988; Hareven, 1987).

Among the European nobility, an alternative definition of family referred not to the parent-child grouping, but to the larger descent group from which claims to privilege and property derived. Starting in the late 17th century, other writers used the word to refer exclusively to a man's offspring, as in the phrase *his family and wife*. Not until the 19th century did the word *family* commonly describe a married couple with their coresident children, distinguished from household residents or more distant kin. This definition spread widely during the 1800s. By the end of the 19th century, the restriction of the word to the immediate, coresidential family was so prevalent that the adjective *extended* had to be added when people wished to refer to kin beyond the household (Williams, 1976).

DIVERSITY IN EMOTIONAL AND SEXUAL ARRANGEMENTS

As my experience with interdisciplinary research on family forms and behaviors grew, I soon realized that diversity extended not just to forms and definitions, but to the emotional meanings attached to families and the psychological dynamics within them. Whereas 17th-century Mediterranean families were organized around the principle of honor, which rested largely on the chastity of the family's women, other groups did not traditionally distinguish between "legitimate" and "illegitimate" children. When Jesuit missionaries told a Montagnais-Naskapi Indian that he should keep tighter control over his wife to ensure that the children she bore were "his," the man replied: "Thou hast no sense. You French people love only your own children; but we love all the children of our tribe" (Leacock, 1980, p. 31; see also Gutierrez, 1991).

What is considered healthy parent-child bonding in our society may be seen as selfishness or pathological isolation by cultures that stress the exchange and fostering of children as ways of cementing social ties. The Zincantecos of southern Mexico do not even have a word to distinguish the parent-child relationship from the house, suggesting that the emotional saliency of the cooperating household unit is stronger than that of blood ties per se. In Polynesia, eastern Oceania, the Caribbean, and the West Indies (and in 16th-century Europe) to offer your child to friends, neighbors, or other kin for adoption or prolonged coresidence was not considered abandonment but a mark of parental love and community reciprocity (Collier, Rosaldo, & Yanigasako, 1982; Peterson, 1993; Stack, 1993).

Modern Americans stress the need for mother-daughter and father-son identification, but in matrilineal societies, where descent is reckoned in the female line, a man usually has much closer ties with his nephews than with his sons. Among the Trobriand Islanders, for instance, a child's biological father is considered merely a relation by marriage. The strongest legal and emotional bonds are between children and their maternal uncles. Conversely, among the patrilineal Cheyenne, mother-daughter relations were expected to be tense or even hostile, and girls tended to establish their closest relationships with their paternal aunts (Collier et al., 1982).

What counts as healthy family dynamics or relationships also varies *within* any given society. Research on contemporary families has demonstrated that parenting techniques or marital relationships that are appropriate to middle-class white families are less effective for families that must cope with economic deprivation and racial prejudice (Baumrind, 1972; Boyd-Franklin & Garcia-Preto, 1994; Knight, Virdin, & Roosa, 1994).

Values about the proper roles and concerns of mothers and fathers differ as well. Today women tend to be in charge of family rituals, such as weddings and funerals. In colonial days, however, this was a father's responsibility, while economic activities were far more central to a colonial woman's identity (and occupied much more of her time) than was child rearing. Contemporary American thought posits an inherent conflict between mothering and paid work, but breadwinning is an integral part of the definition of mothering in many cultural traditions. One study found that "traditional" Mexicanas in the United States experience *less* conflict or guilt in integrating the worlds of home and paid employment than do their Chicana counterparts who have internalized the notions of good mothering portrayed in the American mass media (Calvert, 1992; Gillis, 1996).

Even something as seemingly "natural" as sexual behavior and identity shows amazing variation across time and cultures. Categories of gender and sexuality have not always been so rigidly dichotomous as they are in modern Euro-American culture. Among many Native American societies, for instance, the *berdache* has a spiritual, social, economic, and political role that is distinct from either men's or women's roles. Neither he nor the female counterparts found in other Native American groups can be accurately described by the sexual identity we know as homosexual. Similarly, in traditional African culture, a person's sexual identity was not separable from his or her membership and social role in a family group (Herdt, 1994; Jeater, 1993; Schnarch, 1992; Williams, 1986).

Ever since the spread of Freudian psychiatric ideas at the beginning of the 20th century, Europeans and North Americans have tended to see a person's sexual behavior as the wellspring or driving force of his or her identity. The ancient Greeks, in contrast, thought that dreams about sex were "really" about politics. Until comparatively recently in history, a person's sexual acts were assumed to be separate from his or her fundamental character or identity. Indeed, the term *homosexual* did not come into use until the end of the 19th century. A person could commit a sexual act with a person of the same sex without being labeled as having a particular sexual "orientation." This lack of interest in identifying people by their sexual practices extended to heterosexual behavior as well. In mid-17th century New England, Samuel Terry was several times convicted for sexual offenses, such as masturbating, in public, but this behavior did not prevent his fellow townspeople from electing him town constable (D'Emilio & Freedman, 1988; Padgug, 1989).

Since the early 20th century, most American experts on the family have insisted on the importance of heterosexual intimacy between husband and wife in modeling healthy development for children, yet in the 19th century, no one saw any harm in the fact that the closest bonds of middle-class women were with other women, rather than with their husbands. Men were often secondary in women's emotional lives, to judge from the silence or nonchalance about them in women's diaries and letters, which were saturated with expressions of passion that would immediately raise eyebrows by modern standards of sexual categorization. Although the acceptability of such passionate bonds may have provided cover for sexual relations between some women, these bonds were also considered compatible with marriage. Men, too, operated in a different sexual framework than today. They talked matter-of-factly about sleeping with their best friends, embracing them, or laying a head on a male friend's bosom—all without any self-consciousness that their wives or fiancées might misinterpret their "sexual orientation" (Duberman, Vicinus, & Chauncey, 1989; Faderman, 1981; Rotundo, 1993; Smith-Rosenberg, 1985).

HISTORICAL PERSPECTIVES ON DEFINING THE FAMILY

These anthropological and historical findings about family variability deepened my skepticism about overarching narratives of linear change, such as those proposed by modernization theorists, yet left me uncomfortable with many postmodern writings that failed to incorporate recognition of diversity into an analysis of *patterns* of historical change. On the one hand, the evidence argues against any universal definition of "the" family, whether it is based on structural, functional, or psychological criteria. On the other hand, in almost all societies, families seem to be a basic unit for coordinating personal reproduction and redistribution with larger societal patterns of production and exchange. But there is a tremendous variety in the way families coordinate these functions and deal with their members' physical and emotional needs. The set of relationships, roles, ideologies, and emotional or material exchanges that constitute "the family" can be defined only in the context of a particular society at a specific point in time.

To some authors, this variability allows for an extremely elastic expansion of the term. The editors of this volume, for instance, use the word to cover any group of two or more persons who engage in ongoing intimacy and obligation, whether they do so because of birth, marriage, adoption, or choice. I am inclined, however, to define the word by the kinds of intergenerational relationships, obligations, and rights that are socially and legally sanctioned in a society or subgroup in a society at any point in time.

One objection to defining family in terms of intergenerational relations is that it leaves out childless married couples and denies the benefits of marriage (health insurance, survivors' benefits, and the like) to cohabiting partners, whether of the same or the opposite sex. My interpretation of historical patterns, however, suggests that it may be time to make a theoretical and conceptual distinction between marriage, which organizes mutual services and establishes ongoing rights and obligations between two adults, and family, a unit that organizes intergenerational care, obligations, and redistribution.

It makes sense from both a historical and a humane point of view to argue that our society should recognize as "family" a much wider variety of child-rearing and caregiving arrangements than it currently does and give them all social support. But it would also make sense to question whether marriage should any longer confer exclusive legal privileges or obligations on adults now that it no longer links two larger kin groups into alliances and obligations. Certainly, marriage can remain a powerful way for two individuals to declare their commitment publicly. It is not clear, however, that there is any reason to make health benefits, pensions, and other such rights contingent on a legally sanctioned sexual connection with another person, just as there is no reason that obligations to children should be easier to break if one has not entered into or has dissolved a formal legal contract with another adult.

I raise this issue because one historical trend that seems to run counter to my emphasis on the ubiquity of family diversity is that over the course of the 20th century, marriage has come to organize a smaller and smaller portion of the lives of people in all sections of the population. This situation has occurred partly because of the gradual attenuation of extended kin ties and the state's or market's assumption of the functions of family and partly because elder care and child rearing are increasingly taking place outside the bonds of marriage.

In the United States, for instance, the age of marriage has reached a world historic high for women and tied its previous high of 1890 for men. Thus, young people are living longer outside the institution of marriage than ever before. At the other end of life, a person who reaches age 60 can expect to live another 27 years and is unlikely to be cared for during all this time by a marriage partner. In between, the growing prevalence of divorce and unwed motherhood means that marriage is simply less central to family formation and the organization of interpersonal ties than ever before (Coontz, 1997).

Some people, usually associated with the so-called family values movement, believe that we can and should reverse these trends through a campaign to "reinstitutionalize" marriage. Others think that we cannot turn back the long-range historical tide of alternatives to marriage and must therefore construct interpersonal rights and obligations on a different site. Such contemporary debates flow directly from the study of how families have varied and changed over time and are obviously worth serious discussion. For now, I raise them only to make the point that recognizing the diversity of family history does not preclude seeing patterns of change.

As I discussed earlier, there is no universal definition of family that fits the reality of all cultural groups and historical periods. Yet almost all societies use the term to single out certain biological connections (or imputed biological connections) as having special social weight. If family is defined as a particular *relationship* between social and biological reproduction, it follows that there is unlikely to be only one such relationship in any even moderately complex society. Groups with different positions in the rank or class structure have to reproduce their positions in distinctive ways, both biologically and socially; therefore, they make different demands on families and family members. But because groups and individuals have unequal access to power, resources, or ideology, the relationship between social and biological reproduction that is codified in law and ideology tends to represent the interests and ideals of the dominant members of the society. We need to study the interaction between and within families that are socially legitimated by the dominant structure and those that are constructed by different subgroups, looking for the compromises or contradictions that emerge from the interactions among different families and the larger modes of social reproduction in which they operate. Diversity is not "an intrinsic property of groups that are 'different.'" Instead, it is the product of concrete social relationships that structure the experience of *all* families, albeit "in different ways" (Baca Zinn, 1994, p. 305).

In other words, within any society at any one time, there are always several different types of families. These types of families are best understood not as deviations from a central standard but as *alternative* systems by which groups with different positions in the social structure coordinate their social and personal reproduction. To gain a full understanding of family diversity, we must go beyond collecting separate examples of family variability, as I did in the first part of this chapter. Rather, we must examine the changing dynamics of distinctive but mutually dependent family systems, situated in and shaped by a particular, historically specific articulation of economic, political, and cultural forces and conflicts.

The best way I have found of conceptualizing the relationships among families in any given society is to think of them as bodies circulating within a planetary system. In each place and period, the dominant laws and ideology define one type of family as the center of the social universe. However, many different families make up the system, and they all revolve around the central source of light and heat: the prevailing structure of production, distribution, and exchange of goods or services. Each family type has its own distinctive orbit, rate of rotation, and climactic zones, all affected by its distance from the central source of power and by the competing gravitational pulls to which it is subjected.

In North America, there have been three such broad constellations of family systems. The earliest emerged from the conflict, interaction, and unequal balance of forces among three systems of social reproduction—those of Native American kinship societies, the invading Europeans, and individual

Africans or families who were torn from their own social support networks and brought as captives by the Europeans. The latter two evolved from the evolution and contradictions in the family system established between early European settlement and the war for independence from England.

FAMILIES IN THE CAULDRON OF COLONIZATION

At the time of European exploration of the New World, Native American families in North America orbited around a mode of social reproduction based on kinship ties and obligations. Kinship provided Native Americans with a system of assigning rights and duties on the basis of a commonly accepted criterion—a person's blood relationship (although this relationship might have been fictive) to a particular set of relatives. Kinship rules and marital alliances regulated an individual's place in the overall production and distribution of each group's dominant articles of subsistence and established set patterns in the individual's interactions with others.

Among groups that depended on hunting and gathering, such as those of the northern woods or Great Basin, marriage and residence rules were flexible and informal. In other Native American societies, typically those that had extensive horticulture, people were grouped into different sections, moieties or phratries, and clans, each of which was associated with different territories, resources, skills, duties, or simply personal characteristics. Exogamy, the requirement that an individual marry out of his or her natal group into a different clan or section, assured the widest possible social cooperation by making each individual a member of intersecting kin groups, with special obligations to and rights in each category of relatives. Marriage and residence rules also organized the division of labor by age and gender (Coontz, 1988; Leacock & Lurie, 1971; Spicer, 1962).

Unlike a state system, which makes sharp distinctions between family duties and civil duties, domestic functions and political ones, North American Native Americans had few institutions (prior to sustained contact with Europeans) that were set up on a basis other than kinship. Some groups, such as the Cherokee, might have had a special governing body for times of war, and the influence of such groups was invariably strengthened once Native Americans engaged in regular conflicts with settlers, but most of the time village elders made decisions. There was no opposition between domestic or "private" functions and political or public ones. North American Native Americans had no institutionalized courts, police, army, or other agencies to tax or coerce labor. Kin obligations organized production, distributed surplus products, and administered justice. Murder, for example, was an offense not against the state but against the kin group, and, therefore, it was the responsibility and right of kin to punish the perpetrator. To involve strangers in this punishment, as modern state judicial systems deem best, would have escalated the number of groups and individuals involved in the conflict (Anderson, 1991; Coontz, 1988).

The nuclear family was not a property-holding unit, since resources and land were either available to all or were held by the larger kin corporation, while subsistence tools and their products were made and owned by individuals, rather than families. Its lack of private property meant that the nuclear family had less economic autonomy vis-à-vis other families than did European households. The lack of a state, on the other hand, gave Native American families more political autonomy because people were not bound to follow a leader for any longer than they cared to do so. However, this political autonomy did not seem to create a sense of exclusive attachment to one's "own" nuclear family. The nuclear family was only one of many overlapping ties through which individuals were linked. It had almost no functions that were not shared by other social groupings (Leacock & Lurie, 1971; Spicer, 1962).

Native American kinship systems created their own characteristic forms of diversity. North American Indians spoke more than 200 languages and lived in some 600 different societies with a wide variety of residence, marital, and genealogical rules. Among nomadic foragers, residence rules were flexible and descent was seldom traced far back. Horizontal ties of marriage and friendship were more important in organizing daily life than

were vertical ties of descent. More settled groups tended to have more extensive lineage systems, in which rights and obligations were traced either through the female or the male line of descent. Most of the Great Plains and prairie Indians were patrilineal; matrilineal descent was common among many East Coast groups; the Creeks, Choctaws, and Seminoles of the South; and the Hopi, Acoma, and Zuni groups of the Southwest (Axtell, 1981, 1988; Catlin, 1973; Coontz, 1988; Gutierrez, 1991; Leacock & Luric, 1971; Mindel, Habenstein, & Wright, 1988; Peters, 1995; Snipp, 1989).

Native American family systems produced landuse and fertility patterns that helped maintain the abundance of game and forests that made the land so attractive to European settlers. But they also made the Native Americans vulnerable to diseases brought by the Europeans and their animals, as well as to the Europeans' more aggressive and coordinated methods of warfare or political expansion (Axtell, 1985, 1988; Cronon, 1983).

The impact of European colonization on Native American family systems was devastating. Massive epidemics, sometimes killing 60%–90% of a group's members, devastated kin networks and hence disrupted social continuity. Heightened warfare elevated the role of young male leaders at the expense of elders and women. In most cases, the influence of traders, colonial political officials, and Christian missionaries fostered the nuclear family's growing independence from the extended household, kinship, and community group in which it had traditionally been embedded. In other instances, as with Handsome Lake's revival movement among the Iroquois, Native Americans attempted to adapt European family systems and religious values to their own needs. Either way, gender and age relations were often transformed, while many Native American groups were either exterminated or driven onto marginal land that did not support traditional methods of social organization and subsistence. Native American collective traditions, however, were surprisingly resilient, and Euro-Americans spent the entire 19th century trying to extinguish them (Adams, 1995; Anderson, 1991; Calloway, 1997; Coontz, 1988; Mindel et al., 1988; Peters, 1995).

The European families that came to North America were products of an international mercantile system whose organizing principles of production, exchange, ownership, and land use were on a collision course with indigenous patterns of existence. Europeans also had the support of a centralized state apparatus whose claims to political authority and notion of national interests had no counterweight among Native Americans. Colonial families had far more extensive property and inheritance rights than did Native American Families, but they were also subjected to far more stringent controls by state and church institutions. The redistribution duties of wealthy families, however, were much more limited than those of Native Americans, so there were substantial differences in wealth and resources among colonial families, with the partial exception of those in the New England colonies right from the beginning (Coontz, 1988; Mintz & Kellogg, 1988).

These features of colonial society led to a different kind of family diversity than that among Native Americans. In addition to differences connected to the national, class, and religious origins of the settlers, the sex ratio of different colonizing groups, and the type of agriculture or trade they were able to establish, the colonies were also characterized by larger disparities in the wealth and size of households. Poorer colonists tended to concentrate in propertied households as apprentices, servants, or temporary lodgers.

At the same time as European settlers were destroying the Native American kinship system, they were importing an African kinship system, which they also attempted to destroy. But because the colonists depended on African labor, they had to make some accommodations to African culture and to African American adaptations to the requirements of surviving under slavery. The slaves were at once more subject to supervision and manipulation of their families and more able than Native Americans to build new kinship networks and obligations. They adapted African cultural traditions to their new realities, using child-centered, rather than marriage-centered, family systems; fictive kin ties; ritual coparenting or godparenting; and complex naming patterns that were designed to authenticate extended kin connections, all in the service of building kin ties within the interstices of the slave trade and plantation system. But African American families also had their own characteristic forms of diversity, depending on whether they lived in settlements of free blacks, on large plantations with many fellow slaves, or on isolated small farms in the South (Franklin, 1997; Gutman, 1976; Stevenson, 1996).

Slave families were not passive victims of the traffic in human beings nor organized in imitation of or deference to their masters' values. However, they could never be free of the constraints imposed by their white owners. They emerged out of a complex set of struggles and accommodations between both groups. But slaveowners' families were *also* derived from the dialectic of slavery. Anxieties about social control and racial-sexual hierarchies, fears of alliances between blacks and poor whites, and attempts to legitimate slavery in the face of Northern antislavery sentiment created a high tolerance for sexual hypocrisy; pervasive patterns of violence within white society, as well as against slaves; and elaborate rituals of patriarchy, both in family life and in the community at large (Edwards, 1991; Isaacs, 1982; McCurry, 1995; Mullings, 1997; Stevenson, 1996).

FAMILIES IN THE EARLY COMMERCIAL AND INDUSTRIALIZING ECONOMY

From about the 1820s, a new constellation of family systems emerged in the United States, corresponding to the growth of wage labor, a national market economy, and the specialization of many occupations and professions. Merchants, manufacturers, and even many farmers consolidated production and hired employees to work for a set number of hours, rather than purchased supplies or raw materials from independent producers. Such producers, along with the apprentices and journeymen whom wage workers replaced, lost older routes to self-employment or accession to family farms. At the same time, married women's traditional household production was taken over by unmarried girls working in factories.

In an attempt to avoid becoming wage laborers and to find new professions or sources of self-employment for them and their children, a growing number of middle-class families developed a more private nuclear family orientation, keeping their children at home longer instead of sending them away for training or socialization elsewhere. Meanwhile, immigrants from Europe poured into the growing towns to work in factories or tenement workshops, while westward expansion drew new Mexican and Native American groups into the economy. Such trends in the early development of American capitalism reshaped ethnic traditions and class relations and led to the emergence of "whiteness" as a category that European immigrants could use to differentiate themselves from other groups near the bottom of the economic hierarchy (Johnson, 1978; Jones, 1997; Roediger, 1988; Ryan, 1981).

The gravitational force that was pulling families into new orbits in this period was the emergence of wage labor in the context of competing older values and an inadequately developed set of formal supporting institutions for capitalist production—schools, credit associations, unions, and even a developed consumer industry. Families who sought to escape wage labor by moving west, setting up small businesses, or trying to compete with factory-made goods through household production were just as surely affected by the progress of capitalism as were families who either owned or had to work in the larger workshops and factories that increasingly supplanted apprenticeship arrangements in separate households or farms. At the same time, few families could yet free themselves from some reliance on household production or community sponsorship and social ties.

The gradual separation of work and home—market production and household reproduction—created new tensions between family activities and "economic" ones. Households could no longer get by primarily on things they made, grew, or bartered. However, they could not yet rely on ready-made purchased goods. Even in middle-class homes, the labor required to make purchased goods usable by the families was immense (Strasser, 1982).

These competing gravitational pulls produced a new division of labor among middle-class families and many workers. Men (and in working-class families, children as well) began to specialize in paid

work outside the home. Wives took greater responsibility for child care and household labor. A new ideology of parenting placed mothers at the emotional center of family life and romanticized the innocence of children, stressing the need to protect them within the family circle. What allowed middle-class white families to keep children at home longer and to divert the bulk of maternal attention from the production of clothes and food to child rearing was the inability of many working-class families to adopt such domestic patterns. The extension of childhood and the redefinition of motherhood among the middle class required the foreshortening of childhood among the slaves or sharecropping families who provided cotton to the new textile mills, the working-class women and children whose long hours in the factory made store-bought clothes and food affordable, and the Irish or free African American mothers and daughters who left their homes to work in what their mistresses insisted in defining as a domestic sanctuary, rather than a workplace. In addition to its class limitations, domesticity (along with its corollary, female purity) was constructed in opposition to the way that women of color were defined (Baca Zinn & Eitzen, 1990; Dill, 1998; Glenn, 1992).

Even as many wives gave up their traditional involvement in production for sale or barter, others followed their domestic tasks out of the household and into the factories or small workshops that made up "the sweated trades." Still, as wage labor increasingly conflicted with domestic responsibilities, most families responded by trying to keep one household member near home. Although most wives of slaves and freed blacks continued to participate in the labor force, wives in most other racial and ethnic groups were increasingly likely to quit paid work outside the home after marriage. After the Civil War, freed slaves also attempted to use new norms of sexually appropriate work to resist gang labor, in a struggle with their former masters and current landlords that helped produce the sharecropping system in the South (Hareven, 1976; Franklin 1997; Jones 1985; Lerner, 1969; Mullings 1997).

But these superficially similar family values and gender-role behaviors masked profound differences, since working-class families continued to depend on child labor and support networks of neighbors beyond the family and the work of women within the home or neighborhood varied immensely by class. For example, "unemployed" wives among the working class frequently took in boarders or lodgers, made and sold small articles or foodstuffs, and otherwise kept far too busy with household subsistence tasks to act like the leisured ladies of the upper classes or the hovering mothers of the middle classes (Boydston, 1990; Hareven, 1987).

Among the wealthy, fluid household membership and extended family ties remained important in mobilizing credit, pooling capital, and gaining political connections. In the working class, family forms diverged. Single-person and single-parent households multiplied among the growing number of transient workers. But the early factory system and its flip side, the sweated trades, reinforced the notion of the family as a productive unit, with all members working under the direction of the family head or turning their wages over to him.

After the Civil War, industrialization and urbanization accelerated. As U.S. families adapted to the demands and tensions of the industrializing society, different groups behaved in distinctive ways, but some trends could be observed. It was during this period that American families took on many of the characteristics associated with "the modern family." They became smaller, with lower fertility rates; they revolved more tightly around the nuclear core, putting greater distance between themselves and servants or boarders; parents became more emotionally involved in child rearing and for a longer period; couples oriented more toward companionate marriage; and the separation between home and work, both physically and conceptually, was sharpened (Coontz, 1988; Mintz & Kellogg, 1988).

Yet these trends obscure tremendous differences among and within the changing ethnic groups and classes of the industrializing United States. Between 1830 and 1882, more than 10 million immigrants arrived from Europe. After the Civil War, new professions opened up for middle-class and skilled workers, while job insecurity became more pronounced for laborers. Class distinctions in home furnishings, food, and household labor *widened* in

the second half of the 19th century. There was also much more variation in family sequencing and form than was to emerge in the 20th century. Young people in the 19th century exhibited fewer uniformities in the age of leaving school and home, marrying, and setting up households than they do today. No close integration between marriage and entry into the workforce existed: Young people's status as children, rather than marriage partners, determined when and where they would start work. Family decisions were far more variable and less tightly coordinated throughout the society than they would become in the 20th century (American Social History Project, 1992; Baca Zinn & Eitzen, 1990; Graff, 1987; Modell, 1989).

In addition to this diversity in the life cycle, family forms and household arrangements diverged in new ways. The long-term trend toward nuclearity slowed between 1870 and 1890 when a number of groups experienced an increase in temporary coresidence with other kin, while others took in boarders or lodgers. American fertility fell by nearly 40% between 1855 and 1915, but this average obscures many differences connected to occupation, region, race, and ethnicity. The fertility of some unskilled and semiskilled workers actually *rose* during this period (Coontz, 1988; Hareven, 1987).

Another form of family and gender-role diversity in the late 19th century stemmed from mounting contradictions and conflicts over sexuality, which was increasingly divorced from fertility. In the middle class, birth control became a fact of life, despite agitated attempts of conservatives, such as Anthony Comstock, to outlaw information on contraceptives. In the working class, fertility diverged from sexuality, in another way—not only in the growth of prostitution in the cities, but with the emergence of a group of single working women who socialized with men outside a family setting. The opportunities for unsupervised sexual behavior in the cities also increased the possibilities for same-sex relationships, and even entire subcultures, to develop (D'Emilio & Freedman, 1988).

The changes that helped produce more "modern" family forms, then, started in different classes, meant different things to families who occupied different positions in the industrial order, and did not proceed in a unilinear way. The "modernization" of the family was the result not of some general evolution of "the" family, as early family sociologists originally posited, but of *diverging* and *contradictory* responses that occurred in different areas and classes at various times, eventually interacting to produce the trends we now associate with industrialization. As Katz, Doucet, and Stern (1982, p. 317) pointed out:

> The five great changes in family organization that have occurred are: the separation of home and work place; the increased nuclearity of household structure; the decline in marital fertility; the prolonged residence of children in the home of their parents; and the lengthened period in which husbands and wives live together after their children have left home. The first two began among the working class and among the wage earning segment of the business class (clerks and kindred workers). The third started among the business class, particularly among its least affluent, most specialized, and most mobile sectors. The fourth began at about the same time in both the working and business class, though the children of the former usually went to work and the latter to school.

The fifth trend did not occur until the 20th century and represented a reversal of 19th-century trends, as did the sixth major change that has cut across older differences among families: the reintegration of women into productive work, especially the entry of mothers into paid work outside the home and the immediate neighborhood.

THE FAMILY CONSUMER ECONOMY

Around the beginning of the 20th century, a new constellation of family forms and arrangements took shape, as a consolidated national industrial system and mass communication network replaced the decentralized production of goods and culture that had prevailed until the 1890s. The standardization of economic production, spread of mass schooling into the teenage years, abolition of child labor, growth of a consumer economy, and gradual expansion of U.S. international entanglements created new similarities and differences in people's experience of family life.

In the 1920s, for the first time, a bare majority of children came to live in a male-breadwinner, female-homemaker family, in which the children were in school rather than at work. Numerous immigrant families, however, continued to pull their children out of school to go to work, often arousing intense generational conflicts. African American families kept their children in school longer than any immigrant group, but their wives were much more likely than other American women to work outside the home (Hernandez, 1993).

A major reorientation of family life occurred in the middle classes and in the dominant ideological portrayals of family life at that time. For the 19th-century middle class, the emotional center of family life had become the mother-child link and the wife's networks of female kin and friends. Now it shifted to the husband-wife bond. Although the "companionate marriage" touted by 1920s sociologists brought new intimacy and sexual satisfaction to married life, it also introduced two trends that disturbed observers. One was increased dissatisfaction with what used to be considered adequate relationships. Great expectations, as the historian May (1980) pointed out, could also generate great disappointments. These disappointments took the form of a jump in divorce rates and a change in the acceptable grounds for divorce (Coontz, 1996; May, 1980; Mintz & Kellogg, 1988; Smith-Rosenberg, 1985).

The other was the emergence of an autonomous and increasingly sexualized youth culture, as youths from many different class backgrounds interacted in high schools. The middle-class cult of married bliss and the new romance film industry led young people increasingly to stress the importance of sexual attractiveness and romantic experimentation. At the same time, the model of independent courting activity provided by working-class youths and the newly visible African American urban culture helped spread the new institution of "dating" (Bailey, 1989; D'Emilio & Freedman, 1988)

Another 20th-century trend was the state's greater intervention into the economy in response to the growth of the union movement, industry's need to regulate competition, the expanding international role of the United States, and other related factors. Families became increasingly dependent on the state and decreasingly dependent on neighborhood institutions for regulating the conditions under which they worked and lived. This change created more zones of privacy for some families but more places for state intervention in others. Sometimes the new state institutions tried to impose nuclear family norms on low-income families, as when zoning and building laws were used to prohibit the coresidence of augmented or extended families or children were taken away from single parents. But in other cases, state agencies imposed a female-headed household on the poor, as when single-parent families were the only model that entitled people to receive governmental subsidies (Gordon, 1988; Zaretsky, 1982).

Diversity, however, continued to be a hallmark of American family life. Between 1882 and 1930, more than 22 million immigrants came to America, many of them from southern and Eastern Europe, rather than from the traditional Western European suppliers of labor to the United States. They brought a whole range of new customs, religions, and traditions that interacted with their point of entry into the U.S. economy and with the new ethnic prejudices they encountered. By 1910, close to a majority of all workers in heavy industry were foreign born (Baca Zinn & Eitzen, 1990).

These immigrants enriched urban life and changed the nature of industrial struggle in the United States. They neither "assimilated" to America nor retained their old ways untouched; rather, they used their cultural resources selectively to adapt to shifting institutional constraints and opportunities. For many groups, migration to America set up patterns of life and interaction with the larger mainstream institutions that forged a new cultural identity that was quite different from their original heritage. But this identity, in turn, changed as the socioeconomic conditions under which they forged their family lives shifted (Baca Zinn & Eitzen, 1990; Glenn, 1983; Sanchez, 1993).

Space does not permit me to develop the history of diversity in 20th-century families, but one of the backdrops to the current debate about family life is that for some years there was a seeming reduction in family diversity, especially after restrictions on immigration in the 1920s began to take effect. For the first two-thirds of the 20th century, there was a growing convergence in the age and order in which young people of all income groups and geographic regions left home, left school, found jobs, and got married. The Great Depression, World War II, and the 1950s contributed to the impression of many Americans, even those in "minority" groups, that family life would become more similar over the course of the 20th century. Most families were hurt by the Great Depression, although the impact differed greatly according to their previous economic status. Marriage and fertility rates fell during the 1930s for all segments of the population; desertion rates and domestic violence increased. World War II spurred a new patriotism that reached across class and racial lines. It also disrupted or reshuffled families from all social and ethnic groups, albeit in different ways, ranging from the removal of Japanese Americans to internment camps to the surge in divorce rates as GIs came home to wives and children they barely knew (American Family History Project, 1992; Coontz, 1992; Graff, 1987; Mintz & Kellogg, 1988; see also Chapter 14, in this book).

At the end of the 1940s, for the first time in 60 years, the average age of marriage and parenthood fell, the proportion of marriages ending in divorce dropped, and the birth rate soared. The percentage of women remaining single reached a 100-year low. The percentage of children being raised by breadwinner fathers and homemaker mothers and staying in high school until graduation reached an all-time high. The impression that the United States was becoming more homogeneous was fostered by the intense patriotism and anticommunism of the period, by the decline in the percentage of foreign-born persons in the population, and by powerful new media portrayals of the "typical" American family (Coontz, 1992; May, 1988; Skolnick, 1991).

We now know, of course, that the experience of many families was literally "whited out" in the 1950s. Problems, such as battering, alcoholism, and incest, were swept under the rug. So was the discrimination against African Americans and Hispanics, women, elders, gay men, lesbians, political dissidents, religious minorities, and the handicapped. Despite rising real wages, 30% of American children lived in poverty, a higher figure than today. African American married-couple families had a poverty rate of nearly 50%, and there was daily violence in the cities against African American migrants from the South who attempted to move into white neighborhoods or use public parks and swimming areas (Coontz 1992, 1997; May, 1988).

Yet poverty rates fell during the 1950s as new jobs opened up for blue-collar workers and the government gave unprecedented subsidies for family formation, home ownership, and education of children. Forty percent of the young men who started families at the end of World War II were eligible for veterans' benefits. Combined with high rates of unionization, heavy corporate investment in manufacturing plants and equipment, and an explosion of housing construction and financing options, these subsidies gave young families a tremendous economic jump start, created predictable paths out of poverty, and led to unprecedented increases in real wages. Sociologists heralded the end of the class society, and the popular media proclaimed that almost everyone was now "middle class." Even dissidents could feel that social and racial differences were decreasing. The heroic struggle of African Americans against Jim Crow laws, for example, finally compelled the federal government to begin to enforce the Supreme Court ruling against "separate but equal" doctrines.

Despite these perceptions, diversity continued to prevail in American families, and it became more visible during the 1960s, when the civil rights and women's liberation movements exposed the complex varieties of family experiences that lay behind the Ozzie and Harriet images of the time. In the 1970s, a new set of divisions and differences began to surface. The prolonged expansion of real wages and social benefits came to an end in the 1970s. By 1973, real wages were falling for young families in particular, and by the late 1970s, tax revolts and service cuts had eroded the effectiveness of the government's antipoverty programs that had proliferated in the late 1960s and brought child poverty to an all-time low by 1970. A new wave of immigrants began to arrive, but this time the majority were from Asian, Latin American, and Caribbean countries, rather than from Europe. By the 1980s, racial and ethnic diversity was higher than it had been since the early days of colonization, while it was obvious to most Americans that the reports of the death of class difference had been greatly exaggerated (Coontz, 1992, 1997; Skolnick, 1991)

Race relations were also no longer as clear-cut as in earlier times, despite the persistence of racism. They had evolved "from a strictly-enforced caste system," in which there was unequivocal subordination of all blacks to whites to a more complex "system of power relations incorporating elements of social status, economics, and race" (Allen & Farley, 1986, p. 285). Although long-term residential segregation and discrimination in employment ensured that the deterioration of the country's inner cities would hit African Americans especially hard, resulting in deepening and concentrated poverty, some professional African Americans made impressive economic progress in the decades after the 1960s, leading to a shift in the coding of racism and often to the rediscovery of white ethnicity by Americans who were seeking to roll back affirmative action (Coontz, Parson, & Raley, 1998; Rubin, 1994; Wilson, 1978, 1996).

In one important way, family life has changed in the same direction among all groups. In 1950, only a quarter of all wives were in the paid labor force, and just 16% of all children had mothers who worked outside the home. By 1991, more than 58% of all married women in the United States, and nearly two-thirds of all married women with children, were in the labor force, and 59% of children, including a majority of preschoolers, had mothers who worked outside the home. Women of color no longer have dramatically higher rates of labor force participation than white women, nor do lower-income and middle-income groups differ substantially in the labor force participation of wives and mothers. Growing numbers of women from all social and racial-ethnic groups now combine motherhood with paid employment, and fewer of them quit work for a prolonged period while their children are young (Spain & Bianchi, 1996).

But the convergence in women's participation in the workforce has opened up new areas of divergence in family life. Struggles over the redivision of household labor have created new family conflicts and contributed to rising divorce rates, although they have also led to an increase in egalitarian marriages in which both spouses report they are highly satisfied. Women's new economic independence has combined with other social and cultural trends to produce unprecedented numbers of divorced and unwed parents, cohabiting couples (whether heterosexual, gay, or lesbian), and blended families. Yet each of these family types has different dynamics and consequences, depending on such factors as class, race, and ethnicity (Coontz, 1997; Cowan, Cowan, & Kerig, 1993; Gottfried & Gottfried, 1994; Morales, 1990). Other chapters in this book discuss these areas of diversity among contemporary families.

IMPLICATIONS OF HISTORICAL DIVERSITY FOR CONTEMPORARY FAMILIES

The amount of diversity in U.S. families today is probably no larger than in most periods of the past. But the ability of so many different family types to demand social recognition and support for their existence is truly unprecedented. Most of the con-

temporary debate over family forms and values is not occasioned by the *existence* of diversity but by its increasing *legitimation*.

Historical studies of family life can contribute two important points to these debates. First, they make it clear that families have always differed and that no one family form or arrangement can be understood or evaluated outside its particular socioeconomic context and relations with other families. Many different family forms and values have worked (or not worked) for various groups at different times. There is no reason to assume that family forms and practices that differ from those of the dominant ideal are necessarily destructive.

Second, however, history shows that families have always been fragile, vulnerable to rapid economic change, and needful of economic and emotional support from beyond the nuclear family. *All families experience internal contradictions and conflicts, as well as external pressures and stresses.* Celebrating diversity is no improvement over ignoring it unless we analyze the changing social conditions that affect families and figure out how to help every family draw on its potential resources and minimize its characteristic vulnerabilities.

REFERENCES

Adams, D. (1995). *Education for extinction: American Indians and the boarding school experience, 1877–1928.* Lawrence: University Press of Kansas.

Allen, W., & Farley, R. (1986) The shifting social and economic tides of black America, 1950–1980. *American Review of Sociology, 12.* 277–306.

American Social History Project. (1992). *Who built America? Working people and the nation's economy, politics, culture, and society* (Vols. 1 and 2). New York: Pantheon.

Anderson, K. (1991). *Chain her by one foot: The subjugation of women in seventeenth-century New France.* New York: Routledge.

Axtell, J. (1981). *The Indian peoples of eastern America: A documentary history of the sexes.* New York: Oxford University Press.

Axtell, J. (1985). *The invasion within: The contest of cultures in colonial America.* New York: Oxford University Press.

Axtell, J. (1988). *After Columbus: Essays in the ethno-*

history of colonial North America. New York: Oxford University Press.

Baca Zinn, M. (1990). Feminism, family, and race in America. *Gender & Society, 4,* 68–82.

Baca Zinn, M. (1994). Feminist thinking from racial-ethnic families. In M. B. Zinn & B. T. Dill (Eds.), *Women of color in U.S. society.* Philadelphia: Temple University Press.

Baca Zinn, M., & Eitzen, S. (1990), *Diversity in American families.* New York: HarperCollins.

Bailey, B. (1989) *From front porch to back seat: Courtship in twentieth-century America.* Baltimore: Johns Hopkins University Press.

Baumrind, D. (1972). An exploratory study of socialization effects on black children: Some black-white comparisons. *Child Development, 43,* 261–267.

Berkner, L. (1972). The stem family and the developmental cycle of the peasant household. *American Historical Review, 77,* 398–418.

Boyd-Franklin, N., & Garcia-Preto, N. (1994). Family

therapy: The cases of African American and Hispanic women. In L. Comas-Diaz & B. Greene (Eds.), *Women of color: Integrating ethnic and gender identities in psychotherapy* (pp. 239–264). New York: Guilford Press.

Boydston, J. (1990). *Home and work: Housework, wages, and the ideology of love in the early republic.* New York: Oxford University Press.

Calloway, C. (1997). *New worlds for all: Indians, Europeans, and the remaking of early America.* Baltimore: Johns Hopkins University Press.

Calvert, K. (1992). *Children in the house.* Boston: Northeastern University Press.

Catlin, G. (1973). *Letters and notes on the manners, customs and conditions of the North American Indians.* New York: Dover.

Collier, J., Rosaldo, M., & Yanigasako, S. (1982). Is there a family? New anthropological views. In B. Thorne (Ed.), *Rethinking the family* (pp. 25–39). White Plains, NY: Longman.

Coontz, S. (1988). *The social origins of private life: A history of American families, 1600–1900.* London: Verso.

Coontz, S. (1992). *The way we never were: American families and the nostalgia trap.* New York: Basic Books.

Coontz, S. (1996). Where are the good old days? *Modern Maturity, 34,* 36–43.

Coontz, S. (1997). *The way we really are: Coming to terms with America's changing families.* New York: Basic Books.

Coontz, S., Parson, M., & Raley, G. (Eds.). (1998). *American families: A multicultural reader.* New York: Routledge.

Cowan, P., Cowan, C., & Kerig, P. (Eds.). (1993). *Family, self, and society: Toward a new agenda for family research.* Hillsdale, NJ: Lawrence Erlbaum.

Cronon, W. (1983). *Changes in the land: Indians, colonists, and the ecology of New England.* New York: Hill & Wang.

D'Emilio, J., & Freedman, E. (1988). *Intimate matters: A history of sexuality in America.* New York: Harper & Row.

Dill, B. T. (1998). Fictive kin, paper sons, and *Compadrazgo:* Women of color and the struggle for family survival. In S. Coontz, M. Parson & G. Raley (Eds.), *American families* (pp. 2–19). New York: Routledge.

Duberman, M., Vicinus, M., & Chauncey, G. (1989). *Hidden from history: Reclaiming the gay and lesbian past.* New York: New American Library.

Edwards. L. (1991). Sexual violence, gender, reconstruction, and the extension of patriarchy in Granville County, North Carolina. *North Carolina Historical Review, 68,* 237–260.

Faderman, L. (1981). *Surpassing the love of men: Romantic friendship and love between women from the Renaissance to the present.* New York: William Morrow.

Franklin, D. (1997). *Ensuring inequality: The structural transformation of the African-American family.* New York: Oxford University Press.

Gillis, J. (1996). *A world of their own making: Myth, ritual, and the quest for family values.* New York: Basic Books.

Glenn, E. N. (1983). Split household, small producer, and dual wage-earner. *Journal of Marriage and the Family, 45,* 35–46.

Glenn, E. N. (1992). From servitude to service work: Historical continuities in the racial division of paid reproductive labor. *Signs, 18,* 1–43.

Gordon, L. (1988). *Heroes of their own lives: The politics and history of family violence, Boston 1880–1960.* New York: Viking.

Gottfried, A., & Gottfried, A. (1994) *Redefining families: Implications for children's development.* New York: Plenum.

Graff, H. (Ed.). (1987). *Growing up in America: Historical experiences.* Detroit: Wayne State University Press.

Gutierrez, R. (1991). *When Jesus came, The corn mothers went away: Marriage, sexuality, and power in New Mexico, 1500–1846.* Stanford, CA: Stanford University Press.

Gutman, H. (1976). *The black family in slavery and freedom, 1750–1925.* New York: Pantheon.

Hareven, T. (1976). Women and men: Changing roles. In L. A. Cater, A. F. Scott, & W. Martyna (Eds.), *Women and men: Changing roles, relationships and perceptions Report of a workshop* (pp. 93–118). Palo Alto, CA: Aspen Institute for Humanistic Studies.

Hareven, T. (1987). Historical analysis of the family. In M. B. Sussman & S. K. Steinmetz, (Eds.), *Handbook of marriage and the family.* New York: Plenum.

Hawkes, J. (1973). *The first great civilizations: Life in Mesopotamia, the Indus Valley, and Egypt.* New York: Alfred A. Knopf.

Herdt, G., (Ed.). (1994). *Third sex, Third gender: Beyond sexual dimorphism in culture and History.* New York: Zone.

Hernandez, D. (1993). *America's children: Resources from family, government, and the economy.* New York: Russell Sage Foundation.

Howard, E. A., Heighton, R., Jordan, C., & Gallimore, R.

(1970), Traditional and modern adoption patterns in Hawaii. In V. Carroll, (Ed.), *Adoption in Eastern Oceania*. Honolulu: University of Hawaii Press.

Ingoldsby, B., & Smith, S. (Eds.). (1995). *Families in multicultural perspective*. New York: Guilford Press.

Isaacs, R. (1982). *The transformation of Virginia, 1740–1790*. Chapel Hill: University of North Carolina Press.

Jeater, D. (1993). *Marriage, perversion, and power: The construction of moral discourse in Southern Rhodesia, 1894–1930*. New York: Oxford University Press.

Johnson, P. (1978). *A shopkeeper's millennium: Society and revivals in Rochester, New York, 1815–1837*. New York: Hill & Wang.

Jones, J. (1985). *Labor of love, Labor of sorrow: Black women, work, and the family from slavery to the present*. New York: Basic Books.

Jones, J. (1997). *American work: Four centuries of black and white labor*. New York: W. W. Norton.

Katz, M., Doucet, M., & Stern, M. (1982). *The social organization of industrial capitalism*. Cambridge, MA: Harvard University Press.

Knight, G. P., Virdin, L. M., & Roosa, M. (1994). Socialization and family correlates of mental health outcomes among Hispanic and Anglo-American children. *Child Development, 65*, 212–224.

Leacock, E. (1980). Montagnais women and the program for Jesuit colonization. In M. Etienne & E. Leacock, (Eds.), *Women and colonization: Anthropological perspectives*. New York: Praeger.

Leacock, E., & Lurie, N. O. (1971). *North American Indians in historical perspective*. New York: Random House.

Leibowitz, L. (1978). *Females, males, families: A biosocial approach*. North Scituate, MA: Duxbury Press.

Lerner, G. (1969). The lady and the mill girl: Changes in the status of women in the age of Jackson, 1800–1840. *Midcontinent American Studies Journal, 10*, 5–14.

May, E. T. (1980). *Great expectations: Marriage and divorce in post-Victorian America*. Chicago: University of Chicago Press.

May, E. T. (1988). *Homeward bound: American families in the cold war era*. New York: Basic Books.

McCurry, S. (1995). *Masters of small worlds: Yeoman households, gender relations, and the political culture of the antebellum South Carolina Low Country*. New York: Oxford University Press.

Mindel, C., Habenstein, R., & Wright, R, (Eds.). (1988), *Ethnic families in America: Patterns and variations*. New York: Elsevier.

Mintz, S., & Kellogg, S. (1988). *Domestic revolutions: A social history of American family life*. New York: Free Press.

Modell, J. (1989). *Into one's own: From youth to adulthood in the United States, 1920–1975*. Berkeley: University of California Press.

Morales, E. S. (1990). Ethnic minority families and minority gays and lesbians. In F. W. Bozett & M. B. Sussman (Eds.), *Homosexuality and family relations*. (pp. 217–239) New York: Harrington Park Press.

Morris, P. (1993). Incest or survival strategy? Plebian marriage within the prohibited degrees in Somerset, 1730–1835. In J. C. Fout, (Ed.), *Forbidden history: The state, society, and the regulation of sexuality in modern Europe*. Chicago: University of Chicago Press.

Mullings, L. (1997). *On our own terms: Race, class, and gender in the lives of African-American women*. New York: Routledge.

Padgug, R. (1989). Sexual matters: Rethinking sexuality in history. In M. B. Duberman, M. Vicinus, & G. Chauncey, Jr. (Eds.), *Hidden From History: Reclaiming the gay and lesbian past* (pp. 54–64). New York: New American Library.

Peters, V. (1995). *Women of the earth lodges: Tribal life on the Plains*. North Haven, CT: Archon Books.

Peterson, J. (1993). Generalized extended family exchange: A case from the Philippines. *Journal of Marriage and the Family, 55*, 570–584.

Roediger, D. (1988). *The wages of whiteness: Race and the making of the American working class*. London: Verso.

Rotundo, A. (1993). *American manhood*. New York: Basic Books.

Rubin, L. (1994). *Families on the fault line*. New York: Basic Books.

Ryan, M. (1981). *Cradle of the middle class: The family in Oneida County, New York*. New York: Cambridge University Press.

Sanchez, G. (1993). *Becoming Mexican-American: Ethnicity, culture, and identity in Chicano Los Angeles, 1900–1945*. New York: Oxford University Press.

Schnarch, B. (1992). Neither man nor woman: Berdache—A case for non-dichotomous gender construction. *Anthropologica, 34*, 106–121.

Skolnick, A. (1991). *Embattled paradise: The American family in an age of uncertainty*. New York: Basic Books.

Smith-Rosenberg, C. (1985). *Disorderly women: Visions of gender in Victorian America*. New York: Oxford University Press.

Snipp, M. (1989). *American Indians: The first of this land.* New York: Russell Sage Foundation.

Spain, D., & Bianchi, S. M. (1996). *Balancing act: Motherhood, marriage, and employment among American women.* New York: Russell Sage Foundation.

Spicer, E. H. (1962). *Cycles of conquest: The impact of Spain, Mexico, and the United States on the Indians of the Southwest, 1533–1960.* Tucson: University of Arizona Press.

Stack, C. (1993). Cultural perspectives on child welfare. in M. Minow (Ed.), *Family matters: Readings on family lives and the law* (pp. 344–349). New York: New Press.

Stevenson, B. E. (1996). *Life in black and white: Family and community in the slave South.* New York: Oxford University Press.

Strasser, S. (1982). *Never done: A history of American housework.* New York: Pantheon.

Wilson, W. J. (1978). *The declining significance of race: Blacks and changing American institutions.* Chicago: University of Chicago.

Wilson, W. J. (1996). *When work disappears: The world of the new urban poor.* New York: Alfred A. Knopf.

Williams, R. (1976). *Keywords: A vocabulary of culture and society.* New York: Oxford University Press.

Williams, W. L. (1986). *The spirit and the flesh: Sexual diversity in American Indian culture.* Boston: Beacon Press.

Zaretsky, E. (1982). The place of the family in the origins of the welfare state. In B. Thorne (Ed.), *Rethinking the family* (pp. 188–224). White Plains, NY: Longman.

CHAPTER 3

Diversity of Family Structure:
Economic and Social Influences*

JAY D. TEACHMAN

In this chapter, I address diversity in the demographic structure of American families as shaped by economic and social forces. I place particular emphasis on changes in the economic fortunes of Americans that have altered their ability to realize particular family types. As a family demographer, my interest in the social and economic forces shaping American families was stimulated in 1984 when I heard Preston (1984) give his presidential address at the annual meeting of the Population Association of America (PAA). In his talk, Preston noted a radical shift in the composition of Americans living in poverty—from mostly older individuals to children. Using his talk as a springboard, together with additional reading and thought, convinced me that the structure of the American economy has changed and that this change has serious implications for the way Americans structure their family lives.

Although the economy has changed in many ways, there are three points that strike me as being particularly important for understanding why families are the way they are. First, the average American family has made relatively little economic progress since 1973. In no other time in American history has such a prolonged period of economic stagnation occurred. Although the economic fortunes of American families have marginally improved over the past 25 years, it is apparent that we can no longer expect that, as a matter of course, children will be better off than their parents—the American Dream for a continuously improving future appears to be gone or, at least, on a long hiatus.

Second, although the average change in family income indicates little economic gain, a closer look reveals tremendous diversity in the economic fortunes of American families. The average is the result of the counterbalancing of opposite fortunes. Some families have done quite well, while others have floundered. Families with more education and good labor market skills have flourished, whereas those with little education and poor labor market skills have seen their economic fortunes stagnate or actually decline. Thus, the economic climate facing America's families is not only uncertain, but uneven.

Third, many American families have dealt with economic uncertainty and have kept their standard of living from falling dramatically by the movement of wives and mothers into the labor force. Over the past 20 years, men have lost earning power, and this loss has been largely made up by the participation of women in the labor market. As the economic fate of men has worsened, that of women has improved. To be sure, women still earn much less than do men, but the heterogeneity in their earnings has decreased over time while the heterogeneity of men's earnings has increased. The traditional division of responsibility for economic support has begun to change. Men are no longer the sole breadwinners in most American families.

These three changes trace the outlines of a new economic reality that families in America have been facing. There has been a substantial erosion in well-paying manufacturing jobs that, in the past, allowed men with even limited education to support families with the "traditional" division of labor. While the income of men has stagnated and the country has witnessed increasing inequality between the rich

*Support was provided by grant HD-31723 from the National Institute of Child Health and Human Development.

and the poor, the income of women has grown and has become more equal to that of men (Gottschalk & Danziger, 1993). One important result has been that women have become a critical source of economic support to families. Although this has long been true for African American families, it is now true for the majority of families.

I believe that the changing economic basis of family life and the changes implied for the roles of men and women have altered the processes by which families form and dissolve. One result is increasing diversity in the family experiences of Americans. No longer can it be assumed that American women and men will marry young, bear children, and live their lives with the same partners. Indeed, the definition of what constitutes a family has been called into question.

Changes in the roles of men and women have been most dramatic when it comes to work outside the home. As I note later, the majority of married women now work outside the home. It is less clear that there has been a substantial change in work roles inside the home; most research has indicated that women still perform the majority of household chores (Goldscheider & Waite, 1991). However, the combination of work outside and inside the home has radically altered the amount of work performed by women and therefore the division of labor between men and women.

BACKGROUND

As I mentioned earlier, my interest in family diversity began with Preston's address given at the annual meeting of the PAA. The PAA is an association of demographers, and demographers have had a long-standing interest in the structure of families. For example, demographers have traditionally asked questions like these: How many families are there? How many families have children? What is the income of the average American family? How many families are disrupted by divorce? The basic idea has been to provide a snapshot of American families at a given time. Demographers have also been interested in changes in family structure over time, as well as differences in family structure across major population subgroups.

My training as a demographer gave me the tools to answer the typical questions demographers ask. What Preston's (1984) talk did was to lead me to ask a different type of question. In particular, upon reflection, I was struck by the fact that demographers had little idea why major subgroups of the population have different family experiences. It was clear to me that the next great challenge facing demographers was not simply to describe family structure, but to provide reasonable explanations for changes and diversity in it. It is only with such explanations that demographers could join the growing debate about the future of the family.

To be sure, demographers have always had some idea about why families change. Crude concepts about the family life cycle (Teachman, 1994; Teachman, Polonko, & Scanzoni, 1987) have long been part of the field. Unfortunately, the family life cycle is more of a taxonomy of change than an explanation, and it has limited usefulness for understanding family diversity for population subgroups at similar points in the life cycle. Moreover, it is rooted in mainstream expectations about the patterning of family events. Recognizing these limitations, demographers have begun the struggle to provide better frameworks for understanding the diversity of family life in America.

It would be incorrect to assume that all demographers use the same conceptual framework to explain family change and diversity. However, I believe that my view is not too different from that of a large number of demographers. I begin with a few simple assumptions. First, most Americans want to live their lives in a family (see the next section for my definition of what constitutes a family) and to have children and provide them with a good future. Second, diversity is shaped by the choices that individuals make about family life. Third, these choices are shaped by two major factors: (1) values and (2) external constraints that limit available choices.

Although values are certainly an important consideration in relation to family diversity, my preference is to begin with a consideration of external constraints. On the one hand, I have already specified the major values I believe most Americans hold in common about family life: They want to live in families, have children, and provide them with a secure future. Additional differences in values are likely to affect variations on this major theme. On the other hand, external constraints may alter an individual's ability to satisfy even these basic values.

I am also concerned that values are often used to explain behavior when external constraints are really the culprit. This type of oversight is particularly hurtful when the behavior being examined is central to our value structure. For example, most Americans would agree that it is the responsibility of parents to provide for the well-being of their children. If a particular subgroup has greater difficulty doing so because they are denied access to key resources, does it do us any good to blame their predicament on their poor values? As I describe later, this is the situation that many mother-headed families face. If we ignore the limited resources available to these women, are we any closer to developing policies that will enable them to better provide for their children? I would argue not.

Finally, because I believe that differences in resources can go a long way toward explaining family diversity, at least at a structural level, I pay attention to subgroups who are the most clearly disadvantaged in terms of economic resources—African Americans and mothers who are heads of families. As I show in this chapter, much of the diversity in family structure can be traced to differences in resources, particularly economic resources. If we are to understand how families organize themselves and what the future holds for them, we must understand the economic environment within which choices are being made.

Defining the Family

America is made up of families, not the family. That is, there are many family types: two-parent families, one-parent families, cohabiting couples, gay and lesbian families, and so on. To attempt a definition of families that encompasses all possible variations is a difficult task. However, the assumption underlying my discussion of families is that they represent various ways in which couples in intimate relationships organize themselves to adapt to their social and economic surroundings. I pay particular attention to families as a means of reproduction. As

I discussed earlier, the bearing and rearing of children is an activity that is central to almost all types of families.

Despite my more encompassing definition of the family, I am forced by the availability of data to make use of official statistics (largely from the census or the Current Population Survey) that all assume a legal definition of marriage and the family. The census defines a *family* as "a group of two persons or more (one of whom is a householder) related by birth, marriage or adoption and residing together," *married couple* as a "husband and wife enumerated as members of the same household," and an *unmarried couple* as "two unrelated adults of the opposite sex (one of whom is the householder) who share a housing unit with or without the presence of children under 15 years old" (U.S. Bureau of the Census, 1995a, pp B1–B4). Although these definitions may reflect a conservative view of the family, they are also the result of two methodological challenges. First, the diversity of American families defies categorization into family types that can be easily represented on interview schedules. Second, there is often public opposition to the government obtaining more than limited information about the family lives of Americans.

Even within the official definition of what constitutes a family, I am further limited by the fact that information is often not available for subgroups of the population. For example, because the questions have not been asked, it is difficult to obtain information about Native American or Asian American families (particularly data that allow a perspective across time). The information we have about finely grained subgroups of the American population that may contribute substantially to diversity in family form and function is often based on anecdotal evidence and small, nonrepresentative samples.

I do not mean to say that smaller, nonrepresentative samples are not useful for understanding families. Indeed, much of our understanding about diversity in American families comes from such samples. However, data from nonrepresentative samples cannot provide us with information on levels and trends that can be compared to other groups. Thus, while process may be illustrated well with nonrepresentative samples, structure is not. And for the purposes of this chapter, it is the structure of American families, particularly as it has changed across time and varied across important subgroups of the population, in which I am most interested. Thus, the data that I present indicate changes in officially defined families for relatively large and well-documented population groups—whites, African Americans, and sometimes Hispanics.

Outline of Topics

I begin by considering trends in marriage, divorce, and remarriage and assessing them for the changing context of childbearing and changes in the living arrangements of children. Next, I outline the retreat of men from and the advance of women into the labor market, evaluating these trends within the context of the changing economic fortunes of fam-

ilies. I conclude by assessing the available data for what they may indicate about the decline in family life in America.

When possible, I provide data on whites, African Americans, and Hispanics. I also attempt to provide a deeper understanding of the data by drawing on relevant research findings. The conclusions to be drawn are not always clear except that American families have undergone and are continuing to experience substantial changes.

CHANGES IN MARRIAGE, DIVORCE, AND REMARRIAGE

Long-term shifts in rates of marriage, divorce, and remarriage from 1921–23 to 1987–89 are shown in Figure 3.1. The rate of marriage is defined as first marriages per 1,000 single women aged 15–44. The

FIGURE 3.1
Rates of Marriage, Divorce and Remarriage: 1921–23 to 1987–89

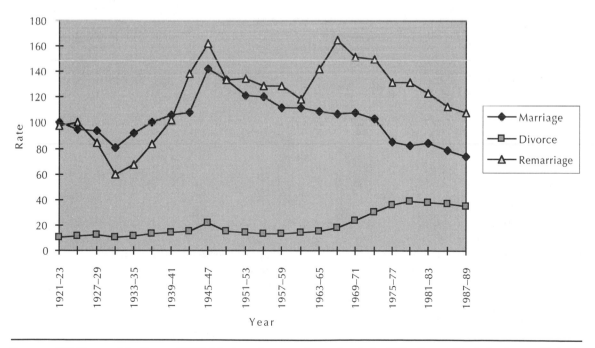

Source: U.S. Bureau of the Census, (1992). Marriage, divorce, and remarriage in the 1990s. *Current Population Reports* (Series P-23, No. 180).

rate of divorce is defined as divorces per 1,000 married women aged 15–44. The rate of remarriage is defined as remarriages per 1,000 widowed and divorced women aged 15–54.

There has been a consistent decline in the rate of marriage since the end of World War II. The high rates of marriage in the 1945–47 period were tied to the end of World War II, the return of veterans to civilian life, and the exit of women from the industrial labor force. In 1989, the rate of marriage was as low or lower than that observed during the Great Depression, and the rate of divorce slowly, but steadily increased over the period covered. The increase in the divorce rate was particularly great during the 1970s but slowed considerably afterward. The rate of remarriage generally followed the decline in the rate of marriage with the exception of an upward spike in remarriage in the first half of the 1960s.

The trends shown in Figure 3.1 indicate a general decline over time in the formation of marriages and an increase over time in the dissolution of marriages. These trends reflect the pattern of change in most Western, industrialized nations (Kammerman, 1995). Rates of marriage and divorce have converged since the late 1940s, with the differential in the 1980s being particularly small. These trends imply that as time passed, a smaller proportion of adults married and remained married to the same persons. In particular, it implies that the context within which childbearing occurs has altered substantially. These are points to which I return later.

Marriage

Figures 3.2 and 3.3 provide a more elaborate description of the changes in marriage that occurred between 1975 and 1994. They depict trends in spe-

FIGURE 3.2
Percentage of Women Aged 20–24 Ever Married

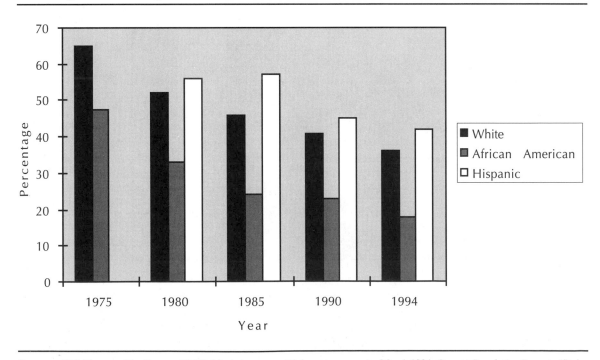

Source: U.S. Bureau of the Census. (1996). Marital status and living arrangements: March 1994, *Current Population Reports*, (Series P-20, No. 484).

FIGURE 3.3
Percentage of Women Aged 35–39 Ever Married

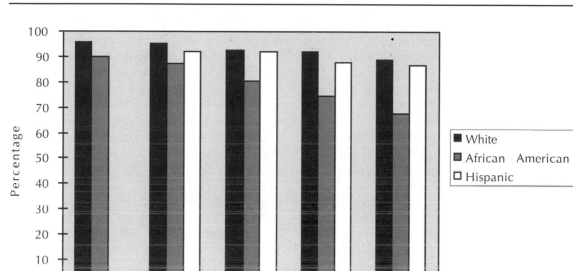

Source: U.S. Bureau of the Census. (1996). Marital status and living arrangements: March 1994, *Current Population Reports*, (Series P-20, No. 484).

cific age groups which are not affected by shifts in the age structure of the American population. This is not true of Figure 3.1. Thus, at least part of the shifts in rates shown in Figure 3.1 can be attributed to changes in age structure. For example, part of the upswing in divorce during the 1970s can be attributed to the substantial increase in marriages of short duration (in which the risk of divorce is high) associated with the first marriages of members of the baby-boom cohort.

Figure 3.2 shows the trend in the percentage of women aged 20–24 by racial-ethnic status who had ever been married. The changes illustrated are dramatic. Among whites, the percentage of women aged 20–24 who were ever married declined by about 28 percentage points between 1975 and 1994. In the 1990s, only slightly more than one-third of the white women in this age group had ever mar-

ried. Among African Americans, the decline was also about 28 percentage points. But because African American women were less likely to be married in the first place, the decline resulted in only about one-fifth of African American women aged 20–24 in the 1990s having been married.

The change observed for Hispanic women is much less dramatic. The percentage of Hispanic women aged 20–24 who were ever married changed little between 1980 and 1985. Between 1985 and 1994, however, Hispanics witnessed about a 14 percentage-point decline in the proportion of women in this age group who were ever married. Still, Hispanic women in the 1990s were more likely than either African American or white women to have formed marriages by age 20–24.

Moving to a point later in the life course, Figure 3.3 shows the trend over time in the percentage of women aged 35–39 by racial-ethnic status who were ever married. Historically, women who did not marry by age 35–39 remained single; thus, these percentages approximate permanent singlehood. Of course, these figures do not represent the percentage of women who form nonmarital unions. As I discuss later, part of the decline in marriage has been matched by an increase in the rate at which nonmarital unions are formed. For whites, there was relatively little change in permanent singlehood from 1975 to 1994. Over 90% of white women ever married. A slightly lower percentage of Hispanic women ever married, and this percentage did not change much over time either.

For African Americans, there has been a much more substantial change in permanent singlehood over time. The percentage of women who were ever married by age 35–39 declined from nearly 90% in 1975 to about two-thirds in 1994. This result implies that nearly 1 in 3 African American women will never form legal marriages. This is an extremely large proportion and indicates a swift retreat from legal marriage in the African American population.

The evidence is consistent in showing a retreat from early marriage for all racial-ethnic groups for which there is reliable information and a decline in ever marriage for African American women. What factors may explain these trends? There are several likely scenarios. The most common explanations in the literature often include some combination of the following.

First, some authors have suggested that the rise of the welfare state has negated the economic role of marriage, particularly for low-income women (Murray, 1984). Why should women marry if they can obtain similar or greater economic support from Aid to Families with Dependent Children (AFDC), food stamps, and Medicaid, particularly if the economic future of their potential husbands is highly uncertain? Although this argument seems to fit the decline in early marriage, especially for low-income women, and the overall retreat from marriage for African American women, few researchers have found consistent evidence that welfare benefits reduce the likelihood of marriage (Moffitt, 1990, 1992; Schultz, 1994). And those who have

found an effect have not found it to be substantively important (Lichter, LeClere, & McLaughlin, 1991; McLanahan & Casper, 1995). Moreover, rates of marriage have continued to decline at the same time as the value of AFDC benefits has declined dramatically (Schultz, 1994). The most consistent evidence for a welfare effect is that it appears to encourage young unmarried women who become pregnant to set up their own households, rather than remain at home with their parents (Moffitt, 1994).

Second, it has been proposed that the increasing value that Americans have placed on individualism has decreased the perceived benefits of marriage (Bellah, Madsen, Swidler, Sullivan, & Tipton, 1985; South, 1992, 1993). While attractive in its simplicity, this argument is difficult to test empirically. Are the views of Americans on marriage changing because people cannot otherwise attain the marital ideals of their parents, or is the change in their marital behavior a result of their changed views toward marriage? As I discuss later, the importance of a change in values about marriage is most often mentioned as an alternative when other sources of change have been considered and found wanting. A change in values as an indicator of the decline in families in America is a topic to which I return at the conclusion of this chapter.

Third, two interrelated arguments concerning the growth in the economic independence of women and the decline in the economic power of men have been proposed. Both arguments assume that one of the major functions of marriage is to provide economic security, particularly for the bearing and rearing of children. Becker (1981) emphasized the exchange between home and market production that is threatened by the growing ability of women to support themselves outside marriage (which reduces their need to exchange home production for the market production of their husbands). Wilson (1987) argued that the decline in job opportunities for young African American men, particularly in inner cities, has sharply eroded the men's ability to form and support families. In line with Wilson's argument, other researchers have documented the declining economic prospects of young men, both African American and white, who came of age in the 1970s and 1980s (Duncan,

Boisjoly, & Smeeding, 1996; Levy & Murnane, 1992).

Taken together, these two arguments appear to offer a promising explanation of changes in marriage across time, including the observed differences between whites and African Americans. The earning power of both white women and African American women increased substantially over the past two decades, while the earning power of white men has stagnated and that of African American men has declined (as discussed later). What has the research found when these changes are juxtaposed with shifts in marriage formation?

McLanahan and Casper (1995) found that for white men, marriage is more common when they are employed, have more education, and have higher incomes, whereas for white women, marriage is less common when they are employed, have more education, and have higher incomes. For African Americans, the economic characteristics of women are not important for predicting marriage, while the economic characteristics of men are less important than for whites. McLanahan and Casper argued that increases in women's earning power explain about 70% of the decline in marriage for white women, but decreases in men's earning power explain only 8% of the decline in marriage for white men. For African Americans, neither the increased earning power of women nor the decreased earning power of men explains much of the decline in marriage.

Moreover, hardly any of the racial difference in the propensity to marry can be explained by race-specific economic characteristics. This finding is consistent with those of other studies (Ellwood & Crane, 1990; Levy & Michael, 1991) that focused on the relative economic position of men and women; that is, racial differences in the relative economic position of men and women cannot explain racial differences in marriage. Thus, the difference between African Americans and whites in marriage, as well as the decline across time in marriage among African Americans, appears to be due to some factor other than the relative earnings of men and women. Accordingly, as I discussed earlier, one is tempted to return to such arguments as differences in the value of marriage to explain race-

specific variations in marital formation. First, additional structural factors affecting marriage need to be considered.

For example, while the characteristics of individuals (e.g., their education and income) are undoubtedly important factors in determining when and if marriage will occur, marital decisions are made in a larger structural context. In particular, it has been argued that the availability of suitable spouses in a local marriage market is an important determinant of marital behavior (Lichter et al., 1991; Lichter, McLaughlin, Kephart, & Landry, 1992; Lloyd & South, 1996; South & Lloyd, 1992). Marriage depends not only on one's personal characteristics, but on the characteristics of one's competitors and on the availability of suitable spouses. Thus, the likelihood of marriage decreases even for individuals with the most desirable traits if there is a shortage of potential spouses with suitable or preferred characteristics.

The evidence on the role of marriage-market conditions indicates the importance of local context. A number of studies have shown that the availability of economically attractive men is positively linked to rates of marriage after individual characteristics are accounted for (Lichter et al., 1991; Lichter et al., 1992; Lloyd & South, 1996; South & Lloyd, 1992). The characteristics of both individuals and the marriage market in which they find themselves are important in determining when and if marriage will occur.

With these results in mind, it is possible that the source of the African American–white differential in marriage may lie in the character of the marriage markets in which the two groups are located, if not their individual characteristics. For instance, African American women tend to live in areas where marriage market conditions are much worse than is the case for white women (Fossett & Kiecolt, 1991; Lichter et al., 1992). Indeed, the true heart of Wilson's (1987) argument is that it is the decline in the pool of "marriageable" men in local marriage markets that has led to the retreat from marriage among African Americans.

Do differences in local marriage markets explain the different marriage behavior of African Americans and whites? To some extent, the answer is yes.

As Lichter et al. (1992) pointed out, differences in local marriage markets do more to explain the differences in marriage than do individual characteristics. However, the explanation is far from perfect. Only about one-fifth of the difference in rates of marriage can be explained by variations in local marriage markets. Similar results have been obtained by other researchers (Mare & Winship, 1991; Testa, Astone, Krogh, & Neckerman, 1991).

Two additional issues illustrate the difficulty in pinpointing racial differences in marriage (and therefore our ability to explain rates of marriage). First, nonmarital cohabitation has increased substantially in recent years. African Americans are much more likely to cohabit nonmaritally than are whites (Shoen & Owens, 1992). Indeed, if one considers nonmarital cohabitation as a marital union, racial differences in marriage are substantially, if not totally, explained (Bumpass, Sweet, & Cherlin, 1991; Qian & Preston, 1993).

If one is willing to consider nonmarital unions, then there are many fewer differences between whites and African Americans in ever having formed a union. However, nonmarital unions are much less stable than marital unions, and African Americans are much less likely than whites to convert nonmarital unions into marriages (Manning & Smock, 1995; Schoen & Owens, 1992). Thus, a consideration of nonmarital unions does not yield similar experiences in the number and duration of unions as does a consideration of legal marriages. Nor is it clear that nonmarital unions fulfill the same functions as marital unions (Brown & Booth, 1996; Nock, 1995; Rindfuss & VandenHeuvel, 1990). Additional research is needed to gain a better understanding of the nature and role of nonmarital unions for various racial and ethnic groups.

A second issue confounding the interpretation of racial differences in marriage is that there is some evidence that more recent cohorts of women have responded differently to their economic independence than did earlier cohorts. That is, whereas early evidence suggested that participation in the labor market and higher wages tended to reduce the likelihood that a woman would marry (Espenshade, 1985; Farley & Bianchi, 1987; Lichter et al., 1991; Teachman, Polonko, & Leigh, 1987), evidence for more recent cohorts of women suggests that the reverse is true (Lichter et al., 1992).

This finding implies that marriage is contextualized not only by local marriage markets but by historical period. Among more recent cohorts of women, financial resources either make women more attractive or allow them to form marriages. In part, this finding is likely to stem from the stagnant or declining economic prospects of young men (Duncan et al., 1996). Since it has become increasingly clear that men's wages are insufficient to provide the economic resources needed for marriage, the economic resources of women have become more important in meeting the basic needs of couples. There is some evidence that this has been the case for African American women much longer than for white women (McLanahan & Casper, 1995).

This pattern suggests that an understanding of changes in marital formation and differences that occur among racial/ethnic groups is likely to rest on a variety of individual and contextual conditions. Thus, although it is tempting to resort to an explanation of trends and differences that relies on shifts in the value of marriage, the evidence is not sufficiently strong to point clearly in this direction. This is not to say that values concerning marriage are not important. South (1992, 1993) found that the desire to marry varies among racial/ethnic groups in a way that is consistent with observed racial/ethnic differences in marriage. However, shifts in values are likely to be closely interwoven with changes in individual and contextual opportunities and constraints. Clearly, we have a long way to go to understand fully the timing and certainty of marriage among Americans.

Divorce

With this caveat in mind, I now shift to a consideration of marital stability. I begin with a simple, yet useful, assumption: If one assumes that marriage is becoming less valued and less important as a source of economic stability and exchange, it makes sense to expect an increase in marital dissolution in addition to a retreat from early marriage. Figure 3.4 indicates that this is the case. The proportion of

FIGURE 3.4
Percentage of Women Aged 40–44 Divorced After First Marriage

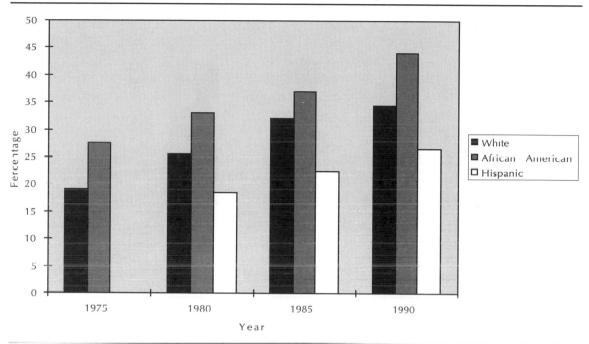

Source: U.S. Bureau of the Census. (1992). Marriage, divorce and remarriage in the 1990s, *Current Population Reports* (Series P-23, No. 180).

first-married women who were divorced from their first marriages by age 40–44 rose from 1975 to 1990 for all racial/ethnic groups (see also the trend in divorce rates in Figure 3.1).

The percentage of women aged 40–44 who were divorced from their first marriages underestimates the percentage of women who were ever divorced. The measure misses women who ended their first marriages at an older age and women who dissolved their second or higher-order marriages. However, trends in divorce are accurately captured by the percentage of this age group who ended their marriages.

For whites, the increase was particularly large from 1975 to 1985 (20%–30%, or 10 percentage points) with some slowing in the 1985–90 period (30%–33%). For African Americans, the increase was more consistent—from slightly less than 30% in 1975 to over 40% in 1990—and for Hispanics the increase was from just less than 20% to around 28%. In all the years in which data are available, Hispanic women were less likely to have ended their first marriages than were white women who, in turn, were less likely to have divorced than were African American women.

Remarriage

Figure 3.5 shows the percentage of women aged 45–49 who remarried after divorce over the period 1975 to 1990 (data are not available for Hispanic women before 1990). For both African Americans and whites, the percentages who remarried declined. The decline for white women was not substantial, and most of the change occurred from 1985 to 1990. For African Americans, the decline was more substantial, although there was little change in the 1985–90 period. In all the periods, the likelihood that an African American woman remarried was less than for a white woman. In 1990, the

FIGURE 3.5
Percentage of Women Aged 45–49 Remarried After Divorce

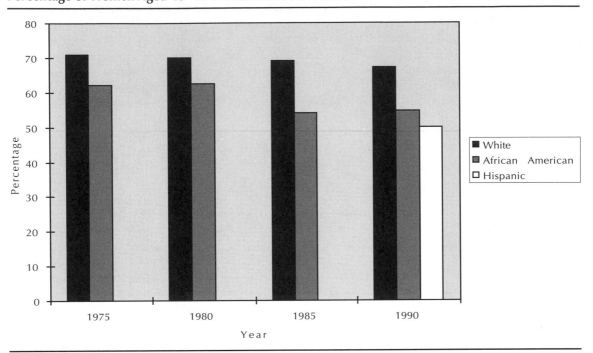

Source: U.S. Bureau of the Census. (1992). Marriage, divorce and remarriage in the 1990s, *Current Population Reports* (Series P-23, No. 180).

remarriage experiences of Hispanic women were closer to those of white women than African American women.

I will not dwell on the rationales that have been put forward concerning changes in the likelihood of divorce and remarriage. It is sufficient to note that most of the arguments concerning changes in these demographic behaviors mirror those put forth for the formation of marriages (Becker, 1981; Becker, Landes, & Michael, 1977; Espenshade, 1985; Grossbard-Shiechtman, 1993; South & Spitze, 1986). This is not to say that all factors related to marital dissolution and remarriage are identical to those for marital formation. Clearly, aspects of marital interaction and experience affect the likelihood of marital dissolution that did not affect marital formation. However, there appear to be elements of common influence, especially with respect to the constraints and opportunities made possible by

changing social and economic conditions. There is even evidence that the characteristics of marriage markets also affect the likelihood of divorce (South & Lloyd, 1995). The bottom line is that there has been a general retreat from early, permanent marriages—a retreat that has been more rapid and extensive for African Americans than for other racial-ethnic groups.

CHANGES IN THE CONTEXT OF CHILDBEARING AND CHILD REARING

The fact that there has been a general retreat from early, stable marriages leaves open the possibility that the context within which childbearing occurs has changed. As American women spend a smaller fraction of their childbearing years being married, the opportunity for nonmarital childbearing increases. Thus, one might suspect that more childbearing is occurring outside marriage than in the past. Indeed, the data indicate that there has been a growing proportion of nonmarital births. In 1992, about 23% of white births occurred outside marriage, compared to 39% of Hispanic births and 68% of African American births, whereas in 1980, these figures were 11% for whites and 56% for African Americans (U.S. Bureau of the Census, 1995a).

Is the increase in the proportion of nonmarital births due to a decline in marital births with no change in nonmarital births? Or is the increase due to an increase in nonmarital births with little change in marital births? To answer these questions, I turn to Figure 3.6, which shows the rates of out-of-wedlock childbearing from 1970 to 1992. These rates reflect the propensity of single women to have children outside marriage.

The changes shown for African American women indicate that the relationship between out-of-wedlock childbearing and the retreat from marriage is not direct—there is at least one intervening relationship. Between 1975 and 1985, when African American women were less likely to marry and more likely to divorce than white women, the rates of African American out-of-wedlock childbearing declined. This pattern suggests that the rise in the proportion of nonmarital births among African Americans was initially driven by a decline in marital fertility. A simplified explanation of this point is that is possible for a rise in the proportion of nonmarital births to be associated largely with rates of out-of-wedlock childbearing even when these rates are declining if the rates of marital childbearing are declining even faster (for a more detailed description of how nonmarital fertility can change over time, see Smith & Cutright, 1988). However, the rate of out-of-wedlock childbearing increased appreciably from 1985 to 1990 for African Ameri-

FIGURE 3.6
Rate of Out-of-Wedlock Childbearing

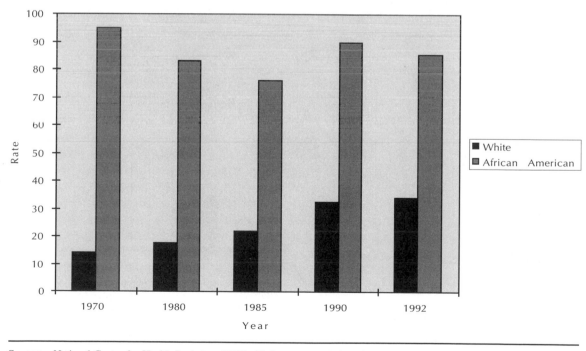

Source: National Center for Health Statistics. (1995). *Births to unmarried mothers: United States, 1980–92* (Series 21, No. 53). Washington, DC: Author.

cans, indicating the growing importance of this component of change for the proportion of births that are nonmarital (National Center for Health Statistics, 1995).

For whites, the rate of out-of-wedlock childbearing increased consistently from 1970 to 1994. Although marital fertility has declined for whites, the increase in nonmarital fertility has played a stronger role in determining the proportion of nonmarital births (National Center for Health Statistics, 1995). The gap between African Americans and whites in the rates of out-of-wedlock childbearing has also narrowed, although the rate for white women remains substantially below that for African American women.

What do rising out-of-wedlock birth rates, combined with the retreat from early, stable marriages, imply for the living arrangements of children? Figure 3.7 presents information relevant to this point. It indicates that the likelihood that a child will be born outside marriage or will spend part of his or her childhood in a single-parent family increased from 1970 to 1994.

In 1970, nearly 90% of white children lived with two parents, compared to slightly less than 80% in 1994. A similar trend occurred for Hispanic children (a decline from just under 80% to about 65%). Over the period being considered, African American children were substantially less likely than the other two groups to live with two parents; the percentage for African American children fell from under 60% in 1970 to about 33% in 1994.

Although these figures indicate substantial changes, they underestimate children's experience with single-parent families. The values shown in Figure 3.7 refer to a series of snapshots taken between 1970 and 1994. Between each of these snapshots, children moved into and out of different

FIGURE 3.7
Percentage of Children Under Age 18 Living with Two Parents

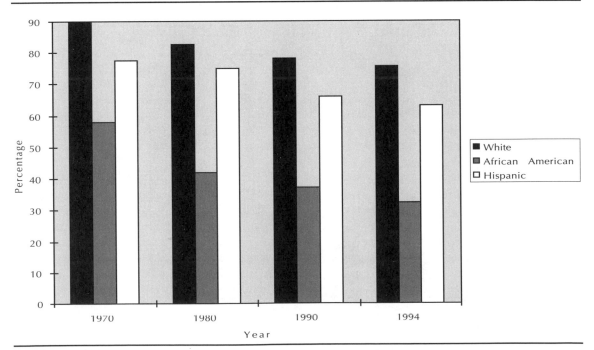

Source: U.S. Bureau of the Census. (1995). Household and family characteristics: March 1994, *Current Population Reports* (Series P-20, No. 483).

family types owing to the formation and dissolution of marriages by their parents (usually their mothers). Taking these life-course changes into account, nearly 50% of white children and two-thirds of African American children are likely to spend part of their childhoods in single-parent families (Bumpass & Sweet, 1989; Martin & Bumpass, 1989).

The combined result of the retreat from marriage and the changing context of childbearing is depicted in Figure 3.8, which shows the change in household composition between 1970 and 1994. In 1970, about 40% of all households consisted of a married couple with at least one child living in the household, whereas in 1990 and 1994, the proportion was about 30%. There were substantial increases in the percentages of households made up

of persons who were living alone and other families with children (mainly households headed by single women). Other, nonfamily households (nonrelated individuals living together) also witnessed a gain across time.

Overall, married-couple households declined as a fraction of all households, from over 70% in 1970 to less than 60% in 1994. The percentage of nonfamily households increased, as did the percentage of families without a married couple. The net result of the changes in marriage, divorce, remarriage, and childbearing discussed earlier is the increased diversity in the types of households in the United States. This diversity would be even greater if the data were available to calculate the percentage in Figure 3.7 so that stepparent families were included as a separate category. Over time, the proportion of

FIGURE 3.8
Household Composition: 1970–94

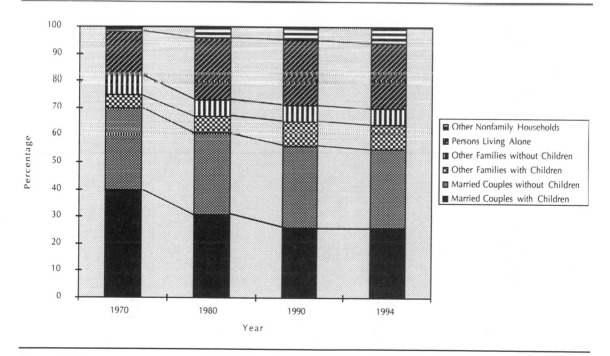

Source: U.S. Bureau of the Census. (1995). Household and family characteristics: March 1994, *Current Population Reports* (Series P-20, No. 483).

married couples with children has included more stepparents.

THE CHANGING ECONOMIC FORTUNE OF AMERICA'S FAMILIES

As I noted earlier, the retreat from marriage and the changing context of childbearing have been accompanied by a substantial shift in the economic fortune of families. I begin the discussion of the economic well-being of America's families by presenting information on their median incomes from 1970 to 1995 (see Figure 3.9). For white families, there was a slight upward shift in median income, from just under $38,000 in 1970 to just under $43,000 in 1995 (in constant 1995 dollars)—a gain of about 13% over a 23-year period, or about

.5 percent per year. This increase hardly reflects a noticeable gain in the affluence of white families.

The median income for African American families also increased slightly between 1970 and 1995 (from about $21,170 to about $25,970, or about 23%). The median income for Hispanic families declined from just under $26,000 in 1970 to about $24,500 in 1995. While Hispanic families earned slightly more than African American families in 1975, this relative ordering had reversed by 1995. Although I do not present detailed information on this point, most of the gain in median income was constrained largely to families in which at least one member has a college education. To give some idea of the educational differences involved, I note that the 1995 median family income in families in which the highest level of education obtained was a

FIGURE 3.9
Median Income of Families: 1970–93

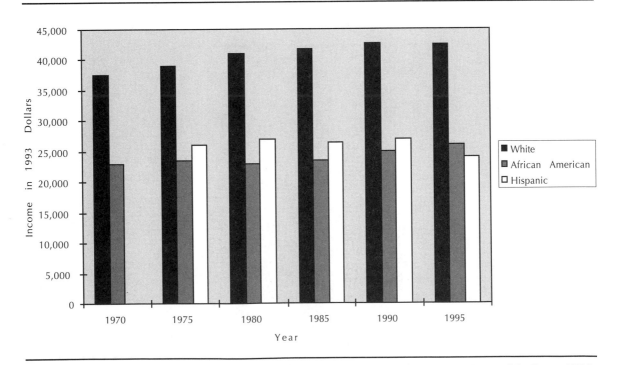

Sources: U.S. Bureau of the Census. (1995). *Statistical Abstract of the United States, 1995*, and U.S. Bureau of the Census. (1996). *Money Income in the United States: 1995. Current Population Reports* (Series P-60, No. 193).

high school degree was $36,751. For families in which the highest level of education obtained by at least one member was a college degree, the 1995 median income was $67,529, or 183% higher.

A different picture of family income is shown in Figure 3.10—income by family type from 1970 to 1995 in constant 1995 dollars. The data indicate that married-couples families in which the wives were in the labor force increased their income from just over $45,000 to $57,000, or about 27%. The data for married-couple families in which the wives were not in the labor force indicate a much lower median income and a slower increase over the 25 year period (from just over $34,000 to just under $40,000, or about 17.5%). These figures suggest that the changes in median family incomes shown in Figure 3.9 were driven, in large part, by increases in the income of married-couple families in which the wives were employed.

Figure 3.10 also shows the poor economic position of families headed by women. Although the median income of these families increased by about 13% from 1970 to 1995, it was still relatively low (slightly over $21,000) in 1995. The median income of male-headed families was higher than that of female-headed families, but the increase was only about 6% over the 25-year period (from about $33,000 to about $35,000).

The increasing importance of women's income to their families can be traced to differences in two factors for men and women: (1) changes in the rate of labor force participation and (2) changes in income. Figure 3.11 outlines the changes in labor force participation for men and women. It indicates a steady decline in the participation of married men in the labor force, from just under 90% in 1960 to under 80% in 1994. In contrast, the proportion of married women in the labor force surged from

FIGURE 3.10
Median Family Income, by Family Type

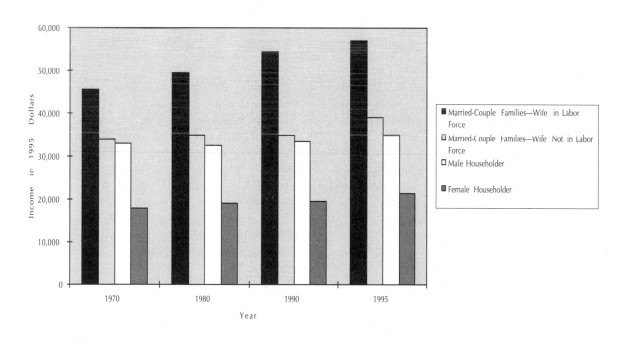

Sources: U.S. Bureau of the Census. (1995). *Statistical Abstract of the United States, 1995*, and U.S. Bureau of the Census. (1996). *Money Income in the United States: 1995. Current Population Reports* (Series P-60, No. 193).

FIGURE 3.11
Labor Force Participation Rates

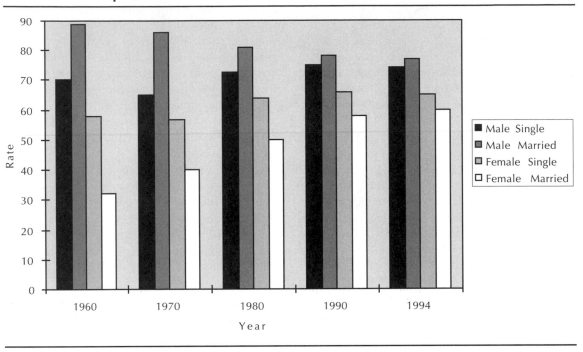

Source: U.S. Bureau of the Census. (1995). *Statistical Abstract of the United States, 1995.*

about 3 out of 10 in 1960 to nearly 6 out of 10 in 1994. These changes mean that married men were 2.8 times more likely than married women to be employed in 1960, but only 1.3 times more likely to be employed in 1994.

Figure 3.11 is also interesting because it indicates a decline in the ability to predict labor force participation based on sex and marital status. In 1960, it was clear that men were more likely to work than women and that marriage increased the likelihood of employment for men but depressed it for women. By 1994, men were still more likely to be employed than women, but the differential had been cut substantially. Married men were also more likely to work for pay than single men, but only by a few percentage points. Married women were less likely to be employed than single women, but the difference had declined from about 27 percentage points to only 8 percentage points. With respect to

participation in the labor force, there is more diversity today than there was in the past.

Figure 3.12 sketches changes in the median incomes of men and women by racial-ethnic group from 1970 to 1995 (in constant 1995 dollars). The median income of white men was about $25,800 in 1970 but only about $23,800 in 1995. A decline in income also occurred for Hispanic men, from about $17,800 in 1975 to about $14,800 in 1995. African American men experienced a virtually flat income trajectory (from about $15,300 in 1970 to about $16,000 in 1995).

For white and African American women, there was a steady increase in median earnings between 1970 and 1995. For white women, the increase was from around $8,300 to around $12,300 and for African American women, from about $7,600 to about $10,900. The income trajectory for Hispanic women was basically flat.

FIGURE 3.12
Median Income of Men and Women With Earnings

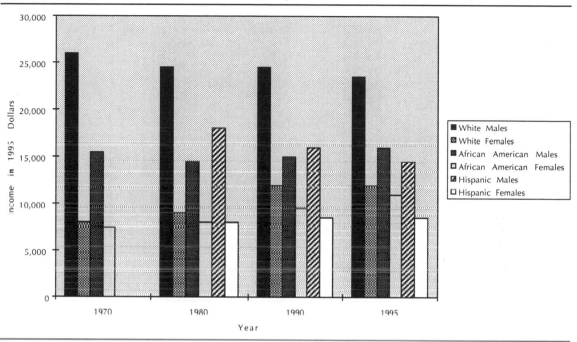

Source: U.S. Bureau of the Census. (1996). Money Income in the United States: 1995, *Current Population Reports* (Series P-60, No. 193).

Although the increases in the median incomes of white and African American women were due to a combination of factors, including more women working full time, full year, and for higher wages, they indicate the growing importance of wives' incomes in families. Not only are women more likely to be bringing home needed income, they are bringing home a greater proportion of their families' total incomes. This point follows from increases in women's incomes, from men's decreased likelihood of being in the labor force, and from men's flat or declining incomes from 1970 to 1995.

While the changes illustrated in Figures 3.9–3.12 outline the increasing economic contributions of women to their families, the figures also suggest substantial changes in the distribution of family income. Has the distribution of family income matched an overall trend toward greater wage inequality in America? (Danziger & Gottschalk,

1993, 1995; Fischer et al., 1996; McFate, Lawson, & Wilson, 1995). Figure 3.13 shows the changes between 1970 and 1995 in the percentages of families who fell into broad income categories.

The major change was the decline in the proportion of middle-income families—from 57.8% of all families to about 47% of all families (10 percentage points). A somewhat surprising finding was that the decline in middle-income families was not the result of more families falling into lower income categories. Rather, it was the result of more families entering higher-income categories. The proportion of higher-income families rose from 27.8% in 1970 to 39% in 1995.

The net result of these shifts is that the income distribution of American families became more heterogeneous from 1970 to 1995. As more and more married women have entered the labor force, there was an increase in the proportion of higher-income families and a consequent decline in the proportion

FIGURE 3.13
Percentage of Families Receiving Income Amounts

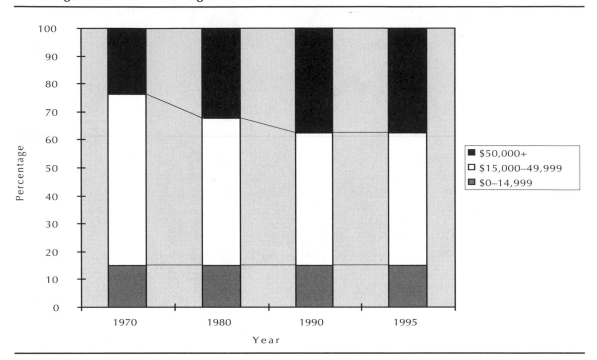

Source: U.S. Bureau of the Census. (1996). Money Income in the United States: 1995, *Current Population Reports* (Series P-60, No. 193).

of middle-income families. What did not change, however, was the percentage of low-income families—about 14% of all families at each point in time.

Some additional data illustrate the growth of income inequality among American families. For example, the poorest fifth of families earned 5.2% of all income in 1980 but only 4.2% in 1993 (U.S. Bureau of the Census, 1995b). In contrast, the richest fifth of families earned 41.5% of all income in 1980, but 46.2% in 1993. The richest 5% of American families increased their share of all income from 15.3% to 19.1% over the same period.

Not only is the distribution of family income becoming more unequal, but the richest families are getting richer and the poorest families are getting poorer. That is, the growth in inequality is not simply the result of rich families gaining income more rapidly than poor families. The upper income limit

for the poorest fifth of families was $17,535 in 1980 (in constant 1993 dollars) but only $16,952 in 1993 (U.S. Bureau of the Census, 1995b). However, the lower limit of the richest fifth of families was $58,871 in 1980 and $66,794 in 1993. Danziger and Gottschalk (1993) reported that in 1989, the real income of families at the 20th percentile was 5% lower than it was in 1969, but for families at the 80th percentile, real income was 19% higher than it was in 1969.

The distribution of income is also closely tied to the characteristics of families. Figure 3.9 indicated a growing disparity between the incomes of African American families and white families. Figure 3.10 showed the growth in the income of married-couple families in which the wives were in the labor force and the stagnation in the income of other family types.

Examining these changes in a systematic fashion, Karoly and Burtless (1995) decomposed the change in income inequality among American families. They reported that family income at the lowest levels fell from 1959 to 1989 for two reasons: (1) the increase in single-parent families headed by women with low skills and low incomes and (2) the increase in income inequality among men, such that the wages of men at the lower end of the distribution fell (see Figure 3.12). Thus, families at the lower end of the income distribution either do not have access to men's earnings or have seen these earnings decrease over time.

At higher levels, family income has grown because of two factors: (1) the substantial growth in the income of men at the upper end of the distribution and (2) the tendency of employed women to be concentrated in higher-income families. The second factor is consistent with increases in the educational homogamy of marriages over time (Mare, 1991), meaning that valued labor market skills are increasingly concentrated in two-earner families.

Karoly (1993) found that income inequality increased more among African American and Hispanic families than among white families. Thus, not only are African American and Hispanic families poorer than white families, they are subject to greater disparity between the incomes of rich and poor families. Moreover, although most of the increase in inequality among white families was the result of substantial gains in the incomes of the rich and much smaller gains in the incomes of the poor, the increase in inequality among African Americans and Hispanics was driven by gains in the incomes of the rich and a decline in the incomes of the poor.

The relatively constant percentage of families in the lowest-income category shown in Figure 3.13 means that there has been little progress toward reducing poverty in America. Figure 3.14 shows the percentage of families with incomes below the poverty line. There are two striking components to this figure. First, there was a substantial reduction in poverty for both African Americans and whites over the decade of the 1960s. The attacks against poverty under President Lyndon Johnson's Great Society programs were quite successful in raising the incomes of the poorest Americans. In just 10

years, the proportion of African Americans whose incomes were under the poverty line fell nearly 20 percentage points. For white Americans, the poverty rate was nearly halved.

The second interesting component of Figure 3.14 is the overwhelming stability of rates of poverty from 1970 to 1994. No racial-ethnic group witnessed progress with respect to the elimination of poverty. For African American families, the rate of poverty remained at about 30%. For Hispanic families, the poverty rate increased from about 23% in 1980 to about 28% in 1994. For white families, the rate was much lower, but remained constant at about 8% to 9%.

DISCUSSION

Clearly, the past quarter century has seen increased diversity in the demographic structure of American families. There has been a retreat from universal early marriage, and among some groups, particularly African Americans, there has been a retreat from marriage altogether. In addition, more and more households are not composed of families, and of family households an increasing proportion are not composed of two parents living with their children. There has been a rapid increase in persons living alone, mother-only families, cohabiting couples, and stepfamilies. It is no longer the case that a child can expect to live his or her childhood with both biological parents. What do these significant shifts in family structure mean for the well-being and future of America's families?

The debate on the meaning of these changes in family structure has been heated. On the one hand, such authors as Popenoe (1988, 1993) believe that the American family is declining, that its influence is waning, and that an increasing number of adults are rejecting the responsibilities of family life. Popenoe argued that recent changes in the family are different from changes that occurred in the past because the nuclear family is breaking up, losing its key functions of child rearing and the provision of affection and companionship. Moreover, a key component of the breakdown in family life is the rapid erosion of normative support for family life. The likely consequences of these changes, according to

FIGURE 3.14
Percentage of Families Below the Poverty Line

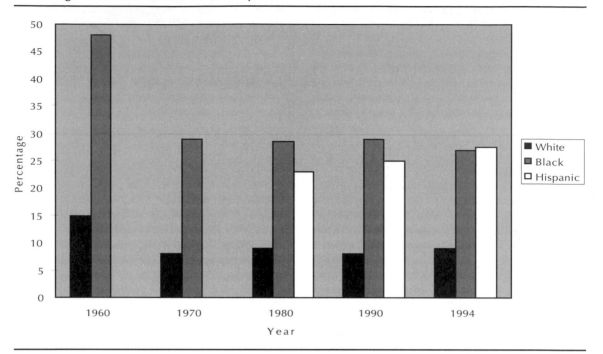

Source: U.S. Bureau of the Census. (1996). Income, Poverty and Valuation of Noncash Benefits: 1994, *Current Population Reports* (Series P-60, No. 189).

Popenoe, is that the well-being of children will suffer, placing subsequent generations of American children at a further risk of negative consequences.

Other authors (Coontz, 1992; Greeley, 1991; Kain, 1990) have taken the perspective that the American family is not declining, it is merely changing. Stacey (1990, 1993) even argued that the decline in the family as we have known it is a good thing because it will end the hegemony of the traditional family that exploited women. Which of these views is correct? Is the American family in decline? And, if so, what does the decline imply for the well-being of Americans?

To begin, the issue of family decline must be placed in context. It is virtually impossible to talk sensibly about it without making assumptions about the value of particular family forms. For example, one must be concerned about which fam-

ily structure is the best for which family members. Does the relationship between family structure and well-being vary according to the stage of the life course being considered?

For some researchers, the value of marriage to adults is of interest. Waite (1995) argued that marriage is beneficial to the health and emotional well-being of men and women. Yet, a number of authors have noted the increasing importance of individuation and secularization in personal fulfillment (Bellah et al., 1985; Lesthaeghe, 1983; Lesthaeghe & Surkyn, 1988). Bumpass (1990) and Sweet and Bumpass (1992) presented data to indicate that many young Americans do not consider marriage an important dimension of their life course.

These are questions that would lead one to qualify statements about the decline of families. But, for the moment, let me consider families from the perspective of children. Have families been less successful in generating child well-being?

With this gauge in mind, it seems clear that there has been a decline in the ability of families to meet the needs of children. I base this assessment on two gross, yet important, demographic indicators: the percentage of children living in poverty and the educational attainment of young adults. I chose these two indicators because they are consistent in indicating a decline in child well-being, can be easily tied to variations in family structure, and are closely linked to long-term well-being beyond childhood (Duncan & Brooks-Gunn, 1997). Moreover, both are amenable to governmental intervention. In the past, public assistance programs and public education had a substantial impact on poverty and educational attainment. More refined measures of psychological functioning generally indicate minor differences according to family type (Amato & Keith, 1991). The recently formed Federal Interagency Forum on Child and Family Statistics has released information on numerous indicators of the well-being of children (U.S. Department of Health and Human Services, 1996). However, it is difficult to tie many of them to variations in family structure.

A higher proportion of children under age 18 were living in poverty in 1994 than in 1970—21.8% versus 15.1% (U.S. Bureau of the Census, 1996). The increase in child poverty is important to note not only because of the spread of unpleasant living conditions that it implies, but because poverty has been linked to a variety of negative outcomes for children, including lower birthweight, greater probability of childhood injury, increased behavioral problems, lower cognitive and academic achievement, and a greater likelihood of out-of-wedlock pregnancy (Duncan & Brooks-Gunn, 1997; Duncan, Brooks-Gunn, & Klebanov, 1994; Huston, 1991; Klerman, 1991; McLeod & Shanahan, 1993; McLoyd & Wilson, 1991). The negative impact of poverty is exacerbated by the fact that younger children are the most likely to be poor, particularly when they live in mother-headed families (U.S. Department of Health and Human Services, 1996) and that poverty experienced before age 6 is particularly detrimental to positive development (Duncan & Brooks-Gunn, 1997).

The second indicator of the decline in the well-being of children is the stagnation in the educational attainment of young adults. Since 1975, the proportion of Americans aged 25–29 who have completed high school has remained constant at about 85% (U.S. Bureau of the Census, 1996). The stagnation in educational attainment is a significant trend, given the importance of education to economic success over the life course. Indeed, over the past 20 years, the value of education has become even more important, since the premium accruing to a college education has increased substantially (Grogger & Eide, 1995; Murphy & Welch, 1993). Individuals with high school degrees have witnessed stagnation and even a decrease in their earning power, while those with a college education have seen their incomes rise consistently.

If one accepts the proposition that the well-being of children has declined in recent years, the next question to ask is whether the increase in family diversity is responsible for the change. With respect to both child poverty and the stagnation in educational achievement, if not other indicators of child well-being, the answer is yes—to a degree. For example, the economic well-being of children is clearly linked to family structure. In particular, children who live with a single mother are much more likely to live in poverty than are children who live with two parents. Thus, the increase in single-parent families over the past two decades has played a role in the increase in child poverty. Gottschalk and Danziger (1993), for example, estimated that over the period 1968–86 increased female headship increased child poverty by 12.9 percentage points among African Americans and 3.0 percentage points among whites.

However, shifts in family structure cannot fully explain all the increase in child poverty. Several researchers have noted the role played by factors like economic stagnation among wage earners (particularly men), increasing inequality in the distribution of earnings, and reduced governmental income transfers (Gottschalk & Danziger, 1993; Haveman & Wolfe, 1994; Huston, 1994). Thus, even without an increase in female headship, rates of child poverty would have increased.

With respect to educational achievement, family

structure has been identified as an important factor. For instance, children who spend some time living in mother-only families are less likely to graduate from high school or attend college (Astone & McLanahan, 1991; Haveman, Wolfe, & Spaulding, 1991; McLanahan & Sandefur, 1994; Sandefur, McLanahan & Wojtkiewicz, 1992). But how much of the relationship can be attributed to family structure itself? McLanahan and Sandefur (1994) noted that half the educational deficit associated with living in a single-parent family can be attributed to the lack of income so often associated with these families. The rest of the deficit can be attributed to low parental involvement, reduced parental supervision, low parental aspirations for children, and residential mobility.

Just as low income is not a necessary result of living in a mother-only family, neither is increased residential mobility. Nor do either of these conditions imply a retreat from family life. And although mother-only families may be at a disadvantage in providing parental supervision, this does not imply a rejection of parental responsibilities and the value of family life. Low parental involvement and aspirations may be better indicators of family decline, but they can explain only a fraction of the negative relationship between living in a mother-only family and failing to complete high school.

A more detailed search reveals that while mother-only families have lower educational expectations for their children and are less able to spend time with their children, there are few other differences in parenting values. It is possible that the lower educational expectations of single mothers are simply a reflection of the meager economic resources at their command. Higher educational expectations may not be reasonable for persons with low incomes.

Several studies have found that there is no consistent patterning of differences according to family type in child-rearing values, mothers' rules for children, maternal support and control, mother-adolescent disagreement, verbal aggression, and physical violence (Acock & Demo, 1994; Amato, 1987; Amato & Keith, 1991). Moreover, differences that do occur are generally small and of little substantive significance. This is not to say that there have not been changes in child-rearing values over time. The evidence suggests that such changes have occurred (e.g., parents want more autonomy for their children), but they have occurred for all families (Alwin, 1986, 1990).

In sum, the evidence that changes in child well-being are due to shifts in family structure or changes in values about child-rearing that can be linked to family structure is weak at best. Much of the linkage between family structure and well-being can be attributed to differences in economic resources or structural constraints on the amount of time that can be spent with children. Although young Americans may place considerable emphasis on personal fulfillment and tend to devalue marriage as an important goal (Bumpass, 1990; Sweet & Bumpass, 1992), they still take child-rearing responsibilities seriously.

Indeed, it is possible to argue that there is remarkable continuity in values and practices related to child-rearing among types of families (Acock & Demo, 1994). By itself, the increasing diversity of family structure does not lead to family decline. How, then, can one make sense of the changes that have occurred to America's families and children? Part of the answer appears to be the rapid shift in the economic environment that families face. As I discussed in this chapter, economic stagnation and growing uncertainty about the economic future has plagued young men, while economic opportunities have increased for young women. These changes have made it extremely difficult for young men and women to achieve the type of family modeled by their parents or grandparents. To some extent, these changes reflect a continuation of long-term shifts in economic production and family roles associated with the Industrial Revolution (Goode, 1963).

In fact, men and women have had to renegotiate taken-for-granted assumptions about the division of economic and household labor, as well as their notions about acceptable economic security. The period of renegotiation has been difficult, as witnessed by the substantial delay in marriage, the rise in the divorce rate, and the declining socioeconomic well-being of children. However, there are small signs that new types of families may be emerging.

For example, women's employment now seems to be encouraging marriage rather than discouraging it (Lichter et al., 1992). Young men also appear to be more willing to accept an egalitarian division of labor, reducing the terrific work burden so often placed on wives in dual-earner families (Goldscheider & Waite, 1991).

At the same time as there is evidence that new families are forming, the most economically deprived Americans still face substantial challenges to marriage. At the extreme, poverty and the lack of economic opportunity remain barriers to a productive and fulfilling family life that is conducive to the well-being of children (Wilson, 1987). The retreat of public support for education and the passage of welfare reform make the future even more uncertain for individuals at the lowest ranks of the income distribution. It is among these individuals that the threat of family decline remains the most salient.

REFERENCES

Acock, A., & Demo, D. (1994). *Family diversity and well-being.* Thousand Oaks, CA: Sage.

Alwin, D. (1986). Religion and parental child-rearing orientations: Evidence of a Catholic-Protestant convergence. *American Journal of Sociology, 92,* 412–440.

Alwin, D. (1990). Cohort replacement and changes in parental socialization values. *Journal of Marriage and the Family, 52,* 347–360.

Amato, P. (1987). Family processes in one-parent, stepparent and intact families: The child's point of view. *Journal of Marriage and the Family, 49,* 327–337.

Amato, P., & Keith, B. (1991). Parental divorce and the well-being of children: A meta-analysis. *Psychological Bulletin, 110,* 26–46.

Astone, N. & McLanahan, S. (1991). Family structure and high school graduation. The role of parental practices. *American Sociological Review, 56,* 309–320.

Becker, G. (1981). *A treatise on the family.* Cambridge, MA: Harvard University Press.

Becker, G., Landes, E., & Michael, R. (1977). An economic analysis of marital instability. *Journal of Political Economy, 85,* 1141–1187.

Bellah, R., Madsen, R., Swidler, A., Sullivan, W., & Tipton, S. (1985). *Habits of the heart: Individualism and commitment in American life.* Berkeley: University of California Press.

Brown, S., & Booth, A. (1996). Cohabitation versus marriage: A comparison of relationship quality. *Journal of Marriage and the Family, 58,* 668–678.

Bumpass, L. (1990). What's happening to the family: Interactions between demographic and institutional change. *Demography, 27,* 483–498.

Bumpass, L., & Sweet, J. (1989). Children's experience in single-parent families: Implications of cohabitation and marital transitions. *Family Planning Perspectives, 21,* 256–260.

Bumpass, L., Sweet, J., & Cherlin, A. (1991). The role of cohabitation in declining rates of marriage. *Journal of Marriage and the Family, 53,* 913–927.

Coontz, S. (1992). *The way we never were: American families and the nostalgia trap.* New York: Basic Books.

Danziger, S., & Gottschalk, P. (Eds.). (1993). *Uneven tides: Rising inequality in America.* New York: Russell Sage Foundation.

Danziger, S., & Gottschalk, P. (1995). *American unequal.* Cambridge, MA: Harvard University Press.

Duncan, G., Boisjoly, J., & Smeeding, T. (1996). Economic mobility of young workers in the 1970s and 1980s. *Demography, 33,* 497–509.

Duncan, G., & Brooks-Gunn, J. (1997). *Growing up poor.* New York: Russell Sage Foundation.

Duncan, G., Brooks-Gunn, J., & Klebanov, P. (1994). Economic deprivation and early-childhood development. *Child Development, 65,* 296–318.

Ellwood, D., & Crane, J. (1990). Family change among African Americans: What do we know? *Journal of Economic Perspectives, 4,* 65–84.

Espenshade, T. (1985). Marriage trends in America: Estimates, implications and underlying causes. *Population and Development Review, 11,* 193–245.

Farley, R., & Bianchi, S. (1987). The growing racial difference in marriage and family patterns (Research report No. 87-107). Ann Arbor: Population Studies Center, University of Michigan.

Fischer, C., Hout, M., Jankowski, M., Lucas, S., Swidler, A., & Voss, K. (1996). *Inequality by design: Cracking the bell curve myth.* Princeton, NJ: Princeton University Press.

Fossett, M., & Kiecolt, J. (1991). A methodological review of the sex ratio: Alternatives for comparative research. *Journal of Marriage and the Family, 53,* 941–957.

Goldscheider, L., & Waite, L. (1991). *New families, no families? The transformation of the American home.* Berkeley: University of California Press.

Goode, W. (1963). *World revolution and family patterns.* New York: Free Press.

Gottschalk, P., & Danziger, S. (1993). Family structure, family size and family income: Accounting for changes in the economic well-being of children, 1968–1986. In S. Danziger & P. Gottschalk (Eds.), *Uneven tides: Rising inequality in America* (pp. 165–194). New York: Russell Sage Foundation.

Greeley, A. (1991). *Faithful attraction: Discovering intimacy, love and fidelity in American marriage.* New York: Tor.

Grogger, J., & Eide, E. (1995). Changes in college skills and the rise in the college wage premium. *Journal of Human Resources, 30,* 280–310.

Grossbard-Shiechtman, S. (1993). *On the economics of marriage: A theory of marriage, labor and divorce.* Boulder, CO: Westview Press.

Haveman, R., & Wolfe, B. (1994). *Succeeding generations: On the effects of investments in children.* New York: Russell Sage Foundation.

Haveman, R., Wolfe, B., & Spaulding, J. (1991). Childhood events and circumstances influencing high school completion. *Demography, 28,* 133–157.

Huston, A. (1991). Children in poverty: Developmental and policy issues. In A. Huston (Ed.), *Children in poverty: Child development and public policy* (pp. 1–22). New York: Cambridge University Press.

Huston, A. (1994). Children in poverty: Designing research to affect policy. *Social Policy Report, 8,* 1–15.

Kain, E. (1990). *The myth of family decline.* Lexington, MA: D. C. Heath.

Kammerman, S. (1995). Gender role and family structure changes in the advanced industrialized West: Implications for social policy. In K. McFate, R. Lawson, & W. Wilson (Eds.), *Poverty, inequality and the future of social policy: Western states in the new world order* (pp. 231–256). New York: Russell Sage Foundation.

Karoly, L. (1993). The trend in inequality among families, individuals, and workers in the United States: A twenty-five year perspective. In S. Danziger & P. Gottschalk (Eds.), *Uneven tides: Rising inequality in America* (pp. 19–97). New York: Russell Sage Foundation.

Karoly, L., & Burtless, G. (1995). Demographic change, rising earnings inequality, and the distribution of personal well-being, 1959–1989. *Demography, 32,* 379–405.

Klerman, L. (1991). *Alive and well? A research and policy review of health programs for poor young children.* New York: National Center for Children in Poverty, Columbia University School of Public Health.

Lesthaeghe, R. (1983). A century of demographic and cultural change in Western Europe: An exploration of underlying dimensions. *Population and Development Review, 9,* 411–436.

Lesthaeghe, R., & Surkyn, J. (1988). Cultural dynamics and economic theories of fertility decline. *Population and Development Review, 14,* 1–45.

Levy, F., & Michael, R. (1991). *The economic future of American families: Income and wealth trends.* Washington, DC: Urban Institute Press.

Levy, F., & Murnane, R. (1992). U.S. earnings levels and earnings inequality: A review of recent trends and proposed explanations. *Journal of Economic Literature, 30,* 1333–1381.

Lichter, D., LeClere, F., & McLaughlin, D. (1991). Local marriage markets and the marital behavior of African American and white women. *American Journal of Sociology, 96,* 843–867.

Lichter, D., McLaughlin, D., Kephart, G., & Landry, D. (1992). Race and the retreat from marriage: A shortage of marriageable men? *American Sociological Review, 57,* 781–799.

Lloyd, K., & South, S. (1996). Contextual influences on young men's transition to first marriage. *Social Forces, 74,* 1097–1119.

Manning, W., & Smock, P. (1995). Why marry? Race and the transition to marriage among cohabitors. *Demography, 32,* 509–520.

Mare, R. (1991). Five decades of educational assortative mating. *American Sociological Review, 56,* 15–32.

Mare, R., & Winship, C. (1991). Socioeconomic change and the decline of marriage for blacks and whites. In C. Jencks & P. Peterson (Eds.), *The urban underclass* (pp. 175–202). Washington, DC: Urban Institute Press.

Martin, T., & Bumpass, L. (1989). Recent trends in marital disruption. *Demography, 26,* 37–51.

McFate, K., Lawson, R., & Wilson, W. (Eds.). (1995). *Poverty, inequality and the future of social policy: Western states in the new world order.* New York: Russell Sage Foundation.

McLanahan, S., & Casper, L. (1995). Growing diversity and inequality in the American family. In R. Farley

(Ed.), *State of the union: America in the 1990s* (Vol. 2, pp. 1–45). New York: Russell Sage Foundation.

McLanahan, S., & Sandefur, G. (1994). *Growing up with a single parent*. Cambridge, MA: Harvard University Press.

McLeod, J., & Shanahan, M. (1993). Poverty, parenting, and children's mental health. *American Sociological Review, 58,* 351–366.

McLoyd, V., & Wilson, L. (1991). The strain of living poor: Parenting, social support, and child mental health. In A. Huston (Ed.), *Children in poverty: Child development and public policy* (pp. 105–135). New York: Cambridge University Press.

Moffitt, R. (1990). The effect of the U.S. welfare system on marital status. *Journal of Public Economics, 41,* 101–124.

Moffitt, R. (1992). Incentive effects of the U.S. welfare system: A review. *Journal of Economic Literature, 30,* 1–61.

Moffitt, R. (1994). Welfare effects on female headship with area effects. *Journal of Human Resources, 29,* 621–636.

Murphy, K., & Welch, F. (1993). Industrial change and the rising importance of skill. In S. Danziger & P. Gottschalk (Eds.), *Uneven tides: Rising inequality in America* (pp. 101–132). New York: Russell Sage Foundation.

Murray, C. (1984). *Losing ground*. New York: Basic Books.

National Center for Health Statistics. (1995). *Births to unmarried mothers: United States, 1980–1992* (Vital and Health Statistics, Series 21–53). Washington, DC: U.S. Government Printing Office.

Nock, S. (1995). A comparison of marriages and cohabiting relationships. *Journal of Family Issues, 16,* 53–76.

Popenoe, D. (1988). *Disturbing the nest: Family change and decline in modern society*. New York: Aldine de Gruyter.

Popenoe, D. (1993). American family decline, 1960–1990: A review and appraisal. *Journal of Marriage and the Family, 55,* 527–555.

Preston, S. (1984). Children and the elderly: Divergent paths for America's dependents. *Demography, 21,* 435–457.

Qian, Z., & Preston, S. (1993). Changes in American marriage, 1972 to 1987: Availability and forces of attraction by age and education. *American Sociological Review, 58,* 482–495.

Rindfuss, R., & VandenHeuvel, A. (1990). Cohabitation: A precursor to marriage or an alternative to being single? *Population and Development Review, 16,* 703–726.

Sandefur, G., McLanahan, S., & Wojtkiewicz, R. (1992). The effects of parental marital status during adolescence on high school graduation. *Social Forces, 71,* 103–121.

Schoen, R., & Owens, D. (1992). A further look at first marriages and first unions. In S. South & S. Tolnay (Eds.), *The changing American family* (pp. 109–114). Boulder, CO: Westview Press.

Schultz, T. (1994). Marital status and fertility in the United States: Welfare and labor market effects. *Journal of Human Resources, 29,* 637–669.

Smith, H., & Cutright, P. (1988). Thinking about change in illegitimacy ratios: United States, 1963–1983. *Demography, 25,* 235–248.

South, S. (1992). For love or money? Sociodemographic determinants of the expected benefits of marriage. In S. South & S. Tolnay (Eds.), *The changing American family* (pp. 171–194). Boulder, CO: Westview Press.

South, S. (1993). Racial and ethnic differences in the desire to marry. *Journal of Marriage and the Family, 55,* 357–370.

South, S., & Lloyd, K. (1992). Marriage opportunities and family formation: Further implications of imbalanced sex ratios. *Journal of Marriage and the Family, 54,* 440–451.

South, S., & Lloyd, K. (1995). Spousal alternatives and marital dissolution. *American Sociological Review, 60,* 21–35.

South, S., & Spitze, G. (1986). Determinants of divorce over the marital life course. *American Sociological Review, 51,* 583–590.

Stacey, J. (1990). *Brave new families: Stories of domestic upheaval in late 20th century America*. New York: Basic Books.

Stacey, J. (1993). Good riddance to "the family": A response to David Popenoe. *Journal of Marriage and the Family, 55,* 545–547.

Sweet, J., & Bumpass, L. (1992). Young adults' views of marriage, cohabitation and family. In S. South & S. Tolnay (Eds.), *The changing American family* (pp. 143–170). Boulder, CO: Westview Press.

Teachman, J. (1994). Household and family demography. In D. Bogue (Ed.), *Reader in methods of population research* (pp. 1173–1245). New York: United Nations Press.

Teachman, J., Polonko, K., & Leigh, G. (1987). Marital timing: Race and sex comparisons. *Social Forces, 66,* 239–268.

Teachman, J., Polonko, K., & Scanzoni, J. (1987). Demography of the family. In M. Sussman & S. Steinmetz (Eds.), *Handbook of marriage and the family* (pp. 3–36). New York: Plenum.

Testa, M., Astone, N., Krogh, M., & Neckerman, K. (1991). Employment and marriage among inner-city fathers. *Annals of the American Academy of Political and Social Science, 501,* 79–91.

U.S. Bureau of the Census. (1995a). *Household and family characteristics: March 1994 (Current Population Reports,* Series P20-483). Washington, DC: U.S. Government Printing Office.

U.S. Bureau of the Census. (1995b). *Statistical abstract of the United States, 1995.* Springfield, VA: National Technical Information Service.

U.S. Bureau of the Census. (1996). *Educational attainment in the United States: March 1995* (Current Population Reports, Series P20-489). Washington, DC: U.S. Government Printing Office.

U.S. Department of Health and Human Services. (1996). *Trends in the well-being of America's children and youth: 1996.* Washington, DC: Office of the Assistant Secretary for Planning and Evaluation.

Waite, L. (1995). Does marriage matter? *Demography, 32,* 483–507.

Wilson, W. J. (1987). *The truly disadvantaged.* Chicago: University of Chicago Press.

PART III
Gender Dynamics in Families

CHAPTER **4**

Gender, Marriage, and Diverse Possibilities for Cross-Sex and Same-Sex Pairs

VIRGINIA RUTTER AND PEPPER SCHWARTZ

WHY WE STUDY GENDER, MARRIAGE, AND OTHER COMMITTED RELATIONSHIPS

Assessing the costs and benefits of marriage—especially with respect to gender—reminds us of the ironic saying, often applied to dining hall cuisine: This food is so bad, and there is not enough of it. From our feminist perspective, there is much about marriage that is disappointing, yet marriage and other committed relationships are what people hunger for and build their lives around. This feminist perspective involves observations about the bold and subtle ways in which social structure and the process of intimate relationships combine to create and support inequalities based on gender, race, ethnicity, class, sexual orientation, and other social status characteristics.

We, too, are hungry fans of marriage: We are both married and dedicated to our relationships as sources of emotional, intellectual, and creative stimulation. We like being married to our partners. But, as this chapter delineates, we are alert to how gender influences intimate relationships and interferes with harmony, equity, and empathy.

One gender issue that is particularly remarkable to us was highlighted for nearly the first time in Blumstein and Schwartz's (1983) study, which observed how gender influences—and, in some ways, defines—intimate relationships not only of cross-sex pairs (as in heterosexual marriage and cohabitation) but of same-sex pairs (as in gay and lesbian couples). In this chapter, we focus on heterosexual and same-sex pairs in committed relationships.

A RESEARCH TRADITION FOR FRAMING GENDER IN RELATIONSHIPS

The American Couples study was conducted at the University of Washington by Pepper Schwartz, a heterosexual, married professor of sociology, and her dear friend and close collaborator, Philip Blumstein, a gay professor of sociology whose lifetime committed relationship ended when he and his partner both died in the early 1990s from AIDS. The legacy of this work has influenced Pepper's continued research and advocacy regarding gender, marriage, and same-sex unions, as well as the work of subsequent students of sociology at the University of Washington, including Virginia Rutter. Virginia's research interest in marriage and intimate relationships emerged from her experience as a journalist and public affairs person in Washington, DC. Her work with policy makers, the media, and family therapists highlighted some of the deficits of research and theory in the area of gender, power, and family issues and whetted her curiosity and taste for social research.

Blumstein and Schwartz's (1983) study was the first to have the following design: a sample of heterosexual cohabitors, heterosexual married couples, gay couples, and lesbian couples who were surveyed and interviewed extensively to understand similarities and differences among types of couples. For example, in what ways are cohabitors similar to married couples? In what ways are lesbian and gay couples different from one another? Blumstein and Schwartz discovered that the pervasive influence of gender on intimate relationships stretches to nearly all people, regardless of sexual orientation, living arrangement, or ethnicity. Since the early 1980s, research on family diversity across sexual orientations has expanded considerably. As Demo and Allen (1996) noted, variations (by sexuality, class, and ethnicity, for example) in how gender influences different types of relationships is key to understanding family diversity; however, there is also a continuity of gender effects across all types of relationships.

Men and women of every sexual orientation experience similar socialization into relationship roles and sexual roles. For example, typically, men are not expected to focus on relationships as the center of their lives, but women are exhorted to do so (Gilligan, 1982; Thompson 1993). Role models for men have tended to stress independence and the provider role and to equate success in work with masculinity and personal success (Bernard, 1981; Coltrane, 1996; Pleck, 1981). Although women's socialization is changing, women are more often trained to link their future identity as adults to good marriages, motherhood, and more modest work achievements (Thurer, 1994). Furthermore, men and women live in a world where they are socialized into heterosexuality, which ties conventions of masculinity and femininity to sexual expression and

social arrangements, especially marriage, that treat heterosexuality as natural and normative (Richardson, 1996). Theoretically, then, men interacting with men and women interacting with women share approaches, reactions, and role expectations (Blumstein & Schwartz, 1983). Members of the opposite sex (as defined in cross-sex pairs) may be expected to bring in certain contributions associated with their gender roles in heterosexual relationships; these roles may be absent in same-sex relationships in which there is no "opposite." Of course, lesbian, gay, and heterosexual partners may seek to resist or reject gendered statuses (Risman & Schwartz, 1989). However, this is a case of the exception supporting the rule. Whether one accepts or rejects gendered norms, the decision-making process serves to acknowledge the power of gendered norms.

THE SOCIAL CONSTRUCTION OF ESSENTIALIST GENDER DIFFERENCE

In our research and writing on marriage, cohabitation, and committed same-sex relationships, we focus on the influence of gender within the context of other statuses (i.e., race, ethnicity, and class). We need to explain our epistemological frame with respect to this "influence" of gender and exactly what we mean by gender.

The influence of gender may be best explained by an example: Think of the debate in the late 1990s about same-sex marriage that captured popular attention and continues to keep legislatures and courts busy. The debate highlights the fundamental importance of gender to conventional, heterosexual marriage. Indeed, legal opponents of same-sex marriage in the 1997 Hawaii case held that for the benefit of society, marriage requires gender differences: Marriage, according to opponents of same-sex marriages, must include a man and a woman who are the proper unit for producing and raising children into a stable, civil society (Gross, 1994). Some opponents hold that marriage really is rooted in a fundamental biological function that requires a sex difference: Procreation, after all, requires a man and a woman (fertility technologies notwithstanding). The debate on same-sex marriage, which we touch on in this chapter but that merits a far more detailed examination than we can provide here, foregrounds the extent to which gender is a critical organizing feature of marriage (see Eskridge, 1996).

The requirement of gender difference stems largely from what we call an essentialist view of sexuality and gender: Men and women were born different and are, by virtue of their biological sex assignment, naturally prepared for the role of either wife or husband, mother or father. These statuses are not, according to essentialists, interchangeable. Essentialists are those who take a biological, sociological, or evolutionary point of view and believe that people's sexual desires and orientations are innate. Such essentialists think that differences in men's and women's behavior are related, above all, to their different biological contributions to reproduction (Buss, 1995; Rossi, 1984). Social impact is minimal.

In contrast, we believe that there is little in the social world that is contingent primarily on biological sex differences. Instead, most of the identities, abilities, interests, and preferences of men and women in intimate relationships are socially constructed and highly influenced by social definitions of masculinity and femininity. Bodies are an important part of the social construction of masculinity and femininity as they are enacted in intimate relationships. Furthermore, the biological roles men and women are assigned in reproduction influence the social experiences of pregnancy, birth, and child-rearing. But the meanings applied to bodies are fundamentally social and tend to be socially constructed to exaggerate biological "sex" differences into social gender differences. For example, the experiences of gender, marriage, and sexuality vary in important ways by class, race, and ethnicity (e.g., how often people opt for marriage or what constitutes power sharing in relationships).

What Are Gender and Gender Difference?

The term *gender* is often used without attention to what it means. Clarity about this central concept aids family scholars who are interested in diversity and will shape everything from the research designs they choose to their editorial decisions. *Gender* is not simply a "politically correct" word for what used to be called sex. *Sex* refers to biological sex assignment. Although some researchers have

debated whether it is even reasonable to identify only two "sexes"—male and female (Kessler & McKenna 1985), we use the term *sex* to refer to male and female, which, most of the time, is a clear-cut biological distinction. In contrast, *gender* refers to the social meanings of masculinity and femininity that are produced through social processes and interactions that produce "men" and "women" (Goffman, 1977; West & Zimmerman, 1987). Thus, sex (whether a subject is male or female) is randomly assigned. However gender, or the status and characteristics of men and women, is not randomly assigned. As fundamental as these definitions seem, it is important to set them forth.

A recent Internet exchange about the editorial policy of an American Psychological Association (APA) journal highlights how far reaching the intellectual confusion about sex and gender is. A psychologist's manuscript had been copyedited for publication, and the copyeditor, following current editorial policy, systematically changed the word *sex* to *gender* without attention to the context or content. The author's attempts to explain that she or he really meant sex as it is assigned at birth, not gender as it is learned in life, were rebuffed. Indeed, in the wake of the episode, the APA executive director vowed to review the editorial policy. If a group of leading scholars and editors have difficulty understanding the difference between these two concepts, it is reasonable to think that intellectuals who are concerned with family and diversity would also benefit from a reminder of how to manage these common terms.

Notions of gender tend to rely on notions of gender difference, which maximize small distinctions into "essential" differences. Many Americans are familiar with the pop-psychology, best-selling view of Gray's (1992) *Men Are from Mars, Women Are from Venus* of gender differences in intimate relationships. A significance of this view is that it implies that fundamental (essentialist) differences between men and women are immutable and can explain the course of intimate relationships, including the joys and problems people experience in intimate relationships. Gender difference from this Mars-and-Venus view is a cause for phenomena in relationships: "She [or he] treats me this way because she [or he] is a woman [or man]." From our point of view, such gender difference is framed as a cause of relationship behavior the same way that saying that a person acts "this" or "that" way because his [or her] sign is Leo or Taurus or Cancer. This Mars-and-Venus view of gender is akin to astrology in its basis in fact and its enormous plasticity (so that whatever is said somehow sounds "right").

In our view of gender, masculinity and femininity are consequences of social interaction, including interactions in intimate relationships. Especially in heterosexual relationships, the cross-sex partners are set up as a contrasting and complementary pair. Sociologist and symbolic interactionist Erving Goffman (1977, p. 324) observed that marriage functions as a kind of "staging ground" for the production of gender:

> In all societies, initial sex-class placement stands at the beginning of a sustained sorting process whereby members of the two classes are subject to differential socialization . . . every society seems to develop its own conception of what is "essential" to, and characteristic of, the two sex classes. . . . Here are ideals of masculinity and femininity, understandings about ultimate human nature which provide grounds . . . for identifying the whole person.

Goffman's "ideals" are what we talk about as "gendered social scripts"—the rules that people carry around in their heads about what they ought to be like as men or women (straight, gay, lesbian, bisexual, transgendered, or intersexed) and what others ought to be like as men or women. Gendered social scripts develop from a learning history that involves everyday interactions with others (Coltrane, 1998; Gagnon & Simon, 1973; Howard & Hollander, 1997). Such scripts involve one's upbringing as a boy or a girl (Chorodow, 1978; Gilligan, 1982) and a person's observations of others that she or he uses to help figure out what the rules and norms for being a boy or a girl are (Goffman, 1977).

Gendered social scripts are also influenced by social structures, including laws, governmental policies, economics, and religious rules (see sections on social control of female sexuality, gender stratification, and gender and the state in Hess & Ferree, 1987). For example, social structure, in the form of laws and courts, dictates that the only legitimate marriages involve cross-sex pairs and bars that privilege from same-sex pairs. Recognizing that these are gendered scripts and the laws of a particular culture—not laws of nature—helps diversify sexual and gender possibilities in intimate relationships.

What makes the study of gender and intimate relationships so interesting and personal is that everyone is subject to gendered social scripts, but no one ever lives up to those expectations. There may be some idea in the ambient culture about what constitutes the ideal, perfectly feminine woman or the ideal, perfectly masculine man. But one compelling aspect of gender in intimate relationships is that hardly anyone has the sense that she or he is doing it right. Some people actively contest gendered scripts that influence intimate relationships (such as peer marriages or polyamorous, i.e., multiple-partner, lesbian communities), but even people who are not concerned with challenging social norms related to gender are still not ever doing it right. Often, when people feel like they are not doing it right, they feel bad about themselves or alienated from their environment or bad about their relationship. For example, unrealistic standards of feminine beauty are considered a key catalyst for anorexia and bulimia. In this case, women feel they are not thin enough to meet the beauty standards for women in U.S. and other Western cultures; in fact, victims of anorexia and bulimia see themselves as fat even when they are thin and continue to starve and purge themselves to become sufficiently thin (Rosen, 1996). It is interesting that these disorders are most common among white, middle-class women. However, rates of anorexia and bulimia are increasing among minority groups (Hsu, 1987) and among men as standards of beauty become more diffuse (Wakeling, 1996).

SOCIAL CONTEXTS OF INTIMATE RELATIONSHIPS

Heterosexual Pairing

Gender scripts are as pervasive as marital scripts in U.S. culture. Three out of every 4 adults in the

United States are married or have been married at some point (Tucker & Mitchell-Kernan, 1995), and 9 out of 10 will marry before they die (Ahlburg & DeVita, 1992). Although rates of marriage have declined in recent decades, the United States continues to be the most marriage (and divorce) prone society in the world. Rates of marriage are higher among whites than among African Americans, partly because of the way gender influences marital practices. Schoen (1995) and others have noted that, in general, African American women, who tend to be more economically self-sufficient than white women, have less to gain from marriage.

One needs simply to scan magazines at a supermarket checkout line to see that the U.S. media perpetuate cultural themes, such as women's desire to marry and men's desire to stay single. But despite the image of the reluctant groom that are captured by headlines like "How to Get Your Man to Stay," men marry eagerly and often. Most men who divorce eventually (and quickly) remarry. However popular marriage bashing may be in bars and locker rooms, most men want to be married more than women do. Across all races and ethnic groups, men desire marriage and remarriage more than do women (Tucker & Mitchell-Kernan, 1995).

The differences in the degree to which men and women in different ethnic groups desire marriage reveal powerful social influences. For example, Latino men want to marry more than other men do, but Latina women are also more favorably disposed toward marriage than other women. African American women are less likely than other women to express an interest in marriage. White men are the least likely to express an interest in marriage or remarriage (although they are still more interested than white women), perhaps because white men, on average, have greater opportunities in life than do men of other racial groups even without the advantage of having wives (Cherlin, 1992; Tucker & Mitchell-Kernan, 1995).

Differences in who actually gets married within different ethnic groups demonstrate that marriage is more of a social than a private institution. Before the 1960s, whites and African Americans had similar profiles in terms of age of marriage and proportion married at any given time. Since then, however,

the flight from marriage has been much greater among African Americans than among whites. On average, African Americans get married later in life, their marriages are shorter in duration, they divorce more frequently, and they are less likely to remarry than are whites (Cherlin, 1992; Glick & Sung-Ling, 1987). The explanation has much to do with gender: By tradition, marriage dictates that the man should be more dominant than the woman in the economic sphere. However, African Americans, more so than whites, have a smaller gender difference in income. Put another way, the employment of African Americans is positively related to marriage rates. Therefore, high rates of unemployment depress the likelihood that African American men will marry (Tucker & Mitchell-Kernan, 1995; Wilson, 1996). African American men, like white men, earn more than women of either race, but for African Americans, the gender difference is smaller. The size of the gender difference is crucial for understanding heterosexual marriage, which tends to be structured around wives' economic dependence on husbands. In the absence of appealing alternative styles of marriage (such as peer, or egalitarian, marriage), minimal gender differences tend to minimize interest in heterosexual marriage.

It makes sense that men like to be married because they benefit a great deal from it in terms of the quality of the lives, mental health, and professional opportunities—considerably more than do women (Cherlin, 1992; Lillard & Waite, 1995; Rutter, 1997). Although the flow of resources between partners is complicated, overall the flow of social, emotional, material, and sexual resources is from wives to husbands. In contrast, while women's occupational attainment and earnings are depressed by marriage, divorce increases their occupational possibilities and earnings, albeit largely out of necessity (Weitzman, 1985). In other words, men gain more from being married than do women, especially among whites. Of course, this flow of resources is not foremost in the minds or hearts of the matrimonial pair.

Even when individuals seek to experience marriage as something other than a social requirement to be done in traditional gender scripts, the rest of the world—social institutions, laws, schools, family, physicians, insurance companies—tends to insist on responding to its participants in the conventional manner (Haas, 1992). For example, outsiders assume that married people have promised sexual fidelity to each other and that they are not available for liaisons with other people (Lawson, 1988). In addition, wives who keep their family names must go out of their way to inform people that they do not wish to be known by their husbands' names. The few husbands who take their wives' family names must make an even greater effort to inform others of this choice because it is nonnormative.

Social norms for gender difference in marriage have nearly irresistible power. A married couple may begin as equal partners, but the marriage sets in motion a wife's duties to the household and children and a husband's duties to earn money for the family. Schwartz's (1994) research on peer, or egalitarian, marriage observed that even when both partners work to earn money (as they do in over half the current marriages), their marriages tend to become polarized by gender. Schwartz used quantitative data from the American Couples study and updated the information with a series of in-depth interviews of couples (from a snowball sample) who believed their marriages were egalitarian. It turned out that the majority of couples who considered themselves to be egalitarian were actually "near peers," that is, they fell into gendered patterns of domestic, economic, and emotional labor even when they did not intend to. The fact that most men earn more than most women tilts the division of responsibilities. In fact, the norm of the man being the provider is so strong that even if the woman has money from her family or earns more than her husband, Schwartz observed, the man is still granted the perks of the provider status.

The same set of assumptions sustains the caretaker "mommy" status. Women carry a greater burden of domestic labor than men do, even when they are employed full time, earn more than their partners, or view the division of labor as fair (Brines, 1994; Hochschild with Machung, 1989; Lennon, 1994). The world, from hospitals to schools, typically assumes that the mother is the primary parent. Through everyday interactions, the traditional roles of men and women are reinforced. The father soon gets the point that he is not considered the primary parent. Thus, despite the feminist critique of marriage in the 1970s and changes in women's status in society (especially their growing representation in the workforce), women and men experience marriage differently.

Heterosexual Cohabitation

Heterosexual cohabitation is similar to marriage in that it tends to be a monogamous relationship for more than a trivial duration and is usually founded on love and the hope for a continued future. Cohabitors differ from married people, however, in that they are less economically dependent on each other and less likely to have children (Bumpass, Sweet, & Cherlin, 1991). In addition, cohabitations are less stable and have a higher break-up rate than marriaged couples. Although heterosexual cohabitors often drift into polarized positions economically and domestically, the division of labor is more equitable than it is among heterosexual married couples (Rindfuss & VandenHeuvel, 1990). Half the married couples are dual earners, but along with income and household data, observational and ethnographic studies have demonstrated that husbands end up being the primary breadwinners and, when children are present, wives end up being the primary parents and domestic laborers (Cowan & Cowan, 1992; DeVault, 1991; Hochschild with Machung, 1989.) Such stark differences are present less often in cohabiting relationships (Blumstein & Schwartz, 1983).

In sum, among heterosexual couples, men tend to have more economic power than women. This power, compounded by cultural "norms" that require men to fulfill patriarchal and provider roles and women to fulfill domestic and caregiving roles, influences the structure of marriages and generates a drift toward traditionalism over time.

Same-Sex Commitment

With no legal institution of marriage available to them, gays and lesbians may feel less societal pressure—or, at least, less family pressure—to move in together, restrict sexual access to others, and make emotional commitments. Nonetheless, the urge to bond with another person is strong, and the majority of gays and lesbians do so. Lesbians and gay men, like heterosexuals, are socialized into the two-by-two world, and their requirements for bonding come from early socialization and a social structure that relies on pairing off. Two surveys reported by Lever (1994, 1995) in the *Advocate,* a national gay and lesbian magazine, indicated that more than 92% of gay men and lesbians favor being in a couple. The *Advocate* surveys were not random samples. Indeed, it is difficult to establish base rates for various aspects of gay and lesbian life because of issues related to being "out" (publicly identified as being gay or lesbian). However, these surveys, which tap an audience that may be more likely to be out, are consistent with the findings of other qualitative and quantitative studies.

As proponents of same-sex marriage have pointed out, no institutional framework exists to help keep same-sex relationships intact. Without the institution of marriage, the idea of lifetime commitment, "'til death [or complicated legal extrication] do you part," is less likely. This is one reason why the idea of marriage has great appeal to same-sex pairs. Almost three-quarters of the lesbians and 85% of the gay men in the *Advocate* surveys said they would legally marry if they were allowed to do so (Lever, 1994, 1995). Some lesbians and gay men have put the right to marry at the top of their political action and advocacy agenda.

Same-sex pairs share most of the burdens of everyday life that influence heterosexuals, but they also experience impediments that are unique to gay men and lesbians. Lesbian couples, for example, are often under more economic pressure than other kinds of couples because, on average, their combined resources are smaller than the combined resources of couples in which at least one man is a contributor (Klawitter & Flatt, 1997). Of course, women who are single parents, whether heterosexual or lesbian, are even more vulnerable to financial problems. Married heterosexual women earn less than paired lesbians (Klawitter & Flatt, 1997), partly because of the drift toward traditionalism among heterosexual pairs. These lower-earning heterosexual women have access to their husbands' resources, at least for the duration of their marriages.

Because they are more discriminated against than heterosexual couples, gay men and lesbians may often and regularly be placed in situations that are stressful to them (Patterson, 1995). Both gay and lesbian couples are rejected more frequently by their "in-laws" and sometimes by their own parents than are other kinds of couples (Kurdek & Schmitt, 1987). Parents sometimes blame their child's lover for his or her homosexuality or continue to treat their son or daughter well but are awkward or unaccommodating toward his or her partner. They may refuse to cooperate in major ways. They may even be openly adversarial, such as by blocking child custody rights for the partner when their son or daughter dies. They can also raise barriers in pettier ways, as when they exclude the gay partner from a family photograph but include heterosexual in-laws and long-term partners without a second thought. Even such seemingly small matters can lead to resentment between partners or to a cut-off from their families (and from any of the emotional and material resources that families provide) or both (Patterson, 1995).

Issues of whether to stay closeted or to come out to the world become relationship pitfalls when the two partners disagree about how to handle them (Patterson & Schwartz, 1994). This dilemma is heightened by the cost of being in or out. A gay man in a mainstream career may seek to remain closeted or discreet about his relationship, but his partner may feel strongly that being out is a political statement. Being closeted or out has economic and political consequences that can make these conflicts intense (Day & Schoenrade, 1997; Kurdek & Schmitt, 1987).

For same-sex pairs, the economics of marriage contrast with those for heterosexual pairs. There is no preconceived provider or caregiver role when partners are both men or both women, nor is there an institutional incentive (such as tax breaks or health insurance coverage for partners) for couples to pair up. Economics do, however, influence same-sex pairs to the extent that money represents power. In particular, money buys mobility and autonomy;

those who have sufficient economic resources have greater economic power to move on from a relationship. (Of course, other kinds of power, including emotional power and cultural power, also influence mobility.) However, gay couples are more likely than lesbian couples to follow traditional patterns of intimate relationships that confer greater domestic privilege in areas such as who does what housework to the higher earner (Kurdek, 1993). For lesbian couples, there is greater conflict with this traditional standard (Blumstein & Schwartz, 1983). When one lesbian partner earns more than the other, the two will seek to balance this apparent power imbalance in other ways in the relationship, including sharing housework evenly (Kurdek, 1993). If they are not successful keeping the power differences at a minimum, lesbians tend to experience higher levels of conflict (Kurdek, 1994).

In sum, social structure provides less stability for same-sex pairs than for heterosexual pairs. But the social structural support for heterosexual pairs has much to do with the investment in gender difference, which is a critical underpinning of the current institution of legal marriage. Gay and lesbian pairs experience this instability differently, too, because of gender differences across types of couples. On average, gay (higher-earning) couples have more economic stability than do lesbian couples. But such pairs also have less subcultural orientation toward stability, security, and monogamy in relationships that generally help sustain lesbian relationships.

POWER AND COMMUNICATION

Demographics, economics, and social structure are not, of course, the only ways to understand gender, power, and intimacy in heterosexual marriages or same-sex pairs. As social researchers, we emphasize combining macrolevel and mesolevel knowledge with microlevel accounts of intimate relationships as the most prudent way to understand intimacy. Thus, we shift to the microlevel of everyday intimate communication and conversation.

One gender-theoretical approach to conversation hypothesizes that men and women use the act of conversing differently (Tannen, 1990). Gendered patterns are identified as dominance (masculine) tactics and support (feminine) tactics. Such dominance tactics as interrupting or steering the conversation reinforce or help to create a hierarchical relationship (Kollock, Blumstein, & Schwartz, 1985). "Masculine" and "feminine" styles of conversing are an example of the social construction of gender and the social promotion of gendered statuses in social interaction. We introduce this theme with an important caveat: These styles are not "essential" differences between men and women but styles that are artifacts of "gendered" social processes.

Research on women's approaches to conversation and problem solving supports the view that women tend to use conversation as part of intimacy more so than do men. Women work to keep conversations going, encourage their interlocutors, fill silences, and ask questions. They seek consensus because it is emotionally rewarding to them (Gilligan, 1982; Thorne, 1993). They tend to take time in conversations to find or create a common ground. Men tend to find the "feminine" supportive style weak; they prefer strong tactics, such as interruption and conversational leadership. Women tend to dislike verbal challenges because they believe they violate intimacy and civility; men persistently prefer to spar. "Masculine" tactics facilitate expeditious decision making and reduce the length of conversations or "debates" (Markman & Kraft, 1989; Tannen, 1990). These characterizations are not news to the reader; in fact, they sound more like a case of "Mars-and-Venus" differences that we eschew, until one considers the social context in which such communication patterns emerge.

Although communication researchers have often associated men with conversational power and women with conversational submission, other researchers have focused on how these gendered styles are consequences of social processes. In particular, Kollock et al. (1985) found that "gendered" styles of communication are more strongly associated with personal power than with gender.

Kollock et al. (1985) hypothesized that power, rather than gender, might be the influential feature in communication strategies, such as dominance and support. To test their hypothesis, they observed conversations between heterosexual, gay, and lesbian couples. They found that the more powerful (by status and commitment to the relationship) speaker had more control over decisions and the decision-making process, regardless of his or her sex. Powerful tactics, including minimal responses (such as "hmm" or "uh-huh") that avoid the effort of substantive verbal exchange and more frequent interruptions, were used with the more powerful (economically and emotionally) partner regardless of whether the partner was a man or a woman. Similarly, the more powerful (not necessarily male) partner did not generally ask for the other's opinions or input by using tag questions (e.g., "This is what I think; what do you think?"), commonly used by the less powerful speaker. Notably, for heterosexual couples, the more powerful partner is often the man, but this is not always the case. For same-sex couples' no "gender" is more powerful because gender is a constant. Economic and emotional statuses vary and thus were indicators of power that were correlated with "powerful" communication strategies.

Demand-Withdraw in Heterosexual Communication

Psychological research in the 1990s has supported the observation about power and gender. Christensen and Heavey (1990) and Christensen and Shenk (1991), who are couples-therapy researchers, closely studied demand-withdraw patterns in observations of distressed couples. They found that couples' conflicts and struggles frequently involve a demand-withdraw communication pattern. A demand-withdraw pattern can be initiated when one party seeks or demands conversation, attention, or focus on a particular project or issue. The other party then responds by withdrawing and may seek to distance himself or herself. Demand-withdraw patterns tend to polarize couples who become entrenched in their positions of demanding and withdrawing. Christensen and Heavy (1990) and Christensen and Shenk (1991), among others, observed that among heterosexual pairs, demand-withdraw patterns fall along expected gender lines (men as withdrawers and women as demanders) about 60% of the time; however, 30% of the time, the

roles are reversed, and another 10% of the time both partners display both strategies. Other research on distressed heterosexual couples (Babcock, Waltz, Jacobson, & Gottman, 1993) suggested that when both partners use both strategies, the husband is more likely to be a batterer.

Same-Sex Couples and Communication

How do these power and gender-related styles of communication influence same-sex couples' communication? Same-sex couples are, by definition, without sex difference and tend to work against gender differences. Thus, in cross-sex couples, power differences are camouflaged by gender difference, but in same-sex couples power differences have no camouflage (or confounding variable) and are therefore more readily evident when they exist. When power differentials and gender are used as distinct predictors of conversational control, power differentials, rather than gender, appear to be better predictors of who maintains conversational control, although gender plays an important role (Kollock et al., 1985; Kurdek, 1994). When it comes to communication styles, a participant's gender has a similar influence on same-sex couples as it does on cross-sex couples. The participant's power within the relationship dictates patterns of influence and accommodation for heterosexual and same-sex couples.

For example, lesbian and gay couples are more likely to aspire to egalitarian relationships, but their conversational styles reflect different strategies for balancing power. Lesbian couples, who tend to be more highly sensitized to power imbalances than are other kinds of couples, may seek to minimize conflict and avoid power plays (Kurdek, 1993), including those in conversations. Instead, conversation is oriented to a shared goal: creating an emotionally close, fulfilling, disclosing conversation. Indeed, of the four kinds of couples (lesbian, gay, married, and cohabiting heterosexual) Kollock et al. studied, lesbians had the lowest rate of attempted interruptions and the fewest conversational challenges. Eschewing conventional power tactics in conversation is a path to (and a result of) egalitarianism for lesbians.

Like other men, gay men are more likely to jockey openly for power. They are more likely to acknowledge rank and its privileges and to use various strategies to claim it. For example, gay men use minimal responses ("yes," "no," "um-humh") during conversations more than do other kinds of couples (Kollock et al., 1985). Whereas the less powerful partner in a heterosexual couple tends to ask "tag questions" (e.g., "What do you think?"), the more powerful partner in a gay couple does so. A man with an obvious economic or power advantage goes out of his way to draw out his less powerful partner and to make him feel his opinion matters and that he has interactive value. Because power and masculinity are prominent issues for gay men, this practice represents an effort to equalize status and curb resentment (Kurdek, 1994).

Although egalitarianism tends to be a goal in same-sex couples, not all same-sex couples who aspire to it achieve it. Conversational problems for lesbians arise from the higher levels of expressiveness that tend to be normative in some woman-to-woman relationships. This emotional intensity can produce an "implosion" from the intensive introspection used in pursuit of emotional issues. Because women typically seek to minimize interpersonal conflict and to attain a consensus, lesbians are more likely to avoid controversial issues or to expect their partners to intuit or know their feelings without conversation (Kurdek, 1994). While emotional expressiveness is high, problem solving may be delayed indefinitely. The avoidance of problems may lead to an accumulation of unresolved or seemingly insurmountable relationship problems (Kurdek, 1994; Peplau, Cochran, Rook, & Padesky, 1978).

In contrast, gay men, like heterosexual men, engage in a low level of disclosure. When the relationship is troubled, this may become "stonewalling" during which no communication occurs. Gay couples may fail to create opportunities to address important relationship issues. Small arguments are avoided, while angry feelings accumulate over time. By the time a problem is addressed, a heated, explosive argument may erupt, and the accumulation of issues and resentment may mean that resolution is much more difficult. The male conversational style may complicate the problem once conflict is identified (Kurdek, 1994). Men are more likely to challenge their partners without listening to them. Furthermore, some gay men view compromise (Berzon, 1988) as a failure of masculinity, so a resolution may be impossible.

A final note about gender, marriage, and communication: We have observed that gender and power combine to influence communication patterns and, by extension, the flow of influence between partners, generating diverse adaptations and problems across types of couples (heterosexual, lesbian, and gay). It is crucial to remember, however, that these styles are produced via social learning and social structure, as we discussed earlier. Although research has indicated that there are socially produced gender differences between heterosexual partners and across types of couples, these differences in communication should not be confused with gender difference in the desire for intimacy. Research on couples communication and the influence of conflict on the likelihood of divorce by Gottman (1994) and others has highlighted that although communication styles and individual techniques for achieving intimacy may differ, there are not gender differences in men's and women's desire for love and closeness. In addition, we have reviewed some of the communication research in an attempt to establish links between the social structural aspects of gender and power in terms of how those aspects shape behavior in microinteractions. Further research on the links between social structural conditions and intimate relationships is important to gain a greater understanding of gender and inequality.

SEXUAL EXPRESSION

In *The Gender of Sexuality* (Schwartz & Rutter, 1998), we elaborated on the links between social structural conditions and the conditions of intimate relationships in accounting for the social construction of gender and sexuality. We also noted that the area of sexuality in intimate relationships is notoriously difficult to study because of the ambivalence and prudery of funders of research (including the U.S. government), research scientists, and the individuals and couples being studied. This ambivalence is part of a general cultural ambivalence about sexuality that spurs debates on sex education and abortion (Jones et al., 1985). When scientific studies are conducted, using mostly self-report measures, there is greater suspicion of reporting bias, partly because of sexual ambivalence and partly because different people have different definitions of what constitutes sex (or any particular sex act). In our writing, we draw from the American Couples study and from the National Health and Social Life Survey (NHSLS) (Laumann, Michael, & Gagnon, 1994), as well as from less scientific surveys conducted by magazines and qualitative and theoretical work that explores issues of sexuality in intimate relationships. In this section we discuss two aspects of sexuality in intimate relationships: sexual initiation and nonmonogamy.

Intimate relationships, whether heterosexual or same-sex, decline in sexual frequency over time. Life intrudes, with issues such as housework, power conflicts, and communication difficulties. Various studies have defined sex differently. For example, the American Couples study defined sex as any genital contact. In any case, committed intimate relationships, not single encounters, are the context in which people have the most sexual activity (Laumann et al., 1994). Actually, gay men and cohabiting heterosexuals start out at a higher rate of sexual frequency than do married or lesbian couples, but the sexual frequency of all four categories declines over time (Blumstein & Schwartz, 1983; Laumann et al., 1994).

What Is Important About Initiation and Refusals?

As important as external influences are, sexual expression is undermined, in part, by the gendered scripts that are related to initiation and refusal. Sexual initiation and refusal are deeply gendered sexual customs that affect sexual frequency. Because leadership and dominance are considered masculine, men are required to take charge in various ways. One simple way of showing masculinity, as it is stereotypically defined, is to be the director of a couple's sex life.

One element of sexual arousal is desire (Schnarch, 1994). Couples may vary in who is in charge of desire. For many men, their desire tends

to be a sexual cue; for many women, their partner's desire tends to be the cue. If men always initiate, they are responding to their own internal signals of desire but are then less often the recipients of lust. When women are mostly the recipients of desire, they must wait for cues from their partners to begin to satisfy their sexual appetites. Women, who are generally taught to wait for men and adjust their mood accordingly, learn to experience their partners' desire as erotic. Although men's and women's sexual passions and propensities are highly diverse, this fundamental script pervades sexual activity and fantasy among heterosexuals (Blumstein & Schwartz, 1983). Thus, a woman may take the sexual initiative, but part of its eroticism is that it is "counternormative" or naughty. A man may enjoy submission, and as Ehrenreich, Hess, and Jacobs (1986) observed, women's sexual pleasure has become increasingly acceptable, but this is often seen as role-playing, not the real thing.

Patterns of Heterosexual Initiation and Refusal. Despite the strong social pressures on men to initiate sex, studies have shown that men want women to initiate more—just not too much. In other words, on average, men want to be wanted, but they do not want to give up the thrill of being the sexually dominant partner. Some data show that a man likes a woman to initiate often but that when she starts to initiate more than he does, his satisfaction decreases (Blumstein & Schwartz, 1983). Women have been given leeway to be sexual, but it is unclear how sexual they can be before reprisal. The self-report surveys still tell a traditional story: Married men report doing more of the initiating than married women in all age groups (Laumann et al., 1994).

The same traditions persist when it comes to refusal. On the one hand, wives are no longer expected to have headaches and forgiven for their lesser interest in sex. On the other hand, refusal is still a woman's tool for controlling or responding to her partner. Similarly, men are not supposed to refuse, even if they are in long-term, perhaps boring, sexual relationships. The politics of modern sexuality profess to give men as much of a right as women to refuse sex, but women sometimes feel extremely rejected when their spouses respond to advances with "I'm too tired." Women see their own right to say "I'm tired" as quite a different thing. The stereotype of men's greater sexual appetite is still alive. A man's refusal is seen as going against his natural instincts, whereas a woman's refusal tends to be interpreted as a reflection of her natural, lesser desire (Ehrenreich et al., 1986).

Initiation and Refusal in Same-Sex Pairs. For same-sex pairs, the initiation-and-refusal issues stem from themes similar to those just described. According to the men-as-initiators custom, gay men should have the most sex and lesbians the least, and there is some truth to that generalization (Blumstein & Schwartz, 1983; Laumann et al., 1994; Lever 1994, 1995). However, other issues complicate the sexual interaction. As with heterosexual pairs, frequency declines over time among gay and lesbian pairs. These trends illustrate that frequency is not dependent on gender. If women's socialization to have less sex were a factor, lesbians would have a pronounced change in sexual frequency, while gay men would not. Nevertheless, gay couples' frequency declines similar to other couples. Gay couples and heterosexual cohabitors start out with higher sexual frequency than lesbian pairs, so the base rates are higher, but over time, all relationship types move toward reduced sexual activity.

Differences between the sexual frequency of gays and lesbians have several ramifications. For instance, in our culture, men—straight and gay— are tantalized with visions of sexual variety. In a number of polls, straight and gay men have tended to rate the desire for variety higher than have women. This preference creates a special challenge for long-term gay relationships. If variety spikes desire, and desire is required for initiation, gay men in a committed relationship (who do not have a variety of partners) may decrease initiation. Without the marital sexual obligation, gay couples must find new ways to cultivate sexual connection. Many do, with sex toys, videos, or outside partners (Huston & Schwartz, 1995), but others allow sexual frequency in a long-term relationship to slide.

Lesbians, like heterosexual women, tend to have been socialized into the custom of initiating sex less often than men and of refusing more often (Risman

& Schwartz, 1989). With lesbian couples, however, if each woman expects to be approached and both wait for the other woman to initiate, inevitably sexual frequency declines. If both women feel comfortable saying no, less sex is likely.

Many lesbians are sensitive about sex as a source of power. Power issues are a common theme for lesbian pairs; this political awareness sometimes is related to a concern about manipulation and hierarchy that appears to be inherent in marriage and other heterosexual relationships. Because many lesbians are in a position to be able to reject the hierarchical nature of heterosexual relationships, they are sensitized to any replication of those patterns in their own homes (Wilton, 1996). A sexually intense partner, especially one who likes sex for its own sake, may be seen as aggressive and unfeeling. Thus, sexual gratification is not considered a right as much as an outgrowth of a good relationship (on a good day in that relationship). "Pushing it" can be seen as a power trip or, even worse, as coercion or rape. In any kind of couple in which sexual aggression is a sensitive issue, sexual initiation can be complicated by the concern that a request will feel like pressure or aggression.

A final observation about gender and sexual initiation in couples comes from a finding in the American Couples study. When gay men were asked who initiates more, each partner was likely to report that he did. In contrast, when lesbians were asked who initiates more, each partner was likely to say that her partner did. Whether straight, gay, or lesbian, partners continue to view initiation as "masculine" and receptivity-refusal as "feminine" (Blumstein & Schwartz, 1983).

Nonmonogamy and Affairs

One problem that many long-term partners fear, even if it never happens to them, is nonmonogamy. We define *nonmonogamy* as a sexual liaison outside a committed relationship that may be a single episode, a long-term affair, or a number of affairs. In this chapter, we do not address emotional affairs—nonsexual, covert involvement, usually with someone at work (see Glass & Wright, 1992). The notion of emotional affairs highlights the notion of the flexibility of the definition of non-monogamy. Among the many aspects of non-monogamy that are understudied and difficult to establish is, What kinds of sex acts fall within the definition of nonmonogamy? Does kissing count? Oral sex? This level of detail tends to be excluded from discussions of nonmonogamy.

Often people refer to extramarital affairs as "cheating," "infidelity," or "adultery" because they believe that for heterosexuals they are a transgression of the marriage vows. Steady relationships are common among gay men and even more so among lesbians (Lever 1994, 1995). Although gay couples and, less often, lesbian couples sometimes have an agreement that nonmonogamy is permissible under discreet and limited circumstances, the vast majority of married and cohabiting heterosexual couples do not.

Heterosexuals and Affairs. Ask most heterosexual married couples why they are monogamous, and they tend to find the question odd. The frequently reply to the effect that, "Why get married, if you don't want to be monogamous?" or, as Pittman (1989) notes, "Even if we fail to practice fidelity, we seem to believe that infidelity should not be tolerated" (p. 29). Quite a few people would quote scripture and the Bible and respond with comments like: Adultery is a sin. It defiles the rules God set forth for marriage (Lawson, 1988). In other words, marriage is fundamentally a closed, stable, social institution. Nonmonogamy generates chaos. Yet, some people do go outside the relationship for sex and intimacy.

Most studies on attitudes toward nonmonogamy show that more than 85% of both men and women say they disapprove of it (Laumann et al., 1994). With such high disapproval ratings, one might assume that nonmonogamy rarely occurs. Some studies have suggested that there is, indeed, a low rate of nonmonogamy. In the NHSLS (Laumann et al., 1994), 79% of the married men and 89% of the married women said they had been monogamous throughout their marriages. These data were collected in nonprivate settings, however, which may have led to underreporting. In addition, nonrandom samples have reported lower rates of monogamy and

higher rates of nonmonogamy—anywhere from 25–30% (Blumstein & Schwartz, 1983; Hunt, 1974) to 50% reported in recent surveys in popular magazines like *Playboy* and *Redbook*. While magazine surveys are not generally touted by social scientists as sources of social knowledge, in the realm of sexual behavior it can be difficult to obtain information—or even governmental funding and permission to collect information—about sexuality. Magazine surveys have the limitations of response bias (as social science surveys often do) and, in some cases, unsophisticated survey construction, yet they have traditionally added valuable pieces to the jigsaw puzzle of sexual behavior and sexual attitudes.

Nevertheless, some groups may be more likely than others to report that they have engaged in nonmonogamy. In fact, research data on rates of extramarital affairs may not be as informative about how much nonmonogamy occurs as they are about the relative likelihood of different groups engaging in it. The NHSLS (Laumann et al., 1994) found that rates of affairs are higher among people in the lowest educational category (did not complete high school) and in the highest educational category (completed a graduate degree). The most conservative group were college graduates. Urban dwellers and people of low professed religiosity were more likely to have affairs than others, and very poor people were more likely to have affairs than richer people. Furthermore, cohabitors had many more affairs than married people, perhaps because of their lesser level of commitment and more frequent exposure to sexual and romantic opportunities. Similarly, people who had multiple marriages were more likely than those who remained in their first marriages to have affairs.

Nonmonogamy has traditionally been tolerated in men more so than in women. Looking at two simple variables, age and gender, suggests some ways that the sexual double standard regarding extramarital sex may have changed or, from another view, how it may have changed only a small amount. In the NHSLS, in the youngest age group (22–33), more women than men said they were nonmonogamous. In the next older groups (34–53), women's rates of nonmonogamy increased at a lower rate than did men's. In the oldest age group (54–63), men's experience with nonmonogamy far out-stripped women's. These statistics suggest a trend: Over time, women have gained license to be non-monogamous (and to admit it in survey interviews), although only the youngest women are more non-monogamous than men in their age group.

There are lifetime effects to observe, as well. As men age, their rates of nonmonogamy increase. Men in the oldest age group in the survey (54–63) are having affairs at three times the rate of women. Of course, this discrepancy is partly due to genera-tion: Men who were raised in the 1940s and 1950s have more "gendered" permission for extramarital sex. But the difference is also due to the way sexual attraction is gendered. In almost all cultures, including the United States, younger women have a higher "market value" in the sexual marketplace than do older women. Younger women's allure to alternative mates and the possibility of "trading up" spouses make them more likely to have affairs. Alternatively, most men's market value increases as they age. This is a common explanation for hyper-gamy—younger women marrying slightly older men. Note that although there is little direct evi-dence, when women are less economically depend-ent and in egalitarian or "peer" marriages, they seem to be both more sexually frank within mar-riage and more likely to engage in nonmonogamy (Schwartz, 1994). They are less dependent, which may increase their likelihood of having a roving eye or reduce the perceived costs of surrendering to transitory temptations.

More often, when it comes to extramarital affairs, the sexual double standard, which involves greater sexual permission to men and greater sexual control of women, flourishes. Men and women real-ize different benefits and costs of sex outside the relationship. Some men's freedom to be sexually aggressive and recreational guarantees that, at least in the heterosexual world, they would have more extramarital sex than women.

Women, on the other hand, have rarely had the power in cross-sex relationships to complain about their partners' behavior. Men's sexual acts outside marriage may be considered deplorable, but they have never been seen as a great trespass until recently and in only a few Western countries. U.S.

law no longer allows men to murder nonmonoga-mous wives with impunity, as it did in the past. However, a wife's trespass often modifies an abu-sive or murderous husband's sentence. In both the criminal and civil version of the O. J. Simpson mur-der trials, the defense lawyers painted the murder victim, Nicole Simpson, as a "party girl" who had slept around and who therefore would have had many potential jealous admirers. The idea was not only an alternative explanation for her murder, but a way of making her a less sympathetic character.

Women are less likely to have sex outside mar-riage, but the reasons are unromantic. First, they are simply more economically insecure than men (Goldin, 1990; Klawitter & Flatt, 1997); their fear of losing economic support for themselves and their children encourages them to have more conserva-tive attitudes about sexuality. Second, women tend to be raised with a concern for "reputation," which has been touted as important for their appeal to men. Third, most women have been told by churches, governments, parents, and schools that their role is to be champions of family values, and many have adjusted their sexuality to that responsi-bility. Finally, women tend to be more physiologi-cally vulnerable to sexually transmitted disease, including HIV, than are heterosexual men (Eng & Butler, 1997). "Free spirits," women who are able to think of sex in recreational terms and who are finan-cially capable of absorbing any fallout from their behavior, are rare, particularly among the married (Laumann et al., 1994).

Both women and men still have powerfully strong feelings against nonmonogamy that are linked to traditional religious values; custom; and, more recently, to the "family values" movement (Pittman, 1994). Women are somewhat more likely than men to be severe critics of nonmonogamy, although the majority of both men and women con-demn it (Laumann et al., 1994). Women, however, are more vulnerable to the economic vicissitudes that follow divorce than men, and so are their dependent children (Cherlin, 1992). Men, with less to lose, are more often supportive of, or at least more complacent about, their own or other men's pecca-dilloes (Pittman, 1994). To the extent that men's and women's views on nonmonogamy contrast, this is an excellent example of how complicated a gendered perspective on sexuality can be. Although sexual norms tend to control women's sexuality more than men's, this control is cast as a benefit to family stability that, in turn, tends to be in the interest of women who, in turn, are more likely to be caretakers of children. Whether marital monogamy helps to stabilize families is an as-yet-unanswered, empirical question. Valuing and emphasizing monogamy, however, is certainly treated as a benefit to families. On the one hand, concern for marital fidelity tends to benefit women, who are less likely to have affairs and more likely to suffer economically if their marriages break up. On the other hand, such conservatism casts women as the stakeholders of virtue, fidelity, and family values, which can undermine a pro-feminist, sex-positive attitude that promotes women's independence and autonomy.

Same-Sex Couples.   Same-sex couples, like cohabiting cross-sex couples, are, in general, more likely to report nonmonogamy than are heterosexual couples (Lever, 1994, 1995). In the 1980s, gay men were highly likely to have extra-relationship sex, calculated as high as 95% in long-term couples. Lesbians also reported that they were more likely to practice nonmonogamy than were heterosexual couples; an estimated 38% of pairs who had been together 2–10 years had engaged in affairs (Blumstein & Schwartz, 1983). With the aging of the population and the tide of concern about sexually transmitted diseases, including HIV, the rate of nonmonogamy slowed in the 1990s, according to the *Advocate* surveys and other public health-focused accounts of gay and lesbian sexual activity.

Monogamy has literally become a life-or-death issue for heterosexuals, lesbians, and bisexuals, but perhaps especially for gay men. Indeed, rates of HIV infection are growing more among heterosexual than gay communities in the United States, but the base rate is still higher among gay men (Eng & Butler, 1997). Although there was a flourishing sex-positive, playful attitude toward sexual expression in gay communities in the 1970s, AIDS and the aging of the gay male population caused a radical reversal in attitudes toward monogamy in the

1990s, when the overwhelming majority endorsed monogamy as a relationship ideal. Partners who are faced with negotiating a monogamy agreement may actually achieve greater solidarity by explicitly establishing shared values. The proliferation of public health campaigns to promote safer sex to gay men has contributed to the revision of gay norms related to monogamy. Furthermore, while the tragic incursion of AIDS has decimated the gay community, it has generated a culture of gay solidarity in the face of everyone's potential mortality and the likelihood of death among one's friends. National cultural events in the United States (such as the touring Broadway play *Angels in America,* which deals with AIDS in the lives of gay men, or the AIDS Quilt, which commemorates AIDS victims in a quilt made of patches memorializing individuals who died) generate art, community activities, and cultural references for the gay community facing AIDS. Movies like *It's My Party* (1996) and *Philadelphia* (1994) have brought the AIDS experience to the mainstream, just as celebrity and community fund-raising events for AIDS research and care have turned AIDS into a mainstream concern.

Even though attitudes toward nonmonogamy for gay men have changed since the AIDS era, behavior lags behind attitudes. For example, in the *Advocate* study, Lever (1995) observed that many self-described "monogamous" couples reported an average of three to five partners in the past year; Blasband and Peplau (1985) observed a similar pattern. Monogamous behavior is influenced by age (younger men are less likely to be monogamous than older men) and by context. Because longer-term relationships tend to be characterized by lower levels of sexual frequency, this situation sometimes makes sexual activity with others more likely. Furthermore, whether a gay relationship is open or closed to nonmonogamy has little impact on satisfaction, commitment, expectations for the future, or degrees of liking or loving their partner (Patterson, 1995).

Lesbians, like heterosexual women, are more likely than men in general to value monogamy, although there are growing communities of lesbians who are challenging this norm. As long ago as 1984, Vance documented "sex-positive" and sexually experimental lesbian communities in *Pleasure and Danger*, and this sex positivity has grown in the 1990s. Nevertheless, certain social structures make nonmonogamy more likely for lesbians than for heterosexual women. For example, the strong friendship networks in which lesbians tend to be embedded make affairs more likely. Conversely, affairs transform friendship networks into "incestuous" and complex settings. Indeed, an affair between friends, rather than strangers, is more likely to threaten the primary relationship. Long-term lesbian couples cite affairs most often as a reason for considering a break-up (Johnson, 1990). Finally, although lesbians tend to prefer monogamy, some subcultures seek to challenge bourgeois images of female sexuality by engaging in noncommitted nonmonogamy.

In summary, nonmonogamy, whether in the context of cross-sex or same-sex relationships (or both) is a dilemma for a particular relationship on the basis of the norms that the partners have established in private for taking other lovers. Social norms regarding nonmonogamy, however, powerfully influence people's apprehension about nonmonogamy.

AGGRESSION: HETEROSEXUALS, GAY MEN, AND LESBIANS

In 1796, British feminist polemicist and novelist Mary Wollstonecraft (1984, pp. 153–154) wrote about a character, Mary, who was a battered wife: "Marriage has bastilled me for life." Indeed, coercion and aggression have traditionally been an inescapable part of the marriage bond. In 18th-century British Common Law, for example, there was the "rule of thumb": Husbands were entitled to beat their wives with a stick not to exceed the width of one's thumb (Finkelhor & Yllo, 1985). Laws and attitudes have changed, but wife battering persists as a method of dominance and control.

Heterosexual Battering

Rates of battering are difficult to determine, and there is a range of estimates. Battering tends to be conducted in private, and the stigma of being bat-

tered may inhibit women from reporting domestic violence. Part of the control function of battering involves husbands' control over wives' communications with anyone outside the home. Jacobson and Gottman (1998) reported that 2 million to 4 million women are battered annually and that nearly one third of severe injuries to women are inflicted by male partners or ex-partners. Although poverty and lower levels of education are risk factors for battering, battering cuts across class lines (Koss et al., 1994; Straus, Gelles, & Steinmetz, 1988).

Unlike communication patterns or patterns of sexual expression, in which gender differences are subtle but detectable, the gender difference with respect to violence in marriage is dramatic. Despite the minor debate about the number of women who are battered, researchers agree that domestic violence is most commonly something that husbands do to wives, not vice versa. Although Straus et al.'s (1988) survey indicated that wives do strike their husbands, such blows are largely defensive and generate few injuries or hospitalizations.

In a longitudinal study of violent couples, Jacobson and Gottman (1998) observed that the crucial factor in understanding violence in couples is to understand the function of such violence (see also Jacobson, 1994; Jacobson, Gottman, Gortner, Berns, & Short, 1996). Wives may strike back, but it is their husbands' violence that instills fear in wives and controls their behavior. Using observational, physiological, and self-report data, Jacobson and Gottman (1998) also discovered a surprising diversity among batterers. In particular, they found that while the majority of batterers are emotionally and physiologically upset and appear to be out of control when they engage in violence, a subset of batterers stay physiologically calm even as they engage in fierce beatings.

Violence in Same-Sex Couples

Same-sex couples are not immune from violent conflict. The presence of violence in same-sex relationships supports the notion that power more than gender influences social practices in intimate relationships, although same-sex battering has been understudied. Early research on gays and lesbians generally ignored this topic (as has much research on heterosexual couples). Indeed, it is difficult to obtain accurate rates of violence, emotional abuse, physical aggression, or systematic battering among more commonly studied heterosexual populations (Koss et al., 1994).

In a survey of 100 lesbian victims of domestic violence, Renzetti (1992) found that battered lesbians generally had higher levels of income, education, and occupational prestige and had made greater contributions to the relationship than had their battering partners. Renzetti hypothesized that violence in these relationships was used to rebalance the distribution of power. Indeed, half the battered women in the study cited power imbalances as the reason for violence, and 68% reported that their partners' dependence was a source of strain in the relationship. The more the battered (higher-earning) lesbians sought independence, the more the abuse occurred. In addition, 70% of the battered lesbians cited jealousy and accusations of non-monogamy as reasons for the abuse.

Walker (1986) noted that lesbians tend to fight back more than heterosexual women, citing the smaller size differential that typically characterizes lesbians relative to that of heterosexual partners. Battered lesbians are also more inclined to leave battering relationships than are battered heterosexual women. Because lesbians are often more evenly matched physically, the outcome of a fight is uncertain. It is more likely for either woman to be the initiator or the active resister than it is for heterosexual women who are more likely to be outmatched physically by their partners.

Renzetti (1992) established that 10%–20% of gay men experience violence similar to heterosexual wife battering. Waterman, Dawson, and Bologna (1989) found that when violence occurs, men are more likely to reciprocate violence than are women. One of the reasons for the higher rates of violence reported by lesbians than by gay men may have to do with beliefs about violence. Lesbians are more likely to be sensitized to the issues of physical aggression and to define more acts as physically aggressive or coercive. In contrast, gay men are more likely to see physical aggression as a normal part of men's reactions to serious disagreements.

The evidence of research on heterosexual and same-sex intimate violence suggests that men and women both have the capacity for violence because violence occurs in lesbian relationships as well as heterosexual and gay relationships. However, physical size makes a difference. It makes men more able to dominate women in heterosexual relationships and same-sex partners more likely to fight back when partners may be more closely matched physically. Whereas gender difference and power difference interact in heterosexual couples to generate the persistence of wife battering as a cultural practice, power and perhaps gendered attitudes toward violence are keys to understand battering among cross-sex couples.

CONTESTING TRADITION: THE CASE OF PEER MARRIAGE

Does marriage have the potential to undermine gendered social norms and conventions? Although social norms are resistant to change, we offer a hopeful vision, which stems partly from our experience studying same-sex committed relationships alongside heterosexual marriages and cohabitation.

As we see it, the dilemma of unfulfilled intimacy and sexual promise in marriage has much to do with the typical absence of equity in marriage. Power imbalance is at the heart of the enactment of gender difference; indeed, couples therapy researchers (who study troubled, rather than normal, relationships) observed that such imbalances are central to marital conflict (Jacobson, 1989).

However, marriage need not be the centerpiece of the institutionalization of gender difference. Research on egalitarian marriage, or peer marriage (Schwartz, 1994), discussed earlier, illustrates that the potential for power sharing, obligation sharing, and resource sharing in marriage is real, though not commonly enacted. Indeed, Blumstein and Schwartz's *American Couples* (1983) study on same-sex pairs provided the initial images of successful egalitarian and pair partnerships. For heterosexuals, pairs with the ambition of egalitarianism often fall short, into the "near-peer" category, but a few are actually in egalitarian relationships.

The typical scenario is heterosexual partners who

believe in equality but do not quite achieve it (Coltrane, 1998). Usually the husband "helps" his wife with the children more, and the woman "helps" her husband make economic decisions. The husband still does the major earning, and the wife is still the primary parent and support staff to the family. The persistence of this imbalance is buttressed by the fact that wives as much as, or more than, husbands, perceive this "helper"-style relationship as fair (Hochschild with Machung, 1989; Lennon, 1994). Alternatively, Gerson (1993) reported that husbands are reluctant to accept wives as coproviders.

In a peer marriage (Schwartz, 1994), the partners have organized their emotional, sexual, economic, and parenting functions with the idea that there are no prescribed jobs or responsibilities. The key to happiness and stability is to experience together, and in much the same way, all the things the marriage needs to accomplish. The model—whether characterized as coparenting, job sharing, or acting as a parenting and working team—is not impossible, although it is rare. In her qualitative and quantitative study of peer, near-peer, and traditional marriages, Schwartz observed that peer marriages do not necessarily consist of ideological pairs who are trying to revise gender-related doctrine. Although many of the spouses in peer marriages in her study did emphasize that they were concerned with the disruptive patterns in their families of origin or previous marriages, they had something more. Peer partners were foremost interested in true friendship with their mates, and it was their interest in friendship and companionship that drove them to revise traditional gendered norms in their marriages.

The gendered quality and power differences of marriage and intimate relationships can influence sexual and other social practices within marriage (such as housework). But peer marriages are resolutely different sexually and socially from nonegalitarian marriages. There are few examples for couples to follow, and special attention must be given to creating and sustaining shared domestic and economic responsibilities. For example, couples who are coprinciples of their own firm and who bring their child to work with them so that they can both give care may not be ordinary, but they do exist. These couples typically have a high level of companionship and mutual respect and a notably minimal amount of residual anger. Equity has its rewards. However, the social world tends to reward and enable traditional marriages far more than nontraditional and peer marriages. For example, poor services for day care and limited family support services send a message that families are better off with stay-at-home mothers (Bane & Jargowsky, 1989; Haas, 1992).

Although peer marriages are rare, studying these couples helps us predict social change as follows: When gendered power differences are minimized and committed partnerships—whether heterosexual or same-sex—use equality, rather than difference, as the governing principle, then satisfaction, shared sexual roles, and commitment can be better sustained. It may be that passion still diminishes over time in such relationships. After all, if passion is often inflamed by tension, fear, uncertainty, and the desire to bridge gaps between people, then equitable marriages will be less passionate. But that does not mean they will be less sexually satisfying. What remains is the desire to give and receive pleasure and love, which is more likely to continue when the relationship is reciprocal in all other ways. Equality in a sexual relationship, like equality in the rest of the relationship, is about comradeship—which may not sound exciting on first blush but is really the highest and best hope for a union to last 50 years or more. At this point, our prediction is yet to be thoroughly tested. Sociologist Barbara Risman (1998) studied families in which equality was integral and concluded that those who are entrenched in gendered scripts are capable of change. Her work is the most recent effort to theorize about, as well as bring evidence to bear on, the possibility of truly changing family and intimate relationships.

Schwartz's (1994) study of peer marriage produced information about couples' sexuality, as well as task sharing. The couples in peer marriages had greater satisfaction but less frequent sexual activity than did the couples in near-peer marriages and far less than the couples in traditional marriages. However, the partners were more balanced on sexual initiation, and there was more experimentation and variety in sexual acts. For example, women in peer marriages were sexually on top (literally) more often than women in traditional relationships. Both men and women in peer marriages said that when one of them did refuse, it was not mistaken as a rejecting gesture. The reduced passion characteristic of peer marriages seems to relate to the burdens of everyday life (which all kinds of couples are subject to), intense work schedules, and perhaps the way sexual imaginations and desires are shaped by our culture. Our cultural sexual imagery nearly always includes gender differences in power and social position. Even in an egalitarian marriage, the spouses continue to be influenced by the sexual traditions that are part of the U.S. culture. Even when the mind says, "I want to find a person who regards me as an equal and does a fair share of everything," the erotic internal script may say, "I want to be 'swept away'" or "I like it when I feel strong and competent and my partner feels helpless and innocent." In time, as old scripts fade, new sexual imagery may become more exciting. In fact, there may be some evidence of it already. Women's and men's magazines often include not only physically fit women, but strong and muscular women. Intelligent, strong women are more likely to be mentioned as erotic symbols than ever before.

Finally, when gender difference fuels power differences in intimate relationships, heterosexual pairs may learn from innovative gay and lesbian couples and families. Gay and lesbian advocates for same-sex marriage seek to gain the institutional privileges held by heterosexual couples in marriage contracts (Stacey, 1996). Skepticism from within gay and lesbian communities regarding same-sex marriage comes from the desire not to reproduce the power differences that have been historically associated with conventional cross-sex marriage. However, gay activists have, in general, rallied around the right to marry—not only as part of an equal rights campaign but in their belief that marriage need not continue in its present, gendered, hierarchical format forever. They consider reform not only possible, but probable.

It is interesting that much of the popular alarm about trends in marriage, divorce, and diversity of family forms is based on the argument that movements toward egalitarianism in marriage are all about individualism and narcissism (e.g., Blanken-

horn 1995; Popenoe 1996; Whitehead, 1993). In ironic contrast, the movement toward same-sex marriage, which has merited attention in this book's focus on family diversity, is an example of just how family-oriented egalitarian pairing can be.

CONCLUSION

Marriage is a special category of intimate relationship; as it now exists, it seems to hinge on and amplify gender difference. In the past several decades, gender difference in marriage has declined, but it has hardly disappeared. Persistent gender difference is not merely a theoretical problem, because gender difference tends to mean power difference. Men and women do not simply have different rules they are expected to follow and different roles they have to play. Men and women have different statuses; that is, they have different levels of power and different privileges and obligations in the social structure. In our examination of same-sex relationships, we have observed that the social practices with respect to gender that generate power differences in heterosexual marriage also influence same-sex relationships.

There are many differences between heterosexual marriage and same-sex commitment. First, same-sex partners continue to have no access to the legal institution of marriage. Second, although same-sex partners are socialized into their gender in a similar way as heterosexual partners, their relationship is not characterized by a sex difference. Third, same-sex partners are subject to homophobia and other social problems associated with being gay or lesbian.

We began this chapter by observing that as fans of marriage, we are nonetheless alert to the gendered burdens that are traditionally attached to marriage. We focused on three specific areas: social structural context, sexual expression, and domestic violence. But a more detailed analysis of parenting, decision making, extended family relationships, housework, and work-and-family conflicts, would tell a similar story. When it comes to economic power, sexual authority, and patterns of abuse, norms of masculinity and femininity generate different experiences for men and women, whether they are in cross-sex or same-sex relationships. But these norms are not so far apart. For example, men and women have the same interest and investment in intimacy that underpins many emotional issues. Men and women sustain sexual expression both in marriages and in committed relationships, and even when men are involved with men or women with women, all partners are subject to sexual decline over time in their relationships, which suggests that passion and desire are not so different for men and women. Although aggression in heterosexual relationships presents the greatest level of gender polarities (men

as aggressors, women as victims), we expect that as women accumulate power in the social structure, the level of abuse will also be reduced (though not extinguished). Trends toward egalitarian marriages point to a reduction in the "gendered" quality of marriage. Furthermore, the institutionalization of same-sex couples into same-sex marriage provides a blueprint for cross-sex pairs: Although biological sex and socially constructed gender cannot be surmounted even in same-sex pairs, these couples actually provide images of the potential for egalitarianism that cross-sex couples have.

REFERENCES

Ahlburg, D. A., & DeVita, C. J. (1992). *New realities of the American family (Population Bulletin,* Vol. 48, No. 2). Washington, DC: Population Reference Bureau.

Babcock, J. C., Waltz, J., Jacobson, N. S., & Gottman, J. M. (1993) Power and violence: The relationship between communication patterns, power discrepancies and domestic violence. *Journal of Consulting and Clinical Psychology, 61,* 40–50.

Bane, M. J., & Jargowsky, P. (1989). The links between government policy and family structure: What matters and what doesn't. In A. J. Cherlin (Ed.), *The changing American family and public policy* (pp. 219–262). Washington, DC: Urban Institute.

Bernard, J. (1981). The good provider role. *American Psychologist 36:* 1–12.

Berzon, B. (1988). *Permanent partners: Building gay and lesbian relationships that last.* New York: E. P. Dutton.

Blankenhorn, D. (1995). *Fatherless America: Confronting our most urgent social problem.* New York: Basic Books.

Blasband, D., & Peplau, L. A. (1985). Sexual exclusivity versus openness in gay male couples. *Archives of Sexual Behavior, 14,* 395–412.

Blumstein, P., & Schwartz, P. (1983). *American couples: Money, work, and sex.* New York: William Morrow.

Brines, J. (1994). Economic dependency, gender, and division of labor at home. *American Journal of Sociology, 100,* 652–660.

Bumpass, L. L., Sweet, J. A., & Cherlin, A. (1991). The role of cohabitation in declining rates of marriage. *Journal of Marriage and the Family, 53,* 913–927.

Buss, D. (1995). Psychological sex differences: Origins through sexual selection. *American Psychologist, 50,* 164–168.

Cherlin, A. (1992). *Marriage, divorce, remarriage* (rev. ed.). Cambridge, MA: Harvard University Press.

Chodorow, N. (1978). *The reproduction of mothering.* Berkeley: University of California Press.

Christensen, A., & Heavey, C. L. (1990). Gender and social structure in the demand/withdraw pattern of marital conflict. *Journal of Personality and Social Psychology, 59,* 73–81.

Christensen, A., & Shenk, J. L. (1991). Communication, conflict, and psychological distance in nondistressed, clinic, and divorcing couples. *Journal of Consulting and Clinical Psychology, 59,* 458–463.

Coltrane, S. (1996). *Family man: Fatherhood, housework, and gender equity.* Oxford, England: Oxford University Press.

Coltrane, S. (1998). *Gender and families.* Thousand Oaks, CA: Pine Forge Press.

Cowan, C. P., & Cowan, P. (1992). *When partners become parents.* New York: Basic Books.

Day, N. E., & Schoenrade, P. (1997). Staying in the closet versus coming out: Relationships between communication about sexual orientation and work attitudes. *Personnel Psychology, 50,* 147–163.

Demo, D., & Allen, K. R. (1996). Diversity within lesbian and gay families: Challenges and implications for family theory and research. *Journal of Social and Personal Relationships, 13,* 415–434.

DeVault, M. (1991). *Feeding the family: The social construction of caring as gendered work.* Chicago: University of Chicago Press.

Ehrenreich, B., Hess, E., & Jacobs, G. (1986). *Remaking love: The feminization of sex.* Garden City, NY: Anchor Press/Doubleday.

Eng, T. R., & Butler, W. T. (Eds.). (1997). *The hidden epidemic: Confronting sexually transmitted diseases.* Washington, DC: National Academy Press.

Eskridge, W. N. (1996). *The case for same-sex marriage: From sexual liberty to civilized commitment.* New York: Free Press.

Finkelhor, D., & Yllo, K. (1985). *License to rape: Sexual abuse of wives.* New York: Free Press.

Gagnon, J. H., & Simon, W. (1973). *Sexual conduct: The social sources of human sexuality.* New York: Aldine de Gruyter.

Gerson, K. (1993). *No man's land.* New York: Basic Books.

Gilligan, C. (1982). *In a different voice.* Cambridge, MA: Harvard University Press.

Glass, S. P., & Wright, T. L. (1992). Justification for extramarital relationships: The association between attitudes, behavior, and gender. *Journal of Sex Research, 29,* 361–387.

Glick, P., & Sung-Ling, T. (1987). Remarriage after divorce: Recent changes and demographic variations. *Sociological Perspectives, 30,* 162–179.

Goffman, E. (1977). The arrangement between the sexes. *Theory and Society, 4,* 301–331.

Goldin, C. (1990). *Understanding the gender gap: An economic history of American women.* New York: Oxford University Press.

Gottman, J. M. (1994). *What predicts divorce.* Hillsdale, NJ: Lawrence Erlbaum.

Gray, J. (1992). *Men are from Mars, women are from Venus.* New York: HarperCollins.

Gross, J. (1994, April 25). After a ruling, Hawaii weighs gay marriages. *New York Times,* p. A1.

Haas, L. (1992). *Equal parenthood and social policy.* Albany: State University of New York Press.

Hess, B. B., & Ferree, M. M. (Eds.). (1987). *Analyzing gender: A handbook of social science research.* Newbury Park, CA: Sage.

Hochschild, A., with Machung, A. (1989). *The second shift.* New York: Viking Press.

Howard, J. A., & Hollander, J. A. (1997). *Gendered situations, gendered selves.* Newbury Park, CA: Sage.

Hsu, L. K. G. (1987). Are eating disorders becoming more common in blacks? *International Journal of Eating Disorders, 6,* 113–124.

Hunt, M. 1974. *Sexual behavior in the 1970s.* Chicago: Playboy Press.

Huston, M., & Schwartz, P. (1995). The relationships of lesbians and gay men. In J. T. Wood & S. Duck (Eds.), *Understudied relationships: Off the beaten track.* Newbury Park, CA: Sage.

Jacobson, N. S. (1989). The politics of intimacy. *Behavior Therapist, 12,* 29–32.

Jacobson, N. S. (1994). Contextualism is dead: Long live contextualism. *Family Process, 33,* 97–100.

Jacobson, N. S., & Gottman, J. M. (1998). *When men batter women: New insights into ending abusive relationships.* New York: Simon & Schuster.

Jacobson, N. S., Gottman, J. M., Gortner, E. T., Berns, S. B., & Shortt, J. W. (1996). Psychological factors in the longitudinal course of battering: When do the couples split up? When does the violence decrease? *Violence and Victims, 11,* 371–392.

Johnson, S. E. (1990). *Staying power: Long term lesbian couples.* Tallahassee, FL: Naiad.

Jones, E. F., Darroch-Forest, J., Goldman, N., Henshaw, S. K., Lincoln, R., Rossof, J. I. Westoff, C. F., & Wulf, D. (1985). Teenage pregnancy in developed countries: Determinants and policy implications. *Family Planning Perspectives, 17,* 53–63.

Kessler, S. J., & McKenna, W. (1985). *Gender: An ethnomethodological approach* (2nd ed.). Chicago: University of Chicago Press.

Klawitter, M. M., & Flatt, V. (1997). *The effects of state and local antidiscrimination policies for sexual orientation.* Unpublished manuscript, University of Washington, Seattle.

Kollock, P., Blumstein, P., & Schwartz P. (1985). Sex and power in interaction: Conversational privileges and duties. *American Sociological Review, 50,* 34–46.

Koss, M. P., Goodman, L. A., Browne, A., Fitzgerald, L. F., Keita, G. P., & Russo, N. F. (1994). *No safe haven: Male violence against women at home, at work, and in the community.* Washington, DC: American Psychological Association.

Kurdek, L. A. (1993). The allocation of household labor in gay, lesbian, and heterosexual married couples. *Journal of Social Issues, 49,* 127–139.

Kurdek, L. A. (1994). Conflict resolution styles in gay, lesbian, heterosexual nonparent, and heterosexual parent couples. *Journal of Marriage and the Family, 56,* 705–722.

Kurdek, L. A., & Schmitt, J. P. (1987). Perceived emotional support from family and friends in members of gay, lesbian, married, and heterosexual cohabiting couples. *Journal of Homosexuality, 14,* 57–68.

Laumann, E. O., Michael, R. T., & Gagnon, J. H. (1994). *The social organization of sexuality: Sex practices in the United States.* Chicago: University of Chicago Press.

Lawson, A. (1988). *Adultery: An analysis of love and betrayal.* New York: Basic Books.

Lennon, M. C. (1994). Relative fairness and the division of housework: The importance of options. *American Journal of Sociology, 100,* 506–531.

Lever, J. (1994, August 23). The 1994 *Advocate* survey of sexuality and relationships: The men. *The Advocate:*

The National Gay & Lesbian Newsmagazine, pp. 17–24.

Lever, J. (1995, August 22). The 1995 *Advocate* survey of sexuality and relationships: The women. *The Advocate: The National Gay & Lesbian Newsmagazine,* pp. 22–30.

Lillard, L. A., & Waite, L. J. (1995). 'Til death do us part: Marital disruption and mortality. *American Journal of Sociology, 100,* 1131–1156.

Markman, H. J., & Kraft, S. (1989). Men and women in marriage: Dealing with gender differences in marital therapy. *Behavior Therapist, 12,* 51–56.

Patterson, D. G. (1995). *Virtual in-laws: Kinship and relationship quality in gay male couples.* Unpublished master's thesis, University of Washington, Seattle.

Patterson, D. G., & Schwartz, P. (1994). The social construction of conflict in intimate same-sex couples. In D. D. Cahn (Ed.), *Conflict in personal relationships.* Hillsdale, NJ: Erlbaum.

Peplau, L. A., Cochran, S., Rook, K., & Padesky, C. (1978). Loving women: Attachment and autonomy in lesbian relationships. *Journal of Social Issues, 34,* 7–27.

Pittman, F. S., (1989). *Private lies: Infidelity and the betrayal of intimacy.* New York: W. W. Norton.

Pittman, F. S. (1994). *Man enough.* New York: Putnam.

Pleck, J. H. (1981). *The myth of masculinity.* Cambridge, MA: MIT Press.

Popenoe, D. (1996). *Life without father.* New York: Free Press.

Renzetti, C. M. (1992). *Violent betrayal: Partner abuse in lesbian relationships.* Newbury Park, CA: Sage.

Richardson, D. (Ed.). (1996). *Theorising heterosexuality.* Buckingham, England: Open University Press.

Rindfuss, R. R., & VandenHeuvel, A. (1990). Cohabitation: A precursor to marriage or an alternative to being single? *Population and Development Review, 16,* 703–726.

Risman, B. (1998). *Gender vertigo: American families in transition.* New Haven, CT: Yale University Press.

Risman, B., & Schwartz, P. (1989). *Gender in intimate relationships.* Belmont, CA: Wadsworth.

Rosen, J. C. (1996). Body image assessment and treatment in controlled studies of eating disorders. *International Journal of Eating Disorders, 20,* 331–343.

Rossi, A. (1984). Gender and parenthood. *American Sociological Review, 49,* 1–19.

Rutter, V. E. (1997). *Wedding belle blues: Marriage, gender and depression.* Unpublished master's thesis, University of Washington, Seattle.

Schnarch, D. (1994). *The sexual crucible.* New York: W. W. Norton.

Schoen, R. (1995). The widening gap between black and white marriage rates: Context and implications. in M. B. Tucker & C. Mitchell-Kernan (Eds.), *The decline of marriage among African Americans.* New York: Russell Sage Foundation.

Schwartz, P. (1994). *Peer marriage.* New York: Free Press.

Schwartz, P., & Rutter, V. E. (1998). *The gender of sexuality: Sexual possibilities.* Thousand Oaks, CA: Pine Forge Press.

Stacey, J. (1996). *In the name of the family: Rethinking family values in the postmodern age.* Boston: Beacon Press.

Straus, M. A., Gelles, R. J., & Steinmetz, S. K. (1988). *Behind closed doors: Violence in the American Family.* Newbury Park, CA: Sage.

Tannen, D. (1990). *You just don't understand: Women and men in conversation.* New York: Ballantine Books.

Thompson, L. (1993). Family work: Women's sense of fairness. *Journal of Family Issues, 12,* 181–196.

Thorne, B. (1993). *Gender play.* New Brunswick, NJ: Rutgers University Press.

Thurer, S. L. (1994). *The myths of motherhood: How culture reinvents the good mother.* Boston: Houghton Mifflin.

Tucker, M. B., & Mitchell-Kernan, C. (Eds.). (1995). *The decline in marriage among African Americans.* New York: Russell Sage Foundation.

Vance, C. S. (1984). *Pleasure and danger: Exploring female sexuality.* Boston: Routledge & Kegan Paul.

Wakeling, A. (1996). Epidemiology of anorexia nervosa. *Psychiatry Research, 62,* 3–9.

Walker, L. (1986). Battered women's shelters and work with battered lesbians. In K. Lobel (Ed.), *Naming the violence: Speaking out about lesbian battering* (pp. 198–201). Seattle, WA: Seal Press.

Waterman, C. K., Dawson, L. J., & Bologna, M. J. (1989). Sexual coercion in gay male and lesbian relationships: Predictions and implications for support services. *Journal of Sex Research, 26,* 118–124.

Weitzman, L., (1985). *The divorce revolution: The unexpected social and economic consequences for women and their children in America.* New York: Free Press.

West, C., & Zimmerman, D. H. (1987). Doing gender. *Gender and Society 1,* 124–151.

Whitehead, B. D. (1993, April). Dan Quayle was right. *Atlantic Monthly,* pp. 47–57.

Wilson, W. J. (1996). *When work disappears: The world of the new urban poor.* New York: Alfred A. Knopf.

Wilton, T. (1996). "Which one's the man? The heterosexualisation of lesbian sex," in D. Richardson (Ed.), *Theorising heterosexuality,* (pp. 125–142). Buckingham, England: Open University Press.

Wollstonecraft, M. (1984). The wrongs of woman. (1796) in G. Kelly (Ed.), *Mary and the wrongs of woman* (pp. 154–155). Oxford England: Oxford University Press. (Original work published 1796)

CHAPTER **5**

Gender and Parent-Child Relationships

GARY W. PETERSON, DENISE ANN BODMAN, KEVIN R. BUSH, AND DEBRA MADDEN-DERDICH

Children in our society are born into ongoing social processes that are laden with "engendered" meanings and experiences (Bem, 1993). The everyday development of children occurs in countless settings, including households, child care centers, schools, neighborhoods, peer groups, and religious institutions, all of which provide engendered socialization environments for the young. Foremost among these contexts are "families," often considered social settings in which gender issues are particularly potent forces in the socialization of children (Ferree, 1991; Peterson & Rollins, 1987; Thompson & Walker, 1995; Thorne, 1987). A basic organizing principle that parents often use to define the social meaning of young children (beginning with newborns) is the interpersonally defined categories "boy" and "girl" (Bornstein, 1995; Ruble & Martin, 1998).

The gender-based social labels for family members ("father," "mother," "son," and "daughter"), when considered together, connote traditional family definitions, despite the decrease of households in which heterosexual parents live together with biologically related offspring. Such two-parent families, in which fathers, but not mothers, work outside the home have declined to a minority status in our society (Teachman, Polonko, & Scanzoni, 1999). The persistence of traditional engendered meanings for family roles is puzzling, however, when viewed in terms of fundamental structural changes that are redefining divorced, stepfamily, dual earner, and lesbian and gay relationships as normative family relationships.

The trend toward fewer traditional nuclear families and the growing acceptance of several "alternative" forms may indicate that family diversity has become "normative" in our society. Although the value of two-parent families need not be dimin-

ished, similar to the biologist's view that complex ecosystems are viable precisely because they adapt, the inevitability of social change is necessary and important to recognize. The fact that no single family form currently predominates does not suggest, as some observers have claimed, that family relationships are endangered (Popenoe, 1993). A more defensible position is that families are changing and adapting to meet the current and emerging demands of a dynamic society (Coontz, 1997). Families have become vital emotional units, based primarily on love and affection, that provide psychological security and nurturance to their members. Increasingly, families in American society cannot be described in terms of specific structural definitions, but exist largely because individuals subjectively define themselves as members of intimate groups that are assigned special significance. Structural definitions are inadequate to encompass the wide array of viable forms that include dual-earner, single-parent, divorced, stepfamily, and lesbian and gay relationships.

Our purpose here is to describe the current research and theory on the meaning of gender for parent-child relationships within diverse family forms. We are particularly concerned with how much this research remains tied to conceptions of gender that are linked to nuclear or two-parent families. An important factor that established the nuclear family as the normative standard was the structural-functional perspective, a theoretical framework that dominated sociology and the study of families during the middle of this century (Parsons & Bales, 1955). Such conceptions of nuclear families and associated meanings about gender became deeply rooted in white middle-class ideals. An important result was the failure to recognize that these relationships and engendered meanings are subject to social change and vary substantially according to racial, ethnic-cultural, and social class membership. Despite the decline in the use of Parsonian theory (Kingsbury & Scanzoni, 1993), however, traditional assumptions about the role of gender in parent-child relationships often continue to shape our definitions of what is thought to be normative. Consequently, a primary goal of this chapter is to determine where functionalist assumptions either implicitly or explicitly continue to guide research on the meaning of gender in parent-child relationships. We also examine how ideas shared by contemporary feminist and symbolic interaction theories can be used to challenge functionalist thought on the engendered nature of these relationships.

Following a brief overview of theories, we explore whether gender (1) is a source of fundamental meaning for children's "active roles" within reciprocal models of parent-child socialization; (2) influences how fathers and mothers identify with and perform parenting roles; (3) shapes how boys and girls are differentially socialized by parents who are performing maternal and paternal roles; and (4) is a source of structure and role expectations for parent-child role relationships within diverse family forms, including dual-earner, divorced, stepfamily, and lesbian and gay relationships. In addition, we provide some personal reflections, evaluate current research, and make recommendations for future work on the meaning of gender within the parent-child relationship.

GENDER THEORY, THE FAMILY, AND PARENT-CHILD RELATIONS

Parsonian Theory

The classic view of gender as a source of social structure in families and parent-child relationships was provided in Parsons and Bales's (1955) version of the structural-functional perspective. Because Parsons's primary concern was the maintenance of social order, he and Bales proposed that a particular family form that existed in the 1950s was a functional necessity for urban industrial society. This "nuclear family" consisted of a heterosexual husband-wife relationship, breadwinner father, home-

maker mother, and dependent children. Parsons and Bales further proposed that a gender-based division of labor was necessary to achieve family stability and the effective socialization of children. Parental roles were gender differentiated and complementary, so that internal harmony could be fostered and families could assume a unified stance toward outside institutions. Fatherhood was viewed primarily as the "instrumental" role, whereas motherhood was viewed as an outgrowth of the "expressive" role. Although fathers were supposed to be in secondary parental roles, as the primary links to the outer society, they were expected to demand mature, achievement-oriented behavior from their children. In contrast, mothers were supposed to be centered within family boundaries and responsible for integrative activities, family solidarity, and the provision of noncontingent love to their children.

The failure to maintain this gender-based division of labor could endanger a child's "appropriate sex-role" development and foster deviant behavior. From the standpoint of society, the purpose of socialization within families (gender socialization, in particular) was to produce adults who fit into the existing role system of society. In the case of gender roles, this meant masculine and feminine gender roles, or collections of social expectations based, in part, on individuals' biological (and gender-differentiated) attributes. Family structures that deviated from the nuclear family model were viewed as threats because they had the potential to disrupt the society's ability to maintain itself through the effective socialization of new members.

The Parsonian basis for conceptualizing children's socialization was the conventional way that the concept of role and its more specific derivative gender role were defined. Sex role or gender role was a construct shared with other frameworks besides functionalism (e.g., social learning theory in psychology) and defined the basis for male-female differences in conforming to socially defined role expectations. As an aspect of social structure, roles were viewed as clusters of expected duties, rights, and obligations that provided guidance for individuals to "role-play" assigned interpersonal "scripts." Therefore, socialization was viewed as a unidirectional process in which parents' primary task was to inculcate social scripts in their children. The result was that conceptions of family life, parent-child relationships, and the larger society allowed for little individuality, negotiation, or social change.

Feminist Theory

Feminist theory contradicts functionalism, is useful for critiquing Parsonian theory, and helps to conceptualize the research on gender influences within the parent-child relationship. Feminist perspectives take issue with many functionalist ideas and caste new light on families, parent-child relationships, and the concept of gender. First, feminist ideas challenge Parsons's elevation of the nuclear family to the standard against which all other forms of intimate relations are compared and deviance is defined. A feminist viewpoint legitimates the "normality" of diverse family forms and recognizes that whatever is defined as a family at a particular time must result from processes of "social construction" during human interaction. Consequently, the family is simply a product of particular sociocultural conditions during a given historical period and is subject to constant social change in meaning and structure. Feminist observers view diverse family forms as having the potential to be effective socialization environments for children, with parenting being only one option within a diverse array of possible intimate relationships (Osmond & Thorne, 1993; Thompson & Walker, 1995; Thorne, 1987).

Feminists have proposed that gender is central to all social institutions and the lives of all individuals and inherently involves issues of power and inequality. Consequently, gender is fundamental in structuring aspects of family life, such as parent-child relationships, fatherhood, motherhood, and childhood. Much of family life and parent-child relationships is shaped by socially constructed divisions of labor within families, many of which result in the differential allocation of resources, responsibilities, and status (Ferree, 1991; Thompson & Walker, 1995). Gender divisions are not as impervious to social change as Parsons argued, but are socially constructed through ongoing social processes conducted by mothers, fathers, boys, and

girls that are referred to as "doing gender" (Ferree, 1991; Thompson & Walker, 1995; West & Zimmerman, 1987). The centrality of gender in feminist thought is qualified only somewhat by the idea that an individual's engendered circumstances may vary, depending upon his or her experiences as a member of a particular social class, racial, or ethnic-cultural group (Osmond & Thorne, 1993).

The concept of sex role, which is based partially in functionalism, has been criticized by feminist scholars for failing to demonstrate that gender permeates all social institutions. Feminist critics have argued that gender role (or sex role) is a primary means of conceptualizing how males and females conform to generalized expectations for either masculine or feminine behaviors. Such conceptions of gender roles have masked both the potential for social change within engendered relationships and the extensive variability within (rather than between) the respective populations of males and females (Bem, 1993; Osmond & Thorne, 1993). More flexible conceptions of engendered relationships exist that are useful for understanding the interpersonal associations structured by parents and children.

Symbolic Interactionist Theory

Several ideas from the symbolic interactionist perspective complement those of feminist thought, offer interpretations contrary to Parsonian views, and provide ideas for critiquing the current research on gender within the parent-child relationship (Hewitt, 1997; LaRossa & Reitzes, 1993; Stryker & Statham, 1985). The first idea, the interactionist conception of role, is substantially different from the functionalist view (LaRossa & Reitzes, 1993). In contrast to the one-way socialization model of functionalism, the symbolic interactionist perspective provides a conception of roles as sets of expectations performed by a person (e.g., a father) interacting with a partner (e.g., a daughter) who, in turn, responds by enacting a reciprocal set of expectations. An interactionist conception of role is more like a general gestalt, rather than a list of specific duties, that induces conforming behavior. Individuals use roles to acquire a general or tentative sense (i.e., a definition of the situation) of another person's behavior so that meaningful responses can be made during interaction. Individuals act within roles, but in a manner that permits greater latitude than actors' assigned roles in a play.

Although roles provide a general sense of social structure, individuals are constantly engaging in interactions that gradually alter patterns of role expectations and create new social organization (Callero, 1986; Hewitt, 1997). Thus, engendered role expectations are flexible and allow for more dynamic parent-child negotiations than is portrayed in functionalist conceptions. Even the more formalized aspects of roles (which collectively are responsible, in part, for social structure) are subject to long-term historical change through (1) large-scale socioeconomic forces and (2) infinite numbers of microlevel (face-to-face) renegotiations that contribute to incremental changes in role relationships among fathers, mothers, boys, and girls.

Another symbolic interactionist idea is that the more salient (or important) roles for individuals usually become central aspects of the "self," often referred to as a person's "identities." Individuals both define themselves and behave in terms of those social expectations with which they are most identified and that have the greatest social meaning for them. Mothers and fathers often identify with and define parental roles as fundamental aspects of their identities, but great individual variation exists in just how intense this investment actually becomes for each mother and father.

Contrary to some critiques of interactionist ideas, role concepts are not simply limited to the rational side of relationships and ignore emotional dimensions (Osmond & Thorne, 1993). Instead, the roles in which we are most invested and through which we define ourselves are deeply laden not only with substantive expectations for behavior but with how we are expected to respond emotionally in various situations. Emotional experiences are not merely physiological responses that are directly evoked by particular persons or specific situations, but are deeply embedded in our role relationships with others, cultural expectations for appropriate responses, and the meanings acquired during social interaction. For example, the physiological responses of mothers

and fathers to the birth and early parenting of a young infant boy or girl often are culturally labeled as the emotions of exhilaration, love, devotion, worry, and anxiety. The exact labels given to similar physiological experiences, however, may vary extensively with the new parent's own history of family relationships and culturally defined role expectations.

Symbolic interactionists also share with feminists the idea that conceptions of unitary gender roles are too narrow, and both theories emphasize that a great variety of social roles are engendered. Roles occupied within families, work settings, and most social institutions are composed of expectations that convey engendered meanings for social behavior (Hewitt, 1997; West & Zimmerman, 1987). Such a diversity of role learning contexts does not negate the possibility that young children develop gender-role stereotypes at early ages that structure social reality in fundamental ways (Fagot, 1995; Ruble & Martin, 1998). Gender stereotypes and the great diversity of engendered roles operate to structure the meanings and behaviors of parents and children at virtually all levels of social organization, including individual, dyadic, familial, extrafamilial, and macrostructural (institutional) levels.

An interactionist perspective views gender as a social "boundary," or a pervasive source of social meaning in society. Gender provides meaning that classifies people, promotes identification, gives cues for interacting with others, and establishes sanctions for those who depart from these cues and expectations (Lamont & Fournier, 1992). Although roles are not scripts and are subject to constant renegotiations (Strauss, 1978), a balanced view recognizes that engendered expectations for many social roles have substantial structuring capacities within the context of flexibility and change. Elements of social structure vary in the extent to which change is prevalent, making it difficult for patterned human behavior to be completely subject to individual renegotiation from the ground level within most relationships. Gender is an important means of structuring parent-child relationships, but is flexible enough for those who wish to challenge some of the conventional assumptions and renegotiate their circumstances. Most parents and their children, however, use at least some of the existing social expectations as general guides (not prescriptions) in negotiating the specific nature of their parental identifications, involvements, and responsibilities that differ by gender.

Locating gender influences primarily within social, rather than biological, origins does not negate the idea that engendered social structure establishes boundaries between the "male and female worlds." These same dynamic social processes and interactions with others help to convey social meaning, provide predictability in relationships, become patterns of social structure, shape our conceptions of reality, and contribute to fundamental aspects of our social identities. Consequently, gender is an important basis for role expectations (and social structure) similar to other fundamental social characteristics, such as race, ethnicity, and social class (LaRossa & Reitzes, 1993; Mead, 1934). The remainder of this chapter examines how symbolic interactionist and feminist ideas differ from functionalist interpretations of how gender shapes parent-child relationships, beginning with the role of children in diverse family forms.

CHILDREN IN ACTIVE, ENGENDERED ROLES

An obvious shortcoming in the current scholarship is the failure to recognize that children have active roles in constructing engendered meanings and role expectations that define how children and parents respond to each other. Instead, most of this literature portrays children as being inducted into social awareness and engendered role expectations through unidirectional socialization, similar to functionalist conceptions of the young being molded into scripted roles (Parsons & Bales, 1955). Unidirectional perspectives propose that socializing agents use strategies that are aimed at inducing children to internalize adult conceptions of religious beliefs, political attitudes, social class attitudes, ethnic identification, and engendered meanings that contribute to social structure (Peterson & Hann, 1999). Children's development is conceptualized in terms of how the adult gender expectations shape their lives (Thorne, 1987), with the young having

little to do with fostering their own engendered role identities and behavior.

The preoccupation with unidirectional models of gender influences is surprising and demonstrates how this area of scholarship lags substantially behind other related topics in conceptualizing how gender socialization occurs within families. A contrasting idea, but a commonsense one, is that children also influence their parents. Socialization influences occur in a reciprocal or bidirectional manner, with children and adolescents taking active roles in negotiating the engendered meaning of their relationships with parents and other adults (see Ambert, 1992; Peterson & Hann, 1999). This view that children are active participants, rather than passive recipients, of socialization is consistent with both the feminist and symbolic interactionist perspectives that humans actively construct meaning, interpret the social world, and actively shape their own development (Mead, 1934; Peterson & Rollins, 1987; Thorne, 1987; West & Zimmerman, 1987). Increased attention must be devoted to understanding how children's gender and their abilities to negotiate engendered relations influence their development and identities, as well as those of their parents.

Research on gender already provides a limited basis for thinking in a reciprocal manner. Perceiving an infant's gender, for example, appears to shape the engendered expectations of parents, which, in turn, influences the different responses that parents direct toward male versus female infants. Newborn sons are often described by parents as better coordinated, more alert, stronger, and hardier than infant daughters, whereas infant daughters are viewed as more beautiful, softer, smaller, less attentive, weaker, and cuter than infant sons. Parental responses to infants that differ by gender include the tendency of boys to receive more rough-and-tumble engagement than girls, especially from fathers (Bornstein, 1995).

Other research has examined the cognitive basis for children to begin actively constructing their own engendered meanings and experiences within the parent-child relationship. Between ages 2 to 3, children acquire *gender schemas,* or abstract theories about each gender and what such conceptualizations imply for their own self-definitions (Bem, 1993; Ruble & Martin, 1998). Gender schemas help govern what children do by directing their attention, biasing their memories, and setting parameters for actions taken in reference to being either a "boy" or a "girl." Rather than simply being incrementally shaped by the environment, young boys and girls use these newly developed gender schemas as cognitive screening mechanisms to selectively remember, forget, accept, or reject information that applies to their own gender. This screened, processed, and organized information may be used to guide decisions as well as behavior. Instead of being shaped into gender-typed toy preferences, for example, young boys can be viewed as actively selecting toys that are labeled and categorized as "boy toys" (e.g., action figures) and rejecting toys that are labeled and categorized as "girl toys" (e.g., dolls) (Ruble & Martin, 1998). Therefore, children's concepts and behavior can be viewed as actively constructing and having an impact on their engendered environment.

Later in development, when the pubertal changes of adolescent girls are under way and more complex feminine role behavior becomes prevalent, the father-daughter relationship is often characterized as distant (Starrels, 1994; Youniss & Smollar, 1985). Engendered meanings about daughters' emerging sexuality may contribute to this distance, but the daughters' gender-role behaviors may also negotiate this circumstance in ways that are not yet understood. Thus, an important objective would be to understand whether fathers of daughters and fathers of sons may have different conceptions of girls and women.

THE ENGENDERED NATURE OF MOTHERHOOD

Motherhood today is characterized by diversity, contradictory images, a complicated array of role involvements, and engendered role expectations (Barnard & Martell, 1995). Women become mothers by choice, the failure to plan, natural childbirth, technological innovations, and adoption. Mothers are married, single, partnered, employed, nonemployed, young, old, rich, and poor. Such diversity in the circumstances of mothers makes functionalist conceptions of maternal expressive roles within nuclear families seem like historical anachronisms. Part of the difficulty in describing the great diversity and reality of motherhood is the extent to which idealized images set high and perhaps unrealistic standards for most women. One of these images, Madonna and Child, conveys the angelic, self-sacrificing, all-loving, and totally accepting vision of motherhood. An equally prevalent image proposes that mothering is rooted in instinctive, perhaps biological, phenomena. According to this view, most mothers are biologically predisposed to parent, have an intuitive grasp of child care, and have corresponding abilities to do so without ambivalence or awkwardness (Boulton, 1983; Chodorow & Contratto, 1982; Thompson & Walker, 1989).

Perhaps the most defining characteristic of motherhood is its engendered nature in the form of disproportionate and distinctive social expectations that women face in performing parental roles. Mothers continue to face gender-role divisions in parenting that are consistent in spirit, if not the exact letter, with functionalist conceptions of expressive roles in nuclear families, even though their everyday lives differ substantially from such classic conceptions. The majority of mothers, for example, work outside the home and are members of families that differ in structure and meaning from the nuclear family. The downside of complex maternal role demands is that mothers have less time and energy for investment (even when they do work outside the home) within the more "prestigious" roles of paid labor markets beyond family boundaries. Mothers' work often occurs as invisible unpaid labor within families, and the relatively low prestige of this work reflects how our status definitions are shaped by the values of a male-dominant culture. In contrast, fathers have more time and energy to perform prestigious (paid) work roles in the public sphere that legitimate their dominance within both family boundaries and the society at large (Chow & Bertheide, 1988).

The irony of traditional gender conceptions is that both historical and current evidence indicate that many circumstances of motherhood may have never corresponded with Parsonian conceptions. Such evidence also illustrates how the engendered meanings of motherhood are modified by the forces of race, ethnic, cultural, and class membership. For example, low-income and ethnic-minority women in our society have long faced the necessity of working outside the home and the corresponding inability to invest themselves exclusively in maternal roles as higher-income women have done (Currie, 1988). Historical accounts demonstrate that the culturally idealized images of stay-at-home mothers, who focus exclusively on children's emotional care in nuclear families, are a recent development, even in Western societies (O'Barr, Pope, & Wyer, 1990). These idealized circumstances remain a culturally privileged model of mothering that is rooted largely in white, Western, patriarchal, and nuclear family traditions. Most mothers, but especially those of low-income, ethnic-minority backgrounds, have been largely unable to attain the ideal of a total investment in motherhood, a circumstance that has increasingly been waning even among middle-class women.

An obvious consequence of persistent gender-based divisions of labor is societal pressure to assign mothers the primary tasks of caring for, interacting with, and socializing the young. Compared to fathers, for example, mothers (1) are more involved in performing parenting roles, (2) are expected to do so by a greater variety of significant others, (3) believe they have (and actually do have in most cases) ultimate responsibility for managing children's lives and schedules, and (4) are more likely than fathers to be blamed when children have problems (Chodorow & Contratto, 1982; McMahon, 1995; Parke, 1995). Motherhood roles remain more central to most women's identities than comparable fatherhood roles are for most men. Such generalizations must be qualified, however, by the wide variation that exists in how much women and men identify with and effectively perform parental roles.

Maternal roles are engendered, in part, through gender-based ideologies that originate within larger social institutions that define role expectations and structure the parental division of labor (Coleman, 1991). Feminist observers have proposed that motherhood's engendered nature is rooted in social definitions conveyed by the ideologies of experts, religious doctrine, the mass media, the popular culture, and the medical establishment (Thompson &

Walker, 1989). Women are commonly believed to be instinctively predisposed to caring for children. Some researchers have further concluded that out-of-home child care totaling more than 40 hours per week may foster insecure attachment in infants (Belsky, 1991). Although disputed by other findings (Field, 1991), such conclusions help to perpetuate the belief that women are biologically programmed for affiliation and are more competent to care for children than are men.

Despite increases in the involvement of mothers beyond family boundaries, many societal interests persist in viewing the meaning of "woman" as virtually synonymous with motherhood roles (Osmond & Thorne, 1993; Thompson & Walker, 1989). This view supports the belief that female identity investment should remain disproportionately within the family and, more specifically, within the parent-child relationship. Ironically, these conceptions have persisted even after women have diversified their role identifications into the larger society much more than men have reciprocated by investing in family roles. Consequently, many mothers have become victims of incomplete social change in which they must respond both to traditional engendered roles (consistent, at least in spirit, with Parsonian conceptions) and to newer expectations for increased role identification beyond family boundaries. The result is a new cultural ideal, the "supermom," in which employed mothers are expected to compensate children for their absence by devoting themselves to their young as much as possible when they are home without appreciably compromising their careers and job standards of performance (Crosby, 1991; Ferree, 1987). Many women who attempt to be supermoms, however, experience role strain, diminished status, and inequality of opportunity in the public sphere. An important way for women to alter these circumstances is to negotiate greater equality with men in the difficult tasks that are associated with caregiving (Baber & Allen, 1992).

THE ENGENDERED NATURE OF FATHERHOOD

Fatherhood consists of a variety of engendered meanings that differentiate what fathers and mothers are expected to do within the breadwinner, companion, care provider, moral guide, protector, disciplinarian, playmate, and coparent roles (Lamb, 1997b; Pleck, 1997). Compared to maternal roles, paternal roles are often described as being less culturally scripted and difficult for boys to learn in the absence of clearly defined role models (Marsiglio, 1995). Therefore, many fathers remain in secondary parenting roles (or "helpers") and are more difficult for children to develop clear images of and to use as role models (Lewis, 1997). In two-parent families in which mothers are not employed, fathers spend only 20% to 25% as much time in direct interaction with children as do mothers and only about a third as much time being accessible to them. Fathers are especially unlikely to have overall responsibility for managing children's environments or for structuring their schedules and setting limits. Fathers' direct interaction and accessibility increases only modestly when mothers work outside the home, while virtually no change occurs in fathers' overall responsibilities for managing children's lives (Lamb, 1997a, 1997b; Parke, 1996; Pleck, 1997). In both historic and current times, fathers have faced fewer social expectations to identify with (or become committed to) parental roles and have spent substantially less time in caregiving and related activities than have mothers (Marsiglio, 1993, 1995).

Comparisons between mothers and fathers indicate, in part, that fathers are behaving consistently with Parsonian conceptions of the instrumental role as the primary links to the larger society and as the secondary or "back-up" parent. Beginning in infancy, fathers are characterized as novel playmates (engaging in rough-and-tumble play), whereas mothers are caretakers (Lamb, 1997a; Parke, 1995). Such patterns of interaction appear consistent with those of middle childhood, during which fathers are more involved in physical-outdoor play interactions, whereas mothers are more involved in caregiving tasks. Fathers engage in fewer punitive episodes, conflictual interactions, negative emotional expressions, and positive emotional communications with children of elementary school age than do mothers (Russell & Russell, 1987; Straus, 1994). These comparatively different patterns of paternal interaction may simply reflect

that fathers spend less time than do mothers with children of all ages (Parke, 1995).

Fathers engage in more leisure-time activities with their adolescents, whereas mothers are again primarily responsible for caretaking. Fathers' relationships with teenagers are characteristically less close than mothers', and fathers are primarily involved in giving practical advice to sons (Collins & Russell, 1991). Teenage daughters are especially inclined to view fathers as distant authority figures, the result being that little interaction occurs in father-daughter relationships (Starrels, 1994; Youniss & Smollar, 1985).

Although such gender differences in parenting certainly hearken back to the Parsonian view of traditional gender-of-parent differences, sufficient evidence also indicates that paternal roles are subject to historical change, substantial variability, and social construction within specific parental relationships. Partly in response to feminist thought and the changing roles of women, the attitudes of men and the general society have changed toward the acceptance of coequal responsibility for parenting roles by fathers (Pleck & Pleck, 1997). Despite arguments that such changes in fatherhood are largely cultural myths (LaRossa, 1988, LaRossa & Reitzes, 1995), the prevailing view is that slow but moderate change has occurred in fathers' identification with and actual performance of coequal parenting roles (Coltrane, 1995; Parke, 1995, 1996).

An important qualification to conclusions about change or stability, however, is that substantial variation exists in paternal role performance. A father's competence in performing roles is predicted by a man's attitudes (motivations) to do so, perceived parental competence, self-confidence in parental roles, supportiveness of the wife, and degree of mother's involvement in work roles, as well as formal supports from the workplace (e.g., parental leave) and other institutions (Lamb, 1997a; Parke, 1995, Pleck & Pleck, 1997).

Modest evidence of greater paternal involvement is further qualified by the fact that coequal parenting is not as prevalent among African American, Hispanic, and Native American fathers. Instead, the movement toward coequal parenting seems fairly localized within samples of highly educated fathers, especially European American fathers with considerable formal education. For example, the economic marginality and discrimination that many ethnic-minority men often face greatly diminishes their abilities to provide for their families and their legitimacy in fatherhood roles (Pleck & Pleck, 1997). A common result within lower-income and ethnic-minority populations (e.g., some lower-income African American fathers), therefore, is diminished paternal involvement in and higher rates of absence from the households in which their children live. A compelling irony is that a growing number of inner-city fathers are retreating from their families precisely at the time that others are becoming more involved in parental roles (Furstenburg, 1995).

Moreover, paternal involvement by any group of men has failed to increase proportionate with the greater involvement of mothers in breadwinner roles outside family boundaries (Hass, 1992). Consequently, current conceptions about the engendered nature of fatherhood remain moderately consistent with functionalist views that fathers are the primary occupants of extrafamilial roles, but only as performers of parenting roles in a secondary sense.

DIFFERENTIAL TREATMENT OF BOYS AND GIRLS IN FAMILIES

Another way that engendered social patterns shape parent-child relationships may occur through the differential manner in which parents treat boys and girls. Differential treatment is rooted in distinctive engendered meanings held by parents who occupy both complementary and gender differentiated roles. The tendencies of parents to socialize their sons and daughters differentially are consistent with functionalist concerns that boys and girls should be prepared for "appropriate" gender roles. The literature on differential treatment proposes that parents enact gender-specific role behavior that socializes children for gender-typed (masculine and feminine) roles that functionalists view as central (or even essential) aspects of nuclear families. Parents are viewed as either overtly or covertly communicating their own gender-stereotyped role expectations that, in turn, affect the motivations, attitudes, self-concepts, role expectations, and role behaviors of children.

Maccoby and Jacklin (1974) were among the first to review the differential treatment literature and concluded that parents' child-rearing practices directed at boys and girls were similar. Systematic gender differences were prevalent in only a few areas: (1) infant boys were more frequent recipients of physical stimulation and encouragement; (2) boys were punished more frequently, (3) boys received more praise, and (4) parents encouraged gender-typed behavior and discouraged cross-gender behavior, especially for boys.

Subsequent reviews by Huston (1983) and Block (1976, 1983) were critical of Maccoby and Jacklin's (1974) conclusions and were more favorably disposed toward differential socialization perspectives. Several examples of differential treatment were identified, such as encouragement of motor activity for boys and nurturant play for girls. Although Huston acknowledged that several areas demonstrated negative or uncertain findings, her overall conclusion was that parents' socialization practices contributed to gender-typed personality characteristics in children. Evidence supported the gender stereotypes that feminine, communal behaviors in daughters were associated with the use of high levels of warmth and moderate-to-high control by parents, whereas masculine, agentic behaviors in sons were associated with high parental demands, control, encouragement of independence, and moderate warmth. Huston concluded that gross motor activities and freedom from adult supervision are fostered in boys, whereas dependence, affectionate behavior, responsive emotions, and assistance with achievement issues are central for girls.

Block's (1976, 1983) criticism of Maccoby and Jacklin's (1974) conclusions included that few studies were concerned with fathers, whom Block assumed would emphasize gender-role socialization more than mothers (a conclusion that received mixed support in subsequent scholarship; see Fagot, 1995; Fagot & Hagan, 1991; Gottfried, Gottfried, & Bathurst, 1995; Lytton & Romney, 1991). Other criticisms focused on Maccoby and Jacklin's tendency to treat most of the reviewed studies equally, despite wide variation in the quality and design of the research. In contrast to the reviews of Block (1976, 1983) and Huston (1983), a recent meta-analysis by Lytton and Romney (1991) found few patterns of differential treatment in the amount of interaction, encouragement of achievement, warmth and responsiveness, encouragement of dependence, restrictiveness-low encouragement of independence, disciplinary strictness, clarity of communication, and use of reasoning. The only socialization areas that displayed significant gender effects were the encouragement of sex-typed activities and the more frequent use of physical punishment with boys.

Fagot (1995), the most recent reviewer, supported Lytton and Romney's (1991) finding of few patterns of consistent sex-determined socialization practices by parents. Although parents were found to provide a somewhat sex-differentiated environment, a predominant socialization pattern was determined more by a child's individuality than by a child's gender.

Current research continues to demonstrate a mixture of findings for differential treatment based on gender and the socialization of children into masculine and feminine roles. Most of the recent work has addressed how parents design the environments (social or physical) and define the responsibilities of children and youths. Illustrative research areas include how parents design environments (e.g., toys and room furnishings) (Pomerieau, Boldoc, Malcuit, & Cosset, 1990), encourage same-sex peer interactions (Fagot & Hagan, 1991), and choose gender-specific names and clothes for their children (Crouter, Manke, & McHale, 1995). Differential treatment is manifested even before birth through the choice of gender-specific names for infants (Bornstein, 1995). Moreover, girls are dressed in pink clothes and given Barbie dolls, while boys are dressed in blue clothes and given action figures. The use of gender-typed names and physical environments may be powerful means of conveying social cues and defining situations that foster traditional gender-role expectations.

Another illustration of differential treatment is research on the engendered division of domestic role activities assigned by parents to older children and adolescents. This research has indicated that boys and girls differ in both the types and amount of domestic role assignments they are expected to perform (Mauldin & Meeks, 1990; White & Brinkerhoff, 1981). On the one hand, girls are more likely to receive domestic role assignments associated with traditional feminine role expectations, such as doing the dishes, caring for younger siblings, cleaning activities, doing the laundry, shopping, and running errands. On the other hand, boys are assigned fewer domestic role expectations associated with feminine roles, but face demands to perform outdoor chores, household maintenance, and car repair (Benin & Edwards, 1990; Blair, 1992; Zill & Peterson, 1982). The social mechanisms assumed to underlie differential socialization are children's modeling of parents' domestic role performances, which often are engendered in ways that correspond fairly closely with functionalist expectations for gender-based divisions of labor (Crouter, Manke, & McHale, 1995; Hoffman & Kloska, 1995). More direct mechanisms involve the assignment of domestic role expectations to sons and daughters on the basis of gender-differentiated criteria that result from the parent's own traditional role expectations. Such practices include gender-based incentives in which parents either pay boys more for doing the same chores as girls or expect girls to perform greater amounts of domestic role activities for the same compensation that boys receive (Goodnow, 1988).

Some of the research findings, however, complicate the interpretation that domestic role activities are assigned to children on the basis of gender. Burns and Homel (1989), for example, found that children's gender-role expectations were unrelated to parents' division of labor in family roles and were more a function of the family's socioeconomic standing. This finding was partially supported by White and Brinkerhoff's (1981) study indicating that more highly educated parents were less inclined to assign children's domestic role expectations on the basis of gender. Moreover, contrary to the expected view, Manke, Seery, Crouter, and McHale (1994) found that dual-earner families were more likely to assign domestic chores to children on the basis of gender than were traditional single-earner families. These surprising results may reflect an efficient decision by full-time employed mothers to reduce their role overload by delegating responsibilities for domestic role performance to daughters, rather than sons, because girls are viewed as being more capable of performing such gender-typed activities. They also suggest that traditional gender-role divisions of labor persist, despite increased maternal employment and redefinitions of instrumental and expressive roles that many assume to be characteristic of dual-earner families.

The differential treatment research, therefore, continues to examine whether parents perform socialization roles in a distinctive manner that influences children to learn traditional masculine versus feminine roles. Despite some consistency with functionalist thought, only a few areas of gender-typed differences are evident in the midst of mixed and/or negative findings. As feminist scholars have argued, insufficient attention has been given to how gender-role expectations have changed historically and have made masculine versus feminine role expectations different in subsequent periods. Furthermore, an inaccurate image has been conveyed that engendered role expectations collect together as a unitary construct (sex role), rather than the view that most (perhaps all) roles that family members occupy are engendered.

PARENT-CHILD GENDER ISSUES IN DIVERSE FAMILY FORMS

Dual-Earner Families

Interest in the engendered nature of parent-child relationships has grown as mothers have increasingly become employed outside the home and dual-earner families, rather than nuclear families, have become the normative pattern in our society (Gottfried & Gottfried, 1994). Much of this work was initially driven by negative assumptions (derived from functionalist or similar perspectives) that maternal employment roles would endanger children's development because expressive roles would be deemphasized. More recently, however, the topics in this area of research have been broadened to include (1) the positive consequences of maternal employment roles for children, (2) how fathers' identification with parental roles often results from increased

maternal involvement in wage labor, and (3) the greater recognition that *both* fathers' and mothers' employment roles may influence men's and women's abilities to parent (Crouter & McHale, 1993). Such issues illustrate how much the engendered division of labor between maternal and paternal roles is subject to renegotiation and redefinition. Contrary to Parsonian conceptions of expressive roles, women have increasingly assumed and become identified with work roles outside their families. These trends also reflect how major social-historical forces (e.g., economic requirements for women to work outside the home) have reshaped the engendered nature of work and family roles occupied by parents (Osmond & Thorne, 1993; Thompson & Walker, 1995).

Parental work outside the home (whether by fathers or mothers) contributes to the economic well-being of mothers, fathers, and children in families (Crouter & McHale, 1993; Gottfried et al., 1995). Besides financial realities, however, a gender bias has often motivated research on parental employment roles, the assumption being that mothers who work outside the home are placing themselves at odds with the maintenance of high-quality role relationships with children. This functionalist perspective was further reinforced by the false presumption that paternal employment roles become problems only when fathers either are unemployed or are employed in low-wage occupations. Despite the persistence of these gender biases, however, current scholarship has struck a better balance in conceptualizing how the paid work roles of both fathers *and* mothers have consequences for parent-child roles and the psychosocial outcomes for children (Gottfried et al., 1995; Menaghan & Parcel, 1990).

Most research on mothers' employment, for example, has found that it has few adverse effects on children (Gottfried et al., 1995; Lerner, 1994), and some research has indicated that positive effects can result (Menaghan & Parcel, 1990; Spitze, 1991). Maternal employment itself is not as strong a predictor of parenting and child outcomes as are other mediating variables, such as satisfaction with work roles, satisfaction with parental roles, aspects of work that conflict with family responsibilities, continuity of employment, amount of time that children are unsupervised after school, and lower work stress (Gottfried et al., 1995; Greenstein, 1995). Mixed results have been found for the influence of maternal employment roles on mother-infant attachment, with some studies indicating no effects (Gottfried et al., 1995) and others suggesting that insecure attachment is more evident among infants of employed mothers (Belsky & Rovine, 1988).

Another issue is how much fathers' involvement in parenting roles has increased as mothers' work roles outside the home have intensified. Some authorities (Gottfried et al., 1995) have argued that there has been a clear trend toward an increased investment in parental roles by fathers in dual-career families as maternal employment has increased, whereas others have been less convinced that substantial changes have occurred in paternal role performance in recent years (LaRossa & Reitzes, 1995). Although fathers have failed to become involved in child care roles proportionate to the growing occupational role investments of mothers, most authorities agree that at least modest increases in paternal role involvement have occurred (Parke, 1995, 1996).

An important means of reconciling this disagreement about the extent of fathers' involvement in parenting roles is to examine different aspects of fathers' roles. Most increases in paternal role involvement have been restricted to "direct activities" (e.g., playing with children) and "accessibility," in the form of being available to assist with child care without having immediate contact. In contrast, fathers have made much less (if any) progress relative to mothers in the "management" of child care, which involves being generally responsible for planning and scheduling child care and a child's daily activities (Lamb, 1997b; Parke, 1995).

Other research has refocused attention from an exclusive concern with mothers' employment roles to how the psychological orientation and personal well-being of *both* mothers and fathers in occupational roles may contribute to the performance of parental roles. Focusing on the consequences of work roles for both parents has removed some of the gender bias in previous research on the interface between work and parent-child roles. The substantive complexities of work-role expectations have been examined, involving degrees of self-direction, flexibility in work patterns, and openness of decision making that parents experience. Studies have found that parents who are employed in work settings with higher substantive complexity in role expectations place greater emphasis on self-direction, autonomy, and nurturance in their performance of parenting roles. Work expectations characterized by lower substantive complexity, on the other hand, foster parents' greater emphasis on obedience to authority, harsh control, and punitiveness (Crouter & McHale, 1993; Greenberger, O'Neil, & Nagel, 1994; Schooler, 1987).

Other identified influences of work-role involvement on parental role performance include increased attention to the sources and consequences of job stress experienced by both mothers and fathers. A focus on the psychological consequences of work for both fathers *and* mothers has helped to remove the gender bias so frequently evident in earlier work. The origins of stress include depersonalization, low wages, poor job conditions, limited advancement opportunities, long hours, job demands, poor conditions, and low job satisfaction (Crouter & McHale, 1993). Parental stress originating from these aspects of work roles may have an impact on the extent to which parents can effectively identify with and perform their child-socialization roles (Piotrkowski, Rapaport, & Rapaport, 1987; Voydanoff, 1990).

Current evidence suggests that as the relative involvement of mothers and fathers in employment roles has changed so, too, have paternal and maternal roles. The remaining inequalities in maternal and paternal role performances (which are considerable) also illustrate how changes in such fundamental social structures (e.g., engendered parental role expectations) are slow and difficult to change. Social forces that define the engendered nature of parental roles are resistant to change, even in the face of major socioeconomic pressures that are redefining the relative amount of time that parents of both genders have available for their children. Gender, as a source of social structure, is at least moderately resistant to individual negotiations, but more amenable to long-term, incremental actions by individuals within countless interpersonal relationships.

Divorced Families

Research on gender in the parent-child relationships of divorcing families continues to focus on issues inspired by functionalist views about the ideal form of engendered family structure. A substantial portion of this research has used the traditional nuclear family as the mythological standard against which divorcing families have been compared. Single-parent families are often viewed, either implicitly or explicitly, as threats to the two-parent family norm of gender-based divisions of labor for domestic and child care roles (see Popenoe, 1993).

Gender-of-parent issues continue to be evident in tendencies to assign blame to mothers for the adverse consequences of divorce that may befall children. Although these consequences should not be taken lightly, current research has found that children often recover from the worst circumstances and outcomes of divorce (Hetherington & Stanley-Hagan, 1995). Moreover, adverse influences that predate divorce, such as conflict and hostility within two-parent families, have often been underestimated in much of the research (Cherlin et al., 1991; Demo, 1992).

Similar to functionalist conceptions of the expressive role, a frequent presumption is that, compared to divorced fathers, divorced mothers identify more with parental roles. This view is supported by the fact that the vast majority of mothers (86%, U.S. Bureau of the Census, 1992) receive primary custody of their children and are substantially more involved in parental roles during and after divorce than are fathers (Hetherington & Stanley-Hagan, 1995). This gender-typed presumption (and probably a reality) about maternal role identification is further supported by the fact that even nonresidential mothers maintain substantial contact with their children and are more sensitive, supportive, and knowledgeable about the children's activities than are nonresidential fathers (Hetherington,

Cox, & Cox, 1982). Nonresidential fathers tend to diminish their involvement in parental roles over time, with only 25% of children from divorced homes seeing their fathers more than once a week and over 33% never seeing their fathers or seeing them only a few times a year (Furstenberg, 1988; Hetherington et al., 1982; Seltzer, 1991).

Current research on divorcing fathers has suggested that many men would ideally like to have either sole or joint custody of their children but often reject these options because they (1) believe that children benefit more from the closer relationships with their mothers, (2) view their job responsibilities as being too inflexible for the demands of parental custody, and (3) wish to avoid exposing their children to prolonged custody battles (Hetherington & Stanley-Hagan, 1995). Compared to mothers, fathers are less confident of their abilities to perform parental roles, and paternal roles tend to be secondary for male identities. Men who assume the added responsibilities of raising children on their own may be perceived as "heroic" (as rising above conventional role expectations), whereas mothers are simply expected to do so as a matter of course. This view is offset somewhat by evidence indicating that the small percentage of fathers who have custody seem no less competent than the custodial mothers and contribute to the postdivorce adjustment of children (Hetherington & Stanley-Hagan, 1995). The small but growing number of custodial fathers, however, are likely to be those who are most identified with and most competent in performing parental roles.

The standard view of the residential mother's circumstance is that she must make role transitions that result from both the psychologically stressful consequences of divorce and the father's disengagement from provider, domestic, and parental roles. As a result, a residential mother must incorporate aspects of the disengaging father's instrumental role (e.g., disciplining children) into her own role performance, cope with a large decrease in income, and build new support networks (Hetherington & Stanley-Hagan, 1995; Kitson & Holmes, 1992). Feelings of anger, anxiety, loneliness, depression, and being overwhelmed increase a custodial mother's risk of psychological problems and foster declines in the quality of the performance of her parental roles (Cohen, 1995). Moreover, divorce is a major contributor to the rapid rise of female-headed families in our society, with consequences that become cumulative when gender, race, and class issues are considered together. The adverse material consequences of divorce, in turn, are often severe in female-headed families, especially in African American and Latino families (see Chapters 12 and 13, this volume). The most important adverse result is that disproportionate numbers of these mothers and children are disenfranchised and live in poverty (National Center for Education Statistics, 1996).

Researchers have found that divorced mothers' and fathers' performance of parenting roles differs. For example, residential fathers report more difficulty than residential mothers managing their households and greater role strain from the difficult tasks of balancing work and parental roles (Greif, 1985). Residential mothers report more problems than residential fathers in disciplining and controlling their children, but seem more capable of monitoring them (Buchanan, Maccoby, & Dornbusch, 1992). Custodial fathers also report greater difficulties in parenting their daughters than their sons (Greif, 1985), especially dealing with their daughters' emotional needs and pubertal changes. Compared to either residential mothers or married parents, residential fathers have been found to foster more flexible child-rearing approaches and gender-role socialization in their children (Lamb, Pleck, & Levine, 1985; Weinraub & Gringlas, 1995). It is important to note, however, that huge variations exist in fathers' and mothers' parenting behaviors and that a significant percentage of nonresidential parents of both genders are involved in their children's lives. Future researchers would do well to examine within-group differences in the parenting practices of divorced mothers and fathers, rather than simply examine gender-of-parent distinctions in the form of group mean differences.

In general, an implicit functionalist assumption in this work is that nuclear families and their heterosexual division of parental responsibilities ought to be the standard against which divorced and single-parent families are judged. Such comparisons fail to recognize the reality of family pluralism in contemporary American society and reify an unattainable standard for most parents and children. Feminist scholars remind us that comparisons between mother-headed and nuclear families involve inherent gender biases and fail to adjust for the reality that single-mother families are at a distinct socioeconomic disadvantage compared to many two-parent families.

Stepfamilies

Much of the research on stepfamilies has been conducted after the decline of structural functional theory, with the result that Parsonian conceptions of gender issues have had a limited influence on conceptualizations of parent-child relations in stepfamilies. Despite the tendency to use two-parent families for comparisons, researchers have recognized that parents and children in stepfamilies may not recapture the same kinds of gender-based role assignments, role identifications, and role performances that exist in idealized images of nuclear families.

Remarriages often result in increasingly large and complex family structures as husbands and/or wives deal with new spouses, ex-spouses, children of different genders, and former in-laws. Children in these families must deal with step- and biological parents, new grandparents of different gender combinations, and step- and half-siblings. Compared to functionalist conceptions of nuclear families, however, the engendered roles of stepparents and the structure of parent-child relationships in stepfamilies are not as clearly delineated by standard role expectations and legal norms in our society (Hetherington & Henderson, 1997; Mahoney, 1994). Instead, role assignments, levels of role identification, and role performances emerge as family members and stepparents balance their distinct family histories and perhaps contradictory engendered expectations for family life. Members of stepfamilies are viewed as socially constructing their own patterns of engendered role relationships in different ways, depending upon the particular combinations of gender of stepparent, gender of biological parent, and gender of child that are involved.

Past role relationships are modified so that step-parents can be incorporated into the redefined family system. New roles and relationships must be negotiated and role-making must be undertaken as family members assign meaning, negotiate order, and define their place within this new social group (Ganong & Coleman, 1994; Strauss, 1978; Turner, 1962). This process of negotiating order involves establishing an orderly set of relationships among people who sometimes have conflicting interests, competing time demands, divided loyalties, and different engendered role expectations. The social meaning of gender complicates these negotiations because the emerging relationship issues differ, depending on the particular genders of the parent, stepparent, and children.

Stepfamilies consisting of a biological mother and a stepfather constitute the vast majority of remarried households. Prior to remarriage, for example, remarried mothers often have close, companionate role relationships with their daughters. After they remarry, however, the mothers must share their commitment, time, and role identifications with their new husbands, a circumstance that may change the daughters' status within the family. Redefining relationships in this manner often leads to resentment by the daughters and increases their conflicts with both their mothers and new stepfathers (Hetherington et al., 1992; Hetherington & Stanley-Hagan, 1995). Moreover, because newly remarried mothers tend to invest themselves in new role relationships (e.g., with their new husbands), they now have less time and energy to perform parental roles. A common result is that they are temporarily less able to monitor and control their sons and daughters. Most remarried mothers eventually restabilize their relationships with their sons and daughters, however (Hetherington et al., 1992).

The gender-based challenge for new stepfather-husbands is the lack of clear expectations for newly assumed parental roles—a different circumstance from the more specified expectations for instrumental roles in nuclear families. The dilemma for stepfathers is to structure clear, appropriate roles without interfering with the biological mothers' role as the primary care providers for the children.

A frequently successful strategy is for stepfathers to ease themselves into parenting roles that are supportive of the mothers without involving themselves in areas in which the children are not receptive. Consequently, the essential task of stepfathers is gradually to legitimate themselves in parenting roles that, from the perspectives of children and adolescents, have moderate authority (Hetherington, 1993; Hetherington & Jodl, 1994).

The task of stepfathers is especially difficult when preadolescent and adolescent stepchildren initially fail to acknowledge their authority, a reality that makes authoritative parenting approaches much less realistic (Hetherington, 1993). Shortly after marriage, stepfathers' effective performance of parental roles has been characterized as that of "polite strangers," with stepfathers being less likely than biological fathers to demonstrate positive affect, negative affect, monitoring behavior, and control with stepchildren (Fine, Voydanoff, & Donnelly, 1993; Hetherington & Jodl, 1994; Kurdek & Fine, 1995). Although some studies have indicated that preadolescent and early adolescent girls have the greatest difficulties adjusting to stepfathers (Hetherington, 1993), other investigations have failed to confirm this pattern (Amato & Keith, 1991).

Perhaps the one person in a stepfamily who faces traditional role expectations similar to functionalist gender norms for parenting is the residential stepmother. Most remarried residential fathers expect that stepmothers will become equally or even more identified with parenting roles than they are (Hetherington & Henderson, 1997; White, 1994). Stepmothers express many reservations about their abilities to identify with and perform parental roles in response to these expectations and to be equally supportive as biological mothers or to practice discipline as effectively as biological fathers (Hetherington & Stanley-Hagan, 1995). However, when stepmothers throw caution to the wind and assume major responsibilities for parenting roles, they often face substantial conflict with their stepchildren, particularly their stepdaughters (Brand, Clingempeel, & Bowen-Woodward, 1988). Moreover, a competitive relationship often develops between the stepmothers and nonresidential (biological) mothers, which prevents the stepmothers from fully identifying with and performing parental roles (Hetherington et al., 1982; White, 1994).

Lesbian and Gay Families

Although lesbian and gay parenthood faces severe discrimination, the fact that it is receiving moderate but growing research attention may indicate that there is a greater tolerance and acceptability of family diversity in our society (Patterson, 1995). Gender issues within the parent-child relationships of lesbian and gay families challenge the basic functionalist assumption that children's socialization should be governed by heterosexual role expectations. Despite deeply rooted resistance to gay and lesbian parenting, the growing visibility of these relationships may indicate how much gender differences in parental roles are gradually being redefined in our society (Demo & Allen, 1996).

Although it challenges basic assumptions, a contradictory trend is the extent to which functionalist concerns about problems associated with lesbian and gay parenting continue to dominate the research on this topic (Patterson & Chan, 1997; Rivera, 1991). These issues often address how violations of heterosexual role expectations for parenthood (1) are associated with the belief that mental health problems may be more prevalent among lesbian and gay parents, (2) result in parental role performances that differ substantially from those of heterosexual parents, (3) inhibit the development of conventional gender-role identifications in children, and (4) result in difficult social (e.g., peer) relationships for children (Patterson, 1995; Patterson & Chan, 1997).

Research on the first issue has found that lesbian and heterosexual mothers do not differ on assessments of self-concept, overall adjustment, and psychiatric status (Falk, 1989; Patterson, 1995). Moreover, few differences exist between gay and heterosexual fathers' parental attitudes and motivations for becoming parents (Bigner & Jacobsen, 1989a, 1989b). Consequently, lesbian and gay parents are not more likely than heterosexual parents to have psychological characteristics that undermine

their identification with or performance of parenting roles.

Lesbian and gay parents also demonstrate patterns of identification with and performance of parental roles similar to or even greater than those of heterosexual mothers and fathers. Specifically, compared to heterosexual mothers, biological mothers who are lesbian tend to view their maternal role as more salient (Patterson, 1995), and gay and lesbian couples share the performance of parental roles more equally than do heterosexual couples (McPherson, 1993; Patterson, 1995). Lesbian mothers appear to be equally warm as and more child centered, more flexible about rules, and more likely to have nontraditional expectations for their daughters than are heterosexual mothers (Hill, 1987). Gay fathers have characterized their parental behavior as warmer, more responsive and rational, and setting limits to a greater extent than have heterosexual fathers (Bigner & Bozett, 1990; Bigner & Jacobsen, 1989a).

Research on gender identity and gender-role behavior has revealed few, if any, differences between children of lesbian or gay parents and children of heterosexual parents (Patterson, 1992; Patterson & Chan, 1997). Evidence does not exist, for example, that children of lesbian and gay parents are any more likely than children of heterosexual parents to develop a lesbian or gay orientation themselves (Baily, Bobrow, Wolfe, & Mikach, 1995; Patterson, 1992). Children of gay and lesbian parents also do not demonstrate more than normal levels of behavioral, emotional, self-concept, or social problems (Patterson, 1992). The most notable problem that has been identified is that some children seek to conceal the sexual orientation of their lesbian or gay parents from their peers (Patterson & Chan, 1997).

The prevailing evidence provides little support for functionalist concerns that nonheterosexual parenting will result in the poor performance of parental roles, the socialization of children for lesbian and gay orientations, or other psychosocial problems. A remaining challenge for research on lesbian and gay parent-child relations is to focus more extensively on sources of variation within these families, rather than comparative strategies using two-parent families as the standard for normality (Demo & Allen, 1996).

Personal Reflections

The ideas that have shaped this chapter—family diversity, gender, and parent-child relationships—are central to the professional and personal lives of all the authors. As the senior author (Gary Peterson), for example, my own views about these issues were deeply influenced by growing up in a low-income family in which the dominant forces were my mother and grandmother. Both were exceptionally strong people who were the dominant forces in our large extended family of more than 200 relatives who resided in or near a small community in rural Nebraska. Mom and Grandma were tough, hard-nosed women who had suffered much during the Great Depression, had limited formal education (also true for the whole family), but had wisdom in ways that higher education cannot provide. They taught me that women could combine the best elements of being assertive, exercising leadership, expressing love, and practicing unqualified devotion to their children and grandchildren. Both spent much of their lives being ravaged by the most severe kind of rheumatoid arthritis (the complications of which ended both their lives), yet both rose above the debilitating pain and seemed to become all the stronger for their suffering. Besides the deepest love, my admiration for them is without limit.

I do not remember girls and boys in our family being dealt with much differently about things that really mattered. Out of economic necessity, most of the women in our extended family worked outside the home before this practice became common. We were taught to work hard and to view our circumstances in a positive way, though perhaps as somewhat unpredictable. Going to college was just a vague idea that no one in our family really understood or had ever thought to attain.

I also do not recall much prejudice being expressed by members of my family, which may stem from the fact that I grew up in a neighborhood that included several Mexican American families who had migrated initially to work in the local sugar beet factory. My mother was adamant about such issues; she repeatedly taught my sister, brother, and me that "we should mind our own business, not judge other people, and accept others for what they are." We were taught to "take yourself seriously," though the greatest virtue was never to "get too damn snooty." These simple precepts were powerful forces in teaching me to be tolerant, to accept diversity, and to have a sense of humility about whether one's choices in life were the "only way" to live. A few judgmental things that I do remember being taught, however, were to have a "healthy distrust" for the rich, the powerful, and the privileged, which provided much impetus for my liberal political leanings in adulthood.

These early experiences greatly influenced how I have tried to deal with bringing up my own children as I transitioned from being married, to being a joint custodial parent following a divorce, to currently being a member of a stepfamily. Formal education simply provided me with a better means of being conscious of my beliefs. As the father of two daughters in high school and a 2-year-old son, I deal with challenges in gender socialization each day.

SUMMARY AND CONCLUSIONS

Research on how gender defines the meaning, structure, and interactions in parent-child relationships involves a mixture of traditional and more recent conceptions. A significant portion of this scholarship suggests that ideas that are either derived from or similar to the structural-functional perspective continue to shape many areas of current research. These functionalist conceptions are used explicitly or implicitly to convey standards for identifying both the "normal" form of the family (the nuclear family) and the engendered nature of parent-child relationships (instrumental and expressive roles). Concepts from two alternative orientations, the symbolic interactionist and feminist frameworks, are helpful in demonstrating how change is occurring, both in the meaning of engendered role expectations and the performance of parent-child roles in diverse family forms.

The influence of functionalist conceptions of gender in parent-child relationships varies from area to area, with perhaps the least effects evident in research on parent-child relations in dual-career and stepfamilies. Even in these areas, however, functionalist influences persist in the form of traditional gender-based assumptions about the parent-child relationship. Mothers who work outside the home, for example, continue to face disproportionate expectations to shoulder expressive aspects of parental roles, while stepmothers often face premature expectations to assume these responsibilities in unrealistic ways.

Furthermore, substantial attention has been devoted to demonstrating how functionalist conceptions of engendered divisions of labor continue to shape ideas about motherhood and fatherhood. Functionalist assumptions are particularly evident in the literature on differential treatment, which examines whether mothers and fathers use distinctive strategies with sons versus daughters to foster traditional gender-role development. Moreover, traditional engendered divisions of labor continue to be the norm against which the experiences of mother-headed (often divorced) families are compared. Functionalist assumptions about gender-based socialization also define the primary focus of research on lesbian and gay parenting, which remains excessively preoccupied with how nonheterosexual relationships are problematic or pathological. Perhaps the most obvious reflection of functionalism, however, is the persistent view that gender socialization is primarily a unidirectional, parent-initiated process, with little recognition given to viewing children as active occupants and creators of engendered roles.

Perspectives like the symbolic interactionist and feminist frameworks provide substantially different conceptions of the engendered nature of parent-child relationships. They include a greater recognition that parenting roles are flexible, gender is constructed, parental role identification varies, active roles for children are engendered, and parent-child roles are reciprocal. They also acknowledge that the quality of parental role performance varies widely and that a greater range of parent-child circumstances are "normative" than simply those in nuclear families.

Therefore, despite the persistence of functionalist assumptions, both the conceptions and realities of motherhood and fatherhood are increasingly being recognized as more complex than the images conveyed by the expressive and instrumental roles of nuclear families. The complexity and reality of social change are illustrated by the gradual renegotiations of engendered relationships between mothers and fathers in dual-career families. Patterns of change are also evident in the increased recognition that engendered parent-child roles in stepfamilies may differ substantially from those of traditional nuclear families.

Future research on gender and parent-child relationships will benefit from greater attention to several issues. First, although a strong theoretical base exists in feminist thought, substantial empirical work is needed to explore how a variety of parent-child roles are engendered rather than conceptualize sets of gender-role expectations as unitary sex roles (or collected together). A broader conception (and empirical examination) of gender is necessary to refocus research away from the search for group mean differences in the attributes of mothers versus fathers and sons versus daughters. A reconceptualization of gender will focus more attention on how variations within, rather than the differences between, each gender shape the nature of parent-child relations. Such alternative perspectives also raise the possibility that parents and children may respond to each other on the basis of a variety of individual attributes and that gender is not a major source of differential meaning and behavior (Fagot, 1995; Ruble & Martin, 1998).

Second, the literature continues to be preoccupied with static models of gender-role socialization that are unidirectional in the sense that parents are viewed as shaping their children. Such static models again reinforce the tendency to view traditional gender-role differences as being immutable and essential for parents and children to demonstrate. Future research should utilize conceptions of engendered role relations that are much more flexible and varied, amenable to historical change, and viewed as reciprocal processes involving dynamic negotiations between active parents *and* active children. Such perspectives also view adaptive relationships between parents and children as occurring in diverse family structures that change over time.

Finally, the need to address new issues will require more diverse empirical and methodological strategies than is prevalent in the current research. Methodological strategies are needed to expand beyond the present preoccupation with group mean comparisons to identify gender differences, cross-sectional or one-shot assessments, and static conceptions of gender roles. Qualitative strategies are necessary to reveal new concepts, acquire in-depth knowledge about, and discover the meanings assigned to engendered parent-child relationships in diverse family forms (Ambert, Adler, Adler, & Detzner, 1995). Behavioral observation approaches should be helpful in examining how engendered relationships are continuously negotiated (or socially constructed) by parents and children within the context of reciprocal interaction. Increased attention to longitudinal designs is required so that developmental changes in engendered relationships within a variety of family circumstances can be charted and more clearly understood. Such strategies should help refocus research attention on the unique circumstances and variation within each family form and engendered pattern of parent-child relationships. An environment can be created, therefore, in which different family forms and gender issues can be examined for their own merits, rather than viewed as necessarily deficient compared to an ideal standard.

REFERENCES

Amato, P. R., & Keith, B. (1991) Parental divorce and adult well-being: A meta-analysis. *Journal of Marriage and the Family, 53,* 43–58.

Ambert, A. (1992). *The effects of children on parents.* New York: Haworth Press.

Ambert, A., Adler, P. A., Adler, P., & Detzner, D. F. (1995). Understanding and evaluating qualitative research. *Journal of Marriage and the Family, 57,* 879–893.

Baber, K., & Allen, K. R. (1992). *Women and families: Feminist reconstructions.* New York: Guilford Press.

Baily, J. M., Bobrow, D., Wolfe, M., & Mikach, S. (1995). Sexual orientation of adult sons of gay fathers. *Developmental Psychology, 31,* 124–129.

Barnard, K. R., & Martell, L. K. (1995). Mothering. In M. H. Bornstein (Ed.), *Handbook of parenting: Vol. 3. Status and social conditions of parenting* (pp. 3–26). Mahwah, NJ: Lawrence Erlbaum.

Belsky, J. (1991). Parental and nonparental child care and children's socioemotional development: A decade in review. In A. Booth (Ed.), *Contemporary families: Looking forward, looking back* (pp. 127–140). Minneapolis, MN: National Council on Family Relations.

Belsky, J., & Rovine, M. J. (1988). Nonmaternal care in the first year of life and the security of infant-parent attachment. *Child Development, 59,* 157–167.

Bem, S. L. (1993). *The lenses of gender: Transforming the debate on sexual inequality.* New Haven, CT: Yale University Press.

Benin, M. H., & Edwards, D. (1990). Adolescents' chores: The difference between dual and single-earner families. *Journal of Marriage and the Family, 52,* 361–373.

Bigner, J. J., & Bozett, F. W. (1990). Parenting by gay fathers. In F. W. Bozett & M. B. Sussman (Eds.), *Homosexuality and family relations* (pp. 155–176). New York: Harrington Park Press.

Bigner, J. J., & Jacobsen, R. B. (1989a). Parenting behaviors of homosexual and heterosexual fathers. In F. W. Bozett (Ed.), *Homosexuality and the family* (pp. 173–186). New York: Harrington Park Press.

Bigner, J. J., & Jacobsen, R. B. (1989b). The value of children to gay and heterosexual fathers. In F. W. Bozett (Ed.), *Homosexuality and the family* (pp. 163–172). New York: Harrington Park Press.

Blair, S. L. (1992). Sex-typing of children's housework. *Youth & Society, 23,* 178–203.

Block, J. H. (1976). Issues, problems, and pitfalls in assessing sex differences: A critical review of the psychology of sex differences. *Merrill-Palmer Quarterly, 22,* 283–308.

Block, J. H. (1983). Differential premises arising from differential socialization of the sexes: Some conjectures. *Child Development, 54,* 1335–1354.

Bornstein, M. H. (1995). Parenting infants. In M. H. Bornstein (Ed.), *Handbook of parenting: Vol. 3. Status and social conditions of parenting* (pp. 3–26). Mahwah, NJ: Lawrence Erlbaum.

Boulton, M. (1983). *On being a mother.* London, England: Tavistock.

Brand, E., Clingempeel, W. G., & Bowen-Woodward, K. (1988). Family relationships and children's psychosocial adjustment in stepmother and stepfamilies. In E. M. Hetherington & J. D. Arasteh (Eds.), *Impact of divorce, single-parenting, and stepparenting on children* (pp. 299–324). Hillsdale, NJ: Lawrence Erlbaum.

Buchanan, C. M., Maccoby, E. E., & Dornbusch, S. M. (1992). Adolescents and their families after divorce: Three residential arrangements compared. *Journal of Research on Adolescence, 2*, 261–291.

Burns, A., & Homel, R. (1989). Gender division of tasks by parents and their children. *Psychology of Women Quarterly, 13*, 113–125.

Callero, P. L. (1986). Toward a Meadian conceptualization of role. *Sociological Quarterly, 27*, 343–358.

Cherlin, A. J., Furstenberg, F. F., Chase-Lansdale, P. L., Kiernan, K. E., Robins, P. K., Morrison, D. R., & Teitler, J. O. (1991). Longitudinal studies on the effects of divorce on children in Great Britain and the United States. *Science, 252*, 1386–1389.

Chodorow, N., & Contratto, S. (1982). The fantasy of the perfect mother. In B. Thorne, with M. Yalom (Eds.), *Rethinking the family: Some feminist questions* (pp. 54–71). New York: Longman.

Chow, E. N., & Bertheide, C. W. (1988). The interdependence of family and work: A framework for family life education, policy, and practice. *Family Relations, 37*, 23–28.

Cohen, O. (1995). Divorced fathers raise their children by themselves. *Journal of Divorce and Remarriage, 23*(1–2), 55–73.

Coleman, M. T. (1991). The division of household labor. In R. L. Blumberg (Ed.), *Gender, family, and economy* (pp. 245–260). Newbury Park, CA: Sage.

Coltrane, S. (1995). The future of fatherhood: Social, demographic, and economic influences on men's family involvements. In W. Marsiglio (Ed.), *Fatherhood: Contemporary theory, research, and social policy* (pp. 255–274). Thousand Oaks, CA: Sage.

Collins, W. A., & Russell, G. (1991). Mother-child and father-child relationships in middle childhood and adolescence: A developmental analysis. *Developmental Review, 11*, 99–136.

Coontz, S. (1997). *The way we really are.* New York: Basic Books.

Crosby, F. J. (1991). *Juggling—The unexpected advantages of balancing career and home for women and their families.* New York: Free Press.

Crouter, A. C., Manke, B. A., & McHale, S. M. (1995). The family context of gender intensification in early adolescence. *Child Development, 66*, 317–329.

Crouter, A. C., & McHale, S. M. (1993). The long arm of the job: Influence of parental work on child rearing. In

T. Luster & L. Okagaki (Eds.), *Parenting: An ecological perspective* (pp. 179–202). Hillsdale, NJ: Lawrence Erlbaum.

Currie, D. (1988). Re-thinking what we do and how we do it: A study of reproductive decisions. *Canadian Review of Sociology and Anthropology, 25*, 231–252.

Demo, D. H. (1992). Parent-child relations: Assessing recent changes. *Journal of Marriage and the Family, 54*, 104–117.

Demo, D., & Allen, K. R. (1996). Diversity within lesbian and gay families: Challenges and implications for family theory and research. *Journal of Social and Personal Relationships, 13*, 415–434.

Fagot, B. I. (1995). Parenting boys and girls. In M. H. Bornstein (Ed.), *Handbook of parenting: Vol. 1. Children and parenting* (pp. 163–183). Mahwah, NJ: Lawrence Erlbaum.

Fagot, B. I., & Hagan, R. (1991). Observations of parent reactions to sex-stereotypes behaviors: Age and sex effects. *Child Development, 62*, 617–628.

Falk, P. J. (1989). Lesbian mothers: Psychosocial assumptions in family law. *American Psychologist, 44*, 941–947.

Ferree, M. M. (1987). The struggles of superwomen. In C. Boss, R. Feldberg, and N. Sokoloff (Eds.), *Hidden aspects of women's work* (pp. 161–180). New York: Praeger.

Ferree, M. M. (1991). Feminism and family research. In A. Booth (Ed.), *Contemporary families* (pp. 103–121). Minneapolis, MN: National Council on Family Relations.

Field, T. (1991). Quality infant day-care and grade school behavior and performance. *Child Development, 62*, 863–870.

Fine, M. A., Voydanoff, P., & Donnelly, B. W. (1993). Relations between parental control and warmth and child well-being in stepfamilies. *Journal of Family Psychology, 7*, 222–232.

Furstenberg, F. F., Jr. (1988). Good dads—bad dads: Two faces of fatherhood. In A. Cherlin (Ed.), *The changing American family and public policy* (pp. 193–218). Washington, DC: Urban Institute.

Furstenberg, F. F., Jr. (1995). Fathering in the inner city: Paternal participation and public policy. In W. Marsiglio (Ed.), *Fatherhood: Contemporary theory, research, and social policy* (pp. 119–147). Thousand Oaks, CA: Sage.

Ganong, L. H., & Coleman, M. (1994). *Remarried family relationships.* Thousand Oaks, CA: Sage.

Goodnow, J. J. (1988). Children's household work: Its nature and functions. *Psychological Bulletin, 103*, 5–26.

Gottfried, A. E., & Gottfried, A. W. (1994). Demography and changing families: Introduction to the issues. In A. E. Gottfried and A. W. Gottfried (Eds.), *Redefining families: Implications for children's development* (pp. 3–8). New York: Plenum.

Gottfried, A. E., Gottfried, A. W., & Bathurst, K. (1995). Maternal and dual-earner employment status and parenting. In M. H. Bornstein (Ed.), *Handbook of parenting: Vol. 4. Biology and ecology of parenting* (pp. 139–161). Mahwah, NJ: Lawrence Erlbaum.

Greenberger, E., O'Neil, R., & Nagel, R. (1994). Parents' concerns about their child's development: Implications for fathers' and mothers' well-being and attitudes toward work. *Journal of Marriage and the Family, 52,* 621–635.

Greenstein, T. N. (1995). Gender ideology, marital disruption, and the employment of married women. *Journal of Marriage and the Family, 57,* 31–42.

Greif, G. (1985). Single fathers rearing children. *Journal of Marriage and the Family, 47,* 185–191.

Haas, L. (1992). *Equal parenthood and social policy.* Albany: State University of New York Press.

Hetherington, M. E. (1993). An overview of the Virginia longitudinal study of divorce and remarriage with a focus on early adolescence. *Journal of Family Psychology, 7,* 1–18.

Hetherington, M. E., Clingempeel, W. G., Anderson, E. R., Deal, J. E., Stanley-Hagan, M., Hollier, E. A., & Linder, M. S. (1992). Coping with marital transitions: A family systems perspective. *Monographs of the Society for Child Development, 57*(2–3, Serial No. 227).

Hetherington, M. E., Cox, M., & Cox, R. (1982). Effects of divorce on parents and children. In M. E. Lamb (Ed.), *Nontraditional families* (pp. 233–288). Hillsdale, NJ: Lawrence Erlbaum.

Hetherington, M. E., & Henderson, S. H. (1997). Fathers in stepfamilies. In M. E. Lamb (Ed.), *The role of the father in child development* (pp. 212–226). New York: John Wiley.

Hetherington, M. E., & Jodl, K. M. (1994). Stepfamilies as settings for child development. In A. Booth & J. Dunn (Eds.), *Stepfamilies: Who benefits? Who does not?* (pp. 55–79). Hillsdale, NJ: Lawrence Erlbaum.

Hetherington, M. E., & Stanley-Hagan, M. (1995). Parenting in divorced and remarried families. In M. H. Bornstein (Ed.), *Handbook of parenting: Vol. 3. Status and social conditions of parenting* (pp. 233–254). Mahwah, NJ: Erlbaum.

Hewitt, J. P. (1997). *Self and society: A symbolic interactionist social psychology.* Needham Heights, MA: Allyn & Bacon.

Hill, M. (1987). Child-rearing attitudes of black lesbian mothers. In Boston Lesbian Psychologies Collective (Eds.), *Lesbian psychologies: Explorations and challenges* (pp. 215–226). Urbana: University of Illinois Press.

Hoffman, L. W., & Kloska, D. D. (1995). Parents' gender-based attitudes toward marital roles and child rearing. *Sex Roles, 32,* 273–295.

Huston, A. C. (1983). Sex typing. In E. M. Hetherington (Ed.), *Handbook of child psychology, socialization, personality, and social development* (Vol. 4, pp. 387–467). New York: John Wiley.

Kingsbury, N., & Scanzoni, J. (1993). Structural-functionalism. In P. G. Boss, W. J. Doherty, R. LaRossa, W. R. Schumm, & S. K. Steinmetz (Eds.), *Sourcebook of family theories and methods: A contextual approach* (pp. 195–217). New York: Plenum.

Kitson, G. C., & Holmes, W. M. (1992). *Portrait of divorce: Adjustment to marital breakdown.* New York: Guilford Press.

Kurdek, L. A., & Fine, M. A. (1995). Mothers, fathers, stepfathers, and siblings as providers of supervision, acceptance, and autonomy to young adolescents. *Journal of Family Psychology, 9,* 95–99.

Lamb. M. E. (1997a). The development of father-infant relationships. In M. E. Lamb (Ed.), *The role of the father in child development* (pp. 104–120). New York: John Wiley.

Lamb. M. E. (1997b). Fathers and child development: An introductory overview and guide. In M. E. Lamb (Ed.), *The role of the father in child development* (pp. 1–18). New York: John Wiley.

Lamb, M. E., Pleck, J. H., & Levine, J. A. (1985). The role of the father in child development: The effects of increased paternal involvement. In B. B. Lahey & A. E. Kazdin (Eds.), *Advances in clinical child psychology* (Vol. 8, pp. 229–266). New York: Plenum.

Lamont, M., & Fournier, M. (1992). *Cultivating differences: Symbolic boundaries and the making of inequality.* Chicago: University of Chicago Press.

LaRossa, R. (1988). Fatherhood and social change. *Family Relations, 37,* 451–457.

LaRossa, R., & Reitzes, D. C. (1993). Continuity and change in middle class fatherhood, 1925–1939: The culture-conduct connection. *Journal of Marriage and the Family, 55,* 455–468.

LaRossa, R., & Reitzes, D. C. (1995). Gendered perceptions of father involvement in early 20th century America. *Journal of Marriage and the Family, 57,* 223–229.

Lerner, J. V. (1994). *Employed mothers and their families.* Newbury Park, CA: Sage.

Lewis, C. (1997). Fathers and preschoolers. In M. E. Lamb (Ed.), *The role of the father in child development* (pp. 121–142). New York: John Wiley.

Lytton, H., & Romney, D. M. (1991). Parents' differential socialization of boys and girls: A meta-analysis. *Psychological Bulletin, 109,* 267–296.

Maccoby, E. E., & Jacklin, C. N. (1974). *The psychology of sex differences.* Stanford CA: Stanford University Press.

Mahoney, M. M. (1994). Reformulating the legal definition of stepparent-child relationship. In A. Booth & J. Dunn (Eds.), *Stepfamilies: Who benefits? Who does not?* (pp. 191–196). Hillsdale, NJ: Lawrence Erlbaum.

Manke, B. A., Seery, B. L., Crouter, A. C., & McHale, S. M. (1994). The three corners of domestic labor. *Journal of Marriage and the Family, 56,* 657–668.

Marsiglio, W. (1993). Contemporary scholarship on fatherhood: Culture, identity, and conduct. *Journal of Family Issues, 14,* 484–509.

Marsiglio, W. (1995). Fathers' diverse life course patterns and roles. Theory and social interventions. In W. Marsiglio (Ed.), *Fatherhood: Contemporary theory, research, and social policy* (pp. 78–101). Thousand Oaks, CA: Sage.

Mauldin, T. & Meeks, C. B. (1990). Sex differences in children's time use. *Sex Roles, 22* (9–10), 537–554.

McMahon, M. (1995). *Engendering motherhood: Identity and self-transformation in women's lives.* New York: Guilford Press.

McPherson, D. (1993). *Gay parenting couples: Parenting arrangements, arrangement satisfaction, and relationship satisfaction.* Doctoral dissertation, Pacific Graduate School of Psychology, Palo Alto, CA.

Mead, G. H. (1934). *Mind, self, and society.* Chicago: University of Chicago Press.

Menaghan, E. G., & Parcel, T. L. (1990). Parental employment and family life: Research in the 1980s. *Journal of Marriage and the Family, 52,* 1079–1098.

National Center for Education Statistics. (1996). *Youth indicators, Indicator 21.* Washington, DC: Author.

O'Barr, J., Pope, D., & Wyer, M. (1990). Introduction. In J. O'Barr, D. Pope, & M. Wyer (Eds.), *Ties that bind: Essays on mothering and patriarchy* (pp. 1–14). Chicago: University of Chicago Press.

Osmond, M. W., & Thorne, B. (1993). Feminist theories: The social construction of gender in families and society. In P. G. Boss, W. J. Doherty, R. W. LaRossa, W. R. Schumm, & S. K. Steinmetz, (Eds.), *Sourcebook of family theories and methods: A contextual approach* (pp. 591–623). New York: Plenum.

Parke, R. D. (1995). Fathers and families. In M. H. Bornstein (Ed.), *Handbook of parenting: Vol 3. Status and social conditions of parenting* (pp. 27–63). Mahwah, NJ: Lawrence Erlbaum.

Parke, R. D. (1996). *Fatherhood.* Cambridge, MA: Harvard University Press.

Parsons, T., & Bales, R. (1955). *Family socialization and interaction process.* New York: Free Press.

Patterson, C. J. (1992). Children of lesbian and gay parents. *Child Development, 63,* 1025–1042.

Patterson, C. J. (1995). Lesbian and gay parenthood. In M. H. Bornstein (Ed.), *Handbook of parenting: Vol 3. Status and social conditions of parenting* (pp. 255–274). Mahwah, NJ: Lawrence Erlbaum.

Patterson, C. J., & Chan, R. W. (1997). Gay fathers. In M. E. Lamb (Ed.), *The role of the father in child development* (pp. 245–260). New York: John Wiley.

Peterson, G. W. & Hann, D. (1999). Socializing children and parents in families. In M. Sussman, S. Steinmetz, & G. W. Peterson (Eds.), *Handbook of marriage and the family* (rev. ed.) (pp. 327–370). New York: Plenum Press.

Peterson, G. W., & Rollins, B. C. (1987). Parent-child socialization. In M. B. Sussman & S. K. Steinmetz (Eds.), *Handbook of marriage and the family* (pp. 471–507). New York: Plenum.

Piotrkowski, C. S., Rapaport, R. N., & Rapaport, R. (1987). Families and work. In M. B. Sussman & S. K. Steinmetz (Eds.), *Handbook of marriage and the family* (pp. 251–284). New York: Plenum.

Pleck, J. H. (1997). Paternal involvement: Levels, sources, and consequences. In M. E. Lamb (Ed.), *The role of the father in child development* (pp. 66–103). New York: John Wiley.

Pleck, E. H., & Pleck, J. H. (1997). Fatherhood ideals in the United States: Historical dimensions. In M. E. Lamb (Ed.), *The role of the father in child development* (pp. 33–48). New York: John Wiley.

Pomerieau, A., Bolduc, D., Malcuit, G., & Cosset, L. (1990). Pink or blue: Environmental gender stereotypes in the first two years of life. *Sex Roles, 22,* 359–367.

Popenoe, D. (1993). American family decline, 1960–1990. A review and appraisal. *Journal of Marriage and the Family, 49,* 527–555.

Rivera, R. (1991). Sexual orientation and the law. In J. C. Gonsiorek & J. D. Weinrich (Eds.), *Homosexuality: Research implications for public policy* (pp. 81–100). Newbury Park, CA: Sage.

Ruble, D. N., & Martin, C. (1998). Gender development. In W. Damon (Series Ed.) & N. Eisenberg (Vol. Ed.), *Handbook of child psychology (5th ed.): Vol. 3. Social, emotional and personality development* (pp. 933–1016). New York: John Wiley & Sons.

Russell, G., & Russell, A. (1987). Mother-child and father-child relationships in middle childhood. *Child Development, 58,* 1573–1585.

Schooler, C. (1987). Psychological effects of complex environments during the life span: A review and theory. In C. Schooler & K. Warner Schaie (Eds.), *Cognitive functioning and social structure over the life course* (pp. 24–29). Norwood, NJ: Ablex.

Seltzer, J. A. (1991). Relationships between fathers and children who live apart: The father's role after separation. *Journal of Marriage and the Family, 53,* 79–101.

Spitze, G. (1991). Women's employment and family relations. In A. Booth (Ed.), *Contemporary families* (pp. 381–404). Minneapolis, MN: National Council on Family Relations.

Starrels, M. E. (1994). Gender differences in parent-child relations. *Journal of Family Issues, 15,* 148–165.

Straus, M. A. (1994). *Beating the devil out of them: Corporal punishment in American families.* New York: Lexington Books.

Strauss, A. (1978). *Negotiations.* San Francisco: Jossey-Bass.

Stryker, S. & Statham, A. (1985). Symbolic interaction and role theories. In G. Lindzey & E. Aaronson (Eds.), *Handbook of social psychology* (Vol. 1, pp. 311–378). New York: Random House.

Teachman, J. D., Polonko, K. A., & Scanzoni, J. (1999). Demography and families. In M. B. Sussman, S. Steinmetz, & G. W. Peterson (Eds.), *Handbook of marriage and the family* (rev. ed., pp. 39–67). New York: Plenum.

Thompson, L., & Walker, A. J. (1989). Gender in families. *Journal of Marriage and the Family, 51,* 845–871.

Thompson, L., & Walker, A. J. (1995). The place of feminism in family studies. *Journal of Marriage and the Family, 57,* 847–866.

Thorne, B. (1987). Re-visioning women and social change: Where are the children? *Gender & Society, 1,* 85–109.

Turner, R. H. (1962). Role-taking: Process vs. conformity? In A. M. Rose (Ed.), *Human behavior and social processes* (pp. 20–40). Boston: Houghton Mifflin.

U. S. Bureau of the Census. (1992). Studies in marriage and the family: Married couple families with children. In *Current Population Reports* (Series P-23, No. 162). Washington, DC: U. S. Government Printing Office.

Voydanoff, P. (1990). Economic stress and family relations: A review of the eighties. *Journal of Marriage and the Family, 52,* 1099–1115.

Weinraub, M., & Gringlas, M. B. (1995). Single parenthood. In M. H. Bornstein (Ed.), *Handbook of parenting: Vol. 3. Status and social conditions of parenting* (pp. 65–88). Mahwah, NJ: Lawrence Erlbaum.

West, L. K., & Zimmerman, D. (1987). Doing gender. *Gender and Society, 1,* 125–151.

White, L. (1994). Stepfamilies over the life course: Social support. In A. Booth & J. Dunn (Eds.), *Stepfamilies: Who benefits? Who does not?* (pp. 109–137). Hillsdale, NJ: Lawrence Erlbaum.

White, L. K., & Brinkerhoff, D. B. (1981). The sexual division of labor: Evidence from childhood. *Social Forces, 60,* 170–181.

Youniss, J., & Smollar, J. (1985). *Adolescent relations with mothers, fathers, and friends.* Chicago: University of Chicago Press.

Zill, N., & Peterson, J. L. (1982). Learning to do things without help. In L. M. Loasa & I. E. Sigel (Eds.), *Families as learning environments for children* (pp. 343–467). New York: Plenum Press.

CHAPTER 6

Gender and Intergenerational Relationships

DEBRA UMBERSON AND ELLEN SLATEN

PERSONAL REFLECTIONS ON FAMILY DIVERSITY

Debra Umberson

In my brief experience as a clinical social worker—my life before I became a sociologist—I found that the disjuncture between ideals about family life and the realities of family life caused a great deal of anxiety and unhappiness for many individuals. This disjuncture seemed to take different forms for mothers and fathers, who experience family and parenthood in unique ways. It was also clear that, most of the time, an individual's psychological distress is closely tied to the conditions of his or her family, as well as the larger social environment—conditions that may include poverty, domestic violence, and the demands of raising young children. I saw that the social environment could benefit individuals, for example, by providing supportive family ties. My interest in how the larger social environment affects family relationships and how family relationships affect individual well-being is what led me to sociology. I wanted to understand better these socially patterned responses to the social environment. I believe that individual differences in well-being are strongly influenced by the social structures to which we are exposed. These social structures are in a continual state of change. Over the family life course, individuals move from one marital status to another, from one stage of parenting to another, and in and out of employment and retirement and experience rises and falls in financial strain and comfort. These social structural arrangements, singly and in combination, shape our experiences and the quality of our lives.

This chapter focuses specifically on gender and intergenerational family relationships. Gender, an indicator of social structural position, shapes one's family relationships in systematic ways, but the relationship between gender and intergenerational relationships further depends on other characteristics of the social environment that will be considered. In a general sense, I adopt a family ecology model in my work, but I do not rigidly adhere to a particular theoretical model. In addition to my belief that structural circumstances shape one's life experiences, I recognize that the meanings of family and of gender vary across racial, socioeconomic, and other groups. In turn, these meanings, or social constructions, influence how individuals form families and particular family structures affect individual well-being. I also view myself as a feminist in that I do not think that current social arrangements between men and women are necessarily adaptive, and I certainly do not believe they are immutable to change.

My early research on family relationships was largely quantitative, relying primarily on secondary analyses of national surveys. This methodological approach allowed me to explore the association between various family structures and individual well-being in the general population. For example, I could assess whether parents or nonparents exhibited higher levels of psychological distress and then identify other factors that might help to explain why one group was more distressed than the other (see, for example, Umberson, 1987, 1992; Umberson & Gove, 1989). The opportunity to study these issues drew me into sociology and away from social work. On the other hand, I wanted more in-depth information from individuals in a survey. I wanted to know more about the processes through which parenting or not parenting contributed to psychological distress. It was this interest that led me to combine my quantitative research with qualitative methods, primarily in-depth interviews. In my current research projects, I combine analyses of large-scale survey data with qualitative analyses of in-depth interview data. Conducting in-depth interviews has reenergized my sociological imagination by reminding me that although I am interested in patterns of structure and outcome in the general population, I am also interested in interpersonal dynamics and individuals.

Ellen Slaten

My interest in studying family caregivers was sparked in the early 1980s when I learned from my mother that two of my cousins were HIV positive. My HIV-infected cousins feared negative reactions from others and opted to keep their diagnoses a secret from all but a few relatives. It saddened me that because of the stigma of AIDS, my cousins did not receive emotional support from more family members. While pursuing graduate work in sociology, I decided to learn as much as I could about HIV and AIDS by attending informational workshops at a local AIDS agency. Attending these workshops led to my involvement in the agency's Buddy Program, which proved to be a life-altering experience. Becoming involved with my buddy and his family strengthened my commitment to write my dissertation on the experiences of family caregivers for those with HIV. At the time, the AIDS caregiving literature tended to treat the caregiving experience as if it was the same for all family members, but I noticed differences in those experiences. I launched a study in which I conducted in-depth interviews with mothers, fathers, sisters, partners, and wives of men with HIV. I found that these family members assumed distinct roles and faced unique strains as they provided care for their loved ones.

The issue of diversity is readily apparent when one studies families of persons with HIV. As I conducted my study, I observed that gay men and their partners forge strong family bonds and consider their relationships to be marriages in all but legal terms. Gay partners and their friends constitute committed family networks, providing countless hours of care to those with HIV. In some instances, HIV-positive gay men have wives, ex-wives, or children who provide a great deal of support. They,

along with the man's current partner, form an extended family of caregivers. Sisters tend to play the important role of confidantes to brothers with HIV and are often the first family members to whom brothers disclose their HIV diagnosis. Mothers engage in the majority of physical caretaking while fathers often specialize in "managing" their sons' illness by handling financial and medical decision-making issues and coordinating outside assistance (Slaten, 1996). I find qualitative methods to be the most appropriate when I explore issues of how family members define and cope with caregiving. In-depth interviews allow family members to describe their daily experiences in their own words and to define the relevant issues in their lives.

DEFINITIONS AND METHODS OF RESEARCH

Intergenerational relationships refer to relationships between the generations. This term, however, is found primarily in the social gerontological literature, where it is used to refer to relationships between adult children and their parents. Other scholars define intergenerational relationships more broadly to include relationships between minor children and parents, between adult children and parents, between children and grandparents or great-grandparents, and between two generations of close kin or nonkin individuals who have a close kinlike relationship (see Chapters 7 and 11, this volume).

That the literatures on parents of minor children and parents of adult children are separate is surprising, considering how much theory and research points to the importance of early childhood experiences in shaping adult experiences. This split is the result partly of the methodological difficulties and complexity inherent in linking childhood and adulthood experiences and partly of general disciplinary divisions, so that some researchers focus on childhood development and others focus on adult development (for an exception and review, see Aquilino, 1997).

In this chapter, we focus on diversity in adults' experiences of intergenerational relationships. We adopt the editors' definition of diversity and describe both intergenerational processes and structural variation in intergenerational processes, especially according to gender. Toward this end, we consider how parents experience relationships with minor and adult children and how adult children experience relationships with parents, with a particular emphasis on the gender of the parents.

Many methodologists point to the importance of triangulated methods—defined as combining different research methodologies in an attempt to draw on the strengths and to address the weaknesses inherent in each approach (Denzin, 1989). Research on intergenerational relationships does not typically rely on triangulated methods. Rather, several distinctive lines of research on intergenerational relationships exist, all of which emphasize gender differences in parenting experiences. First, most research on frequency of contact, support and aid exchanges, and effects of intergenerational relationships on psychological well-being relies primarily on survey research methods and is based on national or community probability samples. These approaches are excellent for documenting associations between variables in a general population; however, they are limited in their ability to reveal insights into relationship dynamics and processes. Second, another line of research is concerned with special populations, such as adult child caregivers of impaired elderly parents. Although most of these studies are also based on survey methods, the samples tend to be small and are typically nonrepresentative. For example, they often exclude men and minorities, as well as individuals of lower socioeconomic status. Third, still another area of research, based primarily on qualitative methods, tends to address issues of process. For example, such studies identify the major types of interactions between givers and recipients of care and frequently rely on homogeneous samples. Future research would benefit from the greater use of triangulated methods that can examine social patterns as well as social processes.

THEORETICAL APPROACHES

Family Ecology Model

It is easy to imagine that a single mother who works full time, lives in poverty, and has her child in an unlicensed family day care facility will experience parenting differently from a married mother who works part time and has a full-time nanny and a high family income. Empirical evidence documents that parenting experiences vary a great deal, depending on one's social context. We work primarily from the family ecology model to emphasize the power of the social structural context to shape individuals' life experiences, including relationships with others. The family ecology perspective suggests that some social structural conditions are inherently more stressful than others, whereas others provide greater financial, personal, and social resources. The strains and resources that characterize an individual's social environment shape the person's life experiences and life outcomes. It is in this way that socially patterned group differences in parenting experiences develop. For example, because structural constraints and opportunities differ for men and women, the strains and resources of parenting are different for men and women. In turn, parenting is a different experience for men and women, with gendered consequences for psychological well-being. We emphasize the dynamic quality of intergenerational relationships and the continual change in the dynamics of intergenerational relationships over time for any person. For example, when men and women shift from one marital status to another, the strains and resources of parenting change. As suggested by family life-course research, the strains and resources of parenting or other family roles differ across cohorts of individuals; for example, becoming a parent during the Great Depression or during the economic boom of the 1950s made the parenting of young children a different experience (Elder, 1997).

The dynamics of intergenerational relationships vary according to many structural features in addition to gender, including socioeconomic status, race, and marital status. Although the primary focus of this chapter is on gender, each of these structural variations are also considered. The family ecology perspective views any stratified structural parameter (e.g., race, socioeconomic status, gender) as having the potential to shape parenting relationships in socially patterned ways. It permits quantitative tests of gender and other group differences in the experience and consequences of parenting. This theoretical perspective is broad in its ability to explain group diversity in parenting experiences; however, it is not typically examined critically, particularly in terms of the socially constructed nature of social phenomena. We adopt the feminist premise that gender is not experienced uniformly across social groups; rather, the meaning and experience of gender varies across individuals and groups and, in turn, influences the nature and consequences of families for individuals. In the next section, we discuss how premises of feminist theory and nonpositivist models may be combined with a family ecology-positivist model to explore gender and family relationships.

Feminist Theory

Whereas the family ecology model emphasizes empirical testing of group differences in parenting experiences, feminist theory focuses more on the socially constructed nature of gendered parenting experiences (Thompson & Walker, 1995). Much early feminist theory developed in response to the cultural belief that only women could mother and that women's instinctive need to mother interfered with their ability to do anything but mother (e.g., Firestone, 1970). Many early feminist theorists sought to break away from biological determinism in an effort to achieve gender equality in society.

Until recently, most feminist theory was formulated by white, middle-class women. These perspectives have been criticized for assuming that women's experiences are universal. For example, Chodorow (1978) explained that adult gender differences in relationship orientations are derived from early childhood experiences, assuming that mothers were the primary caretakers of infants and young children and that distant working fathers lived at home. Chodorow and other feminist theorists contributed greatly to our understanding of gendered parenting experiences by breaking away from biological determinism and offering explanations that centered on social interactions and social imperatives. However, these feminist views have been criticized for considering that all mothers and all families conform to white, middle-class ideals or need to conform to them (Collins, 1994). Such theories tend to reify gender, emphasizing that early

childhood experiences set gender into place in basic and inevitable ways that are immutable over time (Epstein, 1988).

More recent feminist theory has stressed the importance of considering diversity in the experience of motherhood. Historical and present social contexts of mothering differ greatly for women of different races and ethnicities. As Dill (1988) noted, African American and Asian American women and Latinas did not historically experience motherhood as a private sphere separate from the public sphere of work; In fact, employment historically took precedence over motherhood to enable women to protect their children. Stack and Burton (1994) demonstrated that caring for children is not traditionally the sole domain of mothers in the African American community; rather, mothering is often shared with other family and community members. Feminist writing on lesbian mothers has also emphasized that women who fall outside the cultural view of appropriate mothering are devalued as mothers (Allen & Demo, 1995). Recognition of lesbian mothers, as well as racial and class variations in the experience of motherhood, expands feminist theorizing on motherhood. Lewin (1993, p. 3) argued that "motherhood, even more clearly than sexual orientation, defines womanhood, thereby intensifying the already existing birfurcation of women into mothers and nonmothers." Flaks, Ficher, Masterpasqua, and Joseph (1995) found that lesbian parents are more aware of effective parenting skills than are heterosexual parents. They concluded that this greater awareness may be the result of parents' gender, rather than sexual orientation, because women seem to be more aware of such skills.

Perhaps what unites various theoretical views on motherhood under the rubric of feminist theory is the view that the experience of mothering is not determined solely by one's social and material context, as the family ecology perspective indicates. As Glenn (1994, p. 3) stated, in addition to mothering occurring

> within specific social contexts that vary in terms of material and cultural resources and constraints . . . [it] is constructed through men's and women's actions

within specific historical circumstances. Thus agency is central to an understanding of mothering as a social, rather than biological, construct.

Although many researchers working from a family ecology model do not question or criticize the gender status quo, a feminist perspective is compatible with the family ecology model. For example, Epstein (1988) and Johnson (1988) emphasized the powerful influence of structural circumstances on individuals, yet both theorists were critical of the arrangement between the sexes and did not see it as necessary or as immutable. Furthermore, the possibility of social change can be built into the family ecology model. Research has shown that when social conditions are similar for men and women, gender differences in family experiences are greatly reduced or eliminated. For example, Risman (1987) found that men who must assume the role of primary parent following the dissolution of their marriages exhibit the same nurturing behaviors toward their children as do women who are primary caretakers. This finding suggests that similar structural experiences may reduce differences in the family experiences of men and women even when certain family roles continue to be defined differently for and by men and women. In this view, change in social structure produces change in family relationships, and individuals may deliberately seek to alter social structures.

THEORY AND METHODS

Feminist theorists are often critical of researchers who use quantitative methods and define gender as a dichotomous variable. Feminist theory suggests that gender means something different to men and women of different races, classes, nationalities, ages, and so on and reveals the problem of viewing any group who differs from the normatively defined group (e.g., white, male) as deviant or dysfunctional. Although this problem may characterize much research from a family ecology perspective, many feminists who work from this perspective are aware of this tendency and emphasize the importance of avoiding the "deceptive distinctions" implied by the dichotomous (male versus female)

approach (Epstein, 1988; Umberson, Chen, House, Hopkins, & Slaten, 1996).

Much of the difference-versus-similarity concern rests on the types of research methods that family ecology and feminist researchers typically use. Most family ecology research relies on quantitative methods that dichotomize gender into two categories—male and female. Feminist research is more likely to rely on nonquantitative methods that stress the social context and meaning of social phenomena, including gender. In the feminist model, gender is viewed as existing along a continuum, rather than as two discrete categories. Research that combines qualitative and quantitative methods may facilitate the merging of feminist and family ecology approaches to the study of gender and family issues (Demo & Allen, 1996). The advantages of such an approach are discussed later in this chapter.

THE LITERATURES ON MOTHERHOOD AND FATHERHOOD

The most striking difference between the motherhood and fatherhood literatures is that the literature on motherhood is so vast and the literature on fatherhood is so limited. Much of the literature on motherhood is devoted to such issues as why women do all the mothering; whether women's mothering is responsible for gender inequality; how the equalization of parenting would affect gender equality; and the consequences of women's mothering for women, men, and children. The literature on motherhood includes theoretical work, quantitative and qualitative research, writing on personal experiences, and works of fiction. In addition to the sheer bulk of the work on motherhood, one is struck by the emotion in it. Clearly, the writers believe that motherhood matters. Yet, men as fathers have greater structural power and, often, privilege.

The work on fatherhood is much smaller and has a much shorter intellectual history. A number of authors have explored the history of fatherhood, particularly in the United States, although these books tend to describe a white, middle-class version of fatherhood. Although some studies have documented the increasing role of fathers in child rearing, others have lamented the absence or departure of fathers from their children's lives. Furstenberg (1992) referred to the "good dads-bad dads" distinction in arguing that both trends are occurring. Few studies have attempted to theorize about fatherhood. One exception was LaRossa's study (1988), which distinguished between the culture of fatherhood and the way that fatherhood is enacted. It is interesting that the literatures on motherhood and fatherhood have seldom incorporated a full theoretical discussion of parenting by men and women. This separation probably reflects the social construction of science in that motherhood and fatherhood have been viewed as distinctive phenomena. Both researchers and theorists have always worked from the assumption that mothering and fathering are unique, rather than that individuals who parent have something in common.

EMPIRICAL EVIDENCE: DIVERSITY IN INTERGENERATIONAL RELATIONSHIPS

Parenting of an infant, toddler, adolescent, or adult child represents a wide range of experiences. Many studies have concluded that parenting of minor children is characterized by a high level of demands that are conducive to psychological distress in parents—especially mothers (see reviews by Ambert, 1992; McLanahan & Adams, 1987; Ross, Mirowsky, & Goldsteen, 1990). In contrast, research on relationships between parents and adult children has emphasized that intergenerational relationships tend to be mutually supportive and beneficial to psychological functioning—especially for mothers (Rossi & Rossi, 1990; Umberson, 1992). Taken together, these studies suggest that the strains and rewards of parenting change over the family life course, with the relationship improving as children grow older. In fact, several studies have found that parents gain a psychological boost once children become adults and leave the parental home; this boost is also greater for mothers than for fathers (Glenn, 1975; Harkins, 1978).

The empirical research on parent-child relationships provides striking evidence that parenting is a different phenomenon for mothers and fathers over the life course. This gender difference begins with pregnancy for most parents. Biologically, only women can be pregnant and give birth and then, if they so choose, breast-feed their babies. Some theoretical perspectives suggest that these biological differences set the stage for long-term gender differentiation in parenting experiences (Rossi, 1985). Of course, these models ignore how structural forces may modify presumed gender differences in parenting. For example, Risman's (1987) research showed that individuals who assume new structural roles (e.g., men who become primary parents) begin to exhibit behaviors that are consistent with their parenting role, whether or not these behaviors fit gender-typed assumptions. These models also assume a heterosexual-couple model, but research on lesbian mothers has challenged this premise, finding that, among lesbian couples, biological mothers report greater involvement in child care whereas nonbiological mothers spend more hours in paid employment (Patterson, 1995).

The family life-course model is a family ecology model in that it contends that structural influences affect individuals and their relationships. Elder (1997), a leading proponent of this model, emphasized that structural influences can be macro (e.g., historical events, such as extreme economic downturns or wars) or micro (e.g., the division of labor at home). Moen, Erickson, and Dempster-McClain (1997) showed that both micro- and macro-level structural conditions affect individuals. They found that both childhood socialization processes (e.g., mothers' gender-role attitudes during their daughters' childhoods) and life-course experiences (e.g., the gender-role revolution) affect adult daughters' gender attitudes.

The Transition to Parenting

Research on the transition to parenting is often based on a longitudinal design in which parents are studied before and after they give birth to their first child. These studies are typically small and are usually restricted to white, middle-class married couples, although Crohan (1996) found similar effects of the transition on the quality of African American and white marriages. Studies have generally concluded that the transition is associated with a decline in the quality of marriages and psychological well-being and that this decline is greater for women than men (Belsky, Lang, & Rovine, 1985; Cowan & Cowan, 1992; Crohan, 1996). This body of research has shown that women's lives are more affected because they do more of the child care and make more lifestyle accommodations to meet the demands of child rearing, with the latter having a greater impact.

Relationships with Minor Children

In an early study on the transition to parenting, LeMasters (1957) drew an analogy between new parents and soldiers entering combat for the first time. Mothers have consistently been portrayed as the soldiers on the frontline of this combat—in the sense that they do most of the child care and experience more of the strain of parenting. Rich (1976) emphasized the powerful ambivalence that mothers feel as they face the extreme stress, as well as the emotional gratification, of parenting.

Even couples who have been fairly egalitarian in their relationships tend to become more traditional particularly in division of household labor, following the birth of their first children. Substantial evidence exists that mothers shoulder the primary responsibility for child care, even if they are employed outside the home (Nock & Kingston, 1988). It is not surprising, then, that mothers report significantly more demands from minor children than do fathers (Umberson, 1989). The quality and dynamics of relationships with minor children are important to parents, partly because they affect parents' psychological well-being. Positive relationships with minor children are conducive to psychological well-being, while the demands and strains of parenting are associated with diminished psychological well-being (Umberson, 1989). Compared to fathers, mothers perceive that children place more demands on them (Umberson, 1989), and the objective evidence certainly is that mothers shoulder more of the daily tasks of child rearing (Nock & Kingston, 1988). In turn, mothers' perceptions of children's demands partly explain the findings of previous studies that parenting of young

children is more detrimental to the psychological well-being of mothers than of fathers (e.g., Gove & Geerken, 1977; Reskin & Coverman, 1985; Umberson, 1989). Windle and Dimenci (1997) found that men and women had similar levels of parental and occupational stress and that both types of stress contributed to psychological distress equally for men and women. These results are limited, however, because the sample was restricted to white, dual-earner, middle-class, married couples.

Almost all quantitative survey research on relationships with minor children has adopted (either implicitly or explicitly) a family ecology or structural-functionalist approach. The emphasis in these studies is on how structural characteristics of the social environment may modify parenting experiences. Some scholars (e.g., Scott & Alwin, 1989, Simon, 1992) have used a symbolic interactionist approach to indicate that the meaning of parenting influences parenting experiences and the consequences of parenting for individuals. Scott and Alwin concluded that because parenting is more central to the identity of women than of men, it has a greater impact on women's perceptions of parental role strain. Although most studies have stressed that young children are conducive to psychological distress among parents, the degree to which this is the case is influenced by a complex interplay of social and economic factors.

The employment of mothers appears to have little effect on the quality of relationships with minor children (Umberson, 1989). However, under certain conditions, such as having an adequate income (Ross & Huber, 1985) and assistance with housework and child care (Mirowsky & Ross, 1989), it may reduce the psychological distress of having young children. In fact, Ross (1995) found that women who have these resources, along with supportive spouses, actually exhibit better mental health than do married women without children. Unmarried mothers and fathers diverge even more greatly than do married mothers and fathers in their parenting experiences, largely because mothers are much more likely than fathers to have physical custody of their children and fathers are much more likely than mothers to have minimal contact with children (Seltzer, 1991). The reasons for these differences are many and complex but include divergent social norms for mothers and fathers, difficult interactions between parents that impede cooperative parenting (Arendell, 1986, 1995; Demo & Acock, 1996), and structural barriers (e.g., geographic distance) that deter fathers' contact with children (Umberson & Williams, 1993).

Relationships with Adult Children

The quality of intergenerational relationships is as variable when children are adults as it is when they are young, although the dynamics of these relationships take on new dimensions. Whereas relationships with minor children last until the children are 18 years old, relationships with adult children can easily last 30 to 60 years. As a result, the relationships between adult children and their parents have ample opportunities to change over time. They may be characterized by increasingly equal exchanges of support and aid or role reversal as parents age. Overall, the empirical evidence strongly suggests that most adult children and their parents remain involved with one another throughout the life course. Adult children and parents are typically in frequent contact with one another; feel affection for and closeness to one another; and engage in a fairly equal exchange of support and services, for example, social support exchanges and help with tasks (Rossi & Rossi, 1990).

The different roles of mothers and fathers of young children contribute to gender differences in the relationships that parents have with adult children. In a national survey mothers said that their adult children visited and talked with them more often and provide them with more emotional support and reported less dissatisfaction with parenting of adult children than did fathers (Umberson, 1992). It seems that mothers' greater investment in parenting of minor children, even with its attendant demands, may contribute to closer and more positive relationships between children and their mothers later in life. The different roles of mothers and fathers and gendered meanings of parenthood are also reflected in Ryff, Schmutte, and Lee's (1996) work on the impact of adult children's adjustment on their parents. This study found that mothers and

fathers had similar views of how their adult children have turned out (in their interpersonal lives, inner qualities, and educational-career attainment), but that, mothers felt more responsible than the fathers for how their children turned out.

Adult children's motivation for contact with their mothers and fathers may differ as well. Their affection for their mothers is positively associated with the frequency with which they visit their mothers. This is not the case for their fathers, which suggests that adult children maintain contact with their fathers for other reasons, perhaps out of obligation more than affection (Lawton, Silverstein, & Bengtson, 1994). Gender differences are also apparent in studies of adult children's views of intergenerational ties: Daughters report greater closeness to their parents than do sons (Rossi & Rossi, 1990).

Coresidential status of parents and adult children has received a great deal of research attention. Parents and adult children are more likely to coreside because of the adult children's, rather than the parents' needs (Speare & Avery, 1993). Coresidence is more common among African Americans, Latinos, and especially Asians than among whites (Speare & Avery, 1993). Parents whose adult children return to live in their parental homes are generally satisfied with this situation (Aquilino & Supple, 1991), as are the adult children (Ward & Spitze, 1996). Unlike most other aspects of intergenerational relationships, gender differences are minimal. Both sons and daughters provide only modest housework and financial contributions to their parents' households, although daughters do somewhat more housework, and sons are somewhat more likely to pay room and board (Ward & Spitze, 1996). These contributions, or the lack thereof, do not affect the overall quality of their relationships with their parents.

The evidence is clear that the quality of relationships between adult children and parents has significant effects on the psychological well-being of both generations (Umberson, 1992). Supportive relationships between parents and adult children seem to enhance the psychological well-being of both generations, while strained relationships contribute to psychological distress (as measured by symptom checklists; e.g., problems with appetite and sleep patterns, feelings of depression and sadness) for both parents and adult children. Although intergenerational relationships are, on average, generally positive, strained relationships have a greater relative impact on psychological well-being.

Although gender clearly shapes intergenerational experiences, its effects are not uniform within groups of men and women. Gender differences in the experience of parenthood are further differentiated on the basis of marital status, race and ethnicity, and socioeconomic status, as well as other social parameters, including sexual orientation. This diversity in parenting experiences is described next.

Marital Status

Divorced Parents. Whether a parent is divorced or not is one of the most important factors influencing the quality of parent-child relationships, whether the children are minors or adults. Compared to married parents, divorced mothers and fathers report lower-quality relationships (e.g., in terms of parental satisfaction and happiness) with minor children, although probably for different reasons. Most divorced mothers are single parents who live with and have legal custody of their children, whereas most divorced fathers are nonresidential parents. There is a great deal of evidence on the strains of single parenting for divorced mothers (e.g., Arendell, 1986; McLanahan, 1983; Ross & Huber, 1985). Arendell's (1986) qualitative study of white divorced mothers found that economic decline and financial hardship were the most stressful problems these women faced. Several studies (e.g., Peterson, 1996) have shown that the financial status of mothers declines following divorce (from 13% to 35%), while the financial status of fathers improves. Arendell reported that parenting itself was not as difficult a part of divorce for the women in her study as other difficulties–particularly financial hardship and social isolation. Demo and Acock (1996) analyzed national data on the influence of family structure on mothers' well-being in first-married, remarried, continuously single-parent, and divorced families. They concluded that differences in mothers' well-being were not entirely explained by structural factors, such as socioeconomic status.

It seems that married mothers have greater social resources (e.g., social support), whereas single and divorced mothers experience greater life strains (e.g., no relief from parenting responsibilities and dealing with nonresidential fathers).

Divorced fathers have received more research attention than fathers in general. Researchers and policy makers have been concerned with the demographic composition of divorced fathers as a group, the psychological consequences of divorce and noncustodial fathering on fathers and their children, and the qualitative experience of noncustodial fathering. In fact, much of this research has stressed the importance of residential and nonresidential parenting arrangements. The negative attention focused on noncustodial divorced fathers, who are sometimes referred to as "deadbeat dads," stems, in part, from the prevalence of this status. About half the parents who divorce have minor children (National Center for Health Statistics, 1991). Following divorce, custody of children is awarded to mothers about 90% of the time, and most noncustodial fathers do not visit their children regularly (Seltzer, 1991). One survey (Furstenberg & Cherlin, 1991) found that 42% of minor children had not seen their fathers at all during the previous year, and over half of the children had never been in their fathers' homes. Only about 58% of the women with young children who divorce are awarded child support, and only about 60% of the divorced fathers comply with child-support awards (Garfinkel, Oellerich, & Robins, 1991). Research on recent legislation to increase child support enforcement has yielded mixed results (Garfinkel et al., 1991), but has generally suggested that child-support payments can be increased through legal strategies (Teachman, 1991).

In-depth interviews with divorced fathers point to several key sources of parental role strain for divorced men: visitation and child support, relationship problems with the ex-partners, and personal and social identity problems (Arendell, 1995; Umberson & Williams, 1993). Although finances are a concern for many men, qualitative research has found that divorced men often view the payment of child support as optional or as a tool to facilitate control over their ex-wives (Arendell,

1995; Umberson & Williams, 1993). An analysis of national survey data indicated that the strain of parenting after divorce partly explains the higher rates of psychological distress exhibited by divorced fathers than their married counterparts (Umberson & Williams, 1993). Although the divorced father–minor child relationship is typically portrayed as distant and difficult, many divorced fathers manage to maintain relationships with their children. A number of factors are associated with fathers' greater financial support of children: larger child support awards, geographic proximity, regular visitation, not remarrying, and a shorter period in the divorced status (Teachman, 1991).

The difficulties between parents and children that are associated with divorce do not disappear once children become adults. Compared to married parents, divorced parents have reported more relationship strain with their adult children, less emotional support from their children, and more dissatisfaction with adult children (Umberson, 1992). Two types of effects of parental divorce have been addressed in the research literature on the relationships of adult children and their parents: parental divorce during childhood and parental divorce during adulthood. Both types of studies have suggested that the strains of parenting following divorce often remain after children become adults. Research on the first issue is generally based on the assumption that the strains of parenting in the divorced status simply continue after children make the transition from childhood to adulthood. Adult children who grow up in divorced families, compared to those who grow up in intact families, report less contact with parents; fewer exchanges of instrumental and economic support, as well as emotional support; and poorer overall relationships with their parents (for a review, see White, 1994). Zill, Morrison, and Coiro (1993) found that two thirds of a sample of 18 to 22 year olds whose parents were divorced had poor relationships with their fathers and one third had poor relationships with their mothers, about twice the proportion of children from nondivorced families. Booth and Amato's (1994) longitudinal study of the effects of parents' marital quality and divorce during the respondents' childhoods on the parents' relationships with adult children 12 years

later concluded that poor marital quality and conflict interfered with the parents' ability to provide various types of support to their children long before the divorce occurred. In turn, the parents' inability to provide this support undermined the quality of the relationship with children in ways that persisted into adulthood.

Studies on the effects of parental divorce after children are adults have similarly concluded that divorce adversely affects intergenerational relationships, although these effects vary by the gender of the parents and children. Cooney (1994) found that recent parental divorce adversely affects relationships between young, white adult children and their fathers, but not their mothers, and that the relationships between mothers and daughters seem to be especially resilient. These adverse effects on the relationships with fathers may stem, in part, from the greater geographic distance between fathers and adult children following parental divorce (Aquilino, 1994a).

A striking feature of this body of research is gender differences across studies. Although many studies have found that both divorced mothers and divorced fathers have poorer relationships with adult children than do their continuously married counterparts, they have consistently found that fathers' relationships with their children are more adversely affected by divorce than are mothers'. In fact, some studies have noted that adult children's relationships with their mothers, particularly daughters' relationships with their mothers, are not significantly affected by parental divorce. The reasons for these gender differences have not been adequately identified but probably include (1) greater geographic distance of children from their fathers than their mothers (Aquilino, 1994a), (2) mothers' greater propensity to engage in kin-keeping activities and nurturant behavior and lifelong differences in the emotional closeness of children to their mothers and fathers (for a review, see Thompson & Walker, 1995), and (3) children's decisions to maintain a distance from their fathers (Cooney, 1994). Most of the evidence on these points comes from quantitative studies of national or community survey data. Additional qualitative research on later-life divorce and its effects on intergenerational relationships could provide important insights into the processes through which divorce affects relationships with adult children.

The genders of the children also play a role in shaping intergenerational relationships following parental divorce. It appears that "the father-daughter tie is especially vulnerable, whereas the mother-daughter tie is especially resilient" (Booth & Amato, 1994, p. 31). Rossi and Rossi (1990), among other researchers, emphasized the uniquely strong intimate tie between mothers and daughters. On the other hand, feminist theorists have stated that relationships between mothers and daughters should not be romanticized, but should be considered in terms of ambivalence and complexity as well as intensity. Survey research has found that relationships between fathers and sons are less influenced by parents' divorce because fathers and sons have less intimate and more instrumental relationships.

Although the evidence is more limited, it seems that the divorce of an adult child may also affect the nature of intergenerational ties. Umberson (1992) found that divorced children received less emotional support from their mothers and fathers than did married children. However, Spitze, Logan, Deane, and Zerger (1994) observed that divorced adult children differed only slightly from nondivorced children in their intergenerational relationships. They found that divorced daughters received more help from parents, particularly with child care and finances, but that divorced sons' ties to their parents slightly weakened. In fact, married sons with children maintained greater contact with their parents than did divorced sons. Spitze et al. (1994) concluded that the presence of grandchildren and the needs of divorced adult children seem to facilitate intergenerational exchanges. Although some scholars have expressed concern over the possible negative impact of high divorce rates on adult daughters' propensity to assist aging parents, Spitze et al. concluded that an adult daughter's divorce does not decrease the extent to which she helps her parents.

Remarriage Following Divorce. Young adults raised in divorced single-parent families seem to maintain fairly positive relationships with their custodial parents, typically their mothers (White,

1994). The remarriage of custodial mothers also appears to have minimal long-term effects on the quality of the relationships between mothers and children. In fact, when a custodial mother remarries, she seems to have more contact with and a better relationship with her adult children (White, 1994). On the other hand, the remarriage of custodial fathers is associated with poorer relationships between fathers and adult children and less support from parents to children (White, 1994). This gender difference probably occurs because fathers are more likely than mothers to disengage from some family relationships to establish new family ties (Furstenberg, Morgan, & Allison, 1987; Umberson & Williams, 1993).

Widowhood. Although the death of a parent is rare during childhood, it is extremely likely during adulthood. The first experience of parental death is most likely to occur when adult children are middle aged. An average of 13 years typically separates the death of a mother and a father, with fathers more likely to die before mothers (Winsborough, Bumpass, & Aquilino, 1991). The adult child must cope not only with his or her grief over the loss of a parent but with the grief and adjustment of the surviving parent. Most of the empirical research on widowhood and intergenerational relationships is concerned with the role of adult children in facilitating the well-being of widowed parents, and this literature suggests that adult children are central players in this regard. According to Umberson's (1996) national prospective study of parental death and intergenerational relationships, the surviving parents stated that the adult children increased both the frequency of contact with and the amount of emotional support given to them following the death. In this prospective design, individuals were interviewed both before and after the death of one of their parents and compared to a nonbereaved control group. Although levels of contact and emotional support tended to return to predeath levels over time, the adult children appeared to be responding to their parents when the parents needed them the most.

The perspective of adult children has been largely ignored in research on widowhood and intergenerational relationships. An exception was

Aquilino's (1994b) study, which compared a national sample of adult children of widowed parents to adult children of married parents and found gender differences in the effects of parental widowhood on adult children. Aquilino concluded that the death of fathers had little effect on relationships between surviving mothers and adult sons or daughters. However, the death of mothers was associated with a substantial decline in the quality of the relationships between surviving fathers and daughters and a minimal change in the relationships between surviving fathers and sons. Umberson's (1996) prospective analysis of national survey data indicated that the effects of a parent's death on relationships with surviving parents were generally not statistically significant, but, the qualitative component of the study suggested that the death of a parent may lead to a substantial change (either positive or negative) in these relationships. A positive change may occur if the surviving parent and child are more supportive and accepting of one another after the other parent dies, whereas a negative change may occur if the surviving parent begins to place more demands on the child.

The impact of a parent's widowhood on the parent's relationship with an adult child has received substantial research attention, but the impact of the widowhood of an adult child on this relationship has not. However, two studies (Bankoff, 1983; Umberson, 1992) found that parents are more likely to provide financial and emotional support to widowed children than to married children. These results, like those on the divorce of adult children, indicate that parents attempt to provide more support to their adult children in times of greater need.

Nonmarital Relationships.   Ross (1995) argued that, in contemporary U.S. society, it is much more relevant to refer to a continuum of attachment, rather than to marital status, per se, as an indicator of involvement in a relationship. She based her argument partly on the observation that a number of common and important relationship statuses (such as cohabiting, never-married noncohabiting, and gay and lesbian partners with children) are not represented in the usual marital-status categories. With regard to intergenerational exchanges between parents and their cohabiting and never-married adult children with young children, Marks and McLanahan (1993) found that single adults with young children are generally more involved with their parents than are married adults and that women are more involved than are men. They also found that divorced women are more involved with their parents than are never-married women and concluded that this finding may be the result of the greater social recognition and acceptance of divorced parents.

One of the few studies of gay or lesbian parent–adult child relationships was Lewin's (1993) comparative qualitative analysis of intergenerational relationships among lesbian and single heterosexual mothers and their parents. Although strain sometimes arose in lesbian women's relationships with their parents because of the daughters' sexual orientation, Lewin was struck by the more pervasive similarities of the two groups of mothers. Lesbian mothers were as likely as single heterosexual mothers to rely on their parents for practical and emotional support and the receipt of such support.

Although the complexity of understanding diversity in intergenerational relationships is daunting, without expanding research on other family contexts (e.g., cohabiting, lesbian, and gay parents), researchers will not recognize the considerable diversity in intergenerational relationships, along with the particular strengths and weaknesses of various arrangements. Given the pervasive gender differences in intergenerational relationships, one would expect that the unigender parenting that is likely to characterize single-parent and gay-lesbian parenting ties with children would greatly influence the nature of the resulting intergenerational ties. Therefore, research on intergenerational relationships should further explore relationships in pluralistic parent-child contexts.

Race and Ethnicity

Of the few studies that have directly examined racial differences in relationships between parents and minor or adult children, some (e.g., Hogan, Eggebeen, & Clogg, 1993) have suggested that most racial differences in family experiences are due to class differences, and others have found that intergenerational relationships differ only slightly across racial groups. For example, Umberson (1989) found that African American mothers received fewer demands from their minor children than did other mothers, and Kessler and McRae (1982) and Reskin and Coverman (1985) indicated that parenting of minor children is more distressing for white parents than for African American parents. These findings are surprising from a family ecology perspective and in light of the greater prevalence of financial hardship and single parenthood among African Americans than among whites. Ethnographic research has suggested that African American mothers may experience fewer parenting demands because African American grandmothers play a more central role in child rearing than do white grandmothers and single parenting is more accepted in the African American culture (Burton, 1996).

Gender differences in African American parenting are taken as a given in that the majority of African American mothers are single parents (Waite, 1995). Restricted economic opportunities for African American men impose constraints on the ability of fathers to maintain relationships with their children throughout the life course. African American adult children in a national sample reported less frequent contact with their fathers than did white children (Umberson, 1992). Reflecting the central role of African American women in raising children, much of the qualitative research on these families has focused exclusively on mother-child relationships. For example, Burton (1996) emphasized the value systems of African Americans in shaping intergenerational ties and the importance of maternal lineages in African American families. Her ethnographic work revealed a common pattern of mutual aid across generations of African American families, with grandmothers raising grandchildren and daughters caring for great-grandmothers.

One indicator of intergenerational involvement is the coresidential status of parents and adult children. African American, as well as Latino and Asian, parents and adult children are more likely than their white counterparts to share households (Angel & Tienda, 1982). These coresidential patterns may reflect the needs or values of the two gen-

erations. The apparent greater involvement of African American and Latino families is attributed sometimes to greater structural need and sometimes to stronger cultural and familistic values. The lower rates of institutionalization of the elderly among African Americans than among whites is sometimes viewed as evidence of greater family support among African Americans (Dwyer, Barton, & Vogel, 1994).

Few studies on intergenerational relations have explicitly examined race-ethnicity as a variable from the viewpoints of either parents or adult children. With regard to parents, one study found that compared to white parents, African American parents reported that they received less emotional support from their children and experienced greater parental dissatisfaction (Umberson, 1992). Mutran's (1985) analysis of national data on African American and white families concluded that African American parents received more financial and instrumental support from their adult children than did white parents, although, this racial difference was explained largely by the lower socioeconomic status, and presumably the greater needs, of African American parents. In addition, Freeberg and Stein's (1996) study of a small snowball sample of European American, African American, and Mexican American young adults concluded that Mexican American intergenerational relationships are characterized by greater feelings of familism and more helping behavior toward parents. With regard to adult children, Umberson (1992) found that the African American adult children reported that their mothers gave them substantially more emotional support than the white adult children reported.

Although much ethnographic research has suggested that African American and Latino families are characterized by larger and more supportive kin networks, empirical comparisons of these groups with white families have provided little support for cultural differences once socioeconomic differences are taken into account (Hogan et al., 1993; Mutran, 1985). In fact, Hogan et al. argued that the meager financial resources of many African American families may make it even more difficult for these families to meet the needs of multiple generations. Their analysis of national data concluded that African Americans and Latinos were less likely than whites to engage in intergenerational exchanges of instrumental and financial assistance and advice. Although socioeconomic status may be confounded with ethnicity in effects on intergenerational ties among African Americans and Latinos, the evidence points to stronger familism among Asian families, independent of socioeconomic status (Lin & Liu, 1993).

Research on race, ethnicity, and intergenerational relationships has not yielded sufficient comparative information on both the quantitative and qualitative aspects of intergenerational relationships to conclude that cultural differences do or do not exist apart from socioeconomic resources and needs. Therefore, more qualitative and quantitative research is needed and of various ethnic groups' perceptions of parent-child ties and the social contexts of those ties.

Socioeconomic Status

A consistent theme in the literature on minor child–parent relationships is that economic hardship exacerbates the strain of parenting (Ross et al., 1990). In contrast, several studies have provided empirical evidence that parents of lower socioeconomic status have closer and more supportive relationships with their adult children (Rossi & Rossi, 1990; Treas & Bengtson, 1987; Umberson, 1992), perhaps because the needs of these parents lead their children into closer and more reciprocal roles with the parents. Umberson's (1992) analysis of a national sample found that the incomes and education of adult children had little effect on parents' and adult children's reports of the quality of their intergenerational relationships. Other researchers have indicated that education is associated with the greater frequency of contact between parents and adult children, perhaps because of the variation in social norms or the greater resources offered to adult children (see Cooney, 1994). Overall, little is known about differences in intergenerational experiences by class. Education and income are typically control variables in multivariate analyses, rather than central research foci. Studies by Conger, Xiaojia, Elder, Lorenz, and Simons (1994) and

Elder (1997) on the effects of economic hardship on minor child-parent relationships are an exception to this pattern; they found that financial problems undermine the quality of these relationships.

INTERGENERATIONAL CAREGIVING

When individuals become ill, they are most likely to rely on family members for informal caregiving, primarily spouses, or, in the absence of spouses, adult children (Montgomery & Datwyler, 1990; for a review, see Baum & Page, 1991). Adult children also provide care to one parent when the other parent is present, either because additional care is needed or because the other parent's ability to provide care is limited (Stoller, 1983). Parents are most likely to be informal caregivers of their mentally impaired adult children (Greenberg, Seltzer, & Greenley, 1993).

Although family members are better able to cope with and recover from severe physical illnesses and to postpone institutionalization when they receive significant informal support (Sherbourne & Hays, 1990), the provision of such care may generate emotional, social, physical, occupational, and financial strain for the caregivers (Cantor, 1983; Turner & Pearlin, 1989) that are associated with psychological distress (Kahana, Biegel, & Wykle, 1994; Umberson et al., 1996). The availability of social support to caregivers and caregivers' personal resources (such as mastery and self-esteem) play a role in mediating the relationship between caregiving and distress (Pearlin, Mullan, Semple, & Skaff, 1990). Differences in coping responses or in the use of social support may account for why some caregivers fare better than others in similar circumstances.

Women are much more likely than men to assume responsibility for providing direct care (Umberson et al., 1996). Daughters and daughters-in-law are more likely than sons to provide care to their parents or in-laws (Aldous, 1994; Kahana et al., 1994). Sons are less likely to be caregivers even in families with multiple sons, and only daughters are twice as likely to become caregivers as only sons (Coward & Dwyer, 1990). Furthermore sons' contributions to caregiving are considered unimportant by both daughters and sons (Matthews,

1995). When adult children require care, mothers are much more likely than fathers to provide it.

Women and men also provide qualitatively different types of care. Daughters provide more hours of care over longer periods and engage in more daily personal caregiving and household maintenance, whereas sons commit less time to caregiving and are more likely to provide sporadic and long-distance care (Horowitz, 1985; Montgomery & Kamo, 1989). Women (both wives and daughters) may also experience more stress and psychological distress as a result of their caregiving activities (Umberson et al., 1996), including a "loss of self" (Skaff & Pearlin, 1992). Caregivers become engulfed in their roles when they have limited social contacts and occupy a few number roles other than caregiver; this loss of self is associated with a decline in self-esteem, diminished mastery, and increased depression.

Most research on caregiving has focused specifically on daughters as providers and mothers as recipients of care, so little information is available on male caregivers and receivers. Since both sons and daughters are more likely to provide care to same-sex parents (Lee, Dwyer, & Coward, 1993), one reason why daughters greatly outnumber sons as caregivers may be that elderly women greatly outnumber elderly men. Furthermore, Montgomery and Kosloski (1994) found that son caregivers are more likely than daughter caregivers to decide to institutionalize their impaired parents.

Marital Status of Caregivers

Most adult child caregivers are daughters (Noelker & Wallace, 1985; Stone, Cafferata, & Sangl, 1987), and most research that has considered the marital status of caregivers has focused specifically on daughters. Several studies (Allen & Pickett, 1987; Brody, Litvin, Albert, & Hoffman, 1994; Walker, Martin, & Jones, 1992) have found that never-married daughters are more likely than daughters of other marital statuses to provide care to parents, presumably because they have fewer competing demands. Brody et al. (1994) found that never-married women provided 77% of the care to their elderly parents; widowed daughters, 62%; and married, remarried, and separated-divorced daughters,

50%–54%. Elderly parents of married and widowed daughters did not actually receive less care overall; rather, they were more likely to receive care from other formal and informal sources in addition to their daughters, according to Brody et al. Allen and Pickett's (1987) research on lifelong never-married women used a life-course perspective to explain why these women took responsibility for family caregiving. The never-married women in their sample were typically the youngest or only girls in their families and played the essential and historical role of unmarried daughters of keeping their relatives, as well as their family histories, alive. Further qualitative research is needed to determine why unmarried women are more likely than other women to serve as caregivers.

Race and Ethnicity

Most of the research on intergenerational caregiving has been based on white, middle-class samples and has often excluded men, primarily because most caregivers are white and female, and it is difficult and expensive to obtain representative samples of caregivers. Although studies of minority caregivers have suggested that they have unique caregiving experiences, the absence of comparisons with other caregivers makes it difficult to assess actual differences across social groups. Empirical studies have clearly shown that caregiving to parents is common among racial-ethnic groups and that such caregiving is stressful and costly to psychological well-being; however, the current state of this research tells little about racial, ethnic, and class variations in intergenerational caregiving and the consequences of such caregiving. This literature is beginning to focus on both the gratifications and the strains of providing care (see, for example, Allen & Walker, 1992), and if it incorporates racial-ethnic comparisons, may reveal significant diversity in both the rewards and costs of providing informal care.

Horowitz and Reinhard's (1995) study of the provision of family care to relatives with mental illness suggested that ethnic-group values shape perceptions of caregivers' burdens. It found that caregiving is more normative and less stressful for African Americans than for European Americans because African Americans are more involved in intergenerational caregiving for extended kin. The extended helping networks and group-centered values of African Americans may protect them from role strain more than the values of European Americans that focus on nuclear family orientations and reliance on professionals. In a study of 209 parents of severely mentally ill children, Pickett, Uraniak, Cook, and Cohler (1993) found that African American parents had higher self-worth and lower levels of depression than did European American parents. On the other hand, minority families tend to have lower incomes, poorer housing, more chronic diseases, and higher levels of disability than do European American families that may increase the strain of caregiving. Montgomery and Datwyler (1990) argued that minority women face more frequent and intense demands as caregivers because they are often the sole financial providers for their families.

Parents Caring for Adult Children

Most research on intergenerational relationships and caregiving has concentrated on children's provision of care to parents, but about 85% of caregivers of adults with mental illness and mental retardation are parents (Greenberg et al., 1993). Although parents of mentally retarded adults typically have had many years to adjust to their caregiving role, parents of adults with mental illness generally have more problems adjusting to their caregiving role because mental illness is usually of later onset (Greenberg et al., 1993). Seltzer, Krauss, Choi, and Hong (1996) emphasized that many parents of mentally retarded adults experience the parent-child relationship as loving and gratifying, but as they age, many of them worry about the future care of their aging children. Caregiving for adult children is difficult, in part, because of its nonnormative nature and the elements of grief and loss that are associated with lost dreams for children. On the other hand, much of the caregiving role is inherent to the meaning of parenting one's children.

As AIDS has become more prevalent, many parents have also provided some type of care to their adult children with AIDS before their children's death. AIDS is thus a multigenerational family disease, affecting not only the HIV infected but their family members. It has been estimated that one third of persons with AIDS are dependent on older parents for financial, physical, and emotional support (Allers, 1990). These parents may be dealing with infirmities or decreasing capacities of their own and living on fixed incomes and be coping with acceptance of their children's sexual orientation or drug use (Gutheil & Chichin, 1991). Raveis and Siegel (1991) noted that when informal care is initiated in the final stages of AIDS (when persons living with AIDS can no longer care for themselves and "go home to die"), parents are suddenly confronted with enormous demands.

The stigma of AIDS often prevents parents from receiving adequate social support that would help to alleviate some of the strain of caregiving (Powell-Cope & Brown, 1992). This lack of support and the caregivers' felt need to conceal their activities further exacerbate the strain of caregiving for adult children with AIDS (Trice, 1988).

Although parents as caregivers to adult children with AIDS have not received extensive research attention in general, fathers have been grossly underrepresented in such studies. Several studies have suggested that, although other family members may be available, mothers constitute the major source of family care for persons with AIDS in the United States. Schiller (1993) stated that 52% of the 107 participants with AIDS who lived with family members lived with parents, usually their mothers. In interviews with mothers of HIV-positive men, Slaten (1996) found that mothers (1) played the role of health regulator for their gay sons before the sons became infected with HIV by warning them about the threat of HIV and urging them to use condoms; (2) provided intensive, exhausting physical care care, such as bathing and dressing their adult sons; and (3) repressed their feelings of grief to carry out their caregiving responsibilities, often until their sons had died. Interviews with the fathers of HIV-infected men revealed that the fathers became the financial managers of their sons' illness by keeping detailed financial records of medical expenses; engaged in collaborative caregiving by receiving assistance from professionals and volunteers with the provision of physical care; and adopted the role of medical decision maker on behalf of their sons, at times grappling with such difficult issues as whether to discontinue intravenous feeding.

Despite the strains they face, one of the recurrent themes in the literature on caregiving for adult children is that parents would not consider giving up their role as caregivers for their mentally impaired (Seltzer et al., 1996) or HIV-infected children (Trice, 1988). Trice's (1988) study of 24 mothers of HIV-positive men found that those who had provided care to their sons had more panic attacks, hypertension, night terrors, job turnovers, and episodes of uncharacteristic violence than did those who did not provide care. All the mothers who cared for their sons reported that they would do it again, despite the psychological distress they experienced.

Minority families have been hit especially hard by the AIDS pandemic. Boyd-Franklin (1997) asserted that in the African American community, which is experiencing the highest incidence of HIV infection in women and children, it is difficult to find a family that has not been touched by AIDS. For minority group members with HIV, the persistent stigma of AIDS, coupled with rampant homophobia, has contributed to the fear of disclosing the illness. Therefore, many African American grandparents provide care in secrecy to their HIV-infected adult children and grandchildren. Because poor families often are not given access to medical advances or supportive services, such as home health care, their burden may be heavier. Although the impact of AIDS on minority families must be assessed, Boyd-Franklin observed that African Americans tend to distrust researchers and are often reluctant to reveal intimate family issues to them. Thus, researchers face the challenge of acquiring more knowledge about AIDS caregiving in minority families.

CONCLUSIONS

Gender and Intergenerational Relationships

The lifespans of parents and children easily overlap by 50 years or more in contemporary U.S. society. Several types of studies have strongly indicated that parents and children remain closely involved with one another over the life course. Empirical research

has also provided striking and consistent evidence that the genders of parents and children shape the intensity, quality, and psychological consequences of intergenerational relationships. Mothers report greater closeness, more frequent contact, and more parental satisfaction in intergenerational relationships than do fathers and, according to survey research, relationships between mothers and daughters seem to be particularly resilient. Parents and adult children also play important roles in providing informal care to one another for physical and mental impairment. In cases of informal caregiving, there is clear evidence of gender differences: Mothers and daughters are much more likely than fathers and sons to provide the most intensive and personal types of informal care.

Why do these gender differences exist? Although various theoretical perspectives yield possible insights into the gendering of intergenerational relationships, empirical evidence has yet to establish clearly the causes of gender differences in relationship orientations (Finley, 1989; Umberson et al., 1996). The family ecology model suggests that structural circumstances encourage and constrain different behaviors in men and women that foster women's greater involvement in and concern with intergenerational relationships (Epstein, 1988; Johnson, 1988; Umberson et al., 1996). Feminist theory emphasizes the socially constructed nature of gender and family experiences (Thompson & Walker, 1995). Each of these theoretical perspectives recognizes that gendered intergenerational experiences are not monolithic. Rather, men's and women's experiences of intergenerational relationships reflect other structural circumstances, including marital status, socioeconomic status, and racial-ethnic cultural differences, as well as the socially constructed nature of gender and family in different cultures and populations. The diversity in men's and women's experiences as parents and children illustrate these influences and constructions.

Future research and theoretical work should seek to provide fuller explanations for the gendered nature of intergenerational relationships. These explanations should incorporate recognition of both the similarities and differences between men's and women's experiences (Umberson et al., 1996). The growing research interest in fatherhood represents a step in this direction, although theoretical work has not been the central focus of the literature on fatherhood. Research on fatherhood, like research on motherhood, must recognize the diversity of fathers' experiences of parenthood and parenting. Fathers tend to be viewed as "good dads" or "bad dads," and this dualism does not reflect the range of their experiences.

Methods

Theoretical models on gender and family relationships tend to diverge along methodological lines, with feminist theorists advocating the use of qualitative methods and more structurally oriented researchers (including advocates of the family ecology model) promoting the use of quantitative methods. We argue that a strict division between these theoretical perspectives undermines the ability to gain a full understanding of gender and family experiences and only serves to maintain the theoretical divide. We strongly advocate the use of triangulated methods in the study of gender and family. On the one hand, quantitative methods are well suited to document associations between variables in the general population, allowing researchers to see possible similarities and differences between groups of individuals, but they are limited in their ability to reveal insights on gender and family processes. On the other hand, qualitative methods are uniquely suited to revealing such insights, although they are limited in their ability to reveal larger patterns of demographic trends and differences and similarities within the general population. A blending of methods draws on the strengths of each approach and has the potential to reveal corroboration between the two approaches, as well as reasons for any possible differences in conclusions. As was noted about Umberson's (1996) study on parental death and intergenerational ties, our qualitative results suggested reasons for the absence of statistically significant effects. As Demo and Allen (1996, p. 428) stated, "a promising direction [for theoretical development] is to use the insights and applications of both positivist and nonpositivist approaches."

The Family Life Course

The literatures on parenting of minor children and parenting of adult children are almost entirely separate. A significant body of research has relied on retrospective techniques to explore how childhood relationships with parents may influence adult relationships with parents, but such retrospective reports are subject to distortion over time. Because most of this research is cross-sectional in design, it is difficult to draw firm conclusions about this life-course linkage.

Gender differences in parent-child relationships begin when children are born, if not before. Future research and theory should attempt to connect the literatures on childhood and adulthood relationships with parents, emphasizing gender similarities and differences (as well as other group similarities and differences) in these linkages. It is almost certainly the case that later-life gender differences in intergenerational relationships reflect early parent-child experiences. One of the few prospective analyses of childhood-to-adulthood intergenerational experiences concluded that both continuity and change characterize intergenerational relationships over time (Aquilino, 1997). Continuity is especially apparent in that the quality (emotional closeness and control-conflict) of childhood relationships with parents is strongly linked to the quality of those relationships in adulthood. Changes in these relationships are most likely to occur as children's roles change, for example, when they leave home, cohabit or marry, or obtain full-time employment.

The Dynamic Quality of Intergenerational Ties

A clear theme in research on parent-child relationships is that these relationships are constantly changing. As parents and children age and shift from one marital status to another, move to another city or into the same household, obtain or leave jobs, become severely ill, or experience any manner of other common life changes, their relationships are affected. Whether their relationships are affected positively or negatively depends on the available resources and strains that accompany the change, as well as the parents' and children's definitions of family. Both structural conditions and socially constructed aspects of these changes influence the quality and dynamics of intergenerational relationships. Certainly, parent-child ties are central to the lives of parents and children throughout the life course. The considerable diversity that exists across social groups and over time for any given relationship provides a rich area for continuing research and theoretical development.

REFERENCES

Aldous, J. (1994). Someone to watch over me: Family responsibilities and their realization across family lives. In E. Kahana, D. E. Biegel, & M. L. Wykle (Eds.), *Family caregiving across the lifespan* (pp. 42–68). Thousand Oaks, CA: Sage.

Allen, K. R., & Demo, D. H. (1995). The families of lesbians and gay men: A new frontier in family research. *Journal of Marriage and the Family, 57,* 111–127.

Allen, K. R., & Pickett, R. S. (1987). Forgotten streams in the family life course: Utilization of qualitative retrospective interviews in the analysis of lifelong single women's family careers. *Journal of Marriage and the Family, 49,* 517–526.

Allen, K. R., & Walker, A. J. (1992). Attentive love: A feminist perspective on the caregiving of adult daughters. *Family Relations, 41,* 264–289.

Allers, C. T. (1990). AIDS and the older adult. *Gerontologist, 30,* 405–407.

Ambert, A. M. (1992). *The effect of children on parents.* New York: Haworth.

Angel, R. C., & Tienda, M. (1982). Determinants of extended household structure: Cultural pattern or economic need? *American Journal of Sociology, 87,* 1360–1383.

Aquilino, W. S. (1994a). Impact of childhood family disruption on young adults' relationships with parents. *Journal of Marriage and the Family, 56,* 295–313.

Aquilino, W. S. (1994b). Later life parental divorce and widowhood: Impact on young adults' assessment of parent-child relations. *Journal of Marriage and the Family, 56,* 908–922.

Aquilino, W. S. (1997). From adolescent to young adult: A prospective study of parent-child relations during the transition to adulthood. *Journal of Marriage and the Family, 59,* 670–686.

Aquilino, W., & Supple, K. R. (1991). Parent-child relations and parent's satisfaction with living arrangements when adult children live at home. *Journal of Marriage and the Family, 53,* 13–27.

Arendell, T. (1986). *Mothers and divorce.* Berkeley: University of California Press.

Arendell, T. (1995). *Fathers and divorce.* Thousand Oaks, CA: Sage.

Bankoff, E. A. (1983). Aged parents and their widowed daughters: A support relationship. *Journal of Gerontology, 38,* 226–230.

Baum, M., & Page, M. (1991). Caregiving and multigenerational families. *Gerontologist, 31,* 762–769.

Belsky, J., Lang, M., & Rovine, M. (1985). Stability and change across the transition to parenthood: A second study. *Journal of Personality and Social Psychology, 50,* 517–522.

Booth, A., & Amato, P. R. (1994). Parental marital quality, parental divorce, and relations with parents. *Journal of Marriage and the Family, 56,* 21–34.

Boyd-Franklin, N. (1997, June). *Multigenerational issues in African Americans with HIV/AIDS.* Paper presented at the fifth annual NIMH conference on the Role of Families in Preventing and Adapting to HIV/AIDS, Baltimore, MD.

Brody, E., Litvin, S. J., Albert, S. M., & Hoffman, C. J. (1994). Marital status of daughters and patterns of parent care. *Journal of Gerontology, 49,* S95–S103.

Burton, L. (1996). Age norms, the timing of family life transitions, and intergenerational caregiving among American women. *Gerontologist, 36,* 199–208.

Cantor, M. H. (1983). Strain among caregivers: A study of experience in the United States. *Gerontologist, 23,* 597–604.

Chodorow, N. (1978). *The reproduction of mothering.* Berkeley: University of California Press.

Collins, P. H. (1994). Shifting the center: Race, class, and feminist theorizing about motherhood. In E. N. Glenn, G. Chang, & L. R. Forcey (Eds.), *Mothering: Ideology, experience, and agency* (pp. 45–66). New York: Routledge.

Conger, R. D., Xiaojia, G., Elder, G. H., Lorenz, F. O., & Simons, R. L. (1994). Economic stress, coercive family process, and development problems of adolescents. *Child Development, 65,* 541–561.

Cooney, T. M. (1994). Young adults' relations with parents: The influence of recent parental divorce. *Journal of Marriage and the Family, 56,* 45–56.

Cowan, C. P., & Cowan, P. A. (1992). *When partners become parents.* New York: Basic Books.

Coward, R. T., & Dwyer, J. W. (1990). The association of gender, sibling networks composition, and patterns of parent care by adult children. *Research on Aging, 12,* 158–181.

Crohan, S. E. (1996). Marital quality and conflict across the transition to parenthood in African American and white couples. *Journal of Marriage and the Family, 58,* 933–944.

Denzin, N. (1989). *The research act* (3rd ed.). Englewood Cliffs, NJ: Prentice Hall.

Demo, D. H., & Acock, A. C. (1996). Singlehood, marriage and remarriage: The effects of family structure and family relationships on mothers' well-being. *Journal of Family Issues, 17,* 388–407.

Demo, D. H., & Allen, K. R. (1996). Diversity within lesbian and gay families: Challenges and implications of family theory and research. *Journal of Social and Personal Relationships, 13,* 415–434.

Dill, B. T. (1988). Our mothers' grief: Racial ethnic women and the maintenance of families. *Journal of Family History, 13,* 415–431.

Dwyer, J. W., Barton, A. J., & Vogel, W. B. (1994). Area of residence and the risk of institutionalization. *Journal of Gerontology, 49,* S75–S84.

Elder, G. H. (1997). The life course and human development. In R. M. Lerner, (Ed.), *Handbook of Child Psychology, Vol. 1: Theoretical Models of Human Development* (pp. 939–991). New York: John Wiley.

Epstein, C. F. (1988). *Deceptive distinctions: Sex, gender, and the social order.* New Haven, CT: Yale University Press.

Finley, N. (1989). Theories of family labor as applied to gender differences in caregiving for elderly parents. *Journal of Marriage and the Family, 51,* 79–96.

Firestone, S. (1970). *The dialectic of sex.* New York: Bantam Books.

Flaks, D. D., Ficher, I., Masterpasqua F., & Joseph, G. (1995). Lesbians choosing motherhood: A comparative study of lesbian and heterosexual parents and their children. *Developmental Psychology, 31,* 105–114.

Freeberg, A. L., & Stein, C. (1996). Felt obligation towards parents in Mexican-American and Anglo-American young adults. *Journal of Social and Personal Relationships, 13,* 457–471.

Furstenberg, F. F. (1992). Good dads—bad dads: Two faces of fatherhood. In A. S. Skolnick & J. H. Skolnick (Eds.), *Families in Transition* (7th ed., pp. 342–62). New York: HarperCollins.

Furstenberg, F. F., & Cherlin, A. J. (1991). *Divided families: What happens to children when parents part.* Cambridge, MA: Harvard University Press.

Furstenberg, F. F., Morgan, S. P., & Allison, P. D. (1987). Paternal participation and children's well-being after marital dissolution. *American Sociological Review, 52,* 695–701.

Garfinkel, I., Oellerich, D., & Robbins, P. K. (1991). Child support guidelines: Will they make a difference? *Journal of Family Issues, 12,* 404–429.

Glenn, E. N. (1994). Social constructions of mothering: A thematic overview. In E. N. Glenn, G. Chang, & L. R. Forcey (Eds.), *Mothering: Ideology, experience, and agency* (pp. 1–32). New York: Routledge.

Glenn, N. D. (1975). Psychological well-being in the postparental stage: Some evidence from national surveys. *Journal of Marriage and the Family, 37,* 105–110.

Gove, W. R., & Geerken, M. (1977). The effect of children and employment on the mental health of married men and women. *Social Forces, 56,* 66–76.

Greenberg, J. S., Seltzer, M. M., & Greenley, J. R. (1993). Aging parents of adults with disabilities: The gratifications and frustrations of later-life caregiving. *Gerontologist, 33,* 542–550.

Gutheil, I. A., & Chichin, E. R. (1991). AIDS, older people and social work. *Health and Social Work, 16,* 237–244.

Harkins, E. (1978). Effects of empty nest transition on self-report of psychological and physical well-being. *Journal of Marriage and the Family, 40,* 549–556.

Hogan, D. P., Eggebeen, D. J., & Clogg, C. C. (1993). The structure of intergenerational exchanges in American families. *American Journal of Sociology, 98,* 1428–1459.

Horowitz, A. (1985). Family caregiving to the frail elderly. In C. Eisdorfer, M. P. Lawton, & G. L. Maddox (Eds.), *Annual Review of Gerontology and Geriatrics* (Vol. 5, pp. 194–246). New York: Springer.

Horowitz, A. V., & Reinhard, S. C. (1995). Ethnic differences in caregiving duties and burdens among parents and siblings of persons with severe mental illnesses. *Journal of Health and Social Behavior, 36,* 138–150.

Johnson, M. (1988). *Strong mothers, weak wives.* Berkeley: University of California Press.

Kahana, E., Biegel, D. E., & Wykle, M. L. (Eds.). (1994). *Family caregiving across the lifespan.* Thousand Oaks, CA: Sage.

Kessler, R. C., & McRae, J. A. (1982). The effect of wives' employment on the mental health of married men and women. *American Sociological Review, 47,* 216–227.

LaRossa, R. (1988). Fatherhood and social change. *Family Relations, 37,* 451–457.

Lawton, L., Silverstein, M., & Bengtson, V. (1994). Affection, social contact, and geographic distance between adult children and their parents. *Journal of Marriage and the Family, 56,* 57–68.

Lee, G., Dwyer, J., & Coward, R. (1993). Gender differences in parent care: Demographic factors and same gender preferences. *Journal of Gerontology, 48,* S9–S16.

LeMasters, E. E. (1957). Parenthood as crisis. *Marriage and Family Living, 19,* 352–355.

Lewin, E. (1993). *Lesbian mothers.* Ithaca, NY: Cornell University Press.

Lin, C., & Liu, W. T. (1993). Intergenerational relationships among Chinese immigrant families from Taiwan. In H. P. McAdoo (Ed.), *Family ethnicity* (pp. 271–286). Newbury Park, CA: Sage.

Marks, N. F., & McLanahan, S. S. (1993). Gender, family structure, and social support among parents. *Journal of Marriage and the Family, 55,* 481–493.

Matthews, S. H. (1995). Gender and the division of filial responsibility between lone sisters and their brothers. *Journal of Gerontology, 50B,* 312–320.

McLanahan, S. (1983). Family structure and stress: A longitudinal comparison of two-parent and female-headed families. *Journal of Marriage and the Family, 45,* 347–357.

McLanahan, S., & Adams, J. (1987). Parenthood and psychological well-being. *Annual Review of Sociology, 13,* 237–257.

Mirowsky, J., & Ross, C. E. (1989). *Social causes of psychological distress.* New York: Aldine De Gruyter.

Moen, P., Erickson, M. A., & Dempster-McClain, D. (1997). Their mother's daughters? The intergenerational transmission of gender attitudes in a world of changing roles. *Journal of Marriage and the Family, 59,* 281–293.

Montgomery, R., & Datwyler, M. M. (1990, Summer). Women and men in the caregiving role. *Generations,* pp. 34–38.

Montgomery, R., & Kamo, Y. (1989). Parent care by sons and daughters. In J. A. Mancini (Ed.), *Aging parents and adult children* (pp. 213–230). Lexington, MA: D. C. Heath.

Montgomery, R., & Kosloski, K. (1994). A longitudinal analysis of nursing home placement for dependent elders cared for by spouses vs. adult children. *Journal of Gerontology, 49,* S62–S74.

Mutran, E. (1985). Intergenerational family support among blacks and whites: Response to culture or to socioeconomic differences? *Journal of Gerontology, 40,* 382–389.

National Center for Health Statistics. (1991, May 21). Advance report of final divorce statistics, 1988. *Monthly Vital Statistics Report, 39*(12), Suppl. 2. Washington, DC: U.S. Bureau of the Census.

Nock, S. L., & Kingston, P. W. (1988). Time with children: The impact of couples' work-time commitments. *Social Forces, 67,* 59–85.

Noelker, L. S., & Wallace, R. W. (1985). The organization of family care for impaired elderly. *Journal of Family Issues, 6,* 23–44.

Patterson, C. J. (1995). Families of the lesbian baby boom: Parents' division of labor and children's adjustment. *Developmental Psychology, 31,* 115–123.

Pearlin, L. I., Mullan, J. T., Semple, S. J., & Skaff, M. M. (1990). Caregiving and the stress process: An overview of concepts and their measures. *Gerontologist, 30,* 583–594.

Peterson, R. R. (1996). A re-evaluation of the economic consequences of divorce. *American Sociological Review, 61,* 528–536.

Pickett, S. A., Uraniak, D., Cook, J. A., & Cohler, B. (1993). Strength in adversity: Blacks bear burden better than whites. *Professional Psychology-Research and Practice, 24,* 460–467.

Powell-Cope, G. M., & Brown, M. A. (1992). Going public as an AIDS family caregiver. *Social Science and Medicine, 34,* 571–580.

Raveis, V. H., & Siegel, K. (1991, February). The impact of care giving on informal or familial care givers. *AIDS Patient Care,* pp. 39–43.

Reskin, B. F., & Coverman, S. (1985). Sex and race in the determinants of psychophysical distress: A reappraisal of the sex-role hypothesis. *Social Forces, 63,* 1038–1058.

Rich, A. (1976). *Of woman born.* New York: W. W. Norton.

Risman, B. J. (1987). Intimate relationships from a microstructural perspective: Men who mother. *Gender & Society, 1,* 6–32.

Ross, C. E. (1995). Reconceptualizing marital status as a continuum of social attachment. *Journal of Marriage and the Family, 57,* 129–141.

Ross, C. E., & Huber, J. (1985). Hardship and depression. *Journal of Health and Social Behavior, 26,* 312–327.

Ross, C. E., Mirowsky, J., & Goldsteen, K. (1990). The impact of the family on health: The decade in review. *Journal of Marriage and the Family, 52,* 1059–1078.

Rossi, A. S. (1985). Gender and parenthood. In A. S. Rossi (Ed.) *Gender and the life course* (pp. 161–191). New York: Aldine.

Rossi, A. S., & Rossi, P. H. (1990). *Of human bonding.* New York: Aldine de Gruyter.

Ryff, C. D., Schmutte, P. S., & Lee, Y. H. (1996). How children turn out: Implications for parental self-evaluation. In C. D. Ryff & M. M. Seltzer (Eds.), *The parental experience in midlife* (pp. 383–422). Chicago: University of Chicago Press.

Schiller, N. G. (1993). The invisible women: Caregiving and the construction of AIDS health services. *Culture, Medicine and Psychiatry, 17,* 487–512.

Scott, J., & Alwin, D. F. (1989). Gender differences in parental strain: Parental role or gender role. *Journal of Family Issues, 10,* 482–503.

Seltzer, J. A. (1991). Relationships between fathers and children who live apart: The father's role after separation. *Journal of Marriage and the Family, 53,* 79–101.

Seltzer, M. M., Krauss, M. W., Choi, S. C., & Hong, J. (1996). Midlife and later-life parenting of adult children with mental retardation. In C. D. Ryff & Seltzer, M. M. (Eds.), *The parental experience in midlife* (pp. 459–489). Chicago: University of Chicago Press.

Sherbourne, C. D., & Hays, R. D. (1990). Marital status, social support and health transitions in chronic disease patients. *Journal of Health and Social Behavior, 31,* 328–343.

Simon, R. W. (1992). Parental role strains, salience of parental identity, and gender differences in psychological distress. *Journal of Health and Social Behavior, 33,* 25–35.

Skaff, M. M., & Pearlin, L. I. (1992). Caregiving: Role engulfment and the loss of self. *Gerontologist, 32,* 565–664.

Slaten, E. L. (1996). *Stigma, strain, and psychological distress: The experiences of informal caregivers for persons with HIV disease.* Doctoral dissertation, University of Texas, Austin.

Speare, A., & Avery, R. (1993). Who helps whom in older parent-child families. *Journal of Gerontology, 48,* S64–S73.

Spitze, G., Logan, J. R., Deane, G., & Zerger, S. (1994). Adult children's divorce and intergenerational relationships. *Journal of Marriage and the Family, 56,* 279–293.

Stack, C. B., & Burton, L. M. (1994). Kinscripts: Reflections on family, generation, and culture. In E. N. Glenn, G. Chang, & L. R. Forcey (Eds.), *Mothering: Ideology, experience, and agency* (pp. 33–44). New York: Routledge.

Stoller, E. P. (1983). Parental caregiving by adult children. *Journal of Marriage and the Family, 45,* 851–858.

Stone, R., Cafferata, G. L., & Sangle, J. (1987). Caregivers of the frail elderly. *Gerontologist, 27,* 617–626.

Teachman, J. D. (1991). Who pays? Receipt of child support in the United States. *Journal of Marriage and the Family, 53,* 759–772.

Thompson, L., & Walker, A. J. (1995). The place of feminism in family studies. *Journal of Marriage and the Family, 57,* 847–865.

Treas, J., & Bengtson, V. L. (1987). The family in later years. In M. B. Sussman & S. K. Steinmetz (Eds.), *Handbook of marriage and the family* (pp. 625–648). New York: Plenum.

Trice, A. D. (1988). Posttraumatic stress syndrome-like symptoms among AIDS caregivers. *Psychological Reports, 63,* 656–658.

Turner, H. A., & Pearlin, L. I. (1989, Fall). Issues of age, stress, and caregiving. *Generations,* pp. 56–59.

Umberson, D. (1987). Family status and health behaviors: Social control as a dimension of social integration. *Journal of Health and Social Behavior, 28,* 306–339.

Umberson, D. (1989). Relationships with children: Explaining parents' psychological well-being. *Journal of Marriage and the Family, 51,* 999–1012.

Umberson, D. (1992). Relationships between adult children and their parents: Psychological consequences for both generations. *Journal of Marriage and the Family, 54,* 664–685.

Umberson, D. (1996). Demographic position and stressful midlife events: Effects on the quality of parent-child relationships. In C. D. Ryff & M. M. Seltzer (Eds.), *The parental experience in midlife* (pp. 493–532). Chicago: University of Chicago Press.

Umberson, D., Chen, M., House, J. S., Hopkins, K., & Slaten, E. (1996). The effect of social relationships on psychological well-being: Are men and women really so different? *American Sociological Review, 61,* 837–857.

Umberson, D., & Gove, W. R. (1989). Parenthood and psychological well-being: Theory, measurement, and stage in the family life course. *Journal of Family Issues, 10,* 440–462.

Umberson, D., & Williams, C. L. (1993). Divorced fathers: Parental role strain and psychological distress. *Journal of Family Issues, 14,* 378–400.

Waite, L. J. (1995). Does marriage matter? *Demography, 32,* 483–507.

Walker, A. J., Martin, S. S. K., & Jones, L. L. (1992). The benefits and costs of caregiving and care receiving for daughters and mothers. *Journal of Gerontology, 47,* S130–S140.

Ward, R. A., & Spitze, G. (1996). Gender differences in parent-child coresidence experiences. *Journal of Marriage and the Family, 58,* 718–725.

White, L. K. (1994). Growing up with single parents and stepparents: Long-term effects on family solidarity. *Journal of Marriage and the Family, 56,* 935–948.

Windle, M., & Dumenci, L. (1997). Parental and occupational stress as predictors of depressive symptoms among dual-income couples: A multilevel modeling approach. *Journal of Marriage and the Family, 59,* 625–634.

Winsborough, H. H., Bumpass, L. L., & Aquilino, W. S. (1991). *The death of a parent and the transition to old age* (Working paper 39). Madison: Center for Demography and Ecology, University of Wisconsin.

Zill, N., Morrison, D. R., & Coiro, M. J. (1993). Long-term effects of parental divorce on parent-child relationships, adjustment and achievement in young adulthood. *Journal of Family Psychology, 7,* 91–10.

CHAPTER 7

Kinship and Gender

COLLEEN L. JOHNSON

INTRODUCTION

Even a casual reading of the ethnographic literature on families in other cultures conveys to most white middle-class Americans how little we are bound by close interdependent ties to kin. In contrast to our family life, kinship systems in small-scale societies constitute the core social units that perform the functions of most social institutions. My own training in anthropology, which included a strong emphasis on kinship studies, was carried over to studies of ethnic groups in the United States. Like cross-cultural studies, studies of families of Japanese Americans and Italian Americans opened a new perspective about the family in general, one that could no longer be dominated by conceptions that nuclear families are only remotely linked to a wider network of relatives. These studies led to the conclusion that one of the primary differences found in the study of ethnic families lay in their stronger bonds between members of the nuclear family and their extended kin (Johnson, 1974, 1977, 1985). Instead of being limited mostly to close bonds between parents and children, members of these ethnic groups simultaneously maintained active relationships with siblings, aunts and uncles, nieces and nephews, and cousins. We on the research staff often concluded that we were missing out on a whole new type of solidarity, even though we were also free of the onerous obligations and responsibilities that extended family solidarity often entails.

After completing my doctorate and teaching family studies at Syracuse University, I transferred to the Medical Anthropology Program at the University of California in San Francisco, where research was my major activity. California has been noted for its great cultural diversity, particularly in family constellations, and I profited from these

diverse populations. For example, while researching divorcing, white, mostly middle-class families in northern California suburbs and black families in the inner city, I observed how, in the absence of close kin, some individuals spontaneously constructed kinlike networks, some as complex as any in the ethnographic literature. The ego-centered kinship groups that were selectively created out of personal preferences were functioning effectively but differently from conventional kinship groups. Similar processes were identified in research on older blacks who, in the absence of children, constructed kin networks that consisted of distant relatives and fictive kin.

Finally, a recently completed 10-year research project on very old people contributed additional insights about families and their kinship networks. For most older Americans, their families are not equated with their households, so unlike younger people, their "families" are mostly extended "kin." Few of those aged 85 years and older lived in families, many were widowed; and almost one third were without children, yet most needed some family supports. Almost one quarter of the oldest old no longer sustained any family relationship beyond exchanges of Christmas cards and rare telephone calls, so they risked outliving their families. Consequently, in looking at how their needs were being met, my conceptual framework rested upon kinship relationships that were not limited to intergenerational relationships (Johnson, 1993; Johnson & Troll, 1992).

I often selected these research topics because they were compatible with the funding priorities of the National Institutes of Health. Nevertheless, my research projects have always focused on diversity in how people adapt to cultural change, whether molding family life to meet the pressure for assimilation, dealing with family change after divorce, enhancing the family integration of older people, or facing the challenges of minority status and the attendant prejudice and discrimination. In all these areas, relationships beyond generational and sibling bonds were an important unit of study.

The Status of Kinship Research

Researchers in the major disciplines are divided on the conceptual approaches for studying kinship in modern societies. On the one hand, proponents of a cultural approach in anthropology, led by Schneider (1968) have concentrated on abstracting symbols and meanings about kinship and analyzing them separately from the ongoing social interactions. Although useful in understanding the symbolic or definitional aspects of kin relationships, such studies are incomplete without data on the social content of ongoing interactions. On the other hand, sociologists have not usually looked beyond the "modified extended family" (Sussman & Burchinal, 1962), a unit consisting of the family of procreation and orientation. Even then, their interests are mainly in the relationship between parents and children. Historical shifts from a structural-functionalist perspective, however, have had markedly different effects in anthropology and sociology. Whereas kinship research has been revived in anthropology through an infusion of feminist thought, few sociologists now conduct research on relationships beyond those in the nuclear family (e.g., parent-child relationships). Consequently, there are appreciable gaps in our understanding of how kinship relationships are changing in the context of recent structural changes in the American family (Aerts, 1993; Bumpass, 1990; Popenoe, 1993).

The dominant conceptual models of kinship in both sociology and anthropology overlook the major reorganization of our kinship system that has been wrought by divorce and remarriage. Critics have suggested that new kinship models are needed to take into account not only marital change (Johnson, 1989; Johnson & Barer, 1987), but the large number of individuals who are foregoing marriage altogether. Also feminists and gay men and lesbians have devised alternate family forms that make kinship a matter of choice rather than being based on blood and marital ties (Weston, 1991). Moreover, research on the American family and kinship has not really come to terms conceptually with the great variation by race and ethnicity. When race has been analyzed in recent years, it has tended to be a nuisance variable that must be controlled in regression equations (Jackson, 1989).

Psychologists, in contrast to others in the social sciences, have generally concentrated on the individual or the psychological dimensions of dyadic bonds between members of the nuclear family. For example, research on families in later life has been dominated by those who were trained in human development (particularly at the University of Chicago) who tend to focus on intergenerational relationships mainly through a psychological lens (Sprey, 1991). Studies of solidarity (Bengtson, Rosenthal, & Burton, 1990) and attachment (Troll & Fingerman, 1996) have contributed to the understanding of specific family relationships from a social psychological perspective on the interior of kinship relationships, but they have been confined mainly to intergenerational relationships.

The Scope of This Chapter

In preparing this chapter, I found that several intriguing questions arose about basic definitions of the family and kinship network. First, why do most Americans, both scholars and the public in general, use the term *family* to refer to any unit, ranging from a one-parent household to a nuclear family to intergenerational relationships to complex extended families? Does this usage mean that kinship relationships are so murky and ill defined that we do not require a terminology of daily usage that distinguishes various types of relationships? Also why does kinship research rarely go beyond the study of intergenerational relationships? Do these limitations suggest that other relationships are not that important? Or has interest in kinship waned because changes in families in the late 20th century redirected researchers' attention to more pressing social issues?

Understandably, gender is a primary concern in the study of kinship because kinship is most basically determined by relationships between men and women, their procreation, and the socialization of dependent children. Given the wide variety of types of extended families that may be emerging today, definitions of the extended family must be expanded to include those based not only on blood and marriage, but on divorce and remarriage and those with the propensity to create kin out of nonkin. For the purposes of this chapter, *kinship* is defined as being synonymous with the extended family. The term refers to social bonds between those who are related by blood; marriage; or a self-ascribed association that extends beyond the marital dyad, the nuclear family of parents and dependent children, or one-parent households. The kinship system includes lineal relationships formed by intergenerational linkages, collateral relationships linked through siblings and other kin of similar ages, and fictive kin created out of nonkin relationships.

In the conceptions of family and kinship used here, both structural and cultural factors are of relevance. Social structural dimensions refer to the actual resources of families, namely, the members of the family and their kinship relationships, their proximity, and their position in relation to the broader society in terms of social and geographic mobility. In contrast, cultural factors in the study of kinship include definitions of relationships that determine who is related, and in what way (Schneider, 1968). Cultural dimensions also include norms and values that offer directives on obligations and mutual responsibilities and the strength of the attachment among kin.

When one studies the kinship group, as opposed to a nuclear family, boundary is useful as a normative concept that both defines expectations among kin and reflects a process that can be fixed, relatively closed, and exclusive of potential members or open, inclusive, and changeable. Kinship functioning is based on value orientations that determine preferences for closeness to specific members over others. These orientations may involve a lineal emphasis between generations or a collateral emphasis that capitalizes on bonds between siblings and other age

peers or an individualized emphasis based on situations and personal preferences.

In this chapter, I trace the status of kinship research since the 1950s. Because most research on kinship comes from the cross-cultural studies of anthropology and studies of American kinship by sociologists, publications from these fields are emphasized. In analyzing kinship and gender, I also draw upon my own research on kinship among various subgroups in our society. This overview of American kinship research since 1950 found relatively few articles on American kinship in the 1990s other than those on parent–adult child relationships. Consequently, I organized that section historically to provide an overview of American social scientists' waxing and waning interest in this subject during those years. Finally, some possible explanations are presented on the limited research by social scientists in the 1990s, and projections are made on the possible role of kinship in changing family systems in the future.

To avoid an overlap with other chapters in this book, I do not concentrate on kinship in specific ethnic groups except when data on gender and kinship are relevant to the discussion. Kinship studies in gerontology, feminist, and gay and lesbian writings are covered elsewhere in this volume. Also the recent literature on specific kinship dyads is too sparse outside research in gerontology to write extensively about the dynamics of relationships. The exception is the parent–adult child dyad, covered in Chapter 6. Instead, I address the theoretical frameworks or explanatory schemes that have been used in recent decades to interpret and explain gender differentiation in kinship status and roles. In addition, I tentatively suggest how the study of kinship, or the lack thereof, may reflect the dominant interests of family scholars in the nuclear family and the recent difficulty of this family form in remaining the dominant family type.

CROSS-CULTURAL PERSPECTIVES ON KINSHIP

Anthropologists have focused primarily on kinship systems in small-scale societies in which corporate kinship systems perform most societal functions.

Lewis Henry Morgan (1887) was the founder of the anthropological study of kinship in the mid-to-late 19th century. He was a lawyer for the New York Central Railroad, who, in the process of settling land claims with tribes of the Iroquois Nation, began to map kinship patterns of descent and marriage (Peletz, 1995). Morgan concentrated on degrees of relatedness as reflected in kinship terminologies, an approach that resulted, in the next 100 years, in an immense compendia of kinship terms. This taxonomic emphasis, however, failed to inform researchers about the empirical workings of kinship systems.

Social anthropologists in Britain, until recent years, have continued their interest in the social dimensions of kinship with comprehensive ethnographies of cultures in the British Empire. In fact, they have usually identified themselves as the sociologists of small-scale societies. They had an impact on American anthropology, at least until the concept of culture as a system of meanings replaced social paradigms in recent years. Also their earlier studies emphasized the structure and functioning of societies largely from a male perspective with little interest in gender issues.

Biological Basis of Kinship

Despite the debate about the significance of biologically based commonalities, an understanding of kinship principles cross-culturally is incomplete without the recognition of biologically based universals. Studies of the biological basis of kinship have dramatically pointed to gender differences. Fox (1967) evoked the basic facts of life to explain the origins of kinship. The universal facts he succinctly described included these: (1) women have the children, (2) men impregnate women, (3) men have more power than women, and (4) primary kin do not mate with each other—or as he put it—"Gestation, impregnation, domination, and avoidance of incest lie at the root of all social organization" (p. 31). These facts of life have a host of ramifications, for biological fatherhood is difficult to pin down. Consequently, anthropologists define kinship using social criteria, with "blood" relationships in a genetic sense having little to do with it (Barnes,

1973). The father is defined not biologically by the term *genitor*, but by a legal term, *pater*, a social designation that is accompanied by socially mandated rights and responsibilities.

Physical motherhood through the birth process is a directly observable and identifiable event. As Barnes (1973) concluded, the mother-child relationship is based on a birth process that is publicly evident to all observers, and the mother's response to the new infant has innate and biological elements. Fatherhood, in contrast, is not self-evident; no one can state with assurance who impregnated a woman. In fact, some theories of conception have little to do with biological fatherhood, and there is no evidence that men are biologically programmed to respond to the needs of dependent infants.

The Universality of the Nuclear Family

Several decades ago, in their quest for cultural universals, anthropologists identified the nuclear family as a basic building block of social structure, a unit that performs vital functions on a daily basis. Nevertheless, female-headed households were (and remain) common cross-culturally, as well as in this country, which led Adams (1960) to maintain that the most elemental unit is the mother-child dyad, a unit that is more pervasive and more likely to be a universal unit than the nuclear family. In contrast, in some cultures, the nuclear family can be so submerged in a larger kinship unit that it is difficult to identify (Levi-Strauss, 1956). When the nuclear family is given strong functional value, such as in American culture, it is the dominant or preferred form even though its ideal form is not always achievable.

The nuclear family consists of an unstable combination of two dyads, the maternal and the conjugal. The conjugal dyad is the most unstable and weakest link in any kinship structure and thus requires social and economic reinforcements that cross-culturally take the form of dowries or bride-prices. Although the nuclear family is not universally found, attempts to de-emphasize the centrality of this family type have rarely been successful, as in post-Revolution Russia (Geiger, 1968), the kibbutz in Israel (Spiro, 1954), and communal experiments like the Oneida Community (Kephart, 1972). Such attempts were unsuccessful in the long run, some (see, for example, Levi-Strauss, 1956; Malinowski, 1913) have concluded, because the nuclear family is an efficient unit for fulfilling the functional prerequisites of society, such as reproduction and socialization of children.

One also finds wide variation in the significance of marriage. The incest taboo has been a matter of great interest, for that principle forms the very basis of kinship. Mostly through rules of marriage, all cultures control sexuality by the incest taboo, although which relatives who are included in the taboo differ. Nevertheless, the taboo is a normative concept separate from the incidence when the taboo is violated. Given the need to mate outside one's family, Levi-Strauss (1956) viewed women as objects of exchange in building alliances with other kinship groups. Because men cannot mate with their mothers, daughters, and sisters, they must look outside the kinship group for their own mates and those of their sisters. This one-sided emphasis on women marrying out of their own extended families through alliances formed by their male relatives relegates women to the status of commodities who are controlled and traded by the more powerful men (Fox, 1967).

In matrilineal societies, where rules of descent go through women, females are rarely or never more powerful than their male relatives. In those cases, they are beholden to their brothers, not their husbands, who exert control over their procreative functions. Historical studies of Asian societies, however, have pointed out that the "exchange of women" does not necessarily mean that women are completely cut off from their own kin or that they are completely incorporated into their husbands' kinship groups. In Chinese, Indian, and Islamic cultures, women retain rights and obligations with their natal kin (Goody, 1990). In other words, they are not simply pawns in their husbands' extended families.

The most extreme example of matrilineal kinship was found among the Nayars in 19th-century India (Gough, 1952). The interdependence between sisters and brothers was so strong that men outside the lineage were procreators only and played virtu-

ally no role as fathers. The genitor's sole responsibility was to establish a newborn's legitimacy by giving a bolt of cloth to the matrilineage, a token gift that signified the absence of paternal responsibility. Because the genitor's biological contribution was ignored and social fatherhood was barely recognized, the lineage based on the sibling bond in the Nayar culture was strengthened.

Kinship and Interpretive Anthropology

Interest in the social dimensions of kinship has ebbed in recent years as anthropologists have shifted their focus from structure and functioning to the symbolic dimensions of kinship, namely, what people think about kinship and how they define a given person as a relative. This interpretive approach, typified by Schneider's (1968) *American Kinship: A Cultural Account,* resulted in a de-emphasis on actual data about social structure and kinship roles and relationships. In other words, this shift in paradigms entailed a focus on the symbolic importance of relatedness through blood or shared biogenetic substance and through marriage in terms of law or codes of conduct. In its original interpretation, the symbols and meanings were viewed as similar for men and women, a stance challenged by feminist scholars and later reconsidered by Schneider (1980) and Schneider and Smith (1973). Although these ideas have had a great impact on anthropologists, Schneider's large-scale study produced few empirical reports on kinship relationships, except for a privately distributed publication (Schneider & Cottrell, 1975).

This new model of "interpretive anthropology" was consistent with the rise of cultural determinism and its constructions (Geertz, 1973), but the failure to link symbolic systems to the actual lives of individuals limited the application of this approach outside anthropology (Peletz, 1995). Within the field, some critics have called for the renewed study of social relationships. Sheffler (1991) promoted a redirection of kinship studies from symbols to "real social facts." He condemned the intellectual coalition of feminist and symbolic anthropologists that resulted in an alliance that seeks not only, "to denaturalize and deuniversalize, but also to deconstruct and dismantle categories of kinship, marriage, and the family" (p. 361). A prominent example of deconstruction is Collier, Rosaldo, and Yanagisako's (1992, p. 31), a critique of Malinowski's thesis on the universality of the nuclear family that viewed the contemporary family "not as a concrete institution designed to fulfill universal human needs, but as an ideological construct associated with the modern state." Collier et al.'s approach rested not on empirical data, but on rethinking what the family represents symbolically to Americans. The central notion these authors identified in American culture is that the family should be a source of nurturance and an antithesis to the values of the marketplace, a function, they asserted, the family fails to perform.

Feminists' Contributions

Understandably, feminist writing on kinship first strove to diminish gender biases by emphasizing that gender-based role systems are culturally derived and do not stem from biological determination. Two books were of great influence in shifting the interests of anthropologists: *Women, Culture, and Society* (Rosaldo & Lamphere, 1974b), and *Gender and Kinship* (Collier & Yanagisako, 1987). These editors brought together important articles that attempted to rethink basic kinship principles in terms of gender roles and examine universal and culturally specific dimensions of gender. Most of these scholars had been influenced by the interpretive school of which Schneider's work is paramount.

Feminist anthropologists have questioned core concepts at the heart of which were challenges to the gender-based division of labor as a universal phenomenon (Collier & Yanagisako, 1987; Yanagisako & Collier, 1987). Collier and Yanigasako, the principal spokeswomen, called for a rethinking of kinship and gender that goes beyond biological facts of reproduction and its roots in natural gender differences. Rosaldo and Lamphere (1974a) had earlier taken a more moderate view than is found among anthropologists today (Ehrenreich & McIntosh, 1997). They clarified conceptions of biological differences between the sexes by viewing biological factors as constraining, rather than solely

determinative. In contemporary, high-technology societies, for example, biologically determined gender differences are of declining importance because men's greater strength and speed are not required in most contemporary occupations.

Feminists also challenged the pervasive assignment of men to the political-jural domain and women to the domestic sphere that essentially excludes them from power. Collier and Yanigasako (1987), among others, also pointed to the evidence that women performed multiple functions beyond the domestic tasks of childbearing and child rearing. Obviously, this role distinction parallels Parsons' (1949) conceptions of instrumental and expressive functional specialization by gender. At the core of the feminist critique is that the biological functions entailed in women's childbearing and child rearing led to gender dichotomy of male and female roles that oversimplifies women's status in many cultures.

These works, (Collier & Yanagisako, 1987; Rosaldo & Lamphere, 1974b; Yanagisako & Collier, 1987) provide much information on the great diversity in women's roles worldwide. Investigations and commentary also focused on discrepancies between ideology about women's roles in families and the actual practices taking place. In this respect, kinship remains an important area in anthropological studies of gender. As Bergman (1995) noted, kinship studies are intellectually acceptable today in anthropology because they are now phrased in terms of how meanings are culturally constructed. This approach is consistent with the interpretive emphasis in contemporary anthropology.

Anthropologists also have taken on the task of explaining the universal devaluation of women. In asserting that women are subordinate to men in every culture, they have challenged common myths about matriarchy. Ortner's (1973) analysis posed the question, "Are females to males as nature is to culture?" Following a biological perspective, Ortner maintained that one must treat the universal devaluation of women in the context of other cultural universals. One such universal fact is that survival needs are met by transcending nature and one's biological limitations to exercise mastery over one's life. Because women are closer to nature or biological determinants than are men, their bodies and procreative functions have more influence on their social roles and psychic structure, making it difficult for them to transcend nature (Chodorow, 1973, 1978).

Unfortunately, this brief review cannot do justice to the many contributions that anthropologists have made to cross-cultural studies of gender and kinship. One can only conclude that anthropology is one of the few fields that has flourished because of the acceptance of feminist theories (Stacey & Thorne, 1985). More recently, there has been a further shift to Marxist and feminist concerns about social inequality (DiLeonardo, 1991), although attention to social phenomena continues to decline. This trend has paralleled the decreasing influence of structural-functionalism in social anthropology in general, as well as sociology (Peltz, 1995; Verdon, 1980).

INTERDISCIPLINARY STUDY OF KINSHIP AND SOCIAL CHANGE

Ideological biases cloud sociologists' understanding of the traditional extended family versus the nuclear ideal. On the one hand, the passing of the traditional family system is often seen as progressive because the individual is freed from onerous obligations and control by elders (Hareven, 1982). On the other hand, such changes in the family have been described as "the world we have lost" (Laslett, 1965), which refers to the demise of a secure extended family setting with individuals cast adrift to fend for themselves. Such themes about loss of family benefits have been repeated in widely recognized books by Lasch (1979) and Bellah, Madsen, Sullivan, Swidler, and Tipton (1985). Empirically, these critics may feel justified, for worldwide, extended multifunctional households have declined in prominence, and the nuclear family has become increasingly prevalent (Cowgill & Holmes, 1972; Goode, 1963; Hogan & Spencer, 1993; Moore, 1988). In Western Europe and the United States, the ascendence of the nuclear family preceded the industrial revolution even in rural areas (Laslett, 1978).

Hareven (1982) concluded that nostalgic myths about the history of the American family structure have obscured understanding of the contemporary family. These myths maintain that three-generation households and the multifunctional extended kin group broke up with industrialization. Hareven also contended that the beliefs that the nuclear family is defunctionalized is also misleading because the family still retains emotional functions. These transitions from a large, interdependent extended family to a nuclear family household mean that much of one's family life is hidden from the sometimes prying eyes of kin (Laslett, 1978). As a consequence, extended kin have lost much of their knowledge of relatives' lives and hence are less able to exert influence over them. In the process, family members may develop a more individuated than collective value orientation. Along with the decline in traditionalism, these changes entail more personal choices in the selection of mates, marriages based on love and companionship, and neolocal residence after marriage (Moore, 1988).

When one distinguishes between the ideology about the family and its actual structure and functioning, some issues become clarified. For example, the nuclear ideal was part of the ideology of trade unions' advocacy for a family wage that would be sufficient to support a wife and children (Moore, 1988; Stacey, 1990, 1992). Fry (1994) suggested that the ideology regarding family and kinship needs to be analyzed separately from the social organization of kinship. She compared kinship organization in seven cultures, ranging from Bushmen in Africa to upper-middle-class families in Swarthmore, Pennsylvania. She noted that in modern societies, bilateral kinship systems are shaped by economic factors, as well as by ideologies favorable to the individual over the kinship group, whereas collective ideologies are more likely to be found in small-scale societies that are dominated by the interdependence found in multifunctional kinship groups.

Fry (1994) raised an important question: If the ideology of kinship no longer endorses norms of reciprocity and exchange, what are one's obligations to kin? At the American extreme, emotions and sentiments are the prominent cohesive forces underlying what are essentially optional kinship ties. In fact, an ideology based on sentiments may result in a kinship group that is flexible and adaptive in contemporary society, but not necessarily supportive of dependent members. Discrepancies between ideology and practice are also expressed in the insistence on the independence of the nuclear household, when households are often intimately linked socially, economically, and emotionally (Moore, 1988).

Some ethnic groups vary from the nuclear family model. My research with Italian American (Johnson, 1978, 1983c, 1985) and Japanese American families (1974, 1977) showed that the families in both ethnic groups displayed many features of traditionalism, which the respondents referred to as "the old fashioned way." More power and authority lay in the hands of the old over the young and of men over women. The value systems of both groups included a strong emphasis on respect for elders and the precedence of family interests over individual interests. Such traditionalism in both groups also resulted in strong norms of responsibility to parents and other members of the extended family.

Women, Work, and Kinship

The numerous studies on women and work in the context of social change are so diverse and complex that they defy synthesis or generalizations here. In her extensive review of this subject, Moore (1988) concluded that the effects of modernization and urbanization have altered women's relationship to the home, the family, and the workplace. Going beyond Western cultures to examine changes in Africa, South American, and Southeast Asia, however, one finds no obvious link between modernization, urbanization, and the rise of the nuclear family. For instance, the impacts of migration, economic necessity, and the growing number of women who head households undermine any allegation about the increased nuclearization of the family.

Moore (1988) also concluded that when extended or joint families are transplanted to cities, they do not disappear but, instead, change their structure and functioning as they adjust to new circumstances. With the increased employment of women outside the home, new needs are created that an urban version of the traditional family can meet. For example, Rapp (1982) found that women

who moved to a city reported continuity in their kin relationships, although mothers and sisters were replaced by mothers-in-law and sisters-in-law. O'Rand and Agree (1993) pointed out that women in the workforce have altered their gender roles but continue to operate within a moral economy, defined as involving reciprocity among kin in caring for children and the elderly. Rather than a close-knit kinship group that may have existed before migration, however, the transplanted extended family is usually altered in size and household composition to meet the social and economic necessities of urban life.

In urban contexts, changing economic circumstances can either encourage the nuclearization of the family or promote different functions for the extended family. In the latter case, a kinship group may be used as a resource to meet new demands. Such a pattern was common during the migration of blacks from the rural South to the northern cities in this country (Aschenbrenner, 1973; Martin & Martin, 1978) and in the chain migration of southern Italian immigrants (Johnson, 1995b). In more complex societies, social status has acted as an important point of family differentiation (Poster, 1978). While a stronger nuclear family may emerge to conserve the newfound wealth in the middle class, for instance, the poor often cannot afford to abandon interdependent kinship bonds (Farber, 1971).

AN OVERVIEW OF U.S. KINSHIP RESEARCH: 1950 TO 1990

The Debate on the Isolated Nuclear Family

In tracing the interest in kinship among sociologists since the 1950s, one finds a rise and then a decline in research activity on kinship. The decade reviews of the *Journal of Marriage and the Family* offer a good historical record of the shift in interests in kinship. In 1971, Bert Adams wrote an extensive, in-depth review of the status of kinship research in which considerable space was devoted to the debate on whether "the isolated nuclear family" was the dominant form in view of new findings on the importance of kinship.

On the one hand, the isolationists had been influenced by Parsons (1943, 1949), whose work was prominent in the 1950s. This period was known as the familistic era, with high rates of births and marriages and postwar declines in divorce rates. Parsons viewed the nuclear family as adaptive to the occupational needs of contemporary American society. This family type, he maintained, had independent movable assets, its members were free of responsibility to kin, and it was geographically mobile in meeting the needs of national corporations. With many of its functions turned over to other institutions, the nuclear family was functionally specialized in socializing children and in meeting the psychological needs of adults. Its conjugal roles were also specialized: Men fulfilled instrumental needs as the families' representatives to the outside world and women ideally functioned as the emotional centers of the families and were expected to fulfill the important psychological needs of their husbands and children (Parsons, 1965).

With the rise of feminism in the 1960s, Parsons was an early target of criticism. Feminists identified the nuclear family as an instrument of oppression of women and a source of women's exclusion from higher status in the broader society (Friedan, 1963). In response to critics of his isolationist stance, Parsons (1965) followed an anthropological perspective by drawing on evidence that large multifunctional extended families were the norm cross-culturally and concluded that the American family represented an extreme form in terms of its isolation from kin. Earlier, Parsons (1942) had also conceded that structural problems inherent in the nuclear family form had led to the isolation of women and older people from the society at large.

Unheralded and Overheralded Kin Family Networks

During the 1960s, studies began to document the viability of the kinship network. Sussman (1965) pointed out that the evidence for extensive kin involvement was so convincing that further research to establish that fact was no longer needed. Did the discovery of kinship mean that the isolated nuclear family was a concept that was incongruent with reality? Was there an academic cultural lag

between theory and practice? Or could these contradictions be traced to methodological factors or the neglect of cultural diversity? The surveys conducted mostly by sociologists provided measures of kin interactions and kin supports, but they were less informative about the quality of kin interactions, the strength of norms of responsibility, and the nature of the effects of social and geographic mobility.

When confronted with sound studies about the viability of kinship in contemporary society, sociology experienced a relatively brief renaissance in kinship research (Adams, 1971). The findings that kin relations were an important social resource led to formulations about "a kin family network," which was originally labeled "the unheralded feature" of the American family—unheralded because kinship had previously been ignored by most sociologists (Sussman & Burchinal, 1962). The kin family network consists of families of orientation (nuclear families of birth) and families of procreation (those linked by marriage and procreation). These relatives are bound together by affection and personal preferences, rather than by institutionalized rights and obligations.

Because relationships are based, for the most part, on sentiments, the kin family network can function without living in proximity, a factor viewed as an advantage in our mobile society (Litwak, 1965). In this view, kinship connections have not disappeared; rather, they are functional in meeting the needs of an industrial society. In fact, relatives may be supportive in facilitating adjustments to geographic mobility and in linking their kin to job opportunities (Litwak, 1960). Relatives do not impede status achievement or the geographic mobility needed to meet occupational requirements. The major flow of aid occurs from parents to children, rather than the reverse. Because aid is usually disguised as gifts, onerous obligations do not accumulate.

Such enthusiasm for the kin family network began to diminish in the early 1970s, when Gibson (1972) pointed out that most research on the kin family network focused on parents and adult children, not on extended kin. Gibson suggested that the kin family network was an "overheralded kinship concept." About that time, a European conception of kinship relationships as "intimate at a distance" began to be cited to depict kinship relations in this country (Rosenmayr & Krockeis, 1963). Later, Litwak's (1985) work on kin support modified a global acceptance of kin solidarity by conceptualizing a specialization of kinship roles. Litwak distinguished how the nature of the help from kin should be matched to the characteristics of specific kin, such as their proximity and long-term commitment to each other. This analysis led to the conclusion that, with some tasks, face-to-face interaction is not required if a high level of commitment still persists.

The Dwindling Interest in Kinship Research

A decade later, the review in *Journal of Marriage and the Family* by Gary Lee (1980) noted that the quantity of kinship studies had declined, but the scope of research had broadened to include more research on ethnicity and more linkages between kinship and other variables. That the space allotted to this review was less than half that of Adams's (1971) earlier review, led Lee to apologize that the page limitations resulted in a superficial review of the subject. In any case, Lee found that "the isolated nuclear family debate" had finally been put to rest. Kinship ties were still viable, and researchers were actively studying the relationships between kinship and other social variables. For example, black kinship solidarity was found to be linked not only to economic need, but to cultural factors (Aschenbrenner, 1973; Martin & Martin, 1978). Lee (1980) further noted that geographic proximity, more than socioeconomic status, predicted kinship involvements, an anticipated finding because the frequency of social contacts is the major variable used to indicate the level of kinship solidarity. Farber (1971) concluded that kin constituted a lineage and reference group for higher-status groups, but functioned as a source of sociability and mutual aid for those in lower-status groups.

Lee (1980) also examined the possibility that kinship involvements decreased with age, a factor readily attributed to age-related decreases in the pool of kin. In her study of widows, Lopata (1978) noted reservations about the extended kin network. Although children were frequent supporters, she found, most widows did not mention other relatives. The findings on widowhood and kinship integration were unclear, however, probably obscured by Shanas's (1979b) findings from several surveys. Shanas concluded that family abandonment of the aged was a myth, in that 70% of older people lived near a child and 75% of them saw a child at least weekly. She found few widows who were isolated and without families, and only 3% with no surviving relatives. Bedford and Blieszner (1996) suggested there is a lack of mutuality between parents and their adult children, in that adult children tend to refer to their own households as families, making parents "kin," while parents invariably consider their children their "families."

Lee (1980) concluded that it was deceptively tempting to overestimate the role of kin in the lives of older people, for studies were finding that the actual amount of tangible aid between generations was not that large (Gibson, 1972; Lopata, 1978). Shanas (1979a) failed to comment on her own findings that contradicted her thesis that all people had someone to help them; of her housebound respondents, 24% had no family member assisting them. My own research on older people found that while parents are active, children's contributions were mostly in expressive benefits, but children delivered little practical assistance to parents and even less to other kin (Johnson 1983a, 1983b, Johnson & Catalano, 1983). When parents became disabled, however, children increased their supports, but only in rare cases did they provide the round-the-clock, hands-on care that entailed personal sacrifices.

Very old people may willingly disengage from demanding or difficult family relationships when they no longer have the desire or ability to socialize (Johnson & Barer, 1993). In other research, a social selectivity theory has been conceptualized as a pattern of delimiting social relationships as one ages (Carstensen, 1987). In addition, social gerontologists (Bengtson, Rosenthal, & Burton, 1990; George & Gold, 1991) have suggested that the family has become more vertical in structure. Using projections on the effects of demographic shifts, they proposed that with declines in both fertility and mortality, there are increasing concerns about the added generations of older people who will have fewer younger people to care for them. Research on dyadic relationships has generally found that norms of responsibility are not that strong in relationships other than the marital and parent-child dyads (Johnson, 1988b).

Findings from a northern California survey in the late 1970s offer further reservations about the solidarity of the kin family network. Fisher (1982a, 1982b) concluded that nuclear families were not isolated from kin, even though kin were geographically dispersed and rarely listed as helpers. In fact, parents and children are the main kin who consistently assist each other. The relative aloofness to other kin often follows their geographic dispersal, which is a factor related to educational level and urban living. Even with geographic mobility, however, Fisher (1982b) found that contact and support can continue over distance, but such connections are usually limited to relationships between parents and children, rather than to more distant kin. Consequently, kinship relationships beyond generational links consist of voluntary and selective bonds. The contemporary kinship structure is limited in size; its functions lie in their potentialities, and kin are not active in regular routines. After synthesizing these findings, Fisher (1982a) nevertheless concluded that extended kin are crucial strands in the social fabric of individuals' lives. This possibility should be further explored, for kin are the most likely source of identification and sense of family continuity.

In his 1980 decade review of kinship research, Lee concluded that for the majority of Americans, kinship was not the most important part of their lives. He indicated that this may have been what Parsons (1965) meant when he said that from a cross-cultural perspective, the American family is relatively isolated from kin. Although Lee predicted that theoretical advances in kinship research were in the offing, such a contribution did not appear in the 1990 decade review. Undoubtedly a theoretical framework is still missing, for the issue is no longer whether family members are simply isolated from each other, but under what circumstances do close-knit kin ties occur. Needless to say, the study of ethnic diversity may fill this gap (Johnson, 1995a).

To summarize, except for a relatively brief period in the past four decades, the study of kinship was mostly peripheral to the interests of family researchers, whose major focus was on the nuclear family. In fact, in preparing this chapter, I reviewed the 1991–96 issues of *Journal of Marriage and the Family, American Sociological Review,* and *American Journal of Sociology* and found no theoretical or empirical articles on kinship. In the *Journal of Marriage and the Family* in the 1990s, occasional articles on the sibling bond and numerous articles on the parent-adult child relationship appeared, but there were no studies of kinship networks or systems. It is relevant to point out that kinship appears more important to blacks than to whites (Hofferth, 1984; Johnson, 1995b; Johnson & Barer, 1990). Even with the social mobility of black women, collective gains of the extended family have been noted. In contrast, mobility for white women is viewed as an individual achievement (Higginbottam & Weber, 1992).

Three explanations may account for the virtual disappearance of kinship as a theoretical and empirical interest among most American sociologists. The explanation may be that kinship is not important enough to be a subject of widespread research because relatives have a minor role in nuclear family life beyond sentimental or identificational bonds. In fact, this situation may be more the case in the United States, for an international survey found that Americans are less reliant upon kin than are most Europeans (Hogan & Spencer, 1993). Nevertheless, there are still scattered articles on the importance of kin. For example, middle-aged women define their social networks to include the intergenerational bonds, while other relatives are part of a "reunion effect," those seen on the special occasions that bring kin together (Waite & Harrison, 1992). Some people are predisposed to see kin more, for those who see parents frequently also see their siblings more often than the average. Another study (Leigh, 1982) found that kinship interactions over the life span do not vary, a finding that supports the contention about a lifelong predisposition to be either distant or close to kin.

A second explanation may be that research has not ceased but has merely been diverted to other research paradigms, such as social network theories. Ever since social network involvements were linked to health, they have been a key interest of many social and behavioral scientists (Cohen & Syme, 1985). Today, the concept of social networks is commonly used in studies of stress and social support. Although measures of networks may include kin, they are not usually well differentiated in statistical models used to report findings. Thus, such research is not informative about contemporary kinship interactions.

A third explanation may be that attention has been diverted from kinship research to more pressing family problems. In a 1987 issue of the *Journal of Family Issues* that reported on the status of the contemporary family, Edwards referred to the disappearing nuclear family; Booth expressed concern about the effects of divorce and the declining role of fatherhood; and White bluntly stated that the family was falling apart because of disappearing fathers, no-fault divorce, and the rising incidence of childlessness. Most relevant here was Schwartz's discussion of the profound changes taking place in the family that involved a transfer of allegiances from group welfare to individual welfare, factors that Schwartz maintained have led to the declining importance of kinship.

By 1990, when kinship was no longer covered in the decade review of the *Journal of Marriage and the Family,* the table of contents of that journal indicated a deflection away from kinship to the concern about what was happening to the nuclear family. New articles included three on divorce-related issues, two on minorities, and one each on feminism and family violence. Then in 1993, *Journal of Marriage and the Family* published an extensive debate about whether the family's capacity to serve the needs of its members was declining, or whether the family's structure and functioning were merely changing. On the one hand, Poponoe (1993), a proponent of the family-decline stance, maintained that the nuclear family is breaking up, creating serious consequences for children, and perhaps affecting the economic well-being of the family (see also, Longino & Earle, 1996). On the other hand, Stacey (1993) maintained that there is no longer a culturally dominant family form, so it is time to move beyond thinking that it should be the dominant form.

By focusing on an institutional analysis, Aerts (1993) presented an objective interpretation of family change. She traced one source of change to the decreasing institutional reinforcements of the nuclear family as we have known it. Moreover, family changes are increasingly becoming institutionalized, so what was once considered a variant pattern is now considered normative. Three changes have been institutionalized: the optional status of marriage, the legitimation of the employment of mothers, and the erosion of fatherhood. Staccy contended that these changes reflect the changing position of women because of higher education and employment. With the liberalization of laws on marriage and divorce, along with career advancement, women have more freedom to determine their matrimonial and reproductive futures.

With these changes, recent definitions of the family first eliminated children, leaving nonprocreative partnerships as legal families. Subsequently, social agencies used a more minimalist approach, eliminating husbands as a necessary component of families. With in-vitro fertilization, even biological mothers have become surrogates without a future role with children (Robertson, 1991). Some gay and lesbian couples have developed their own kinship system on the basis of new childbirth technologies or relatives by adoption (Allen, 1997). In other words, the family forms that were considered deviant only a few decades ago are now more acceptable. Along with new birth technology and a high rate of adoption, biological connections are no longer a requirement for family formation (Modell, 1994).

RETHINKING KINSHIP RESEARCH

Qualitative Urban Studies

To this point, this review has not dealt with the classic kinship studies that influenced sociologists' thinking about extended families in the past. Methodologically, qualitative research on kinship has contributed insights on the contexts in which kinship activities flourish, a contribution that is most applicable today. These studies are in a minority, however, for most kinship research in Western societies has been based on large-scale sociological surveys in which the frequency of contact and the exchange of aid are the primary indicators of kinship involvement. Because few studies on the qualities of kinship relationships at the theoretical level are available, understanding of the daily workings of kin groups must rely on a few qualitative studies. Stack's (1974) *All Our Kin* is a classic example of how the ethnographic method taps kinship processes and the formation of helping networks among young black mothers. Young and Wilmott's (1957) classic book, *Family and Kinship in East London,* provides rich accounts of close-knit kinship bonds between "Mum" and her daughters in working-class London. These dyads are at the core of extended family life, but the kinlike relationships in the neighborhood were also important social bonds. This ethnographic account vividly portrayed how the break-up of urban neighborhoods and resettlement in suburban housing estates diminished kin solidarity and resulted in the greater isolation of nuclear households.

Elizabeth Bott's (1971) *Family and Social Network* went beyond these descriptive works to study the dynamics of kinship networks in interaction with gender-role differentiation in the family. In her intensive study of 20 families, Bott developed a theory that distinguished between connected and loose-knit networks. Connected kin networks were constellations in which network members were acquainted not only with one individual but also with each other. This type of network was compared with loose-knit networks, in which a member had social ties with individuals from multiple sources, including the family, neighborhood, and the workplace, most of whom were unacquainted with each other. Bott identified how members of connected networks were more influenced by kinship norms and ideology because they were less influenced by new ideas from contexts outside their kin networks. Members of connected kin networks differed from members of loose-knit networks in several key respects. In terms of internal family processes, husbands and wives in close-knit networks had a more segregated division of labor, with women being the family and kinship custodians and men emphasizing work associates and male peer-group activity. The main conceptual contribution of Bott's work lay in viewing each extended family as a system of interacting parts each of which could be examined in relation to the whole. This work was one of the first to apply the concept of network to the study of contemporary kinship, a concept now widely used in family studies.

Collateral Versus Lineal Bonds

We may need new concepts in the study of kinship organization as one means of interpreting cultural diversity. For example, variations in the emphasis upon vertical, collateral, or individuated social ties have been identified as a basic value orientation inherent in any society (Fry, 1994; Kluckhohn, 1968; Nakane, 1970). These orientations are not mutually exclusive. Although all cultures have these categories of relationships, one type tends to be stressed over others and ultimately influences the organization of the family and its extensions. These preferences are determined by norms of reciprocity, responsibility, and interdependence among specific kinship relationships. In the process, the boundaries of a family and kinship group are defined through the inclusion or exclusion of potential kin. When the organizational principle is based on the link between parents and children, collateral relatives are usually less important. In contrast, the collateral principle of organization stresses horizontal ties of the same generation who are more or less equivalent in status. It maximizes bonds between siblings so that when sibling solidarity exists, other collateral relationships develop among cousins and the children of siblings.

Thus, larger helping networks may develop in kinship systems with a collateral emphasis (Johnson & Barer, 1995). Cross-cultural research supports this conclusion; the principle of "the unity of the sibling group" refers to one means by which individuals are linked to members of the kinship group (Radcliffe-Brown, 1952). In kinship systems that adhere to this principle, a parent's sibling, although recognized as distinct from a parent, is in the same category as a parent. Thus, the parent's siblings' relatives are genealogically closer than in systems in which this principle is absent. Radcliffe-Brown (1952, p. 66) concluded, "A very large number of collateral relationships of different degrees of relationships can be brought together under a limited number of categories." In Oceania, siblingship is as important as descent and marriage in determining the social organization of the kinship system. In such societies, sibling solidarity encourages an extension of the size of the kinship group (Marshall, 1981; Peletz, 1995).

In two studies of older blacks, both inner-city blacks aged 65 and older and a more economically diverse sample of blacks aged 85 years and older, (Johnson & Barer, 1990, 1995) found strong sibling solidarity in the kinship system. Such bonds most likely grew out of the shared deprivations experienced in childhood and later the chain migration of siblings to northern urban areas. The very old childless blacks who survived into their 80s, were significantly more integrated into supportive kin networks than were their white counterparts (Johnson & Barer, 1995). These differences were traced to the supports, not from siblings who were themselves old or deceased, but from siblings' children, who performed the supportive activities that children ordinarily provide to parents.

Another variant of this principle is found in Italian American immigrant families (Johnson, 1982), in which siblings tended to pool their resources to adapt to the demands of their new situation, often living and working near each other. With adults being distracted with their long work hours, the siblings formed a parental coalition to deal with a coalition of children, namely, brothers and sisters and their cousins, who at the same time developed strong bonds among each other. Many continued these close ties into adulthood, a continuity that eventually led to a solidarity among cousins (Johnson 1983b, 1985). A chain process may occur, in which sibling solidarity is one source of expansion in the number of close kin. Nevertheless, this collaterality may rest on demographic factors. In terms of geographic and social mobility, when siblings live at a distance, strong bonds between aunts and nieces and nephews and between cousins may not develop during childhood, so they fail to form in

adulthood. Also with declining fertility, the future size of the sibling group may decrease and result in a smaller pool of siblings and their children in old age (Hagestad, 1992).

Feminism and American Kinship Research

Feminist theorists have offered fresh perspectives on families and kinship networks in our society as well as cross-culturally (Osmond & Thorne, 1993). Unfortunately, the status of these theories seems to be bound up with the status of women in sociology, a field that is responsible for most American kinship research. Feminists are attempting to dislodge gender and family issues from their marginalized position in sociology to the center of sociological research. They are contesting the dualistic thinking about gender issues, such as the public or male domains versus private or female domains and the instrumental versus expressive functional distinctions. Although female scholars have made important contributions to studies of family violence, single-parent families, and employment and family life, feminist thought has had little influence on the field as a whole (Ferree, 1990). Unlike its counterpart in anthropology, feminist writing in sociology has received no serious critiques, and there have been few attempts to integrate feminist writing into family theories. Such neglect comes at a time when women are increasingly employed outside the home; heading households; and, as kin keepers, orchestrating kinship affairs.

Instead, female family researchers have been marginalized from mainstream sociology. Stacey and Thorne (1985) suggested that the professional marginalization of women may stem from the empiricist bias in sociology. It seems that the academic fields in which female scholars have made the most advances, such as in anthropology and literary criticism, use a symbolic interpretive framework, an approach that is more receptive to female interests. Stacey and Thorne also concluded that sociologists have yet to deal with the dichotomy between the male-dominated public domain and the female-dominated private domestic domain. With this old-fashioned distinction in place, there has been little integration of family research into the study of occupations, status attainment, and other important areas of social research. Thus, family matters tend to be women's concerns, and, at the practical level, the position of women in the field may also be a source of their problems with status attainment in their professional lives.

If male sociologists are so dominant over their female colleagues in sociology, then it is useful to examine their own comments about their power. Goode (1992) concluded that few men have experienced the direct effects of the women's movement, a situation he traced to deeply rooted cultural traditions. Drawing upon a theory of superordination, he stated that contemporary attacks on male privilege will ultimately fail because without sufficient pressure, men will not give up their favored status. Even though polls in the 1980s showed significant changes in men's attitudes toward women's roles, Goode concluded that the ideology underlying these attitudes is not being translated into changes in actual behaviors.

In a different vein, Morgan (1990) suggested that the phrase, *men and families,* strikes a discordant note because of men's marginal family status. The long-held picture of unemployed or retired men being out of place at home still persists and may be related to the vagueness of men's biological connection to their families. In any case, there is much research on gender differences, such as in marital satisfaction, but except for the recent interest in domestic violence, little attention has been paid to men's status and roles in families. Morgan also suggested that the marginalization of women in sociology may be traced to the feminists' identification of the family domain as women's problem, not men's. These gender distinctions, either real or imagined, may deemphasize the authenticity of men's contributions to the study of the family.

CONCLUSIONS AND FUTURE PROJECTIONS ON GENDER AND KINSHIP

From the perspectives of this chapter on gender and kinship, the dominant configuration of the contemporary kinship system includes, first, that its ideal form is bilateral, meaning that both paternal and maternal lines are of equal importance. In reality,

however, there is a strong matrilateral bias. Because data so convincingly document this finding and most often come from interviews with women, the field has been referred to as "wives family sociology" (Safilios-Rothschild, 1969). Women are usually viewed as better informants about family life because they orchestrate kin involvements, and strong bonds between mothers and daughters ensure a continuity in kinship bonds among women.

Women's ascendance in kinship groups will only increase if the divorce rate remains high because custody of children is ordinarily granted to mothers. My research on grandparenting during adult children's divorces found that female-linked kinship ties were retained not only between grandmothers and their divorced daughters, but between them and their former daughters-in-law. These ties often persisted after their sons' divorces (Johnson, 1988a, 1989). The grandmothers maintained that they shared with former daughters-in-law a biological link to grandchildren, one that could not be broken with divorce. In fact, paternal grandmothers sometimes maintained allegiances with their former daughters-in-law even at the expense of their relationships with their sons. Thus, they capitalized upon female-linked bonds to remain close to their grandchildren and often to compensate for their sons' deficiency as fathers. When sons remarried and wanted their mothers to recognize the new marriages by giving at least equal time to the new wives, some grandmothers faced competing loyalties between their former and new daughters-in-law. If they continued a coalition with their former daughters-in-law, the mother-son relationship was usually conflictual, and they were usually more distant from any children of their sons' second marriages.

The dominance of women in the kinship system is also evident in the diminishing importance or even dissolution of the father-child relationship after divorce. In interviews with the children of divorce, Johnson, Schmidt, and Klee (1988) found that only 58% identified their fathers as a member of their families, and only 23% said they were close to their fathers. These findings are consistent with a national survey that reported that half the divorced fathers had no contact with their children one year after the divorce (Furstenberg, Nord, Peterson, & Zill, 1983).

Why, then, is the male link to the family so tenuous? As was noted earlier, kinship systems in small-scale societies function to affirm and solidify the father's status and roles and in the process assure men's conformity to family interests. In contrast, the American kinship group is noted for its flexibility and normative vagueness about such rights and responsibilities. Consequently, a legal apparatus is necessary to affirm and reinforce the father's role (Johnson et al., 1988). However, these laws are not always enforced, so there is no assurance that the responsibilities of fatherhood are performed in our society. It is also important to note that men do not necessarily abandon family life altogether, for they are more likely than their ex-wives to remarry. There is evidence that stepfathers are more able than stepmothers to transfer their allegiances from biological children to stepchildren. This evidence is consistent with Barnes's (1973) thesis that women's roles are linked to nature, while men's roles are more varied and culturally defined.

As a second dominant feature of American kinship, the parent-child bond is the most important relationship and one that persists after children become adults. The study of this relationship and intergenerational relationships in general essentially constitutes the bulk of the kinship research today. Rossi and Rossi (1990) surveyed norms of obligation and, it is not surprising, found that the strongest obligation was between parents and children. The obligation was somewhat less strong for siblings and children-in-law and was progressively weaker for stepchildren, parents-in-law, and other relatives. The roles of siblings and secondary relatives, such as in-laws, cousins, nieces, and nephews, are barely of passing interest to most family researchers. Such a hierarchy of interest will probably continue and will most likely be even more dominated by the female-linked mother-daughter tie. After stating that, it is important to note the high potential for conflicts and tension in mother-daughter relationships because this close-knit relationship has a heavy emotional content that can undermine its quality (Fingerman, 1996). Consequently, there are considerable constraints to a harmonious relationship between parents and children, particularly among those who are in frequent interaction (Hess & Waring, 1978).

Third, studies have long emphasized the normative flexibility inherent in American kinship, but such flexibility usually means the absence of explicit rights and obligations that lead to strong multifunctional kinship systems. For example, when distant kin become important social ties, they may be treated as friends and thus are removed from the obligations and responsibilities of kinship roles that are prescribed by age and birth (Allan, 1989). In the case of Western kinship systems, relationships are often based on positive sentiments, affection, voluntary reciprocal exchanges, and equal status, all of which are characteristics of friendship (Johnson, 1983b; Wood & Robertson, 1978). Given the individual's freedom to define the family as he or she chooses, it becomes necessary to ask, What maintains the family and its extensions? Perhaps Riley's (1983, p. 439) description of the family in later life as a "latent web of continually shifting linkages that provide the opportunity for activating and intensifying close family relationships" was accurate. In other words, the viability of kinship may be in its potentialities to be "on hold" until needs or personal preference arise (Johnson, 1993).

To review the configurations of the kinship system in the United States, most scholars recognize that the dominant family model in contemporary America differs cross-culturally from other family systems. The nuclear family is a discrete unit in residence, property ownership, and income and is functionally separate from occupational, educational, and religious institutions. Relationships between parents and children are the dominant bond, while siblings and other kin are relatively unimportant as sources of sociability and support (Fisher, 1982a; Lee, 1980). In working-class families and some ethnic groups, kin are in more frequent contact with each other. Finally, women are more involved than men in kinship affairs (Adams, 1971; DiLeonardo, 1992; Lee, 1980). A dominant characteristic of kinship relationships in contemporary society is the voluntary, not obligatory, nature of the bonds. The optional quality of kinship relations results in few clear expectations and weak norms of responsibility for kin.

In this review, I have referred to the lagging interest in kinship except in the study of intergenerational relationships. In anthropology, however, an infusion of feminist theory has revived interest in the subject as researchers have called for a rethinking of basic gender differences in the division of labor. Such contributions have not been common in sociology because research on kinship has almost ceased altogether. This situation probably results in the conclusion that kinship relationships are not important in American family life, at least among those outside ethnic and minority-group families.

Most likely, women will continue to dominate kinship affairs. With a continued high rate of divorce, their domination may even increase as fathers become more peripheral to family life or they transfer their allegiances to new families. Reconstituted families may offer innovative arrangements as parents and grandparents multiply with divorce and remarriage. If single mothering continues to be common, we can anticipate an increase in grandparents assuming the role of surrogate parents, often against their will. Finally, the high rates of immigration, much of it from Third World countries, will bring more traditional families into this country who recognize and incorporate kin into the lives of their nuclear families. Consequently, in this dynamic period of family change, the significance of kin will probably change in given contexts.

At the same time, three kinds of changes are occurring that may enhance the importance of kin in the future. First, at the macrolevel, there is a worldwide movement of populations to urban areas and new countries. Over some years now, there has been a decline in the incidence of large multifunctional extended families, but most new immigrants come to the United States through the family reunification program. Extended kin are likely to play an important role in adaptation to the new environment, particularly because women still participate in a moral economy that features reciprocity among kin. Second, at the micro level, changes in marital rates, household composition, and single parenting are occurring, all of which may create a greater need for kin. The late 20th century witnessed a dynamic period of change that most likely will have an impact upon the kinship system. Finally, integral to contemporary changes in the family, new family forms are emerging that transcend previous bases of kinship as formed by blood and marriage, so that relationships are being redefined as a matter of choice or need.

REFERENCES

Adams, B. (1971). Isolation, function and beyond: American kinship in the 1960s. *Journal of Marriage and the Family.* Minneapolis, MN: National Council of Family Relations.

Adams, R. (1960). The nature of the family. In G. Dole & R. Carneiro (Eds.), *Essays in the science of culture.* New York: Crowell.

Aerts, E. (1993). Bringing the institution back in. In P. A. Cowan, D. Field, D. A. Hansen, A. Skolnick, & G. E. Swanson (Eds.), *Family, self, and society* (pp. 3–42). Hillsdale, NJ: Lawrence Erlbaum.

Allan, G. A. (1989). *Friendship: Developing a sociological perspective.* Newbury Park, CA: Sage.

Allen, K. (1997). Lesbian and gay families. In T. Arendell (Ed.), *Contemporary parenting* (pp. 196–218). Thousand Oaks, CA: Sage.

Aschenbrenner, J. (1973). Extended families among black Americans. *Journal of Comparative Family Studies, 4,* 257–268.

Barnes, J. (1973). Genetrix: Genitor: Nature: Culture? In J. Goody (Ed.), *Character of kinship* (pp. 61–73). Cambridge, England: Cambridge University Press.

Bedford, V. H., & Blieszner, R. (1996). Personal relationships in later life. In S. Duck (Ed.), *Handbook of personal relationships* (2nd ed., pp. 523–539). New York: John Wiley.

Bellah, R., Madsen, R., Sullivan, W., Swidler, A., & Tipton, S. (1985). *Habits of the Heart.* Berkeley: University of California Press.

Bengtson, V., Rosenthal, C., & Burton, L. (1990). Families and aging: Diversity and heterogeneity. In R. Binstock & L. George (Eds.), *Handbook of aging and the social sciences* (3rd ed., pp. 263–287). San Diego, CA: Academic Press.

Bergman, J. (1995). The persistence of kinship: Contributions to feminist anthropology. *Anthropological Quarterly, 68,* 234–240.

Booth, A. (1987). The state of the American family. *Journal of Family Issues, 8,* 429–430.

Bott, E. (1971). *Family and social network.* New York: Free Press.

Bumpass, L. (1990). What's happening to the family? Interactions between demographic and institutional change. *Demography, 27,* 483–498.

Carstensen, L. L. (1987). Age-related changes in social activity. In L. L. Carstensen & B. A. Edelstein (Eds.), *Handbook of clinical gerontology* (pp. 222–237). New York: Pergamon.

Chodorow, N. (1974). Family structure and feminine personality. In M. Rosaldo & L. Lamphere (Eds.), *Woman, culture, and society* (pp. 43–66). Stanford, CA: Stanford University Press.

Chodorow, N. (1978). *The reproduction of mothering: Psychoanalysis and the sociology of gender.* Berkeley: University of California Press.

Cohen, S., & Syme, S. (1985). *Social support and health.* Orlando, FL: Academic Press.

Collier, J., Rosaldo, M., & Yanagisako, S. (1992). Is there a family? New anthropological views. In B. Thorne & M. Yalom (Eds.), *Rethinking the family: Some feminist questions* (pp. 31–48). Boston: Northeastern University Press.

Collier, J., & Yanagisako, S. (Eds.). (1987). *Gender and kinship: Essays toward a unified analysis.* Stanford, CA: Stanford University Press.

Cowgill, D. O., & Holmes, L. D. (1972). *Aging and modernization.* New York: Appleton-Century-Crofts.

DiLeonardo, M. (Ed.). (1991). *Gender at the crossroads of knowledge: Feminist anthropology in the postmodern era.* Berkeley: University of California Press.

DiLeonardo, M. (1992). The female world of cards and holidays: Women, families, and the work of kinship. In B. Thorne & M. Yalom (Eds.), *Rethinking the family: Some feminist questions* (pp. 246–261). Boston: Northeastern University Press.

Edwards, J. (1987). Changing family structure and youthful well-being: Assessing the future. *Journal of Family Issues, 8,* 394–421.

Ehrenreich, B., & McIntosh, J. (1997 June 9). The new creationism: Biology under attack. *The Nation,* pp. 11–16.

Farber, B. (1971). *Kinship and class: A midwestern study.* New York: Basic Books.

Ferree, M. M. (1990). Beyond separate spheres: Feminism and family research. *Journal of Marriage and the Family, 52,* 866–884.

Fingerman, K. L. (1996). Sources of tension in the aging mother and adult daughter relationship. *Psychology and Aging, 11,* 591–606.

Fisher, C. (1982a). The dispersion of kin in modern society: Contemporary data and historical speculation. *Journal of Family History, 7,* 353–375.

Fisher, C. (1982b). *To dwell among friends: Personal networks in town and country.* Chicago: University of Chicago Press.

Fox, R. (1967). *Kinship and marriage: An anthropological perspective.* Baltimore, MD: Penguin.

Friedan, B. (1963). *The feminine mystique.* New York: W. W. Norton.

Fry, C. (1994). Kinship and individuation: Cross-cultural perspectives on intergenerational relations. In V. Bengtson, W. Schale, & L. Burton (Eds.), *Intergenerational issues in aging* (pp. 126–155). New York: Springer.

Furstenberg, F. F., Nord, C. W., Peterson, J. L., & Zill, N. (1983). The life course of children of divorce: Marital disruption and parental contact. *American Sociological Review, 48,* 656–668.

Geertz, C. (1973). *The interpretation of cultures.* New York: Basic Books.

Geiger, H. (1968). The fate of the family in Soviet Russia: 1917–1944. In N. Bell & E. Vogel (Eds.), *A modern introduction to the family* (pp. 48–67). New York: Free Press.

George, L., & Gold, D. (1991). Life course perspectives on intergenerational and generational connections. In S. Pfeifer & M. Sussman (Eds.), *Families: Intergenerational and generational connections* (pp. 67–68). New York: Haworth Press.

Gibson, G. (1972). Kin family network: Overheralded structure in past conceptualizations of family function. *Journal of Marriage and the Family, 34,* 13–23.

Goode, W. (1963). *World revolution and family patterns.* New York: Free Press.

Goode, W. (1992). Why men resist. In B. Thorne & M. Yalom (Eds.), *Rethinking the family: Some feminist questions* (pp. 287–310). Boston: Northeastern University Press.

Goody, J. (1990). *The oriental, the ancient and the primitive: Systems of marriage and the family in pre-industrial societies of Eurasia.* New York: Cambridge University Press.

Gough, E. (1952). Changing kinship usages in the setting of political and economic change among the Nayar of

Malabar. *Journal of the Royal Anthropological Institute, 82,* 71–88.

Hagestad, G. O. (1992). Family networks in an ageing society: Some reflections and explorations. In W. J. A. van den Heuvel, R. Illsley, A. Jamieson, & C. P. M. Knipscheer (Eds.), *Opportunities and challenges in an aging society* (pp. 44–52). Amsterdam: North Holland.

Hareven, T. (1982). American family in transition: Historical perspectives on change. In A. Walsh (Ed.), *Normal family processes* (pp. 446–466). New York: Guilford Press.

Hess, B., & Waring, J. (1978). Parent and child in late life: Rethinking the relationship. In R. M. Lerner & G. B. Spanier (Eds.), *Child influences in marital and family interaction.* New York: Academic Press.

Higginbotham, E., & Weber, L. (1992). Moving up with kin and community: Upward mobility for black and white women. *Gender and Society, 6,* 416–440.

Hofferth, S. L. (1984). Kin networks, race and family structures. *Journal of Marriage and the Family, 46,* 791–806.

Hogan, D. P., & Spencer, L. J. (1993). Kinship structure and assistance in an aging society. In G. Maddox & M. Lawton (Eds.), *Annual review of gerontology and geriatrics: Vol. 13. Kinship, aging, and social change.* New York: Springer.

Jackson, J. (1989). Race, ethnicity, and psychological theory [Guest editorial]. *Journal of Gerontology: Psychology, 44,* P1–P2.

Johnson, C. L. (1974). Gift giving and reciprocity among the Japanese Americans. *American Ethnologist, 1,* 295–308.

Johnson, C. L. (1977). Interdependence, reciprocity and indebtedness: An analysis of Japanese American kinship relations. *Journal of Marriage and the Family, 39,* 351–363.

Johnson, C. L. (1978). Family support systems of elderly Italian Americans. *Journal of Minority Aging, 3,* 34–41.

Johnson, C. L. (1982). Sibling solidarity: Its origins and functioning in Italian American families. *Journal of Marriage and the Family, 44,* 155–167.

Johnson, C. L. (1983a). Dyadic family relations and social supports. *The Gerontologist, 23,* 377–383.

Johnson, C. L. (1983b). Fair-weather friends and rainy-day kin: An anthropological analysis of old age friendships. *Urban Anthropology, 12,* 103–123.

Johnson, C. L. (1983c). Interdependence and aging in Italian American families. In J. Sokolovsky (Ed.), *Growing old in different societies: Cross-cul-*

tural perspectives (pp. 92–103). New York: Duxbury Press.

Johnson, C. L. (1985). *Growing up and growing old in Italian-American families.* New Brunswick, NJ: Rutgers University Press.

Johnson, C. L. (1988a). *Ex-familia: Grandparents, parents and children adjust to divorce.* New Brunswick, NJ: Rutgers University Press.

Johnson, C. L. (1988b). Relationships among family members and friends in later life. In R. M. Milardo (Ed.), *Families and social networks.* Newbury Park, CA: Sage.

Johnson, C. L. (1989). In-law relationships in the American kinship system: The impact of divorce and remarriage. *American Ethnologist, 16,* 87–99.

Johnson, C. L. (1993). The prolongation of life and the extension of family relationships: The families of the oldest old. In P. A. Cowan, D. Field, D. A. Hansen, A. Skolnick, & G. E. Swanson (Eds.), *Family, self, and society* (pp. 317–330). Hillsdale, NJ: Lawrence Erlbaum.

Johnson, C. L. (1995a). Cultural diversity in the late life family. In R. Blieszner & V. Bedford (Eds.), *Handbook of aging and the family.* Westport, CT: Greenwood Press.

Johnson, C. (1995b). Determinants of adaptation of oldest old black Americans. *Journal of Aging Studies, 9,* 231–244.

Johnson, C. L., & Barer, B. M. (1987). Marital instability and changing kinship networks of grandparents. *The Gerontologist, 27,* 330–335.

Johnson, C. L., & Barer, B. M. (1990). Families and social networks among older innercity blacks. *The Gerontologist, 30,* 726–733.

Johnson, C. L., & Barer, B. M. (1993). Coping and a sense of control among the oldest-old. *Journal of Aging Studies, 7,* 67–80.

Johnson, C. L., & Barer, B. M. (1995). Childlessness in late late life: Comparisons by race. *Journal of Cross Cultural Gerontology, 9,* 289–306.

Johnson, C. L., & Catalano, D. J. (1983). A longitudinal study of family supports to impaired elderly. *The Gerontologist, 23,* 612–618.

Johnson, C. L., Schmidt, C., & Klee, L. (1988). Conceptions of parentage and kinship among children of divorce. *American Anthropologist, 90,* 24–32.

Johnson, C. L., & Troll, L. (1992). Family functioning in late late life. *Journal of Gerontology, Social Sciences, 47,* 566–572.

Kephart, W. (1972). The experimental family organization: An historico-cultural report on the Oneida community. In M. Gordon (Ed.), *The nuclear family in crisis: The search for an alternative* (pp. 59–77). New York: Harper & Row.

Kluckhohn, F. R. (1968). Variations in the basic values of family systems. In N. W. Bell & E. F. Vogel (Eds.), *A modern introduction to the family* (pp. 319–330). New York: Free Press.

Lasch, C. (1979). *Haven in a heartless world: The family besieged.* New York: W. W. Norton.

Laslett, B. (1978). Family membership, past and present. *Social Problems, 25,* 476–490.

Laslett, P. (1965). *The world we have lost.* New York: Charles Scribner's Sons.

Lee, G. (1980). Kinship in the seventies: A decade review of research and theory. *Journal of Marriage and the Family, 42,* 923–936.

Leigh, G. (1982). Kinship interaction over the family life span. *Journal of Marriage and the Family, 44,* 197–208.

Levi-Strauss, C. (1956). The family. In H. Shapiro (Ed.), *Man, culture and society.* New York: Oxford University Press.

Litwak, E. (1960). Geographic mobility and extended family cohesion. *American Sociological Review, 25,* 9–21.

Litwak, E. (1965). Extended kin relations in an industrial democratic society. In E. Shanas & G. Streib (Eds.), *Social structure and the family: Intergenerational relations.* Englewood Cliffs, NJ: Prentice Hall.

Litwak, E. (1985). *Helping the elderly: The complementary roles of informal networks and formal systems.* New York: Guilford Press.

Longino, C., & Erle, T. (1996). Who are the grandparents at the century's end? *Generations, 20,* 13–16.

Lopata, H. (1978). Contributions of extended families to the support systems of metropolitan area widows: Limitations of the modified kin network. *Journal of Marriage and the Family, 40,* 355–364.

Malinowski, B. (1913). *The family among Australian aborigines.* London: University of London Press.

Marshall, M. (Ed.). (1981). *Siblingship in Oceania: Studies in the meaning of kin relations.* Ann Arbor: University of Michigan Press.

Martin, E. P., & Martin, J. (1978). *The black extended family.* Chicago: University of Chicago Press.

Modell, J. S. (1994). *Kinship with strangers.* Berkeley: University of California Press.

Moore, H. (1988). *Feminism and anthropology.* Minneapolis: University of Minnesota Press.

Morgan, D. (1990). Issues of critical sociological theory: Men in families. In J. Sprey (Ed.), *Fashioning family theory: New approaches* (pp. 67–106). Newbury Park, CA: Sage.

Morgan, L. H. (1887). *Ancient society.* New York: Henry Holt.

Nakane, C. (1970). *Japanese society.* Berkeley: University of California Press.

O'Rand, A., & Agree, E. (1993). Kin reciprocities, the familial corporation, and other moral economies: Workplace, family, and kin in the modern global context. In G. Maddox & M. Lawton (Eds.), *Annual review of gerontology and geriatrics: Vol. 13. Kinship, aging, and social change* (pp. 75–95). New York: Springer.

Ortner, S. (1974). Is female to male as nature is to culture? In M. Rosaldo & L. Lamphere (Eds.), *Woman, culture, and society* (pp. 67–88). Stanford, CA: Stanford University Press.

Osmond, M. W., & Thorne, B. (1993). Feminist theories: The construction of gender in families and society. In P. B. Boss, W. J. Doherty, R. LaRossa, W. R. Schumm, & S. Steinmetz (Eds.), *Sourcebook of family theories and methods* (pp. 591–623). New York: Plenum.

Parsons, T. (1942). Age and sex in the social structure of the United States. *American Sociological Review, 7,* 604–616.

Parsons, T. (1943). The kinship system of the contemporary United States. *American Anthropologist, 45,* 22–38.

Parsons, T. (1949). The social structure of the family. In R. Ashen (Ed.), *The family: Its function and destiny.* New York: Harper & Row.

Parsons, T. (1965). The normal American family. In S. Farber, P. Mustaccho, & R. Watson, (Eds.), *Man and civilization: The family's search for survival* (pp. 31–50). New York: McGraw-Hill.

Peletz, M. (1995). Kinship studies in late twentieth-century anthropology. *Annual Review of Anthropology, 24,* 343–372.

Popenoe, D. (1993). American family decline, 1960–1990: A review and appraisal. *Journal of Marriage and the Family, 55,* 527–555.

Poster, M. (1978). *Critical theory of the family.* London: Macmillan.

Radcliffe-Brown, A. (1952). *Structure and function in primitive society.* New York: Free Press.

Rapp, R. (1982). Family and class in contemporary America: Notes toward an understanding of ideology. In B. Thorne & M. Yalum (Eds.), *Rethinking the family* (pp. 168–187). New York: Longman.

Riley, M. (1983). The family in an aging society: A matrix of latent relationships. *Journal of Family Issues, 4,* 439–454.

Robertson, A. F. (1991). *Beyond the family: The social organization of human reproduction.* Berkeley: University of California Press.

Rosaldo, M., & Lamphere, L. (1974a). Introduction. In M. Rosaldo & L. Lamphere (Eds.), *Woman, culture, and society* (pp. 1–16). Stanford, CA: Stanford University Press.

Rosaldo, M., & Lamphere, L. (Eds.). (1974b). *Woman, culture, and society.* Stanford, CA: Stanford Unversity Press.

Rosenmayr, L., & Krockeis, E. (1963). Propositions for a sociological theory of aging and the family. *International Social Science Journal, 15,* 410–426.

Rossi, A. S., & Rossi, P. H. (1990). *Of human bonding: Parent-child relations across the life course.* New York: Aldine de Gruyter.

Safilios-Rothschild, L. C. (1969). Family sociology or wives' family sociology. *Journal of Marriage and the Family, 31,* 290–301.

Schneider, D. M. (1968). *American kinship: A cultural account.* Chicago: University of Chicago Press.

Schneider, D. M. (1980). Twelve years later: An afterword. In D. M. Schneider, *American kinship: A cultural account* (2nd ed.) (pp. 118–124). Chicago: University of Chicago Press.

Schneider, D. M., & Cottrell, D. B. (1975). *The American kin universe: A geneological study.* Chicago: Department of Anthropology, University of Chicago Press.

Schneider, D. M., & Smith, R. (1973). *Class differences and sex roles in American kinship and family structure.* Englewood Cliffs, NJ: Prentice Hall.

Schwartz, P. (1987). The family as a changed institution. *Journal of Family Issues, 8,* 455–459.

Shanas, E. (1979a). The family as a support system in old age. *The Gerontologist, 19,* 169–174.

Shanas, E. (1979b). Social myth as hypothesis: The case of family relationships of older people. The *Gerontologist, 19,* 3–9.

Sheffler, H. (1991). Sexism and naturalism in the study of kinship. In M. DiLeonardo (Ed.), *Gender at the crossroads of knowledge: Feminist anthropology in the postmodern era.* Berkeley: University of California Press.

Spiro, M. (1954). Is the family universal? *American Anthropologist, 56,* 839–846.

Sprey, J. (1991). Studying adult children and parents. *Families: Intergenerational and generational connections: Pt. 2. Marriage and Family Review, 16*(3–4), 221–236.

Stack, C. (1974). *All our kin.* New York: Harper & Row.

Stacey, J. (1990). *Brave new families: Stories of domestic upheaval in the late twentieth century.* New York: Basic Books.

Stacey, J. (1992). Backward toward the postmodern family: Reflections on gender, kinship, and class in the Silicon Valley. In B. Thorne & M. Yalom (Eds.), *Rethinking the family* (pp. 91–118). Boston: Northeastern University Press.

Stacey, J. (1993). Good riddance to "the family": A response to David Popenoe. *Journal of Marriage and the Family, 55,* 545–547.

Stacey, J., & Thorne, B. (1985). The missing feminist revolution in sociology. *Social Problems, 32,* 303–316.

Sussman, M. (1965). Relations of adult children with their parents. In E. Shanas & G. F. Streib (Eds.), *Social structure and the family* (Pp. 62–92). Englewood Cliffs, N.J: Prentice Hall.

Sussman, M., & Burchinal, L. (1962). Kin family network: Unheralded structure in current conceptualizations of family functioning. *Marriage and Family Living, 24,* 231–240.

Troll, L. & Fingerman, K. L. (1996). Connections beween parents and their adult children. In C. Magai & S. H. McFaddon (Eds.), *Handbook of emotions, adult development and aging* (pp. 185–200). New York: Academic Press.

Verdon, M. (1980). From the social to the symbolic equation: The progress of idealism in contemporary anthropological representations of kinship, marriage, and the family. *Canadian Review of Sociology and Anthropology, 17,* 315–329.

Waite, L., & Harrison, S. (1992). Keeping in touch: How women in mid-life allocate social contacts among kith and kin. *Social Forces, 70,* 637–655.

Weston, K. (1991). *Families we choose; Lesbians, gays, Kinship.* New York: Columbia University Press.

White, L. (1987). Freedom versus constraint. *Journal of Family Issues, 8,* 468–470.

Wood, V., & Robertson, J. (1978). Friendship and kinship interaction: Differential effects on the morale of the elderly. *Journal of Marriage and the Family, 40,* 367–375.

Yanagisako, S. & Collier, J. (1987). Toward a unified analysis of gender and kinship. In In J. F. Collier & S. J. Yanagisako (Eds.), *Gender and kinship* (pp. 14–50). Stanford, CA: Stanford University Press.

Young, M. & Wilmott, P. (1957). *Family and kinship in East London.* Baltimore, MD: Penguin.

PART IV
Family Structure and Family Diversity

CHAPTER **8**

*Diversity Within Single-Parent Families**

Single-parent families are common in the United States today, but they have always been part of our social landscape. About one-fourth of children born around the turn of the 19th century experienced the death of a parent before they reached age 15 (Uhlenberg, 1980), and another 7% or 8% experienced parental separation or divorce (Furstenberg & Cherlin, 1991). Most people believed then—as they do now—that being a single parent is difficult and that children develop best when they grow up with two parents. But in recent decades, single parenthood has been transformed from a private misfortune into a social issue—an issue that has become the focus of a good deal of media attention, public debate, and social policy.

Several factors are responsible for the emergence of single parenthood as a social issue. First, because of declines in parental mortality during the 20th century, the percentage of children growing up with single parents reached an all-time low in the years following World War II (Popenoe, 1995). The stable, two-parent family of the 1950s, with its breadwinner father and homemaker mother, became an idealized family form, not only in popular culture, but in

sociological theory (Parsons & Bales, 1955). However, single-parent families became more common again during the 1960s, and the percentage of children living with single parents more than doubled between 1970 and 1995 (U.S. Bureau of the Census, 1996, Table 81). On the basis of current trends, demographers project that more than one-half the children born in the 1990s will spend time in single-parent households (Bianchi, 1995; Bumpass & Sweet, 1989)—a figure higher than at any time in U.S. history. The large number of children involved, coupled with a nostalgia for the family of the 1950s, has led many people to believe that the American family is in a state of crisis and that an entire generation of children is in danger (see Popenoe, 1995, for a statement of this position).

Another factor that contributed to the emergence of single-parent families as a social issue was the change in the *cause* of single parenthood. The death of one parent was the most common route to this family form in the past, but the percentage of single-parent families formed in this manner declined dramatically during the 20th century. The increase in single parenthood since the 1960s was fueled, at first, by an increase in parental divorce and, more recently, by a growth in the percentage of children born outside marriage (Bianchi, 1995). Although the death of a parent is usually unintended, marital dis-

---

*I thank the editors of this volume, Katherine Allen, David Demo, and Mark Fine, along with Stacy Rogers, for their helpful comments on an earlier version of this chapter.

149

solution and nonmarital birth usually result from individuals' choices. For this reason, some people see the growth in single-parent families as a *moral* problem—a problem reflecting a hedonistic culture in which parents place a higher priority on their own needs than on those of their children (Glenn, 1996).

Single parenthood is also controversial because it is related to the changing status of women. Most (85%) single-parent families are headed by mothers. From a feminist perspective, the rise in the number of single mothers can be viewed as an indicator of women's growing economic power. Large increases in women's employment, as well as modest increases in women's wages, have made it easier for women to leave unhappy marriages or bear children outside marriage (Spain & Bianchi, 1996). But the risk of living in poverty is also high for single mothers. Although economic hardship often precedes the formation of single-parent households, most single mothers are poor because women earn less than men, many fathers pay little or no child support, and public assistance is meager. For these reasons, the growth in single-mother families has led to an increase in poverty among women and children in the United States (Bianchi, 1995; Eggebeen & Lichter, 1991; Garfinkel & McLanahan, 1986; McLanahan & Booth, 1989). The growth of single-mother families, therefore, presents a paradox: On the one hand, it reflects women's growing economic power, but on the other hand, it reflects the economic vulnerability of many mothers and their children.

A final factor involved in the transformation of single parenthood into a social issue is the striking racial difference in the prevalence of single-parent families. Demographers (Bianchi, 1995; Bumpass & Sweet, 1989) estimate that 36% of white children will live with a single parent versus 80% of African American children. The racial gap is especially large for nonmarital births: 24% of births among whites are to unmarried mothers, compared with 69% of births among African Americans (U.S. Bureau of the Census, 1996, Table 91). Some observers (see, for example, Moynihan, 1965, 1986) have argued that the prevalence of this family form among African Americans is part of a culture of poverty that perpetuates an underclass. In contrast, Wilson (1987) posited that the increased rate of nonmarital births among African American women is due to a decline in the economic prospects (and, hence, marriage potential) of African American men in recent decades. Alternatively, others (Burton & Bengtson, 1985; Staples & Johnson, 1993; Taylor, 1994) have claimed that single-parent families are a reflection of an Afro-centric cultural tradition in which extended kin networks—not just parents—care for children. The debate over whether the African American family structure is a cause of poverty, a consequence of poverty, or simply a continuation of an African cultural tradition has not been resolved.

For the reasons just noted, single parenthood has become one of the most controversial issues of our time. To inform the public debate, social scientists have conducted hundreds of studies comparing the economic resources, parental adjustment, parent-child relationships, and well-being of children in single-parent and two-parent families. This body of research has yielded a great deal of valuable information. But a major limitation of this work has been the tendency to combine all single-parent families into one category, thus obscuring the variability of resources and outcomes *within* single-parent families.

This chapter does not present information on how single parents and their children differ from married parents and their children; rather I discuss the variability that exists within the category of single-parent families. I address this issue by describing data from the U.S. Bureau of the Census on single-parent families, reviewing empirical studies on family and child outcomes, and presenting new analyses of data from the 1987–88 National Survey of Families and Households. First, however, I offer some thoughts on family diversity, definitions of family, and my conceptual framework.

BACKGROUND

Reflections on Family Diversity

Diversity is a term that is richly loaded with connotative meanings—some negative and some positive. On the one hand, it refers to dissimilarity, which suggests the possibility of misunderstanding and conflict, as when two groups clash over opposing goals or compete for scare resources. On the other hand, it refers to variety and interdependence, which suggests choice, personal freedom, and strength, as when companies diversify their products to protect against market fluctuations or people with different backgrounds pool their knowledge to solve a problem. These two views of diversity, one threatening and one benign, underlie most people's thinking about the increasing diversification of family life in the United States.

As a social scientist, I am interested in family diversity for two reasons. First, the growth of family diversity is one of the most remarkable social transformations of the 20th century. Massive increases in nonmarital births, cohabitation, divorce, remarriage, and other family variations during the past 30 years in the United States have affected the most intimate details of people's daily experiences. I want to understand the growth in family diversity because it is an immense, objective, indisputable social fact that touches the lives of virtually everyone in this country. No other social institution has changed as much as the family in recent decades. As a researcher, it is exciting to work "where the action is."

I also find that studying family diversity provides insights into the values that exist within our culture. The notion of diversity is consistent with the fundamental values that underlie our democratic institutions: freedom of individuals to pursue their private goals (provided that they do no harm to others), tolerance of differences, and respect for the dignity of all people. Of course, these principles are not always applied in practice. Before the 1967 Supreme Court ruling (*Loving v. Virginia*), some states refused to recognize marriages between African Americans and whites (Glendon, 1989). Similarly, the current refusal of all state legislatures to recognize marriages among gays and lesbians is contrary to the democratic values of freedom, tolerance, and respect. Studying family diversity, therefore, provides insights into the manner in which our basic values guide—and often fail to guide—our political and legal institutions, as well as our private behavior.

Defining Families

Because no single definition of *family* captures its full complexity, I find it useful to adopt two definitions. First, I sometimes rely on the U.S. Bureau of the Census's (1996, p. 6) definition as "two or more people related by birth, marriage, or adoption and residing together in a household." This definition is useful for researchers because the census bureau has been collecting information on families since the middle of the 19th century, and the definition allows researchers to study how families have changed over long periods. This definition also has the advantage of counting as families many groups *other than* the traditional two-parent family, including a single parent and a child, a grandparent and a grandchild, and two adult siblings, provided that they live together. Unfortunately, it leaves out other important groups that many people would consider to be families, such as cohabiting couples (both heterosexual and same-sex) and families spread across more than one household.

In addition to the census bureau's structural definition of the family (based on biology, legal ties, and residence), I find it useful to adopt a definition based on functional and emotional aspects of relationships. Most people, when asked to define family, refer to characteristics like love, trust, mutual helping, and commitment. On the basis of these everyday, implicit understandings, it is possible to define families as people who relate to one another in "familylike" ways, that is, through loving, trusting, and helping one another within the context of long-term relationships. In this sense, family members may not be related through birth, marriage, or adoption and may not reside in the same household (see Weston, 1991 on the distinction between biological and chosen families).

Adopting a definition based on feelings and characteristics of relationships leads to some interesting implications. Consider a child who, following her parents' divorce, lives with her mother but maintains a close relationship with her noncustodial father. When asked to list family members, she is likely to mention her father as well as her mother. The mother, in contrast, is unlikely to view her exhusband as a family member. Thus, although the mother and child are members of the same household, they are members of *overlapping* families. In this situation, the mother probably defines herself as a single parent, even though the child interacts frequently with two functioning parents. This example suggests that from a child's perspective, some single-parent *families* should be reclassified as single-parent *households*.

In spite of the complexities involved, I rely on the U.S. Bureau of the Census's definition of families in this chapter for two reasons. First, it allows me to present national census data to describe the degree of diversity that exists within households headed by single parents. Second, it permits me to use survey data (in which the household is the unit sampled) to determine how outcomes for single parents and their children (who reside together) vary with multiple dimensions of diversity. Therefore, in this chapter, a single-parent family refers to a household that contains at least one child under age 18, one biological or adoptive parent, and no stepparent.

Conceptual Framework

Although researchers have used a variety of conceptual frameworks to understand single-parent families, much of my own research has relied on a straightforward perspective based on *resources* and *stressors* (Amato, 1995). This perspective assumes that people's well-being depends on the quantity and quality of resources at their disposal. Resources can reside in the individual (knowledge, self-efficacy), in interpersonal relationships (emotional support, practical assistance), and in the larger social and physical environment (the quality of schools, supportive governmental policies). In general, the well-being of single parents and their children is positively related to the quantity and quality of resources available to them.

Stressors—circumstances that tax people's resources and exceed their ability to cope—represent risk factors for negative outcomes among parents and children. Research has indicated that members of single-parent families are exposed to more stressors than are members of two-parent families (McLanahan, 1983; McLanahan & Booth, 1989). These multiple stressors include economic hard-

ship, discrimination in housing, frequent moving, having sole responsibility for children's supervision, the lack of affordable child care, and living in unsafe neighborhoods. All things being equal, the well-being of single parents and their children is negatively related to the number and severity of stressors to which they are exposed.

Depending on their access to resources, however, some members of single-parent families are relatively vulnerable to the ill effects of stress, whereas others are relatively resilient. Single parents with low-paying jobs and weak social support, for example, are less able to cope with the rigors of single parenthood than are those with high-paying jobs and strong social support. Single parents' and children's outcomes, therefore, can be understood by considering the mix of resources and stressors in their lives, that is, by viewing these families in a larger social and physical context (Hetherington & Blechman, 1996).

It is also useful to think about single-parent families in terms of their location in the social structure. U.S. society is stratified by gender, race-ethnicity, and class—factors that have an impact on people's access to resources as well as their exposure to stressors. Because of this fundamental inequality, single parents who are male, white, and well educated have certain advantages over single parents who are female, African American or Latino, and poorly educated, respectively. Other factors that are likely to affect the mix of resources and stressors in the lives of single parents include marital status (divorced, separated, never married, or widowed), age, and residing alone versus residing with kin.

In summary, not all single-parent families are alike. The characteristics of single parents (such as gender, race-ethnicity, and education) determine the mix of resources and stressors in their lives. Resources (such as income) and stressors (such as residential instability), in turn, determine whether single parents and their children experience positive or negative outcomes.

VARIATIONS WITHIN SINGLE-PARENT FAMILIES

To reveal variability within the category of single-parent families, I present recent data from the U.S.

Bureau of the Census on the gender, race, education, age, and living arrangements of single parents. To maintain consistency, I discuss each trend from the perspective of children.

Parental Gender

Figure 8.1 shows the percentage of children in the United States living with two parents, mothers only, fathers only, and neither parent. It reveals two well-known trends: Children are more likely to live with single mothers than single fathers, and the percentage of children living with a single parent increased between 1970 and 1995. The rate of increase, however, was greater for single fathers than single mothers. During this time, the percentage of children living with single mothers doubled (from 11% to 23%), whereas the percentage living with single fathers quadrupled (from 1% to 4%). Of all the children who were living with single parents, only 8% lived with fathers in 1970, but this figure rose to 15% in 1995.

Because 1 out of every 7 children in a single-parent household lives with a father, it is misleading to think exclusively of single parents as mothers. Indeed, in 1995, over 2.5 million children lived with single fathers. Yet, except for a handful of studies (see, for example, Eggebeen, Snyder, & Manning, 1996; Grief, 1985; Meyer & Garasky, 1993; Risman, 1986), most research has focused on single mothers and omitted single fathers. Researchers may not pay attention to single fathers because they think that single mothers are more vulnerable than single fathers, and, hence, are more deserving of study. In addition, single fathers have been more difficult to locate than single mothers, although this

FIGURE 8.1
Percentage of Children in Four Family Structures: 1970–95

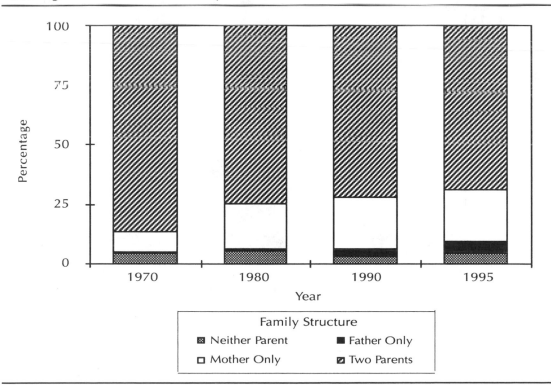

Source: U.S. Census Bureau (1996).

situation is changing as their numbers increase. The relative neglect of single fathers may also be due to the tendency to equate parenting with mothers. This tendency is consistent with the tendency for researchers to devote less time to fathers than to mothers, although fatherhood appears to be an area of future research growth.

Race and Ethnicity

Figure 8.2 shows the percentage of children in 1995 in three broad racial categories (based on the parent's race) as defined by the U.S. Bureau of the Census (black, white, and other) by family structure. The other category is a combination of Asian, Pacific Islander, and Native American. The figure

reveals that, in 1995, 35% of the children in mother-only households and 19% of the children in father-only households were black, compared with less than 8% of the children in two-parent households. This difference reflects the fact that blacks are more likely than whites to have nonmarital births or to divorce. Nevertheless, the majority of children who lived with single mothers (60%) and single fathers (77%) were white in 1995.

The U.S. Bureau of the Census also publishes information on people of Hispanic origin, who can be from any racial group, although about 91% of Hispanics are considered to be white (following the census bureau's terminology). In 1995, 17% of the children who were living with single parents were of Hispanic origin, compared with 13% of the chil-

FIGURE 8.2
Percentage of Children in Three Racial Groups by Family Structure: 1995

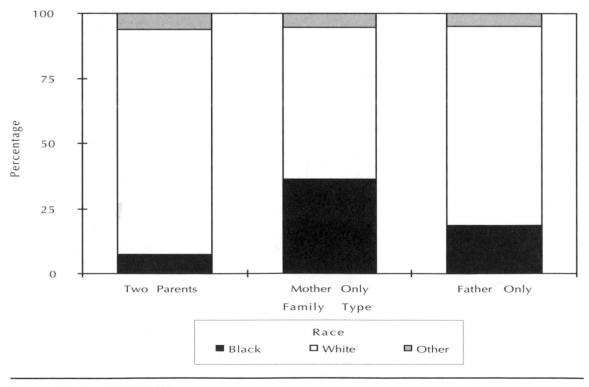

Source: U.S. Census Bureau (1996).

dren who were living with married parents. This broad category, however, obscures diversity within this ethnic group. Single parenthood is most common among Puerto Ricans, least common among Cubans, and intermediate among Mexican Americans (Bean & Tienda, 1992).

Parental Education

Figure 8.3 shows the percentage of children in different types of families who were living with parents with different levels of education in 1995. In two-parent households, the parent can be either the mother or father, depending on which parent completes the census bureau's questionnaire and is therefore designated as the householder. Note that the children in single-parent families were less likely than those in two-parent families to be living with parents who were college graduates and were more likely to be living with parents who dropped out of high school. This situation is true for children who were living with single fathers as well as for those who were living with single mothers, although single fathers are slightly better educated, on average, than single mothers.

The educational differences between single and married parents reflect the fact that poorly educated people are more likely than well-educated people to

FIGURE 8.3
Percentage of Children Living With Parents With Different Levels of Education by Family Structure: 1995

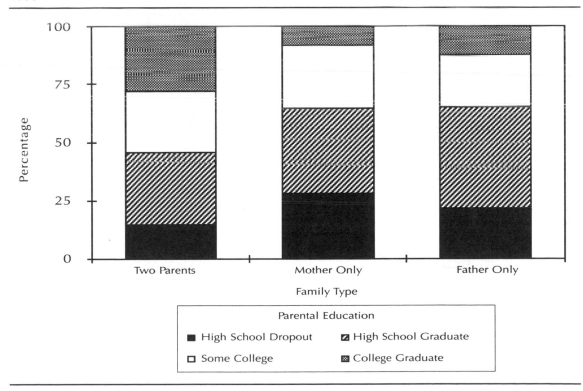

Source: U.S. Census Bureau (1996).

have children outside marriage or to divorce. In addition, teenage childbearing makes it more difficult to finish high school or attend college (Furstenberg, 1976). Nevertheless, Figure 8.3 reveals that a substantial minority of single parents are well educated. Thirty-six percent of children with single mothers and 35% of children with single fathers have parents who attended college, and 8% of children with single mothers and 12% of children with single fathers have parents who are college graduates; only a minority of children in single-parent families (about one fourth) have parents who are high school dropouts. These data indicate that, although single parents are less well educated than are married parents, a substantial proportion have

educational resources that may help them cope successfully with the demands of single parenthood.

Marital Status

Figure 8.4 shows the percentage of children living with single mothers by the mothers' marital status. (A similar breakdown was not available for single fathers.) Note that the percentage of children who were living with never-married mothers rose substantially between 1970 and 1995. Most of this shift reflects the increasing rate of nonmarital births in the United States, although some of it is due to technical refinements that allowed the census bureau to identify never-married mothers more accurately

FIGURE 8.4
Percentage of Children Living With Single Mothers by Mother's Marital Status: 1970–95

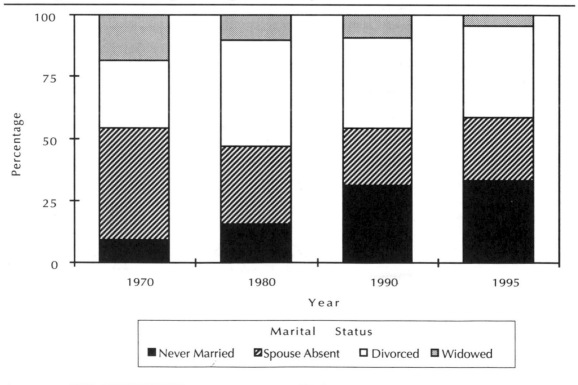

Source: U.S. Census Bureau (1996).

(Bianchi, 1995). The figure also shows an increase in the percentage of children who were living with divorced mothers, along with a decline in the percentage of children who were living with mothers with absent spouses. This change reflects the spread of no-fault divorce since the 1970s to all 50 states. The relative ease of obtaining a divorce led to a decline in the number of children with separated parents and a corresponding increase in the number with divorced parents. In addition, Figure 8.4 shows a decline in the percentage of children who were living with widowed single mothers; this trend reflects the expansion of the other causes of single parenthood, as well as modest decreases in mortality rates among middle-aged men (U.S. Bureau of the Census, 1996, Table 122).

Although not shown in the figure, these trends also vary with race. Increases in the percentage of never-married mothers occurred among all races, but the largest increase was among blacks. As of 1995, most black single mothers (56%) were never married, whereas most white single mothers (72%) were divorced or had an absent spouse (U.S. Bureau of the Census, 1996, Table 81.)

Parental Age

Figure 8.5 shows the percentage of children in different types of families who were living with parents of different ages in 1995. The figure reveals that single mothers and fathers tended to be younger than married parents. For example, among

FIGURE 8.5
Percentage of Children Living With Parents of Different Ages by Family Structure: 1995

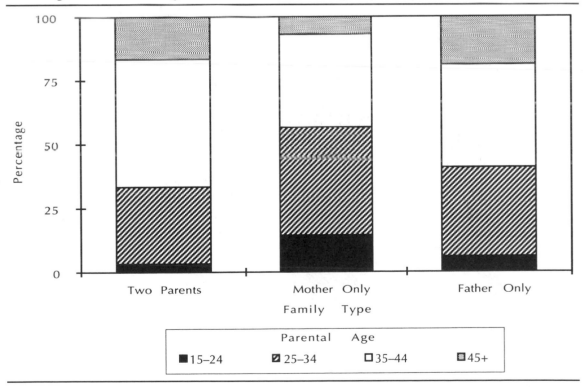

Source: U.S. Census Bureau (1996).

the children with married parents, only 3% had parents younger than 25, compared 15% of the children with single mothers and 7% of the children with single fathers. Nevertheless, most single parents had reached a mature age. Among the children who were living with single mothers, 44% had mothers older than 35, and among the children who were living with single fathers, 59% had fathers older than 35. Much public debate has focused on young single mothers, especially teenagers, who are especially vulnerable because of their economic dependence and lack of life experience. However, as the figure shows, a substantial proportion of the single parents were older and, consequently, had

greater economic and personal resources on which to draw.

Living Arrangements

Figure 8.6 shows the percentage of children who were living with unmarried mothers in three types of households—with no other adults present, with nonkin present, and with kin present—in 1990. (Comparable data were were not available for single fathers.) To construct this figure, I omitted children living with "single" mothers and cohabiting partners because these cases are more like two-parent families than single-parent families in many

FIGURE 8.6
Percentage of Children in Unmarried-Mother Families Residing With Kin and Nonkin by Mothers' Race: 1990

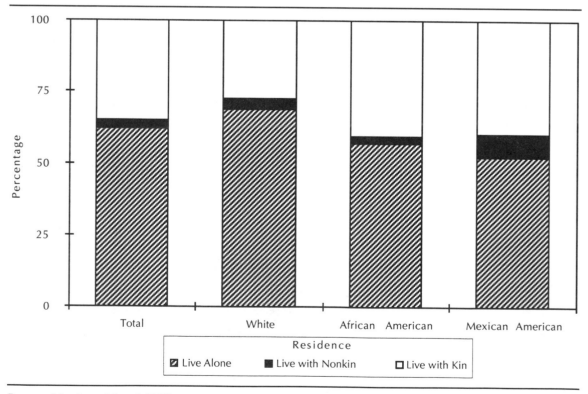

Source: Manning and Smock (1997).

respects. The bar on the far left indicates that most children (62%) were living with single mothers and no other adults, 34% were living with kin, and 4% were living with nonkin (see also Manning & Smock, 1997): In contrast, although not shown in the figure, only 17% of the children in two-parent families were living with other adults, either kin or nonkin (Bianchi, 1995). These data indicate that children with single mothers are considerably more likely than children with married mothers to share accommodations with adult kin.

Many observers have noted that residing with kin is especially prevalent among African Americans—a factor that is often cited as one of the strengths of African American families (Stack, 1974; Staples & Johnson, 1993; Taylor, Chatters, & Jackson, 1993). For these reasons, it is instructive to consider the situations of whites and blacks separately.

Figure 8.6 indicates that black children with single mothers were more likely than white children with single mothers to reside with kin (40% versus 27%, respectively)—a finding that is consistent with the notion of strong kin support among African American families. (There is little racial difference in the percentage of children living with nonkin.) Figure 8.6 also reveals, however, that a substantial proportion (44%) of Mexican American children were residing with single mothers and adult kin—a figure that is even higher than for blacks. And although not shown in the figure, 44% of Asian children with single mothers were also living with adult kin. These data suggest that strong kin support is a characteristic not only of black families, but of Mexican American and Asian families as well.

Single mothers of all races are more likely than married mothers to be living with other adults because they benefit from pooling income and having ready access to emotional support, companionship, and assistance with child care—all of which are valuable resources. Nevertheless, in spite of the frequency of sharing accommodation, Figure 8.6 reveals that the majority of children with single mothers—black as well as white—were *not* living with kin or other adults in 1990. Of course, because black mothers are more likely than white mothers to be single, they are more likely overall than white mothers to live with their parents or other relatives. But if we restrict our view to single parents, then blacks are only somewhat more likely than whites to be living in the homes of kin.

The fact that the majority of all single mothers and their children live in their own households suggests that most single mothers value their independence and prefer living on their own, if possible. This conclusion is consistent with the finding that in states with the most generous public assistance benefits, single mothers are the least likely to be living in the homes of kin (Garfinkel & McLanahan, 1986). This conclusion is also consistent with another fact: The percentage of children living with grandparents declined throughout the 20th century—a trend that is true for children of all races and for children in single-parent, as well as in two-parent families (Hernandez, 1993).

Summary

Single parents vary considerably with regard to gender, race and ethnicity, education, marital status, age, and living arrangements. Although more children live with single mothers than with single fathers, fathers make up a significant and growing proportion of single-parent families. Blacks are more likely than whites to live in single-parent families, but the majority of single-parent families are white. Although single parents are more likely than married parents to be high school dropouts, a sizable proportion are college graduates. Nonmarital birth is an increasing cause of single parenthood, but single parents have a variety of marital statuses. Single parents are younger, on average, than married parents; however, the majority are in their 30s or 40s. Finally, many single parents reside with kin, but the majority, both blacks and whites, live in their own households.

THE WELL-BEING OF SINGLE PARENTS AND THEIR CHILDREN *Question -*

The conceptual framework in this chapter states that such factors as gender, race, education, marital status, age, and kin residence affect the mix of resources and stressors in the lives of single parents and their children. In this section, I examine the implications of these variations for income (a key resource) and residential instability (a key stressor). I also examine the implications of these factors for three types of outcomes: parents' psychological well-being and health, the quality of parent-child relationships, and children's behavior.

Because relatively few studies have examined variations among single-parent families, I supplement the literature with a new analysis of a large, national data set: the National Survey of Families and Households (NSFH). To create the NSFH, researchers at the University of Wisconsin collected information in 1987–88 from a probability sample of over 13,000 households (Sweet, Bumpass, & Call, 1988). Unfortunately, even a data set as large as the NSFH captures only a handful of people in certain groups of interest, such as Native Americans, Asians, and gays and lesbians. Because it is not possible to draw reliable statistical inferences when sample sizes are small, I omitted these groups from consideration. My analysis is based on 1,515 single parents who were *not* in cohabiting relationships at the time of the survey. I excluded cohabiting couples because they are more like two-parent families, in many respects, than like single-parent families.

Economic Well-being

Income is a key resource for parents, allowing them to afford educational toys, travel, private lessons, and other commodities that facilitate children's educational attainment. Poverty, in contrast, increases the number of stressors with which parents and children must cope, including hunger, inadequate housing, and dangerous neighborhoods. Previous studies (Bianchi, 1995; Hernandez, 1993; Lino, 1995; McLanahan & Booth, 1989; Teachman & Paasch, 1994) have consistently found that single parents have fewer economic resources and are more likely to be poor than are married parents. Qualitative research (Arendell, 1986) has also indicated that most single mothers experience considerable economic hardship following divorce.

Studies (Hao, 1996; Meyer & Garasky, 1993) have also shown, however, that single-parent families vary in their standards of living. Single fathers, for example, earn more income, have more accumulated assets, and are less likely to be poor than are single mothers. Similarly, qualitative research (Richards & Schmiege, 1993) has indicated that single mothers report more financial problems than do single fathers, suggesting that single mothers experience greater adversity. In relation to race, Garfinkel and McLanahan (1986) found that white single mothers have more income than African American single mothers (except among the never married, for whom racial differences are negligible). In addition, Garfinkel and McLanahan stated that widowed mothers tend to have the highest incomes, followed, in turn, by those who are divorced, separated, and never married. Hao (1996) found an identical rank order in relation to single mothers' accumulated wealth. In an Australian study, Amato and Partridge (1987) noted that widowed mothers report fewer economic problems and are more likely to own their own homes than are divorced mothers. In relation to living arrangements, young single mothers who remain in their mothers' homes are less likely to go on welfare than are those who live on their own, presumably because they benefit from their mothers' economic resources (Brooks-Gunn & Furstenburg, 1986).

To gain further insight into these variations, I relied on two indicators of economic well-being in the NSFH. The first indicator was the single parent's annual income from all sources, and ranged from $0 to over $100,000. Because the distribution was severely skewed, I collapsed the top 1% of scores at the 99th percentile ($65,000). This procedure decreased the skewness substantially, thus making the data amenable to regression analysis.

The second indicator consisted of family income (the combined income of all family members in the household) divided by the poverty threshold for the family in 1988. Poverty thresholds were based on the number of related adults and children living together. Economists usually refer to this statistic as an income-to-needs ratio. These ratios ranged from 0 to 8.61. Once again, I collapsed the top 1% of scores before I conducted the main analysis. The resulting mean was 1.54, indicating that the income of the average single-parent family was only 54% above the poverty line. To place this figure in perspective, the mean for two-parent families was 4.05, and only 7% of single-parent families had income-to-needs ratios of this magnitude or higher.

Table 8.1 shows the annual incomes (column 1) and income-to-needs ratios (column 2) of single parents by the six dimensions of diversity. The figures in the table are adjusted means, derived from an analysis of covariance. For example, the figures

in rows 1 and 2 (column 1) are the mean income levels one would expect if mothers' and fathers' other characteristics (race, education, marital status, age, and living arrangements) were distributed identically. The significance tests indicate whether the categorical variable is related, overall, to the economic well-being variables.

Column 1 reveals that the incomes of single parents who were fathers, college graduates, divorced, aged 35 years or older, and living alone were the highest, and the incomes of single parents who were mothers, high school dropouts, separated or

TABLE 8.1
Single Parents' Economic Well-being and Residential Mobility, by Six Dimensions of Family Diversity

Dimension	Parent's Total Income	Family's Income Needs Ratio	Moves in Past Five Years
Gender			
Female	$11,200***	1.43***	1.73***
Male	$16,896	2.69	1.19
Race			
African American	$11,322	1.32***	1.24***
White	$12,644	1.69	1.89
Latino	$12,539	1.44	1.52
Education			
High school dropout	$7,362***	.97***	1.07
High school graduate	$11,449	1.38	1.53
Some college	$14,265	1.84	1.61
College graduate	$24,966	3.03	1.47
Marital Status			
Separated	$10,321***	1.18***	1.80**
Divorced	$14,533	1.72	1.83
Widowed	$11,838	1.49	1.35
Never married	$10,497	1.47	1.40
Age			
15–24	$6,580***	1.11***	2.66***
25–34	$11,467	1.34	1.97
35–44	$16,103	1.76	.92
45+	$14,549	1.93	.59
Living Arrangement			
With kin	$9,333**	1.75	.56***
Alone	$12,618	1.53	1.84
Grand mean	$12,213	1.54	1.63
(SD)	($11,593)	(1.43)	(2.11)

* Overall difference across categories is significant at $p < .05$.
** Overall difference across categories is significant at $p < .01$.
*** Overall difference across categories is significant at $p < .001$.

Source: 1987–88 National Survey of Families and Households. Sample size = 1,515.

never married, aged 24 years or younger, and living with kin were the lowest. The role of education in determining income was especially noteworthy, with college graduates earning $24,966 per year compared with $7,362 for high school dropouts. The fact that those who were living with kin earned less than those who were living on their own suggests that economic necessity is a motive for sharing a residence.

Column 2 shows that the highest standard of living was found among single parents who were fathers, white, college graduates, divorced, and aged 45 years or older, whereas the lowest standard of living was found among single parents who were mothers, African American, high school dropouts, separated, and aged 24 years or younger. Once again, the effect of education was striking: The typical single parent without a high school diploma lived slightly below the poverty threshold, whereas the typical single parent with a college education lived far above the poverty threshold. Finally, it is noteworthy that, although single parents who were living with kin had less personal income, their mean income-to-needs ratio was no lower than that of other single parents (because of the additional income contributed by other adult relatives in the household). This finding suggests that sharing accommodations with kin is an effective strategy of single parents for improving their standard of living.

Overall, 47% of the single parents in the sample lived in poverty. To see how poverty varied with the six characteristics shown in Table 8.1, I created a logistic multiple regression model to estimate the probability of being poor for certain groups of parents. The sharpest differences appeared for gender and education. For example, a single mother with the modal characteristics in the sample (that is, white, a high school graduate, divorced, aged 27–34, and living alone) had a .49 probability of being poor, compared to only .17 for a single father with the same characteristics. In relation to *education,* a single mother without a high school degree who was divorced, aged 27–34, and living alone had a .72 probability of being poor; in contrast, a single mother who was identical in other respects but had a college degree had only a .17 probability of being poor.

I also estimated the probability of poverty for individuals who jointly occupied the least-advantaged categories (African American, high school dropout, separated, under age 25, and living alone) and for those who jointly occupied the most advantaged categories (white, college graduate, divorced, 45 years or older, and living with kin). For the most disadvantaged group, the probability of being poor was .96 for a single mother and .86 for a single father. In contrast, for the most advantaged group, the probability of being poor was .10 for a single mother and .02 for a single father. These dramatic differences indicate that living in poverty is extremely likely for some single parents and their children, but extremely unlikely for others. More generally, these results demonstrate that the effects of gender, race, and class (along with the other dimensions of diversity) can combine to create a substantial disadvantage for some parents and their children.

Residential Instability

Moving is not only stressful (particularly if it is involuntary), but disruptive of parents' and children's social networks and access to community resources. For children, moving often involves changing schools, which can have a negative impact on their school performance (McLanahan & Sandefur, 1994). Compared with married parents, single parents are more likely to be renters, have housing that is smaller and of poorer quality, and spend a greater proportion of their incomes on housing (Bianchi, 1995; Lino, 1995). Consequently, single parents are more likely than married parents to relocate because they can no longer afford their current accommodations, are evicted, or are dissatisfied with their homes or neighborhoods (McLanahan & Sandefur, 1994).

Table 8.1 (column 3) presents information on the frequency of moves during the previous five years. In the NSFH sample, the number of moves ranged from 0 to 20, but only 8% of the single parents moved five or more times (that is, once per year or more often). The typical single parent moved one to two times during this period. Those who moved the most often were mothers, white, separated or divorced, relatively young, and living alone. Moving was especially common among single parents aged 24 or younger, who moved about four times as often as those aged 45 or older. Single parents who lived alone moved about three times as often as those who lived with kin. These results indicate that single parents vary considerably in the extent to which they and their children must deal with the stress of moving.

Psychological Well-being and Health

How psychological well-being and health may vary among single parents is not well understood. Some studies have found no gender differences in adjustment to divorce (Booth & Amato, 1991). In relation to race, a few studies have suggested that divorce has fewer negative consequences for African American adults than for white adults (Kitson & Morgan, 1991). As for education, Acock and Demo (1994) found that single mothers' education is positively related to self-esteem and health, and Booth and Amato found that education is positively associated with psychological well-being following divorce. With regard to marital status, Acock and Demo found no differences between divorced and never-married mothers on measures of psychological well-being and health. However, Amato and Partridge (1987) found that widowed mothers are more likely than divorced mothers to report feeling depressed or tired and that older single mothers report more health problems than do younger single mothers.

Table 8.2 presents data on three indicators of parents' psychological and physical well-being. The first is a self-rating of overall life happiness on a 7-point scale (from 1 = *not very happy* to 7 = *very happy*). The second is a 10-item depression scale, based on the number of days during the previous week that the respondents had various symptoms of depression. Scores range from 1 to 7, with high scores indicating greater levels of depression. The third is a self-rating of overall physical health on a 5-point scale (1 = *very poor,* 5 = *excellent*).

The bottom row of Table 8.2 indicates that the typical single parent reported being moderately happy and healthy and described relatively few

symptoms of depression. Given the difficulties of raising children alone, as well as the low standard of living of many single parents, one might have expected more negative results. Furthermore, these generally positive ratings did not vary significantly with single parents' gender or race.

Education was negatively associated with depression and positively associated with physical health, with high school dropouts reporting the poorest outcomes and college graduates reporting the best. College graduates also reported the most happiness, although this difference was not significant. Other investigators have noted that well-educated individuals, in general, tend to have better mental health, not only because they have more economic resources, but because they have a greater sense of control over their lives (Ross & Wu, 1995).

Marital status was related to two outcomes, with separated parents showing the lowest level of happiness and the highest level of depression. Some recently separated parents may be suffering from the aftermath of marital disruption, and other parents may find the state of being separated (as opposed to divorced) to be ambiguous and, hence, stressful. Although widowed parents also reported a relatively low level of happiness, they reported the lowest level of depression.

Age was related to depression, with symptoms being the highest among those aged 24 or younger and the lowest among those aged 35 to 44. In addition, older respondents reported the poorest physical health.

Relatives can be a source of friction for single parents, as well as a source of support. Indeed, some studies have found that tension can outweigh the benefits of involvement with kin, especially when kin interfere with parenting (Milardo, 1987). In contrast, others have emphasized the beneficial aspects of living with kin, especially for African American single mothers (Wilson, 1989). Consistent with this latter view, the NSFH data indicate that single parents who lived with other adult relatives reported greater happiness and physical health and fewer symptoms of depression than those who lived alone. Living with kin can lighten the economic burdens of single parents and provide ready access to social

TABLE 8.2
Single Parents' Psychological Well-being, by Six Dimensions of Family Diversity

Dimension	Happiness	Depression	Health
Gender			
Female	4.99	1.76	3.94
Male	5.11	1.64	4.00
Race			
African American	5.01	1.85	3.98
White	4.99	1.71	3.96
Latino	5.16	1.55	3.82
Education			
High school dropout	5.02	2.09***	3.75***
High school graduate	4.93	1.80	3.95
Some college	5.07	1.44	4.04
College graduate	5.16	1.31	4.35
Marital Status			
Separated	4.67***	2.04**	3.95
Divorced	5.05	1.72	3.95
Widowed	4.76	1.59	3.97
Never married	5.17	1.65	3.95
Age			
15–24	5.09	1.95*	4.00*
25–34	5.06	1.75	3.97
35–44	4.96	1.55	3.97
45+	4.84	1.80	3.77
Living Arrangement			
With kin	5.24*	1.40*	4.08*
Alone	4.96	1.80	3.92
Grand Mean	5.01	1.74	3.95
(SD)	(1.40)	(1.57)	(.84)

* Overall difference across categories is significant at $p < .05$.
** Overall difference across categories is significant at $p < .01$.
*** Overall difference across categories is significant at $p < .001$.

Source: 1987–88 National Survey of Families and Households. Sample size = 1,515.

support and assistance with child care. These results suggest that the benefits of living with kin outweigh the costs for many single mothers.

Parent-Child Relationships

Qualitative research yields a mixed picture of parent-child relationships in single-parent families: Some studies have found that tense relationships are common, especially following divorce or parental remarriage (Wallerstein & Kelly, 1980), whereas others have found that many children (especially adolescents) develop close relationships with single parents, sometimes acting as confidants (Lewin, 1993; Weiss, 1979). One study (Buchanan, Maccoby, & Dornbusch, 1996) indicated that rela-

tionships in which adolescents become confidants of single parents are not harmful, provided that the adolescents do not feel burdened and responsible for the parents.

How do parent-child relationships vary with characteristics of single-parent families? In relation to gender, Risman (1986) found that most single fathers feel comfortable as parents and have close relationships with their children. Similarly Buchanan et al. (1996) found that although most adolescents feel close to their residential parents, regardless of the parents' gender, both sons and daughters feel somewhat closer to their single mothers than to their single fathers. Consistent with this latter finding, Downey and Powell (1993) found that children of both genders report a more supportive home environment if they live with single mothers than with single fathers. In contrast, Luepnitz (1982) and Santrock and Warshak (1979) found few differences between single mothers and single fathers in their affective involvement with children.

In relation to marital status, Acock and Demo (1994) observed few differences between divorced mothers' and never-married mothers' relationships with children, but Demo and Acock (1993) noted that divorced mothers seem to assign more chores to their children than do never-married mothers. Sack (1985) found that divorced parents are more likely than widowed parents to use harsh punishment. In relation to age, common sense suggests that younger parents have fewer parenting skills than do older parents. However, Furstenberg (1976) found that the age of unmarried mothers is unrelated to their satisfaction with parenting or to their performance as parents. Finally, some evidence suggests that having extended kin in the household improves the parenting skills of single mothers (Wilson, 1989) and the amount of control and supervision these mothers exercise over their children (Dornbusch et al., 1985; Thomson, McLanahan, & Curtin, 1992).

To explore this issue further, Table 8.3 presents data on single parents' relationships with children. The first column refers to parents' ratings of how often they have talks with their children (from 1 = *rarely* to 6 = *almost every day*). The second and third columns indicate how often parents praise and

TABLE 8.3
Single Parents' Relationships With Children, by Six Dimensions of Family Diversity

Dimension	Talk	Praise	Hug	Feel Close	TV Rules
Gender					
Female	4.67**	3.60***	3.71***	6.24*	.98*
Male	4.22	3.35	3.35	6.02	.80
Race					
African American	4.53	3.52	3.58**	6.38***	.98
White	4.67	3.61	3.74	6.10	.94
Latino	4.71	3.61	3.62	6.44	.89
Education					
High school dropout	4.47***	3.53***	3.57**	6.19	.82***
High school graduate	4.58	3.54	3.70	6.27	.94
Some college	4.76	3.64	3.74	6.19	1.04
College graduate	4.97	3.74	3.78	6.25	1.21
Marital Status					
Separated	4.68	3.61***	3.72	6.18	.98
Divorced	4.60	3.64	3.65	6.26	.92
Widowed	4.69	3.49	3.76	6.24	1.04
Never married	4.62	3.43	3.63	6.21	1.02
Age					
15–24	4.53	3.55	3.78	6.28	.85
25–34	4.75	3.57	3.70	6.22	1.03
35–44	4.60	3.59	3.66	6.26	.91
45+	4.46	3.57	3.58	6.15	.99
Living Arrangement					
With kin	4.72	3.68	3.72	6.26	.83
Alone	4.63	3.58	3.67	6.23	.96
Grand Mean	4.63	3.58	3.67	6.23	.96
(SD)	(1.31)	(.58)	(.61)	(1.04)	(.48)

* Overall difference across categories is significant at $p < .05$.
** Overall difference across categories is significant at $p < .01$.
*** Overall difference across categories is significant at $p < .001$.

Source: 1987–88 National Survey of Families and Households. Sample size = 1,515.

hug their children, respectively (from 1 = *never* to 4 = *very often*). The fourth column shows parents' ratings of how close they feel to their children on a 7-point scale (from 1 = *not very close* to 7 = *very close*). For this particular item, parents provided separate ratings for each child in the household, so I used the mean rating across all children. Finally, the fifth column reflects the extent to which parents have rules about (1) how much television their children can watch, and (2) what types of television programs their children can watch (from 0 = *no rules,* 1 = *rules about amount or type of programs,* 2 = *rules about both*). Although not shown in the table, the analysis controlled for the number of children in the family, the age of the youngest child in the family, and whether the parent had a teenage child.

Table 8.3 shows that single mothers reported talking with, praising, and hugging their children more frequently than did single fathers and felt closer to their children. At the same time, single mothers were more likely than single fathers to regulate their children's television use. And although not reported in the table, single mothers spent more time with their children and provided more help with homework, although these trends were only marginally significant ($p < .10$). These results suggest that single mothers behave in a more authoritative fashion than do single fathers, that is, by combining warmth and firm (but not coercive) control—a combination generally associated with positive child outcomes (Maccoby & Martin, 1983).

The results for race were mixed. On the one hand, the African American single parents reported hugging their children the least often. On the other hand, the African American and Hispanic parents reported feeling closer to their children than did the white parents. Overall, these results suggest that there are no consistent racial differences in parent-child relationships.

The results for education were straightforward: Education was positively associated with talking with, praising, and hugging children. In addition, well-educated parents were more likely to regulate their children's television viewing than were poorly educated parents. And although not reported in the table, education was positively associated with

helping children with homework ($p < .05$) and negatively associated with hitting or spanking children ($p < .05$). This pattern indicates that education facilitates authoritative parenting among single parents, although it does not affect feelings of closeness to children.

Children's Behavior

Although many studies have compared children in two-parent and single-parent families, few have considered how children's outcomes vary within single-parent families. Buchanan et al. (1996) found no differences in depression or school performance between adolescents who lived with their mothers and those who lived with their fathers; however, the adolescents reported more behavioral problems (such as substance use) when they lived with their fathers. Downey and Powell (1993) indicated that children in single-father families outperformed children in single-mother families on standardized achievement tests. But with income controlled, children in single-mother families did better; this finding suggests that if mothers had the same economic resources as fathers, then children in single-mother families would outperform children in single-father families. In contrast, McLanahan and Sandefur (1994) found no differences between single-mother and single-father families in children's educational attainment, a finding that is consistent with reviews of the literature by Amato and Keith (1991) and Warshak (1986).

In relation to race, Acock and Demo (1994) noted that white single mothers reported lower child well-being than did African American single mothers. Similarly, McLanahan and Sandefur (1994) found, after controlling for parents' education, that white offspring from single-parent families were more likely to drop out of high school than were African American offspring. These results suggest that African American children adjust better than white children to life in single-parent families, although the explanation for this difference is not clear.

Consistent evidence exists for parental education. Acock and Demo (1994), Elder and Russell (1994), and McLanahan and Sandefur (1994) all showed that education among single mothers is positively correlated with children's global well-being, socioemotional development, and academic performance. Several studies (such as Amato & Keith, 1991; McLanahan & Sandefur, 1994) have suggested that children with widowed parents suffer fewer problems than do children with divorced parents and children born outside marriage. Cooksey (1997) found that children with divorced mothers have higher cognitive scores than do children with never-married mothers.

Furstenberg (1976) found that unmarried mothers' age is unrelated to children's behavioral problems. In relation to living arrangements, two studies (Dornbusch et al., 1985; Kellam, Ensminger, & Turner, 1977) showed that children are better adjusted when extended kin are present in their households. Stolba and Amato (1993) found that mothers rated their adolescent children's behavior more positively when they lived with an additional adult, primarily when the additional adult was a grandparent of the same gender as the child. Other studies, however, did not support the notion that the presence of extended kin in the household improves children's outcomes (McLanahan & Sandefur, 1994).

As part of the NSFH, parents were asked whether any of their children had the following problems: repeating a grade in school, seeing the child's teacher or principal because of a problem at school, running away from home, getting in trouble with the police, seeing a doctor or therapist about an emotional problem, and being especially difficult to raise. To simplify the analysis, I summed the number of problems to produce an overall score ranging from 0 to 6. It should be noted that reports of problems were relatively uncommon, with the average single parent reporting about one problem for his or her children, overall.

Although not shown in a table, this indicator was related significantly to three characteristics of single parents. First, white parents reported more problems than did African American or Latino parents ($p < .05$), a result that is consistent with the finding, noted earlier, that white parents report feeling slightly less close to their children than do other single parents. It is possible that white children have more problems because single-parent families are more normative among African Americans or because African American single parents receive stronger support from their kin. Second, parental education was negatively associated with the number of problems reported by parents ($p < .01$). This finding is consistent with the trend, noted earlier, for well-educated parents to have authoritative relationships with children. If well-educated single parents tend to behave in an authoritative fashion, then it is not surprising that they report relatively few behavioral problems among their children. Third, parents who lived with other adult kin reported fewer problems, although this finding was true only for adolescents ($p < .05$).

Summary

Most of the results of my analysis of the NSFH data are consistent with previous studies of single parents. But because previous studies are few in number, the present results help to consolidate certain findings and extend others.

Parental Gender. Compared with single mothers, single fathers have more resources and experience fewer sources of stress, as reflected in their higher incomes, higher standards of living, and greater residential stability. Of course, single fathers are still disadvantaged relative to married fathers, because their standard of living is only two-thirds that of married fathers. Single mothers are even worse off, however, because their standard of living is only about half that of single fathers. But in spite of their greater economic hardship, single mothers appear to be as happy with their lives, no more depressed than, and as healthy as single fathers. Furthermore, single mothers seem to have more authoritative relationships with their children, as reflected in more talking, praise, affection, and rule setting. From a child's perspective, therefore, it seems that single fathers tend to offer greater economic resources, whereas single mothers tend to offer greater interpersonal resources. That both types of resources are important for children's development may explain why single mothers' and single fathers' reports of their children's behavioral problems do not differ.

Race and Ethnicity. Racial and ethnic variations among single parents are not pronounced. African American single parents have the lowest income-to-needs ratio but the highest level of residential stability. In contrast, white single parents have the highest income-to-needs ratio but the lowest level of residential stability. Latinos fall between the other two groups on both outcomes. No differences are apparent among whites, African Americans, and Latinos on measures of parents' happiness, depression, and health. Although children are likely to benefit from the higher standard of living found in white households, they may experience disruption and tension associated with frequent moving. Perhaps partly for this reason, white parents report more behavioral problems in their children than do African American or Latino parents.

Parental Education. Parental education is one of the strongest predictors of well-being. Highly educated single parents earn more money and have a higher standard of living than do poorly educated single parents. Perhaps because they have more economic resources, highly educated single parents also experience fewer symptoms of depression, have better health, describe more authoritative relationships with their children, and report fewer behavioral problems in their children.

Marital Status. Divorced parents are the most successful economically, whereas separated parents are the least successful. However, both divorced and separated parents tend to move more often than do widowed or married parents. Separated parents also report the lowest levels of personal happiness and the most symptoms of depression. Separated parents may find themselves in an ambiguous social status, may still be emotionally attached to their spouses, and may not have had time to recover from the emotional strain of the disrupted relationship. Furthermore, many separated mothers may not yet have had a child-support award. Nevertheless, in spite of these differences, parents' marital status has few implications for parent-child relationships or children's behavioral problems.

Parental Age. Younger single parents appear to have fewer resources and more sources of stress than do older single parents. Younger single parents, compared with their older counterparts, earn less income, have a lower standard of living, and move more frequently. Given these findings, it is not surprising that they also report the most symptoms of depression. Their relationships with their children, however, do not appear to suffer.

Living Arrangements. Single parents who live with kin tend to earn less money than do other single parents, but their standard of living is no lower than that of other single parents. Single parents who live with kin also report greater happiness, less depression, and better physical health, perhaps because of the emotional support and companionship provided by other adults in their households. Finally, single parents who live with kin report few behavioral problems among their adolescent children, probably because of the greater supervision available in extended households—especially at a time when children are the most difficult to monitor. Of course, sharing accommodations with kin can also be a source of stress: Households may be crowded, grandparents may feel burdened, and kin may interfere with the parents' child-rearing methods. Because single parents can move out, however, the cases of coresidence in the NSFH data may be ones in which intergenerational ties were especially strong and harmonious in the first place. Overall, these results indicate that living with kin provides beneficial resources to at least some single parents and their children.

CONCLUSIONS

In this chapter, I have explored how several variations within single-parent families are related to resources, stressors, personal well-being, the quality of family relationships, and child outcomes. Unfortunately, certain types of single-parent families are largely absent from the research literature. For example, little is known about gay and lesbian single parents and how their experiences may differ from those of heterosexual single parents. One exception is the study by Lewin (1993), which showed that lesbian single mothers experience some concerns that heterosexual single mothers do not share (for example, the fear that their children will be ostracized). Lewin also found, however, that lesbian single mothers are similar to their heterosexual counterparts in many others ways (for instance, in the extent to which they rely on their own parents for support).

Furthermore, relatively little is known about single parenthood among racial-ethnic groups other than African Americans and whites, including Mexican Americans, Puerto Ricans, Cuban Americans, Asian Americans, and Native Americans. With regard to the latter group, Native American single parents tend to have less education, lower rates of labor force participation, higher rates of welfare use, and a greater likelihood of being poor than do married Native American parents (Yellowbird & Snipp, 1994). But how the particular characteristics of Native American culture affect the dynamics of single parenthood is unclear. In a rare study of young, single Navaho mothers, Dalla and Gamble (1997) found that those who were the most committed to parenting also had a strong desire to pass their cultural heritage on to their children. More qualitative, descriptive studies, as well as quantitative, comparative studies, are necessary to understand the similarities and differences in the experiences and situations of single parents in these underrepresented racial and ethnic groups.

Understanding the variability within single-parent families is important, not only to gain a deeper conceptual understanding of family diversity, but also to guide the formulation of social policy. A focus on resources and stressors suggests that some single parents are in greater need of assistance than are others. Policy initiatives can be targeted more effectively if policy makers have a better understanding of which families are the most at risk of various problems and which families are coping well.

For example, the analysis of the NSFH data in this chapter indicates that educational attainment is a strong predictor of the economic well-being of single mothers. Education also predicts higher psychological well-being, better parent-child relationships, and fewer behavioral problems among children. Kates (1995) indicated that attending college is an effective way for single parents to escape poverty. Current welfare policies allow single parents two years before their benefits are discontinued—an insufficient time to complete a bachelor's degree. Given the importance of education, it makes sense to extend the period of public assistance, provided that single parents are pursuing college degrees and making reasonable progress. This change would be in the interest of the state as well, because research has shown that single mothers with college degrees are rarely forced to rely on public assistance (Burtless, 1977).

The present results also suggest that children in single-father families have a considerably higher standard of living than do children in single-mother families. This difference reflects the continued gender stratification of U.S. society, with women earning less than men. Many of the disadvantages experienced by children with single mothers will be ameliorated only when women, in general, achieve parity with men in earnings. In the meantime, programs that raise the income earning potential of poor single mothers, especially ones that combine job training, subsidized child care, health benefits, and tax credits to supplement low wages, are necessary (Edin & Lein, 1996; Larner, Terman, & Behrman, 1997).

In spite of economic disadvantage, children who live with single mothers experience more authoritative parenting than do children who live with single fathers. Although most single fathers appear to be competent parents, many are handicapped by their relative lack of involvement in child care before they became single parents. As I noted earlier, the number of single-father families is increasing. Consequently, many men need to recognize that one day they may have primary responsibility for the care of their children, either as single custodial fathers or as fathers with joint physical custody. Educational programs that encourage men to share child care with women would not only be fair to employed married mothers, but also would improve the well-being of children in *all* types of families.

REFERENCES

Acock, A. C., & Demo, D. H. (1994). *Family diversity and well-being.* Thousand Oaks, CA: Sage.

Amato, P. R. (1995). Single parent households as settings for children's development, well-being, and attainment: A social network/resources perspective. *Sociological Studies of Children, 7,* 19–47.

Amato, P. R., & Keith, B. (1991). Parental divorce and the well-being of children: A meta-analysis. *Psychological Bulletin, 110,* 26–46.

Amato, P. R., & Partridge, S. (1987). Widows and divorcees with dependent children: Material, personal, family, and social well-being. *Family Relations, 36,* 316–320.

Arendell, T. (1986). *Mothers and divorce: Legal, economic, and social dilemmas.* Berkeley: University of California Press.

Bean, F. D., & Tienda, M. (1992). *The Hispanic population of the United States.* New York: Russell Sage Foundation.

Bianchi, S. M. (1995). The changing demographic and socioeconomic characteristics of single-parent families. *Marriage and Family Review, 20,* 71–97.

Booth, A., & Amato, P. R. (1991). Divorce and psychological stress. *Journal of Health and Social Behavior, 32,* 396–407.

Brooks-Gunn, J., & Furstenburg, F. F., Jr. (1986). The children of adolescent mothers: Physical, academic, and psychological outcomes. *Developmental Review, 6,* 224– 251.

Buchanan, C. M., Maccoby, E. E., & Dornbusch, S. M. (1996). *Adolescents after divorce.* Cambridge, MA: Harvard University Press.

Bumpass, L., & Sweet, J. (1989). Children's experiences in single-parent families: Implications of cohabitation and marital transitions. *Family Planning Perspectives, 21,* 256–260.

Burtless, G. T. (1997). Welfare recipients' job skills and employment prospects. *The Future of Children, 7,* 39–51.

Burton, L. M., & Bengtson, V. L. (1985). Black grandmothers: Issues of timing and continuity of roles. In V. L. Bengtson & J. F. Robertson (Eds.), *Grandparenthood* (pp. 61–77). Beverly Hills, CA: Sage.

Cooksey, E. C. (1997). Consequences of young mothers' marital histories for children's development. *Journal of Marriage and the Family, 59,* 245–261.

Dalla, R. L., & Gamble, W. C. (1997). Exploring factors related to parenting competence among Navajo teenage mothers: Dual techniques of inquiry. *Family Relations, 46,* 113–121.

Demo D. H., & Acock, A. C. (1993). Family diversity and the division of domestic labor: How much have things really changed? *Family Relations, 42,* 323–331.

Dornbusch, S. M., Carlsmith, J. M., Bushwall, S. J., Ritter, P. L., Leiderman, H., Hastorf, A. H., & Gross, R. T. (1985). Single parents, extended households, and the control of adolescents. *Child Development, 56,* 326–341.

Downey, D., & Powell, B. (1993). Do children in single-parent households fare better living with same-sex parents? *Journal of Marriage and the Family, 55,* 55–71.

Edin, K., & Lein, L. (1996). Work, welfare, and single mothers' economic survival strategies. *American Sociological Review, 61,* 253–266.

Eggebeen, D. J., & Lichter, D. T. (1991). Race, family structure, and changing poverty among American children. *American Sociological Review, 56,* 801–817.

Eggebeen, D. J., Snyder, A. R., & Manning, W. D. (1996). Children in single father families in demographic perspective. *Journal of Family Issues, 17,* 441–465.

Elder, G. H., & Russell, S. T. (1994). Academic performance and future aspirations. In R. L. Simons (Ed.), *Understanding differences between divorced and intact families* (pp. 176–192). Thousand Oaks, CA: Sage.

Furstenberg, F. F., Jr. (1976). *Unplanned parenthood.* New York: Free Press.

Furstenberg, F. F., Jr., & Cherlin, A. (1991). *Divided families: What happens to children when parents part.* Cambridge, MA: Harvard University Press.

Garfinkel, I., & McLanahan. S. (1986). *Single mothers and their children.* Washington, DC: Urban Institute.

Glendon, M. A. (1989). *The transformation of family law.* Chicago: University of Chicago Press.

Glenn, N. D. (1996). Values, attitudes, and the state of American marriage. In D. Popenoe, J. B. Elshtain, & D. Blankenhorn (Eds.), *Promises to keep: Decline and renewal of marriage in America* (pp. 15–34). Lanham, MD: Rowman & Littlefield.

Grief, G. L. (1985). *Single fathers.* Lexington, MA: Lexington Books.

Hao, L. (1996). Family structure, private transfers, and the economic well-being of families with children. *Social Forces, 75,* 269–292.

Hernandez, D. (1993). *America's children.* New York: Russell Sage Foundation.

Hetherington, E. M., & Blechman, E. A. (Eds.). (1996). *Stress, coping, and resiliency in children and families.* Mahwah, NJ: Lawrence Erlbaum.

Kates, E. (1995). Escaping poverty: The promise of higher education. *Social Policy Report, Society for Research in Child Development, 9,* 1–21.

Kellam, S. G., Ensminger, M. E., & Turner, R. J. (1977). Family structure and the mental health of children. *Archives of General Psychiatry, 34,* 1012–1022.

Kitson, G. C., & Morgan, L. A. (1991). The multiple consequences of divorce. In A. Booth (Ed.), *Contemporary families: Looking forward, looking back* (pp. 150–161). Minneapolis, MN: National Council on Family Relations.

Larner, M. B., Terman, D. L., & Behrman, R. E. (1997). Welfare to work: Analysis and recommendations. *The Future of Children, 7,* 4–19.

Lewin, E. (1993). *Lesbian mothers: Accounts of gender in American culture.* Ithaca, NY: Cornell University Press.

Leupnitz, D. A. (1982). *Child custody.* Lexington, MA: D. C. Health.

Lino, M. (1995). The economics of single parenthood: Past research and future directions. *Marriage and Family Review, 20,* 99–114.

Maccoby, E., & Martin, J. (1983). Socialization in the context of the family: Parent-child interaction. In P. H. Mussen (Series Ed.) & E. M. Hetherington (Vol. Ed.), *Handbook of child psychology: Vol. 4. Socialization, personality, and social development* (4th ed., pp. 1–101). New York: John Wiley.

Manning, W. D., & Smock, P. J. (1997). Children's living arrangements in unmarried-mother families. *Journal of Family Issues, 18,* 526–544.

McLanahan, S. S. (1983). Family structure and stress: A longitudinal comparison of two-parent and female-headed families. *Journal of Marriage and the Family, 45,* 347–357.

McLanahan, S. S., & Booth, K. (1989). Mother-only families: Problems, prospects, and politics. *Journal of Marriage and the Family, 51,* 557–580.

McLanahan, S. S., & Sandefur, G. (1994). *Growing up with a single parent.* Cambridge, MA: Harvard University Press.

Meyer, D. R., & Garasky, S. (1993). Custodial fathers: Myths, realities, and child support policies. *Journal of Marriage and the Family, 55,* 73–87.

Milardo, R. M. (1987). Changes in social networks of women and men following divorce: A review. *Journal of Family Issues, 8,* 78–96.

Moynihan, D. P. (1965). *The Negro family: The case for notional action.* Washington DC: Office of Policy Planning and Research, U.S. Department of Labor.

Moynihan, D. P. (1986). *Family and nation.* San Diego, CA: Harcourt Brace Jovanovich.

Parsons, T., & Bales, R. F. (1955). *Family socialization and interaction process.* Glencoe, IL: Free Press.

Popenoe, D. (1995). *Life without father.* New York: Free Press.

Richards, L. N., & Schmiege, C. J. (1993). Problems and strengths of single-parent families. *Family Relations, 42,* 277–285.

Risman, B. J. (1986). Can men "mother"? Life as a single father. *Family Relations, 35,* 95–102.

Ross, C. E., & Wu, C. (1995). The links between education and health. *American Sociological Review, 60,* 719–745.

Sack, W. H. (1985). The single-parent family and abusive child punishment. *American Journal of Orthopsychiatry, 55,* 252–259.

Santrock, J. W., & Warshak, R. A. (1979). Father custody and social development in boys and girls. *Journal of Social Issues, 35,* 112–135.

Spain, D., & Bianchi, S. M. (1996). *Balancing act: Motherhood, marriage, and employment among American women.* New York: Russell Sage Foundation.

Stack, C. (1974). *All our kin: Strategies for survival in a Black community.* New York: Harper & Row.

Staples, R., & Johnson, L. B. (1993). *Black families at the crossroad.* San Francisco: Jossey-Bass.

Stolba, A., & Amato, P. R. (1993). Extended single-parent households and children's behavior. *Sociological Quarterly, 34,* 543–549.

Sweet, J., Bumpass, L., & Call, V. (1988). *The design and content of the National Survey of Families and Households* (Working Paper NSFH-1). Madison: Center for Demography and Ecology, University of Wisconsin.

Taylor, R. J. (1994). Black American families. In R. L. Taylor (Ed.), *Minority families in the United States: A multicultural perspective* (pp. 19–46). Englewood Cliffs, NJ: Prentice Hall.

Taylor, R. J., Chatters, L. M., & Jackson, J. S. (1993). A profile of familial relations among three-generation black families. *Family Relations, 42,* 332–341.

Teachman, J. D., & Paasch, K. M. (1994). Financial impact of divorce on children and their families. *Future of Children, 4,* 61–83.

Thomson, E., McLanahan, S. S., & Curtin, R. B. (1992). Family structure, gender, and parental socialization. *Journal of Marriage and the Family, 54,* 378–378.

Uhlenberg, P. 1980. Death and the family. *Journal of Family History, 5,* 313–320.

U.S. Bureau of the Census. (1996). *Statistical Abstract of the United States: 1996* (116th ed.). Washington, DC: U.S. Government Printing Office.

Wallerstein, J. S., & Kelly, J. B. (1980). *Surviving the breakup: How children and parents cope with divorce.* London: Grant McIntyre.

Warshak, R. A. (1986). Father-custody and child development: A review and analysis of psychological research. *Behavioral Sciences and the Law, 4,* 185–202.

Weiss, R. S. (1979). *Going it alone: The family life and social situation of the single parent.* New York: Basic Books.

Weston, K. (1991). *Families we choose.* New York: Columbia University Press.

Wilson, M. N. (1989). Child development in the context of the Black extended family. *American Psychologist, 44,* 380–385.

Wilson, W. J. (1987). *The truly disadvantaged.* Chicago: University of Chicago Press.

Yellowbird, M., & Snipp, C. M. (1994). American Indian families. In R. L. Taylor (Ed.), *Minority families in the United States: A multicultural perspective* (pp. 179–201). Englewood Cliffs, NJ: Prentice Hall.

CHAPTER 9

Diversity Among Stepfamilies

E. Mavis Hetherington and Margaret Stanley-Hagan

A common assumption is that a stable family headed by two biological parents who have a strong positive marriage; support one another's parenting; and provide an authoritative parenting environment, characterized by warmth and involvement, supervision and firm discipline, and low conflict is a protective environment for children that reduces their vulnerability as they negotiate normative developmental challenges. A related popular perception is that children who are denied the opportunity to develop within such a traditional, two-parent family are doomed to live troubled lives. However, recent research on parents and children in never-married and divorced single-parent families and in stepfamilies has shown that this doom and gloom perception does not fit the real experiences of many children of single and remarried parents. Critical to children's well-being is the quality of the parenting environment provided by residential parents, regardless of whether the parents are single parents or partners in first marriages or stepfamilies. Also critical is the degree to which the children are exposed to and a part of high-conflict or abusive family relationships. In other words, family processes and the qualities of relationships are more important than family structures to the understanding of family and individual adjustment.

The negative perceptions of single-parent families and stepfamilies are due, in part, to early studies that focused on the overrepresentation of children, first, from single-parent households and later from stepfamily households in clinical populations and on the higher average rates of poor adjustment and greater psychopathology in children from these families in comparison to children in first-marriage families. However, early research was often methodologically limited, if not flawed. Longitudinal studies that could assess how families adjust

over time to each family transition were rare. Some researchers failed to measure or account for the period between the family transition and the time of assessment. Others examined family relationships, circumstances, and outcomes only in the early months of the formation of single-parent families or stepfamilies. Problems noted were assumed to be characteristic of all families with like marital structures. The focuses of analyses were often on differences between the average adjustment of parents and children in first-marriage families and their counterparts in what were considered to be nontraditional families. Again, it was not uncommon for statistical averages to be generalized to all parents and children. Largely ignored were the magnitudes of differences and the variabilities in family circumstances and relationships and in individual adjustment, both in the months immediately following family transitions and over time.

Divorce and remarriage do introduce and reintroduce stresses and risks associated with changing family roles, relationships, and circumstances (Hetherington, 1993). Each marital transition is marked by a period of disorganization, followed by a gradual restabilization of the family system and the definition of roles and relationship processes that make family life somewhat predictable. Restabilization, sometimes into a salutary pattern of family relationships, sometimes into a more dysfunctional pattern, typically takes two or three years for newly divorced families (Hetherington, 1989), but as long as five to seven years for stepfamilies (Cherlin & Furstenberg, 1994). Remarried couples divorce more rapidly and at higher rates than do couples in first marriages. That is, 60% of remarried couples divorce, and divorce rates are 50% higher in stepfamilies than in those in which no stepchildren are present (Tzeng & Mare, 1995). Thus, many members of stepfamilies face the risks associated with multiple family transitions, often with little opportunity for a period of stabilization between transitions.

In recent years, however, researchers have come to recognize great variations in the responses of adults and children to both divorce and remarriage. The course of adaptation to a family transition involves complex interactions among risks and protective factors that are often unique to each family and family member and differ at different points in the family transition. Adaptation trajectories are affected by multiple interacting factors, such as the individual characteristics of parents and children; the quality and stability of family relationships; the availability and quality of extended family supports; family histories; and the experience of concurrent changes in financial resources, employment or school, and residence. For example, children may suffer behavioral and emotional problems when they move from a two-parent family to a single-parent family, particularly if the family experiences multiple concurrent stressors like high conflict and a decline in financial resources or if the single parent is unable to provide a positive, supportive parenting environment (Hetherington, 1989; Hetherington et al., 1992). The addition of a stepparent may upset the equilibrium of a stabilized single-parent family, be met with resistance from children, and lead to disrupted family relations (Hetherington et al., 1992). On the other hand, the adjustment and general well-being of the parent and children may improve when they move from a highly conflicted, dysfunctional two-parent family to a well-functioning single-parent family or from a stressed and troubled single-parent family to a more harmonious stepfamily with greater resources (Amato, 1993; Amato & Keith, 1991a; Amato, Loomis, & Booth, 1995; Emery, 1998; Furstenberg & Cherlin, 1991; Zill, Morrison, & Coiro, 1993). Stepparents can provide practical support in the forms of finances and help with household tasks and child care. They also can become an important source of emotional support for both their spouses and stepchildren.

The focus of this chapter is on the diversity of experiences, family processes, and adjustment of family members in stepfamilies. Included are descriptions of different family histories that lead to diversity in the forms that stepfamilies take. We discuss the variability in the adjustment of individual family members and the complex individual characteristics and immediate and extended family relationships that affect adjustment trajectories. Again, the picture that emerges is one of complex interactions among potential risks and potential protective factors. Identified are ways in which stepfamily life parallels life in most families and ways in which stepfamily life can be unique. However, we turn our attention first to the theoretical perspectives that have guided, to varying degrees, the thinking and research of those who are interested in families, particularly stepfamilies.

PERSPECTIVES ON STEPFAMILIES

Although research on remarriage and stepfamilies has accelerated rapidly since 1980, it is only recently that substantial efforts have been made to build and test alternative theories on remarriage and stepfamilies (Ganong & Coleman, 1994). No single theory is preeminent in guiding research on stepfamilies, although family systems theory dominates clinical conceptualizations and practice. Most researchers combine perspectives and test hypotheses on the basis of multiple theories in their work, and many theories are interrelated. The most prevalent theories are deficit theories, sociobiological theories, personality theories, social-role theories, social-exchange theories, ecological theories, risk-and-resilience theories, and cognitive developmental theories.

Deficit Theory

As we noted in the introduction to this chapter, much of the early research on stepfamilies was based on the view that the normative and desirable family form was a nuclear family composed of a homemaker mother and a father (in a first marriage) who was the economic provider and their biological children. Deviations from this family form were assumed to be dysfunctional and to lead to problems in family relationships and deficits in the adjustment of children. Conservative contemporary family theorists, such as Popenoe (1994), who have proposed a "new familism" emphasizing family obligation and putting children first, have argued that they are not suggesting a return to a traditional nuclear family because they emphasize equal rights, power, and men's and women's commitments to work. However, although they bolster their arguments with evolutionary theory and role theory, the concerns they express about divorce and remarriage, single mothers, the absence of fathers, and stepparents' lack of investment in stepchildren suggest that they are deficit theorists in new guises.

Sociobiological Theory

This position emphasizes that human beings use reproductive strategies that increase the chances of the survival of their genes into the next generation and, hence, that parents are more invested in nurturing and protecting biological offspring than stepchildren and other nonbiologically related children. Daly and Wilson (1989, p. 83) stated that "Parental investment is a precious resource and selection must favor those parental psyches that do not squander it on nonrelatives." However, even sociobiologists who emphasize evolutionary processes would not say that warm, caring relationships cannot develop among stepkin; rather, they would emphasize that the special nature of the bond between biological parents and children makes it more difficult for unrelated parents and children to attain love and commitment.

Attachment theory, which also is based on evolutionary principles (Bowlby, 1969), would lead to similar predictions about difficulties or delays in stepparents and stepchildren forming close relationships. When behaviors of parents and infants that have evolved to promote bonding and survival of the young do not occur at the time of the formation of specific attachments in the first year, close parent-child relationships are less likely to develop. Thus, the development of a strong attachment between a stepparent and a child may be more difficult when the remarriage occurred when the child was older.

With the emphasis on procreation and sexual competitiveness in evolutionary theory, it has also

been hypothesized that puberty will trigger sexual competition between stepchildren and their parents. It has been suggested that, in the most common type of stepfamily involving a biological mother and a stepfather, the adolescent stepdaughter will be the most disruptive member of the family system and that this type of stepfamily will be most unstable (Van den Berghe, personal communication, cited in White, 1994).

Personality Theory ③

Some individuals have personality characteristics that place them at an increased risk for marital discord, instability, multiple marital transitions, and other adverse life experiences (Capaldi & Patterson, 1991; Simons, Johnson, & Lorenz, 1996). Psychological problems, such as emotionality, depression, and antisocial behavior, may precipitate difficulties in social relationships, especially in intimate relationships. Moreover, adults with these problems often select maladjusted partners, which increases their risk of marital dysfunction and dissolution. Finally, personality problems in parents that lead to marital difficulties and multiple marital transitions are also associated with inept parenting practices and behavioral problems in children. Problems in the parents' and children's adjustment are, to some extent, genetically associated (Plomin & Rendes, 1991). Thus, there may be a genetic substrate underlying links between personality problems in parents, marital instability and multiple transitions, disrupted parent-child relationships, and deviant behavior in children (Jockin, McGue, & Lykken, 1996; McGue & Lykken, 1992).

Social Role Theory 4

It has been proposed that in remarriage, the roles of stepparents with stepchildren are poorly defined (Cherlin, 1978). The behavioral norms and responsibilities of stepparents are not institutionalized, and both the normative and legal obligations of stepparents and stepchildren are considerably fewer than those of biological parents and children (Fine, 1994; White, 1994). Thus, role ambiguity will contribute to more difficulties and less consensus in negotiating family relationships in stepfamilies, and members of stepfamilies will be less effective in providing support to each other (White, 1994).

Social Exchange Theory

According to social exchange theory, individuals in relationships seek to maximize their resources and benefits and minimize their losses. The things exchanged or valued may include money, social and emotional support, physical appearance, sex, services like housework or child care, social status, education, and property. Costs may include debts; having children from a previous marriage; or undesirable personal attributes, such as alcoholism, physical abusiveness, low education, poor health, or few social skills. The spouses are continuously comparing the costs and benefits of their relationships to the costs and benefits of other possible relationships. These costs and benefits are ever changing as the spouses become less attractive, lose their jobs, become more educated, or increase in status or income. Remarried spouses are more practical and less romantic in what they value in relationships (Furstenberg & Spanier, 1984). Remarried women may value economic resources more because of the financial decline many experience following divorce. Both remarried men and women may value the emotional, social, and child-rearing support their spouses provide. However, because of personality traits, beliefs about relationships, or previous marital experiences, they may also be less willing to tolerate costs and more willing to divorce to seek equity. Also, unless they are young, they may face a more limited remarriage pool with fewer good marital matches available (Booth & Edwards, 1992).

Family Systems Theory

Family systems theorists emphasize that the whole family system and the relationships and functioning of subsystems and individual family members are altered when a stepfamily is formed. The greater complexity found in stepfamilies requires definitions of external boundaries involving who is or is not a member of the stepfamily and of internal boundaries involving rules about roles, alliances,

and membership in the stepfamily (Bray & Berger, 1993; Ganong & Coleman, 1994; McGoldrick & Carter, 1989; O'Connor, Hetherington, & Reiss, 1998). When families go through a transition, such as a remarriage, that involves multiple changes, stresses, and reorganization, there is a period of disruption and destabilization in family relationships and functioning, followed gradually by the emergence of a new homeostasis that may differ from that found in nuclear families in first marriages with biological children (Bray & Berger, 1993; Hetherington & Jodl, 1994). It is also possible that a homeostasis may never occur because of the fluidity of stepfamily boundaries and the frequently altering composition that occurs in stepfamilies.

Ecological Theory

Ecological theorists propose that the functioning of families, including stepfamilies, is influenced by the interaction of the family with other social systems, the larger social cultural and historical context in which it is embedded, and the overarching beliefs and values of the society (Avenevoli, Sessa, & Steinberg, 1999; Bronfenbrenner, 1986). Families in different ecological niches respond differently to remarriage and living in a stepfamily. Moreover, ecologies are dynamic, and ecological changes in residence, neighborhoods, schools, and friendship and kin networks occur following remarriage. Finally, historical changes in acceptance, beliefs, and the frequency of marital transitions influence adjustment to remarriage.

Risk-and-Resilience Theory

Remarriage and the formation of stepfamilies involve notable life changes and an increase in both positive and negative life events (Hetherington, Cox, & Cox, 1985). Remarriage can present an escape from poverty for single mothers and an opportunity to form new, gratifying supportive relationships that can promote the well-being of children and adults. It can offer a ready-made family for stepparents who want and enjoy children. However, it also can lead to increased stress, problems in family relationships, and anger and acrimony that undermine the happiness, health, and adjustment of family members (Bray & Berger, 1993; Hetherington, 1989; Hetherington & Jodl, 1994). There is great diversity in the response to remarriage and life in a stepfamily that depends on the balance between individual, familial, and extrafamilial vulnerability and protective factors (Hetherington, 1989, 1991; Werner, 1993).

Cognitive-Developmental Theory

A recent model of stepfamily adjustment, introduced by Fine and Kurdek (1994), focuses on the perceptions, attributions, expectancies, assumptions, and standards relative to stepfamily life that are constructed by stepfamily members. It suggests that the congruence in cognitions among family members influences family functioning. Cognitions about stepfamilies become clearer, more realistic, and balanced and more agreed upon over time in well-functioning stepfamilies but not in dysfunctional ones.

Most of these theories are complementary, but deficit and sociobiological theories, by postulating prototypes of family relationships, differ most from the other perspectives. Moreover, most of these theories are not limited to stepfamilies; their implications for family functioning and the well-being of family members are applicable to all families. As we do in this chapter, it is common for researchers today to draw upon multiple perspectives to provide frameworks for their work. For example, a researcher may use family systems theory to describe relationships among marital and stepparent-stepchild subsystems and the risk-and-resiliency model to address whether the qualities of family relationships undermine or support individual adjustment. Many of the results described in this chapter reflect the evolution and integration of the theories that guide current research.

Question 2

DIVERSITY IN THE NUMBER OF TRANSITIONS AND FAMILY STRUCTURES

Changes in divorce and remarriage rates over the past three decades indicate that many children today are simultaneously negotiating developmental challenges and those associated with repeated family reorganizations. The risks to both parents' and children's adjustment increase when the stability of family relationships is challenged by the loss of a family member through separation or divorce or the addition of new members through remarriage.

The demographics of divorce and remarriage reveal the diversity in both the number and types of transitions experienced by many adults and their children. The 1960s witnessed a dramatic increase in the divorce rate (Simons, 1996) and, to a lesser extent, a rise in births to single mothers. Although the divorce rate stabilized in the 1970s and has decreased slightly since then, just under half the marriages in the United States end in divorce, and 1 million children experience their parents' divorce each year (National Center for Health Statistics, 1997). Approximately 75% of men and 66% of women eventually remarry, and, as a result, the stepfamily has become the fastest-growing family type in the United States (U.S. Bureau of the Census, 1992). About half the children whose parents divorce will experience the transition into stepfamilies within four years of the separation, and 1 out of 10 children will experience at least two divorces of their residential parents before they turn 16 (Furstenberg, 1988). When rates of parental cohabitation are added to the count, the actual number of family reorganizations is even higher, because cohabitation is increasingly becoming a substitute for remarriage (Cherlin & Furstenberg, 1994; Ganong & Coleman, 1994).

The national divorce and remarriage figures mask important differences among racial and ethnic groups. African Americans are more likely than whites to bear children outside marriage; are less likely to marry; and, if married, are more likely to divorce (Demo & Acock, 1996; Tzeng & Mare, 1995; U.S. Bureau of the Census, 1992). In contrast, Hispanic whites are less likely than non-Hispanic whites to divorce after they separate. Even this trend masks differences among Hispanic Americans of different national origins. For example, divorce rates are about the same for Mexican Americans, Cuban Americans, and Anglo Americans, about 25%, but the rate for Puerto Ricans is 40%.

Both Hispanic and African American parents are less likely to remarry than are non-Hispanic whites, who make up 80% of the stepfamilies in the United States (Cherlin, 1992; Larson, 1992).

Often overlooked in the literature are the stepfamilies in which the parents and/or stepparents are gay or lesbian. Definitive numbers are unavailable, but researchers have noted that, as a result of the social movements of the past few decades (e.g., the women's movement and the gay lights movement) and the growing tolerance of family models that are different from the traditional heterosexual model, more gay and lesbian adults are seeking to become parents (Benkov, 1994). Family demographers have also suggested that a small but significant number of previously married adults are gay or lesbian parents (Benkov, 1994; Crosbie-Burnett & Helmbrecht, 1993). For these individuals, entry into intimate relationships marks the establishment of stepfamilies about which little is known.

For those in remarried families, diversity is noted not only in the number of transitions the families experience, but in the structures the families may take. Adults may or may not have been previously married, and their former relationships may have ended with the death of their spouses, a breakdown in cohabitation, or divorce. For children, the residential parents, nonresidential parents, or both may remarry. When both parents remarry, the resultant linked family system (Jacobson, 1982), or binuclear family (Ahrons, 1979), is made complex by the presence of residential or nonresidential stepsiblings and biologically and nonbiologically related extended family members, such as grandparents and stepgrandparents. Nearly 50% of new stepfamilies form blended households with children from both the wives' and husbands' previous relationships (Ganong & Coleman, 1994), and slightly more than half the remarried parents have children with their new spouses, which adds halfsiblings to their families (Bridgwood & Savage, 1993). The sheer complexity of the potential kin networks in stepfamilies represents not only a marked deviation from the composition of first marriage families, but a need to regard each stepfamily as unique in its definition and thus its challenges (Booth & Edwards, 1992; Bray, 1988; Bray, Berger,

& Boethal, 1994; Burrell, 1995; Cherlin & Furstenberg, 1994).

DIVERSE DEFINITIONS OF FAMILY

Regardless of structure, stepfamily formation offers unique challenges to family members. Unlike couples in first marriages, couples in stepfamilies work to establish positive and strong marital relationships in the presence of children. Parents may need to adjust their relationships with residential and nonresidential children. Stepparents must establish relationships with their stepchildren. Stepchildren must adjust to the addition of the stepparents and often stepsiblings, while coping with complex networks of kin and stepkin outside the households. All this is accomplished simultaneously and with limited guiding norms (Cherlin, 1978; Giles-Sims, 1984; Keshet, 1990).

The ability of the stepfamily to negotiate these tasks successfully may be related to how the remarried adults and their children and stepchildren define *family*. Research has suggested that expecting a stepfamily to fit the model of a first-marriage family or even a media-generated model of an ideal family can precipitate or exacerbate problems (Bray & Berger, 1993; Visher & Visher, 1990). Stepfamilies who successfully negotiate the challenges of family formation recognize that instant love among immediate and extended family members and instant family cohesion are difficult, if not impossible, to attain in any new family (Visher & Visher, 1990). These stepfamily members also recognize that the dynamics of relationships within stepfamilies may be different from those that are typical in first-marriage families. For example, stepparents may need to adopt parenting roles that are qualitatively different from those assumed by biological parents. Compared to the types of parenting observed in biological parent-child relationships, those associated with positive adjustment and deviant behavior in stepchildren may differ. Moreover, compared to first-married couples, who typically have the opportunity to develop martial relationships before they integrate children into their family systems, stepfamilies may have less clearly defined boundaries between concurrently developed marital and parent-child subsystems. In first marriages, the marital relationships may be the cornerstone of good family functioning; in stepfamilies, relationships between children and their parents or stepparents may be more salient.

The stepfamily's boundaries must also be flexible to accommodate relationships with nonresidential parents or children and extended family members, many of whom are not biologically related to the residential children. Given that each stepfamily is unique in the complexity of its immediate and extended family relationships and the absence of role or relationship norms, it is understandable that building a sense of family takes time. Stepfamily members who recognize this fact may be more open to defining roles and relationships that are adaptive to their unique circumstances and are likely to find the challenges in this process less frustrating.

INDIVIDUAL ADJUSTMENT: VULNERABILITY AND RESILIENCE

The course of adaptation to remarriage involves complex, dynamic interactions among risks and protective factors that are unique to each family, change at different points in the family transition, and differ for adults and children at different ages. In our discussion, we focus on some of the individual, family, and extrafamilial factors that contribute to the well-being or adjustment problems of members of stepfamilies. Despite the diversity in stepfamily structures, the primary targets of research have been stepfather families that are formed when single custodial mothers remarry. Although researchers have begun to investigate other stepfamily types, far less is known about stepmother families, blended families in which both partners bring custodial children to the marriage, or stepfamilies that are formed when parents cohabit before or instead of getting married. The discussions of individual adjustment and stepfamily relationships reflect this research balance.

Adjustment of Adults

Most of the stepfamily research to date has focused on children's adjustment, rather than the adjustment of parents and stepparents. A few studies have found evidence that, compared to their counterparts in first-marriage families, remarried parents and stepparents tend to be more depressed and report more health problems (Hetherington et al., 1992). However, when found, differences in the health and general well-being of adults in first and later marriages are small in magnitude and most evident when stepfamilies are newly forming.

Across different family structures, similar associations are found between the adjustment of adults and the quality of family relationships. Both remarried biological fathers and stepfathers fare better when they are satisfied with their marriages and are involved in family decision making (Ganong & Coleman, 1994). Women, too, report better health and general well-being when they are satisfied with their marriages. However, in contrast to men, women's well-being is linked to the number of children. The more children in the home, the more likely mothers and stepmothers are to report health problems, a gender difference that is due, perhaps, to the greater involvement of women in child care. It is interesting that, compared to remarried fathers and stepfathers, remarried mothers and stepmothers report better health when they are less responsible for decision making. It may be that, in the absence of stepfamily norms and in the face of stresses associated with complex stepfamily relationships, adherence to a traditional marital model in which the husband takes the lead in decision making is adaptive for some remarried couples. However, there is evidence that the degree to which mothers invite or tolerate the stepfathers' involvement in child rearing varies from family to family (Hetherington et al., 1992; Hetherington & Stanley-Hagan, 1995). Some mothers expect and encourage the stepfathers' involvement in discipline, whereas others report that they have mixed feelings or actively discourage the stepfathers' involvement in parenting. More research is needed to test the applicability of the traditional gender roles as they apply to stepfamilies, particularly whether perceptions of involvement in decision making include or exclude child-rearing decisions.

Stepmothers appear to have the most difficult time. Like biological mothers and fathers and stepfathers, their health is positively related to their perceptions that there marriages are positive and supportive (Ganong & Coleman, 1994). However, the more involved stepmothers are in the care and discipline of stepchildren, the worse their perceived health tends to be. Again, traditional roles may offer an explanation for this association. According to the traditional gender-role model, both women and their spouses expect that the women will assume primary child care responsibilities (Fine, Voydanoff, & Donnelly, 1993; Thomson, McLanahan, & Curtin, 1992; Whitsett & Land, 1992). However, as we previously noted, instant love and instant closeness are myths. A stepmother's efforts to discipline and control her stepchildren may be met with hostile resistance or withdrawal by them. The likelihood that the stepchildren will do so appears to increase if the biological father decreases his involvement in parenting and if the nonresidential mother is an involved parent.

In general, the evidence suggests that some newly remarried parents and stepparents experience psychological and physical problems that may be the result of stressful times as single parents, the stresses associated with the family transition, or both. However, research on restabilized stepfamilies has indicated that, with the possible exception of some stepmothers, adults in stepfamilies are no more likely to experience problems in well-being than are adults in other families and that the formation of new meaningful intimate relations enhances the adjustment of divorced parents (Hetherington & Jodl, 1994). However, although there is little evidence that being in a stepfamily promotes psychopathology in remarried adults, there is evidence that depression, antisocial behavior, and neuroticism contribute to marital dissolution and multiple marital transitions (Capaldi & Patterson, 1991; Jockin et al., 1996; Simons et al., 1996).

Adjustment of Children *Question ③*

Although the results of both cross-sectional and longitudinal studies indicate a pattern of greater problems for children in stepfamilies than in first-marriage families, these differences are relatively modest and have become smaller as marital transitions have become more common (Amato & Keith, 1991a). In addition, for most children, disruptions in well-being are neither severe nor long lasting. Researchers who have compared the mean ratings of the adjustment of children in stepfamilies to that of children in first-marriage families have found that the former are more likely to exhibit behavioral and emotional problems, poorer academic achievement, lower social competence and social responsibility, and lower self-esteem (Amato & Keith 1991a; Bray, 1988; Bray & Berger, 1993; Dawson, 1991; Fine, Kurdek, & Hennigen, 1991; Fine et al., 1993; Hetherington, 1993; Hetherington et al., 1992; Hetherington & Jodl, 1994). Children in stepfamilies may also have more problems in their relationships with parents, siblings, and peers in childhood, adolescence, and adulthood (Amato & Keith, 1991b; Hetherington, in press). In addition, problems may continue long after the remarriage has occurred; young adults from divorced and remarried families are more likely to be in unstable marriages, to report less general well-being, to have more behavioral problems, and to have lower educational and socioeconomic attainment than are those from first-marriage families (Hetherington, in press). The adjustment of children in stepfamilies appears more similar to that of children in divorced, single-parent families than to that of children in first-marriage families (Amato & Keith, 1991a; Cherlin & Furstenberg, 1994).

It is important to repeat that this summary is based on mean differences and does not address the variability in children's responses. Many children do exhibit disruptions in their adjustment and well-being as families struggle with the initial challenges of family transitions, and some children experience pervasive or recurring adjustment difficulties long after their families have restabilized. About 20% to 25% of the children in divorced, single-parent families and stepfamilies, versus 10% in first-marriage families, experience significant or enduring adjustment problems (Hetherington, 1989, 1991; Hetherington et al., 1992; Hetherington & Jodl, 1994; McLanahan & Sandefur, 1994; Zill et al., 1993). Thus, most children adapt over time, are resilient in coping with their parents' marital transitions, and eventually develop into reasonably competent individuals who function within the normal ranges of adjustment (Emery & Forehand, 1994).

In summary, the pattern of adjustment problems documented in the literature suggests that the stresses associated with family transitions place children at risk, but that there is variability among children's responses and in the responses of individual children over time. Factors related to the variations in the severity, timing, and duration of children's problems include their temperament, age, gender, race, and preexisting adjustment difficulties

Temperament. Children may have characteristics that increase their risk of or protect them from adverse consequences of their parents' marital transitions. Those who have difficult temperaments or behavioral problems may elicit negative responses from their parents when they are stressed and may be less able to cope with parental negativity when it occurs (Hetherington, 1989, 1991). In addition, these children may not have the skills needed to identify potential sources of support or gain support from others. On the other hand, children who have easy temperaments; are intelligent, socially mature, and responsible; and exhibit few behavioral problems are more likely to evoke positive responses and social support and to maximize the use of available resources (Hetherington, 1989; Werner, 1988).

Age. Although evidence of a sensitive period in adjusting to divorce is equivocal, researchers have found that the younger the child is at the time of remarriage, the more easily the child establishes a positive relationship with a stepparent (Hetherington, 1993; Perry, 1995). However, children who are young when their parents divorce are more likely than older children and adolescents to experience not only life in a stepfamily but also a second divorce (Thomson, 1994). Thus, the young child may initially profit from an emotional attachment formed to a stepparent only to experience the risks to adjustment associated with repeated periods of family disequilibrium and with the loss of, first, a biological parent and then a stepparent.

Early adolescence appears to be an especially difficult time in which to have a remarriage occur because children are coping with the normative developmental challenges of balancing attachment with the need for greater social and economic autonomy, of coping with physical maturing and sexual fantasies and needs, and of forming romantic relationships (Hetherington et al., 1992; Hetherington & Jodl, 1994). Some young adolescents who have lived with single parents attain early autonomy and are used to having a role in family decision making and little adult supervision. These young teenagers, particularly girls, often view new stepparents as a threat to these freedoms and to their relationship with their biological parents (Hetherington et al., 1992; Hetherington & Jodl, 1994).

For young adolescent girls, the physical maturation and increased sexual feelings and fantasies that accompany puberty may contribute to tense relationships with stepfathers. Many biological fathers and daughters are uncomfortable and become more distant as the daughters go through puberty; in families with nonbiologically related stepfathers, this discomfort may become more acute. In addition, this discomfort may be exacerbated by the fact that girls in stepfather families attain puberty earlier than those in first-marriage families, and early physical maturing is associated with greater parent-daughter conflict in all families (Hetherington & Jodl, 1994). In newly forming stepfather families, stepfather-stepdaughter conflict may be exacerbated by the concurrent stresses of early puberty and new family relationships.

Even for offspring whose parents had remarried earlier and who may have been adjusting well, the challenges of adolescence and young adulthood may trigger problems in adjustment (Amato & Keith, 1991a, 1991b; Bray & Berger, 1993; Demo & Acock, 1996; Hetherington, 1993, in press; Hetherington & Jodl, 1994). A small but significant proportion of adolescents in stepfamilies continue to exhibit behavioral problems similar to those found in childhood and are more likely to drop out of school, to be unemployed, to associate with antisocial peers, to be involved in delinquent activities and substance abuse, to become sexually active earlier, and to have children outside marriage (Amato & Keith, 1991a; Demo & Acock, 1996; Hetherington et al., 1992; McLanahan & Sandefur, 1994).

Unfortunately, for some adolescents, problems do not end when they enter adulthood. Adults from remarried families are, on average, less satisfied with their lives, have more adjustment problems, attain lower socioeconomic attainment, and are more likely to be on welfare than are those from first-marriage families (Amato & Keith, 1991b; Hetherington, in press; McLanahan & Sandefur, 1994). In addition, compared to their counterparts who grew up in first-marriage families, young spouses who were raised in single-parent families and stepfamilies have marital interactions that are characterized by more reciprocated, escalating negative exchanges; denial; belligerence; criticism; contempt; and less effective problem-solving strategies (Hetherington, in press). Youth who spend a significant proportion of their early developmental years in single-parent families and stepfamilies are more likely than their peers later to experience marital instability themselves (Bumpass, Martin, & Sweet, 1991), perhaps because they model their parents' inept conflict resolution styles (Hetherington, in press).

Gender.   When gender differences in children's responses to parents' remarriage appear, they are more likely to be found among preadolescents than among adolescents. In a meta-analysis of the effects of marital transitions on children's adjustment, Amato and Keith (1991a) concluded that an involved stepfather benefits the well-being of stepsons but has no effect on or exacerbates the problems of stepdaughters. Boys, especially preadolescent boys, are more likely than girls to accept (Brand, Clingempeel, & Bowen-Woodward, 1988) and benefit from being in stepfather families (Amato & Keith, 1991a; Hetherington, 1993; Hetherington & Jodl, 1994; Lindner-Gunnoe, 1993; Zill et al., 1993). For boys who often have difficult or conflicted, coercive relationships with their single mothers or who have little or no contact with their fathers, a close relationship with their stepfathers can provide support and a positive role model

(Hetherington, 1993). However, as suggested in the discussion of age effects, girls seem to have more trouble adjusting to the entry of either stepfathers or stepmothers (Brand et al., 1988; Hetherington et al., 1992; Hetherington et al., 1985; Schaffer, 1990). A single mother and her daughter are more likely to have developed a close, companionate relationship, sharing confidences and responsibilities for housework and the care of younger children. A stepfather may be seen as a threat to this intimate relationship. Furthermore, as with sons, daughters in single-parent families grow up faster and have greater autonomy and power than do those in two-parent nondivorced families. Stepparents who attempt to curtail their freedoms are likely to face resentment.

Thus, relationships between stepparents and stepchildren, particularly stepdaughters, are often described as lacking in warmth and high in coercion (Hetherington et al., 1992; Hetherington & Jodl, 1994). Adolescent stepdaughters may not always engage in overt conflict, but they may exhibit contemptuous, nonresponsive, and ignoring behavior toward their stepfathers. For example, compared to daughters and fathers in first-marriage families, stepdaughters have been observed to communicate one third less to their stepfathers (Vuchinich, Hetherington, Vuchinich, & Clingempeel, 1991). Given the gender differences in preadolescents' responses to stepparents, it is not surprising that close relationships with stepfathers are more likely to reduce antisocial behavior and enhance the achievement of stepsons than stepdaughters (Amato & Keith, 1991a; Hetherington, 1993; Lindner-Gunnoe, 1993). Furthermore, compared to preadolescent boys, preadolescent girls are more likely to experience sustained problems in their relationships with both stepfathers (Hetherington, 1993; Hetherington et al., 1992; Hetherington & Jodl, 1994; Vuchinich et al., 1991) and stepmothers (Brand et al., 1988) and are at a greater risk of poor adjustment (Lee, Burkham, Zimiles, & Ladewski, 1994).

Race.   Some researchers have suggested that living in stepfamilies may be more beneficial for African American youth than white youth. In contrast to the higher risks of school drop-out and adolescent parenthood experienced by white adolescents in stepfamilies, African American males are no more likely to drop out of school and African-American females no more likely to become parents when they live in stepfamilies than when they live in first-marriage families (McLanahan & Sandefur, 1994). Given the low remarriage rates among African American families, the parents who remarry may be atypical (Fine, McKenry, Donnelly, & Voydanoff, 1992). There is evidence that those who remarry have higher levels of education and more resources than do those who do not remarry. Thus, racial differences in children's well-being may be related more to family resources and differences in parenting than to family structure. On the other hand, McLanahan and Sandefur (1994) suggested that African American youth who live in disorganized neighborhoods with few financial or social resources may benefit from the income, monitoring, and role models provided by involved stepfathers. If this is the case, the low remarriage rates among African American families mean that the youth are less likely to encounter the potential benefits of stepfathers.

Preexisting adjustment problems. There is now evidence from the results of a few longitudinal studies that the adjustment problems exhibited by some adults and children following divorce or remarriage may not be the result solely of family transitional stress but represent a continuation of problems that were evident before each transition. For example, according to what has been called the marital selectivity hypothesis, some adults may have characteristics that place them at an increased risk for problematic social relationships, inept parenting, decreased psychological well-being and to multiple marital transitions (Capaldi & Patterson, 1991; Larson & Holman, 1994; Simons et al., 1996). Adults who later divorce are more likely than those in emotionally satisfying first marriages to be depressed, alcoholic, or antisocial prior to divorce (Amato, 1993; Capaldi & Patterson, 1991; Forgatch, Patterson, & Ray, 1995). They are also more likely to have maladaptive beliefs about marital relation-

ships; to exhibit poor problem-solving and conflict-resolution skills; and to engage in reciprocal negative spousal exchanges characterized by contempt, denial, withdrawal, and both negative affect and attributions (Gottman, 1993, 1994; Gottman & Levenson, 1992; Matthews, Wickrama, & Conger, 1996). These personal attributes and relationship styles not only predict initial divorce but increase the risk of multiple marital failures. This is not meant to suggest that all adults who divorce or remarry exhibit these problems. Again, divorce can be an adaptive response to a high-conflict, abusive, and unsatisfying marital relationship, and remarriage can provide economic, emotional, and social support for single parents and children.

Some researchers have also reported that, when the adjustment of children preceding parental divorce is controlled, the degree of adjustment problems noted after the divorce is greatly reduced (Block, Block, & Gjerde, 1986; 1988; Cherlin et al., 1991). An extension of this hypothesis is that the behavioral and emotional problems observed in children of remarried couples may be the result of experiences of conflict, loss, poverty, and negative change in divorced families, rather than a response to the new family transition (Furstenberg, 1988). It is notable that the economic advantages and possible support of stepparents in remarried families are not reflected in more positive adjustment in stepchildren over that found in children in mother-headed single-parent families. It may be that the effects of the experiences in divorced or single-parent families are difficult to overcome or that the new socioemotional challenges in stepfamilies counter the benefits of remarriage. Adjustment problems typically increase in the period immediately following each family transition. The adjustment problems of children in newly forming stepfamilies are greater than those exhibited not only by children in first-marriage families (Hetherington et al., 1992), but by children in longer-remarried stabilized stepfamilies and in stabilized divorced families (Hetherington & Jodl, 1994).

Although children who experience parental divorce and remarriage are more likely than children in first-marriage families to encounter conflict and periods of diminished parenting, conflict and poor parenting are not limited to single-parent and stepfamily households. If close parent-child relationships and authoritative parenting can be sustained, children are better adjusted in divorced or remarried families than in conflict-ridden first-marriage families.

FAMILY RELATIONSHIPS

When family relationships are relatively positive and mutually supportive, other risk factors are less likely to compromise parents' or children's adjustment. Thus, recent research has targeted the quality of family relationships and family processes that may moderate or mediate the impact of life in a stepfamily on individual well-being and how they may differ or be similar in first marriages and remarriages (Amato & Keith, 1991a; Fine & Kurdek, 1992; Fine et al., 1993; Hetherington et al., 1992).

Marital Relationships

Perhaps because of their previous marital experiences and the practical realities of immediate child care responsibilities, newly remarried spouses view their relationships as less romantic and more egalitarian with respect to fulfilling both childcare and household jobs than do spouses in first marriages (Furstenberg, 1987; Giles-Sims, 1984, 1987). Although remarried spouses report levels of marital satisfaction similar to those expressed by spouses in first marriages (Hetherington et al., 1992; Hetherington & Jodl, 1994), observational studies have shown that interactions between spouses in stepfamilies often differ from those between spouses in first marriages (Bray & Berger, 1993; Hetherington, 1993; Hetherington et al., 1992; Hetherington & Jodl, 1994). Spouses in stepfamilies tend to be freer in expressing criticisms and anger. The openness observed by researchers is acknowledged by the spouses themselves, who report that they are open in confronting conflict (Bray & Berger, 1993; Giles-Sims, 1984, 1987; Hetherington, 1993). For couples who are negotiating the concurrent challenges of establishing their own relationships and changing or developing relationships with children, this openness may be a way of confronting problems and disagreements as they arise and thus may be adaptive.

Harmonious, satisfying marriages benefit the partners in both first marriages and remarriages. Over time, the support received from their spouses helps to relieve psychological and physical problems that may have developed in response to the stresses of single parenting. Moreover, strong, positive marital relationships in stepfamilies have been found to be related to better relations between parents and children and between stepparents and stepchildren (Bray & Berger, 1993; Fine & Kurdek, 1995; Hetherington et al., 1992; Hobart, 1988; Visher & Visher, 1988). One notable exception to this pattern of positive associations is found in some families with preadolescent stepdaughters. Again, both preadolescent boys and preadolescent girls often initially resist the entry of stepparents but preadolescent boys are more likely than preadolescent girls eventually to accept and benefit from their relationships with stepfathers, and this relationship is enhanced by a close marital relationship (Amato & Keith, 1991a; Hetherington, 1993; Hetherington et al., 1992; Hetherington & Jodl, 1994). Preadolescent stepdaughters are more likely to respond negatively to the entry of stepparents, and their resistance tends to be higher if they have had a close relationship with their residential parents and if the marital relationship is close. In adolescence, in contrast to preadolescence, a satisfying marital relationship is associated with greater acceptance of stepfathers by both stepdaughters and stepsons. A strong marital bond may be perceived by stepdaughters as a protective buffer against inappropriate intimacy in the stepfather-stepdaughter relationship.

Regardless of children's ages and genders, many parents and stepparents report that child-rearing issues and parenting roles and behavior are common areas of disagreement in their marriages. Furthermore, the presence of a hostile child or a child with behavioral problems can erode the quality of the marital relationship in a stepfamily. However, in spite of differences in building the marital and stepparent-stepchild relationships concurrently and the higher risk of marital dissolution for remarried couples, the differences between conjugal relationships in remarried and first-married couples are typically small in magnitude (Booth & Edwards, 1992).

Residential Parents and Their Children *Question 4*

As we noted earlier, it is not uncommon for newly remarried residential parents to feel slightly depressed and preoccupied as they cope with the challenges of establishing their marital relationships while working to adjust their relationships with their children. Thus, in the months immediately following remarriage, residential mothers are often less involved with their children, engage in less monitoring and control, and are more negative than are mothers in first marriages who have children of comparable ages (Bray & Berger, 1991, 1993; Hetherington, 1993; Hetherington et al., 1992). In turn, negative mother-child interactions are related to more disengagement, dysfunctional family roles, poorer communication, and less cohesion in stepfamilies (Bray, 1990). Over time, as the stepfamilies restabilize, mothers reengage in parenting, and their monitoring improves and eventually comes to resemble that of mothers in first-marriage families, except when the children are early adolescents (Bray & Berger, 1991; Hetherington, 1993; Hetherington et al., 1992; Hetherington & Jodl, 1994). When the remarriage occurs while the children are early adolescents, there is an increased risk of long-term problems in the mother-child relationship. The decreases in warmth, monitoring, and control and increases in conflict that characterize parent-child relationships in almost all families as they negotiate the children's transition to adolescence (Hetherington, 1993) can be exacerbated in stepfamilies who are faced with adjusting to a new remarriage. Maternal monitoring and control eventually stabilize in these families but at levels lower than those in first-marriage families or in stepfamilies that formed when the children had not yet reached or had passed the early adolescent years.

Although the number of father-headed families in the United State has tripled since 1974 (Meyer & Garasky, 1993), fathers with full custody of their children are still relatively rare and represent only about 14% of divorced fathers. Residential fathers remarry more rapidly than do residential mothers but experience similar disruptions in their relationships with their children, particularly their daughters (Clingempeel, Brand, & Ievoli, 1984). Initially, fathers may be more likely than mothers to expect their new spouses to assume a primary chid care role and adjust their parenting to accommodate this expectation (Hetherington & Stanley-Hagan, 1995). However, as family relations stabilize over time, relationships between remarried fathers and their residential children eventually become similar to those between fathers and children in first marriage families (Hetherington & Jodl, 1994).

Question 4

Nonresidential Parents and Their Children

Despite recent social changes, marked by greater paternal involvement in child rearing and an increase in the number of fathers who seek child custody at the time of divorce, there are still relatively few nonresidential mothers. However, nonresidential mothers are more than twice as likely to remain in contact with their children and to be active parents than are nonresidential fathers (Hetherington, 1993; Hetherington & Jodl, 1994; Lindner-Gunnoe, 1993). The continued positive involvement of these mothers can be an important resource for their children and is associated with fewer behavioral problems and greater achievement, especially in daughters (Lindner-Gunnoe, 1993). Although nonresidential mothers tend to exhibit slightly less control and monitoring than either divorced, residential mothers or mothers in first-marriage families, they are warm and supportive and arrange their work and living arrangements to accommodate the needs of their children (Hetherington & Jodl, 1994). Children have reported that their relationships with their nonresidential mothers remain close and that they are able to communicate and confide in their mothers (Lindner-Gunnoe, 1993). Unfortunately, the bonds that children feel with their nonresidential mothers may make them resist their stepmothers' overtures, and some children have reported conflicted loyalties toward their mothers and residential stepmothers (Furstenberg, 1987; Lindner-Gunnoe, 1993; Santrock, Sitterle, & Warshak, 1988).

The involvement and quality of parenting exhibited by nonresidential fathers differs from that of nonresidential mothers. Although contact rates between nonresidential fathers and their children are improving (Dillon & Emery, 1996; Maccoby & Mnookin, 1992), compared to nonresidential mothers, fathers are still more likely to disengage (Furstenberg, 1988; Hetherington & Jodl, 1994; Lindner-Gunnoe, 1993). Over 20% of children have no contact with their nonresidential fathers or see them only a few times a year, and only about 25% of children have weekly visits with their fathers (Dillon & Emery, 1996).

Nonresidential fathers are less adept than nonresidential mothers in controlling and monitoring their children's behavior (Lindner-Gunnoe, 1993). Wanting their time with their children to be pleasant and fun, they are more likely to establish friendly, recreationally oriented relationships than parenting relationships with their children (Bray & Berger, 1993; Furstenberg & Cherlin, 1991; Lindner-Gunnoe, 1993; Hetherington, 1991, 1993). Recreational fathers are more likely to avoid confrontations and are less likely to exert control and discipline. Differences in the roles adopted by nonresidential fathers versus mothers may explain why children report that nonresidential mothers are more interested in and informed about their activities, more supportive and sensitive, and more responsive to their needs than are nonresidential fathers (Lindner-Gunnoe, 1993). Moreover, the differences in relationships may explain why children feel closer to their nonresidential mothers than to their nonresidential fathers, why children feel freer to discuss their problems and interests with their nonresidential mothers (Lindner-Gunnoe, 1993), and why nonresidential mothers have more influence over their children's development, especially that of their daughters (Brand et al., 1988; Lindner-Gunnoe, 1993).

Perhaps because nonresidential fathers assume a less active role in control and discipline than do nonresidential mothers, their continued involvement is less likely to conflict with the residential stepfathers' efforts to establish authoritative relations with the children (Hetherington, 1993; Hetherington & Jodl, 1994; White, 1994). The positive involvement of both nonresidential fathers and stepfathers may be beneficial for children by providing additional support and, especially for boys, two male role models (Hetherington, 1993; Hetherington & Jodl, 1994; Lindner-Gunnoe, 1993). However, regardless of the genders of parents and children or the quality of parenting, most children report that they feel closer to their nonresidential parents than to their stepparents.

Researchers have found that a father's involvement in parenting prior to the divorce is a poor predictor of his continued contact with nonresidential children after the divorce. Some formerly uninvolved fathers may be motivated to become more active when faced with the threat of losing their relationships with their nonresidential children. However, other fathers who were involved, competent parents may find intermittent contact painful and withdraw. It is equally difficult to predict a nonresidential father's involvement after he remarries on the basis of his relations with his children during his time as a single parent. Some researchers have found that affective and time commitments made by stepfathers to stepchildren may occur at the expense of the stepfathers' involvement with their own nonresidential children (Mott, 1990; Papernow, 1994; White, 1994). However, other researchers have found that balancing the needs and demands of residential stepchildren and nonresidential biological children creates a great deal of stress for newly remarried men. Some fathers reduce the stress by choosing to remain more involved with their own children and less involved with their stepchildren (Clingempeel, Colyar, & Hetherington, 1994). Differences in the degree to which fathers who remarry become involved parents of their stepchildren may reflect differences in the degree to which the men were engaged parents before their remarriage. Those who remain involved with their own children may find it difficult to justify the time and emotional investment needed to establish and maintain relationships with their new stepchildren. Those who were relatively uninvolved with their children may be more willing to make the effort to become involved stepparents.

Residential Stepparents and Stepchildren

Both stepfathers and stepmothers report that they want their new marriage to be successful (Brand et al., 1988; Bray & Berger, 1993; Hetherington, 1993; Kurdek & Fine, 1993). However, the entry of a new stepparent disrupts the family system and is sometimes met with initial resistance, if not overt hostility, from stepchildren, especially stepdaughters. As residential stepfathers try to ingratiate themselves with their stepchildren in the early months of their relationships, they appear to behave more like polite strangers than parents. In comparison to biological fathers in first marriages, stepfathers are attentive, but report feeling less closeness and rapport with stepchildren. They are also less negative, monitoring, and controlling with their stepchildren (Bray & Berger, 1992; Hetherington et al., 1992). Biological fathers are more likely than newly married stepfathers not only to be warm and supportive but to criticize and intervene in their children's behavior over such issues as manners, cleanliness, homework, chores, and obedience.

The family-type differences in paternal relationships with children are reflected in the differential treatment of biological children and stepchildren in blended stepfamilies. Parents are more involved and committed and perform more child care tasks with biological children than with stepchildren (Henderson, Hetherington, Mekos, & Reiss, 1996; Hetherington & Jodl, 1994). Thus, in blended families, stepfathers may provide less warmth, support, monitoring, and control to stepchildren than they do to their own residential children (Henderson et al., 1996; Marsiglio, 1991, 1992).

Findings of greater conflict in stepparent-stepchild relationships are inconsistent. However, that such conflict can escalate in a small number of families with disastrous consequences is reflected in the fact that the rate of physical abuse by stepfathers is seven times higher than the rate by biological fathers (Wilson, Daly, & Weghorst, 1980), and stepfathers' rates of homicide of stepchildren are 100 times higher. However, these differential rates are most marked for infants and preschool children (Daly & Wilson, 1996).

Even in long-established stepfamilies, disengaged parenting remains the most common parenting style of stepfathers, and only a small subset of stepfathers manage eventually to establish active, authoritative relationships with their stepchildren. Those who do establish relationships with more parental control and positive discipline, in addition to warmth and support, are more likely to be dealing with less resistant, younger stepchildren. Research has suggested that stepfathers initially do best when they establish warm, supportive friendships with their stepchildren and engage in control and discipline only through their support of mothers' parenting efforts (Bray & Berger, 1993; Fine et al., 1993; Hetherington et al., 1992; Hetherington & Jodl, 1994; Kelly, 1992). Stepfathers who refrain from taking an active role in discipline report having not only better relations with their stepchildren, but higher marital satisfaction. More authoritative parenting can be displayed only gradually, and in many stepfamilies, particularly those with adolescents, may not be attained at all (Bray & Berger, 1993).

Although few differences have been found between the adjustment of children living with stepfathers and that of children living with stepmothers (Coleman & Ganong, 1990; Fine & Kurdek, 1992; Fine et al., 1992), stepmothers have an even more difficult time integrating into stepfamilies than do stepfathers (Clingempeel et al., 1984; Furstenberg, 1987; MacDonald & DeMaris, 1996; Santrock et al., 1988). As we noted in our discussion of stepmothers' adjustment, one explanation has been that stepmothers, like mothers in first marriages, expect and are expected by their new husbands to assume the primary caretaker role (Whitsett & Land, 1992), including the role of disciplinarian (Fine et al., 1993; Ihinger-Tallman, 1988; Thomson et al., 1992). MacDonald and DeMaris (1996) found, however, that stepmothers experience more difficulties in their relationships with stepchildren even when the amount of time they devote to child care responsibilities is controlled. This finding suggests that qualities other than simple involvement in child care shape stepmother-stepchild relationships.

In contrast to the myth of the wicked stepmother, stepmothers are no more likely to criticize or to use coercive strategies to control their stepchildren's than their biological children's behavior (Henderson et al., 1996; Hetherington & Jodl, 1994). However, they are less positive and engage in less monitoring and control of their stepchildren's behaviors than do other mothers. Stepchildren often view their stepmothers as uninvolved and unsupportive (Santrock et al., 1988) and their relationships with their stepmothers are more stressful than those reported by children of stepfathers (Furstenberg, 1987). These perceptions may be a response to their stepmothers' lack of involvement and support; however, it also may be that stepmothers who are faced with uninvolved and unsupportive stepchildren respond by disengaging themselves.

The likelihood that stepmothers and stepchildren will be able to establish positive emotional attachments may depend on the involvement of the biological parents. Children find it difficult to balance their relationships with their biological mothers and their stepmothers, particularly when their biological mothers maintain contact and remain involved with them (Furstenberg, 1987). In addition, the stepmother-stepchild relationship tends to be more positive when a child's father does not encourage the stepmother to assume the role of disciplinarian and remains responsible for supervising and controlling his child's behavior (Fine & Kurdek, 1992).

Sibling Relationships

The impact of sibling relationships on child adjustment in remarried families has been found to parallel the associations evident between parent-child relations and child adjustment. Greater social competence and responsibility in children are associated with warm, supportive sibling relationships, and antisocial behavior is associated with sibling rivalry and aggression (Hetherington et al., 1992; Hetherington & Jodl, 1994). Thus, sibling relationships that are warm and supportive may help to protect children from the adverse outcomes associated with unstable parent-child relationships and difficult stepparent-stepchild relationships that are typical during the early months of stepfamily formation. Unfortunately, the few studies that have examined sibling relationships have found that they may suffer from an unstable family history. Less involved, harsher parenting is associated with rivalrous, aggressive, and nonsupportive sibling relationships in single-parent and remarried families (Conger & Conger, 1996; Hetherington, 1991, 1993; Hetherington et al., 1992). Early in remarriages, relationships between full- and half-siblings in stepfamilies are less warm and supportive and more contentious and rivalrous than are sibling relations in first-marriage families (Hetherington, 1989, 1993; Hetherington & Jodl, 1994). In a stepfamily, the relationship between two sons from the mother's previous marriage is less supportive than is the relationship between two daughters, and a positive relationship between sisters can serve as a protective factor against the development of behavioral problems when they encounter adversity (Hetherington & Jodl, 1994). In contrast, in a stabilized, long-remarried stepfamily, the relationship between biologically related siblings appears both more positive and involved but also more aggressive and rivalrous than the relationship between unrelated stepsiblings in a blended family (Hetherington & Jodl, 1994). Although there is a risk that stepsiblings will become disengaged, many residential stepsiblings form successful, friendly satellite relationships (Ihinger-Tallman, 1988) that provide both companionship and support. Disengagement or friendship may be more likely than rivalry between residential stepsiblings because both stepsiblings can justify any differential treatment by parents and stepparents. The stepsiblings may expect more affection and support from their biological parent than from their stepparent.

Summary

In summary, the changes in family relationships that accompany remarriage can support or undermine adults' and children's efforts to adapt to their new family situation. A critical factor for adults is their ability to establish a positive marital relationship that is strong enough to accommodate the challenges of children's adjustment problems and their own potential disagreements about issues related to new roles and responsibilities. The difficulties in establishing such a relationship are reflected in the rapidity of divorce and the 60% divorce rate among remarried couples.

Critical factors associated with children's adjustment continue to include the qualities of their relationships with residential and nonresidential biological parents and stepparents and with siblings, although individual variations associated with age, gender, temperament-personality, and ethnicity also occur. In most stepfamilies, relationships between the biological parents and children during the early stages of family formation are more disrupted and conflicted and the parenting is less authoritative. However, over time, these relationships stabilize, and with the possible exception of families with early-adolescent children, come to resemble those that are typical in first-marriage families. Stepparents usually remain less authoritative and more disengaged from stepchildren than they are with their own children in blended families or than biological parents are in first-marriage families. However, a parenting model that includes high warmth and support, little direct discipline, and support for the biological parent's child-rearing practices may be adaptive for stepparents. Such a model allows stepparents and stepchildren eventually to develop strong, supportive relationships that are not in conflict with those that the children maintain with actively involved nonresidential parents (Bray & Berger, 1993; Coleman & Ganong, 1990; Fine et al., 1993).

EXTENDED FAMILY AND EXTRAFAMILIAL SUPPORTS

The most effective support for children from single-parent, remarried, and first-marriage families are authoritative parents (Hetherington, 1989, 1993; Hetherington et al., 1992; Hetherington & Jodl, 1994; Steinberg, Mounts, Lamborn, & Dornbusch, 1991). However, support systems outside the immediate family also play a role in buffering children from possible adverse consequences of family transitions. For example, researchers have found that when parents or stepparents are unable to provide an authoritative family environment, an authoritative school environment may, to some extent, protect against the development of problems in adjustment (Hetherington, 1993; Hetherington &

Jodl, 1994). Children in remarried families whose parents or stepparents are not authoritative demonstrate improved academic achievement and social responsibility and fewer behavioral problems when they have teachers who are warm and responsive, provide control in a structured classroom environment, and make age-appropriate maturity demands of the children (Hetherington, 1993).

Relationships with extended family members, such as grandparents, may provide similar support and comfort with the added benefit of the closeness found in a stable attachment relationship. Although researchers have found that grandparents, especially maternal grandparents, can become more actively involved in the family lives of their adult children and grandchildren and provide practical, financial, and emotional support after the adult children divorce (Cherlin & Furstenberg, 1986; Giles-Sims & Crosbie-Burnett, 1989; Ihinger-Tallman & Pasley, 1987; Kennedy & Kennedy, 1993), less is known about the supportive function of grandparent-grandchild relationships after the grandchildren become part of stepfamilies. It has been suggested that the continued close involvement of a grandparent may interfere with the newly reconstituted family's attempts to establish relationships between new stepparents and stepsiblings and integrate new family members into the family system (Wilks & Melville, 1990). However, a retrospective study that compared the qualities of grandparent-grandchild relationships of young adults who grew up in first-marriage families to those of young adults who grew up in divorced, single-parent, and remarried families found evidence that the emotional and practical support provided by grandparents may increase in salience with each family transition (Kennedy & Kennedy, 1993). It has been suggested that a child's or adolescent's association with a biological grandparent can be important during a time when relationships with parents are changing and relationships with stepparents are new (Ihinger-Tallman & Pasley, 1987; Kennedy & Kennedy, 1993; Wilks & Melville, 1990).

Even less is known about the possible supportive functions of children's relationships with stepgrandparents than with grandparents (Bray & Berger, 1993; Giles-Sims & Crosbie-Burnett, 1989), but what little is known indicates that the stepgrandparent and stepgrandchild can develop a close, positive relationship that is beneficial to both. Some stepgrandparents have difficulty accepting or building relationships with stepgrandchildren (Kornhaber, 1996). The reasons for stepgrandparents' difficulties establishing positive bonds may include problems with overcoming grief at the breakdown of their adult children's marriages and the loss of their relationships with their former daughters-in-law or sons-in-law, accepting and building relationships with their adult children's new spouses, and defining what their roles as stepparents and stepgrandparents should be in the absence of social norms (Henry, Ceglian, & Ostrander, 1993). Generally, however, stepgrandchildren's perceptions of their stepgrandparents are positive (Furstenberg & Spanier, 1984; Trygstad & Sanders, 1989), and most stepgrandparents express a desire to become part of their stepgrandchildren's lives.

The likelihood that stepgrandparents and stepgrandchildren will develop a positive emotional attachment has been found to be associated with several factors. Stepgrandparents are more likely to initiate relations with the stepchildren when they are satisfied with their adult children's new marital relationships and have begun to establish positive relationships with their adult children's new spouses (Trygstad & Sanders, 1989). In addition, like stepparents, stepgrandparents need to recognize the children's existing relationships with biological grandparents and slowly integrate themselves into the lives of their stepgrandchildren without assuming an authority role or expecting immediate acceptance (Kornhaber, 1996). Regardless of family dynamics, a positive emotional bond in a steprelationship that parallels that found between biological grandparents and grandchildren is more likely to occur when the stepchildren are young at the time of the remarriage and other biological grandchildren are not available (Cherlin & Furstenberg, 1994; Johnson, 1985; Kornhaber, 1996).

Grandparents can provide the added benefits associated with a stable family relationship and, over time, stepgrandparents can become important sources of guidance and emotional support. During the transition into stepfamily life, some children and adolescents may seek support through relationships with caring adults outside the immediate fam-

ily (Chapman, 1991). Child care centers and schools that provide a supportive and stable environment and responsive teachers, coaches, or parents of friends can offer children the security, comfort, and validation of self-worth they need as they cope with the changing family relationships and roles that accompany divorce and remarriage (Hetherington & Anderson, 1988; Hetherington et al., 1992; Hetherington & Jodl, 1994).

SOCIAL RISK FACTORS AND SOCIAL POLICIES

The absence of clear norms to guide the expression of affection for stepchildren and how or even whether a stepparent should exert parental authority or responsibilities are major sources of stress to new stepparents (Peek, Bell, Waldren, & Sorrell, 1988). Furthermore, the absence of social norms may lead to disparate expectations among family members. Over half the biological parents and stepparents think that stepparents should share childrearing responsibilities equally with parents and play an active parenting role (Giles-Sims, 1984; Marsiglio, 1992), but their stepchildren often believe that stepparents should not act as parents (Visher & Visher, 1988). Conflict over the role of stepparents is associated with lower parenting satisfaction among stepparents, as well as lower marital and family satisfaction (Kurdek & Fine, 1991).

The absence of social norms and the ambiguity expressed by family members may be exacerbated by the absence of a legal parental status for stepparents. Thus, policies that are designed to help stepparents and stepchildren establish legal relationships and responsibilities with each other (Fine, 1989, 1994; Jaff, 1988; Mahoney, 1984, 1989, 1994; Melton, 1991; Polikoff, 1990) and that preserve the rights and responsibilities of both residential and nonresidential parents are needed (Fine, 1994; Brooks-Gunn, 1994). For example, rather than adopt stepchildren, which would terminate the rights of the nonresidential parent, a stepparent could share a legal but limited coparenting relationship with the stepchild's residential parent. The stepparent might be allowed gain access to his or her stepchildren's academic records or respond to concerns raised by teachers, but not have the right to take the stepchild out of the geographic region without the parent's authorization. New policies must be flexible to respond to the special needs and diversity of stepfamilies (Fine, 1994) and sensitive to the points that some stepparents may not choose to assume a parenting role or that to do so may not be in the best interests of the child. Also, policies need to consider that in some families a continued relationship following divorce can be positive for both stepparents and stepchildren (Fine, 1994). The provision of legal status to stepparents would help legitimate step relationships. It could result in stepparents' increased commitment to their stepchildren, reassure the stepchildren that the step relationship is not transitory, and help both adults and children to achieve a clearer family identity.

SUMMARY AND CONCLUSION

Since the beginning of our careers, we have been interested in how children and families cope with challenging life situations. We have been struck by the great diversity in adjustment exhibited by children and families who are coping with both normative life transitions, such as adolescence, and with nonnormative life transitions like parental divorce and remarriage. Although we started out being interested in divorce and life in single-parent families, because we do only longitudinal research, we also rapidly became interested in stepfamilies and the complex and varied trajectories of family transitions, structures, roles, and relationships that occur over time. Despite early researchers' use of a deficit model that views any family that deviates from the so-called traditional married, two parent-family as deficient, we have been impressed by the resilience and adaptability of families and their members in diverse families forms.

There is a growing recognition and acceptance that both in the early months of family formation and once restabilized, stepfamilies may differ from other types of families in their patterns of functioning, organization, and relationships. Relationship processes that are adaptive for stepfamilies may differ from those that are adaptive for single-parent or first-marriage families. However, in most families, mutual positive family relationships, low conflict, and supportive, involved parenting or relationships

with adults are associated with positive outcomes and resilience in children. All families experience some circumstances, such as changes of jobs and schools, geographic moves, illnesses, births, and deaths that can place members at risk of behavioral and emotional problems. Each stepfamily, with its own unique history and configuration of immediate and extended family relationships, faces additional challenges that can place all family members at risk of problems but that can also offer opportunities for growth. The disruptions in parenting that may accompany remarriage may deny children the benefit of a protective authoritative parenting environment as a new member is added to the family, relationships with nonresidential and extended family members are adjusted, and family relationships are altered to accommodate new roles and responsibilities. However, families do restabilize over time. Few differences are noted between the parenting of biological parents in long-established remarried families and in first marriage families with one exception: families whose children were early adolescents at the time of the remarriage. Moreover, although there is evidence that problems reemerge or develop for some children in late adolescence and adulthood, the majority of children suffer no severe or lasting problems associated with divorce and remarriage.

Research on adjustment in remarried families using risk-and-resilience models that draw on systems, developmental, and ecological perspectives is just beginning. That much of what is known about relationships and adjustment in stepfamilies is based on studies of white stepfather families is not surprising, given that stepfather families make up the largest proportion of remarried families. As a result of this focus, far less is known about the relationships and adjustment trajectories in other types of stepfamilies, including those with residential stepmothers and those that occur in other racial and ethnic groups. More longitudinal research is needed to investigate diverse developmental trajectories, family relationships, and processes in stepfamilies with less common structures, including not only stepmother families, but mixed or blended stepfamilies, families headed by single parents who marry for the first time, and families headed by cohabiting adults. Given evidence of a positive association between the number of family transitions experienced and the risk of problems in children's adjustment (Amato & Booth, 1991), researchers need to examine the impact of multiple family transitions on adults and children. Regardless of the targets of future studies, care must be taken to examine various adaptive trajectories associated with marital transitions, to avoid the trap of equating differences with deficits, and to focus on the protective factors that contribute to resilience.

REFERENCES

Ahrons, C. R. (1979). The binuclear family: Two households, one family. *Alternative Lifestyles, 2,* 499–515.

Amato, P. R. (1993). Children's adjustment to divorce: Theories, hypothesis, and empirical support. *Journal of Marriage and the Family, 55,* 23–38.

Amato, P. R., & Booth, A. (1991). Consequences of parental divorce and marital unhappiness for adult well-being. *Social Forces, 69,* 895–914.

Amato, P. R., & Keith, N. (1991a). Parental divorce and adult well-being: A meta-analysis. *Journal of Marriage and the Family, 53,* 43–58.

Amato, P. R., & Keith, N. (1991b). Parental divorce and the well-being of children: A meta-analysis. *Psychology Bulletin, 110,* 26–46.

Amato, P. R., Loomis, L. S., & Booth, A. (1995). Parental divorce, marital conflict, and offspring well-being during early adulthood. *Social Forces, 73,* 895–915.

Avenevoli, S., Sessa, F. M., & Steinberg, L. (1999). Family structure, parenting practices, and adolescent adjustment: An ecological examination. In E. M. Hetherington (Ed.), Coping with divorce, single parenting, and remarriage: A risk and resiliency perspective. (pp. 65–90). Hillsdale, NJ: Lawrence Erlbaum.

Benkov, L. (1994). *Reinventing the family: Lesbian and gay parents.* New York: Crown.

Block, J. H., Block, J., & Gjerde, P. F. (1986). The personality of children prior to divorce: A prospective study. *Child Development, 57,* 827–840.

Block, J. H., Block, J., & Gjerde, P. F. (1988). Parental functioning and the home environment in families of divorce: Prospective and concurrent analyses. *Journal of the American Academy of Child and Adolescent Psychiatry, 27,* 207–213.

Booth, A., & Edwards, J. N. (1992). Starting over: Why remarriages are more unstable. *Journal of Family Issues, 13,* 179–194.

Bowlby, J. (1969). *Attachment and loss 1: Attachment.* London: Hogarth Press.

Brand, E., Clingempeel, W. G., & Bowen-Woodward, K. (1988). Family relationships and children's adjustment in stepmother and stepfather families. In E. M. Hetherington & J. D. Arasteh (Eds.), *Impact of divorce, single parenting, and stepparenting on children* (pp. 299–324). Hillsdale, NJ: Lawrence Erlbaum.

Bray, J. H. (1988). Children's development during early remarriage. In E. M. Hetherington & J. Arasteh (Eds.), *The impact of divorce, single parenting, and stepparenting on children* (pp. 279–298). Hillsdale, NJ: Lawrence Erlbaum.

Bray, J. H. (1990, August). *The developing family 2: Overview and previous findings.* Paper presented at the annual meeting of the American Psychological Association, Boston.

Bray, J. H., & Berger, S. H. (1991). Developmental issues in stepfamilies research project: Family relationships and parent-child interactions. *Journal of Family Psychology, 7,* 76–90.

Bray, J. H., & Berger, S. H. (1992). Nonresidential family-child relationships following divorce and remarriage. In C. E. Depner & J. H. Bray (Eds.), *Nonresidential parenting: New vistas in family living* (pp. 243–256). Newbury Park, CA: Sage.

Bray, J. H., & Berger, S. H. (1993). Developmental Issues in Stepfamilies Research Project: Family relationships and parent-child interactions. *Journal of Family Psychology, 7,* 76–80.

Bray, J. H., Berger, S. H., & Boethal, C. L. (1994). Role integration and marital adjustment in stepfather families. In K. Pasley & M. Ihinger-Tallman (Eds.), *Stepparenting: Issues in theory, research, and practice* (pp. 69–86). Westport, CT: Greenwood Press.

Bridgood, A., & Savage, D. (Eds.). (1993). *General Household Survey.* London: Her Majesty's Stationery Office.

Bronfenbrenner, U. (1986). Ecology of the family as a context for human development: Research perspectives. *Developmental Psychology, 22,* 723–742.

Brooks-Gunn, J. (1994). Research on stepparenting families: Integrating disciplinary approaches and informing policy. In A. Booth & J. Dunn (Eds.), *Stepfamilies: Who benefits? Who does not?* (pp. 167–189). Hillsdale, NJ: Lawrence Erlbaum.

Bumpass, L. L., Martin, T. C., & Sweet, J. A. (1991). The impact of family background and early marital factors on marital disruption. *Journal of Family Issues, 12,* 22–42.

Burrell, N. A. (1995). Communication patterns in stepfamilies: Redefining family roles, themes, and conflict styles. In M. A. Fitzpatrick & A. L. Vangelisti (Eds.), *Explaining family interactions* (pp. 290–309). Thousand Oaks, CA: Sage.

Capaldi, D. M., & Patterson, G. R. (1991). Relations of parental transitions to boys' adjustment problems: 1. A linear hypothesis. 2. Mothers at risk for transitions and unskilled parenting. *Developmental Psychology, 27,* 489–504.

Chapman, S. F. (1991). Attachment and adolescent adjustment to parental remarriage. *Family Relations, 40,* 232–237.

Cherlin, A. (1978). Remarriage as an incomplete institution. *American Journal of Sociology, 84,* 634–649.

Cherlin, A. (1992). *Marriage, divorce, remarriage: Social trends in the U.S.* Cambridge, MA: Harvard University Press.

Cherlin, A., & Furstenberg, F. F. (1986). *The new American grandparent: A place in the family, a life apart.* New York: Basic Books.

Cherlin, A., & Furstenberg, F. F. (1994). Stepfamilies in the United States: A reconsideration. In J. Blake & J. Hagen (Eds.), *Annual review of sociology* (pp. 359–381). Palo Alto, CA: Annual Reviews.

Cherlin, A., Furstenberg, F. F., Chase-Lansdale, P. L., Kiernan, K. E., Robins, P. K., Morrison, D. R., & Teitler, J. O. (1991). Longitudinal studies of effects of divorce in children in Great Britain and the United States. *Science, 252,* 1386–1389.

Clingempeel, W. G., Brand, E., & Ievoli, R. (1984). Stepparent-stepchild relationships in stepmother and stepfather families. *Child Development, 57,* 474–484.

Clingempeel, W. G., Colyar, J. J., & Hetherington, E. M. (1994). Toward a cognitive dissonance conceptualization of stepchildren and biological children loyalty conflicts: A construct validity study. In K. Pasley & M. Ihinger-Tallman (Eds.), *Stepparenting: Issues in theory, research, and practice* (pp. 151–173). Westport, CT: Greenwood Press.

Coleman, M., & Ganong, L. H. (1990). Remarriage and stepfamily research in the 1980s: Increased interest in an old family form. *Journal of Marriage and the Family, 52,* 925–940.

Conger, R. D., & Conger, K. J. (1996). Sibling relationships. In R. Simons & Associates (Eds.), *Understanding differences between divorced and intact families: Stress, interaction and child outcome* (pp. 104–124). Thousand Oaks, CA: Sage.

Crosbie-Burnett, M., & Helmbrecht, L. (1993). A descriptive empirical study of gay male stepfamilies. *Family Relations, 42,* 256–262.

Daly, M., & Wilson, M. (1989). The Darwinian psychology of discriminative parental solicitude. *Nebraska Symposium on Motivation* (pp. 211–234). Lincoln: University of Nebraska Press.

Daly, M., & Wilson, M. I. (1996). Violence against stepchildren. *Current Directions in Psychological Science, 5*(3), 77–81.

Dawson, D. A. (1991). Family structure and children's health and well-being: Data from the 1988 National Health Interview Survey on Child Health. *Journal of Marriage and the Family, 53,* 573–584.

Demo, D. H., & Acock, A. C. (1996). Family structure, family process, and adolescent well-being. *Journal of Research on Adolescence, 6,* 457–488.

Dillon, P. A., & Emery, R. E. (1996). Divorce mediation and resolution of child custody disputes: Long-term effects. *American Journal of Orthopsychiatry, 66,* 131–140.

Emery, R. E. (1998). *Marriage, divorce, and children's adjustment.* Newbury Park, CA: Sage.

Emery, R. E., & Forehand, R. (1994). Parental divorce and children's well-being: A focus on resilience. In R. J. Haggerty, L. R. Sherrod, N. Garmezy, & M. Rutter (Eds.), *Stress, risk, and resilience in children and adolescents* (pp. 64–99). Cambridge, England: Cambridge University Press.

Fine, M. A. (1989). A social science perspective on stepfamily law: Suggestions for legal reform. *Family Relations, 38,* 53–58.

Fine, M. A. (1994). Social policy pertaining to stepfamilies: Should stepparents and stepchildren have the option of establishing a legal relationship? In A. Booth & J. Dunn (Eds.), *Stepfamilies: Who benefits? Who does not?* (pp. 197–204). Hillsdale, NJ: Lawrence Erlbaum.

Fine, M. A., & Kurdek, L. A. (1992). The adjustment of adolescents in stepfather and stepmother families. *Journal of Marriage and the Family, 54,* 725–736.

Fine, M. A., & Kurdek, L. A. (1994). A multidimensional cognitive developmental model of stepfamily adjustment. In K. Pasley & M. Ihinger-Tallman (Eds.), *Stepparenting: Issues in theory, research and practice* (pp. 15–32). Westport, CT: Greenwood Press.

Fine, M. A., & Kurdek, L. A. (1995). Relation between marital quality and (step)parent-child relationship quality for parents and stepparents in stepfamilies. *Journal of Family Psychology, 9,* 216–223.

Fine, M. A., Kurdek, L. A., & Hennigen, L. (1991). Family structure, perceived clarity of (step)parent roles, and perceived self-competence in young adolescents. *Family Perspective, 25,* 261–282.

Fine, M. A., McKenry, P. C., Donnelly, B. W., & Voydanoff, P. (1992). Perceived adjustment of parents and children: Variations by family structure, race, and gender. *Journal of Marriage and the Family, 54,* 118–127.

Fine, M. A., Voydanoff, P., & Donnelly, B. W. (1993). The relations between parental control and warmth and child well-being in stepfamilies. *Journal of Family Psychology, 7,* 222–232.

Forgatch, M. S., Patterson, G. R., & Ray, J. A. (1995). Divorce and boys' adjustment problems: Two paths with a single model. In E. M. Hetherington & E. A. Blechman (Eds.), *Stress, coping, and resiliency in children and families* (pp. 67–105). Mahwah, NJ: Lawrence Erlbaum.

Furstenberg, F. F., Jr. (1987). The new extended family: The experience of parents and children after remarriage. In K. Pasley & M. Ihinger-Tallman (Eds.), *Remarriage and stepparenting: Current research and theory* (pp. 42–61). New York: Guilford Press.

Furstenberg, F. F., Jr. (1988). Child care after divorce and remarriage. In E. M. Hetherington & J. D. Arasteh (Eds.), *Impact of divorce, single parenting, and stepparenting on children* (pp. 245–261). Hillsdale, NJ: Lawrence Erlbaum.

Furstenberg, F. F., Jr., & Cherlin, A. (1991). *Divided families: What happens to children when parents part.* Cambridge, MA: Harvard University Press.

Furstenberg, F. F., & Spanier, G. B. (1984). *Recycling the family: Remarriage after divorce.* Beverly Hills, CA: Sage.

Ganong, L. H., & Coleman, M. (1994). *Remarried family relationships.* Thousand Oaks, CA: Sage.

Giles-Sims, J. (1984). The stepparent role: Expectations, behavior, and sanctions. *Journal of Family Issues, 5,* 116–130.

Giles-Sims, J. (1987). Social exchange in remarried families. In K. Pasley & M. Ihinger-Tallman (Eds.), *Remarriage and stepparenting today: Current research and theory* (pp. 141–163). New York: Guilford Press.

Giles-Sims, J., & Crosbie-Burnett, M. (1989). Stepfamily research: Implications for policy, clinical interventions and further research. *Family Relations, 38,* 19–23.

Gottman, J. M. (1993). A theory of marital dissolution and stability. *Journal of Family Psychology, 7,* 57–75.

Gottman, J. M. (1994). *What predicts divorce?* Hillsdale, NJ: Lawrence Erlbaum.

Gottman, J. M., & Levenson, R. W. (1992). Marital processes predictive of later dissolution: Behavior, physiology and health. *Journal of Personality and Social Psychology, 63,* 221–233.

Henderson, S. H., Hetherington, E. M., Mekos, D., & Reiss, D. (1996). Stress, parenting, and adolescent psychopathology in nondivorced and stepfamilies: A within-family perspective. In E. M. Hetherington & E. H. Blechman (Eds.), *Stress, coping, and resiliency in children and families* (pp. 39–66). Mahwah, NJ: Lawrence Erlbaum.

Henry, C. S., Ceglian, C. P., & Ostrander, D. L. (1993). The transition to stepgrandparenthood. *Journal of Divorce and Remarriage, 3,* 25–44.

Hetherington, E. M. (1989). Coping with family transitions: Winners, losers, and survivors. *Child Development, 60,* 1–14.

Hetherington, E. M. (1991). Families, lies, and videotapes. *Journal of Research on Adolescence, 1,* 323–348.

Hetherington, E. M. (1993). An overview of the Virginia longitudinal study of divorce and remarriage with a focus on early adolescence. *Journal of Family Psychology, 7,* 1–18.

Hetherington, E. M. (in press). Social capital and the development of youth from nondivorced, divorced, and remarried families. In A. Collins (Ed.), *Relationships as developmental contexts: The 29th Minnesota Symposium on Child Psychology.* Mahwah, NJ: Lawrence Erlbaum.

Hetherington, E. M., & Anderson, E. R. (1988). The effects of divorce and remarriage on early adolescents and their families. In M. D. Levine & E. R. McAnarmey (Eds.), *Early adolescent transitions* (pp. 49–67). Lexington, MA: D. C. Heath.

Hetherington, E. M., Clingempeel, W. G., Anderson, E. R., Deal, J., Stanley-Hagan, M., Hollier, E. A., & Lindner, M. (1992). Coping with marital transitions: A family systems perspective. *Monographs of the Society for Research in Child Development, 57*(2–3, Serial No. 227).

Hetherington, E. M., Cox, M., & Cox, R. (1985). Long term effects of divorce and remarriage on the adjustment of children. *Journal of the American Academy of Child Psychiatry, 24,* 518–530.

Hetherington, E. M., & Jodl, K. M. (1994). Stepfamilies as settings for child development. In A. Booth & J. Dunn (Eds.), *Stepfamilies: Who benefits? Who does not?* (pp. 55–79). Hillsdale, NJ: Lawrence Erlbaum.

Hetherington, E. M., & Stanley-Hagan, M. (1995). Parenting in divorced and remarried families. In M. Bornstein (Ed.), *Handbook of parenting* (pp. 233–255). Mahwah, NJ: Lawrence Erlbaum.

Hobart, C. W. (1988). The family system in remarriage: An exploratory study. *Journal of Marriage and the Family, 50,* 649–661.

Ihinger-Tallman, M. (1988). Research on stepfamilies. *Annual Review of Sociology, 14,* 25–48.

Ihinger-Tallman, M., & Pasley, K. (1987). *Remarriage.* Beverly Hills, CA: Sage.

Jacobson, D. S. (1982, August). *Family structure in the age of divorce.* Paper presented at the annual meeting of the American Psychological Association, Washington, DC.

Jaff, J. (1988). Wedding bell blues: The position of unmarried people in American law. *Arizona Law Review, 30,* 207–242.

Jockin, V., McGue, M., & Lykken, D. T. (1996). Personality and divorce: A genetic analysis. *Journal of Personality and Social Psychology, 71,* 288–299.

Johnson, C. L. (1985). Grandparenting options in divorcing families: An anthropological perspective. In V. L. Bengston & J. F. Robertson (Eds.), *Grandparenthood* (pp. 81–96). Beverly Hills, CA: Sage.

Kelly, P. (1992). Healthy stepfamily functioning. *Journal of Contemporary Human Services, 73,* 579–587.

Kennedy, G. E., & Kennedy, C. E. (1993). Grandparents: A special resource for children in stepfamilies. *Journal of Divorce and Remarriage, 19,* 45–68.

Keshet, J. K. (1990). Cognitive remodeling of the family: How remarried people view stepfamilies. *American Journal of Orthopsychiatry, 60,* 196–203.

Kornhaber, A. (1996). *Contemporary grand parenting.* Thousand Oaks, CA: Sage.

Kurdek, L. A., & Fine, M. A. (1991). Cognitive correlates of adjustment for mothers and stepfathers in stepfather families. *Journal of Marriage and the Family, 53,* 565–572.

Kurdek, L. A., & Fine, M. A. (1993). Parent and nonparent residential family members as providers of warmth, support, and supervision to young adolescents. *Journal of Family Psychology, 7,* 245–249.

Larson, J. H. (1992, July). Understanding stepfamilies. *American Demographic,* 36–40.

Larson, J. H., & Holman, T. B. (1994). Premarital predictors of marital quality and stability. *Family Relations, 43,* 228–237.

Lee, V. E., Burkam, D. T., Zimiles, H., & Ladewski, B. (1994). Family structure and its effect on behavioral and emotional problems in young adolescents. *Journal of Research on Adolescence, 4,* 405–437.

Lindner-Gunnoe, M. L. (1993). *Noncustodial mothers'*

and fathers' contributions to the adjustment of adolescent stepchildren. Doctoral dissertation, University of Virginia, Charlottesville.

Maccoby, E. E., & Mnookin, R. H. (1992). *Dividing the child: Social and legal dilemmas of custody.* Cambridge, MA: Harvard University Press.

MacDonald, W. L., & DeMaris, A. (1996). Parenting stepchildren and biological children: The effects of stepparents' gender and new biological children. *Journal of Family Issues, 17,* 5–25.

Mahoney, M. M. (1984). Support and child aspects of the stepparent-child relationship. *Cornell Law Review, 70,* 38–79.

Mahoney, M. M. (1989). Stepfamilies in the law of intestate succession and wills. *University of California at Davis Law Review, 22,* 917–950.

Mahoney, M. M. (1994). Reformulating the legal definition of the stepparent-stepchild relationship. In A. Booth & J. Dunn (Eds.), *Stepfamilies: Who benefits? Who does not?* (pp. 191–196). Hillsdale, NJ: Lawrence Erlbaum.

Marsiglio, W. (1991). Paternal engagement activities with minor children. *Journal of Marriage and the Family, 53,* 973–986.

Marsiglio, W. (1992). Stepfathers with minor children living at home: Parenting perceptions and relationship quality. *Journal of Family Issues, 13,* 195–214.

Matthews, L. S., Wickrama, K. A. S., & Conger, R. D. (1996). Predicting marital instability from spouse and observer reports of marital interaction. *Journal of Marriage and the Family, 58,* 641–655.

McGoldrick, M., & Carter, E. A. (1989). Forming a remarried family. In A. Carter & M. McGoldrick (Eds.), *The family cycle: A framework for family therapy* (pp. 399–429). New York: Gardner.

McGue, M., & Lykken, D. T. (1992). Genetic influence on risk of divorce. *Psychological Science, 6,* 368–373.

McLanahan, S., & Sandefur, G. (1994). *Growing up with a single parent: What hurts, what helps.* Cambridge, MA: Harvard University Press.

Melton, R. L. (1991). Legal rights of unmarried heterosexual and homosexual couples and evolving definitions of family. *Journal of Family Law, 29,* 497–517.

Meyer, D. R., & Garasky, S. (1993). Custodial fathers: Myths, realities, and child support policy. *Journal of Marriage and the Family, 55,* 73–89.

Mott, F. L. (1990). When is a father really gone? Paternal-child contact in father absent homes. *Demography, 27,* 499–517.

National Center for Health Statistics. (1997). Births, marriages, and deaths for 1996. *Monthly Vital Statistics*

Report, 45(12). Hyattsville, MD: National Center for Health Statistics.

O'Connor, T. B., Hetherington, E. M., & Reiss, D. (1998). Family systems and adolescent development: Shared and nonshared risk and protective factors in nondivorced and remarried families. *Development and Psychopathology, 10,* 353–375.

Papernow, P. L. (1994). The stepfamily cycle: An experimental model of stepfamily development. *Family Relations, 33,* 355–363.

Peek, C., Bell, N., Waldren, T., & Sorrell, G. (1988). Patterns of functioning in families of remarried and first married couples. *Journal of Marriage and the Family, 50,* 699–708.

Perry, B. (1995). Step-parenting: How vulnerable are stepchildren? *Educational and Child Psychology, 12,* 58–70.

Plomin, R., & Rendes, R. (1991). Human behavioral genetics. *Annual Review of Psychology, 42,* 161–190.

Polikoff, N. D. (1990). This child does have two mothers: Redefining parenthood to meet the needs of children in lesbian-mother and other nontraditional families. *Georgetown Law Journal, 78,* 459–575.

Popenoe, D. (1994). The evolution of marriage and the problems of stepfamilies: A biosocial perspective. In A. Booth & J. Dunn (Eds.), *Stepfamilies: Who benefits? Who does not?* (pp. 2–27). Hillsdale, NJ: Lawrence Erlbaum.

Santrock, J. W., Sitterle, K. A., & Warshak, R. A (1988). Parent-child relationships in stepfather families. In P. Bronstein & C. P. Cowan (Eds.), *Fatherhood today: Men's changing role in the family* (pp. 144–165). New York: John Wiley.

Schaffer, H. R. (1990). *Making decisions about children: Psychological questions and answers.* Oxford, England: Basil Blackwell.

Simons, R. L. (1996). The effect of divorce on adult and child adjustment. In R. Simons & Associates (Eds.), *Understanding differences between divorced and intact families: Stress, interaction, and child outcome* (pp. 3–20). Thousand Oaks, CA: Sage.

Simons, R. L., Johnson, C., & Lorenz, F. O. (1996). Family structure differences in stress and behavioral predispositions. In R. Simons & Associates (Eds.), *Understanding differences between divorced and intact families: Stress, interaction, and child outcome* (pp. 45–63). Thousand Oaks, CA: Sage.

Steinberg, L., Mounts, N., Lamborn, S., & Dornbusch, S. (1991). Authoritative parenting and adolescent adjustment across varied ecological niches. *Journal of Research on Adolescence, 1,* 19–36.

Thomson, E. (1994). Settings and development from a demographic point of view. In A. Booth & J. Dunn (Eds.), *Stepfamilies: Who benefits? Who does not?* (pp. 89–96). Hillsdale, NJ: Lawrence Erlbaum.

Thomson, E., McLanahan, S. S., & Curtin, R. B. (1992). Family structure, gender, and parental socialization. *Journal of Marriage and the Family, 54,* 368–378.

Trygstad, D. W., & Sanders, G. F. (1989). The significance of stepgrandparents. *International Journal of Aging and Human Development, 29,* 117–132.

Tzeng, J. M., & Mare, R. D. (1995). Labor market and socioeconomic effects on marital stability. *Social Science Research, 24,* 329–351.

U.S. Bureau of the Census (1992). Marriage, divorce, and remarriage in the 1990s. *Current Population Reports* (pp. 23–180). Washington, DC: U.S. Government Printing Office.

Visher, E. B., & Visher, J. S. (1988). *Old loyalties, new ties.* New York: Brunner/Mazel.

Visher, E. B., & Visher, J. S. (1990). Dynamics of successful stepfamilies. *Journal of Divorce and Remarriage, 14,* 3–11.

Vuchinich, S., Hetherington, E. M., Vuchinich, R. A., & Clingempeel, W. G. (1991). Parent and child interaction and gender differences in early adolescents' adaptation to stepfamilies. *Developmental Psychology, 27,* 618–626.

Werner, E. E. (1988). Individual differences, universal needs: A 30-year study of resilient high-risk infants. *Zero to Three: Bulletin of National Center for Clinical Infant Programs, 8,* 1–15.

Werner, E. E. (1993). Risk, resiliency and recovery: Perspectives from the Kauaii longitudinal study. *Development and Psychopathology, 54,* 503–515.

White, L. (1994). Stepfamilies over the life course: Social support. In A. Booth & J. Dunn (Eds.), *Stepfamilies: Who benefits? Who does not?* (pp. 109–138). Hillsdale, NJ: Lawrence Erlbaum.

Whitsett, D., & Land, H. (1992). The development of a role strain index for stepparents. *Families in Society: The Journal of Contemporary Human Services, 73,* 14–22.

Wilks, C., & Melville, C. (1990). Grandparents in custody and access disputes. *Journal of Divorce, 13,* 1–14.

Wilson, M. I., Daly, M., & Weghorst, S. J. (1980). Household composition and the risk of child abuse and neglect. *Journal of Biosocial Science, 12,* 333–340.

Zill, N., Morrison, D. R., & Coiro, M. J. (1993). Long-term effects of parental divorce and parent-child relationships, adjustment, and achievement in young adulthood. *Journal of Family Psychology, 7,* 91–103.

CHAPTER 10

Lesbian, Gay, and Bisexual Families

RITCH C. SAVIN-WILLIAMS AND KRISTIN G. ESTERBERG

A *Newsweek* cover story, "Gay Families Come Out," noted that "same-sex parents are trying to move out of the shadows and into the mainstream. Will they— and their kids—be accepted?" (Kantrowitz, 1996, p. 50). The answer, at least for the parents, appears to be an encouraging, though cautious, yes. On the basis of recent national polls, the majority of Americans (57%) believe that lesbians and gays are equal to heterosexuals in their parenting abilities, although only 36% are willing to extend their acceptance to favor adoption rights for same-sex couples.

Gay and lesbian families are not defined solely, however, by the presence of children. Just as it is impossible to describe a unitary heterosexual family, so it is implausible to assume that there is a single homogeneous lesbian or gay family. Traditional notions of family suggest that lesbian and gay families consist of two same-sex parents and their children. Clearly, this is not an adequate definition. As Stacey (1996) argued, a "real" lesbian-gay family does not exist because *all* families are potential candidates, if one means a family with at least one gay, lesbian, or bisexual member. By examining the diversity of lesbian and gay families, we can thus problematize traditional notions of family.

The following vignettes, based on real-life families who are familiar to us, bring into sharp focus several issues involved in defining lesbian and gay families.

- A bisexual woman with a history of serial relationships with women and men legally marries a man. Her early-adolescent niece lives with them much of the time. Several years later, the wife invites a lesbian with whom she would like to be involved to move into the home. The lesbian joins her lover's household, creating a four-member family (three adults and one child).

- A gay couple in their 30s who have lived together for eight years invites other single gays to join their family as adults with whom they are sexually involved. The couple anticipates that eventually these men will move out of their family to create another family, with which they may be involved. Currently, they have a three-member family (three adults) and have little or no interest in including children in their family.

- A gay couple, one aged 35 and the other aged 65, have been together for eight years. Anticipating his earlier death, the older legally adopted the younger to ensure full legal rights for the couple. They have had a church wedding ceremony, bought a house together, regularly entertain both gay and straight couples, and have no aspirations eventually to add children to their family.[1]

- A lesbian gave birth to a son, whom she conceived through alternative insemination. They live with her female lover. The child lives part of the week with his two mothers and the rest of the week with the gay sperm donor-father and his male lover. The family intends to add another child to their extended household, with the other woman becoming pregnant with sperm from the nonbiological father.

- A lesbian and her female ex-lover are raising their daughter. The three do not live together. The daughter is the biological child of the ex-lover, but her nonbiological mother has legal and physical custody.

- Two gay men who have lived together for over 10 years have opened their home to foster chil-

---

[1]Elovitz (1995) noted that such "adult adoptions" have frequently been disallowed as being "outside of the scope of adoption laws." Still, some gay men and lesbians have been attracted to such adoptions as a way of providing at least some legal protections for their relationships.

dren. They consider their immediate family to include themselves; their foster children; and the mother of one of the men, who lives with them.

- A lesbian couple adopted a newborn girl in an open adoption. Because of state law, only one of the women could have legal custody. The daughter continued to have regular contact with her birth mother after the adoption. When the girl was 5, her two mothers separated, and she went to live with the mother who had legal custody; the girl remains close to her other adoptive mother and her birth mother. Shortly thereafter, her legal mother became romantically involved with a woman who had three adopted sons. The girl thinks of herself as having three stepsiblings and four mothers: her birth mother, two "real" mothers, and a stepmother.

- A gay man in his 60s who lives alone has spent every Sunday and holiday for the past 10 years with his chosen family—another gay man and two lesbians. The four count on each other for emotional and sometimes financial support. They vacation together, plan elaborate holiday meals together, and speak to each other on the phone or in person nearly every day.

- A group of gay street kids relies on an older gay man, whom they call "the mother," for emotional support, small loans, and an occasional overnight stay. "The mother" has helped literally hundreds of street kids in this way, providing whatever he can in the way of food, shelter, and support.

- Three siblings, two 16-year-old identical twin brothers and an 18-year-old sister, are "out" in the local high school. Their father remains married to their mother, although he lives with his male lover of two years. The children report that their mother is now "hanging out all the time with her feminist friends," and they believe she may be a lesbian.

- A gay college junior, the only child of a wealthy East Coast couple, disclosed to his parents that he was gay and had AIDS. The couple did not reveal the son's status to his grandparents or other extended family members but declared

their commitment to him. He died two weeks later.

As these vignettes make clear, lesbian, bisexual, and gay families vary widely. They may or may not include children; they may be—but are most likely not—legally recognized; and they may include chosen kin, as well as biologically or legally recognized kin. Lesbian and gay family members may not even live together. We believe that all these situations are indeed examples of *families*. Although we may not necessarily agree with all the choices these families make, we applaud them for their willingness to expand traditional boundaries and to create life circumstances for themselves that meet their needs and those they love the most.

Just as some mainstream Americans are willing to acknowledge the existence of lesbian and gay families, so some researchers and clinicians are learning to accept lesbian-gay families as a legitimate topic of exploration. Three recent reviews (Allen & Demo, 1995; Demo & Allen, 1996; Laird, 1993) provided an overview of the issues that have been investigated, the many and varied gaps in our knowledge, and the significance of studying lesbian-gay families for theories of families, the health of families, and public policies that affect both lesbian and gay individuals and families.

It is difficult to know where or how to begin a new review of lesbian-gay families, given the excellence of previous efforts. Our focus here is not to duplicate these previous authors' feats, but to review more systematically the *empirical knowledge* that is currently available about these families. In the process, we also highlight our *lack* of knowledge and indicate where future research is needed. In some areas, such as research on the impact of having a lesbian or gay parent, there is considerable empirical research; in others, such as the transition of gays and lesbians to parenthood, almost no research has been published. Finally, we consider some of the current policy debates, including how family policies might better serve the diversity of lesbian-gay families.

In any review of lesbian-gay families, the issue of what constitutes a family must be addressed first. Certainly, lesbian and gay couples and individuals who parent children would be considered families, but our concern in this chapter is much broader. We extend our discussion to include

- families in which parents are heterosexual but the children are lesbian, gay, or bisexual

- children of lesbian and gay parents and how these children have fared, both psychologically and socially

- lesbian and gay adults who are making the decision to parent and the relationships they have with each other

- public policies that have, with relatively few exceptions, neglected the needs of gay and lesbian families

Whenever possible and relevant, we note issues of gender, race, and class and bring siblings, chosen kin, and extended family members into the discussion. We do not claim that this chapter represents a comprehensive review of the relevant literature; for example, we do not discuss families in which one adult discloses to a married spouse that he or she is gay or lesbian or adult intergenerational relationships in which the adult child is lesbian or gay and the parent is heterosexual.

In sharp contrast to much social science research, including research on homosexuality, that takes men as the standard, most of the literature on lesbians and gays as parents has focused on lesbians (see, for example, Lewin, 1993; Pollack & Vaughn, 1987). We have much greater gaps in our knowledge of gay fathers than of lesbian mothers. Empirical research into lesbian and gay families of color is nearly nonexistent (Hill's 1987 chapter on black lesbian mothers is one exception), and studies rarely consider issues of economic class.

First, we discuss our personal and theoretical perspectives on gay and lesbian families. Next, we focus on intrafamilial dynamics, when the adults are presumed heterosexuals and the children are not and when the adults are gay, lesbian, or bisexual and the children are (presumably) not. Issues include youths disclosing their sexuality to family members; parents' and siblings' reactions to that disclosure; the importance of parents to sexual-

minority youths; the effects on children of having lesbian or gay parents; the dynamics of lesbian or gay couples (both with and without children); and lesbian, gay, and bisexual adults who decide to parent. The final section includes issues that affect lesbian and gay families with children and presents a brief discussion of the debates on same-sex marriage and domestic partnerships and how these policies affect the variety of lesbian and gay families.

PERSPECTIVES

Esterberg's Personal and Theoretical Perspective

My primary academic research has focused on issues of identity and community among lesbians and bisexual women. Trained as a sociologist and influenced by feminist and social constructionist accounts of gender and sexuality, I have studied lesbian and bisexual women's narrative constructions of their identities, the stories they tell about who they are and how they came to be that way (Esterberg, 1997). Lesbians' and bisexual women's intimate relationships with other women are an important component of their constructions of the self; in fact, one identity account stressed the importance of love relationships with women in constructing a lesbian identity (Esterberg, 1994). Yet women do not construct their identities in isolation; lesbian communities are an important site for the evolution of lesbian and bisexual identities (Esterberg, 1997; Krieger, 1982; Lockard, 1985; Ponse, 1978).

My research on lesbian communities highlights their importance for the women involved. Some authors (see, for example, Krieger, 1982; Wolf, 1979) have discussed communities as being "like" families, with both the support and the boundary issues families involve. I argue, however, that the metaphor of family is not always appropriate for theorizing about lesbian communities, although families may be constructed in them; rather, lesbian communities are best seen as sets of overlapping social circles (Esterberg, 1997). Still, within these contexts, the variety of lesbian, gay, and bisexual families is apparent (see Weston, 1991, for an outstanding discussion of lesbians, gays, and kinship; see also Ainslie & Feltey, 1991). This research, combined with my own lesbian parenting, my participation in a lesbian mothers' support network, and my political activism, has sparked my scholarly interest in lesbian and gay families. I am particularly interested in identity constructions among lesbian mothers, both those who chose to parent after they came to see themselves as lesbian or bisexual and those who saw themselves as parents first (see also Lewin, 1993). I am also concerned with the legal and social constraints that lesbian and gay families face; the ways in which traditional definitions of family discount the realities of lesbian and gay family life; and how laws and social policies often work to the detriment of lesbians, gays, and children.

Savin-Williams's Personal and Theoretical Perspective

As a developmental and clinical psychologist, my academic focus has been on adolescent peer relationships and the ways in which they affect psychological and social adjustment. When I discovered in 1981 that my life would be a better experience by being overtly gay (see Savin-Williams, 1993, for an account of this experience), my teaching, research, and clinical interests converged on sexual-minority youths. Now, I primarily investigate the ways in which poor peer relationships, which include verbal and physical harassment, affect the mental health of youths with same-sex attractions and the diversity in the developmental trajectories of sexual-minority youths. Although peer relations are clearly of significant consideration, I have come to recognize, largely through my clinical work, the far greater dynamic gravity of the relationships that youths have—or do not have—with family members. For example, although youths may first disclose to a best friend and be "out" to most in their social world, they do not consider themselves to be *really* out until they tell their parents. The more significant the parent, the more critical her (usually) or his reactions are for a youth's self-acceptance and personal happiness. This realization has led me to refocus my research attention to the relationships that

sexual-minority youths have with their families (Savin-Williams, 1998a, 1998b, in preparation; Savin-Williams & Dubé, 1998).

Clinically, my primary concern is with increasing the stability and healthy functioning of sexual-minority individuals; insofar as doing so includes exploring family dynamics, I am concerned with families. This partiality is a result of my perception that relative to the heterosexual members of these families, gay constituents have far fewer sources of affirmation and support. Thus, I use whatever clinical, research, and teaching tools that work to increase knowledge, sensitivities, and healthy functioning, whether of the family unit or individual members in it. Anonymous questionnaires, psychometrically validated research instruments, behavioral observations, and in-depth interviews are research methods that I use to gain a better understanding of sexual-minority individuals within their family context.

Previous Research

In their excellent review of research on gay and lesbian families, Demo and Allen (1996, p. 422) noted the critical need for research that captures "multiple and divergent vantage points on family boundaries, histories, rules, rituals and related dynamics." They were convinced that these issues had been largely ignored by investigators of lesbian-gay families:

> There have been no studies designed to describe relationships that lesbians or gay men have with their grandparents, grandchildren, nieces, nephews, aunts, uncles or other extended kin. Family level analyses, incorporating multiple intra- and intergenerational perspectives, remain largely unexplored . . . thus restricting our understanding of how these families function, how they define their boundaries, make decisions, divide labor, resolve conflicts, experience and cope with internal and external stressors, indeed, how they legitimate their very existence. (p. 421)

We disagree, to some extent, with this dire assessment of research on lesbian and gay families. For example, the issue of a child's disclosure of her or his sexuality to parents and siblings has been investigated from the perspectives of youths and, to a lesser extent, parents and siblings; however, no study has examined the multiple perspectives of the effects of disclosure on a child's individual development, the adults' perceptions of themselves as parents, or family interactions *in the same family*. For example, Boxer, Cook, and Herdt (1991) interviewed over 200 gay youths and 50 parents, but these 50 were not the parents of any of the interviewed youths. In fact, the two groups represented different populations: youths from an inner-city lesbian-gay community center and parents from an upper-middle-class, suburban parents' group. Most of the youths (70%) were racial-ethnic minorities, yet few of the parents were other than white, and most were of a different generation than the youths' parents.

When the sexual orientation of the principals is reversed and the adults are lesbian, bisexual, or gay and the children are presumed to be heterosexual, considerable research has expanded our knowledge of lesbian and gay families. Although much is known about the impact on children of being raised by lesbian (usually) or gay adults, little information is available, except from personal narratives, about the effects on the adults of having children and about intrafamilial relationships under such situations. This lack of information has not, of course, stopped advice-giving tracts from speculating on how the adults should behave in these situations. Again, in these family constellations, little is known about the roles or impact of the extended family members, such as grandparents, stepfamily members, aunts, uncles, and cousins of the children or adults.

Other options, such as families in which all members, adults and children, are lesbian, gay, or bisexual or in which a grandparent or another extended family member is a sexual minority and other family members are heterosexual are rarely conceived, let alone subjected to empirical investigation. The psychological and sociological study of lesbian and gay families needs to be considerably more advanced before this level of analysis can be undertaken. In this regard, our view is consistent with Demo and Allen (1996). Nevertheless, a start has been made, and it is this literature that we review. When a particular research area is slighted,

a brief summary and references of recent reviews of the literature are provided.

The primary focus in the next section is on family dynamics in which adults are presumed to be heterosexuals and children are lesbian, gay, or bisexual.[2] This review is an extensive one, in large part because of the burgeoning research interest in this area and because of the clinical needs of both the youths and their families.

WHEN PARENTS ARE HETEROSEXUAL AND CHILDREN ARE GAY

The Youth-Parent Relationship

Few researchers have investigated the complexities of the relationships that sexual-minority youths have with their parents. Instead, they have focused on the difficulties that youths have disclosing to parents and the parents' reactions on discovering their children's sexual identities. The limited empirical evidence suggests, it is surprising to note, given the popular literature and personal narratives of children (see, for example, Heron, 1994) and adults (Griffin, Wirth, & Wirth, 1986), that the gay child-heterosexual parent relationship, especially the child-mother relationship, is generally positive and satisfying.

Although it is not possible to estimate the exact percentage of youths who have disclosed their same-sex attractions to their parents, surveys have found that 40% to 75% of youths have disclosed to their mothers and 30% to 55% have disclosed to their fathers (Savin-Williams, 1998a). Parents are seldom the first to know about their daughters' or sons' same-sex attractions, and mothers are usually told before fathers. The most consistent conclusion that can be drawn from a review of the literature is the existence of a cohort effect (Savin-Williams, 1998b). With each passing year, a greater percentage of youths are disclosing to their parents. Whether this trend will be reversed, given the current political climate, is uncertain. Information on when youths disclose this information, how they share it, and why they decide to disclose is even

[2]For a more complete discussion of these issues, see Savin-Williams (1998a, 1998b, in preparation) and Savin-Williams & Dubé (1998).

more sparse. A parent may be the first to know or the last; she or he may be told directly, perhaps within the context of a family meeting, or become suspicious because of a son's or daughter's gender-atypical behavior or interests. Finally, the effects that disclosure to parents have on the self-evaluations of sexual-minority youths or their parents have not been systematically or definitively explored.

Some youths do not expect their parents to react positively to their disclosure (Savin-Williams, 1994). They fear they will be expelled from their families, so they choose to postpone, possibly indefinitely, telling their parents about their sexuality. For example, in a sample of youths in support groups (Pilkington & D'Augelli, 1995), slightly over 60% had experienced some degree of verbal or physical harassment from a family member. Significantly more girls than boys were physically assaulted, and mothers (22%) were the most frequent abusers, followed by brothers (15%), fathers (14%), and sisters (9%).

Youths may not want to disclose simply because they do not want either to disappoint or hurt their parents or to place them in an awkward position with relatives and neighbors (Savin-Williams, in preparation). Youths may also fear the long-term effects that such disclosures would have on their status in their immediate and extended families. When the physical and emotional danger of disclosing is real, the only viable alternative for youths may be to mislead and lie to parents. The other possibility, that the anticipated family crisis may not be as traumatic in reality as it appears in the youths' fantasies, must also be seriously considered when sexual-minority youths are deciding whether they should disclose to their parents.

Indeed, in several studies, youths who had not disclosed to their parents expected, perhaps for realistic reasons, a more negative reaction than that received by the youths who had disclosed. In one study, over half the nondisclosers expected their mothers to be intolerant or rejecting, and nearly two thirds expected the same reactions from their fathers (D'Augelli & Hershberger, 1993). These percentages contrast markedly from those who had disclosed to their parents: Only 20% of the mothers and 28% of the fathers were intolerant or rejecting.

Despite their expectations, relatively few of the nondisclosers (about 5%) expressed the fear that they would suffer physical harm from their parents or would be thrown out of the homes if they were more open about their sexuality (D'Augelli & Hershberger, 1993; Herdt & Boxer, 1993; Pilkington & D'Augelli, 1995).

Regardless of whether youths have disclosed, their relationships with their mothers have been reported to be considerably better than those with their fathers (Ben-Ari, 1995; Cramer & Roach, 1988; Herdt & Boxer, 1993; Savin-Williams, 1989, 1990). For example, nearly 60% of the boys and 50% of the girls who came to a youth-serving agency in Chicago had positive or very positive relationships with their mothers, but only 30% of the boys and 24% of the girls had similarly positive relationships with their fathers (Herdt & Boxer, 1993). In another study (Savin-Williams, 1989), perceived satisfaction with the relationships and contact with parents were greater for mothers than for fathers for both sons and daughters. These data probably differ little from heterosexual children's relative preference for their mothers versus their fathers.

Maintaining good relations in their families is clearly a high priority among many sexual-minority youths. In one study (Savin-Williams, 1990), nearly 60% of the lesbian and gay college students who did not live at home had at least weekly contact by phone, mail, or visit with their mothers; comparable percentages with fathers were 33% (daughters) and 42% (sons). Hershberger and D'Augelli (1995) suggested that youths actively seek the support of their families when they experience victimization and that the families extend support when the youths are harassed or distressed.

Only one investigation (Savin-Williams, 1989) attempted to predict the nature of the parent-child relationship on the basis of the characteristics of the youths, parents, and their relationship. Lesbian and bisexual women who were most satisfied with their relationships with their parents maintained the most contact with them, disclosed to them their same-sex orientations, established high levels of self-esteem (true for maternal relationships only), and had married parents (paternal relationships only). For gay and bisexual sons, frequent contact with parents, high self-esteem, young parents (maternal relationships only), and fathers who knews their sons' sexual orientations predicted high satisfaction with the son-parent relationship. The significance of the mothers' youthfulness may indicate a cohort effect; young mothers would more likely have been raised at a time when the visibility of homosexuality encouraged greater openness and tolerance of same-sex attractions.

The long-term effect of disclosure on youths' relationships with their parents is an increasingly important issue because more youths are telling their parents at a sufficiently young age to have extended postdisclosure relations with parents while they are still living at home. The literature says little about sexual-minority youths' relationships with their siblings, grandparents, and extended family members. Sexual-minority youths may disclose to nonparent relatives, but little is known about when and how they do so or the reactions the youths receive. Acceptance from siblings is considerably more common than rejection, although the support that sexual-minority youths receive from their brothers and sisters is less positive than the support they receive from peers, equal to the support they receive from their mothers, and more than the support they receive from their fathers. Although some individuals report that they will never be fully out until their grandparents are dead, they may be relinquishing potential sources of support and guidance from grandparents who could assume an intermediary role in salvaging the integrity and coherency of the family. Thus, if youths do not disclose to extended family members, some of whom may also be gay or lesbian, they may lose sources of information and acceptance (Savin-Williams, 1998a).

Racial-Ethnic Minority Youths

The relationships that sexual-minority youths have with their parents have rarely been empirically explored separately by race or ethnicity, despite the fact that many studies on sexual-minority youths include large numbers of racial-ethnic minority youths (see, for example, D'Augelli & Hershberger, 1993; Herdt & Boxer, 1993; Telljohann & Price, 1993). Studies of parents appear to be prima-

rily of whites. Yet, family dynamics are likely to be different for racial-ethnic minority youths. For example, minority family constellations may emphasize a greater integration of the extended family within the ethnic support system. The family often "constitutes a symbol of their basic roots and the focal point of their ethnic identity" (Morales, 1983, p. 9). To tell their parents about their same-sex attractions, racial-ethnic minority youths may risk their association, identification, and support within their extended communities, which may be of far greater significance than it is for white youths.

Given the emotional centrality of the extended family, some racial-ethnic minority youths with same-sex attractions may believe that they can never publicly disclose their sexual identities because they do not want to humiliate or bring shame to their parents in the eyes of their close-knit, multigenerational extended families (Greene, 1994; Tremble, Schneider, & Appathurai, 1989). Indeed, Garnets and Kimmel (1993) observed that Asian, African American, and Latino gays and lesbians disclose to their families at lower rates than do white youths. However, Chan (1989) reported that 80% of the Chinese, Japanese, and Korean young adults in her study disclosed to a family member, usually a sister; only one quarter disclosed to their parents. Thus, disclosing to a sibling may serve an important function for sexual-minority youths—to gain some measure of acceptance and support and perhaps assistance in coming out to parents. The parents may have their suspicions, as Loiacano's (1989) African American informants described, but they may conspire in this silence, hesitant to publicly acknowledge their bisexual, lesbian, or gay children to avoid embarrassing relatives and their ethnic communities.

Because an extremely weak empirical base of support underlies much of the discourse on race, ethnicity, and sexual orientation, caution must be emphasized in accepting without further investigation any generalizations about the uniqueness or sameness of racial-ethnic minority gay, lesbian, and bisexual youths and their families. In describing the experiences of racial-ethnic minority youth disclosure to parents, issues of variability must be considered. Not all racial-ethnic groups are similar to each other and distinct from the majority culture in the same way. Within each racial-ethnic group, families have distinct functions and structures because of their histories, religious values, and immigration status.

Parental Reactions

Parents may have early "suspicions" that their sons or daughters are not heterosexual. Over one quarter of the parents in one study reported that they suspected that their children were gay or lesbian before they found out (Robinson, Walters, & Skeen, 1989). Some confronted their children with their belief or arranged for them to be in gender-typical activities; others waited, hoping nervously that another fate would befall their children. More commonly, although the data to support this assumption are inconclusive, many parents never suspect that their children are not heterosexual and thus are shocked when they are told or discover the children's sexual orientation.

Responses, such as shock, refusal to believe the information, or dismissal of the children's homosexuality as a phase indicate that parents have accepted myths and stereotypes of gay people and the kind of life they are "condemned" to live. Or they may believe that homosexuality will become an exaggerated feature in their children's lives and that they will be shamed and humiliated when other family members, friends, religious leaders, coworkers, or neighbors learn the "family secret" (Bernstein, 1990; DeVine, 1984; Hammersmith, 1987). To thwart this "public scandal," parents may distance themselves from their spouses, extended families, friends, and religious communities, isolating themselves from others and thus preempting the ostracism they feel will inevitably come. They may selectively edit details about their sons or daughters with cryptic references and mysterious glances and demand that the children tell no one else, perhaps even the other parent. The fewer who know, the safer the parents feel. Religious parents may pray for a conversion, and others may send the children to psychotherapists in futile attempts to proselytize or cure.

Several studies have explicitly assessed the range of initial family reactions to disclosure.

Savin-Williams (1998a) reported that nearly half the mothers of gay and bisexual college students responded with disbelief, denial, or negative comments, such as "It won't last," and half the fathers reacted with silence or disbelief. In contrast, 60% of the siblings were supportive. Furthermore, 18% of the parents responded with acts of intolerance, attempts to convert the children to heterosexuality, and verbal threats to cut off financial or emotional support. Only 11% of the mothers, 3% of the fathers, and 2% of the siblings responded with threats of rejection, uncontrolled emotional outbursts, or other severely negative reactions. None of the youths was evicted from the home, and only one was physically attacked by his father. It should be kept in mind, however, that these data are based on the reports of youths, not of their parents.

Ben-Ari (1995) investigated small samples of gay and lesbian young adults and parents who were not, however, the parents of the youths in the study. The young adults reported that their parents' most frequent initial reaction was shock, followed closely by shame, guilt, and acknowledgment; rejection was the least-common reaction. Compared to the young adults' ratings, the parents reported higher levels of shock and guilt and greater acknowledgment and acceptance. Participants in both samples agreed that the mothers felt greater anger and guilt, that fathers were more likely to deny and reject, and that the two did not differ on shame or acknowledgment. However, because the parents and the young adults were not related, it is difficult to ascertain if the differential responses of the two samples were related to different perceptions of the same event or to the fact that the two samples were drawn from two different populations.

In a cross-national survey of over 400 parents in support groups for families of lesbians, gays, and bisexuals, almost two thirds reported that their initial response was negative, with grieflike reactions, and nearly half experienced guilt (Robinson et al., 1989). Because the sample consisted overwhelmingly of mothers, these figures reflect the reactions of mothers more than fathers.

According to Ben-Ari (1995), parental reactions can be attributed, in part, to the parents' lack of exposure to homosexuality. Many parents reported that they had no understanding of homosexuality, held common stereotypes, or never thought about it. As parents move away from their initial shock and mourn the loss of their heterosexual children, some anger, guilt, and grief may linger, but silent tolerance begins to emerge among some parents. They may feel guilty for not recognizing their children's "condition" early enough to change the outcome or for being the kind of parents who "cause" children to be gay or lesbian. Others may search for an external cause, such as a bad second parent, early sexual abuse, an "alternative" peer group, or a gay teacher as a way to project blame and thus abate feelings of guilt.

The adjustment period may be relatively brief. One month after the disclosure, both the youths and parents in Ben-Ari's study (1995) reported decreases in shock, denial, guilt, and rejection and marked increases in acknowledgment and acceptance. The focus shifted from attempts to alter the children's sexuality to understanding the possible implications of the children's being gay, lesbian, or bisexual. The parents may mourn the inevitable loneliness they assume their children will experience in old age or believe that they will never have a stable relationship, will be childless, or will face discrimination that results in a clandestine, unhappy life. The most important concerns of the parents in Ben-Ari's (1995) study were, in descending order, negative social attitudes, lack of a family life, a harder lifestyle, and fear of AIDS. Because of fear that they will lose their place in the children's lives, many parents are motivated to accept their children's sexual orientation (Boxer et al., 1991; Robinson et al., 1989).

Empirical investigations have found that many parents integrate their children's sexuality into family life. In one sample, 97% of the parents eventually came to accept their sexual-minority children (Robinson et al., 1989). Although the findings of this study are limited in their generalizability to other parents, they offer hope to parents who struggle with their children's homosexuality or bisexuality. Other studies have supported this view: Relationships with parents often deteriorate following disclosure but significantly improve thereafter (Ben-Ari, 1995; Cramer & Roach, 1988; Muller, 1987). It is unclear from the empirical literature how parents move toward acceptance of their gay and

lesbian children and why other parents fail to resolve their dilemmas with their children. Recognizing and integrating the child's and family's new identities require time, trust, flexibility, and stamina.

Youths, however, are less likely than parents to perceive a positive change in the parent-child relationship following disclosure. For example, Ben-Ari (1995) reported that following disclosure, 66% of the lesbian and gay young adults thought that their relationships with their mothers improved, but only 44% thought so about their relationships with their fathers. The parents were strikingly more likely to report improvement: 84% of the mothers and 63% of the fathers.

The differences between the two generations' perceptions of postdiscovery reactions may be real or may be related to the characteristics of the populations sampled. For example, in all but a few cases, the parents were recruited from parents' support groups; perhaps because of this membership, they were more likely to have adapted positively to the reality of having lesbian or gay children. Many of the youths were also from support groups, both community and university based, and may have joined because of problems they were having with their parents.

One other important development *for parents* was articulated in Boxer et al.'s (1991, pp. 83–84) interviews. The parents spoke of an inner process of self-questioning that the discovery elicited, "an opportunity for growth and personal development, coincident with transitions in middle age." Many believed that going through this process made them more socially and culturally enlightened.

In the studies reviewed in this section, few researchers directly asked parents about their lives as parents of bisexual, lesbian, or gay children. Much of what is known was derived from asking youths to report on their parents and, as Ben-Ari (1995) noted, these subjective reports are not always consistent with those of parents. The potential for distortion thus poses a significant risk. Studies that include parents are usually based on samples of parents in support groups, which limits the generalizability of the results to parents who are not in support groups. As a result, little is known about parents who struggle alone or with the assistance of friends and relatives. Other fertile areas of inquiry are the factors—including personal characteristics, sociodemographic factors, and relationship qualities—that predict the reactions that parents will have to the disclosure of their children's sexual orientation and whether parents' reactions vary by the sex of the children (for a review, see Savin-Williams, in preparation).

WHEN PARENTS ARE LESBIAN, GAY, OR BISEXUAL

Transition to Parenthood

Considerable data have been collected about the children of lesbian or gay parents, and a growing body of research has examined dyadic relationships within lesbian and gay couples. Yet almost no research has focused on issues related to the transition to parenthood for lesbian, gay, or bisexual parents—a topic that has been of considerable interest to social scientists regarding heterosexual parents (see, for example, Belsky & Rovine, 1990; Cowan & Cowan, 1992). Researchers have investigated how the timing of entrance into marriage and parenting affects heterosexual parents' satisfaction with their relationships, divorce, and children's well-being, as well as gender relations within heterosexual families. But this body of research has little to say about lesbian and gay families. Studies have not, by and large, considered how lesbians and gays enter into and negotiate family life, including the stressors and supports they encounter. Although scholars (see, for example, Polikoff, 1990) have acknowledged that parenting issues are different for those who become parents within the context of heterosexual marriages from the issues for those who choose parenting within the context of a lesbian or gay relationship, little rigorous, empirical work has examined the daily realities of lesbian, gay, and bisexual family life. On the other hand, a number of edited volumes contain personal narratives and advice aimed at prospective lesbian and gay parents (Arnup, 1995; Martin, 1993; Pies, 1988; Pollack & Vaughn, 1987). These books provide rich anecdotal evidence of the problems, issues, and joys of lesbian and gay family life and are particularly valuable to those who are in the early stages of thinking about parenting.

At the individual level, many issues need to be considered.

- What does it mean to be a lesbian or gay parent within the context of a legal and social system that declares that being lesbian or gay and a parent is incompatible? How do lesbian and gay parents simultaneously construct sexual identities and parenting identities, and how do these identity constructions vary, depending on the circumstances?

- How do lesbian and gay parents negotiate the institutions that child rearing brings to them, such as child care settings and schools? How are lesbian and gay parents—and their institutions—affected by these interactions?

- In what ways is the transition to parenthood both similar to and different from that of heterosexual parents? How do lesbian and gay relationships change with the addition of children, in terms of satisfaction with the relationship, the division of household labor, commitment to equality, and other factors?

- What sources of support are available to lesbian and gay parents from families of origin, chosen kin, and lesbian and gay communities? (Ainslie & Feltey; 1991; Weston, 1991).

Few studies have addressed these issues. Although Slater (1995) mapped a "family life cycle" for lesbian couples based on clinical evidence, she did not focus primarily on couples with children. Several studies have considered sources of support for lesbian mothers. Levy (1989) argued that being open about their lesbian identity may be a source of stress for lesbian mothers, in part because of the legal restrictions that lesbian mothers face. In her study, unlike Lewin's (1993), lesbian parents more often sought support from partners and other lesbians than from their families of origin. In their small-scale study, Ainslie and Feltey (1991) similarly found that lesbian communities were sources of support for the feminist lesbian parents in their sample. Little work has examined the interaction of lesbian and gay parents with educational institutions. Casper and Schultz's (1996) descriptive study of 17 parents is one exception.

Clearly, further research on these and related issues is needed.

Dyadic Relations within Gay and Lesbian Couples

Although there is little research on intergenerational family processes among lesbians and gay men, the literature on the relationships of same-sex couples is much further developed. Several large-scale studies of lesbian and gay couples have been undertaken during the past 17 years. Blumstein and Schwartz's (1983) classic study of 12,000 individuals in both same-sex and heterosexual couples (married and cohabitating) investigated how the couples managed money, work, and sexuality. Among their many findings was a high commitment to equality among lesbian couples. Although all types of couples tended to have at least one member who was relationship centered, lesbian couples tended to be more relationship centered than other couples. Gay and lesbian couples shared more leisure activities than heterosexual couples, which may be important in enhancing levels of satisfaction; those who spent more time together were more satisfied with their relationships. In general, Blumstein and Schwartz found that gender was important in all types of couples; in a number of respects, lesbians were more similar to heterosexual women than to gay men, who, in turn, were more similar to heterosexual men than to lesbians (see also Bailey, Gaulin, Agyei, & Gladue, 1994, for a discussion of sex differences in sexual behavior and fantasy, jealousy, status, preference for partners, and attractiveness).

Bryant and Demian's (1994) national survey of 1,266 primarily white, well-educated lesbian and gay couples provided basic data on such issues as social support, finances, children, legal arrangements, and relationship rituals. Although the goal was primarily descriptive, Bryant and Demian also explored the correlates of relationship quality. For women, the quality of their relationships was positively related to the quality of sexual interactions, commitment to the relationship, joint income, and having executed legal protections (such as wills or powers of attorney) but negatively associated with abusive behaviors and having big arguments. For men, the quality of their relationships was associated with the same things, along with the practice of relationship rituals, and was negatively associated with the breaking of sexual agreements.

Using longitudinal data from lesbian, gay, and heterosexual couples, Kurdek (1988, 1991a, 1991b, 1992, 1994, 1995) published a series of excellent articles on the quality and stability of relationships, social support, and the allocation of household labor. His research is notable for its use of longitudinal data and comparisons with heterosexual married and cohabitating couples, when appropriate. The findings as a whole underscore the somewhat greater importance of equality for lesbian partners than for gay partners. Both lesbian and gay couples were more likely to split household tasks equitably than were heterosexual married couples. The correlates of satisfaction with the relationship were similar for lesbians and gay men, although these correlates changed somewhat over time. For both lesbians and gays, over time, the importance of ideal attachment decreased; changes in commitment to the relationship were explained by discrepancies between current and ideal levels of equality (Kurdek, 1995).

In a unique study (Patterson, 1995a) of 66 lesbian mothers and their 37 children aged 4–9, biological and nonbiological mothers did not differ in their satisfaction with the relationship or in their belief that household labor and decision-making should be equally shared by both partners. The partners maintained this egalitarian division of labor except in the domain of child care, which was more often the responsibility of the birth mother, and paid employment, in which nonbiological mothers reported spending more time. These differences, however, were considerably less stark than is typically found in heterosexual couples. The lesbian couples encouraged and provided opportunities for their children to have considerable contact with their grandparents and other extended family members, especially aunts and uncles.

Although the research on gay couples who are fathers is far more limited, McPherson (1993) found that such couples were more likely than their heterosexual counterparts to report an even distribution of child care and household chores and to be satisfied with the division of labor. The gay couples were also more likely to express satisfaction with their relationships, especially in terms of cohesion and expression of affection.

After reviewing 20 studies of lesbian individuals and couples, Schreurs (1993) concluded that gender is more important than sexual orientation in shaping sexuality. Similar to heterosexual women and unlike gay and heterosexual men, lesbians indicated that emotional closeness was more often a reason to have sex than arousal or the desire for an orgasm. Monogamy was also more often valued and enacted, sex was less frequent, and the other's satisfaction was more often considered in a sexual situation by the lesbian couples (see also Blumstein & Schwartz, 1983; Kurdek, 1995). Lesbian partners were equal to gay and heterosexual partners in their evaluations of the relevance of sexuality in their lives and the importance of sexual compatibility in their emotional relationships, but were less likely to communicate with each other about sexuality. However, Deenen, Gijs, and van Naerssen (1994), among others, found that gay partners value the emotional aspects of their relationships above sexual satisfaction.

Peplau, Veniegas, and Campbell's (1996) and Kurdek's (1995) reviews of the body of research on lesbian and gay couples concluded that when compared with heterosexual couples, lesbian and gay partners reported the following:

- An equal desire to be in committed, enduring romantic relationships.

- Comparable levels of feeling attracted to their partners, satisfaction with the relationships, and less difficulty breaking up when serious problems develop.

- An equal valuing of egalitarian relationships, although whether such relationships were enacted varied from study to study, and a rejection of the traditional husband-wife, masculine-feminine division of labor in favor of flexibility and sharing of housework, household expenses, and roles. Lesbian couples more than gay couples equally shared household labor.

- Similar levels and kinds of conflicts (e.g., over finances, driving styles, and affection and sex) but with unique ones related to gender (merger for lesbians, competition for gay men), sexual

orientation (disclosure to family members), and race-ethnicity (strong conflict when extended family ties were strong).

- Similar predictors of satisfaction with and stability of relationships, such as interdependence and problem-solving abilities. Most studies reported relatively high levels of satisfaction among their respondents.

In sum, the body of research is fairly well developed in its coverage of a number of issues: satisfaction with relationships, issues of equality, and conflict. Although earlier studies tended to compare lesbians and gays with heterosexuals, many studies have also examined differences and similarities between lesbians and gay men. Relatively little research, however, has focused on issues specific to lesbian and gay couples with children. Whether the relationships of lesbian and gay couples change in predictable ways with the addition of children has yet to be demonstrated.

Children with Lesbian or Gay Parents

Significant research attention has been paid to the *children* of lesbian and gay parents. Over 20 scholars have reviewed what is known about the effects on children of having lesbian or gay parents (see Murphy & Rodríques-Nogués, 1995, for an annotated bibliography). Many of these studies were published during the 1980s and early 1990s, when custody cases regarding the children of lesbian or gay adults were entering the judicial system.[3] Much of this literature has taken a defensive stance, aiming to document that lesbian (and, less often, gay) parents are just as capable as heterosexual parents. Despite the assumption by many judges and child welfare officials that lesbian and gay parents are unfit, this research has incontrovertibly shown the parenting abilities of lesbian and gay adults.

Patterson (1992; 1995b, 1995c, 1996) has become the most recent and persistent of these reviewers. She noted that much of this literature is based on small-scale studies of children raised by

---

[3]Custody cases involving lesbian and gay parents did not, of course, begin in the 1980s. As Pollack (1987) noted, the 1975 case of Mary Jo Risher, who lost custody of her 9-year-old son, was well publicized in the media.

divorced lesbian mothers who were once in heterosexual marriages. Recently, research has expanded to include never-married lesbian and bisexual women who decide, with or without same-sex partners, to become parents by giving birth through donor insemination or by adopting. Relatively few studies have included gay men with children, perhaps because men cannot physically bear children and are seldom granted custody in divorce proceedings or because they are extremely reticent to disclose their status publicly for fear of losing all contact with their children, who are likely to be living with their biological mothers as the result of the general judicial bias against granting custody to men (Barrett & Robinson, 1990; Patterson & Chan, 1997).

All the reviewers found little or no empirical evidence to support the conclusion that children who are raised by lesbian and gay parents have any deficits as the result of living in lesbian or gay families (for a meta-analysis of the research, see Allen & Burrell, 1996). Despite the fears of judges and child welfare workers, children of lesbian or gay parents are no more likely than children of heterosexual parents to identify as lesbian, gay, or bisexual. Other research, also limited in scope, has indicated that there is no difference between children who are raised by lesbian or gay versus heterosexual parents regarding gender identity, sex-role behavior, self-concept, intelligence, personality characteristics, behavioral problems, peer relations, and likelihood of being sexually abused. For example, Patterson and Chan (1997, p. 258) concluded: "There is little evidence to suggest that children of gay fathers are any more likely to encounter difficulties in the development of their own sexual identities, to be the victims of sexual abuse, or for that matter, to be placed at any significant disadvantage relative to otherwise similar children of heterosexual fathers." Children of divorced lesbian mothers often have contact with other adults, including their fathers, male friends of their lesbian mothers, and their mothers' lesbian partners and female friends. Allen and Burrell (1996, p. 19) concluded:

The results demonstrate no differences on any measures between the heterosexual and homosexual parents regarding parenting styles, emotional adjustment,

and sexual orientation of the child(ren). In other words, the data fail to support the continuation of a bias against homosexual parents by any court.

Although reviewers have suggested that investigations of gay fathers are needed, as are large-scale studies of children born to lesbian and bisexual women, the political implications of such research need to be considered. Is the goal of this research to compare lesbian and gay families with heterosexual ones? If so, for what purpose? If not, is the goal to compare gay and lesbian families? White versus racial-ethnic families? Upper-class versus working-class families? To characterize ideal conditions for establishing and maintaining gay families? Most of the research to date has attempted to show that lesbian parents are, essentially, similar to heterosexual parents; this research has been used, with mixed success, in court cases and custody challenges. But Pollack (1987), among others (including Stacey, 1996), argued that the emphasis on similarities between lesbian and gay parents and heterosexual parents does not, ultimately, well serve lesbian-gay parents and their children. What is needed is research that considers the particular strengths that children who live in lesbian and gay households may develop, including a greater appreciation of diversity; a willingness to challenge traditional sex-role stereotypes, and an ability to fashion creative, healthy, nurturing family relationships despite legal restraints.

However, some judges disregard the empirical evidence in their custody decisions. The highly publicized cases of Sharon Bottoms, the Virginia mother who lost custody of her son because of her sexual orientation, and Mary Ward, a Florida mother who lost custody to her ex-husband, a convicted murderer, highlight the intractability of homophobic stereotypes among some in the child welfare system. Still, many judges have drawn on social science research in making their decisions, thus emphasizing the importance of high-quality empirical research. We agree with the assumption made by the First Circuit Court of the State of Hawaii in the *Baehr v. Miike* case (Chang, 1996) regarding same-sex marriages. The court argued that it is incumbent on defendants of the status quo to prove that the sexual orientation of parents is in and of itself an indicator of parental fitness. The sexual orientation of parents automatically disqualifies them from being good, fit, loving or successful parents. (p. 35)

For too long, custody, adoption, and visitation decisions have been on the basis of myth and prejudice. It is time for those who believe that lesbian, gay, and bisexual individuals should be disqualified from parenting because of their alleged adverse effects on children to *prove their case.*

POLICY ISSUES

Legal Issues

Several excellent reviews of the legal literature related to gay and lesbian families are available. The National Center for Lesbian Rights has long advocated for lesbian families; its guide (1990) provides information on basic legal issues facing lesbian families (see also Editors of the Harvard Law Review, 1989; de LaMadrid, 1991). Legal scholar Polikoff (1990) noted that legal issues for "intentional" lesbian families are notably different from those of lesbians who gave birth or adopted in the context of heterosexual marriages, in which custody and visitation issues may be paramount. When a lesbian or gay parent is challenged in court by a hostile heterosexual parent, the lesbian or gay parent is likely to lose. As Barrett and Robinson (1990) argued, it is almost impossible for gay men to obtain custody of their children if it is contested, and even visitation rights may be denied or sharply curtailed. Lesbian and gay parents have been required to live apart from their same-sex partners and to sever contact with lesbian and gay communities to maintain custody or visitation rights.

For children born to two (or more) lesbian or gay parents, other issues emerge. As Polikoff (1990) argued, two legal assumptions work to undermine nontraditional families. The law typically requires that the child have one parent of each sex; the two persons identified as mother and father have all rights and responsibilities, and all others have none. Returning to the vignettes with which we began this chapter, we see that this assumption undermines many of the families created by lesbians, gays, and bisexuals. Although a few states and localities grant second-parent adoptions, in which a coparent has been allowed to adopt the child legally without the birth or adoptive parent giving up legal rights to the child, for most lesbian and gay parents this is not an option simply because of the legal code of the state or locality in which they reside. Also, second-parent adoption will not necessarily help support all family forms lesbians and gays have created, such as families consisting of two lesbian mothers and two gay fathers.

The result is that many of those who have functioned as parents since the birth or adoption of their children have no legal relationship to the children. While this situation may affect families on a day-to-day basis (for example, when one parent is denied the right to make legal or medical decisions for her or his child), the effect can be devastating in the case of the break-up of the parents or the death of the legal parent. Polikoff (1990) reviewed the legal literature on this issue and found that, when a couple dissolves their relationship and the legal parent decides to terminate the relationship between her (typically) or his child and a nonlegal parent, the courts are hesitant to establish the rights of the nonlegal parent. If the legal parent dies, at least some precedents for granting custody of the child to the nonlegal parent usually exist. Still, custody is not certain, especially when a relative of the legal parent contests it. In these cases, grandparents and siblings of the legal parent have greater legal standing than the one who has actually done the day-to-day parenting. To our knowledge, no research has examined how the lack of legal recognition affects power in the parents' relationship or the quality of parent-child relationships. Especially as the number of intentional lesbian and gay families increases, such research will be crucial for a greater understanding of how the law supports—or, more often, fails to support—lesbian and gay families.

Same-Sex Marriages and Domestic Partnerships

Although a full review of the issues involved in same-sex marriages and domestic partnerships is well beyond the scope of this chapter, we briefly consider these issues as we close this chapter. In his review of the law regarding the legal consequences of same-sex marriage, Chambers (1996, pp. 447–448) concluded:

> Laws that treat married persons in a different manner than they treat single persons permeate nearly every field of social regulation in this country—taxation, torts, evidence, social welfare, inheritance, adoption, and on and on. . . . [I]n some significant respects the remaining distinctive laws of marriage are better suited to the life situations of same-sex couples than they are to those of the opposite-sex couples for whom they were devised; and, most broadly, that the package of rules relating to marriage, while problematic in some details and unduly exclusive in some regards, are a just response by the state to the circumstances of persons who live together in enduring, emotionally based attachments. Legal marriage, somewhat surprisingly to a person long dubious of the state's regulation of nonviolent private relationships, has much to be said for it.

Chambers noted three central categories of benefits that are denied same-sex couples because of their inability to legally marry:

- recognition of affective or emotional bonds that most spouses feel for each other—decision-making powers granted if one partner becomes incompetent, immigration preference for spouses, and protection of confidential communication between spouses

- recognition of marriage as an ideal or most appropriate context for raising children—laws pertaining to custody, adoption, foster care, and stepparenting

- recognition of the economic arrangements between partners and the couple and the state—laws regulating taxes, inheritance, governmental benefits, joint property, and health insurance

Same-sex marriages, advocates argue, would provide for the legal and social recognition of lesbian and gay relationships. Just as children who are born in the context of heterosexual marriages are presumed to be the legal children of both parents, so would children who are born in the context of same-sex marriages.[4] Lambda Legal Defense and Education Fund lists numerous benefits that accrue to legally married partners: the right to file joint tax returns, the right to share joint parenting rights (along with custody and visitation on divorce), the ability to obtain wrongful death benefits for a surviving partner and children, the right to inherit automatically in the absence of a will, and so forth. Badgett and Goldfoot (1996) cited the advantages of social approval, increased recognition of the relationship, and access to spousal benefits. These benefits, including access to spouses' health and insurance benefits, life insurance, pensions, and social security, can be substantial.

Yet, economic benefits are not the only reason some lesbians and gays seek legal marriage. Marriage is also a symbolic event, which may explain why numerous gays and lesbians have chosen religious marriage or commitment ceremonies that have no legal standing. Marriage normalizes (or, in the words of Eskridge, 1996, "civilizes") gay and lesbian relationships. As Mohr (1996) argued, this is why right-wing opposition to same-sex marriage has been so intense.

Same-sex marriage would certainly not be a panacea for all lesbian and gay families, since only those families that most closely resemble the heterosexual model would be included. As feminist critics, such as Polikoff (1990), have pointed out, extending marriage to same-sex couples would primarily benefit middle-class and wealthy couples (for example, those who have estates to be taxed) and exclude individuals who are single. For critics such as Polikoff, the political goal should be to uncouple economic benefits (like health insurance) from marriage relationships. Rather than allow some nontraditional couples "in," the goal should be to provide benefits to all, regardless of their relationship status (for a thoughtful reflection and, at times, a rebuttal to this position, see Chambers, 1996). Others, however, have argued that poor and working-class lesbians and gays, who may be unable to pay for the full range of legal protections that a private attorney can afford (such as wills and

---

[4]Whether this would actually be the case and how adoptions would be handled are, of course, matters of speculation.

powers of attorney), may benefit most from same-sex marriage.

Citing public hostility to same-sex marriage, other activists have contended that the time is not yet propitious for gaining same-sex marriage rights. Domestic partnerships provide at least some of the legal and economic benefits that accrue to married couples. Indeed, a number of municipalities and corporations have begun to offer domestic-partnership benefits. Although these benefits are not, by and large, transferable (and, unlike benefits to married couples, are taxable), they at least provide some measure of protection for gay and lesbian partnerships.

Clearly, there is much research to be done on lesbian, gay, and bisexual families. Although the literature in some areas is fairly well developed (such as on the effects on children of having lesbian or gay parents), in other areas, the research questions have hardly been conceived. Comparisons of the impact of living in a relatively hostile environment with a more accepting one have not even been attempted. More generally, research on the potential strengths of lesbian, gay, and bisexual families has been far less often conducted. Yet answers to these questions may be of the most use to those who are actually living in lesbian, gay, and bisexual families. As the public (and scholars) increasingly pay attention to lesbian and gay families, it is imperative that researchers take into account the diversity of lesbian and gay family life. It is equally important that we forge stronger links between social research and public policy. As our knowledge about lesbian, gay, and bisexual families increases, so should the possibilities for equitable treatment of these families in law, clinical practice, and social policy.

REFERENCES

Ainslie, J., & Feltey, K. (1991). Definitions and dynamics of motherhood and family in lesbian communities. *Marriage and Family Review, 17,* 63–85.

Allen, K. R., & Demo, D. H. (1995). The families of lesbians and gay men: A new frontier in family research. *Journal of Marriage and the Family, 57,* 111–127.

Allen, M., & Burrell, N. (1996). Comparing the impact of homosexual and heterosexual parents on children: Meta-analysis of existing research. *Journal of Homosexuality, 32,* 19–35.

Arnup, K. (1995). *Lesbian parenting: Living with pride and prejudice.* Charlottetown, Canada: Gynergy Books.

Badgett, M. V. L., & Goldfoot, J. A. (1996). For richer, for poorer: The freedom to marry debate. *Angles: The Policy Journal of the Institute for Gay and Lesbian Strategic Studies, 1,* 1–4.

Bailey, J. M., Gaulin, S., Agyei, Y., & Gladue, B. A. (1994). Effects of gender and sexual orientation on evolutionarily relevant aspects of human mating psychology. *Journal of Personality and Social Psychology, 66,* 1081–1093.

Barrett, R., & Robinson, B. (1990). *Gay fathers.* Lexington, MA: Lexington Books.

Belsky, J., & Rovine, M. (1990). Patterns of marital change across the transition to parenthood. *Journal of Marriage and the Family, 52,* 885–903.

Ben-Ari, A. (1995). The discovery that an offspring is gay: Parents', gay men's, and lesbians' perspectives. *Journal of Homosexuality, 30,* 89–112.

Bernstein, B. (1990). Attitudes and issues of parents of gay men and lesbians and implications for therapy. *Journal of Gay & Lesbian Psychotherapy, 1,* 37–53.

Blumstein, P., & Schwartz, P. (1983). *American couples: Money, work, sex.* New York: Morrow.

Boxer, A. M., Cook, J. A., & Herdt, G. (1991). Double jeopardy: Identity transitions and parent-child relations among gay and lesbian youth. In K. Pillemer & K. McCartney (Eds.), *Parent-child relations throughout life* (pp. 59–92). Hillsdale, NJ: Lawrence Erlbaum.

Bryant, A. S., & Demian. (1994). Relationship characteristics of American gay and lesbian couples: Findings from a national survey. *Journal of Gay and Lesbian Social Services, 1,* 101–117.

Casper, V., & Schultz, S. (1996). Lesbian and gay educators: Initiating conversations. In R. C. Savin-Williams & K. M. Cohen (Eds.), *The lives of lesbians, gays, and bisexuals: Children to adults* (pp. 305–330). Fort Worth, TX: Harcourt Brace.

Chambers, D. L. (1996). What if? The legal consequences of marriage and the legal needs of lesbian and gay male couples. *Michigan Law Review, 95,* 447–491.

Chan, C. S. (1989). Issues of identity development among Asian American lesbians and gay men. *Journal of Counseling and Development, 68,* 16–20.

Chang, K. S. C. (1996, December 3). Findings of fact and conclusions of law, *Baehr v. Miike*. Circuit Court of the First Circuit, State of Hawaii (pp. 1–46).

Cowan, C. P., & Cowan, P. A. (1992). *When partners become parents*. New York: Basic Books.

Cramer, D. W., & Roach, A. J. (1988). Coming out to mom and dad: A study of gay males and their relationships with their parents. *Journal of Homosexuality, 15,* 79–91.

D'Augelli, A. R., & Hershberger, S. L. (1993). Lesbian, gay, and bisexual youth in community settings: Personal challenges and mental health problems. *American Journal of Community Psychology, 21,* 421–448.

Deenen, A. A., Gijs, L., & van Naerssen, A. X. (1994). Intimacy and sexuality in gay male couples. *Archives of Sexual Behavior, 23,* 421–431.

de LaMadrid, G. (1991). *Lesbians choosing motherhood: Legal implications of donor insemination and co-parenting.* San Francisco: National Center for Lesbian Rights.

Demo, D. H., & Allen, K. R. (1996). Diversity within lesbian and gay families: Challenges and implications for family theory and research. *Journal of Social and Personal Relationships, 13,* 415–434.

DeVine, J. L. (1984). A systemic inspection of affectional preference orientation and the family of origin. *Journal of Social Work & Human Sexuality, 2,* 9–17.

Editors of the Harvard Law Review. (1989). *Sexual orientation and the law.* Cambridge, MA: Harvard University Press.

Elovitz, M. (1995). Adoption by lesbian and gay people: The use and misuse of social science research. *Duke Journal of Gender Law & Policy, 2.*

Eskridge, W. (1996). *The case for same-sex marriage.* New York: Free Press.

Esterberg, K. (1997). *Lesbian and bisexual identities: Constructing communities, constructing selves.* Philadelphia: Temple University Press.

Garnets, L. D., & Kimmel, D. C. (1993). Lesbian and gay male dimensions in the psychological study of human diversity. In L. D. Garnets & D. C. Kimmel (Eds.), *Psychological perspectives on lesbian and gay male experiences* (pp. 1–51). New York: Columbia University Press.

Greene, B. (1994). Ethnic minority lesbians and gay men: Mental health and treatment issues. *Journal of Consulting and Clinical Psychology, 62,* 243–251.

Griffin, C. W., Wirth, M. J., & Wirth, A. G. (1986). *Beyond acceptance: Parents of lesbians and gays talk about their experiences.* Englewood Cliffs, NJ: Prentice Hall.

Hammersmith, S. K. (1987). A sociological approach to counseling homosexual clients and their families. *Journal of Homosexuality, 14,* 173–190.

Herdt, G., & Boxer, A. (1993). *Children of Horizons: How gay and lesbian teens are leading a new way out of the closet.* Boston: Beacon Press.

Heron, A. (Ed.) (1994). *Two teenagers in twenty: Writings by gay and lesbian youth.* Boston: Alyson.

Hershberger, S. L., & D'Augelli, A. R. (1995). The impact of victimization on the mental health and suicidality of lesbian, gay, and bisexual youths. *Developmental Psychology, 31,* 65–74.

Hill, M. (1987). Child-rearing attitudes of black lesbian mothers. In Boston Lesbian Psychologies Collective (Ed.), *Lesbian psychologies: Explorations and challenges* (pp. 215–226). Urbana: University of Illinois Press.

Kantrowitz, B. (1996, November 4). Gay families come out. *Newsweek,* pp. 50–57.

Krieger, S. (1982). *The mirror dance: Identity in a woman's community.* Philadelphia: Temple University Press.

Kurdek, L. A. (1988). Perceived social support in gays and lesbians in cohabiting relationships. *Journal of Personality and Social Psychology, 54,* 504–509.

Kurdek, L. A. (1991a). Correlates of relationship satisfaction in cohabiting gay and lesbian couples: Integration of contextual, investment, and problem-solving models. *Journal of Personality and Social Psychology 61,* 910–922.

Kurdek, L. A. (1991b). The dissolution of gay and lesbian couples. *Journal of Social and Personal Relationships, 8,* 265–278.

Kurdek, L. A. (1992). Relationship stability and relationship satisfaction in cohabiting gay and lesbian couples: A prospective longitudinal test of the contextual and interdependence models. *Journal of Social and Personal Relationships, 9,* 125–142.

Kurdek, L. A. (1993). The allocation of household labor in gay, lesbian, and heterosexual married couples. *Journal of Social Issues, 49,* 127–139.

Kurdek, L. A. (1994). The nature and correlates of relationship quality in gay, lesbian, and heterosexual cohabiting couples: A test of the individual difference, interdependence, and discrepancy models. In B. Greene & G. Herek (Eds.), *Lesbian and gay psychology: Theory, research, and clinical applications* (pp. 133–155). Thousand Oaks, CA: Sage.

Kurdek, L. A. (1995). Lesbian and gay couples. In A. R. D'Augelli & C. J. Patterson (Eds.), *Lesbian, gay, and bisexual identities over the lifespan: Psychological perspectives* (pp. 243–261). New York: Oxford University Press.

Laird, J. (1993). Lesbian and gay families. In F. Walsh (Ed.), *Normal family processes* (2nd ed., pp. 282–328). New York: Guilford Press.

Lambda Legal Defense and Education Fund. 120 Wall Street, Suite 1500. New York, NY 10005.

Levy, E. (1989). Lesbian motherhood and social support. *Affilia, 4,* 40–53.

Lewin, E. (1993). *Lesbian mothers: Accounts of gender in American culture.* Ithaca, NY: Cornell University Press.

Lockard, D. (1985). The lesbian community: An anthropological approach. *Journal of Homosexuality, 11,* 83–95.

Loiacano, D. K. (1989). Gay identity issues among black Americans: Racism, homophobia, and the need for validation. *Journal of Counseling and Development, 68,* 21–25.

Martin, A. (1993). *The lesbian and gay parenting handbook.* New York: HarperPerennial.

McPherson, D. (1993). *Gay parenting couples: Parenting arrangements, arrangement satisfaction, and relationship satisfaction.* Doctoral dissertation. Pacific Graduate School of Psychology, Palo Alto, CA.

Mohr, R. (1996). *The stakes in the gay marriage wars.* Unpublished manuscript.

Morales, E. S. (1983, August). *Third World gays and lesbians: A process of multiple identities.* Paper presented at the 91st annual conference of the American Psychological Association, Anaheim, CA.

Muller, A. (1987). *Parents matter: Parents' relationships with lesbian daughters and gay sons.* Tallahasse, FL: Naiad Press.

Murphy, B. C., & Rodríques-Nogués, L. (Eds.) (1995). *Lesbian and gay parenting: A resource for psychologists.* Washington, DC: American Psychological Association.

National Center for Lesbian Rights. (1990). *Lesbian mother litigation manual.* San Francisco: National Center for Lesbian Rights.

Patterson, C. J. (1992). Children of lesbian and gay parents. *Child Development, 63,* 1025–1042.

Patterson, C. J. (1995a). Families of the lesbian baby boom: Parents' division of labor and children's adjustment. *Developmental Psychology, 31,* 115–123.

Patterson, C. J. (1995b). Lesbian mothers, gay fathers, and their children. In A. R. D'Augelli & C. J. Patterson (Eds.), *Lesbian, gay, and bisexual identities over the lifespan: Psychological perspectives* (pp. 262–290). New York: Oxford University Press.

Patterson, C. J. (1995c). Summary of research findings. In B. C. Murphy & L. Rodríques-Nogués (Eds.), *Lesbian and gay parenting: A resource for psychologists* (pp. 1–12). Washington, DC: American Psychological Association Press.

Patterson, C. J. (1996). Lesbian and gay parents and their children. In R. C. Savin-Williams & K. M. Cohen (Eds.), *The lives of lesbians, gays, and bisexuals: Children to adults* (pp. 274–304). Fort Worth, TX: Harcourt Brace.

Patterson, C. J., & Chan, R. W. (1997). Gay fathers. In M. E. Lamb (Ed.) *The role of the father in child development* (pp. 245–250). New York: John Wiley.

Peplau, L. A., Veniegas, R. C., & Campbell, S. M. (1996). Gay and lesbian relationships. In R. C. Savin-Williams & K. M. Cohen (Eds.), *The lives of lesbians, gays, and bisexuals: Children to adults* (pp. 250–273). Fort Worth, TX: Harcourt Brace.

Pies, C. (1988). *Considering parenthood.* Minneapolis, MN: Spinsters Ink.

Pilkington, N. W., & D'Augelli, A. R. (1995). Victimization of lesbian, gay, and bisexual youths in community settings. *Journal of Community Psychology, 23,* 33–56.

Polikoff, N. (1990). This child does have two mothers: Redefining parenthood to meet the needs of children in lesbian-mother and other nontraditional families. *Georgetown Law Journal, 78,* 459–515.

Pollack, S. (1987). Lesbian mothers: A lesbian-feminist perspective on research. In S. Pollack & J. Vaughn (Eds.), *Politics of the heart: A lesbian parenting anthology* (pp. 316–324). Ithaca, NY: Firebrand Books.

Pollack, S., & Vaughn, J. (1987). *Politics of the heart: A lesbian parenting anthology.* Ithaca, NY: Firebrand Books.

Ponse, B. (1978). *Identities in the lesbian world: The social construction of self.* Westport, CT: Greenwood Press.

Robinson, B. E., Walters, L. H., & Skeen, P. (1989). Response of parents to learning that their child is homosexual and concern over AIDS: A national study. *Journal of Homosexuality, 18,* 59–80.

Savin-Williams, R. C. (1989). Coming out to parents and self-esteem among gay and lesbian youths. *Journal of Homosexuality, 18,* 1–35.

Savin-Williams, R. C. (1990). *Gay and lesbian youth: Expressions of identity.* New York: Hemisphere.

Savin-Williams, R. C. (1993). Personal reflections on coming out, prejudice, and homophobia in the academic workplace. In L. Diamant (Ed.), *Homosexual issues in the workplace* (pp. 225–241). New York: Harrington Park Press.

Savin-Williams, R. C. (1994). Verbal and physical abuse as stressors in the lives of lesbian, gay male, and bisexual youths: Associations with school problems, running away, substance abuse, prostitution, and suicide. *Journal of Consulting and Clinical Psychology, 62,* 261–269.

Savin-Williams, R. C. (1998). *". . . and then I became gay:" Young men's stories.* New York: Routledge.

Savin-Williams, R. C. (1998a). The disclosure to families of same-sex attractions by lesbian, gay, and bisexual youths. *Journal of Research on Adolescence, 8,* 49–68.

Savin-Williams, R. C. (1998b). Lesbian, gay, and bisexual youths' relationships with their parents. In C. J. Patterson & A. R. D'Augelli (Eds.), *Lesbian, gay, and bisexual identities in families: Psychological perspectives.* (pp. 75–98). New York: Oxford University Press.

Savin-Williams, R. C. (in preparation). *Gay youths and their families.* Manuscript under contract with American Psychological Association Press, Washington, DC.

Savin-Williams, R. C. & Dubé, E. M. (1998). Parental reactions to their child's disclosure of a gay/lesbian identity. *Family Relations, 47,* 7–13.

Schreurs, K. M. G. (1993). Sexuality in lesbian couples: The importance of gender. *Annual Review of Sex Research: An Integrative and Interdisciplinary Review, 4,* 49–66.

Slater, S. (1995). *Lesbian family life cycle.* New York: Free Press.

Stacey, J. (1996). *In the name of the family: Rethinking family values in the postmodern age.* Boston: Beacon Press.

Telljohann, S. K., & Price, J. P. (1993). A qualitative examination of adolescent homosexuals' life experiences: Ramifications for secondary school personnel. *Journal of Homosexuality, 26,* 41–56.

Tremble, B., Schneider, M., & Appathurai, C. (1989). Growing up gay or lesbian in a multicultural context. *Journal of Homosexuality, 17,* 253–267.

Weston, K. (1991). *Families we choose: Lesbians, gays, kinship.* New York: Columbia University Press.

Wolf, D. (1979). *The lesbian community.* Berkeley: University of California Press.

CHAPTER 11

Older Adults and Their Families

VICTORIA HILKEVITCH BEDFORD AND ROSEMARY BLIESZNER

OUR PERSONAL COMMITMENT TO THE STUDY OF DIVERSITY

Victoria Hilkevitch Bedford

The diversity movement shares with postmodernism and relativism a challenge to the status quo. Those who are cynical about these movements miss an important point: They lend a perspective that provides an opportunity to expose exclusionary practices, whether they occur on the personal, local, national, or global level. Psychological research reveals that humans are hardwired to create in- and out-groups. They do so instantaneously when they divide on such trivial matters as overestimating and underestimating dots on a slide (Tajfel, Billib, Bundy, & Flament, 1971). An interesting question is whether by accepting a broad range of family types, for instance, into the legal system, it is possible to change human nature. If people come to accept diversity in families, will they simply transfer the tendency to create groupings of "us" and "them" in new arenas? I would like to think there are less destructive contexts in which to express this tendency.

In a sense, my research in family studies and gerontology has been devoted to correcting the injustice of exclusion. I have chosen to study family relationships that are traditionally unacknowledged by scholars—adult siblings and the families of old people. Family scholars, practitioners, and policy analysts have been locked into a vertical-centric intergenerational and nuclear family bias irrespective of the reality of family life. Consequently, sibling relationships are marginalized or ignored, and old people are considered, at best, appendages to other people's families (Bedford, 1996; Bedford & Blieszner, 1997; Bedford & Gold, 1989).

Looking back at how I was drawn to these topics, I suspect my personal experiences with both exclusion and privilege may have fueled my interests. Although I have enjoyed the privilege of the dominant white race and of birth into a well-educated middle-class family, I also know what it means to live on the fringe of society because of my political genealogy (my parents were political radicals of the 1930s), religious identity (non-Christian), gender, family experience (as a twin with a closely spaced older sister, my siblings have always been as essential to my original family experience as my parents), and nonmainstream research with respect to my discipline, psychology. In each of these positions, central to my identity at one time or another, I have experienced lack of institutional recognition by the dominant culture in which I live. For example, although I live in a region of the country where much of community and family life is organized around religious holidays, as a member of a minority religion (Judaism), I am nevertheless expected to file an Absence from Campus Form to celebrate my most sacred holidays.

Without diversity there is the danger of stagnation, cognitive numbing, and destructive group processes, such as groupthink (Janis, 1982). Therefore, enriching the scope and depth of family studies by uncovering marginalized family relationships has been a highly satisfying research quest.

Rosemary Blieszner

I do not recall when my career focus crystallized on adult family and friend relationships, but certainly I recognized early the importance of deep friendships and supportive family for fostering my personal development and sustaining my psychological well-being (Blieszner, 1994). Although I was enrolled in an excellent program in human development and family studies at Penn State, in at least one respect I was at the margins of the inquiry that was dominant there at the time: The gerontologists addressed individual-level development in adulthood and old age, and the family scholars focused on dating and early marriage relationships. No one examined friendship. My choice to investigate older adult friendships for my dissertation necessitated an independent and integrative approach to theory and methods. Convinced of the value of studying development over time both to understand aging processes and to illuminate ways of enhancing development, my goal was to articulate the application of principles of individual development to the investigation of relationship interaction patterns and processes. My focus on older adult friendships stemmed further from the fact that so little research had been done on what appeared to be, at least potentially, a crucial relationship.

The knowledge I have gained about heterogeneity in aging contributes to my appreciation of diversity and the need to incorporate notions of diversity in all my work. Various experiences associated with gender, class, and racial-ethnic groups yield different outcomes across the life course, but even those with similar backgrounds can end up traveling different pathways through adulthood. Linking gerontology to family studies has further reinforced the importance of acknowledging diversity. It is impossible to analyze family interaction processes and the connections among families and other societal entities without attending to the ages of family members, their resources, and their places in the social fabric. Diversity among aging families has not been as widely addressed as heterogeneity among aged individuals, probably because the study of aging families is relatively newer. Working in family studies—especially seeking to describe influences on family interaction patterns when some members are old—also keeps my professional attention focused on diversity.

I came to this academic worldview from an interdisciplinary educational history. My undergraduate education was in home economics and my Master's and doctoral degrees were in human development and family studies, which is a contemporary derivative of home economics. I agree with Thompson's (1990) assessment that home economics was one of the foremothers of feminist family studies. I harken to the philosophical underpinnings of that discipline and embrace its liberating goal of improving the quality of life for all individuals and families. This end is also expressed in the life-span developmental perspective that stresses not only descriptions and explanations of influences on development, but using that information to optimize lived experiences (Baltes, Reese, & Nesselroade, 1977).

My entire career has been devoted to this goal. Like research on aged family relationships, the study of adults' and, especially, elders' friendship has a relatively short history, perhaps because friendship was traditionally deemed a peripheral relationship. Yet I have been privileged to discover many exciting and important elements of friendship that demonstrate its significance in people's lives. The recent scholarly emphasis on the significance of everyday life by feminists (such as Smith, 1987), gerontologists (like, Altergott, 1988), and family scholars (including Daly, 1996) suggests that once-peripheral topics are becoming central, lending legitimacy to the study of close ties among family and friends. I see this movement as positive because a greater understanding of close relationship processes and outcomes can contribute to more effective means of enhancing the life experiences of all people.

Purpose

In our personal statements, we recognized in ourselves feelings of being excluded or marginalized within specific domains of life. In this chapter on older adults and their families, we use these experiences to imagine what it feels like to be an old family member in a society that equates family life with household membership. Because most old people in America live alone or as couples, apart from their children, grandchildren, siblings, any parents who are still living, and other relatives, they have often been forgotten by family scholars, family therapists, and policy makers. It was a major breakthrough, therefore, when parent-child relationships in adulthood were first recognized by family scholars (Troll, 1971). More recently, the grandparent-grandchild bond has gained attention owing to the high incidence of surrogate parenting by grandparents (Burton, Dilworth-Anderson, & Merriwether-deVries, 1995; Robertson, 1995). Vertical bonds of old people with siblings, cousins, and the children of these relationships continue to elude attention, although research on siblings has gained some ground in recent years. Almost nothing is known about old people's ties to in-laws or relationships with fictive kin (but see, for example, Kivett, 1989, on the former and Allen, 1989, on the latter).

In this chapter, we advance research on families in later life by encouraging scholars to consider the diversity of old age kin relationships from the points of view of old people and other family members. By way of introduction, we define what we mean by *family,* propose a framework that has the potential to encompass the wide range of family experiences available to old people and their relatives, and explain some of the meaning of old age. In the second part of the chapter, we address specific aspects of diversity in families with aged members. In conclusion, we recommend future directions for the study of families inclusive of a focus on old people.

DEFINING FAMILY

To integrate old people into family studies, a more inclusive definition of *family* is needed. Family scholars often seem to forget that families have old members. Traditional definitions of family describe the nuclear family as composed of two parents (male and female) and dependent children (Johnson, 1995b). Elsewhere (Bedford & Blieszner, 1997, p. 526) we addressed in some detail the rationale for a definition of *family* that is broader than is typically given in family studies textbooks and implied in family research that ignores elders: "A family is a set of relationships determined by biology, adoption, marriage, and, in some societies, social designation and existing even in the absence of contact or affective involvement and, in some cases, even after the death of certain members." Such an improved definition, broader even than the

one provided by this volume's editors (see Chapter 1), is necessary to acknowledge that elders are family members; to recognize the diverse ways in which elders define and execute family relationships; and to account for demographic trends resulting in family relationships that did not exist in the past. For example, increased longevity affords new opportunities for young and old alike to know members of more generations than ever before.

We encourage family researchers to avoid the bias inherent in, for example, viewing adult children as belonging to their parents' family but their parents as belonging merely to the adult children's extended kinship system, rather than to their family per se. This bias assumes a nonmutuality of interaction and influence that is not supported by family gerontology research. Moreover, our definition allows for the possibility of latent or potential family relationships. Some old people take great comfort in feeling confident that their siblings, for example, would come to their aid should help be necessary, even though they rarely seek assistance from siblings (Bedford, 1995). Others identify family relationships that are personally significant although devoid of contact or severely weakened (Johnson, 1993) or relationships with family members who are deceased (Bedford & Blieszner, 1997).

CONCEPTUAL FRAMEWORK

Family Structure

Having established an inclusive definition of family, we ask how old people experience relationships with their family members and how those who are not old experience interactions with their old relatives. We assume these experiences are as varied as the individuals themselves, but as social scientists whose job it is to advance knowledge and inform practitioners, policy makers, and family life educators, it behooves us to identify patterns in these relationships to aid the task of summarizing the literature. However, as soon as we impose a framework on the data to assist us in accomplishing that goal, we run the risk of becoming exclusionary or judgmental. We attempt, therefore, to choose elements of existing frameworks that advance the universal characteristics of families and allow for multiple particularistic options within them. Specifically, we borrow from the family development (Rodgers & White, 1993) and life-course models (Bengtson & Allen, 1993) by expanding the notion of the linear progression of one kind of family's career (nuclear, heterosexual, two-parent, multiple minor children) into a model that combines features of both a flowchart and a time line. Such a perspective encompasses multiple relational possibilities and types of outcomes over time and in response to any kind of event. Some features of the model are schematized in Figure 11.1. To illustrate this perspective, we selected a common family event, (designated Event 1), but almost any event would do. Next we progressed both backward and forward in time, considering the different possibilities that may have led to the event and that may eventuate from it. In this section, we focus on family positions and who occupies them.

Our focal event is the entry of a child into a family, which could be preceded by marriage or not; could occur through birth, foster care, or adoption; and could happen to a gay, lesbian, bisexual, or heterosexual couple; a single parent; or a chosen family collective. The parent or parents might be young adults, middle-aged, or elderly at the time of the child's entrance. The figure depicts a rich variety of potential relations who may make up the family who is receiving the child. These relatives vary by generation (including collaterals at each generation), source of tie (biological, fictive, and legal), sexual orientation, and whether they are living or dead. Fictive kin (also known as play, social, and chosen kin) frequently occupy particular family positions that correspond to specific roles, such as sibling, aunt, and mother. They may substitute for or duplicate others who occupy these positions, or fulfill partial functions of these positions (Cicirelli, 1994). Legal ties are those that are formalized through adoption, marriage, and foster arrangements. Surely the child's and the family's experiences would vary, depending on which combination of circumstances described the family context into which the child came.

In our model, we consider the implications of this event for the family positions of each family member. To answer the question fully, our integration of the family development and life-course perspectives demands that we address the effects of a child's entry into a family from the viewpoints of both lineage (intergenerational) and intragenerational transitions.

Multiple Generational Transitions

With a child's entry into a family, parents become parents for the first time, or parents of siblings for the first time, or parents of a son or a daughter or second son or daughter, and so forth. That is, parents may experience births of different children differently because of changes in the family context, as well as the idiosyncratic meaning these events may have for particular parents. Consequently, we have eliminated from our model preconceived notions as to which of the multiple occurrences of an event affects the family most significantly (such as the launching of the first child). Family members of other generations are also affected by the child's entry. Parents of the child's parents become grandparents, and their parents become great-grandparents. Siblings of these elders become great- or great-great aunts or uncles.

Our model also acknowledges intragenerational changes related to family events. With a child's entry into a family, parents' siblings become aunts or uncles of a niece or nephew for the first time or the nth time. Previously born children gain a sibling (or cousin), which affects the particular birth order and gender composition of the family constellation. We do not assume that the first such role transition is more significant than a later one. For example, to an older child, a younger sibling of a particular gender might have special meaning, regardless of the gender of other siblings, or perhaps becoming an aunt of a niece has special meaning that supersedes becoming an aunt for the first time of a nephew.

We could depict similar paths of potential effects with the exit of family members, whether through divorce, emancipation of children, relocation, or death. Some exits are only temporary, until the next visit or reunion, whereas death signifies a permanent end of the face-to-face interaction. In either case, exits of family members have multiple effects

FIGURE 11.1
Conceptual Framework

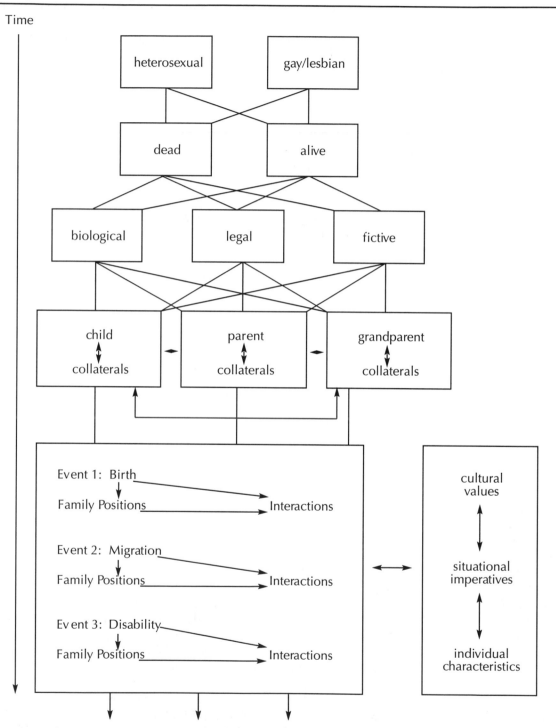

on members of the same and other generations, just as entrances do. Similarly, we could illustrate diverse potential effects on multiple generations in families related to other kinds of events, such as unemployment, winning the lottery, or entering family therapy. Life events that occur to given family members are likely to have impacts on many other relatives, including the old ones.

The flowchart of the family's history and experiences could branch off in many directions over time. For example, the child's entry may be followed by divorce and remarriage by one or more parents, adding other children to the family or not, with a host of potential repercussions for intra- and intergenerational relations.

This broad framework represents a dynamic megastructure of possible family forms and their development through multiple layers of time. As such, it should serve at least as a reminder of the diverse pathways that family development can take and the multiple identities of the potential family players. Casting a broad net in this way is important if old people's place in family life is to be considered, whether by their presence or absence. Adding, deleting, or changing the elements on the flowchart causes other elements, some of which signify the oldest members of the family, to change. Next we consider the processual aspect of the model, namely, how individuals (of any age) are affected by and affect family interaction in contrast to how family structure may be affected.

Family Interaction

Events affect interactions among family members as well as family positions. Other influences on family interaction that are depicted in Figure 11.1 are a change in family position, cultural values (as well as constraints and opportunities afforded by social and historical influences more generally), situational imperatives, and person variables (demographic characteristics, personality, spiritual resources, biological features). As can be seen in the figure, influences are invariably bidirectional. The bidirectional arrows between generations and their collaterals schematize the influences of changes in family members and their behaviors on one another.

From the perspective of elders, their behavior,

feelings, and thoughts are influenced by their interactions with family members and the myriad other conditions and situations described. Because interactions are bidirectional, the old person's influence on family members must also be considered, and this influence in turn, affects how these members influence the old person. Also, as posed in the life-course model (Bengtson & Allen, 1993), interactions do not progress only sequentially in time; participants in the interactions respond to memories of interactions with each other and to anticipations of future interactions.

In an effort to sample some dimensions of diversity in the experiences of older adults and their families along these dimensions, we turn to examples in the literature of intra- and intergenerational relationship experiences that vary by culture. We show how cultural values and the two remaining events depicted in Figure 11.1 (migration and disability) influence family interaction. First, however, we introduce one more source of variation to the picture of older adults and their families—diversity in old age.

Diversity in Old Age

The term *old age* generally marks the latter half of the maximum human life span of roughly 120 years. Because the concept of *age* signifies a continuum, designating one stage, such as old age, inappropriately reifies one interval along this continuum and creates an artificial sense of discontinuity from the previous years of life, when, in fact, many continuities persist throughout the life course. For instance, one's sense of self-identity appears to show a high level of consistency, in contrast to the myriad physical changes that are likely to occur in old age (Kaufman, 1986). Nevertheless, for the sake of our discussion, we need to place boundaries on the part of the life cycle that is our focus as we acknowledge that old age is not a monolithic concept.

Old age is functionally highly diverse both among and within individuals. Scholars who try to dispel the myth that old age is a monolithic experience divide it into arbitrary subsets of, say, 10-year age intervals beginning at 55 or 60 and extending to 100 or older. More meaningful, however, are subdividisions based on functional age, not chronological years. For example, Neugarten and Hagestad (1976) noted the emergence of a young-old group, as distinguished from the old-old on the basis of health and vigor, ability to live independently, and extent of community involvement. Later, Streib and Binstock (1990) identified another emergent subgroup called the oldest old, characterized by high rates of illness and frailty. These subgroup designations tend to be correlated with age, but not perfectly. One person aged 65 may be functionally quite old because of multiple limiting health conditions, while another aged 85 may be functionally young-old because he or she has no major health limitations. Thus, chronological age and functional ability should not be equated.

Aging is multidimensional; changes in physical capacity may affect cognitive functioning or the expression of personality characteristics. Aging is also multidirectional. For example, at the same time as a person may experience stability or growth in certain aspects of relational competence, such as the ability to garner social support, other aspects, like the ability to reciprocate certain social exchanges, may decline because of concomitant changes in health and independent functioning (Hansson & Carpenter, 1994). Both gains and losses occur along the pathway toward the end of life (Baltes, 1987; Baltes & Graf, 1996), illustrating within-person change over time.

Aging also reflects many between-person differences in development over time. Old people differ from one another on many sociocultural dimensions. They differ in the contemporary socioeconomic conditions in which they live and, depending on when they were born, on the historical context in which they matured. These divergent experiences lead to cohort identities that change with every generation, so that each cohort of old people differs from the previous one, which challenges efforts to generalize about old people across time. These differences account for the varying experiences of family life across cohorts and generations.

Hargrave and Anderson (1992, p. 3) pointed out that "aging does not happen just to individuals, it happens to families right along with their elder members." This coaging by family members involves changes elicited by the elders themselves, as when family members respond to the needs of elders with caregiving, resource reallocation, and new forms of emotional sustenance. Coaging proceeds along the family life cycle with respect to other family members as well as the elder. Dyadic relationships, families, and social networks are not static, but change over time as the persons involved experience their own development, changes in significant others, and myriad life events (Antonucci & Akiyama, 1995; Ryff & Seltzer, 1995).

RACIAL AND ETHNIC DIVERSITY IN OLDER ADULTS' FAMILIES

Thus far, we have presented a definition of family that includes older members and a conceptual framework that encompasses both families' structures and their interaction processes, noting especially the implications of these aspects of family life for the involvement of elderly members. Furthermore, we outlined some sources of diversity among old people, which also have implications for family life. We turn now to examples from the literature on aging and families that illustrate components of the conceptual framework, focusing on diversity in both collateral and intergenerational relationships. Then we use the model to formulate suggestions for further research.

Each illustrative study attends to certain subcomponents of the framework, leaving other components implicit, instead of addressing them explicitly. For example, studies that involve comparisons across racial ethnic groups highlight sources of diversity that are due to social context, but do not necessarily simultaneously address diversity rooted in differences in personality, physical aging, historical period, or birth order. We mention this fact to acknowledge that few studies can assess the full range of sources of diversity. Rather, understanding increases as the entire body of literature grows. The important point to us is that family research projects should include old people.

Collateral Relationships in Old Age

Most adults have siblings and, assuming that their parents had siblings who had children, most adults have cousins. Collateral kin include these siblings and cousins and the children of these intragenerational kin. Nieces, nephews, and their children are potential social resources in old age. Nearly all the literature on collaterals, particularly in later life, focuses on sibling relationships.

Although most of the literature on adult siblings is limited to biological ones, siblings can also be adopted, share one biological parent (half siblings), share no biological parent (stepsiblings), have neither legal nor biological links (fictive or socially designated siblings), or be linked by marriage (siblings-in-law). Several recent surveys of the literature on adult siblings appear elsewhere and are not reviewed here (see Bedford, 1995, 1996; Bedford & Avioli, 1996; Cicirelli, 1996). This review focuses on the diversity of collateral family relationships with respect to black American siblings and siblings in several non-Western societies.

Cultural Values as Context

Cross-cultural diversity in both the structure and process of sibling relationships in old age may be understood by considering the cultural value context in which the relationships occur. We have drawn examples from research on American blacks, Asians (Chinese and Japanese), and South Asians (from India, Bangladesh, Pakistan, Nepal, Bhutan, and Sri Lanka).

Black Americans

On the basis of an analysis by Dilworth-Anderson, Burton, and Johnson (1993), "survival and overcoming" (p. 637) are the prime organizing principles for the structure and interactions of black American families (see also Stack, 1974). The marginalization of blacks (as well as Native Americans) can be differentiated from that of other minority groups by the "extreme cruelty and bondage" (Dilworth-Anderson et al., p. 637) to which they have been subjected throughout their history in America. Because of the strength that is found in numbers and the need to share resources to survive and overcome adversity, differentiation of self is limited among American blacks. Instead, one's sense of self is equivalent to that of the group; individuals identify with the extended family unit. Two strategies that appear to guarantee an extensive family system are a strong emphasis on the collateral form of family organization (Johnson, 1995a) and fictive kin relations that are comparable to legally sanctioned and biological kin (Stack, 1974). Both mechanisms would seem to have important consequences for sibling relationships in later life.

Johnson (1995a) compared childless black and white oldest old persons (aged 85 and older) who were living in San Francisco. Her studies demonstrated that the strategies for survival proved successful. By placing more emphasis on collateral relationships, the blacks had more contact with relatives and received more support from them. They were also more likely than whites to have a family member available as a caregiver. Furthermore, in another study (Johnson, 1994) that included oldest old black persons who had children, survival was demonstrated through measures of well-being. Although the blacks perceived their health to be poorer than the whites did, they were functionally no more disabled and had better morale than the whites.

A few investigators have tried to determine whether black and white sibling relationships differ and, if so, the source of the difference (black culture versus differences in demographic characteristics). The expectations in these various studies, given the importance of collateral kin in black societies for survival, were that (1) help exchanges between black siblings would occur more frequently than between white siblings, (2) association patterns between them would differ, and (3) blacks would have more positive types and fewer negative types of sibling relationships. Unfortunately, most empirical research on the relationships of black siblings does not address the structural differences in the designation of siblings. Studies either do not specify what kind of siblings are studied (see, for example, Suggs, 1989) or require respondents to refer only to biological and adoptive siblings (see, for instance, Gold, 1990). Keeping this caveat in mind, we next discuss the results of studies that tested these expectations.

Help. Using data from the 1980 Panel Study of Income Dynamics, Taylor, Chatters, and Mays (1988) identified demographic characteristics associated with blacks' use of parents, children, siblings, in-laws, and nonkin in an emergency. For this sample of mostly urban, uneducated, poor people, ranging in age from 17 to 94, because age was not a significant predictor of who is sought for emergency assistance, one could safely assume that the results are relevant to older adults. The highest percentage of respondents (24%) said they would seek emergency assistance from parents and siblings. Unmarried respondents were more likely to nominate siblings for emergency aid than were married respondents. Compared with the whites and Hispanics in the sample, the blacks were more likely to nominate siblings. Also, consistent with their focus on survival, the blacks were more likely than the whites to seek emergency assistance from a broad base of helpers (parents, siblings, nonkin, and children); the whites tended to rely on a single family member.

Association.   In a study of black and white elders in rural North Carolina who were asked about their relationship with their most contacted sibling, Suggs (1989) compared association patterns (the frequency with which older adults interacted with their siblings) in 13 activities across the two racial-groups. The two groups had in common the top four activities and two predictors: They associated more with their sibling if they helped each other and if they lived together. Differences in predictors of association were that the whites interacted more with their sibling when they shared the same values, whereas among the blacks, the younger the sibling and the higher the respondent's education level, the more frequent the contact. It appears, therefore, that, for whites, association was concerned with commonalities in values, whereas for blacks, it was concerned with their demographic characteristics relative to one another.

Types of Relationships.   Gold (1990) used a convenience sample of urban and suburban, well-educated, old blacks and whites with an average age in their mid-70s. She classified the respondents' relationship with each sibling using a five-category typology: intimate, congenial, loyal, apathetic, and hostile. The results indicated that dyads of black

siblings clustered around more positive types of relationships than did dyads of white siblings. Gender differences were striking in these black-white comparisons: In the hostile and apathetic categories, most of the whites were brother pairs and cross-sex pairs. For the blacks, no brothers were named in these negative sibling types; the few cases found in these categories were sister pairs. Interpreting these results in terms of values to survive and overcome, the lack of men in negative dyads makes sense because it would be counterproductive for men to engage in in-fighting.

Non-Western Societies

Value systems of other cultures are likely to affect the structure and nature of sibling relationships in later life. Although we focus on cultures within the United States in this chapter, we now consider briefly sibling relationships in other countries. Studies on blacks show that strong collateral ties are highly adaptive in late life because of the interdependence available from a large pool of family and chosen family resources that is not typical of whites. Because of the lack of contemporary empirical data from other countries about sibling relationships in later life, we sought examples of family structures that might be adaptable for elderly family members in various cultures, including the United States. Where life expectancy allows family members to grow old together, elders in societies that support strong collateral ties have a network of family relationships that is similar to that of blacks in America—siblings' and cousins' children and grandchildren—even after the death of the old person's generation of family members. In contrast, it is likely that more lineally structured societies result in a poverty of familial relationships available in old age, the reduced availability of support for old people, and lower life satisfaction (Johnson, 1994). We turn to lineally and collaterally structured societies in other countries to examine some variations of each form and the origins of these variations. We invite readers to consider whether the adaptations that these contrasting structures once served continue to be adaptive in view of the demographic changes toward an increasing proportion of old people in both developed and developing societies (Kinsella, 1995).

The Confucian concept of filial piety, well known in Chinese and Japanese societies, reflects a highly lineal society based on primogeniture. Traditionally, the oldest son and his family of procreation lived with his parents; other siblings were excluded. This practice made sense because farms were too small to divide. Even in modern Japan, whose Constitution dictates the equal distribution of inheritance, people do what they wish, and some primogeniture continues. A different picture of the importance of collateral ties among the Japanese emerged when they immigrated to Hawaii (depicted as Event 2 in Figure 11.1). Like many immigrations, these were spearheaded by siblings. As a result of this sibling migration, despite their strong lineal origins, the Japanese Americans who settled in Hawaii developed strong extended family ties (Johnson, 1977), illustrating the fluidity of family organization in response to situational imperatives.

Collateral bonds in Asian societies also broaden our perspective on the meaning of gender in family relationships. In many Asian societies, the social structures are organized around the sibling tie. Whereas the sister-sister bond is the strongest in Western societies (Cicirelli, 1994), this tie often dissolves in Asian societies if sisters separate geographically to live with their in-laws. The sister-brother (cross-sibling) bond, on the other hand, is so strong that it forms the basis of family organization. These primary cross-sex sibling bonds are found mainly in nonindustrial societies, such as in South Asia (Nuckolls, 1993), Oceania (Marshall, 1983) and the Philippines (Peterson, 1990).

An example of such a society is the matrilineal one, in which women's brothers dominate. The ascendance of women's brothers was an adaptive response to warrior societies, such as the Nayar of India, where raiding soldiers impregnated women. It made sense that brothers performed parental duties as social fathers under these circumstances (Gough, 1959). Even though such marriages were outlawed in India under British colonial rule in the 19th century, this and related family structures persist.

Cross-sex sibling relationships have been depicted as complementary (Peterson, 1990), in contrast to same-sex sibling relationships, which are often depicted as substitutable (Johnson, 1982). Complementarity (where one member completes the other in the functions they provide) is seen throughout South Asia. For instance, brothers are obliged to provide material support to their sisters, who provide their brothers with nurturance and affection (Kolenda, 1993). Sibling interdependence is a common theme in South Asian societies. Often, this interdependence is structured by ordinal position instead of, or in addition to, gender. In parts of India, the order of marriage follows birth order, and the desirability of older siblings' marriages contributes to younger siblings' status when they marry. An undesirable marriage by an older sibling ensures that subsequent marriages by younger siblings will be similarly undesirable. In contrast to European American sibling relationships, then, the sibling roles of many Indian adults are structured by sex and birth order. Whereas such dependence contrasts with the values of autonomy and individuality in many Western societies, it exposes the ethnocentric bias of Western social scientists who pathologize the interdependence of siblings as parental or self-sacrificing (Peterson, 1990). A more accepting view of siblings' interdependence may foster more frequent and more satisfying caretaking of siblings in later life (Bedford, 1996).

In sum, an examination of sibling relationships in minority and non-Western cultures provides an opportunity for family scholars and practitioners to reevaluate their assumptions about family structure, normalcy, and values. These insights should lead to creative research agendas that are relevant to the rich ethnic mix of families in the United States and to the dramatic social upheavals that confront families as they move into the new millennium.

INTERGENERATIONAL RELATIONSHIPS OF OLD PEOPLE

As seen in Figure 11.1, generations interact with one another and are influenced by one another through these interactions and through the events that happen to one or more members of any generation. Studies of the oldest old (Johnson, 1993) have shown that the family members with whom an old person interacts need not be living but, rather, can be represented symbolically by a photograph or a grave site. No doubt, similar relationships would be found among younger family members if they were asked about them.

Intergenerational relationships accomplish such functions as long-term socialization for various roles, leisure and companionship, instrumental and emotional support, advice, and development of a sense of family history. In many cases, these interactions represent reciprocal exchanges, with members of both older and younger generations in the family giving and receiving across these domains. The ways of interacting across the generations are varied, reflecting, for example, personal preferences and dispositions, cultural values, and relational competence. Intergenerational relationships can result in harmony or conflict, security or worry. It is important to recognize temporal considerations: Functions and processes change as family members develop and grow older. In this section, we focus on the most researched topic of intergenerational relationships: support given to frail elderly family members (Event 3 in Figure 11.1).

Support exchanged across the generations in a family takes many forms, of which caring for frail members and assisting with household tasks are representative. Not all old people, of course, are dependent on intergenerational care. Some are busy providing care to even older members of the family. Others can manage on their own. But with increasing age comes the likelihood of increasing frailty. Thus, a common form of intergenerational assistance is care provided by younger persons to older frail ones.

In the United States, family members provide the majority of the care that frail elderly people receive (Dwyer & Coward, 1992). Most givers and receivers of care are women, a pattern that holds true across racial-ethnic and class lines, as well as across rural and urban areas of the country (Elder, Rudkin, & Conger, 1995; Stone, Cafferata, & Sangl, 1987). The commitment to family mentioned in relation to adult sibling relationships among blacks can also be found in relation to caregiving for family elders (Strom, Collinsworth, Strom, & Griswold, 1995). In Morycz's (1993)

study, the blacks were more likely to exchange numerous aspects of care and support across the generations than were the whites. Although both the blacks and the whites reported that caring for a disabled older family member was burdensome, when the focus was on caring for a family member with Alzheimer's disease, the blacks felt less stress and strain than did the whites. Apparently, the flexibility of blacks' extended family system enables caregivers to call upon others for help and thereby avoid some of the role overload and exhaustion that white caregivers are likely to experience.

The cross-cultural research of Keith et al. (1994) further illustrates how the intersections of family structure, cultural values, and social institutions influence the provision of care to elderly family members. It is a good example of similarities and diversity in a form of family interaction (elder care) across several cultures. (Additional examples of intergenerational caregiving in various other countries can be found in Hareven, 1996). Keith et al. (1994) compared groups in four regions of the world: !Kung and Herero groups in Botswana, southern Africa; residents of Clifden, on the western Atlantic coast of Ireland, and of Blessington, just outside Dublin; citizens of blue-collar Momence, Illinois, and of upper-middle-class, suburban Swarthmore, Pennsylvania; and elders living in Hong Kong. The following thumbnail sketches show how many circumstances, beyond affectional ties, influence the extent and sources of assistance given to elders.

The !Kung elders rely for their care on relatives and traditional healers who live in their own hamlets; they do not use formal health services even if they are available via mobile clinics. Old people in Herero do make use of available Western-type health care. In addition, they receive care from a variety of relatives, including daughters or daughters-in-law who live in the same households or distant relatives by marriage. In some cases, children are fostered to older persons specifically to provide care. The researchers detected no resentment from the caregivers; in fact, many boasted about the care they gave to older adults.

Most old people in Clifden use formal care. Half the sample also reported that they received care from a member of their household, and 40% cited nonhousehold relatives and nonrelatives as helpers. One tenth of the respondents, however, stated that they had no one available to help them; apparently, many younger people emigrate and therefore are not available to help. Also in this community, many men never marry; thus, 30% of men aged 40–65 are unmarried, which is why there is no immediate-family-support for many of them. Similarly, in Blessington, 15% of the older adults reported having no source of help, whereas 39% cited a household member, 45% mentioned relatives living elsewhere, and 16% cited nonrelatives. Although 42% live alone (compared to 30% of the elderly respondents in Clifden), most elderly members of this community had relatives living nearby whom they saw often. The authors noted that a recent increase in emigration may change this pattern of social contact and assistance.

In Momence, older adults must travel to larger cities for formal health care. Over half the participants (56%) reported receiving help from a relative. Men were more likely than women to state that they required no help and were more likely to use paid help. The most common family caregiver was a spouse. In Swarthmore, too, 50% of the respondents (70% of the men and 38% of the women) stated that they had help available, with most mentioning a relative living in their household, such as a spouse or daughter. Formal services are available, but at a distance, such that many old people must rely on younger people for transportation. The local senior citizen transportation service requires riders to make reservations a week in advance, which limits the usefulness of the service for unexpected visits to health care providers.

Finally, elderly citizens of Hong Kong obtain their health care from public outpatient clinics. Doing so requires waiting in line for a long time; attending specialty clinics for routine vision and dental checkups requires booking appointments at least six months in advance. Since Chinese herbalists are readily accessible with no waiting in line, many elderly persons visit them for minor ailments. Within the family, there is a specific order of caregiving responsibility, depending on the recipient's sex. Help to older women is given primarily by children (including daughters-in-law) who live in the same household (although the authors found that all residents of the household were involved in caregiving), followed by relatives living in other households, friends, and neighbors. Men rarely help with caregiving, even when they are present in the household. Older men receive care primarily from their wives, followed by children in the household, other relatives, and friends or neighbors. If Hong Kong elders have living children, they have almost no chance of being admitted to a nursing home, which provides virtually free care to those without children to help them.

The differences in the availability and use of formal services and the norms and expectations for family assistance varied across the seven study sites, yet some commonalities emerged. In all the study communities, the majority of frail family elders relied on their relatives for day to day assistance. In some cases, caregiving relatives could use formal services as additional resources, but in others, caregivers provided all the help that the elders obtained. Older people without helpers were disadvantaged compared to those with family caregivers available.

Some elderly people are able to acquire additional family helpers. In an unusual approach to analyzing intergenerational support, Gladstone and Westhues (1998) investigated the outcomes of adoption reunions between persons aged 20–77, who were adopted earlier in life, and their birth families. Although not all reunited relationships proved comfortable and close, the authors noted that adoptees and members of their birth family who successfully negotiated a reunion now have additional family resources to draw upon should the need for help arise.

FUTURE DIRECTIONS

Publication of the *Handbook on Aging and the Family* in 1995 (Blieszner & Bedford, 1995) heralded the "coming-of-age" of the field of family gerontology (Troll, 1995, p. xi). Other books (such as Bahr & Peterson, 1989; Szinovacz, Ekerdt, & Vinick, 1992) have also brought the perspective of older family members to family scholars. Our proposed model provides a framework by which to gauge how well we are progressing in representing the rich variety of old people, families, and cultures in which this perspective can be understood. It also points to suggestions for future research. In the remaining section of this chapter, we address the experiences of older family members in a few of the atypical family forms. We include families that engage dead or absent members, families with gay and lesbian members, and families with an impaired younger family member. These examples demonstrate the value of examining many different types of families to further the understanding of family interaction patterns involving old members. Perhaps these examples will stimulate in readers other ideas for extending family gerontology research.

Families with Symbolic or Absent Members

Using a community-dwelling population of oldest-old persons (aged 85–104) in San Francisco, Johnson (1993) uncovered a complex variety of late-life family structures and roles. She identified four family types: the functioning family, with explicit statuses, roles, and norms; the potential family, with latent, flexibly-defined roles; the family as a vessel of sentiment, with inactive roles and no reciprocity, which functions mainly in terms of memories; and the attenuated family, in which old persons have outlived their relatives and thus have no family structure or roles to perform. Only the functional family corresponds remotely to traditional conceptions of families in that face-to-face interaction is ongoing. The potential family is activated in a crisis or for special occasions. The family as a vessel of sentiment exists primarily in the hearts and minds of old persons, whose family photos are the primary source of what passes for family interaction. The attenuated family is virtually erased from memory, in some cases to avoid the pain of loss, and in others as the result of permanent rifts, loss of contact and feeling, and deaths of all members. The identification of these family types brings to awareness variations on a common dimension of family life, but one that has escaped notice. This dimension may be labeled the abstractness of family members

owing to physical absence through death or lack of concrete communication.

Families with Impaired Adult Children

By taking the perspective of old family members, yet another kind of family experience in old age has been discovered. These experiences involve old parents whose child care duties endure because of their offspring's developmental disabilities or mental health limitations. Providing intensive care to and supervision of adult children is a nonnormative family experience that does not necessarily lead to nonnormative outcomes (Greenberg, Seltzer, & Greenley, 1993). For example, parents of mentally retarded adult children remain socially integrated, derive pleasure from seeing the world through their children's eyes, and find a continued purpose in life, even though they have not accomplished, and may never complete, the normative family task of launching their adult children. This line of research illustrates a form of family diversity that is easily overlooked when the lives of older family members are not fully investigated.

Families with Gay or Lesbian Members

Another subpopulation is gays and lesbians. Family scholars have begun to address families that include gays and lesbians, but little is known about the families of old people with gay or lesbian children. A small literature on long-term gay and lesbian relationships exists (for a review, see Huyck, 1995), but the responses of parents of gays and lesbians, particularly in old age, have not been examined much (but see a new review of this literature by Savin-Williams & Dubé, 1998). We know that offspring who are gay or lesbian often create their own fictive families in adolescence, particularly when their parents are not accepting of their sexual orientation (Scrivner, 1995). We recommend that researchers conduct studies that trace what becomes of the family life of parents of gays and lesbians as they become old. Parents who have accepted their children's sexual orientation may have kin who shun them. It is important to find out whether these parents' family networks in later life are truncated because of such ostracism. It would also be useful to find out how old people adapt to the challenges that are presented. For instance, which families overcome their initial aversions? Do old people compensate for the loss of expected family interactions? How does the family handle absent family members at celebrations and holidays?

In each of these three illustrative arenas of family research, taking new perspectives and asking new questions contributes to uncovering more diversity among families with elderly members than might have been assumed to exist in the past. Each case also leads to new research topics and questions that await further inquiry.

CONCLUSION

In our model, we have attempted to ensure that the influences and experiences of older family members are accounted for. We hope we have heightened readers' consciousness of old family members so that they will be included in the analysis of every form of postmodern family. Family therapists are making important strides in this direction as well (for a review of their theories, see Hanna & Hargrave, 1997). We have widened the scope of the intergenerational frameworks, however, by including horizontal (collateral) relationships in addition to vertical (intergenerational) ones to their multiple-household perspective. We have also discussed a greater range of influences that affect family interaction and that family interactions influence. Finally, we have attempted to deconstruct families into highly inclusive entities with the hope that older generations of family members will occupy a permanent place in the consciousness of family scholars and practitioners.

In keeping with our ongoing research goals related to analyzing the family experiences of old people and the many involvements of older adults in the lives of their family members, we aimed to provide a prototypical conceptual framework with empirical examples that address multiple aspects of heterogeneity among older adults and their families. Our intention was also to advocate for gerontologists to pay greater attention to family experiences and family scholars to recognize older adults as significant family members. Toward these ends, we showed the usefulness of a broader definition of *family*, explained why elders are a heterogeneous group, and demonstrated extensive diversity in both intra- and intergenerational family relationships.

REFERENCES

Allen, K. R. (1989). *Single women/family ties: Life histories of older women.* Newbury Park, CA: Sage.

Altergott, K. (1988). *Daily life in later life: Comparative perspectives.* Newbury Park, CA: Sage.

Antonucci, T. C., & Akiyama, H. (1995). Convoys of social relations: Family and friendships within a life span context. In R. Blieszner & V. H. Bedford (Eds.), *Handbook of aging and the family* (pp. 355–371). Westport, CT: Greenwood Press.

Bahr, S. J., & Peterson, E. T. (Eds.). (1989). *Aging and the family.* Lexington, MA: Lexington Books.

Baltes, P. B. (1987). Theoretical propositions of life-span developmental psychology: On the dynamics between growth and decline. *Developmental Psychology, 23,* 611–626.

Baltes, P. B., & Graf, P. (1996). Psychological aspects of aging: Facts and frontiers. In D. Magnussen (Ed.), *The lifespan development of individuals: Behavioral, neurobiological, and psychosocial perspectives* (pp. 427–460). Cambridge, England: Cambridge University Press.

Baltes, P. B., Reese, H. W., & Nesselroade, J. R. (1977). *Life-span developmental psychology.* Monterey, CA: Brooks/Cole.

Bedford, V. H. (1995). Sibling relationships in middle and old age. In R. Blieszner & V. H. Bedford (Eds.), *Handbook of aging and the family* (pp. 201–222). Westport, CT: Greenwood Press.

Bedford, V. H. (1996). Sibling interdependence in adulthood and old age. In T. H. Brubaker (Ed.), *Vision 2010: Families and aging* (pp. 18–19, 43). Minneapolis, MN: National Council on Family Relations.

Bedford, V. H., & Avioli, P. S. (1996). Affect and sibling relationships in adulthood. In C. Malatesta-Magai & S. McFadden (Eds.), *Handbook of emotion, adult development, and aging* (pp. 423–539). New York: Academic Press.

Bedford, V. H., & Blieszner R. (1997). Personal relationships in later-life families. In S. Duck (Ed.), *Handbook of personal relationships* (2nd ed., pp. 523–539). Chichester, England: John Wiley.

Bedford, V. H., & Gold, D. T. (Eds.). (1989). Siblings in old age: A forgotten relationship [Special issue]. *American Behavioral Scientist, 33*(1).

Bengtson, V. L., & Allen, K. R. (1993). The life course perspective applied to families over time. In P. G. Boss, W. J. Doherty, R. LaRossa, W. W. Schumm, & S. K. Steinmetz (Eds.), *Sourcebook of family theories and methods* (pp. 469–499). New York: Plenum.

Blieszner, R. (1994). Feminist perspectives on friendship: Intricate tapestries. In D. L. Sollie & L. A. Leslie (Eds.), *Gender, families, and close relationships: Feminist research journeys* (pp. 120–141). Thousand Oaks, CA: Sage.

Blieszner, R., & Bedford, V. H. (Eds.). (1995). *Handbook of aging and the family.* Westport, CT: Greenwood Press.

Burton, L. M., Dilworth-Anderson, P., & Merriwether-deVries, C. (1995). Context and surrogate parenting among contemporary grandparents. *Marriage and Family Review, 20,* 349–366.

Cicirelli, V. G. (1994). Sibling relationships in cross-cultural perspective. *Journal of Marriage and the Family, 56,* 7–20.

Cicirelli, V. G. (1996). *Sibling relationships across the life span.* New York: Plenum.

Daly, K. J. (1996). *Families and time: Keeping pace in a hurried culture.* Thousand Oaks, CA: Sage.

Dilworth-Anderson, P., Burton, L. M., & Johnson, L. B. (1993). Reframing theories for understanding race, ethnicity, and families. In P. G. Boss, W. J. Doherty, R. LaRossa, W. W. Schumm, & S. K. Steinmetz (Eds.), *Sourcebook of family theories and methods* (pp. 627–646). New York: Plenum.

Dwyer, J. W., & Coward, R. T. (Eds.). (1992). *Gender, families, and eldercare.* Newbury Park, CA: Sage.

Elder, G. H., Jr., Rudkin, L., & Conger, R. D. (1995). Intergenerational continuity and change in rural America. In V. L. Bengtson, K. W. Schaie, & L. M. Burton (Eds.), *Adult intergenerational relations: Effects of societal change* (pp. 30–60). New York: Springer.

Gladstone, J., & Westhues, A. (1998). Adoption reunions: A new side to intergenerational family relationships. *Family Relations, 47,* 177–184.

Gold, D. T. (1990). Late-life sibling relationships: Does race affect typological distribution? *The Gerontologist, 30,* 741–748.

Gough, K. (1959). The Nayars and the definition of marriage. *Journal of the Royal Anthropological Institute, 89,* 23–34.

Greenberg, J. S., Seltzer, M. M., & Greenley, J. R. (1993). Aging parents of adults with disabilities: The gratifications and frustrations of later-life caregiving. *The Gerontologist, 33,* 542–550.

Hanna, S. M., & Hargrave, T. D. (1997). Integrating the process of aging and family therapy. In T. D. Hargrave, & S. M. Hanna (Eds.), *The aging family: New visions in theory, practice and reality* (pp. 19–38). New York: Brunner Mazel.

Hansson, R. O., & Carpenter, B. N. (1994). *Relationships in old age: Coping with the challenge of transition.* New York: Guilford Press.

Hareven, T. K. (Ed.). (1996). *Aging and generational relations over the life course: A historical and cross-cultural perspective.* Berlin: Walter de Gruyter.

Hargrave, T. K., & Anderson, W. T. (1992). *Finishing well: Aging and reparation in the intergenerational family.* New York: Brunner/Mazel.

Huyck, M. H. (1995). Marriage and close relationships of the marital kind. In R. Blieszner & V. H. Bedford (Eds.), *Handbook of aging and the family* (pp. 181–200). Westport, CT: Greenwood Press.

Janis, I. L. (1982). *Groupthink: Psychological studies of policy decisions and fiascoes* (2nd ed.). Boston: Houghton Mifflin.

Johnson, C. L. (1977). Interdependence, reciprocity and indebtedness: An analysis of Japanese American kinship relations. *Journal of Marriage and the Family, 39,* 351–363.

Johnson, C. L. (1982). Sibling solidarity: Its origin and functioning in Italian-American families. *Journal of Marriage and the Family, 44,* 155–165.

Johnson, C. L. (1993). The prolongation of life and the extension of family relationships: The families of the oldest old. In P. A. Cowan, D. Field, D. A. Hansen, A. Skolnick, & G. E. Swanson (Eds.), *Family, self, and society: Toward a new agenda for family research* (pp. 317–330). Hillsdale, NJ: Lawrence Erlbaum.

Johnson, C. L. (1994). Differential expectations and realities: Race, socioeconomic status and health of the oldest-old. *International Journal of Aging and Human Development, 38,* 13–27.

Johnson, C. L. (1995a). Childlessness and kinship organization: Comparisons of very old whites and blacks. *Journal of Cross Cultural Gerontology, 10,* 289–306.

Johnson, C. L. (1995b). Cultural diversity in the late-life family. In R. Blieszner & V. H. Bedford (Eds.), *Handbook of aging and the family* (pp. 307–331). Westport, CT: Greenwood Press.

Kaufman, S. R. (1986). *The ageless self: Sources of meaning in late life.* New York: Meridian.

Keith, J., Fry, C. L., Glascock, A. P., Ikels, C., Dickerson-

Putman, J., Harpending, H. C., & Draper, P. (1994). *The aging experience: Diversity and commonality across cultures.* Thousand Oaks, CA: Sage.

Kinsella, K. (1995). Aging and the family: Present and future demographic issues. In R. Blieszner & V. H. Bedford (Eds.), *Handbook of aging and the family* (pp. 32–56). Westport, CT: Greenwood Press.

Kivett, V. R. (1989). Mother-in-law and daughter-in-law relations. In J. A. Mancini (Ed.), *Aging parents and adult children* (pp. 17–32). Lexington, MA: Lexington Books.

Kolenda, P. (1993). Sibling relations and marriage practices: A comparison of north, central, and south India. In C. W. Nuckolls (Ed.), *Siblings in South Asia: Brothers and sisters in cultural context* (pp. 103–141). New York: Guilford Press.

Marshall, M. (1983). *Siblingship in Oceania* (Monograph No. 8). New York: University Press of America.

Morycz, R. (1993). Caregiving families and cross-cultural perspectives. In S. H. Zarit, L. I. Pearlin, & K. W. Schaie (Eds.), *Caregiving systems: Formal and informal helpers* (pp. 67–73). Hillsdale, NJ: Lawrence Erlbaum.

Neugarten, B. L., & Hagestad, G. O. (1976). Age and the life course. In R. H. Binstock and E. Shanas (Eds.), *Handbook of aging and the social sciences* (pp. 35–55). New York: Van Nostrand Reinhold.

Nuckolls, C. W. (Ed.). (1993). *Siblings in South Asia: Brothers and sisters in cultural context.* New York: Guilford Press.

Peterson, J. T. (1990). Sibling exchanges and complementarity in the Philippine Highlands. *Journal of Marriage and the Family, 52,* 441–451.

Robertson, J. F. (1995). Grandparenting in an era of rapid change. In R. Blieszner & V. H. Bedford (Eds.), *Handbook of aging and the family* (pp. 243–260). Westport, CT: Greenwood Press.

Rodgers, R. H., & White, J. M. (1993). Family development theory. In P. G. Boss, W. J. Doherty, R. LaRossa, W. W. Schumm, & S. K. Steinmetz (Eds.), *Sourcebook of family theories and methods* (pp. 225–254). New York: Plenum.

Ryff, C. D., & Seltzer, M. M. (1995). Family relations and individual development in adulthood and aging. In R. Blieszner & V. H. Bedford (Eds.), *Handbook of aging and the family* (pp. 95–113). Westport, CT: Greenwood Press.

Savin-Williams, R. C., & Dubé, E. M. (1998). Parental reactions to their child's disclosure of a gay/lesbian identity. *Family Relations, 47,* 7–14.

Scrivner, R. (1995, August). *Revisioning the family: Lesbians, gays, and family life.* Paper presented at the 103rd annual convention of the American Psychological Association, New York.

Smith, D. E. (1987). *The everyday world as problematic: A feminist sociology.* Boston: Northeastern University Press.

Stack, C. (1974). *All our kin.* New York: Harper & Row.

Stone, B., Cafferata, G. L., & Sangl, J. (1987). Caregivers of the frail elderly: A national profile. *The Gerontologist, 27,* 616–626.

Streib, G. F., & Binstock, R. H. (1990). Aging and the social sciences: Changes in the field. In R. H. Binstock & L. K. George (Eds.), *Handbook of aging and the social sciences* (3rd ed., pp. 1–16). San Diego: Academic Press.

Strom, R., Collinsworth, P., Strom, S., & Griswold, D. (1995). Strengths and needs of black grandparents. In J. Hendricks (Ed.), *The ties of later life* (pp. 195–207). Amityville, NY: Baywood.

Suggs, P. K. (1989). Predictors of association among siblings: A black/white comparison. *American Behavioral Scientist, 33,* 70–80.

Szinovacz, M., Ekerdt, D. J., & Vinick, B. H. (Eds.). (1992). *Families and retirement.* Newbury Park, CA: Sage.

Tajfel, H., Billib, M. G., Bundy, R. P., & Flament, C. (1971). Social categorization and intergroup behavior. *European Journal of Social Psychology, 1,* 149–178.

Taylor, R. J., Chatters, L. M., & Mays, V. M. (1988). Parents, children, siblings, in-laws, and non-kin as sources of emergency assistance to black Americans. *Family Relations, 37,* 298–304.

Thompson, P. J. (1990, November). *Home economics: Foremother of feminist family studies?* Paper presented at the annual meeting of the National Council on Family Relations, Seattle.

Troll, L. E. (1971). The family of later life: A decade review. *Journal of Marriage and the Family, 33,* 263–290.

Troll, L. E. (1995). Foreword. In R. Blieszner & V. H. Bedford (Eds.), *Handbook of aging and the family* (pp. xi–xx). Westport, CT: Greenwood Press.

PART V

Racial, Ethnic, and Cultural Diversities in Families

CHAPTER **12**

Diversity Within African American Families

RONALD L. TAYLOR

PERSONAL REFLECTIONS

My interest in African American families as a topic of research was inspired more than two decades ago by my observation and growing dismay over the stereotypical portrayal of these families presented by the media and in much of the social science literature. Most of the African American families I knew in the large southern city in which I grew up were barely represented in the various "authoritative" accounts I read and other scholars frequently referred to in their characterizations and analyses of such families. Few such accounts have acknowledged the regional, ethnic, class, and behavioral diversity within the African American community and among families. As a result, a highly fragmented and distorted public image of African American family life has been perpetuated that encourages perceptions of African American families as a monolith. The 1986 television documentary *A CBS Report: The Vanishing Family: Crisis in Black America,* hosted by Bill Moyers, was fairly typical of this emphasis. It focused almost exclusively on low-income, single-parent households in

inner cities, characterized them as "vanishing" non-families, and implied that such families represented the majority of African American families in urban America. It mattered little that poor, single-parent households in the inner cities made up less than a quarter of all African American families at the time the documentary was aired.

As an African American reared in the segregated South, I was keenly aware of the tremendous variety of African American families in composition, lifestyle, and socioeconomic status. Racial segregation ensured that African American families, regardless of means or circumstances, were constrained to live and work in close proximity to one another. Travel outside the South made me aware of important regional differences among African American families as well. For example, African American families in the Northeast appeared far more segregated by socioeconomic status than did families in many parts of the South with which I was familiar. As a graduate student at Boston University during the late 1960s, I recall the shock I experienced upon seeing the level of concentrated poverty among African American families in Roxbury, Massachusetts, an experience duplicated in travels to New York, Philadelphia, and Newark. To be sure, poverty of a similar magnitude was prevalent throughout the South, but was far less concentrated and, from my perception, far less pernicious.

As I became more familiar with the growing body of research on African American families, it became increasingly clear to me that the source of a major distortion in the portrayal of African American families in the social science literature and the media was the overwhelming concentration on impoverished inner-city communities of the Northeast and Midwest to the near exclusion of the South, where more than half the African American families are found and differences among them in family patterns, lifestyles, and socioeconomic characteristics are more apparent.

In approaching the study of African American families in my work, I have adopted a *holistic* perspective. This perspective, outlined first by DuBois (1898) and more recently by Billingsley (1992) and Hill (1993), emphasizes the influence of historical, cultural, social, economic, and political forces in shaping contemporary patterns of family life among African Americans of all socioeconomic backgrounds. Although the impact of these external forces is routinely taken into account in assessing stability and change among white families, their effects on the structure and functioning of African American families are often minimized. In short, a holistic approach undertakes to study African American families *in context*. My definition of the *family,* akin to the definition offered by Billingsley (1992), views it as an intimate association of two or more persons related to each other by blood, marriage, formal or informal adoption, or appropriation. The latter term refers to the incorporation of persons in the family who are unrelated by blood or marital ties but are treated as through they are family. This definition is broader than other dominant definitions of families that emphasize biological or marital ties as defining characteristics.

This chapter is divided into three parts. The first part reviews the treatment of African American families in the historical and social sciences literatures. It provides a historical overview of African American families, informed by recent historical scholarship, that corrects many of the misconceptions about the nature and quality of family life during and following the experience of slavery. The second part examines contemporary patterns of marriage, family, and household composition among African Americans in response to recent social, economic, and political developments in the larger society. The third part explores some of the long-term implications of current trends in marriage and family behavior for community functioning and individual well-being, together with implications for social policy.

THE TREATMENT OF AFRICAN AMERICAN FAMILIES IN AMERICAN SCHOLARSHIP

As an area of scientific investigation, the study of African American family life is of recent vintage. As recently as 1968, Billingsley, in his classic work *Black Families in White America,* observed that African American family life had been virtually ignored in family studies and studies of race and ethnic relations. He attributed the general lack of interest among white social scientists, in part, to their "ethnocentrism and intellectual commitment to peoples and values transplanted from Europe" (p. 214). Content analyses of key journals in sociology, social work, and family studies during the period supported Billingsley's contention. For example, a content analysis of 10 leading journals in sociology and social work by Johnson (1981) disclosed that articles on African American families constituted only 3% of 3,547 empirical studies of American families published between 1965 and 1975. Moreover, in the two major journals in social work, only one article on African American families was published from 1965 to 1978. In fact, a 1978 special issue of the *Journal of Marriage and the Family* devoted to African American families accounted for 40% of all articles on these families published in the 10 major journals between 1965 and 1978.

Although the past two decades have seen a significant increase in the quantity and quality of research on the family lives of African Americans, certain features and limitations associated with earlier studies in this area persist (Taylor, Chatters, Tucker, & Lewis, 1990). In a review of recent research on African American families, Hill (1993) concluded that many studies continue to treat such families in superficial terms; that is, African American families are not considered to be an important unit of focus and, consequently, are treated peripherally or omitted altogether. The assumption is that African American families are automatically treated in all analyses that focus on African Americans as individuals; thus, they are not treated in their own right. Hill noted that a major impediment to understanding the functioning of African American families has been the failure of most analysts to use a theoretical or conceptual framework that took account of the totality of African American family life. Overall, he found that the preponderance of recent studies of African American families are

> (a) fragmented, in that they exclude the bulk of Black families by focusing on only a subgroup; (b) ad hoc, in that they apply arbitrary explanations that are not derived from systematic theoretical formulations that have been empirically substantiated; (c) negative, in that they focus exclusively on the perceived weaknesses of Black families; and (d) internally oriented, in that they exclude any systematic consideration of the role of forces in the wider society on Black family life (p. 5).

THEORETICAL APPROACHES

The study of African American families, like the study of American families in general, has evolved through successive theoretical formulations. Using white family structure as the norm, the earliest studies characterized African American families as impoverished versions of white families in which the experiences of slavery, economic deprivation, and racial discrimination had induced pathogenic and dysfunctional features (Billingsley, 1968). The classic statement of this perspective was presented by Frazier, whose study, *The Negro Family in the United States* (1939), was the first comprehensive analysis of African American family life and its transformation under various historical conditions—slavery, emancipation, and urbanization (Edwards, 1968).

It was Frazier's contention that slavery destroyed African familial structures and cultures and

gave rise to a host of dysfunctional family features that continued to undermine the stability and well-being of African American families well into the 20th century. Foremost among these features was the supposed emergence of the African American "matriarchal" or maternal family system, which weakened the economic position of African American men and their authority in the family. In his view, this family form was inherently unstable and produced pathological outcomes in the family unit, including high rates of poverty, illegitimacy, crime, delinquency, and other problems associated with the socialization of children. Frazier concluded that the female-headed family had become a common tradition among large segments of lower-class African American migrants to the North during the early 20th century. The two-parent male-headed household represented a second tradition among a minority of African Americans who enjoyed some of the freedoms during slavery, had independent artisan skills, and owned property.

Frazier saw an inextricable connection between economic resources and African American family structure and concluded that as the economic position of African Americans improved, their conformity to normative family patterns would increase. However, his important insight regarding the link between family structure and economic resources was obscured by the inordinate emphasis he placed on the instability and "self-perpetuating pathologies" of lower-class African American families, an emphasis that powerfully contributed to the pejorative tradition of scholarship that emerged in this area. Nonetheless, Frazier recognized the diversity of African American families and in his analyses, "consistently attributed the primary sources of family instability to external forces (such as racism, urbanization, technological changes and recession) and not to internal characteristics of Black families" (Hill, 1993, pp. 7–8).

During the 1960s, Frazier's characterization of African American families gained wider currency with the publication of Moynihan's *The Negro Family: The Case for National Action* (1965), in which weaknesses in family structure were identified as a major source of social problems in African American communities. Moynihan attributed high rates of welfare dependence, out-of-wedlock births, educational failure, and other problems to the "unnatural" dominance of women in African American families. Relying largely on the work of Frazier as a source of reference, Moynihan traced the alleged "tangle of pathology" that characterized urban African American families to the experience of slavery and 300 years of racial oppression, which, he concluded, had caused "deep-seated structural distortions" in the family and community life of African Americans.

Although much of the Moynihan report, as the book was called, largely restated what had become conventional academic wisdom on African American families during the 1960s, its generalized indictment of all African American families ignited a firestorm of criticism and debate and inspired a wealth of new research and writings on the nature and quality of African American family life in the United States (Staples & Mirande, 1980). In fact, the 1970s saw the beginning of the most prolific period of research on African American families, with more than 50 books and 500 articles published during that decade alone, representing a fivefold increase over the literature produced in all the years since the publication of DuBois's (1909) pioneering study of African American family life (Staples & Mirande, 1980). To be sure, some of this work was polemical and defensively apologetic, but much of it sought to replace ideology with research and to provide alternative perspectives for interpreting observed differences in the characteristics of African American and white families (Allen, 1978).

Critics of the deficit or pathology approach to African American family life (Scanzoni, 1977; Staples, 1971) called attention to the tendency in the literature to ignore family patterns among the majority of African Americans and to overemphasize findings derived from studies of low-income and typically problem-ridden families. Such findings were often generalized and accepted as descriptive of the family life of all African American families, with the result that popular but erroneous images of African American family life were perpetuated. Scrutinizing the research literature of the 1960s, Billingsley (1968) concluded that when the majority of African American families was con-

sidered, evidence refuted the characterization of African American family life as unstable, dependent on welfare, and matriarchal. In his view, and in the view of a growing number of scholars in the late 1960s and early 1970s, observed differences between white and African American families were largely the result of differences in socioeconomic position and of differential access to economic resources (Allen, 1978; Scanzoni, 1977).

Thus, the 1970s witnessed not only a significant increase in the diversity, breadth, and quantity of research on African American families, but a shift away from a social pathology perspective to one emphasizing the resilience and adaptiveness of African American families under a variety of social and economic conditions. The new emphasis reflected what Allen (1978) referred to as the "cultural variant" perspective, which treats African American families as different but legitimate functional forms. From this perspective, "Black and White family differences [are] taken as given, without the presumption of one family form as normative and the other as deviant." (Farley & Allen, 1987, p. 162). In accounting for observed racial differences in family patterns, some researchers have taken a *structural perspective,* emphasizing poverty and other socioeconomic factors as key processes (Billingsley, 1968). Other scholars have taken a *cultural approach,* stressing elements of the West African cultural heritage, together with distinctive experiences, values, and behavioral modes of adaptation developed in this country, as major determinants (Nobles, 1978; Young, 1970). Still others (Collins, 1990; Sudarkasa, 1988) have pointed to evidence supporting both interpretations and have argued for a more comprehensive approach.

Efforts to demythologize negative images of African American families have continued during the past two decades, marked by the development of the first national sample of adult African Americans, drawn to reflect their distribution throughout the United States (Jackson, 1991), and by the use of a variety of conceptualizations, approaches, and methodologies in the study of African American family life (Collins, 1990; McAdoo, 1997). Moreover, the emphasis in much of the recent work has not been the defense of African American family forms, but rather the identification of forces that have altered long-standing traditions. The ideological paradigms identified by Allen (1978) to describe the earlier thrust of Black family research—cultural equivalence, cultural deviance, and cultural variation—do not fully capture the foci of this new genre of work as a whole (Tucker & Mitchell-Kernan, 1995, p. 17).

Researchers have sought to stress balance in their analyses, that is, to assess the strengths and weaknesses of African American family organizations at various socioeconomic levels, and the need for solution-oriented studies (Hill, 1993). At the same time, recent historical scholarship has shed new light on the relationship of changing historical circumstances to characteristics of African American family organization and has underscored the relevance of historical experiences to contemporary patterns of family life.

AFRICAN AMERICAN FAMILIES IN HISTORICAL PERSPECTIVE

Until the 1970s, it was conventional academic wisdom that the experience of slavery decimated African American culture and created the foundation for unstable female-dominated households and other familial aberrations that continued into the 20th. century. This thesis, advanced by Frazier (1939) and restated by Moynihan (1965), was seriously challenged by the pioneering historical research of Blassingame (1972), Furstenberg, Hershberg, and Modell (1975), and Gutman (1976), among others. These works provide compelling documentation of the centrality of family and kinship among African Americans during the long years of bondage and how African Americans created and sustained a rich cultural and family life despite the brutal reality of slavery.

In his examination of more than two centuries of slave letters, autobiographies, plantation records, and other materials, Blassingame (1972) meticulously documented the nature of community, family organization, and culture among American slaves. He concluded that slavery was not "an all-powerful, monolithic institution which strip[ped] the slave of any meaningful and distinctive culture, family life,

religion or manhood" (p. vii). To the contrary, the relative freedom from white control that slaves enjoyed in their quarters enabled them to create and sustain a complex social organization that incorporated "norms of conduct, defined roles and behavioral patterns" and provided for the traditional functions of group solidarity, defense, mutual assistance, and family organization. Although the family had no legal standing in slavery and was frequently disrupted, Blassingame noted its major role as a source of survival for slaves and as a mechanism of social control for slaveholders, many of whom encouraged "monogamous mating arrangements" as insurance against runaways and rebellion. In fashioning familial and community organization, slaves drew upon the many remnants of their African heritage (e.g., courtship rituals, kinship networks, and religious beliefs), merging those elements with American forms to create a distinctive culture, features of which persist in the contemporary social organization of African American family life and community.

Genovese's (1974) analysis of plantation records and slave testimony led him to similar conclusions regarding the nature of family life and community among African Americans under slavery. Genovese noted that, although chattel bondage played havoc with the domestic lives of slaves and imposed severe constraints on their ability to enact and sustain normative family roles and functions, the slaves "created impressive norms of family, including as much of a nuclear family norm as conditions permitted and . . . entered the postwar social system with a remarkably stable base" (p. 452). He attributed this stability to the extraordinary resourcefulness and commitment of slaves to marital relations and to what he called a "paternalistic compromise," or bargain between masters and slaves that recognized certain reciprocal obligations and rights, including recognition of slaves' marital and family ties. Although slavery undermined the role of African American men as husbands and fathers, their function as role models for their children and as providers for their families was considerably greater than has generally been supposed. Nonetheless, the tenuous position of male slaves as husbands and fathers and the more visible and nontraditional roles assumed by female slaves gave rise to legends of matriarchy and emasculated men. However, Genovese contended that the relationship between slave men and women came closer to approximating gender equality than was possible for white families.

Perhaps the most significant historical work that forced revisions in scholarship on African American family life and culture during slavery was Gutman's (1976) landmark study, *The Black Family in Slavery and Freedom.* Inspired by the controversy surrounding the Moynihan report and its thesis that African American family disorganization was a legacy of slavery, Gutman made ingenious use of quantifiable data derived from plantation birth registers and marriage applications to re-create family and kinship structures among African Americans during slavery and after emancipation. Moreover, he marshaled compelling evidence to explain how African Americans developed an autonomous and complex culture that enabled them to cope with the harshness of enslavement, the massive relocation from relatively small economic units in the upper South to vast plantations in the lower South between 1790 and 1860, the experience of legal freedom in the rural and urban South, and the transition to northern urban communities before 1930.

Gutman reasoned that, if family disorganization (fatherless, matrifocal families) among African Americans was a legacy of slavery, then such a condition should have been more common among urban African Americans closer in time to slavery—in 1850 and 1860—than in 1950 and 1960. Through careful examination of census data, marriage licenses, and personal documents for the period after 1860, he found that stable, two-parent households predominated during slavery and after emancipation and that families headed by African American women at the turn of the century were hardly more prevalent than among comparable white families. Thus "[a]t all moments in time between 1860 and 1925 . . . the typical Afro-American family was lower class in status and headed by two parents. That was so in the urban and rural South in 1880 and 1900 and in New York City in 1905 and 1925" (p. 456). Gutman found that the two-parent family was just as common among the poor as among the more

advantaged, and as common among southerners as those in the Northeast. For Gutman, the key to understanding the durability of African American families during and after slavery lay in the distinctive African American culture that evolved from the cumulative slave experiences that provided a defense against some of the more destructive and dehumanizing aspects of that system. Among the more enduring and important aspects of that culture are the enlarged kinship network and certain domestic arrangements (e.g., the sharing of family households with nonrelatives and the informal adoption of children) that, during slavery, formed the core of evolving African American communities and the collective sense of interdependence.

Additional support for the conclusion that the two-parent household was the norm among slaves and their descendants was provided by Furstenberg et al. (1975) from their study of the family composition of African Americans, native-born whites, and immigrants to Philadelphia from 1850 to 1880. From their analysis of census data, Furstenberg et al. found that most African American families, like those of other ethnic groups, were headed by two parents (75% for African Americans versus 73% for native whites). Similar results are reported by Pleck (1973) from her study of African American family structure in late 19th-century Boston. As these and other studies (Jones, 1985; White, 1985) have shown, although female-headed households were common among African Americans during and following slavery, such households were by no means typical. In fact, as late as the 1960s, three fourths of African American households were headed by married couples (Jaynes & Williams, 1989; Moynihan, 1965).

However, more recent historical research would appear to modify, if not challenge, several of the contentions of the revisionist scholars of slavery. Manfra and Dykstra (1985) and Stevenson (1995), among others, found evidence of considerably greater variability in slave family structure and in household composition than was reported in previous works. In her study of Virginia slave families from 1830 to 1860, Stevenson (1995) discovered evidence of widespread matrifocality, as well as other marital and household arrangements, among antebellum slaves. Her analysis of the family histories of slaves in colonial and antebellum Virginia revealed that many slaves did not have a nuclear "core" in their families. Rather, the "most discernible ideal for their principal kinship organization was a malleable extended family that provided its members with nurture, education, socialization, material support, and recreation in the face of the potential social chaos the slavemasters' power imposed" (1995, p. 36).

A variety of conditions affected the family configurations of slaves, including cultural differences among the slaves themselves, the state or territory in which they lived, and the size of the plantation on which they resided. Thus, Stevenson concluded that

> the slave family was not a static, imitative institution that necessarily favored one form of family organization over another. Rather, it was a diverse phenomenon, sometimes assuming several forms even among the slaves of one community. . . . Far from having a negative impact, the diversity of slave marriage and family norms, as a measure of the slave family's enormous adaptive potential, allowed the slave and the slave family to survive. (p. 29)

Hence, "postrevisionist" historiography emphasizes the great diversity of familial arrangements among African Americans during slavery. Although nuclear, matrifocal, and extended families were prevalent, none dominated slave family forms. These postrevisionist amendments notwithstanding, there is compelling historical evidence that African American nuclear families and kin-related households remained relatively intact and survived the experiences of slavery, Reconstruction, the Great Depression, and the transition to northern urban communities. Such evidence underscores the importance of considering recent developments and conditions in accounting for changes in family patterns among African Americans in the contemporary period.

CONTEMPORARY AFRICAN AMERICAN FAMILY PATTERNS

Substantial changes have occurred in patterns of marriage, family, and household composition in the United States during the past three decades, accompanied by significant alterations in the family lives of men, women, and children. During this period, divorce rates have more than doubled, marriage rates have declined, fertility rates have fallen to record levels, the proportion of "traditional" families (nuclear families in which children live with both biological parents) as a percentage of all family groups has declined, and the proportion of children reared in single-parent households has risen dramatically (Taylor, 1997).

Some of the changes in family patterns have been more rapid and dramatic among African Americans than among the population as a whole. For example, while declining rates of marriage and remarriage, high levels of separation and divorce, and higher proportions of children living in single-parent households are trends that have characterized the U.S. population as a whole during the past 30 years, these trends have been more pronounced among African Americans and, in some respects, represent marked departures from earlier African American family patterns. A growing body of research has implicated demographic and economic factors as causes of the divergent marital and family experiences of African Americans and other populations.

In the following section, I examine diverse patterns and evolving trends in family structure and household composition among African Americans, together with those demographic, economic, and social factors that have been identified as sources of change in patterns of family formation.

Diversity of Family Structure

Since 1960, the number of African American households has increased at more than twice the rate of white households. By 1995, African American households numbered 11.6 million, compared with 83.7 million white households. Of these households, 58.4 million white and 8.0 million African American ones were classified as family households by the U.S. Bureau of the Census (1996), which defines a *household* as the person or persons occupying a housing unit and a *family* as consisting of two or more persons who live in the same household and are related by birth, marriage, or adoption. Thus, family households are households maintained by individuals who share their residence with one or more relatives, whereas non-family households are maintained by individuals with no relatives in the housing unit. In 1995, 70% of the 11.6 million African American households were family households, the same proportion as among white households (U.S. Bureau of the Census, 1996). However, nonfamily households have been increasing at a faster rate than family households among African Americans because of delayed marriages among young adults, higher rates of family disruption (divorce and separation), and sharp increases in the number of unmarried cohabiting couples (Cherlin, 1995; Glick, 1997).

Family households vary by type and composition. Although the U.S. Bureau of the Census recognizes the wide diversity of families in this country, it differentiates between three broad and basic types of family households: married-couple or husband-wife families, families with female householders (no husband present), and families with male householders (no wife present). Family composition refers to whether the household is *nuclear*, that is, contains parents and children only, or *extended*, that is, nuclear plus other relatives.

To take account of the diversity in types and composition of African American families, Billingsley (1968; 1992) added to these conventional categories *augmented* families (nuclear plus nonrelated persons), and modified the definition of nuclear family to include *incipient* (a married couple without children), *simple* (a couple with children), and *attenuated* (a single parent with children) families. He also added three combinations of augmented families: *incipient extended augmented* (a couple with relatives and nonrelatives), *nuclear extended augmented* (a couple with children, relatives, and nonrelatives), and *attenuated extended augmented* (a single parent with children, relatives, and nonrelatives). With these modifications, Billingsley identified 32 different kinds of nuclear, extended, and augmented family households among African Americans. His typology has been widely used and modified by other scholars (see, for example, Shimkin, Shimkin, & Frate, 1978; Stack, 1974). For example, on the basis of Billingsley's typology, Dressler, Haworth-Hoeppner, and Pitts (1985) developed a four-way typology with 12

subtypes for their study of household structures in a southern African American community and found a variety of types of female-headed households, less than a fourth of them consisting of a mother and her children or grandchildren.

However, as Staples (1971) pointed out, Billingsley's typology emphasized the household and ignored an important characteristic of such families—their "extendedness." African Americans are significantly more likely than whites to live in extended families that "transcend and link several different households, each containing a separate . . . family" (Farley & Allen, 1987, p. 168). In 1992, approximately 1 in 5 African American families was extended, compared to 1 in 10 white families (Glick, 1997). The greater proportion of extended households among African Americans has been linked to the extended family tradition of West African cultures (Nobles, 1978; Sudarkasa, 1988) and to the economic marginality of many African American families, which has encouraged the sharing and exchange of resources, services, and emotional support among family units spread across a number of households (Stack, 1974).

In comparative research on West African, Caribbean, and African American family patterns, some anthropologists (Herskovits, 1958; Sudarkasa, 1997) found evidence of cultural continuities in the significance attached to coresidence, formal kinship relations, and nuclear families among black populations in these areas. Summarizing this work, Hill (1993, pp. 104–105) observed that, with respect to

co-residence, the African concept of family is not restricted to persons living in the same household, but includes key persons living in separate households. . . . As for defining kin relationships, the African concept of family is not confined to relations between formal kin, but includes networks of unrelated [i.e., "fictive kin"] as well as related persons living in separate households. . . . [According to] Herskovits (1941), the African nuclear family unit is not as central to its family organization as is the case for European nuclear families: "The African immediate family, consisting of a father, his wives, and their children, is but a part of a larger unit. This immediate family is generally recognized by Africanists as belonging to a local relationship group termed the 'extended family.'"

Similarly, Sudarkasa (1988) found that unlike the European extended family, in which primacy is given to the conjugal unit (husband, wife, and children) as the basic building block, the African extended family is organized around blood ties (consanguineous relations).

In their analysis of data from the National Survey of Black Americans (NSBA) on household composition and family structure, Hatchett, Cochran, and Jackson (1991) noted that the extended family perspective, especially kin networks, was valuable in describing the nature and functioning of African American families. They suggested that the "extended family can be viewed both as a family network in the physical-spatial sense and in terms of family relations or contact and exchanges. In this view of extendedness, family structure and function are interdependent concepts" (p. 49). Their examination of the composition of the 2,107 households in the NSBA resulted in the identification of 12 categories, 8 of which roughly captured the "dimensions of household family structure identified in Billingsley's typology of Black families (1968)— the incipient nuclear family, the incipient nuclear extended and/or augmented nuclear family, the simple nuclear family, the simple extended and/or augmented nuclear family, the attenuated nuclear family, and the attenuated extended and/or augmented family, respectively" (p. 51). These households were examined with respect to their *actual kin networks,* defined as subjective feelings of emotional closeness to family members, frequency of contact, and patterns of mutual assistance, and their *potential kin networks,* defined as the availability or proximity of immediate family members and the density or concentration of family members within a given range.

Hatchett et al. (1991) found that approximately 1 in 5 African American households in the NSBA was an extended household (included other relatives— parents and siblings of the household head, grandchildren, grandparents, and nieces and nephews). Nearly 20% of the extended households with children contained minors who were not the head's; most of these children were grandchildren, nieces, and nephews of the head. The authors suggested that "[t]hese are instances of informal fostering or adoption—absorption of minor children by the kin network" (p. 58).

In this sample, female-headed households were as likely to be extended as male-headed households. Hatchett et al. (1991) found little support for the possibility that economic hardship may account for the propensity among African Americans to incorporate other relatives in their households. That is, the inclusion of other relatives in the households did not substantially improve the overall economic situation of the households because the majority of other relatives were minor children, primarily grandchildren of heads who coresided with the household heads' own minor and adult children. Moreover, they stated, "household extendedness at both the household and extra-household levels appears to be a characteristic of black families, regardless of socioeconomic level" (p. 81), and regardless of region of the country or rural or urban residence.

The households in the NSBA were also compared in terms of their potential and actual kin networks. The availability of potential kin networks varied by the age of the respondent, by the region and degree of urban development of the respondent's place of residence, and by the type of household in which the respondent resided (Hatchett et al., 1991). For example, households with older heads and spouses were more isolated from kin than were younger households headed by single mothers, and female-headed households tended to have greater potential kin networks than did individuals in nuclear households. With respect to region and urbanicity, the respondents in the Southern and North Central regions and those in rural areas had a greater concentration of relatives closer at hand than did the respondents in other regions and those in urban areas. However, proximity to relatives and their concentration nearby did not translate directly into actual kin networks or extended family functioning:

> Complex relationships were found across age, income, and type of household. From these data came a picture of the Black elderly with high psychological connectedness to family in the midst of relative geographical and interactional isolation from them. The image of female single-parent households is, on the

other hand, the reverse or negative of this picture. Female heads were geographically closer to kin, had more contact with them, and received more help from family but did not perceive as much family solidarity or psychological connectedness. (Hatchett et al., 1991, p. 81)

The nature and frequency of mutual aid among kin were also assessed in this survey. More than two thirds of the respondents reported receiving some assistance from family members, including financial support, child care, goods and services, and help during sickness and at death. Financial assistance and child care were the two most frequent types of support reported by the younger respondents, whereas goods and services were the major types reported by older family members. The type of support the respondents received from their families was determined, to some extent, by needs defined by the family life cycle.

In sum, the results of the NSBA document the wide variety of family configurations and households in which African Americans reside and suggest, along with other studies, that the diversity of structures represents adaptive responses to the variety of social, economic, and demographic conditions that African Americans have encountered over time (Billingsley, 1968; Farley & Allen, 1987).

Although Hatchett et al. (1991) focused on extended or augmented African American families in their analysis of the NSBA data, only 1 in 5 households in this survey contained persons outside the nuclear family. The majority of households was nuclear, containing one or both parents with their own children.

Between 1970 and 1990, the number of all U.S. married-couple families with children dropped by almost 1 million, and their share of all family households declined from 40% to 26% (U.S. Bureau of the Census, 1995). The proportion of married-couple families with children among African Americans also declined during this period, from 41% to 26% of all African American families. In addition, the percentage of African American families headed by women more than doubled, increasing from 33% in 1970 to 57% in 1990. By 1995, married-couple families with children constituted 36% of all African American families, while single-parent families

represented 64% (U.S. Bureau of the Census, 1996). The year 1980 was the first time in history that African American female-headed families with children outnumbered married-couple families. This shift in the distribution of African American families by type is associated with a number of complex, interrelated social and economic developments, including increases in age at first marriage, high rates of separation and divorce, male joblessness, and out-of-wedlock births

Marriage, Divorce, and Separation

In a reversal of a long-time trend, African Americans are now marrying at a much later age than are persons of other races. Thirty years ago, African American men and women were far more likely to have married by ages 20–24 than were white Americans. In 1960, 56% of African American men and 36% of African American women aged 20–24 were never married; by 1993, 90% of all African American men and 81% of African American women in this age cohort were never married (U.S. Bureau of the Census, 1994).

The trend toward later marriages among African Americans has contributed to changes in the distribution of African American families by type. Delayed marriage tends to increase the risk of out-of-wedlock childbearing and single parenting (Hernandez, 1993). In fact, a large proportion of the increase in single-parent households in recent years is accounted for by never-married women maintaining families (U.S. Bureau of the Census, 1990).

The growing proportion of never-married young African American adults is partly a result of a combination of factors, including continuing high rates of unemployment, especially among young men; college attendance; military service; and an extended period of cohabitation prior to marriage (Glick, 1997; Testa & Krogh, 1995; Wilson, 1987). In their investigation of the effect of employment on marriage among African American men in the inner city of Chicago, Testa and Krogh (1995) found that men in stable jobs were twice as likely to marry as were men who were unemployed, not in school, or in the military. Hence, it has been argued that the feasibility of marriage among African Americans in recent decades has decreased because the precarious economic position of African American men has made them less attractive as potential husbands and less interested in becoming husbands, given the difficulties they are likely to encounter in performing the provider role in marriage (Tucker & Mitchell-Kernan, 1995).

However, other research has indicated that economic factors are only part of the story. Using census data from 1940 through the mid-1980s, Mare and Winship (1991) sought to determine the impact of declining employment opportunities on marriage rates among African Americans and found that although men who were employed were more likely to marry, recent declines in employment rates among young African American men were not large enough to account for a substantial part of the declining trend in their marriage rates. Similarly, in their analysis of data from a national survey of young African American adults, Lichter, McLaughlin, Kephart, and Landry (1992) found that lower employment rates among African American men were an important contributing factor to delayed marriage—and perhaps to nonmarriage—among African American women. However, even when marital opportunities were taken into account, the researchers found that the rate of marriage among young African American women in the survey was only 50% to 60% the rate of white women of similar ages.

In addition to recent declines in employment rates, an unbalanced sex ratio has been identified as an important contributing factor to declining marriage rates among African Americans. This shortage of men is due partly to high rates of mortality and incarceration of African American men (Kiecolt & Fossett, 1995; Wilson & Neckerman, 1986). Guttentag and Secord (1983) identified a number of major consequences of the shortage of men over time: higher rates of singlehood, out-of-wedlock births, divorce, and infidelity and less commitment among men to relationships. Among African Americans, they found that in 1980 the ratio of men to women was unusually low; in fact, few populations in the United States had sex ratios as low as those of African Americans. Because African American women outnumber men in each

of the age categories 20 to 49, the resulting "marriage squeeze" puts African American women at a significant disadvantage in the marriage market, causing an unusually large proportion of them to remain unmarried. However, Glick (1997) observed a reversal of the marriage squeeze among African Americans in the age categories 18 to 27 during the past decade: In 1995, there were 102 African American men for every 100 African American women in this age range. Thus, "[w]hereas the earlier marriage squeeze made it difficult for Black women to marry, the future marriage squeeze will make it harder for Black men" (Glick, 1997, p. 126). But, as Kiecolt and Fossett (1995) observed, the impact of the sex ratio on marital outcomes for African Americans may vary, depending on the nature of the local marriage market. Indeed, "marriage markets are local, as opposed to national, phenomena which may have different implications for different genders . . . [for example,] men and women residing near a military base face a different sex ratio than their counterparts attending a large university" (Smith, 1995, p. 137).

African American men and women are not only delaying marriage, but are spending fewer years in their first marriages and are slower to remarry than in decades past. Since 1960, a sharp decline has occurred in the number of years African American women spend with their first husbands and a corresponding rise in the interval of separation and divorce between the first and second marriages (Espenshade, 1985; Jaynes & Williams, 1989). Data from the National Fertility Surveys of 1965 and 1970 disclosed that twice as many African American couples as white couples (10% versus 5%) who reached their 5th wedding anniversaries ended their marriages before their 10th anniversaries (Thornton, 1978), and about half the African American and a quarter of the white marriages were dissolved within the first 15 years of marriage (McCarthy, 1978). Similarly, a comparison of the prevalence of marital disruption (defined as separation or divorce) among 13 racial-ethnic groups in the United States based on the 1980 census revealed that of the women who had married for the first time 10 to 14 years before 1980, 53% of the African American women, 48% of the Native American women, and 37% of the non-Hispanic white women were separated or divorced by the 1980 census (Sweet & Bumpass, 1987).

Although African American women have a higher likelihood of separating from their husbands than do non-Hispanic white women, they are slower to obtain legal divorces (Cherlin, 1996). According to data from the 1980 census, within three years of separating from their husbands, only 55% of the African American women had obtained divorces, compared to 91% of the non-Hispanic white women (Sweet & Bumpass, 1987). Cherlin speculated that, because of their lower expectations of remarrying, African American women may be less motivated to obtain legal divorces. Indeed, given the shortage of African American men in each of the age categories from 20 to 49, it is not surprising that the proportion of divorced women who remarry is lower among African American than among non-Hispanic white women (Glick, 1997). Overall, the remarriage rate among African Americans is about one fourth the rate of whites (Staples & Johnson, 1993).

Cherlin (1996) identified lower educational levels, high rates of unemployment, and low income as importance sources of differences in African American and white rates of marital dissolution However, as he pointed out, these factors alone are insufficient to account for all the observed difference. At every level of educational attainment, African American women are more likely to be separated or divorced from their husbands than are non-Hispanic white women. Using data from the 1980 census, Jaynes and Williams (1989) compared the actual marital-status distributions of African Americans and whites, controlling for differences in educational attainment for men and women and for income distribution for men. They found that when differences in educational attainment were taken into account, African American women were more likely to be "formerly married than White women and much less likely to be living with a husband" (p. 529). Moreover, income was an important factor in accounting for differences in the marital status of African American and white men. Overall, Jaynes and Williams found that socioeconomic differences explained a significant amount of the variance in

marital status differences between African Americans and whites, although Bumpass, Sweet, and Martin (1990) noted that such differences rapidly diminish as income increases, especially for men. As Glick (1997) reported, African American men with high income levels are more likely to be in intact first marriages by middle age than are African American women with high earnings. This relationship between income and marital status, he stated, is strongest at the lower end of the income distribution, suggesting that marital permanence for men is less dependent on their being well-to-do than on their having the income to support a family.

As a result of sharp increases in marital disruption and relatively low remarriage rates, less than half (43%) the African American adults aged 18 and older were currently married in 1995, down from 64% in 1970 (U.S. Bureau of the Census, 1996). Moreover, although the vast majority of the 11.6 million African Americans households in 1995 were family households, less than half (47%) were headed by married couples, down from 56% in 1980. Some analysts expect the decline in marriage among African Americans to continue for some time, consistent with the movement away from marriage as a consequence of modernization and urbanization (Espenshade, 1985) and in response to continuing economic marginalization. But African American culture may also play a role. As a number of writers have noted (Billingsley, 1992; Cherlin, 1996), blood ties and extended families have traditionally been given primacy over other types of relationships, including marriage, among African Americans, and this emphasis may have influenced the way many African Americans responded to recent shifts in values in the larger society and the restructuring of the economy that struck the African American community especially hard.

Such is the interpretation of Cherlin (1992, p. 112), who argued that the institution of marriage has been weakened during the past few decades by the increasing economic independence of women and men and by a cultural drift "toward a more individualistic ethos, one which emphasized self-fulfillment in personal relations." In addition, Wilson (1987) and others described structural shifts in the economy (from manufacturing to service industries as a source of the growth in employment) that have benefited African American women more than men, eroding men's earning potential and their ability to support families. According to Cherlin, the way African Americans responded to such broad socio-cultural and economic changes was conditioned by their history and culture:

> Faced with difficult times economically, many Blacks responded by drawing upon a model of social support that was in their cultural repertoire. . . . This response relied heavily on extended kinship networks and de-emphasized marriage. It is a response that taps a traditional source of strength in African-American society: cooperation and sharing among a large network of kin. (p. 113)

Thus, it seems likely that economic developments and cultural values have contributed independently and jointly to the explanation of declining rates of marriage among African Americans in recent years (Farley & Allen, 1987).

Single-Parent Families

Just as rates of divorce, separation, and out-of-wedlock childbearing have increased over the past few decades, so has the number of children living in single-parent households. For example, between 1970 and 1990, the number and proportion of all U.S. single-parent households increased threefold, from 1 in 10 to 3 in 10. There were 3.8 million single-parent families with children under 18 in 1970, compared to 11.4 million in 1994. The vast majority of single-parent households are maintained by women (86% in 1994), but the number of single-parent households headed by men has more than tripled: from 393,000 in 1970 to 1.5 million in 1994 (U.S. Bureau of the Census, 1995).

Among the 58% of African American families with children at home in 1995, more were one-parent families (34%) than married-couple families (24%). In 1994, single-parent families accounted for 25% of all white family groups with children under age 18, 65% of all African American family groups, and 36% of Hispanic family groups (U.S. Bureau of the Census, 1995).

Single-parent families are created in a number of ways: through divorce, marital separation, out-of-

wedlock births, or death of a parent. Among adult African American women aged 25–44, increases in the percentage of never-married women and disrupted marriages are significant contributors to the rise in female-headed households; for white women of the same age group, marital dissolution or divorce is the most important factor (Demo, 1992; Jaynes & Williams, 1989). Moreover, changes in the living arrangements of women who give birth outside marriage or experience marital disruption have also been significant factors in the rise of female-headed households among African American and white women. In the past, women who experienced separation or divorce, or bore children out of wedlock were more likely to move in with their parents or other relatives, creating subfamilies; as a result, they were not classified as female headed. In recent decades, however, more and more of these women have established their own households (Parish, Hao, & Hogan, 1991).

An increasing proportion of female-headed householders are unmarried teenage mothers with young children. In 1990, for example, 96% of all births to African American teenagers occurred outside marriage; for white teenagers, the figure was 55% (National Center for Health Statistics, 1991). Although overall fertility rates among teenage women declined steadily from the 1950s through the end of the 1980s, the share of births to unmarried women has risen sharply over time. In 1970, the proportion of all births to unmarried teenage women aged 15–19 was less than 1 in 3; by 1991, it had increased to 2 in 3.

Differences in fertility and births outside marriage among young African American and white women are accounted for, in part, by differences in sexual activity, use of contraceptives, the selection of adoption as an option, and the proportion of premarital pregnancies that are legitimated by marriage before the children's births (Trusell, 1988). Compared to their white counterparts, African American teenagers are more likely to be sexually active and less likely to use contraceptives, to have abortions when pregnant, and to marry before the babies are born. In consequence, young African American women constitute a larger share of single mothers than they did in past decades. This development has serious social and economic consequences for children and adults because female-headed households have much higher rates of poverty and deprivation than do other families (Taylor, 1991b).

Family Structure and Family Dynamics

As a number of studies have shown, there is a strong correspondence between organization and economic status of families, regardless of race (Farley & Allen, 1987). For both African Americans and whites, the higher the income, the greater the percentage of families headed by married couples. In their analysis of 1980 census data on family income and structure, Farley and Allen (1987) found that "there were near linear decreases in the proportions of households headed by women, households where children reside with a single parent, and extended households with increases in economic status" (p. 185). Yet, socioeconomic factors, they concluded, explained only part of the observed differences in family organization between African Americans and whites. "Cultural factors—that is, family preferences, notions of the appropriate and established habits—also help explain race differences in family organization" (p. 186).

One such difference is the egalitarian mode of family functioning in African American families, characterized by complementarity and flexibility in family roles (Billingsley, 1992; Hill, 1971). Egalitarian modes of family functioning are common even among low-income African American families, where one might expect the more traditional patriarchal pattern of authority to prevail. Until recently, such modes of family functioning were interpreted as signs of weakness or pathology because they were counternormative to the gender-role division of labor in majority families (Collins, 1990). Some scholars have suggested that role reciprocity in African American families is a legacy of slavery, in which the traditional gender division of labor was largely ignored by slaveholders, and Black men and women were "equal in the sense that neither sex wielded economic power over the other" (Jones, 1985, p. 14). As a result of historical experiences and economic conditions, traditional gender distinctions in the homemaker and provider roles have been less rigid in African American families

than in white families (Beckett & Smith, 1981). Moreover, since African American women have historically been involved in the paid labor force in greater numbers than have white women and because they have had a more significant economic role in families than their white counterparts, Scott-Jones and Nelson-LeGall (1986, p. 95) argued that African Americans "have not experienced as strong an economic basis for the subordination of women, either in marital roles or in the preparation of girls for schooling, jobs, and careers."

In her analysis of data from the NSBA, Hatchett (1991) found strong support for an egalitarian division of family responsibilities and tasks. With respect to attitudes toward the sharing of familial roles, 88% of the African American adults agreed that women and men should share child care and housework equally, and 73% agreed that both men and women should have jobs to support their families. For African American men, support for an egalitarian division of labor in the family did not differ by education or socioeconomic level, but education was related to attitudes toward the sharing of family responsibilities and roles among African American women. College-educated women were more likely than were women with less education to support the flexibility and interchangability of family roles and tasks.

Egalitarian attitudes toward familial roles among African Americans are also reflected in child-rearing attitudes and practices (Taylor, 1991a). Studies have indicated that African American families tend to place less emphasis on differential gender-role socialization than do other families (Blau, 1981). In her analysis of gender-role socialization among southern African American families, Lewis (1975) found few patterned differences in parental attitudes toward male and female roles. Rather, age and relative birth order were found to be more important than gender as determinants of differential treatment and behavioral expectations for children. Through their socialization practices, African American parents seek to inculcate in both genders traits of assertiveness, independence, and self-confidence (Boykin & Toms, 1985; Lewis, 1975). However, as children mature, socialization practices are adapted to reflect "more closely the structure of expectations and opportunities provided for Black men and women by the dominant society" (Lewis, 1975, p. 237)—that is, geared to the macrostructural conditions that constrain familial role options for African American men and women.

However, such shifts in emphasis and expectations often lead to complications in the socialization process by inculcating in men and women components of gender-role definitions that are incompatible or noncomplementary, thereby engendering a potential source of conflict in their relationships. Franklin (1986) suggested that young African American men and women are frequently confronted with contradictory messages and dilemmas as a result of familial socialization. On the one hand, men are socialized to embrace an androgynous gender role within the African American community, but, on the other hand, they are expected to perform according to the white masculine gender-role paridigm in some contexts. According to Franklin, this dual orientation tends to foster confusion in some young men and difficulties developing an appropriate gender identity. Likewise, some young African American women may receive two different and contradictory messages: "One message states, 'Because you will be a Black woman, it is imperative that you learn to take care of yourself because it is hard to find a Black man who will take care of you.' A second message . . . that conflicts with the first . . . is 'your ultimate achievement will occur when you have snared a Black man who will take care of you'" (Franklin, 1986, p. 109). Franklin contended that such contradictory expectations and mixed messages frequently lead to incompatible gender-based behaviors among African American men and women and conflicts in their relationships.

Despite the apparently greater acceptance of role flexibility and power sharing in African American families, conflict around these issues figures prominently in marital instability. In their study of marital instability among African American and white couples in early marriages, Hatchett, Veroff, and Douvan (1995) found young African American couples at odds over gender roles in the family. Anxiety over their ability to function in the provider role was found to be an important source of instability in the marriages for African American husbands, but not for white husbands. Hatchett (1991) observed that

marital instability tended to be more common among young African American couples if the husbands felt that their wives had equal power in the family and if the wives felt there was not enough sharing of family tasks and responsibilities. Hatchett et al. (1991) suggested that African American men's feelings of economic anxiety and self-doubt may be expressed in conflicts over decisional power and in the men's more tenuous commitment to their marriages vis-à-vis African American women. Although the results of their study relate to African American couples in the early stages of marriage, the findings may be predictive of major marital difficulties in the long term. These and other findings (see, for example, Tucker & Mitchell-Kernan, 1995) indicate that changing attitudes and definitions of familial roles among young African American couples are tied to social and economic trends (such as new and increased employment opportunities for women and new value orientations toward marriage and family) in the larger society.

African American Families, Social Change, and Public Policy

Over the past three decades, no change in the African American community has been more fundamental and dramatic than the restructuring of families and family relationships. Since the 1960s, unprecedented changes have occurred in rates of marriage, divorce, and separation; in the proportion of single and two-parent households and births to unmarried mothers; and in the number of children living in poverty. To be sure, these changes are consistent with trends for the U.S. population as a whole, but they are more pronounced among African Americans, largely because of a conflux of demographic and economic factors that are peculiar to the African American community.

In their summary of findings from a series of empirical studies that investigated the causes and correlates of recent changes in patterns of African American family formation, Tucker and Mitchell-Kernan (1995) came to several conclusions that have implications for future research and social policy. One consistent finding is the critical role that sex ratios–the availability of mates play in the formation of African American families. Analyzing aggregate-level data on African American sex ratios in 171 U.S. cities, Sampson (1995) found that these sex ratios were highly predictive of female headship, the percentage of married couples among families with school-age children, and the percentage of African American women who were single. In assessing the causal effect of sex ratios on the family structure of African Americans and whites, he showed that the effect is five times greater for the former than the latter. Similarly, Kiecolt and Fossett's (1995) analysis of African American sex ratios in Louisiana cities and counties disclosed that they had strong positive effects on the percentage of African American women who were married and had husbands present, the rate of marital births per thousand African American women aged 20–29, the percentage of married-couple families, and the percentage of children living in two-parent households.

Another consistent finding is the substantial and critical impact of economic factors on African American family formation, especially men's employment status. Analyses by Sampson (1995) and Darity and Myers (1995) provided persuasive evidence that economic factors play a major and unique role in the development and maintenance of African American families. Using aggregate data, Sampson found that low employment rates for African American men in cities across the United States were predictive of female headship, the percentage of women who were single, and the percentage of married-couple families among family households with school-age children. Moreover, comparing the effect of men's employment on the family structure of African American and white families, he found that the effect was 20 times greater for African Americans than for whites. Similar results are reported by Darity and Myers, who investigated the effects of sex ratio and economic marriageability—Wilson and Neckerman's (1986) Male Marriageability Pool Index—on African American family structure. They found that, although both measures were independently predictive of female headship among African Americans, a composite measure of economic and demographic factors was a more stable and effective predictor. Moreover, Sampson found that the strongest independent effect of these factors on family structure was observed among African American families in poverty. That is, "the lower the sex ratio and the lower the male employment rate the higher the rate of female-headed families with children and in poverty" (p. 250). It should be noted that neither rates of white men's employment nor white sex ratios was found to have much influence on white family structure in these analyses, lending support to Wilson's (1987) hypothesis regarding the structural sources of family disruption among African Americans.

Although the findings reported here are not definitive, they substantiate the unique and powerful effects of sex ratios and men's employment on the marital behavior and family structure of African Americans and point to other problems related to the economic marginalization of men and family poverty in African American communities. Some analysts have predicted far-reaching consequences for African Americans and for society at large should current trends in marital disruption continue unabated. Darity and Myers (1996) predicted that the majority of African American families will be headed by women by the beginning of the next decade if violent crime, homicide, incarceration, and other problems associated with the economic marginalization of African American men are allowed to rob the next generation of fathers and husbands. Moreover, they contended, a large number of such families are likely to be poor and isolated from the mainstream of American society.

The growing economic marginalization of African American men and their inability to provide economic support to families have contributed to their increasing estrangement from family life (Bowman, 1989; Tucker & Mitchell-Kernan, 1995) and are identified as pivotal factors in the development of other social problems, including drug abuse, crime, homicide, and imprisonment, which further erode their prospects as marriageable mates for African American women.

In addressing the structural sources of the disruption of African American families, researchers have advanced a number of short- and long-term proposals. There is considerable agreement that increasing the rate of marriage alone will not significantly improve the economic prospects of many poor African American families. As Ehrenreich (1986) observed, given the marginal economic position of poor African American men, impoverished African American women would have to be married to three such men—simultaneously—to achieve an average family income! Thus, for many African American women, increasing the prevalence of marriage will not address many of the problems they experience as single parents.

With respect to short-term policies designed to address some of the more deleterious effects of structural forces on African American families, Darity and Myers (1996) proposed three policy initiatives that are likely to produce significant results for African American communities. First, because research has indicated that reductions in welfare benefits have failed to stem the rise in female-headed households, welfare policy should reinstate its earlier objective of lifting the poor out of poverty. In Darity and Myers's view, concerns about the alleged disincentives of transfer payments are "moot in light of the long-term evidence that Black families will sink deeper into a crisis of female headship with or without welfare. Better a world of welfare-dependent, near-poor families than one of welfare-free but desolate and permanently poor families" (p. 288). Second, programs are needed to improve the health care of poor women and their children. One major potential benefit of such a strategy is an improvement in the sex ratio because the quality of prenatal and child care is one of the determinants of sex ratios. "By assuring quality health care now, we may help stem the tide toward further depletion of young Black males in the future" (p. 288). A third strategy involves improvements in the quality of education provided to the poor, which are key to employment gains.

Although these are important initiatives with obvious benefits to African American communities, in the long term, the best strategy for addressing marital disruptions and other family-related issues is an economic–labor market strategy. Because much of current social policy is ideologically driven, rather than formulated on the basis of empirical evidence, it has failed to acknowledge or address the extent to which global and national changes in the economy have conspired to marginalize significant segments of the African American population, both male and female, and deprive them

of the resources to form or support families. Although social policy analysts have repeatedly substantiated the link between the decline in marriages among African Americans and fundamental changes in the U.S. postindustrial economy, their insights have yet to be formulated into a meaningful and responsive policy agenda. Until these structural realities are incorporated into governmental policy, it is unlikely that marital disruption and other adverse trends associated with this development will be reversed.

There is no magic bullet for addressing the causes and consequences of marital decline among African Americans, but public policies that are designed to improve the economic and employment prospects of men and women at all socioeconomic levels have the greatest potential for improving the lot of African American families. Key elements of such policies would include raising the level of education and employment training among African American youth, and more vigorous enforcement of antidiscrimination laws, which would raise the level of employment and earnings and contribute to higher rates of marriage among African Americans (Burbridge, 1995). To be sure, many of the federally sponsored employment and training programs that were launched during the 1960s and 1970s were plagued by a variety of administrative and organizational problems, but the effectiveness of some of these programs in improving the long-term employment prospects and life chances of disadvantaged youth and adults has been well documented (Taylor et al., 1990).

African American families, like all families, exist not in a social vacuum but in communities, and programs that are designed to strengthen community institutions and provide social support to families are likely to have a significant impact on family functioning. Although the extended family and community institutions, such as the church, have been important sources of support to African American families in the past, these community support systems have been overwhelmed by widespread joblessness, poverty, and a plethora of other problems that beset many African American communities. Thus, national efforts to rebuild the social and economic infrastructures of inner-city communities would make a major contribution toward improving the overall health and well-being of African American families and could encourage more young people to marry in the future.

Winning support for these and other policy initiatives will not be easy in a political environment that de-emphasizes the role of government in social policy and human welfare. But without such national efforts, it is difficult to see how many of the social conditions that adversely affect the structure and functioning of African American families will be eliminated or how the causes and consequences of marital decline can be ameliorated. If policy makers are serious about addressing conditions that destabilize families, undermine communities, and contribute to a host of other socially undesirable outcomes, new policy initiatives, such as those just outlined, must be given higher priority.

REFERENCES

Allen, W. (1978). The search for applicable theories of black family life. *Journal of Marriage and the Family, 40,* 117–129.

Beckett, J., & Smith, A. (1981). Work and family roles: Egalitarian marriage in black and white families. *Social Service Review, 55,* 314–326.

Billingsley, A. (1968). *Black families in white America.* Englewood Cliffs, NJ: Prentice Hall.

Billingsley, A. (1992). *Climbing Jacob's ladder: The enduring legacy of African American families.* New York: Simon & Schuster.

Blassingame, J. (1972). *The slave community.* New York: Oxford University Press.

Blau, Zena. (1981). *Black children/white socialization.* New York: Free Press.

Bowman, P. J. (1989). Research perspectives on black men: Role strain and adaptation across the life cycle. In R. L. Jones (Ed.), *Black adult development and aging* (pp. 117–150). Berkeley, CA.: Cobb & Henry.

Bowman, P. J. (1995). Commentary. In M. B. Tucker & C. Mitchell-Kernan (Eds.), *The decline in marriage among African Americans* (pp. 309–321). New York: Russell Sage Foundation.

Boykin, A. W., & Toms, F. D. (1985). Black child socialization: A conceptual framework. In H. P. McAdoo & J. L. McAdoo (Eds.), *Black children* (pp. 33–54). Beverly Hills, CA: Sage.

Bumpass, L., Sweet, J., & Martin, T. C. (1990). Changing patterns of remarriage. *Journal of Marriage and the Family 52,* 747–756.

Burbridge, L. C. (1995). Policy implications of a decline in marriage among African Americans. In M. B. Tucker & C. Mitchell-Kernan (Eds.), *The decline in marriage among African Americans* (pp. 323–344). New York: Russell Sage Foundation.

Cherlin, A. (1992). *Marriage, divorce, remarriage* (rev. ed.). Cambridge, MA: Harvard University Press.

Cherlin, A. (1995). Policy issues of child care. In P. Chase-Lansdale & J. Brooks-Gunn, (Eds.), *Escape from poverty* (pp. 121–137). New York: Cambridge University Press.

Cherlin, A. (1996). *Public and private families.* New York: McGraw-Hill.

Collins, P. (1990). *Black feminist thought.* Boston, MA.: Unwin Hyman.

Darity, W., & Myers, S. (1995). Family structure and the marginalization of black men: Policy implications. In M. B. Tucker & C. Mitchell-Kernan (Eds.), *The decline in marriage among African Americans* (pp. 263–308). New York: Russell Sage Foundation.

Demo, D. (1992). Parent-child relations: Assessing recent changes. *Journal of Marriage and the Family, 54,* 104–117.

Dressler, W., Haworth-Hoeppner, S., & Pitts, B. (1985). Household structure in a southern black community. *American Anthropologist, 87,* 853–862.

DuBois, W. E. B. (1898). The study of the Negro problem. *Annals, 1,* 1–23.

DuBois, W. E. B. (1909). *The Negro American family.* Atlanta: Atlanta University Press.

Edwards, G. F. (1968). *E. Franklin Frazier on race relations.* Chicago: University of Chicago Press.

Ehrenreich, B. (1986, July–August). Two, three, many husbands. *Mother Jones,* 8–9.

Espenshade, T. (1985). Marriage trends in America: Estimates, implications, and underlying causes. *Population and Development Review, 11,* 193–245.

Farley, R., & Allen, W. (1987). *The color line and the quality of life in America.* New York: Oxford University Press.

Franklin, C. (1986). Black male–Black female conflict: Individually caused and culturally nurtured. In R. Staples (Ed.), *The black family* (3rd ed., pp. 106–113). Belmont, CA: Wadsworth.

Frazier, E. F. 1939. *The Negro family in the United States.* Chicago: University of Chicago Press.

Furstenberg, F., Hershberg, T., & Modell, J. (1975). The origins of the female-headed black family: The impact of the urban experience. *Journal of Interdisciplinary History, 6,* 211–233.

Genovese, E. (1974). *Roll Jordan roll: The world slaves made.* New York: Pantheon.

Glick, P. (1997). Demographic pictures of African American families. In H. McAdoo (Ed.), *Black families* (3rd. ed., pp. 118–138). Thousand Oaks, CA.: Sage.

Gutman, H. (1976). *The black family in slavery and freedom, 1750–1925.* New York: Pantheon.

Guttentag, M., & Secord, P. F. (1983). *Too many women.* Beverly Hills, CA.: Sage.

Hatchett, S. (1991). Women and men. In J. Jackson (Ed.), *Life in black America* (pp. 84–104). Newbury Park, CA.: Sage.

Hatchett, S., Cochran, D., & Jackson, J. (1991). In J. Jackson (Ed.), *Life in black America* (pp. 46–83). Newbury Park, CA: Sage.

Hatchett, S., Veroff, J., & Douvan, E (1995). Marital instability among black and white couples in early marriage. In M. B. Tucker & C. Mitchell-Kernan (Eds.), *The decline in marriage among African Americans* (pp. 177–218). New York: Russell Sage Foundation.

Hernandez, D. J. (1993). *America's children.* New York: Russell Sage.

Herskovits, M. J. (1958). *The myth of the Negro past* (Beacon Paperback No. 69). Boston: Beacon Press.

Hill, R. (1971). *The strengths of black families.* New York: Emerson Hall.

Hill, R. (1993). *Research on the African American family: A holistic perspective.* Westport, CT: Auburn House.

Jackson, J. (Ed.). (1991). *Life in black America.* Newbury Park, CA: Sage.

Jaynes, G., & Williams, R. (1989). *A common destiny: Blacks and American society.* Washington, DC: National Academy Press.

Johnson, L. B. (1981). Perspectives on black family empirical research: 1965–1978. In H. P. McAdoo (Ed.), *Black families* (pp. 252–263). Beverly Hills, CA: Sage.

Jones, J. (1985). *Labor of love, labor of sorrow: Black women, work, and the family from slavery to the present.* New York: Basic Books.

Kiecolt, K., & Fossett, M. (1995). Mate availability and marriage among African Americans: Aggregate-and individual-level analysis. In M. B. Tucker & C. Mitchell-Kernan (Eds.), *The decline in marriage among African Americans* (pp. 121–135). New York: Russell Sage Foundation.

Lewis, D. (1975). The black family: Socialization and sex roles. *Phylon, 36,* 221–237.

Lichter, D. T., McLaughlin, D. K., Kephart, G., & Landry, G. (1992). Race and the retreat from marriage: A shortage of marriageable men? *American Sociological Review, 57,* 781–799.

Manfra, J. A. & Dykstra, R. P. (1985). Serial marriage and the origins of the black stepfamily: The Rowanty evidence. *Journal of American History, 7,* 18–44.

Mare, R., & Winship, C. (1991). Socioeconomic change and the decline of marriage for blacks and whites. In C. Jencks & P. E. Peterson (Eds.), *The urban underclass* (pp. 175–204). Washington, DC: Brookings Institute.

McAdoo, H. P. (Ed.). (1997). *Black families* (3rd ed.). Thousand Oaks, CA: Sage.

McCarthy, J. (1978). A comparison of the probability of the dissolution of first and second marriages. *Demography, 15,* 345–359.

Moynihan, D. P. (1965). *The Negro family: The case for national action.* Washington, DC: U.S. Government Printing Office.

National Center for Health Statistics. (1991). *Monthly Vital Statistics Report* (Vol. 35, No. 4, Suppl.). Washington, DC: U.S. Department of Health and Human Services.

Nobles, W. (1978). Toward an empirical and theoretical framework for defining black families. *Journal of Marriage and the Family, 40,* 679–688.

Parish, W. L., Hao, L. & Hogan, D. P. (1991). Family support networks, welfare, and work among young mothers. *Journal of Marriage and the Family, 53,* 203–215.

Pleck, E. (1973). The two-parent household: Black family structure in late nineteenth-century Boston. In M. Gordon (Ed.), *The American family in socio-historical perspective* (pp. 152–178). New York: St. Martin's Press.

Sampson, R. J. (1995). Unemployment and unbalanced sex ratios: Race-specific consequences for family structure and crime. In M. B. Tucker & C. Mitchell-Kernan (Eds.), *The decline in marriage among African Americans* (pp. 229–254). New York: Russell Sage Foundation.

Scanzoni, J. (1977). *The black family in modern society.* Chicago: University of Chicago Press.

Scott-Jones, D., & Nelson-LeGall, S. (1986). Defining black families: Past and present. In E. Seidman & J. Rappaport (Eds.), *Redefining social problems* (pp. 83–100). New York: Plenum.

Shimkin, D., Shimkin, E. M., & Frate, D. A. (Eds.). (1978). *The extended family in black societies.* The Hague, the Netherlands: Mouton.

Smith, A. W. (1995). Commentary. In M. B. Tucker & C. Mitchell-Kernan (Eds.), *The decline in marriage among African Americans* (pp. 136–141). New York: Russell Sage Foundation.

Stack, C. (1974). *All our kin.* New York: Harper & Row.

Staples, R. (1971). Toward a sociology of the black family: A decade of theory and research. *Journal of Marriage and the Family, 33,* 19–38.

Staples, R., & Johnson, L. B. (1993). *Black families at the crossroads.* San Francisco: Jossey-Bass.

Staples, R., & Mirande, A. (1980). Racial and cultural variations among American families: A decennial review of the literature on minority families. *Journal of Marriage and the Family, 42,* 157–173.

Stevenson, B. (1995). Black family structure in colonial and antebellum Virginia: Amending the revisionist perspective. In M. B. Tucker & C. Mitchell-Kernan (Eds.), *The decline in marriage among African Americans* (pp. 27–56). New York: Russell Sage Foundation.

Sudarkasa, N. (1988). Interpreting the African heritage in Afro-American family organization. In H. P. McAdoo (Ed.), *Black families* (pp. 27–42). Newbury Park, CA: Sage.

Sudarkasa, N. (1997). African American families and family values. In H. P. McAdoo (Ed.), *Black families* (pp. 9–40). Thousand Oaks, CA: Sage.

Sweet, J., & Bumpass, L. (1987). *American families and households.* New York: Russell Sage Foundation.

Taylor, R. L. (1991a). Child rearing in African American families. In J. Everett, S. Chipungu, & B. Leashore (Eds.), *Child welfare: An Africentric perspective* (pp. 119–155). New Brunswick, NJ: Rutgers University Press.

Taylor, R. L. (1991b). Poverty and adolescent black males: The subculture of disengagement. In P. Edelman & J. Ladner (Eds.), *Adolescence and poverty: Challenge for the 1990s* (pp. 139–162). Washington, DC: Center for National Policy Press.

Taylor, R. L. (1997). Who's parenting? Trends and patterns. In T. Arendell (Ed.), *Contemporary parenting: Challenges and issues* (pp. 68–91). Thousand Oaks, CA: Sage.

Taylor, R. J., Chatters, L., Tucker, M. B., & Lewis, E. (1990). Developments in research on black families: A decade review. *Journal of Marriage and the Family, 52,* 993–1014.

Testa, M., & Krogh, M. (1995). The effect of employment on marriage among black males in inner-city Chicago. In M. B. Tucker & C. Mitchell-Kernan (Eds.), *The decline in marriage among African Americans* (pp. 59–95). New York: Russell Sage Foundation.

Thornton, A. (1978). Marital instability differentials and interactions: Insights from multivariate contingency table analysis. *Sociology and Social Research, 62,* 572–595.

Trusell, J. (1988). Teenage pregnancy in the United States. *Family Planning Perspectives, 20,* 262–272.

Tucker, M. B., & Mitchell-Kernan, C. (1995). Trends in African American family formation: A theoretical and statistical overview. In M. B. Tucker & C. Mitchell-Kernan (Eds.), *The decline in marriage among African Americans* (pp. 3–26). New York: Russell Sage Foundation.

U.S. Bureau of the Census. (1990). Marital status and living arrangements: March 1989. *Current Population Reports* (Series P-20, No. 445). Washington, DC: U.S. Government Printing Office.

U.S. Bureau of the Census. (1994). Marital status and living arrangements: March 1993. *Current Population Reports* (Series P-20, No. 478). Washington, DC: U.S. Government Printing Office.

U.S. Bureau of the Census. (1995). Household and family characteristics: March 1994. *Current Population Reports* (Series P-20, No. 483). Washington, DC: U.S. Government Printing Office.

U.S. Bureau of the Census. (1996). *Statistical abstract of the United States: 1996.* Washington, DC: U.S. Government Printing Office.

White, D. G. (1985). *Ain't I a woman? Female slaves in the plantation South.* New York: W. W. Norton.

Wilson, W. J. (1987). *The truly disadvantaged: The inner city, the underclass and public policy.* Chicago: University of Chicago Press.

Wilson, W. J., & Neckerman K. (1986). Poverty and family structure: The widening gap between evidence and public policy issues. In S. Danziger & D. Weinberg (Eds.), *Fighting poverty: What works and what doesn't* (pp. 232–259). Cambridge, MA: Harvard University Press.

Young, V. H. (1970). Family and childhood in a southern Negro community. *American Anthropologist, 72,* 269–288.

CHAPTER 13

Diversity Within Latino Families: New Lessons for Family Social Science

MAXINE BACA ZINN AND BARBARA WELLS

Who are Latinos? How will their growing presence in U.S. society affect the family field? These are vital questions for scholars who are seeking to understand the current social and demographic shifts that are reshaping society and its knowledge base. Understanding family diversity is a formidable task, not only because the field is poorly equipped to deal with differences at the theoretical level, but because many decentering efforts are themselves problematic. Even when diverse groups are included, family scholarship can distort and misrepresent by faulty emphasis and false generalizations.

Latinos are a population that can be understood only in terms of increasing heterogeneity. Latino families are unprecedented in terms of their diversity. In this chapter, we examine the ramifications of such diversity on the history, boundaries, and dynamics of family life. We begin with a brief look at the intellectual trends shaping Latino family research. We then place different Latino groups at center stage by providing a framework that situates them in specific and changing political and economic settings. Next, we apply our framework to each national origin group to draw out their different family experiences, especially as they are altered by global restructuring. We turn, then, to examine family structure issues and the interior dynamics of family living as they vary by gender and generation. We conclude with our reflections on studying Latino families and remaking family social science. In this chapter, we use interchangeably terms that are commonly used to describe Latino national-origin groups. For example, the terms Mexican American, Mexican, and Mexican-origin population will be used to refer to the same segment of the Latino population. Mexican-origin people may also be referred to as Chicanos.

INTELLECTUAL TRENDS, CRITIQUES, AND CHALLENGES

Origins

The formal academic study of Latino families originated in the late 19th and early 20th centuries with studies of Mexican immigrant families. As the new social scientists of the times focused their concerns on immigration and social disorganization, Mexican-origin and other ethnic families were the source of great concern. The influential Chicago School of Sociology led scholars to believe that Mexican immigration, settlement, and poverty created problems in developing urban centers. During this period, family study was emerging as a new field that sought to document, as well as ameliorate, social problems in urban settings (Thomas & Wilcox, 1987). Immigrant families became major targets of social reform.

Interwoven themes from race relations and family studies gave rise to the view of Mexicans as particularly disorganized. Furthermore, the family was implicated in their plight. As transplants from traditional societies, the immigrants and their children were thought to be at odds with social requirements in the new settings. Their family arrangements were treated as cultural exceptions to the rule of standard family development. Their slowness to acculturate and take on Western patterns of family development left them behind as other families modernized (Baca Zinn, 1995).

Dominant paradigms of assimilation and modernization guided and shaped research. Notions of "traditional" and "modern" forms of social organization joined the new family social science's preoccupation with a standard family form. Compared to mainstream families, Mexican immigrant families were analyzed as traditional cultural forms. Studies of Mexican immigrants highlighted certain ethnic lifestyles that were said to produce social disorganization. Structural conditions that constrained families in the new society were rarely a concern. Instead, researchers examined (1) the families' foreign patterns and habits, (2) the moral quality of family relationships, and (3) the prospects for their Americanization (Bogardus, 1934).

Cultural Preoccupations

Ideas drawn from early social science produced cultural caricatures of Mexican families that became more exaggerated during the 1950s, when structural functionalist theories took hold in American sociology. Like the previous theories, structural functionalism's strategy for analyzing family life was to posit one family type (by no means the only family form, even then) and define it as "the normal family" (Boss & Thorne, 1989). With an emphasis on fixed family boundaries and a fixed division of roles, structural functionalists focused their attention on the group-specific characteristics that deviated from the normal or standard family and predisposed Mexican-origin families to deficiency. Mexican-origin families were analyzed in isolation from the rest of social life, described in simplistic terms of rigid male dominance and pathological clannishness. Although the earliest works on Mexican immigrant families reflected a concern for their eventual adjustment to American society, the new studies virtually abandoned the social realm. They dealt with families as if they existed in a vacuum of backward Mexican traditionalism. Structural functionalism led scholars along a path of cultural reductionism in which differences became deficiencies.

The Mexican family of social science research (Heller, 1966; Madsen, 1964; Rubel, 1966) presented a stark contrast with the mythical "standard family." Although some studies found that Mexican family traditionalism was fading as Mexicans became acculturated, Mexican families were stereotypically and inaccurately depicted as the chief cause of Mexican subordination in the United States.

New Directions

In the past 25 years, efforts to challenge myths and erroneous assumptions have produced important changes in the view of Mexican-origin families. Beginning with a critique of structural functionalist accounts of Mexican families, new studies have successfully challenged the old notions of family life as deviant, deficient, and disorganized.

The conceptual tools of Latino studies, women's studies, and social history have infused the new scholarship to produce a notable shift away from cultural preoccupations. Like the family field in general, research on Mexican-origin families has begun to devote greater attention to the "social situations and contexts that affect Mexican families" (Vega, 1990, p. 1015). This "revisionist" strategy has moved much Latino family research to a different plane—one in which racial-ethnic families are understood to be constructed by powerful social forces and as settings in which different family members adapt in a variety of ways to changing social conditions.

Current Challenges

Despite important advances, notable problems and limitations remain in the study of Latino families. A significant portion of scholarship includes only Mexican-origin groups (Massey, Zambrana, & Bell, 1995) and claims to generalize the findings to other Latinos. This practice constructs a false social reality because there is no Latino population in the same sense that there is an African American population. However useful the terms *Latino* and *Hispanic* may be as political and census identifiers, they mask extraordinary diversity. The category Hispanic was created by federal statisticians to provide data on people of Mexican, Cuban, Puerto Rican, and other Hispanic origins in the United States. There is no precise definition of group membership, and Latinos do not agree among themselves on an appropriate group label (Massey, 1993). While many prefer the term *Latino,* they may use it interchangeably with *Hispanic* to identify themselves (Romero, 1996). These terms are certainly useful for charting broad demographic changes in the United States, but when used as panethnic terms, they can contribute to misunderstandings about family life.

The labels Hispanic or Latino conceal variation in the family characteristics of Latino groups whose differences are often greater than the overall differences between Latinos and non-Latinos (Solis, 1995). To date, little comparative research has been conducted on Latino subgroups. The systematic disaggregation of family characteristics by national-origin groups remains a challenge, a necessary next step in the development of Latino family research.

We believe that the lack of a comprehensive knowledge base should not stand in the way of building a framework to analyze family life. We can use the burgeoning research on Latinos in U.S. social life to develop an analytical, rather than just a descriptive, account of families. The very complexity of Latino family arrangements begs for a unified (but not unitary) analysis. We believe that we can make good generalizations about Latino family diversity. In the sections that follow, we use a structural perspective grounded in intergroup differences. We make no pretense that this is an exhaustive review of research. Instead, our intent is to examine how Latino family experiences differ in relation to socially constructed conditions.

CONCEPTUAL FRAMEWORK

Conventional family frameworks, which have never applied well to racial-ethnic families, are even less useful in the current world of diversity and change. Incorporating multiplicity into family studies requires new approaches. A fundamental assumption guiding our analysis is that Latino families are not merely an expression of ethnic differences but, like all families, are the products of social forces.

Family diversity is an outgrowth of distinctive patterns in the way families and their members are embedded in environments with varying opportunities, resources, and rewards. Economic conditions and social inequalities associated with race, ethnicity, class, and gender place families in different "social locations." These differences are the key to understanding family variation. They determine labor market status, education, marital relations,

and other factors that are crucial to family formation.

Studying Latino family diversity means exposing the structural forces that impinge differently on families in specific social, material, and historical contexts. In other words, it means unpacking the structural arrangements that produce and often require a range of family configurations. It also requires analyzing the cross-cutting forms of difference that permeate society and penetrate families to produce divergent family experiences. Several macrostructural conditions produce widespread family variations across Latino groups: (1) the sociohistorical context; (2) the structure of economic opportunity; and (3) global reorganization, including economic restructuring and immigration.

The Sociohistorical Context

Mexicans, Puerto Ricans, Cubans, and other Latino groups have varied histories that distinguish them from each other. The timing and conditions of their arrival in the United States produced distinctive patterns of settlement that continue to affect their prospects for success. Cubans arrived largely between 1960 and 1980; a group of Mexicans indigenous to the Southwest was forcibly annexed into the United States in 1848, and another has been migrating continually since around 1890; Puerto Ricans came under U.S. control in 1898 and obtained citizenship in 1917; Salvadorans and Guatemalans began to migrate to the United States in substantial numbers during the past two decades.

The Structure of Economic Opportunity

Various forms of labor are needed to sustain family life. Labor status has always been the key factor in distinguishing the experiences of Latinos. Mexicans, Puerto Ricans, Cubans, and others are located in different regions of the country where particular labor markets and a group's placement within them determine the kind of legal, political, and social supports available to families. Different levels of structural supports affect family life, often producing various domestic and household arrangements. Additional complexity stems from gendered labor markets. In a society in which men are still assumed to be the primary breadwinners, jobs generally held by women pay less than jobs usually held by men. Women's and men's differential labor market placement, rewards, and roles create contradictory work and family experiences.

Global Reorganization, Including Economic Restructuring and Immigration

Economic and demographic upheavals are redefining families throughout the world. Four factors are at work here: new technologies based primarily on the computer chip, global economic interdependence, the flight of capital, and the dominance of the information and service sectors over basic manufacturing industries (Baca Zinn & Eitzen, 1998). Latino families are profoundly affected as the environments in which they live are reshaped and they face economic and social marginalization because of underemployment and unemployment. Included in economic globalization are new demands for immigrant labor and the dramatic demographic transformations that are "Hispanicizing" the United States. Family flexibility has long been an important feature of the immigrant saga. Today, "Latino immigration is adding many varieties to family structure" (Moore & Vigil, 1993, p. 36).

The macrostructural conditions described earlier provide the context within which to examine the family experiences of different Latino groups. They set the foundation for comparing family life across Latino groups. These material and economic forces help explain the different family profiles of Mexicans, Puerto Ricans, Cubans, and others. In other words, they enable sociologists to understand how families are bound up with the unequal distribution of social opportunities and how the various national-origin groups develop broad differences in work opportunities, marital patterns, and household structures. However, they do not explain other important differences in family life that cut across national-origin groups. People of the same national origin may experience family differently, depending on their location in the class structure as unemployed, poor, working class or professional; their location in the gender structure as female or male;

and their location in the sexual orientation system as heterosexual, gay, lesbian, or bisexual (Baca Zinn & Dill, 1996). In addition to these differences, family life for Latinos is shaped by age, generation living in the United States, citizenship status, and even skin color. All these differences intersect to influence the shape and character of family and household relations.

While our framework emphasizes the social context and social forces that construct families, we do not conclude that families are molded from the "outside in." What happens on a daily basis in family relations and domestic settings also constructs families. Latinos themselves—women, men, and children—have the ability actively to shape their family and household arrangements. Families should be seen as settings in which people are agents and actors, coping with, adapting to, and changing social structures to meet their needs (Baca Zinn & Eitzen, 1996).

Sociohistorical Context for Family Diversity Among Mexicans

Families of Mexican descent have been incorporated into the United States by both conquest and migration. In 1848, at the end of the Mexican War, the United States acquired a large section of Mexico, which is now the southwestern United States. With the signing of the Treaty of Guadalupe Hidalgo, the Mexican population in that region became residents of U.S. territory. Following the U.S. conquest, rapid economic growth in that region resulted in a shortage of labor that was resolved by recruiting workers from Mexico. So began the pattern of Mexican labor migration that continues to the present (Portes & Rumbaut, 1990). Some workers settled permanently in the United States, and others continued in cycles of migration, but migration from Mexico has been continuous since around 1890 (Massey et al., 1995).

Dramatic increases in the Mexican-origin population have been an important part of the trend toward greater racial and ethnic diversity in the United States. The Mexican population tripled in size in 20 years, from an estimated 4.5 million in 1970 to 8.7 million in 1980 to 13.5 million in 1990

(Rumbaut, 1995; Wilkinson, 1993). At present, approximately two thirds of Mexicans are native born, and the remainder are foreign born (Rumbaut, 1995). Important differences are consistently found between the social experiences and economic prospects of the native born and the foreign born (Morales & Ong, 1993; Ortiz, 1996). While some variation exists, the typical Mexican migrant to the United States has low socioeconomic status and rural origins (Ortiz, 1995; Portes & Rumbaut, 1990). Recent immigrants have a distinct disadvantage in the labor market because of a combination of low educational attainment, limited work skills, and limited English language proficiency. Social networks are vital for integrating immigrants into U.S. society and in placing them in the social class system (Fernandez-Kelly & Schauffler, 1994). Mexicans are concentrated in barrios that have social networks in which vital information is shared, contacts are made, and job referrals are given. But the social-class context of these Mexican communities is overwhelmingly poor and working class. Mexicans remain overrepresented in low-wage occupations, especially service, manual labor, and low-end manufacturing. These homogeneous lower-class communities lack the high-quality resources that could facilitate upward mobility for either new immigrants or second- and later-generation Mexicans.

The common assumption that immigrants are assimilated economically by taking entry-level positions and advancing to better jobs has not been supported by the Mexican experience (Morales & Ong, 1993; Ortiz, 1996). Today's Mexican workers are as likely as ever to be trapped in low-wage unstable employment situations (Ortiz, 1996; Sassen, 1993). Studies (Aponte, 1993; Morales & Ong, 1993; Ortiz, 1996) have found that high labor force participation and low wages among Mexicans have created a large group of working poor. Households adapt by holding multiple jobs and pooling wages (Velez-Ibañez & Greenberg, 1992).

Mexicans are the largest Latino group in the United States; 6 of 10 Latinos have Mexican origins. This group has low family incomes, but high labor force participation rates for men and increasing rates for women. Mexicans have the lowest educational attainments and the largest average household size of all Latino groups (See Table 13.1 and Figure 13.1 for between-group comparisons.)

Puerto Ricans

The fortunes of Puerto Rico and the United States were joined in 1899 when Puerto Rico became a U.S. possession in the aftermath of Spain's defeat in the Spanish-American War. Puerto Ricans are U.S. citizens and, as such, have the right to migrate to the

TABLE 13.1
Social and Economic Population Characteristics

	Median Income	Poverty	% Female Head of Household	Labor Force Participation		High School Graduate	Average Household
				Male	Female		
Mexican	23,609	29.6	19.9	80.9	51.8	46.5	3.86
Puerto Rican	20,929	33.2	41.2	70.6	47.4	61.3	2.91
Cuban	30,584	13.6	21.3	69.9	50.8	64.7	2.56
Central/South American	28,558	23.9	25.4	79.5	57.5	64.2	3.54
Other Hispanic	28,658	21.4	29.5			68.4	
All Hispanic	24,313	27.8	24	79.1	52.6	53.4	2.99
All U.S.	38,782	11.6	12	75	58.9	81.7	2.65
	1994	1994	1995	1995	1995	1995	1995

Sources: US Bureau of the Census, Statistical Abstract of the United States: 1996 (116th ed.) Washington, D.C.: U.S. Government Printing Office, 1996, Tables 53,68,241,615,622,723,738.

FIGURE 13.1
Social and Economic Population Characteristics

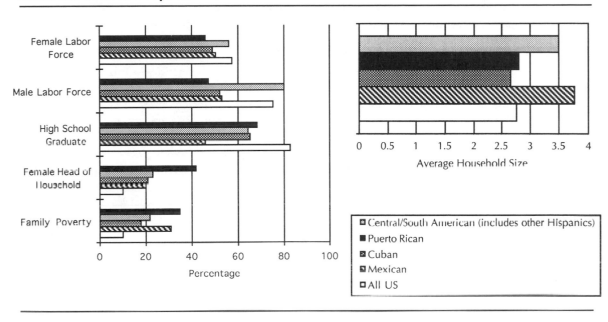

mainland without regulation. A small stream of migrants increased dramatically after World War II for three primary reasons: high unemployment in Puerto Rico, the availability of inexpensive air travel between Puerto Rico and the United States, and labor recruitment by U.S. companies (Portes & Rumbaut, 1990). Puerto Ricans were concentrated in or near their arrival point—New York City—although migrant laborers were scattered throughout the Northeast and parts of the Midwest. They engaged in a variety of blue-collar occupations; in New York City, they were particularly drawn into the textile and garment industries (Torres & Bonilla, 1993). The unique status of Puerto Rico as a commonwealth of the United States allows Puerto Ricans to engage in a circulating migration between Puerto Rico and the mainland (Feagin & Feagin, 1996).

Puerto Ricans are the most economically disadvantaged of all major Latino groups. The particular context of Puerto Ricans' entry into the U.S. labor market helps explain this group's low economic status. Puerto Ricans with limited education and low occupational skills migrated to the eastern seaboard

to fill manufacturing jobs (Ortiz, 1995); their economic well-being was dependent on opportunities for low-skill employment (Aponte, 1993). The region in which Puerto Ricans settled has experienced a major decline in its manufacturing base since the early 1970s. The restructuring of the economy means that, in essence, the jobs that Puerto Ricans came to the mainland to fill have largely disappeared. Latinos who have been displaced from manufacturing have generally been unable to gain access to higher-wage service sector employment (Carnoy, Daly, & Ojeda, 1993).

Compared to Mexicans and Cubans, Puerto Ricans have the lowest median family incomes and the highest unemployment and poverty rates. Puerto Ricans also have a high rate of female-headed households.

Cubans

The primary event that precipitated the migration of hundreds of thousands of Cubans to the United States was the revolution that brought Fidel Castro to power in 1959. This revolution set off several waves of immigration, beginning with the former economic and political elite and working progressively downward through the class structure. Early Cuban immigrants entered the United States in a highly politicized cold-war context as political refugees from communism. The U.S. government sponsored the Cuban Refugee Program, which provided massive supports to Cuban immigrants, including resettlement assistance, job training, small-business loans, welfare payments, and health care (Dominguez, 1992; Perez-Stable & Uriarte, 1993). By the time this program was phased out after the mid-1970s, the United States had invested nearly $1 billion in assistance to Cubans fleeing from communism (Perez-Stable & Uriarte, 1993, p.155). Between 1960 and 1980, nearly 800,000 Cubans immigrated to the United States (Dominguez, 1992).

The Cuban population is concentrated in south Florida, primarily in the Miami area, where they have established a true ethnic enclave in which they own businesses; provide professional services; and control institutions, such as banks and newspapers (Perez, 1994). The unique circumstances surrounding their immigration help explain the experience of Cubans. U.S. government supports facilitated the economic successes of early Cuban immigrants (Aponte, 1993, Fernandez-Kelley & Schauffler, 1994). High rates of entrepreneurship resulted in the eventual consolidation of an enclave economy (Portes & Truelove, 1987).

Immigrants, women, and minorities have generally supplied the low-wage, flexible labor on which the restructured economy depends (Morales & Bonilla, 1993). However, Cubans "embody a privileged migration" in comparison to other Latino groups (Morales & Bonilla, 1993, p. 17). Their social-class positions, occupational attainments, and public supports have insulated them from the effects of restructuring. Yet Cubans in Miami are not completely protected from the displacements of the new economic order. As Perez-Stable and Uriarte (1993) noted, the Cuban workforce is polarized, with one segment moving into higher-wage work and the other remaining locked in low-wage employment.

Cuban families have higher incomes and far lower poverty rates than do other major Latino groups. Cubans are the most educated major Latino group and have the smallest average household size.

Other Latinos

In each national-origin group discussed earlier, one finds unique socioeconomic, political and historical circumstances. But the diversity of Latinos extends beyond the differences between Mexican Americans, Cuban Americans, and mainland Puerto Ricans. One finds further variation when one considers the experiences of other Latino national-origin groups. Although research on "other Latinos" is less extensive than the literature cited earlier, we consider briefly contexts for diversity in Central American and Dominican families.

Central Americans. Political repression, civil war, and their accompanying economic dislocations have fueled the immigration of a substantial number of Salvadorans, Guatemalans, and Nicaraguans since the mid-1970s (Hamilton & Chinchilla, 1997). The U.S. population of Central Americans more than doubled between the 1980 and 1990 censuses and now outnumbers Cubans (U.S. Bureau of the Census, 1993). These Latinos migrated under difficult circumstances and face a set of serious challenges in the United States (Dorrington, 1995). Three factors render this population highly vulnerable: (1) a high percentage are undocumented (an estimated 49% of Salvadorans and 40% of Guatemalans), (2) they have marginal employment and high poverty rates, and (3) the U.S. government does not recognize them as political refugees (Lopez, Popkin, & Telles, 1996).

The two largest groups of Central Americans are Salvadorans and Guatemalans, the majority of whom live in the Los Angeles area. Lopez et al.'s (1996) study of Central Americans in Los Angeles illumined the social and economic contexts in which these Latinos construct their family lives. In general, the women and men have little formal education and know little English, but have high rates of labor force participation. Salvadorans and Guatemalans are overrepresented in low-paying service and blue-collar occupations. Salvadoran and Guatemalan women occupy a low-wage niche in private service (as domestic workers in private homes). Central Americans, especially the undocumented who fear deportation and usually have no access to public support, are desperate enough to accept the poorest-quality, lowest-paying work that Los Angeles has to offer. These immigrants hold the most disadvantageous position in the regional economy (Scott, 1996). Lopez et al. predicted that in the current restructured economy, Central Americans will continue to do the worst of the "dirty work" necessary to support the lifestyles of the high-wage workforce.

Dominicans. A significant number of Dominicans began migrating to the U.S. in the mid 1960s. What Grasmuck and Pessar (1996) called the "massive displacement" of Dominicans from their homeland began with the end of Trujillo's 30-year dictatorship and the political uncertainties that ensued. Dominican immigrant families did not fit the conventional image of the unskilled, underemployed peasant. They generally had employed breadwinners who were relatively well educated by Dominican standards; the majority described themselves as having urban middle-class origins (Mitchell, 1992).

The Dominican population is heavily concentrated in New York City. They entered a hostile labor market in which their middle class aspirations were to remain largely unfulfilled because the restructured New York economy offers low-wage, marginal, mostly dead-end employment for individuals without advanced education (Torres & Bonilla, 1993). Dominicans lacked the English language competence and educational credentials that might have facilitated their upward mobility (Grasmuck & Pessar, 1996). More than two thirds of the Dominican-origin population in the United States is Dominican born. As a group, Dominicans have high rates of poverty and female-headed families. Approximately 4 in 10 family households are headed by women.

THE STRUCTURE OF ECONOMIC OPPORTUNITY

Latino families remain outside the economic mainstream of U.S. society. Their median family income stands at less than two thirds the median family income of all U.S. families (U.S. Bureau of the Census, 1996). But the broad designation of "Latino" obscures important differences among national-origin groups. In this section, we explore variations in the structure of economic opportunity and consider how particular economic contexts shape the lives of different groups of Latino families.

Class, Work, and Family Life

A number of studies (see, for example, Cardenas, Chapa, & Burek, 1993; Grasmuck & Pessar, 1996; Lopez et al., 1996; Ortiz, 1995; Perez, 1994) have documented that diverse social and economic contexts produce multiple labor market outcomes for Latino families. The quality, availability, and stability of wage labor create a socioeconomic context in which family life is constructed and maintained. Cuban American families have fared far better socioeconomically than have other Latino families. Scholars consistently cite the role of the Cuban enclave in providing a favorable economic context with advantages that other groups have not enjoyed (Morales & Bonilla, 1993; Perez, 1994; Perez-Stable & Uriarte, 1993). Cuban families have the highest incomes, educational attainments, and levels of upper-white-collar employment. Puerto Rican, Mexican, and Central American families cluster below Cubans on these socioeconomic indicators, with Puerto Ricans the most disadvantaged group.

The structure of Mexican American economic opportunity stands in sharp contrast to that of Cubans. Betancur, Cordova, and Torres (1993) documented the systematic exclusion of Mexicans from upward-mobility ladders, tracing the incorporation of Mexican Americans into the Chicago economy to illustrate the historic roots of the concentration of Mexicans in unstable, poor-quality work. Throughout the 20th century Mexican migrants have constituted a transient workforce that has been continually vulnerable to fluctuations in the labor market and cycles of recruitment and deportation. Betancur et al.'s study highlighted the significance of the bracero program of contract labor migration in institutionalizing a segmented market for labor. The bracero program limited Mexican workers to specific low-status jobs and industries that prohibited promotion to skilled occupational categories. Mexicans were not allowed to compete for higher-status jobs, but were contracted to fill only the most undesirable jobs. Although formal bracero-era regulations have ended, similar occupational concentrations continue to be reproduced among Mexican American workers.

The effects of these diverging social-class and employment contexts on families are well illustrated by Fernandez-Kelly's (1990) study of female garment workers—Cubans in Miami and Mexicans in Los Angeles—both of whom placed a high value on marriage and family; however, contextual factors shaped differently their abilities to sustain marital relationships over time. Fernandez-Kelly contended that the conditions necessary for maintaining long-term stable unions were present in middle-class families but were absent in poor families. That is, the marriages of the poor women were threatened by unemployment and underemployment. Among these Mexican women, there was a high rate of poor female-headed households, and among the Cuban women, many were members of upwardly mobile families.

Women's Work

Several studies (Chavira-Prado, 1992; Grasmuck & Pessar, 1991; Lamphere, Zavella, Gonzales & Evans, 1993; Stier & Tienda, 1992; Zavella, 1987) that have explored the intersection of work and family for Latinas have found that Latinas are increasingly likely to be employed. Labor force participation is the highest among Central American women and the lowest among Puerto Rican women, with Mexican and Cuban women equally likely to be employed. Not only do labor force participation rates differ by national origin, but the meaning of women's work varies as well. For example, Fernandez-Kelly's (1990) study demonstrated that for Cuban women, employment was part of a broad family objective to reestablish middle-class status. Many Cuban immigrants initially experienced downward mobility, and the women took temporary jobs to generate income while their husbands cultivated fledgling businesses. These women often withdrew from the workforce when their families' economic positions had been secured. In contrast, Mexican women in Los Angeles worked because of dire economic necessity. They were drawn into employment to augment the earnings of partners who were confined to secondary-sector work that paid less than subsistence wages or worse, to provide the primary support for their households. Thus, whereas the Cuban women expected to work temporarily until their husbands could resume the role of middle-class breadwinner, the Mexican women worked either because their partners could not earn a family wage or because of the breakdown of family relationships by divorce or abandonment.

GLOBAL REORGANIZATION

Economic Restructuring

The economic challenges that Latinos face are enormous. A workforce that has always been vulnerable to exploitation can anticipate the decline of already limited mobility prospects. A recent body of scholarship (see, for example, Lopez et al., 1996; Morales & Bonilla, 1993; Ortiz, 1996) has demonstrated that the restructuring of the U.S. economy has reshaped economic opportunities for Latinos.

Torres and Bonilla's (1993) study of the restructuring of New York City's economy is particularly illustrative because it focused on Puerto Ricans, the Latino group hit hardest by economic transformations. That study found that restructuring in New York City is based on two processes that negatively affect Puerto Ricans. First, stable jobs in both the public and private sectors have eroded since the 1960s because many large corporations that had provided long-term, union jobs for minorities left the New York area and New York City's fiscal difficulties restricted the opportunities for municipal employment. Second, the reorganization of light manufacturing has meant that new jobs offer low wages and poor working conditions; new immigrants who are vulnerable to exploitation by employers generally fill these jobs. The restructuring of the economy has resulted in the exclusion or withdrawal of a substantial proportion of Puerto Ricans from the labor market (Morales & Bonilla, 1993).

Families are not insulated from the effects of social and economic dislocations. Research that has tracked this major social transformation has considered how such changes affect family processes and household composition (Grasmuck & Pessar, 1996; Lopez et al., 1996; Rodriguez & Hagan, 1997). What Sassen (1993) called the "informalization" and "casualization" of urban labor markets will, in the end, shape families in ways that deviate from the nuclear ideal. The marginalization of the Puerto Rican workforce is related not only to high unemployment and poverty rates, but to high rates of nonmarital births and female-headed households (Fernandez-Kelly, 1990; Morrissey, 1987).

Contrasting the experience of Dominicans to that of Puerto Ricans indicates that it is impossible to generalize a unitary "Latino experience" even within a single labor market—New York City. Torres and Bonilla (1993) found that as Puerto Ricans were displaced from manufacturing jobs in the 1970s and 1980s, new Dominican immigrants came into the restructured manufacturing sector to fill low-wage jobs. Dominicans were part of a pool of immigrant labor that entered a depressed economy, was largely ineligible for public assistance, and was willing to accept exploitative employment. Grasmuck and Pessar (1991, 1996) showed how the incorporation of Dominicans into the restructured New York economy has affected families. Although the rate of divorce among early immigrants was high, relationships have become increasingly precarious as employment opportunities have become even more constrained. Currently, rates of poverty and female-headed households for Dominicans approximate those of Puerto Ricans (Rumbaut, 1995).

*A **Latino Underclass**?* Rising poverty rates among Latinos, together with the alarmist treatment of female-headed households among "minorities," have led many policy makers and media analysts to conclude that Latinos have joined inner-city African Americans to form part of the "underclass." According to the underclass model, inner-city men's joblessness has encouraged nonmarital childbearing and undermined the economic foundations of the African American family (Wilson, 1987, 1996). Researchers have also been debating for some time whether increases in the incidence of female-headed households and poverty among Puerto Ricans are irreversible (Tienda, 1989). Recent thinking, however, suggests that applying the underclass theory to Latinos obscures more than it reveals and that a different analytical model is needed to understand poverty and family issues in each Latino group (Massey et al., 1995). Not only do the causes of poverty differ across Latino communities, but patterns of social organization at the community and family levels produce a wide range of responses to poverty. According to Moore and Pinderhughes (1993), the dynamics of poverty even in the poorest Latino barrios differ in fundamental ways from the conventional portrait of the underclass. Both African Americans and Puerto Ricans have high rates of female-headed households. However, Sullivan's (1993) research in Brooklyn indicated that Puerto Ricans have high rates of cohabitation and that the family formation processes that lead to these household patterns are different from those of African Americans. Other case studies have underscored the importance of family organization. For example, Velez-Ibañez (1993) described a distinctive family form among poor Mexicans of South Tucson—cross-class household clusters surrounded by kinship networks that stretch beyond neighborhood boundaries and provide resources for coping with poverty.

Immigration

Families migrate for economic reasons, political reasons, or some combination of the two. Immigration offers potential and promise, but one of the costs is the need for families to adapt to their receiving community contexts. A growing body of scholarship has focused on two areas of family change: household composition and gender relations.

Household Composition. Immigration contributes to the proliferation of family forms and a variety of household arrangements among Latinos (Vega, 1995). Numerous studies have highlighted the flexibility of Latino family households. Chavez (1990, 1992) identified transnational families, binational families, extended families, multiple-family households, and other arrangements among Mexican and Central American immigrants. Landale and Fennelly (1992) found informal unions that resemble marriage more than cohabitation among mainland Puerto Ricans, and Guarnizo (1997) found binational households among Dominicans who live and work in both the United States and the Dominican Republic. Two processes are at work as families adapt their household structures. First, family change reflects, for many, desperate economic circumstances (Vega, 1995), which bring some families to the breaking point and leads others to expand their household boundaries. Second, the transnationalization of economies and labor has created new opportunities for successful Latino families; for example, Guarnizo noted that Dominican entrepreneurs sometimes live in binational households and have "de facto binational citizenship" (p. 171).

Immigration and Gender. Several important studies have considered the relationship between immigration and gender (Boyd, 1989; Grasmuck & Pessar, 1991; Hondagneu-Sotelo, 1994). In her study of undocumented Mexican immigrants, Hondagneu-Sotelo (1994) demonstrated that gender shapes migration and immigration shapes gender relations. She found that family stage migration, in which husbands migrate first and wives and children follow later, does not fit the household-strategy model. Often implied in this model is the assumption that migration reflects the unanimous and rational collective decision of all household members. However, as Hondagneu-Sotelo observed, gender hierarchies determined when and

under what circumstances migration occurred; that is, men often decided spontaneously, independently, and unilaterally to migrate north to seek employment. When Mexican couples were finally reunited in the United States, they generally reconstructed more egalitarian gender relations. Variation in the form of gender relations in the United States is partially explained by the circumstances surrounding migration, such as the type and timing of migration, access to social networks, and U.S. immigration policy.

FAMILY DYNAMICS ACROSS LATINO GROUPS

Familism

Collectivist family arrangements are thought to be a defining feature of the Latino population. Presumably, a strong orientation and obligation to the family produces a kinship structure that is qualitatively different from that of all other groups. Latino familism, which is said to emphasize the family as opposed to the individual, "is linked to many of the pejorative images that have beset discussions of the Hispanic family" (Vega, 1990, p. 1018). Although themes of Latino familism figure prominently in the social science literature, this topic remains problematic owing to empirical limitations and conceptual confusion.

Popular and social science writing contain repeated descriptions of what amounts to a generic Latino kinship form. In reality, a Mexican-origin bias pervades the research on this topic. Not only is there a lack of comparative research on extended kinship structures among different national-origin groups, but there is little empirical evidence for all but Mexican-origin families. For Mexican-origin groups, studies are plentiful (for reviews, see Baca Zinn, 1983; Vega, 1990, 1995), although they have yielded inconsistent evidence about the prevalence of familism, the forms it takes, and the kinds of supportive relationships it serves.

Among the difficulties in assessing the evidence on extended family life are the inconsistent uses of terms like *familism* and *extended family system*.

Seeking to clarify the multiple meanings of familism, Ramirez and Arce (1981) treated familism as a multidimensional concept comprised of such distinct aspects as structure, behavior, norms and attitudes, and social identity, each of which requires separate measurement and analysis. They proposed that familism contains four key components: (1) demographic familism, which involves such characteristics as family size; (2) structural familism, which measures the incidence of multigenerational (or extended) households; (3) normative families, which taps the value that Mexican-origin people place on family unity and solidarity; and (4) behavioral familism, which has to do with the level of interaction between family and kin networks.

Changes in regional and local economies and the resulting dislocations of Latinos have prompted questions about the ongoing viability of kinship networks. Analyzing a national sample of minority families, Rochelle (1997) argued that extended kinship networks are declining among Chicanos, Puerto Ricans, and African Americans. On the other hand, a large body of research has documented various forms of network participation by Latinos. For three decades, studies have found that kinship networks are an important survival strategy in poor Mexican communities (Alvirez & Bean, 1976; Hoppe & Heller, 1975; Velez-Ibañez, 1996) and that these networks operate as a system of cultural, emotional, and mental support (Keefe, 1984; Mindel, 1980; Ramirez, 1980), as well as a system for coping with socioeconomic marginality (Angel & Tienda, 1982; Lamphere et al., 1993).

Research has suggested, however, that kinship networks are not maintained for socioeconomic reasons alone (Buriel & De Ment, 1997). Familistic orientation among Mexican-origin adults has been associated with high levels of education and income (Griffith & Villavicienco, 1985). Familism has been viewed as a form of social capital that is linked with academic success among Mexican-heritage adolescents (Valenzuela & Dornbusch, 1994).

The research on the involvement of extended families in the migration and settlement of Mexicans discussed earlier (Chavez, 1992; Hondagneu-Sotelo, 1994; Hondagneu-Sotelo & Avila, 1997) is profoundly important. In contrast to the prevailing view that family extension is an artifact of culture, this research helps one understand that the structural flexibility of families is a social construction. Transnational families and their networks of kin are extended in space, time, and across national borders. They are quintessential adaptations—alternative arrangements for solving problems associated with immigration.

Despite the conceptual and empirical ambiguities surrounding the topic of familism, there is evidence that kinship networks are far from monolithic. Studies have revealed that variations are rooted in distinctive social conditions, such as immigrant versus nonimmigrant status and generational status. Thus, even though immigrants use kin for assistance, they have smaller social networks than do second-generation Mexican Americans who have broader social networks consisting of multigenerational kin (Vega, 1990). Studies have shown that regardless of class, Mexican extended families in the United States become stronger and more extensive with generational advancement, acculturation, and socioeconomic mobility (Velez-Ibañez, 1996). Although an assimilationist perspective suggests that familism fades in succeeding generations, Velez-Ibañez found that highly elaborated second-and third-generation extended family networks are actively maintained through frequent visits, ritual celebrations, and the exchange of goods and services. These networks are differentiated by the functions they perform, depending on the circumstances of the people involved.

Gender

Latino families are commonly viewed as settings of traditional patriarchy and as different from other families because of machismo, the cult of masculinity. In the past two decades, this cultural stereotype has been the impetus for corrective scholarship on Latino families. The flourishing of Latina feminist thought has shifted the focus from the determinism of culture to questions about how gender and power in families are connected with other structures and institutions in society. Although male dominance remains a central theme, it is understood as part of the ubiquitous social ordering of women and men. In the context of other forms of difference, gender exerts a powerful influence on Latino families.

New research is discovering gender dynamics among Latino families that are both similar to and different from those found in other groups. Similarities stem from social changes that are reshaping all families, whereas differences emerge from the varied locations of Latino families and the women and men in them. Like other branches of scholarship on Latino families, most studies have been conducted with Mexican-origin populations. The past two decades of research have shown that family life among all Latino groups is deeply gendered. Yet no simple generalizations sum up the essence of power relations.

Research has examined two interrelated areas: (1) family decision making and (2) the allocation of household labor. Since the first wave of "revisionist works" (Zavella, 1987) conducted in the 1970s and 1980s (Baca Zinn, 1980; Ybarra, 1982), researchers have found variation in these activities, ranging from patriarchal role-segregated patterns to egalitarian patterns, with many combinations in between. Studies have suggested that Latinas' employment patterns, like those of women around the world, provide them with resources and autonomy that alter the balance of family power (Baca Zinn, 1980; Coltrane & Valdez, 1993; Pesquera, 1993; Repack, 1997; Williams, 1990; Ybarra, 1982; Zavella, 1987). But, as we discussed earlier, employment opportunities vary widely, and the variation produces multiple work and family patterns for Latinas. Furthermore, women's employment, by itself, does not eradicate male dominance. This is one of the main lessons of Zavella's (1987) study of Chicana cannery workers in California's Santa Clara Valley. Women's cannery work was circumscribed by inequalities of class, race, and gender. As seasonal, part-time workers, the women gained some leverage in the home, thereby creating temporary shifts in their day-to-day family lives, but this leverage did not alter the balance of family power. Fernandez-Kelly and Garcia's (1990) comparative study of women's work and family patterns among Cubans and Mexican Americans found strikingly different configurations of power. Employed women's newfound rights are often contradictory. As Repack's study (1997) of Central American immigrants revealed, numerous costs and strains accompany women's new roles in a new landscape. Family relations often became contentious when women pressed partners to share domestic responsibilities. Migration produced a situation in which women worked longer and harder than in their countries of origin.

Other conditions associated with varying patterns in the division of domestic labor are women's and men's occupational statuses and relative economic contributions to their families. Studies by Pesquera (1993), Coltrane and Valdez (1993), and Coltrane (1996) found a general "inside/outside" dichotomy (wives doing most housework, husbands doing outside work and sharing some child care), but women in middle-class jobs received more "help" from their husbands than did women with lower earnings.

"Family power" research should not be limited to women's roles, but should study the social relations between women and men. Recent works on Latino men's family lives have made important strides in this regard (Coltrane & Valdez, 1993; Shelton & John, 1993). Still, there is little information about the range and variety of Latino men's family experiences (Mirande, 1997) or of their interplay with larger structural conditions. In a rare study of Mexican immigrant men, Hondagneu-Sotelo and Messner (1994) discussed the diminution of patriarchy that comes with settling in the United States. They showed that the key to gender equality in immigrant families is women's and men's relative positions of power and status in the larger society. Mexican immigrant men's status is low owing to racism, economic marginality, and possible undocumented status. Meanwhile, as immigrant women move into wage labor, they develop autonomy and economic skills. These conditions combine to erode patriarchal authority.

The research discussed earlier suggested some convergences between Latinos and other groups in family power arrangements. But intertwined with the shape of domestic power are strongly held ideals about women's and men's family roles. Ethnic gender identities, values, and beliefs contribute to gender relations and constitute an important but little understood dimension of families. Gender may also be influenced by Latinos' extended family networks. As Lamphere et al. (1993) discovered, Hispanas in Albuquerque were living in a world made up largely of Hispana mothers, sisters, and other relatives. Social scientists have posited a relationship between dense social networks and gender segregation. If this relationship holds, familism could well impede egalitarian relations in Latino families (Coltrane, 1996; Hurtado, 1995).

Compulsory heterosexuality is an important component of both gender and family systems. By enforcing the dichotomy of opposite sexes, it is also a form of inequality in its own right, hence an important marker of social location. A growing literature on lesbian and gay identity among Latinas and Latinos has examined the conflicting challenges involved in negotiating a multiple minority status (Alarcon, Castillo, & Moraga, 1989; Almaguer, 1991; Anzaldua, 1987; Carrier, 1992; Moraga, 1983; Morales, 1990). Unfortunately, family scholarship on Latinos has not pursued the implications of lesbian and gay identities for understanding family diversity. In fact, there have been no studies in the social sciences in the area of sexual orientation and Latino families (Hurtado, 1995). But although the empirical base is virtually nonexistent and making *families* the unit of analysis no doubt introduces new questions (Demo & Allen, 1996), we can glean useful insights from the discourse on sexual identity. Writing about Chicanos, Almaguer (1991) identified the following obstacles to developing a safe space for forming a gay or lesbian identity: racial and class subordination and a context in which ethnicity remains a primary basis of group identity and survival. "Moreover Chicano *family life* [italics added] requires allegiance to patriarchal gender relations and to a system of sexual meanings that directly mitigate against the emergence of this alternative basis of self identity" (Almaguer, p. 88). Such repeated references to the constraints of ethnicity, gender, and sexual orientation imposed by Chicano families (Almaguer, 1991; Moraga, 1983) raise important questions. How do varied family

contexts shape and differentiate the development of gay identities among Latinos? How do they affect the formation of lesbian and gay families among Latinas and Latinos? This area is wide open for research.

Children and Their Parents

Latinos have the highest concentration of children and adolescents of all major racial and ethnic groups. Nearly 40% of Latinos are aged 20 or younger, compared to about 26% of non-Hispanic whites (U.S. Bureau of the Census, 1996). Among Latino subgroups, the highest proportions of children and adolescents are among Mexicans and Puerto Ricans and the lowest among Cubans (Solis, 1995).

Latino socialization patterns have long held the interest of family scholars (Martinez, 1993). Most studies have focused on the child-rearing practices of Mexican families. Researchers have questioned whether Mexican families have permissive or authoritarian styles of child rearing and the relationship of childrearing styles to social class and cultural factors (Martinez, 1993). Patterns of child rearing were expected to reveal the level of acculturation to U.S. norms and the degree of modernization among traditional immigrant families. The results of research spanning the 1970s and 1980s were mixed and sometimes contradictory.

Buriel's (1993) study brought some clarity to the subject of child-rearing practices by situating it in the broad social context in which such practices occur. This study of Mexican families found that child-rearing practices differ by generation. Parents who were born in Mexico had a "responsibility-oriented" style that was compatible with their own life experience as struggling immigrants. U.S.-born Mexican parents had a "concern-oriented" style of parenting that was associated with the higher levels of education and income found among this group and that may also indicate that parents compensate for their children's disadvantaged standing in U.S. schools.

Mainstream theorizing has generally assumed a middle-class European-American model for the socialization of the next generation (Segura &

Pierce, 1993). But the diverse contexts in which Latino children are raised suggest that family studies must take into account multiple models of socialization. Latino children are less likely than Anglo children to live in isolated nuclear units in which parents have almost exclusive responsibility for rearing children and the mothers' role is primary. Segura and Pierce contended that the pattern of nonexclusive mothering found in some Latino families shapes the gender identities of Latinos in ways that conventional thinking does not consider. Velez-Ibañez & Greenberg (1992) discussed how the extensive kinship networks of Mexican families influence child rearing and considered the ramifications for educational outcomes. Mexican children are socialized into a context of "thick" social relations. From infancy onward, these children experience far more social interaction than do children who are raised in more isolated contexts. The institution of education—second only to the family as an agent of socialization—is, in the United States, modeled after the dominant society and characterized by competition and individual achievement. Latino students who have been socialized into a more cooperative model of social relations often experience a disjuncture between their upbringing and the expectations of their schools (Velez-Ibañez & Greenberg, 1992).

Social location shapes the range of choices that parents have as they decide how best to provide for their children. Latino parents, who are disproportionately likely to occupy subordinate social locations in U.S. society, encounter severe obstacles to providing adequate material resources for their children. To date, little research has focused on Latino fathers (Powell, 1995). Hondagneu-Sotelo and Avila's (1997) study documented a broad range of mothering arrangements among Latinas. One such arrangement is transnational mothering, in which mothers work in the United States while their children remain in Mexico or Central America; it is accompanied by tremendous costs and undertaken when options are extremely limited. The researchers found that transnational mothering occurred among domestic workers, many of whom were live-in maids or child care providers who could not live with their children, as well as mothers who could

better provide for their children in their countries of origin because U.S. dollars stretched further in Central America than in the United States. Other mothering arrangements chosen by Latinas in the study included migrating with their children, migrating alone and later sending for their children, and migrating alone and returning to their children after a period of work.

Intrafamily Diversity

Family scholars have increasingly recognized that family experience is differentiated along the lines of age and gender (Baca Zinn & Eitzen, 1996; Thorne, 1992). Members of particular families—parents and children, women and men—experience family life differently. Scholarship that considers the internal differentiation of Latino families is focused on the conditions surrounding and adaptations following immigration.

While immigration requires tremendous change of all family members, family adaptation to the new context is not a unitary phenomenon. Research has found patterns of differential adjustment as family members adapt unevenly to an unfamiliar social environment (Gold, 1989). Gil and Vega's (1996) study of acculturative stress in Cuban and Nicaraguan families in the Miami area identified significant differences in the adjustment of parents and their children. For example, Nicaraguan adolescents reported more initial language conflicts than did their parents, but their conflicts diminished over time, whereas their parents' language conflicts increased over time. This difference occurred because the adolescents were immediately confronted with their English language deficiency in school, but their parents could initially manage well in the Miami area without a facility with English. The authors concluded that family members experience "the aversive impacts of culture change at different times and at variable levels of intensity" (p. 451).

Differential adjustment creates new contexts for parent-child relations. Immigrant children who are school-aged generally become competent in English more quickly than do their parents. Dorrington (1995) found that Salvadoran and Guatemalan children often assume adult roles as they help their parents negotiate the bureaucratic structure of their new social environment; for example, a young child may accompany her parents to a local utility company to act as their translator.

Immigration may also create formal legal distinctions among members of Latino families. Frequently, family members do not share the same immigration status. That is, undocumented Mexican and Central American couples are likely, over time, to have children born in the United States and hence are U.S. citizens; the presence of these children then renders the "undocumented family" label inaccurate. Chavez (1992, p. 129) used the term *binational family* to refer to a family with both members who are undocumented and those who are citizens or legal residents.

Not only do family members experience family life differently, but age and gender often produce diverging and even conflicting interests among them (Baca Zinn & Eitzen, 1996). Both Hondagneu-Sotelo's (1994) and Grasmuck and Pessar's (1991) studies of family immigration found that Latinas were generally far more interested in settling permanently in the United States than were their husbands. In both studies, the women had enhanced their status by migration, while the men had lost theirs. Hondagneu-Sotelo noted that Mexican women advanced the permanent settlement of their families by taking regular, nonseasonal employment; negotiating the use of public and private assistance; and forging strong community ties. Grasmuck and Pessar observed that Dominican women tried to postpone their families' return to the Dominican Republic by extravagantly spending money that would otherwise be saved for their return and by establishing roots in the United States.

DISCUSSION AND CONCLUSION

The key to understanding diversity in Latino families is the uneven distribution of constraints and opportunities among families, which affects the behaviors of family members and ultimately the forms that family units take (Baca Zinn & Eitzen, 1996). Our goal in this review was to call into question assumptions, beliefs, and false generalizations about the way "Latino families are." We examined Latino families not as if they had some essential characteristics that set them apart from others, but as they are affected by a complex mix of structural features.

Our framework enabled us to see how diverse living arrangements among Latinos are situated and structured in the larger social world. Although this framework embraces the interplay of macro-and microlevels of analysis, we are mindful that this review devoted far too little attention to family experience, resistance, and voice. We do not mean to underestimate the importance of human agency in the social construction of Latino families, but we could not devote as much attention as we would have liked to the various ways in which women, men, and children actively produce their family worlds. Given the sheer size of the literature, the "non-comparability of most contemporary findings" and the lack of a consistent conceptual groundwork" (Vega, 1990, p. 102), we decided that what is most needed is a coherent framework within which to view and interpret diversity. Therefore, we chose to focus on the impact of social forces on family life.

The basic insights of our perspective are sociological. Yet a paradox of family sociology is that the field has tended to misrepresent Latino families and those of other racial ethnic groups. Sociology has distorted Latino families by generalizing from the experience of dominant groups and ignoring the differences that make a difference. This is a great irony. Family sociology, the specialty whose task it is to describe and understand social diversity, has marginalized diversity, rather than treated it as a central feature of social life (Baca Zinn & Eitzen, 1993).

As sociologists, we wrote this chapter fully aware of the directions in our discipline that hinder the ability to explain diversity. At the same time, we think the core insight of sociology should be applied to challenge conventional thinking about families. Reviewing the literature for this chapter did not diminish our sociological convictions, but it did present us with some unforeseen challenges. We found a vast gulf between mainstream family sociology and the extraordinary amount of high-quality scholarship on Latino families. Our review took us far beyond the boundaries of our discipline, making us "cross disciplinary migrants" (Stacey, 1995). We found the new literature in diverse and unlikely locations, with important breakthroughs emerging in the "borderlands" between social science disciplines. We also found the project to be infinitely more complex than we anticipatcd. The extensive scholarship on three national-origin groups and "others" was complicated by widely varying analytic snapshots. We were, in short, confronted with a kaleidoscope of family diversity. Our shared perspective served us well in managing the task at hand. Although we have different family specializations and contrasting family experiences, we both seek to understand multiple family and household forms that emanate from structural arrangements.

What are the most important lessons our sociological analysis holds for the family field? Three themes offer new directions for building a better, more inclusive, family social science. First, understanding Latino family diversity does not mean simply appreciating the ways in which families are different; rather, it means analyzing how the formation of diverse families is based on and reproduces social inequalities. At the heart of many of the differences between Latino families and mainstream families and the different aggregate family patterns among Latino groups are structural forces that place families in different social environments. What is not often acknowledged is that the same social structures—race, class, and other hierarchies—affect *all* families, albeit in different ways. Instead of treating family variation as the property of group difference, recent sociological theorizing (Baca Zinn, 1994; Dill, 1994; Glenn, 1992; Hill Collins, 1990, 1997) has conceptualized diverse family arrangements in *relational* terms, that is, mutually dependent and sustained through interaction across racial and class boundaries. The point is not that family differences based on race, class, and gender simply coexist. Instead, many differences in family life involve relationships of domination and subordination and differential access to material resources. Patterns of privilege and subordination

characterize the historical relationships between Anglo families and Mexican families in the Southwest (Dill, 1994). Contemporary diversity among Latino families reveals *new* interdependences and inequalities. Emergent middle-class and professional lifestyles among Anglos and even some Latinos are interconnected with a new Latino servant class whose family arrangements, in turn, must accommodate to the demands of their labor.

Second, family diversity plays a part in different economic orders and the shifts that accompany them. Scholars have suggested that the multiplicity of household types is one of the chief props of the world economy (Smith, Wallerstein, & Evers, 1985). The example of U.S.-Mexican cross-border households brings this point into full view. This household arrangement constitutes an important "part of the emerging and dynamic economic and technological transformations in the region" (Velez-Ibañez, 1996, p. 143). The structural reordering required by such families is central to regional economic change.

Finally, the incredible array of immigrant family forms and their enormous capacity for adaptation offer new departures for the study of postmodern families. "Binational," "transnational," and "multinational" families, together with "border balanced households" and "generational hopscotching," are arrangements that remain invisible even in Stacey's (1996) compelling analysis of U.S. family life at the century's end. And yet the experiences of Latino families—flexible and plastic—as far back as the late 1800s (Griswold del Castillo, 1984), give resonance to the image of long-standing family fluidity and of contemporary families lurching backward and forward into the postmodern age (Stacey, 1990). The shift to a postindustrial economy is not the only social transformation affecting families. Demographic and political changes sweeping the world are engendering family configurations that are yet unimagined in family social science.

These trends offer new angles of vision for thinking about family diversity. They pose new opportunities for us to remake family studies as we uncover the mechanisms that construct multiple household and family arrangements.

REFERENCES

Alarcon, N., Castillo, A., & Moraga, C. (Eds.). (1989). *Third woman: The sexuality of Latinas.* Berkeley, CA: Third Woman.

Almaguer, T. (1991). Chicano men: A cartography of homosexual identity and behavior. *Differences: A Journal of Feminist Cultural Studies, 3,* 75–100.

Alvirez, D., & Bean, F. (1976). The Mexican American family. In C. Mindel & R. Habenstein (Eds.), *Ethnic families in America* (pp. 271–292). New York: Elsevier.

Angel, R., & Tienda, M. (1982). Determinants of extended household structure: Cultural pattern or economic need? *American Journal of Sociology 87,* 1360–1383.

Anzaldua, G. (1987). *Borderlands/La Frontera: The new meztiza.* San Francisco: Spinsters, Aunt Lute Press.

Aponte, R. (1993). Hispanic families in poverty: Diversity, context, and interpretation. *Families in Society: The Journal of Contemporary Human Services, 36,* 527–537.

Baca Zinn, M. (1980). Employment and education of Mexican American women: The interplay of modernity and ethnicity in eight families. *Harvard Educational Review, 50,* 47–62.

Baca Zinn, M. (1983). "Familism among Chicanos: A theoretical review." *Humboldt Journal of Social Relations 10,* 224–238.

Baca Zinn, M. (1994). Feminist rethinking from racial-ethnic families. In M. Baca Zinn & B. T. Dill (Eds.), *Women of color in U.S. society* (pp. 303–312). Philadelphia: Temple University Press.

Baca Zinn, M. (1995). Social science theorizing for Latino families in the age of diversity. In R. E. Zambrana (Ed.), *Understanding Latino families* (pp. 177–187). Thousand Oaks, CA: Sage.

Baca Zinn, M., & Dill, B. T. (1996). Theorizing difference from multiracial feminism. *Feminist Studies, 22,* 321–332.

Baca Zinn, M., & Eitzen, D. S. (1993). The demographic transformation and the sociological enterprise. *American Sociologist, 24,* 5–12.

Baca Zinn, M., & Eitzen, D. S. (1996). *Diversity in families* (4th ed.). New York: HarperCollins.

Baca Zinn, M., & Eitzen, D. S. (1998). Economic restructuring and systems in inequality. In M. L. Andersen & P. H. Collins (Eds.), *Race, class and gender* (3rd ed., pp. 233–237). Belmont, CA: Wadsworth.

Betancur, J. J., Cordova, T., & Torres, M. L. A. (1993). Economic restructuring and the process of incorporation of Latinos into the Chicago economy. In R. Morales & F. Bonilla (Eds.), *Latinos in a changing U.S. economy: Comparative perspectives on growing inequality* (pp. 109–132). Newbury Park, CA: Sage.

Bogardus, A. (1934). *The Mexican in the United States.* Los Angeles: University of Southern California Press.

Boss, P., & Thorne, B. (1989). Family sociology and family therapy. In M. McGoldrick, C. M. Anderson, & F. Walsh (Eds.), *Women in families* (pp. 78–96). New York: W. W. Norton.

Boyd, M. (1989). Family and personal networks in international migration: Recent developments and new agendas. *International Migration Review, 23,* 638–670.

Buriel, R. (1993). "Childrearing orientations in Mexican American families: The influence of generation and sociocultural factors. *Journal of Marriage and the Family, 55,* 987–1000.

Buriel, R., & De Ment, T. (1997). Immigration and sociocultural change in Mexican, Chinese, and Vietnamese American families. In A. Booth, A. C. Crouter, & N. Landale (Eds.), *Immigration and the family: Research and policy on U.S. immigrants* (pp. 165–200). Mahway, NJ: Lawrence Erlbaum.

Cardenas, G., Chapa, J., & Burek, S. (1993). The changing economic position of Mexican Americans in San Antonio. In R. Morales & F. Bonilla (Eds.), *Latinos in a changing U.S. economy: Comparative perspectives on growing inequality* (pp. 160–183). Newbury Park, CA: Sage.

Carnoy, M., Daley, H. M., & Ojeda, R. H. (1993). The changing economic position of Latinos in the U.S. labor market since 1939. In R. Morales & F. Bonilla (Eds.), *Latinos in a changing U.S. economy: Comparative perspectives on growing inequality* (pp. 28–54). Newbury Park, CA: Sage.

Carrier, J. (1992). Miguel: Sexual life history of a gay Mexican American. In G. Herdt (Ed.), *Gay culture in America* (pp. 202–224). Boston: Beacon Press.

Chavez, L. R. (1990). Coresidence and resistance: Strategies for survival among undocumented Mexicans and Central Americans in the United States. *Urban Anthropology, 19,* 31–61.

Chavez, L. R. (1992). *Shadowed lives: Undocumented immigrants in American society.* Forth Worth, TX: Holt, Rinehart, & Winston.

Chavira-Prado, A. (1992). Work, health, and the family:

Gender structure and women's status in an undocumented migrant population. *Human Organization, 51,* 53–64.

Coltrane, S. (1996). *Family man.* New York: Oxford University Press.

Coltrane, S., & Valdez, E. O. (1993). Reluctant compliance: Work-family role allocation in dual earner Chicano families. In J. Hood (Ed.), *Men, work, and family* (pp. 151–175). Newbury Park, CA: Sage.

Demo, D. H., & Allen, K. R. (1996). Diversity within gay and lesbian families: Challenges and implications for family theory and research. *Journal of Social and Personal Relationships, 13,* 415–434.

Dill, B. T. (1994). Fictive kin, paper sons, and compadrazgo: Women of color and the struggle for survival. In M. Baca Zinn & B. T. Dill (Eds.), *Women of color in U.S. society* (pp. 149–169). Philadelphia: Temple University Press.

Dominguez, J. I. (1992). Cooperating with the enemy? U.S. immigration policies toward Cuba. In C. Mitchell (Ed.), *Western hemisphere immigration and United States foreign policy* (pp. 31–88). University Park, PA: Pennsylvania State University Press.

Dorrington, C. (1995). Central American refugees in Los Angeles: Adjustment of children and families. In R. Zambrana (Ed.), *Understanding Latino families: Scholarship, policy, and practice* (pp. 107–129). Thousand Oaks, CA: Sage.

Feagin, J. R., & Feagin, C. B. (1996). *Racial and ethnic relations.* Upper Saddle River, NJ: Prentice Hall.

Fernandez-Kelly, M. P. (1990). Delicate transactions: Gender, home, and employment among Hispanic women. In F. Ginsberg & A. L. Tsing (Eds.), *Uncertain Terms* (pp. 183–195). Boston: Beacon Press.

Fernandez-Kelly, M. P., & Garcia, A. (1990). Power surrendered and power restored: The politics of home and work among Hispanic women in southern California and southern Florida. In L. Tilly & P. Gurin (Eds.), *Women and politics in America* (pp. 130–149). New York: Russell Sage Foundation.

Fernandez-Kelly, M. P., & Schauffler, R. (1994). Divided fates: Immigrant children in a restructured U.S. economy. *International Migration Review, 28,* 662–689.

Gil, A. G., & Vega, W. A. (1996). Two different worlds: Acculturation stress and adaptation among Cuban and Nicaraguan families. *Journal of Social and Personal Relationships, 13,* 435–456.

Glenn, E. N. (1992). From servitude to service work: Historical continuities in the racial division of paid reproductive labor. *Signs: Journal of Women in Culture and Society, 18,* 1–43.

Gold, S. J. (1989). Differential adjustment among new immigrant family members. *Journal of Contemporary Ethnography, 17,* 408–434.

Grasmuck, S., & Pessar, P. R. (1991). *Between two islands: Dominican international migration.* Berkeley: University of California Press.

Grasmuck, S., & Pessar, P. (1996). Dominicans in the United States: First- and second-generation settlement, 1960–1990. In S. Pedraza & R. G. Rumbaut (Eds.), *Origins and destinies: Immigration, race, and ethnicity in America* (pp. 280–292). Belmont, CA: Wadsworth.

Griffith, J., & Villavicienco, S. (1985). Relationships among culturation, sociodemographic characteristics, and social supports in Mexican American adults. *Hispanic Journal of Behavioral Science, 7,* 75–92.

Griswold del Castillo, R. (1984). *La familia.* Notre Dame, IN: University of Notre Dame Press.

Guarnizo, L. E. (1997). Los Dominicanyorks: The making of a binational society. In M. Romero, P. Hondagneu-Sotelo, & V. Ortiz (Eds.), *Challenging fronteras: Structuring Latina and Latino lives in the U.S.* (pp. 161–174). New York: Routledge.

Hamilton, N., & Chinchilla, N. S. (1997). Central American migration: A framework for analysis. In M. Romero, P. Hondagneu-Sotelo, & V. Ortiz (Eds.), *Challenging fronteras: Structuring Latina and Latino lives in the U.S.* (pp. 81–100). New York: Routledge.

Heller, C. (1996). *Mexican American youth: Forgotten youth at the crossroads.* New York: Random House.

Hill Collins, P. (1990). *Black feminist thought: Knowledge, consciousness and the politics of empowerment.* Boston: Unwin Hyman.

Hill Collins, P. (1997). African-American women and economic justice: A preliminary analysis of wealth, family, and black social class. Unpublished manuscript, Department of African American Studies. University of Cincinnati.

Hondagneu-Sotelo, P. (1994). *Gendered transitions: Mexican experiences of migration.* Berkeley: University of California Press.

Hondagneu-Sotelo, P., & Avila, E. (1997). "I'm here, but I'm there": The meanings of transnational motherhood. *Gender and Society, 11,* 548–571.

Hondagneu-Sotelo, P., & Messner, M. A. (1994). Gender displays and men's power: The "new man" and the Mexican immigrant man. In H. Brod & M. Kaufman (Eds.), *Theorizing masculinities* (pp. 200–218). Newbury Park, CA: Sage.

Hoppe, S. K., & Heller, P. L. (1975). Alienation, familism and the utilization of health services by Mexican-

Americans. *Journal of Health and Social Behavior 16*, 304–314.

Hurtado, A. (1995). Variations, combinations, and evolutions: Latino families in the United States. In R. E. Zambrana (Ed.), *Understanding Latino families* (pp. 40–61). Thousand Oaks, CA: Sage.

Keefe, S. (1984). Deal and ideal extended familism among Mexican Americans and Anglo Americans: On the meaning of "close" family ties. *Human Organization 43*, 65–70.

Lamphere, L., Zavella, P., & Gonzales F., with Evans, P. B. (1993). *Sunbelt working mothers: Reconciling family and factory.* Ithaca, NY: Cornell University Press.

Landale, N. S., & Fennelly, K. (1992). Informal unions among mainland Puerto Ricans: Cohabitation or an alternative to legal marriage? *Journal of Marriage and the Family 54*, 269–280.

Lopez, D. E., Popkin, E., & Telles, E. (1996). Central Americans: At the bottom, struggling to get ahead. In R. Waldinger & M. Bozorgmehr (Eds.), *Ethnic Los Angeles* (pp. 279–304). New York: Russell Sage Foundation.

Madsen, W. (1973). *The Mexican-Americans of south Texas.* New York: Holt, Rinehart & Winston.

Martinez, E. A. (1993). Parenting young children in Mexican American/Chicago families. In H. P. McAdoo (Ed.), *Family ethnicity: Strength in diversity* (pp. 184–194). Newbury Park, CA: Sage.

Massey, D. S. (1993). Latino poverty research: An agenda for the 1990s. Items, *Social Science Research Council Newsletter, 47*(1), 7–11.

Massey, D. S., Zambrana, R. E., & Bell, S. A. (1995). Contemporary issues for Latino families: Future directions for research, policy, and practice. In R. E. Zambrana (Ed.), *Understanding Latino families* (pp. 190–204). Thousand Oaks, CA: Sage.

Mindel, C. H. (1980). Extended familism among urban Mexican-Americans, Anglos and blacks. *Hispanic Journal of Behavioral Sciences 2*, 21–34.

Mirande, A. (1997). *Hombres y machos: Masculinity and Latino culture.* Boulder, CO: Westview Press.

Mitchell, C. (1992). U.S. foreign policy and Dominican migration to the United States. In C. Mitchell (Ed.), *Western hemisphere immigration and United States foreign policy* (pp. 89–123). University Park: Pennsylvania State University Press.

Moore, J. W., & Pinderhughes, R. (Eds.). (1993). *In the barrios: Latinos and the underclass debate.* New York: Russell Sage Foundation.

Moore, J. W., & Vigil, J. D. (1993). Barrios in transition. In J. W. Moore & R. Pinderhughes (Eds.), *In the barrios: Latinos and the underclass debate* (pp. 27–50). New York: Russell Sage Foundation.

Moraga, C. (1983). *Loving in the war years: Lo que nunca paso por sus labios.* Boston: South End Press.

Morales, E. S. (1990). Ethnic minority families and minority gays and lesbians. In F. W. Bozett & M. B. Sussman (Eds.), *Homosexuality and family relations* (pp. 217–239). New York: Harrington Park Press.

Morales, R., & Ong, P. M. (1993). The illusion of progress: Latinos in Los Angeles. In R. Morales & F. Bonilla (Eds.), *Latinos in a changing U.S. economy: Comparative perspectives on growing inequality* (pp. 55–84). Newbury Park, CA: Sage.

Morales, R., & Bonilla, F. (1993). Restructuring and the new inequality. In R. Morales & F. Bonilla (Eds.), *Latinos in a changing U.S. economy: Comparative perspectives on growing inequality* (pp. 1–27). Newbury Park, CA: Sage.

Morrissey, M. (1987). Female-headed families: Poor women and choice. In N. Gerstel & H. Gross (Eds.), *Families and work* (pp. 302–314). Philadelphia: Temple University Press.

Ortiz, V. (1995). The diversity of Latino families. In R. Zambrana (Ed.), *Understanding Latino families: Scholarship, policy, and practice* (pp. 18–30). Thousand Oaks, CA: Sage.

Ortiz, V. (1996). The Mexican-origin population: Permanent working class or emerging middle class? In R. Waldinger & M. Bozorgmehr (Eds.), *Ethnic Los Angeles* (pp. 247–277). New York: Russell Sage Foundation.

Perez, L. (1994). Cuban families in the United States. In R. L. Taylor (Ed.), *Minority families in the United States: A multicultural perspective.* Englewood Cliffs, NJ: Prentice Hall.

Perez-Stable, M., & Uriarte, M. (1993). Cubans and the changing economy of Miami. In R. Morales & F. Bonilla (Eds.), *Latinos in a changing U.S. economy: Comparative perspectives on growing inequality* (pp. 133–159). Newbury Park, CA: Sage.

Pesquera, B. M. (1993). In the beginning he wouldn't lift even a spoon: The division of household labor. In A. de la Torre & B. M. Pesquera (Eds.), *Building with our hands* (pp. 181–198). Berkeley: University of California Press.

Portes, A., & Rumbaut, R. G. (1990). *Immigrant America: A portrait.* Berkeley: University of California Press.

Portes, A., & Truelove, C. (1987). Making sense of diversity: Recent research on Hispanic minorities in the

United States. *Annual Review of Sociology, 13,* 357–385.

Powell, D. R. (1995). Including Latino fathers in parent education and support programs: Development of a program model. In R. E. Zambrana (Ed.), *Understanding Latino families* (pp. 85–106). Thousand Oaks, CA: Sage.

Ramirez, O. (1980, March). Extended family support and mental health status among Mexicans in Detroit. *Micro, Onda, LaRed, Monthly Newsletter of the National Chicano Research Network,* p. 2.

Ramirez, O., & Arce, C. H. (1981). The contemporary Chicano family: An empirically based review. In A. Baron, Jr. (Ed.), *Explorations in Chicano Psychology* (pp. 3–28). New York: Praeger.

Repack, T. A. (1997). New rules in a new landscape. In M. Romero, P. Hondagneu-Sotelo, & V. Ortiz (Eds.), *Challenging fronteras: Structuring Latina and Latino lives in the U.S.* (pp. 247–257). New York: Routledge.

Rochelle, A. (1997). *No more kin: Exploring race, class, and gender in family networks.* Thousand Oaks, CA: Sage.

Rodriguez, N. P., & Hagan, J. M. (1997). Apartment restructuring and Latino immigrant tenant struggles: A case study of human agency. In M. Romero, P. Hondagneu-Sotelo, & V. Ortiz (Eds.), *Challenging fronteras: Structuring Latina and Latino lives in the U.S.* (pp. 297–309). New York: Routledge.

Romero, M. (1997). Introduction. In M. Romero, P. Hondagneu-Sotelo, & V. Ortiz (Eds.), *Challenging fronteras: Structuring Latina and Latino lives in the U.S.* (pp. xiii–xix). New York: Routledge.

Rubel, A. J. (1966). *Across the tracks: Mexican Americans in a Texas city.* Austin: University of Texas Press.

Rumbaut, R. G. (1995). *Immigrants from Latin America and the Caribbean: A socioeconomic profile* (Statistical Brief No. 6). East Lansing: Julian Samora Research Institute, Michigan State University.

Sassen, S. (1993). Urban transformation and employment. In R. Morales & F. Bonilla (Eds.), *Latinos in a changing U.S. economy: Comparative perspectives on growing inequality* (pp. 194–206). Newbury Park, CA: Sage.

Scott, A. J. (1996). The manufacturing economy: Ethnic and gender divisions of labor. In R. Waldinger & M. Bozorgmehr (Eds.), *Ethnic Los Angeles.* New York: Russell Sage Foundation.

Segura, D. A., & Pierce, J. L. (1993). Chicana/o family structure and gender personality: Chodorow, familism, and psychoanalytic sociology revisited. *Signs,* 19, 62–91.

Shelton, B. A., & John, D. (1993). Ethnicity, race, and difference: A comparison of white, black, and Hispanic men's household labor time. In J. Hood (Ed.), *Men, work, and family* (pp. 1–22). Newbury Park, CA: Sage.

Smith, J., Wallerstein, I., & Evers, H. D. (1985). *The household and the world economy.* Beverly Hills, CA: Sage.

Solis, J. (1995). The status of Latino children and youth: Challenges and prospects. In R. E. Zambrana (Ed.), *Understanding Latino families* (pp. 62–84). Thousand Oaks, CA: Sage.

Stacey, J. (1990). *Brave new families: Stories of domestic upheaval in late twentieth century America.* New York: Basic Books.

Stacey, J. (1995). Disloyal to the disciplines: A feminist trajectory in the border lands. In D. C. Stanton & A. Stewart (Eds.), *Feminisms in the academy* (pp. 311–330). Ann Arbor: University of Michigan Press.

Stacey, J. (1996). *In the name of the family: Rethinking family values in the postmodern age.* Boston: Beacon Press.

Stier, H., & Tienda, M. (1992). Family, work, and women: The labor supply of Hispanic immigrant wives. *International Migration Review, 26,* 1291–1313.

Sullivan, M. L. (1993). Puerto Ricans in Sunset Park, Brooklyn: Poverty amidst ethnic and economic diversity. In J. W. Moore & R. Pinderhughes (Eds.), *In the barrios: Latinos and the underclass debate* (pp. 1–26). New York: Russell Sage Foundation.

Thomas, D., & Wilcox, J. E. (1987). The rise of family theory. In M. B. Sussman & S. Steinmetz (Eds.), *Handbook of marriage and the family* (pp. 81–102). New York: Plenum.

Thorne, B. (1992). Feminism and the family: Two decades of thought. In B. Thorne & M. Yalom (Eds.), *Rethinking the family: Some feminist questions* (pp. 3–30). Boston: Northeastern University Press.

Tienda, M. (1989). Puerto Ricans and the underclass debate. *Annals of the American Association of Political and Social Sciences, 501,* 105–119.

Torres, A., & Bonilla, F. (1993). Decline within decline: The New York perspective. In R. Morales & F. Bonilla (Eds.), *Latinos in a changing U.S. economy: Comparative perspectives on growing inequality* (pp. 85–108). Newbury Park, CA: Sage.

U.S. Bureau of the Census. (1993). *1990 census of the population: Persons of Hispanic origin in the United States.* Washington, DC: U.S. Government Printing Office.

U.S. Bureau of the Census. (1996). *Statistical abstract of the United States: 1996.* Washington DC: U.S. Government Printing Office.

Valenzuela, A., & Dornbusch, S. (1994). Familism and social capital in the academic achievement of Mexican origin and Anglo adolescents. *Social Science Quarterly, 75,* 18–36.

Vega, W. (1990). Hispanic families in the 1980s: A decade of research. *Journal of Marriage and the Family, 52,* 1015–1024.

Vega, W. A. (1995). The study of Latino families: A point of departure. In R. E. Zambrana (Ed.), *Understanding Latino families* (pp. 3–17). Thousand Oaks, CA: Sage.

Velez-Ibañez, C. (1993). U.S. Mexicans in the borderlands: Being poor without the underclass. In J. Moore & R. Pinderhughes (Eds.), *In the barrios: Latinos and the underclass debate* (pp. 195–220). New York: Russell Sage Foundation.

Velez-Ibañez, C. (1996). *Border visions.* Tucson: University of Arizona Press.

Velez-Ibañez, C. G., & Greenberg, J. B. (1992). Formation and transformation of funds of knowledge among U.S.-Mexican households. *Anthropology and Education Quarterly, 23,* 313–335.

Williams, N. (1990). *The Mexican American family: Tradition and change.* Dix Hills, NY: General Hall.

Wilkinson, D. (1993). Family ethnicity in America. In H. P. McAdoo (Ed.), *Family ethnicity: Strength in diversity* (pp. 15–59). Newbury Park, CA: Sage.

Wilson, W. J. (1987). *The truly disadvantaged: The inner city, the underclass, and public policy.* Chicago: University of Chicago Press.

Wilson, W. J. (1996). *When work disappears: The world of the new urban poor.* New York: Alfred A. Knopf.

Ybarra, L. (1982). When wives work: The impact on the Chicano family. *Journal of Marriage and the Family, 44,* 169–178.

Zavella, P. 1987. *Women's work and Chicano families: Cannery workers of the Santa Clara Valley.* Ithaca, NY: Cornell University Press.

CHAPTER 14

Diversity Within Asian American Families

MASAKO ISHII-KUNTZ

Because the image of Asians as "foreigners" is pervasive, it is easy to forget that Asians have been a significant presence in the United States for more than a century. Chinese, mostly male laborers, dominated the first large-scale Asian immigration to the United States from the 1850s to 1880s. Japanese male laborers replaced these Chinese as a result of anti-Chinese agitation and violence throughout the western United States in the early 1900s. The Filipino population in the United States rose rapidly between 1920 and 1930. With the 1965 immigration law that abolished the quota system, there has been a dramatic increase in Asian immigration in the past three decades (Immigration and Naturalization Service, 1995). Prominent among the new arrivals have been Koreans and Southeast Asian refugees.

Today, the term *Asian American* applies to members of over 28 subgroups who have been classified as a single group because of their common ethnic origins in Asia, similar physical appearance, and similar cultural values (Barringer, Gardner, & Levin, 1993). The classification of a multitude of groups under the single rubric of Asian American masks important differences among and within groups. Asian Americans are culturally and experientially diverse; they differ in immigration experiences (Chan, 1991; Takaki, 1989), occupational skills (Shu & Satele, 1977), cultural values and beliefs (Kitano & Daniels, 1988), religion, primary language, income, education, average age (Barringer et al., 1993; Jiobu, 1988), and ethnic identity (Ishii-Kuntz, 1994c; Sue & Kirk, 1973). Their families' experiences vary considerably by ethnic background, class, gender, sexual orientation, and age (Ishii-Kuntz, 1997a, 1997c). To speak of the Asian American family is to ignore the great diversity in the forms, lifestyles, and experiences of such families. This chapter focuses on the complexities and similarities within American families of Asian ancestry and discusses how the family experiences of the various Asian-origin groups are and have been systematically influenced by gender, class, ethnicity, and other dimensions of social stratification.

PERSONAL REFLECTIONS ON FAMILY DIVERSITY

Western observers have commonly thought of Japanese families as traditional, with a sharp division of labor between husbands and wives and a strong emphasis on interdependence among family members. However, my own family experiences in Japan were different from the expectations surrounding the "typical" Japanese family. Although my father had an extremely demanding full-time job, he actively participated in child care and housework while my mother spent most of her time pursuing her career.

My parents also encouraged me to be self-sufficient, rather than dependent on them. Lunch making was a good example of this emphasis throughout my childhood. In Japan, making *obentos* (boxed lunches) is one of the most important tasks of mothers. Customarily, these *obentos* are highly crafted elaborations of food: a multitude of miniature portions, artistically designed and precisely arranged, in a container that is sturdy and cute. Many mothers are dedicated to making nutritional and tasty-looking *obentos* for their children's school lunches (Allison, 1991). Japanese women who can make beautiful *obentos* are often considered to be "good" mothers. In fact, some child care centers have *obento* photo contests to award mothers who can make the most nutritional and appealing lunches for their children. Japanese women's magazines are also filled with photos and recipes of the most attractive *obento* menus for children.

I was perhaps the only child in my Japanese elementary school who prepared her or his own *obento* because my mother refused to participate in this art. As a child, I was well aware of the unattractive appearance of my *obento* and was sometimes too embarrassed to open my lunch at school. Looking back, however, it was not the appearance of my *obento* that I was worried about, but the negative impression that my *obento* gave my teachers and peers about my mother. In Japanese society, where "uniqueness" is not readily accepted and appreciated (Chiba, 1985), my *obento* symbolized the out-of-group orientation of my family life. My embarrassment about *obentos,* however, disappeared quickly when I moved to the United States in my teens. I still remember how happy I was to see my new American friends eating a variety of lunches, none as attractive as the *obentos* of my peers in Japan.

As I was discovering the diversity of American society initially through school lunches, I also became acutely aware of my Asian heritage. I was no longer part of the majority. In Japan, I always thought that my parents were different from other Japanese parents, but I discovered that they were also different from the parents of my American friends. For example, my parents never expressed their concerns and opinions about any school-related issues, such as the assignment of teachers. I sometimes wondered why some children changed teachers at the beginning of the school year. I soon discovered that it was possible for them to do so because their parents complained to the school principal, whereas my parents would never have thought of doing such a thing.

My encounters with family diversity continued during my college years in Washington state, when I started making American friends of Asian ancestry. The Asian American student association to which I belonged consisted not only of Japanese Americans but of students with Chinese, Korean, and Filipino backgrounds. Although we shared a sense of being a minority in the United States, the heritage our ancestors brought to the United States was richly diverse. Asian Americans are often classified as a group with similar physical features and cultural values, but each Asian American group brings with it diverse family experiences. Despite the model-minority image surrounding Asian Americans (Kitano & Daniels, 1988), some of my Asian American friends came from poor families, and others never excelled academically. At the same time, despite the ideal image of tight-knit Asian families (Ishii-Kuntz, 1997a, 1997c), a good number of my Asian American friends' parents were divorced or separated. Furthermore, although the image of obedient Asian American children was prevalent, many of my Asian American peers had severe conflicts with their parents. My personal experiences, therefore, helped me realize the superficial nature of the images that the American public has of Asian Americans and their families.

These early experiences had a significant impact on my decision to become a sociologist with a strong interest in diverse family lives. As a sociologist and an Asian immigrant in the United States, I felt compelled to study diverse family experiences among Asian Americans. Moreover, I felt responsible for debunking various myths surrounding Asian Americans and their families so that the American public, educators, and practitioners could gain a better understanding of the rich heritage of, as well as the history of discrimination against, Asian Americans.

THEORETICAL APPROACHES TO STUDYING ASIAN AMERICAN FAMILIES

Social anthropologists view behavior as a manifestation of, or a vehicle for conveying, culture (Lebra, 1982). In the past, Asian American families were frequently studied using this cultural perspective, which dates back to the teaching of Confucianism (see Glenn & Yap, 1994; Takagi, 1994). Many anthropological studies (see, for example, Caudill, 1952; Connor, 1976) have focused on how the continuity of Asian cultural values shaped Asian American family relationships and contributed to Asian Americans' work ethic. Such values include familism, which emphasizes the importance of family over the individual, and filial piety, which enforces respect for the elderly and reverence for tradition. Cultural theorists have pointed to the low divorce rates among Asian Americans and close ties between generations (shown in high rates of intergenerational coresidence) as indicators of family stability, and they have argued that these patterns can be explained by the continuity of such unique Asian cultural values as familism and filial piety. Cultural explanations have been used to study Asian American families much more frequently than African American and Latino families, which have been studied primarily from historical, economic, and political perspectives (Stanfield, 1993).

The cultural approach reflects an assimilationist bias in the study of race relations, and it is extremely limited for studying diversity within Asian American families, primarily because of its tendency to view culture as a constant, rather than a variable that changes across historical periods and over generations. Cultural theorists have argued that since Asian Americans share the unique cultural heritage rooted in Confucianism, they are likely to have similar family experiences. For example, the prevalence of three-generational households among many Asian American populations can be seen as a manifestation of the important Confucianistic concept of filial piety. Yet Asian American family experiences are diverse because they have been influenced by such factors as socioeconomic status, immigration history, generational status, age, gender, and nativity, to name just a few.

In contrast to a cultural theory, a critical theory that focuses on the constraints imposed on Asian American families takes into account the legal, political, and institutional structures surrounding Asian Americans and their families (Glenn & Yap, 1994; Takagi, 1994). Using this perspective, we can examine how such factors as immigration policies and institutional structures that control labor markets have influenced the formation, functions, structures, and relationships of Asian American families. A critical perspective differs from a cultural per-

spective in the following four ways. First, a critical theory argues for understanding Asian American families in their social and historical contexts. When we examine the social and historical contexts, we must consider a set of interrelated factors, such as race, gender, class, and other forms of stratification.

Second, unlike a cultural theory, which views Asian American families as cohesive and stable units, a critical theory views families as a frequent source of conflict. In her study of Issei (first-generation) and Nisei (second-generation) domestic workers, Glenn (1986) described a contradictory experience of Japanese American women. The Japanese American family is a social unit that must struggle against external forces like racism; thus, all family members must work together to fight against discrimination. At the same time, however, the family is an organization that subjugates women by placing them at the bottom of the family hierarchy and authority. This contradictory experience of Japanese American women has created conflict in their families.

Third, because a cultural theory has been used to explain the "success" stories of Asian Americans, it considers assimilation to be the ultimate goal of immigrants. Stated another way, a cultural theory defines the "success" of immigrants in terms of the immigrants' level of assimilation and acculturation into the mainstream culture. Instead of focusing on the "success" aspect of Asian Americans, a critical theory explains why it is difficult for some groups of Asian Americans to achieve economic parity with European Americans. Fourth, whereas a cultural theory aims to explain the common experiences among Asian Americans, a critical theory allows us to examine the diversity that exists within Asian American families and the various changes that are taking place in Asian American families.

Cultural and critical theories can be further contrasted in terms of the gender relations in Asian American families. Assuming a continuity of values, cultural theorists view gender hierarchies as a reflection of Confucianistic values that emphasize men's superiority and women's obedience to their husbands. This theory, however, falls short of explaining why, among some Asian American groups like Japanese Americans, there has been a trend toward more egalitarian relations between wives and husbands (Espiritu, 1996; Ishii-Kuntz, 1997c; Takagi, 1994). Using a critical perspective, I argue that the gender hierarchy that has existed in Asian American families has been a product of such factors as husbands' and wives' differential earning power and a gender gap in educational attainment. Historical evidence indicates that changes in family structure and relationships have been driving forces in the lessening of gender inequality in the home. For example, more than 40,000 Japanese on the Pacific Coast, along with their 70,000 American-born children—who were U.S. citizens—were removed from their homes and incarcerated in "relocation camps" during World War II. As a consequence, the economic and social basis for Issei men's authority and security was abruptly taken away, which ironically gave many Japanese American wives and daughters more freedom and power than they had before the incarceration (Broom & Kitsuse, 1956; Nakano, 1990).

From a critical perspective, Asian American families play an active role in maintaining family functions and relations. Individual family members are not only the recipients of various legal, political, and institutional forces, but active participants in shaping their family lives. In adopting a critical perspective, I challenge several traditional assumptions of Asian American families. First, I question the view that Asian American families exist in their own tight-knit communities and are thus immune to "outside" forces, since it is known, for example, that Asian American families have been greatly influenced by restrictive immigration laws and the history of racial discrimination. Second, I assume that individual family members play an active role in forming and shaping their families. Rather than simply having inherited cultural values, Asian Americans have actively and skillfully used their cultural heritage as resources for survival. Third, I challenge the image of Asian American families as being ideal and free of conflicts. Recent research (see Espiritu, 1996) has shown that interest and investments in the family are not equal among family members. Conflicts arise over many family issues, including the division of household labor and child care (Takagi, 1994).

The challenges of a critical perspective against the traditional views of Asian American families are in line with feminist critiques of family studies (see Ferree, 1990; Glenn, 1987; Thompson & Walker, 1989). Feminist scholars have stressed that families are neither separate from wider systems of male domination nor automatically solitary in their own right (Ferree, 1990). Furthermore, feminist perspectives are extremely helpful and useful in understanding a variety of Asian American family experiences. The proposition that gender is continuously being constructed to advance a variety of individual and group goals is central to West and Zimmerman's (1987) concept of "doing gender." According to this view, being a man or woman socially is not a natural or inevitable outgrowth of biological features, but an achievement of routinized conduct. For example, a father who actively participates in child care may have little in common with other men who are not involved with their children, although they are both men biologically. Instead, these involved fathers may think and behave in ways similar to women who "mother" (Risman, 1987).

Similarly, Asian American family experiences are constructed through members' daily interaction with each other and with people in the outside world. Just because one is born into an Asian American family does not mean that one's values, beliefs, and family experiences will be identical to those of other Asian Americans. Rather, these experiences are constructed by social and historical situations that surround the families because these situations provide the concrete resources and constraints that shape family interactions. Feminist perspectives are critical in that they view families as fully integrated into wider systems of economic and political power and recognize the sometimes conflicting interests of family members. Perhaps the only diversion of feminist perspectives from that of a critical theory is the feminists' focus on gender as a central tool with which to study family interaction and relationships.

DEFINITION OF FAMILY

Families encompass a wide range of experiences and issues, so it is extremely difficult to provide a single definition of *family*. The difficulty is rooted in the fact that even though every person is a member of a family (if only in a biological sense), there is no universal definition of *the family*. This difficulty is particularly evident when families are viewed cross-culturally because there is a substantial variety in family arrangements worldwide. In light of this variability, it is important to define *family* as broadly as possible to encompass diverse experiences.

Most official definitions of *family* emphasize blood ties, adoption, or marriage as criteria for membership and value the functions of procreation and socialization of offspring. The U.S. Bureau of the Census (quoted in Barringer et al., 1993, p. 136) uses the term *family* to mean "a group of two or more persons related by birth, marriage, or adoption and residing together in a household." This definition is extremely limited when one considers various family forms that exist in different cultures and subcultures. For example, many Americans form families without legal marriage, and in other countries, such as Brazil, the Constitution recognizes that a family arrangement can exist outside legal marriage (Goldani, 1990). In many families, the members do not necessarily reside together in the same households, as exemplified by Japanese salaried men who live apart from their families owing to their frequent relocation (Ishii-Kuntz, 1993, 1994a). In addition, Asian Americans frequently accommodate recently immigrated distant relatives or friends into their households (Chan, 1991). Thus, a definition of *family* that is based on strict membership criteria and specific functions excludes many of primary groups that have family-like qualities, including child-free couples; couples whose children no longer live at home; and unmarried heterosexual, gay, or lesbian couples with children.

Given all these shortcomings concerning the conventional definition of the family, it is not especially useful to think of the family in terms of specific memberships created by marriage, birth, and adoption or according to a single function, such as the procreation or socialization function. Instead, I suggest a broad relational perspective that focuses on how two or more people view their relationship. Stated simply, families consist of people who view themselves as being committed to caring for one another. Whether these groups of people are recognized as families by the legal or larger social systems, the concept of family applies to those whose relationships are based on commitment or obligation (Ferree, 1990). This definition is similar to the concept of the wider family (Marciano & Sussman, 1991), which views families as social constructions that emerge from various forms of obligatory and committed relationships. Because the commitment and obligation to care for others are important ingredients of wider families, these families are not constrained by the structures, normative patterns, and legal obligations of traditional families.

This broad view of families is particularly useful for studying immigrant Asian families, some of whom may live with nonrelative adults and children and may feel committed to caring for them. It is also more inclusive than the conventional definition of the family because it encompasses units, such as Chinese American split households (Glenn, 1983) and Japanese relocation families (Ishii-Kuntz, 1994a), in which the family members live apart on a more or less permanent basis.

FAMILY PROCESS AND DYNAMICS

Couple Relations

Little has been written about the dynamics of couple relations among Asian Americans. Most of what has been written focuses on the hierarchical nature of the husband-wife relationship, with the husband maintaining an irreproachably authoritative, strict, dignified, and aloof relationship to the wife and children (Lee & Cynn, 1991; Sue, 1989a, 1989b; Sue & Morishima, 1982). Responsible for providing for the economic well-being of their families, many Asian American fathers feel obligated to be the leaders and the principal disciplinarians in the families (Shon & Ja, 1982). Therefore, many fathers are usually seen as stern, distant, and less approachable than mothers.

In contrast, many Asian American women believe that their family role is to monitor the emotional well-being of their families (Lee & Cynn, 1991). The mother is usually the parent who is the most involved in nurturing children; listening when the children have problems; and communicating the children's needs, concerns, and desires to the father (Shon & Ja, 1982). Consequently, children usually report feeling emotionally closer to their mothers than their fathers (Shon & Ja, 1982). For many mothers, the most important bond is likely to be with their children, rather than with their husbands; for husbands, the strongest bond is likely to be with *their* mothers (Lee, 1982). Traditionally, many Asian American wives are publicly subordinate to their husbands, but privately they are not so demure (Kim, 1991).

Not all Asian American families maintain traditional hierarchical relationships between husbands and wives. At least some intraethnic variations among Asian American men and women are due to differences in generations and time since immigration. It seems that as succeeding generations of Asian Americans become more exposed to the mainstream culture, their couple relations become more like those of most white middle-class American families (Uba, 1994). For example, the discrepancies between women's and men's duties and privileges, though still existent, are not so glaring among Japanese and Chinese Americans who were more or less well established economically in the United States before the 1965 immigration law changes (Huang & Ying, 1989). In addition, although Korean men still maintain greater power in their relationships with their wives, many are more egalitarian, as shown by their active participation in child care (Yu & Kim, 1983).

Almost one third of American-born Chinese women are professionals or managers, and more than half of them are technical, sales, or administrative support workers (U.S. Bureau of the Census, 1992). Younger Chinese American husbands and wives are thus coequal breadwinners (Glenn & Yap, 1994). Research has also shown that among contemporary Japanese American families, many of whom are Sansei (third generation), there is a trend toward greater equality between men and women in the family, as evidenced by a more equal division of household labor (Nakano, 1990; Takagi, 1994). Nakano, for example, concluded that Sansei husbands are taking much more responsibility in the household than did their fathers, as shown in the following comments by a Sansei woman: "Now that [my husband] has started a home-based consulting business, it allows him to take Angela to daycare and pick her up three days a week. This shared responsibility on [his] part is the only way I make it day to day as a working mom" (p. 230). In contrast, although the employment rates of Vietnamese women in the United States are relatively high (Haines, 1986), the economic activities of women have not taken on primary significance compared with those of men (Kibria, 1994). In summary, the relationship between men and women in acculturated Asian American families is more egalitarian than that in families whose presence in the United States is relatively new.

Until the 1994 publication of *Amerasia's* special issue on Asian American gay men and lesbians, little had been known about gay and lesbian families among Americans of Asian ancestry. Moreover, Asian Americans have been historically desexualized: Sexualities among them have rarely been the topic of investigation (see Chin & Chan, 1972 for a critique). In this respect, Takagi's (1994) convincing description of the struggle between lesbian and Asian American identities is a significant departure from more conventional approaches to studying Asian Americans. Takagi argued that although both identities are socially constructed, the lesbian identity has the option of "coming out" or "staying in" the closet, whereas the Asian American identity has no such option because of its obvious visibility. Asian American lesbians could also experience "quadruple jeopardy oppression"—class, race, gender, and sexual orientation. Takagi concluded, however, that "marginalization is not as much about the quantities of experiences as it is about [the] qualities of experience" (p. 3).

Given the complexities associated with Asian American intermarriage (Sung, 1990), I speculate that the dynamics of couple relations take on added complexity in interracial gay and lesbian relationships. Although the literature in this area seems to suggest that partnerships among Asian American gays and lesbians are more egalitarian than those among Asian American heterosexual couples, further research on this issue is sorely needed.

Although a cultural perspective can be used to

explain traditional gender relationships, it is limited in explaining the emerging trend toward egalitarianism among Asian American couples and in describing the relationships among Asian American gay and lesbian couples. In contrast, using a critical perspective, one can infer that the high labor force participation of Japanese American women has had the effect of creating greater economic equality between men and women in Japanese American families.

Parent-Child Relationships

The structure and quality of parent-child relationships vary across Asian American groups. Much of this variation comes from the diverse immigration experiences of Asians and the discriminatory practices they have encountered in the United States. For these reasons, it is important to present some historical background that has influenced these relationships among Asian Americans.

Early Chinese male immigrants were forced to live separately from their wives and children who were left behind in China. In these split households (Glenn, 1983), children rarely had opportunities to interact with their father. Because many years passed between visits, children were spaced far apart, and the father was often middle aged or elderly when the youngest child was born. Thus, the age difference increased the formality and distance of the relationship. Japanese American experiences are in stark contrast. Because the Japanese government in the early 1900s was concerned with the problems of prostitution, gambling, and drunkenness among Japanese male immigrants, it promoted the emigration of Japanese women to the United States. Many Japanese men resorted to "picture-bride marriages," in which the partners knew each other only through the exchange of photographs before marriage. In contrast, since many Japanese American couples started their families together in the United States, both parents are usually present in Japanese American households. Their relationships with their children are characterized by close supervision; the passing on of family values that were prevalent in Japan; and, at the same time, the encouragement of their children to assimilate into

the mainstream culture (Ishii-Kuntz, 1997c; Yamamoto & Kubota, 1983).

Japanese American parent-child relationships, however, were forced to undergo major changes when Japanese Americans were interned during World War II. Caudill (1952) observed that Japanese American children were valued for both their potential to help their parents in the future and, in the case of sons, their ability to carry on the family line. However, these expectations more or less disappeared after the war largely because of the loss of parental authority during the internment (Ishii-Kuntz, 1997c). It is clear that this historically significant event affected eventual parent-child relationships among Japanese Americans. Reduced parental supervision and authority gave Nisei more independence in their decision making, and many of them formed separate households from those of their parents (Ishii-Kuntz, 1997c).

Although contemporary Asian American parenting does not seem to differ significantly from that of European Americans, some studies (Hsu, Tseng, Ashton, McDermott, & Char, 1985; Tsui & Schultz, 1988) have found that Asian American parenting is unique in terms of its communication styles. For example, Japanese American families value and rely on indirect and nonverbal communication more than do European Americans, frequently communicating through gestures, facial expressions, intonations, and the volume of speech, rather than through direct statements (Hsu et al., 1985). Asian American parents may communicate with silent looks unnoticed by observers. Many Asian American parents express their disapproval with a look that may appear to the outside observer as a glance but that may convey a great deal (such as, anger, disappointment, and pride) to the children (Uba, 1994).

Other studies on parent-child relationships (see, for example, Fong, 1973; Ho, 1976) have reported that Asian American children are expected to comply with familial and social authority to the point of sacrificing their own desires and ambitions. For example, Chiu (1987) found that Chinese American mothers often select their children's playmates, and Yao (1985) found that the parents of Asian American children from various groups in Grades 5–11 reported having more influence than the children's peers over the selection of their children's clothing, extracurricular activities, and course of study. Receiving the approval and avoiding the displeasure of authority figures are major concerns in the lives of Filipino Americans (Santos, 1983). However, commanding respect for authority is difficult once a Filipino family comes to the United States. Social, cultural, and occupational dislocations make parents in the new society unsure of themselves, and their children consider them less credible guides to functioning in new social situations (Santos, 1983).

Cultural theorists argue that being loyal to and making sacrifices for parents and showing respect for elders are behaviors that are valued in Asian cultures. Thus, when Asian American children are obedient to parents, they are seen as continuing the cultural values of their ancestors (Chiu, 1987; Ho, 1976). When problems and conflicts between parents and children arise, cultural theorists contend that it is an indication of a cultural gap between the two generations caused by the assimilation of the younger generation into the new culture.

In addition to cultural discontinuities, intergenerational conflicts may be derived from other sources, as is evident from the results of some studies on Korean American children and their immigrant parents (Hurh, 1990; Min & Min, 1992; Yu & Kim, 1983). Using questionnaires, Min and Min (1992) reported that Korean American children who are proficient in the Korean language have closer relationships with their parents than do their peers who are not. The effect of language fluency on the closeness of Korean American parent-child relationships is much greater than that of similarities in cultural values between parents and children. Stated another way, a language gap lessens the amount of communication and creates emotional distance between the generations.

Although there is an emerging interest in the relationships between parents and their lesbian daughters or gay sons, little is known about them (see Crosbie-Burnett, Foster, Murray, & Bowen, 1996), and even less is known about the relationships of Asian American parents with lesbian or gay children. What is known is that Asian American parents experience many of the same processes as

do their European American counterparts before, when, and after their children's lesbian or gay identities are disclosed (Hom, 1994). Because many of the parents whom Hom studied came to accept their children's sexual orientations, parent-child relationships were not necessarily adversely affected. However, the Asian American parents were concerned about how their ethnic communities would feel about lesbians and gay men. Other studies (Chan, 1989; Wooden, Kawasaki, & Mayeda, 1983) have reported the identity struggles of Asian American lesbians and gay men and the family pressure toward academic and occupational achievement.

Intergenerational Relations

It is not surprising that research has generally indicated that Asian Americans tend to have strong commitments to family and to care of their elderly parents (Connor, 1974; Kamo & Zhou, 1994). Studies have also shown that, compared with European Americans, Asian Americans, in general, tend to live closer to (Kamo & Zhou, 1994), feel more obligated to (Osako & Wong, 1986), provide more financial aid to (Ishii-Kuntz, 1993), and interact more frequently with their parents (Ishii-Kuntz, 1993; Osako, 1976). Many younger Asian American adults are expected to live with their families until they marry, elderly parents tend to live with family members rather than in nursing homes, and family members of all age levels are typically integrated into family activities (Johnson, 1977; Kamo & Zhou, 1994). Using data from the 1980 census, public use micro data sample (PUMS), Kamo and Zhou (1994) inferred that the prevalence of the coresidence of Chinese American and Japanese American elderly parents and their married adult children is strongly influenced by the traditional values of filial piety.

Although several recent studies (see, for example, Kamo & Zhou, 1994; Leonetti, 1983) have found a higher rate of intergenerational coresidence among Asian Americans than among European Americans, there are also variations. Among Japanese Americans, for example, retired Nisei, unlike Issei-generation parents, generally do not want to live with their children (Ishii-Kuntz, 1997c; Osako & Wong, 1986). Ishii-Kuntz (1993) also reported that contemporary Japanese Americans are less likely to exchange resources between generations than are Chinese, Filipino, and Korean Americans. Compared to Japanese and Chinese Americans, the filial obligations of Korean American adult children have a significant, positive effect on their emotional support for their elderly parents (Ishii-Kuntz, 1997b).

Filial obligation has a differential impact on the provision of support, depending on structural and economic factors (Ishii-Kuntz, 1997b). Analyzing data on 421 Chinese, Japanese, and Korean Americans, Ishii-Kuntz (1997b) found that adult children who live close to their elderly parents and report a higher level of filial obligation are much more likely to provide financial assistance to their parents than are children who live farther away from and feel little obligation to their parents. Ishii-Kuntz (1997b) concluded that the impact of filial obligation on an adult child's support for his or her elderly parents can be better explained by taking into account such structural and social factors as income and residential proximity than by considering cultural variables alone.

Relations With Extended and Chosen Kin

Research has generally indicated that Asian American families are more cohesive than are European American families (Conner, 1977; McDermott et al., 1984). A number of researchers have noted that Chinese, Filipino, and Japanese Americans tend to have strong commitments to family (Connor, 1974; Morris, 1990; Tsui & Schultz, 1988). These strong commitments are usually measured by attitudes toward intrafamilial sharing of thoughts and feelings. For example, McDermott et al. reported that Japanese American parents thought that family members should share their deepest thoughts more than did European American parents, the latter giving more emphasis to individual family members' right to privacy. Japanese American parents also thought that family members should discuss important family decisions more than did European American parents.

There is also evidence of cohesiveness in the extended Asian American family. Cohesion can be assessed by examining the amount of support that individuals receive from their families and the amount of interaction among extended and chosen kin. For example, nuclear and extended Samoan American family members tend to see each other frequently (at least once a week), and Samoan American adult children may live with their parents, siblings, and other kin even after marriage (Ablon, 1976). A study of Asian American families with developmentally disabled children found that these families received more child care support from relatives than did their European American counterparts (Nihira, Mink, & Shapiro, 1991).

The conventional explanation for the cohesion generally found in Asian American families has been that Asian American values emphasize family solidarity. Familial solidarity has been defined by the interdependence of family members; hierarchical relationships in the family; and orientation to the family as a whole, rather than to the individual members (Uba, 1994). Other indications of family solidarity among Asian Americans include the belief that one's behavior reflects on oneself and on one's nuclear and extended families over generations and Confucian ethics emphasizing filial piety (Ho, 1990). However, cohesion can also be viewed as reflecting a familial response to external pressures on the family. For example, an immigrant family that is coping with adaptation to American society or racism can find solace, strength, succor, and identity by affiliating closely within the family (Uba, 1994). The emphasis on cohesion could also reflect the historical need for all members of an Asian American family to work together and cooperate to contribute to the financial support and functioning of the family. Therefore, a critical perspective that incorporates external forces, such as racism, can provide a broader explanation than can a cultural perspective.

COMMONALITIES AND DIFFERENCES AMONG ASIAN AMERICAN FAMILIES

Asian Americans come from all social classes and occupations, including physicians, teachers, businesspersons, custodians, farmers, and laborers. Yet, they have collectively acquired the image of highly successful immigrants (Kitano & Daniels, 1988). Their low rates of divorce and juvenile delinquency and high rates of intergenerational coresidence and children's educational and occupational success corroborate the picture of the Asian American family as being the "ideal family" (Ishii-Kuntz, 1993, 1997a, 1997c). Although these images refer to Asian Americans as a group, in reality, it is difficult to define *Asian Americans* because they come from diverse backgrounds. Social scientists often perpetuate these images by referring to Asian Americans as a single entity and emphasizing their similarities. These similarities are based not merely on Asian Americans' appearance and countries of origin, but their individual and family experiences in the United States, where all Asian Americans share the Asian minority status. Next, I discuss the commonalities and differences in the experiences of Asian American families, using gender, race, and class as dimensions for organizing my discussion. I also compare the family experiences of Asian Americans with those of other populations in the United States.

Commonalities

Asian Americans share many experiences that have affected their family structures and relationships. First, despite their passive image, Asian American women have commonly played a central role in their families. For example, they have been extremely active in maintaining culture by transmitting folk legends and family histories to children (Glenn & Yap, 1994). As portrayed in Amy Tan's novel, *Joy Luck Club,* ties between Asian American women, especially mothers and daughters, are the bonds that hold families together. Asian American women were and are the kin keepers—the vital links between families and schools, churches, and ethnic and such immigrant organizations as *Kenjinkai* (an association comprised of immigrants from the same prefecture in Japan) (Nakano, 1990). They are active in the community, partly because they see such activity as an extension of their responsibilities as mothers (Yap, 1989).

It is also important to recognize that except for a few refugee-turned-immigrant groups, Asian American women are active in the labor force (Takagi, 1994). According to the 1990 U.S. census, approximately 60% of Asian American women aged 16 and over (and 72.3% of Filipino women) participated in the labor force, compared to 56% of the women in the general population (U.S. Bureau of the Census, 1993). Although the average earnings of Asian American women still lag far behind those of men, the high labor force participation of Asian American women has created greater economic equality between men and women in the families. Greater economic equality, in turn, offers women the possibility of a greater choice in partnerships and less dependence in marriage.

However, it is important to acknowledge that Asian American women's high labor force participation also reflects the fact that more Asian American women are compelled to work because the male members of their families earn such low wages (Espiritu, 1996). Employed Asian American women have a higher median income than do employed white women, but as a group they also have superior educational qualifications and live in localities in which wages are higher (Chan, 1991). Despite their generally high educational level, Asian American women receive lower returns for their education than do white women, and the disparity between their returns and those of white men is even greater (Barringer et al., 1993; Yamanaka & McClelland, 1994). For example, among highly educated women, both Asian American and white women faced a gender gap, earning only about 70% of the salaries of white men with similar backgrounds. But Asian American women fared worse than their white counterparts: Only 31% of Asian Americans, compared with 48% of whites were professionals, and 19% of Asian Americans versus 23% of whites were in the managerial class (Ong & Hee, 1994). In other words, the earnings and career positions of Asian American women are not commensurate with their years of schooling.

Second, although contemporary Asian immigrants obviously differ from the descendants of the first wave of Asian immigrants in several significant ways, both groups face or have faced considerable antagonism and racial discrimination in the United States. The Chinese were the first group of Asians who were faced with insurmountable hostility in the United States (Chan, 1991; Ishii-Kuntz, 1997a). Although many Chinese Americans overcame the hostility by achieving educational and occupational success, various forms of discrimination still exist (Chan, 1991). Post-1965 immigrants, many of whom are refugees from Southeast Asia, continue to experience hostility from host communities in the United States (Chan, 1991). The case of the Hmong who settled in Wisconsin is a good example of such hostility; numerous anti-Hmong incidents have been reported, including hostile telephone calls and violent crimes against Hmong families (Hein, 1994).

The increase in hate crimes against Asian Americans as individuals or groups (Takaki, 1989), indicates that high levels of racial antagonism persist. For example, hostility and hatred toward Japanese in the United States surfaced in the 1982 murder of Vincent Chin, a Chinese American in Detroit who was beaten to death by two white men, an auto worker and his stepson, after they mistakenly believed Chin was Japanese (Chan, 1991). In 1990, a group of white men in La Crosse, Wisconsin, beat two Japanese exchange students who they believed to be Hmong (Hein, 1994). From these cases, it is clear that any Asian American can become a target of hostility because many Americans make no effort to distinguish among Asian American groups.

In addition to individuals and national-origin groups, Asian American families have also been subjected to external hostility. A cultural theorist may explain strong bonds in Asian American families by emphasizing group harmony and the solidarity of Asian cultures. However, when external hostilities against Asian Americans are considered, these strong bonds are created not because of cultural values alone, but as mechanisms for surviving in American society.

Many Asian American families have also been strongly embedded in the supportive networks of their ethnic communities. For example, in the early 1900s, Asian ethnic communities played an integral part in the lives of families by providing support for newly arrived immigrants and families who were

experiencing hardships, such as poverty or the death of an immediate family member (Yanagisako, 1985). These networks can be seen as a product of Asian Americans' common experience of facing hostility in the host country and as a collective mechanism for resisting such hostility.

Third, the model-minority image adds a tremendous amount of pressure for high academic achievement among Asian American children and their families. For instance, parents' and teachers' expectations that Asian American children will excel in the classroom increases the stress that these children feel. In fact, suicide rates among Asian American youths tend to be much higher than those of European American youths. Yu, Chang, Liu, and Fernandez (1989) reported that suicide accounts for 16.8% and 19% of the deaths of 15-to 24-year-old Chinese and Japanese Americans, respectively, compared with 11.9% of the deaths of European Americans in the same age group.

In addition, few Asian American families use mental health and other counseling services (Gim, Atkinson, & Kim, 1991; Gim, Atkinson, & Whiteley, 1990). Their failure to do so may be due, in part, to the fact that many professionals tend to consider Asian American families "problem-free" and that Asian American families are likely to believe that their problems should be solved within their families.

Differences

In this section, I review the literature that points to intraethnic differences among Asian American families. First, with regard to class differences, there is a considerable gap between highly educated and disadvantaged Asian American families (Espiritu, 1996; Toji & Johnson, 1992). Japanese and Chinese Americans are reported to have achieved economic parity with European Americans (Wong & Hirschman, 1983), but studies of Southeast Asian refugees in the United States have painted a gloomier picture (Chan, 1991; Haines, 1986; Uba, 1994). In California, where some 40% of the Southeast Asian refugees live, about half remain on public assistance (Chan, 1991). The gap in economic standing is also clear. In 1990, whereas only 3.4% of Japanese, 5.2%

of Filipino, and 11.1% of Chinese families in the United States were living in poverty, the comparable figures for Vietnamese, Cambodians, Laotians, and Hmong were 23.8%, 42.1%, 32.2%, and 61.8%, respectively (U.S. Bureau of the Census, 1993). Family functions and relationships among these refugee families are constrained by severe economic hardship.

Second, Asian American families' experiences differ significantly, depending on the recency of immigration. Except for the Japanese American population, only 32.4% of whom are foreign born, more than half the Chinese (69.3%), Filipino (64.4%), Korean (72.7%), and Vietnamese (79.9%) in the United States are foreign born (U.S. Bureau of the Census, 1993). Such high proportions of recent immigrants have significant implications for family organization, community stability, and integration among Asian American populations, as well as for their economic progress in American society. It is not surprising that in many recently immigrated families, the main languages used at home are most likely not to be English. For example, in 84% of Chinese, 81.6% of Korean, and 93.8% of Vietnamese American households, the primary language spoken was their native language (U.S. Bureau of the Census, 1993). Immigrant parents with limited English ability are disadvantaged in various ways. For instance, children who learn English much more quickly than their parents frequently play the role of facilitator and translator for their parents, increasing the newly arrived Asian parents' dependence on them (Chan, 1991).

The recency of immigration has a significant impact on family structure and relationships as well. In general, the percentage of extended family households decreases with the duration of residence in the United States (Barringer et al., 1993). According to the 1990 census, Vietnamese Americans reported a much larger percentage of other relatives living in their households than did other Asian American groups. Marital stability is also negatively related to the duration of residence, with Japanese Americans exhibiting a higher divorce rate than other Asian American groups (Barringer et al., 1993). Takagi (1994) also noted that the greater economic independence of Japanese American

women may be one explanation for the higher percentage of divorced Japanese women than men. In addition, a higher rate of interracial marriage is reported among more established Asian American groups, such as Japanese and Chinese, than among recent immigrants from Asia (Barringer et al., 1993; Kitano, 1994; Kitano & Kikumura, 1980). Asian Americans who recently immigrated to the United States also tend to rely on their family members for emotional support more frequently than do established Asian Americans (Haines, Rutherford, & Thomas, 1981; Kibria, 1994).

Furthermore, in Asian American populations, reasons for immigration are strongly related to social-class standing. Southeast Asian refugees, particularly the second-wave refugees who arrived after 1978, are a largely disadvantaged group. In a study of the economic progress of 11 immigrant groups, Chiswick (1979) concluded that refugees face the steepest barriers to achieving economic success because they are less likely to be a self-selected labor force than are economic migrants. Their numbers include many nonemployables: young children, the elderly, religious and political leaders, and people in poor mental and physical condition (Portes & Rumbaut, 1990). Many refugee-turned-immigrant families live in poverty (Toji & Johnson, 1992). Because economic hardship has serious consequences for white parents and children in that it decreases the quality of marriages (Conger, Ge, & Lorenz, 1994) and increases children's productive roles in family economics (Elder, Foster, & Ardelt, 1994), it can be speculated that immigrant families in poverty experience many similar family problems and dynamics.

Comparisons With Other American Families

When ethnic minority families are studied, they are frequently compared with American families of European origin. In fact, scholars who conduct studies on ethnic minority issues with no comparative white samples or populations are often criticized (Stanfield, 1993). The emphasis on such comparisons makes it necessary for many researchers to apply theories and methodologies that have been used to study European American families (Ishii-

Kuntz, 1994b). Research on Asian Americans and their families has been no exception. Comparisons between European Americans and Asian Americans have been particularly popular in studies of assimilation and acculturation (see, for example, Hirschman & Wong, 1981; Nee & Wong, 1985). In these studies, Asian Americans' educational and economic achievements have been compared with those of whites. These comparisons are insightful, but they fail to identify the problems and experiences that Asian Americans and their families share with families of other ethnic minority groups.

First, although they are less diverse in composition than Asian American populations, both African American and Latino populations are characterized by a variety of subgroups, cultures, and nationalities. African American populations include sizable numbers of Haitian, Jamaican, Trinidadian, other West Indian, and African peoples, and Latino populations include Mexicans, Puerto Ricans, Cubans, Dominicans, Salvadorians, Columbians, and other Central and South Americans. Therefore, as is the case with Asian American families, it is difficult to describe "the African American family's" or "the Latino family's" experiences (see Chapters 12 and 13 in this book). For example, intraethnic diversity is found in the degree of male-dominated authority in Asian American and Latino families as Baca Zinn (1994) and Chow (1987) noted; earlier studies described both Asian American and Latino families as male-dominated, with fathers having absolute power over family members. More recent writings (such as Baca Zinn, 1994; Glenn & Yap, 1994; Takagi, 1994) have refuted this stereotype. Moreover, the degree of male domination in the family varies considerably across Asian American and Latino populations and is more commonly found among recent immigrant families in both Asian and Latino populations.

Second, the alteration in traditional family functioning and organization among many minority families is a result of the external hostility that these families have commonly experienced. How the extreme form of hostility influenced minority families is illustrated in African American slavery and Japanese American internment. Although these two events occurred in different periods of American history, their eventual impact on African American and Japanese American families has been similar. Jones (1985) contended that egalitarianism in African American family functioning is a legacy of slavery, during which the traditional gender division of labor was largely ignored by slaveholders, and African American men and women were equal in the sense that neither sex wielded economic power over the other. Likewise, it can be argued that the breakdown of traditional gender roles among Japanese American families was facilitated by their internment during World War II. Several scholars (see, for example, Broom & Kitsuse, 1956; Osako, 1976) have pointed out that Japanese Americans' internment experience chipped away the internal structure of prewar Japanese American families. For example, Issei (first-generation) parental authority that existed before the war was further undermined by the loss of status and authority of the unemployed Issei in the internment camps. As a result, the Nisei (second-generation) children, both boys and girls, were granted more independence in social activities in the camps. In contrast to Issei families, younger Nisei families are characterized by relative egalitarianism, shared decision making, and companionship between husbands and wifes (Glenn, 1986). Thus, the breakdown in traditional family organization can be traced to internment and related sociohistorical events.

Third, within each ethnic minority population, there are considerable differences among the subgroups in socioeconomic status. Despite overall progress, improvements in the economic status of African Americans over the past 25 years have been uneven, which has created greater diversity in African American communities and accentuated differences in socioeconomic status (Taylor, 1994). Whereas some segments of the African American community made dramatic economic gains relative to general European American populations during this period, others fell further behind (Farley, 1984). A similar gap is found among Asian American populations: More established groups, such as Japanese and Chinese, have higher socioeconomic status while many groups of refugee-turned-immigrants, such as Hmongs, live in poverty. Thus, African American and Asian American families are increasingly divided into two groups: affluent "middle class" families, composed of better educated individuals who are moving into high-status occupations that guarantee economic security and a prosperous lifestyle, and "underclass" families, composed of individuals who are locked in a vicious circle of poverty, intermittent employment, and dependence on welfare (Espiritu, 1996; Wilson, 1987).

Fourth, Asian American women share similar experiences with other ethnic minority women in educational attainment and labor force participation. Although Asian American women earn considerably less than do their male counterparts, they have become increasingly better educated and earn more money than their peers in previous generations (Espiritu, 1996). This trend is also seen among Latina and African American women (Baca Zinn, 1994; Taylor, 1994). At the same time, Asian American women in disadvantaged families share similar experiences with their African American and Latina counterparts. That is, like many ethnic, poor, and working-class women, disadvantaged Asian women view employment as an opportunity to raise their families' living standards, not as the path to fulfillment or even upward mobility idealized by the white feminist movement (Espiritu, 1996). Hence, employment is viewed as an extension of their family obligations—of their roles as mothers and wives (Kim & Hurh, 1988; Romero, 1992).

Finally, the percentage of extended family households among ethnic minority families is higher than that of white families. According to the 1990 U.S. census (U.S. Bureau of the census, 1992), among Asian Americans, Vietnamese reported the largest percentage (14.3%) and Japanese reported the lowest percentage (4.8%) of other relatives in the household. These figures were appreciably higher than for whites (3.3%), but African Americans (9.5%) and Latinos (7.2%) fell somewhere between.

INTERSECTIONS OF RACE, GENDER, AND CLASS

The problems of race, gender, and class are closely intertwined in the lives of Asian American men, women, and children. To examine in greater detail how the intersections of gender, class, and race affect Asian American families, I describe the experiences of Asian American women in the disadvantaged class.

As I discussed earlier, the contemporary Asian American population includes a sizable proportion of men and women with little education, poor skills, and little or no ability to speak English. According to the 1990 U.S. census, 18% of Asian American men and 26% of Asian American women aged 25 and over had less than a high school diploma. The median income for those with less than a high school diploma was $18,000 for the men and $15,000 for the women in 1990. A large segment of this disadvantaged population, even when employed full time, full year, had less than $10,000 in earnings (Ong & Hee, 1994). The disadvantaged Asian American population is largely a product of immigration: Almost 90% of them are immigrants (Ong & Hee, 1994).

Of these immigrants, Southeast Asian refugees, particularly the second wave of refugees who arrived after 1978, are severely disadvantaged. In 1990, the overall economic status of Southeast Asian Americans was characterized by unstable, minimum-wage employment; dependence on welfare; and participation in the informal economy (Gold & Kibria, 1993). Furthermore, the majority has less than a high school diploma (64%) and the highest rates of joblessness of any Asian American group (33% for men and 58% for women). In addition, Southeast Asian Americans have the highest rate of dependence on welfare of any ethnic or racial group in the United States (Ong & Umemoto, 1994).

The typical pattern of a disadvantaged dual-worker family is a husband who works as waiter, cook, janitor, or store helper and a wife who works for a garment shop or on an assembly line (Espiritu, 1996). It is interesting that while the most disadvantaged Asian American men have extremely limited choices of jobs, their wives seem to have more employment options. Among these options, the garment industry is a top employer, followed by the microelectronics industry and food canneries. In these labor-intensive industries, immigrant women are more employable than men because of the patri-archal and racist assumptions that women can afford to work for less, do not mind dead-end jobs, and are more suited physiologically to certain kinds of detailed and routine work.

Because immigrant men are unable to earn suffi-cient incomes, women's earnings make up an equal or greater share (than men's) of the family income. Because the wages each earn are low, only by pool-ing incomes can a husband and wife earn enough to support a family (Glenn, 1983). These shifts in resources have challenged the patriarchal authority of Asian immigrant men (Luu, 1989), but they have not resulted in a restructuring of the old family sys-tem (Kibria, 1993). That is, Asian immigrants still believe that men should be the heads of households, despite the economic contributions of women. In her study of Vietnamese American families, Kibria (1993) argued that Vietnamese American women (and children) walk an "ideological tightrope," struggling both to preserve the traditional family system and to enhance their power within their fam-ilies. According to Kibria, the traditional family system is valuable to Vietnamese American women because it offers them economic protection and gives them authority, as mothers, over the younger generation.

For many disadvantaged Asian American women, the family and the traditional patriarchy within it are simultaneously a base of resistance to racial and class oppression and an instrument for gender subordination (Glenn, 1986). Constrained by their social-structural location in the dominant society, disadvantaged Asian American women may accept certain components of the old male-domination system to have strong, intact families—an important source of support to sustain them in the world of wage labor (Glenn, 1986). These women also preserve the traditional family system, though in a tempered form, because they value the promise of male economic protection. Although migration may have equalized the economic resources of working-class men and women, women's earnings continue to be too meager to sus-tain women's independence from men (Kibria, 1993).

The experiences of the most disadvantaged Asian American women show that the family serves as a place both to generate power to fight against external oppression and to perpetuate gender inequality. Although these images seem to be con-tradictory, they are routinely and socially con-structed in the women's daily lives. For the most economically disadvantaged women, their family lives and gender relations are structured largely by economic constraints as well as cultural factors.

CONCLUSIONS

It is difficult to speak of a singular Asian American family experience. A narrow definition of the fam-ily thus cannot be applied when describing various forms and experiences of Asian American families. In addition, this family diversity cannot be fully explained using a cultural theory that assumes that family experiences among Asian Americans are homogeneous. If cultural norms and values are shared by Asians Americans, as a cultural theorist would assume, one could expect only slight varia-tions across gender, class, and race among Asian Americans. In contrast, critical and feminist theo-ries provide an opportunity to view Asian American family diversity as it is affected by gender, class, race and other forms of social stratification.

In tracing the diversity within Asian American families, I discussed several important forms of diversity. One is that the formation and mainte-nance of Asian American families have been pro-foundly influenced by the immigration history and external hostility that Asian Americans have faced in the United States. The associations between Japanese Americans' wartime internment and the breakdown of the family organization and the influ-ence of immigration on the disadvantaged lives of the Asian American underclass are two important examples.

Second, Asian American family diversity is reflected in the differential experiences of men and women in different social classes. As I discussed earlier, despite their increased resources many Southeast Asian refugee women are still reluctant to reject their husbands' authority. For disadvan-taged Asian American women, then, the family is a mechanism in which gender subordination is maintained. In contrast, middle-class Asian American women who are employed as professionals have a bargaining chip to negotiate for their husbands' greater involvement in household labor (Hondagneu-Sotelo, 1994; Kibria, 1993).

Asian Americans will experience further intraethnic diversity as rates of interracial marriage continue to increase and generational differences divide the experiences of immigrant parents and native-born children. For example, it is now diffi-

cult to describe a "typical" Japanese American family experience (Takagi, 1994), primarily because of a generational difference between Nisei and Sansei (third-generation) Japanese Americans and high rates of interracial marriage. Generational conflicts have also been reported among immigrant Korean parents and their Korean-born and native-raised children (Hurh, 1990). These changes indicate that each Asian American population will continue to experience its own family diversity.

REFERENCES

Ablon, J. (1976). The social organization for an urban Samoan community. In E. Gee (Ed.), *Counterpoint: Perspectives on Asian America* (pp. 401–412). Los Angeles: Regents of the University of California.

Allison, A. (1991). Japanese mothers and obentos: The lunch-box as ideological state apparatus. *Anthropological Quarterly, 64,* 195–208.

Baca Zinn, M. (1994). Adaptation and continuity in Mexican-origin families. In R. L. Taylor (Ed.), *Minority families in the United States: A multicultural perspective* (pp. 64–81). Englewood Cliffs, NJ: Prentice Hall.

Barringer, H. R., Gardner, R. W., & Levin, M. J. (1993). *Asian and Pacific Islanders in the United States.* New York: Russell Sage Foundation.

Broom, L., & Kitsuse, J. I. (1956). *The managed casualty.* Berkeley: University of California Press.

Caudill, W. (1952). Japanese-American personality and acculturation. *Genetic Psychology Monographs, 45,* 3–102.

Chan, C. S. (1989). Issues of identity development among Asian-American lesbians and gay men. *Journal of Counseling & Development, 68,* 16–20.

Chan, S. (1991). *Asian Americans: An interpretive history.* Boston: Twayne.

Chiba, A. (1985). *Chotto okashiizo, Nihonjin* [A bit strange, Japanese]. Tokyo: Shincho Bunko.

Chin, F., & Chan, J. P. (1972). Racist love. In R. Kostelanetz (Ed.), *Seeing through shuck* (pp. 65–79). New York: Ballantine Books.

Chiswick, B. (1979). The economic progress of immigrants: Some apparently universal patterns. In W. Fellner (Ed.), *Contemporary economic problems* (pp. 357–399). Washington, DC: American Enterprise Institute.

Chiu, L.-H. (1987). Child-rearing attitudes of Chinese, Chinese American, and Anglo-American mothers. *International Journal of Psychology, 22,* 409–419.

Chow, E. N.-L. (1987). The development of feminist consciousness among Asian American women. *Gender and Society, 1,* 284–299.

Conger, R. D., Ge, X.-J., & Lorenz, F. O. (1994). Economic stress and marital relations. In R. D. Conger & G. H. Elder, Jr. (Eds.), *Families in troubled times: Adapting to change in rural America* (pp. 187–203). New York: Aldine De Gruyter.

Connor, J. W. (1974). Acculturation and family continuities in three generations of Japanese Americans. *Journal of Marriage and the Family, 36,* 159–165.

Connor, J. W. (1976). Persistence and change in Japanese American value orientations. *Ethos, 4,* 1–44.

Connor, J. W. (1977). *Tradition and change in three generations of Japanese Americans.* Chicago: Nelson-Hall.

Crosbie-Burnett, M., Foster, T. L., Murray, C. I., & Bowen, G. L. (1996). Gays and lesbians' families of origin: A social-cognitive-behavioral model of adjustment. *Family Relations, 45,* 397–403.

Elder, G. H., Jr., Foster, E. M., & Ardelt, M. (1994). Children in the household economy. In R. D. Conger & G. H. Elder, Jr. (Eds.), *Families in troubled times: Adapting to change in rural America* (pp. 127–146). New York: Aldine De Gruyter.

Espiritu, Y. L. (1996). *Asian American women and men.* Thousand Oaks, CA: Pine Forge Press.

Farley, R. (1984). *Blacks and whites: Narrowing the gap.* Cambridge, MA: Harvard University Press.

Ferree, M. M. (1990). Beyond separate spheres: Feminism and family research. *Journal of Marriage and the Family, 52,* 866–884.

Fong, S. (1973). Assimilation and changing social roles of Chinese Americans. *Journal of Social Issues, 29,* 115–127.

Gim, R. H., Atkinson, D. R., & Kim, S. (1991). Asian American acculturation, counselor ethnicity and cultural sensitivity, and rating of counselor. *Journal of Counseling Psychology, 38,* 57–62.

Gim, R. H., Atkinson, D. R., & Whiteley, S. (1990). Asian-American acculturation, severity of concerns, and willingness to see a counselor. *Journal of Counseling Psychology, 37,* 281–285.

Glenn, E. N. (1983). Split household, small producer and dual wage earner: An analysis of Chinese-American family strategies. *Journal of Marriage and the Family, 45,* 35–46.

Glenn, E. N. (1986). *Issei, Nisei, war bride: Three generations of Japanese women in domestic service.* Philadelphia: Temple University Press.

Glenn, E. N. (1987). Gender and the family. In B. Hess & M. M. Ferree (Eds.), *Analyzing gender* (pp. 348–380). Newbury Park, CA: Sage.

Glenn, E. N., & Yap, S. G. H. (1994). Chinese American families. In R. L. Taylor (Ed.), *Minority families in the United States: A multicultural perspective* (pp. 115–145). Englewood Cliffs, NJ: Prentice Hall.

Gold, S., & Kibria, N. (1993). Vietnamese refugees and blocked mobility. *Asian and Pacific Migration Review, 2,* 27–56.

Goldani, A. M. (1990). Changing Brazilian families and the consequent need for public policy. *International Social Science Journal, 42,* 523–538.

Haines, D. (1986). Vietnamese women in the labor force: Continuity or change? In R. J. Simon & C. B. Brettell (Eds.), *International migration: The female experience* (pp. 62–75). Totowa, NJ: Rowman & Allenheld.

Haines, D., Rutherford, D., & Thomas, P. (1981). Family and community among Vietnamese refugees. *International Migration Review, 15,* 310–319.

Hein, J. (1994). From migrant to minority: Hmong refugees and the social construction of identity in the United States. *Sociological Inquiry, 64,* 281–306.

Hirschman, C., & Wong, M. G. (1981). Trends in socioeconomic achievement among immigrant and native-born Asian-Americans, 1960–1976. *Sociological Quarterly, 22,* 495–514.

Ho, C. K. (1990). An analysis of domestic violence in Asian American communities: A multicultural approach to counseling. *Women and Therapy, 9,* 129–150.

Ho, M.-K. (1976). Social work with Asian Americans. *Social Casework, 57,* 195–201.

Hom, A. Y. (1994). Stories from the homefront: Perspectives of Asian American parents with lesbian daughters and gay sons. *Amerasia, 20,* 19–32.

Hondagneu-Sotelo, P. (1994). *Gendered transition: Mexican experiences in immigration.* Berkeley: University of California Press.

Hsu, J., Tseng, W-S., Ashton, G., McDermott, J., Jr., & Char, W. (1985). Family interaction patterns among Japanese-American and Caucasian families in Hawaii. *American Journal of Psychiatry, 142,* 577–581.

Huang, L. N., & Ying, Y.-W. (1989). Chinese American children and adolescents. In J. T. Gibbs, L. N. Huang, & Associates (Eds.), *Children of color: Psychological interventions with minority children* (pp. 30–66). San Francisco: Jossey-Bass.

Hurh, W. M. (1990). The 1.5 generation: A paragon of Korean-American pluralism. *Korean Culture, 22,* 21–30.

Immigration and Naturalization Service. (1995). *Statistical yearbook of the Immigration and Naturalization Service.* Washington, DC: U.S. Government Printing Office.

Ishii-Kuntz, M. (1993, November). *Intergenerational relationships among Asian Americans.* Paper presented at the annual meeting of the National Council on Family Relations, Baltimore, MD.

Ishii-Kuntz, M. (1994a). The Japanese father: Work demands and family roles. In J. C. Hood (Ed.), *Men, work and family* (pp. 45–67). Newbury Park, CA: Sage.

Ishii-Kuntz, M. (1994b, November). *Methodological challenges to studying ethnic minority families.* Paper presented at the annual meeting of the National Council on Family Relations, Minneapolis, MN.

Ishii-Kuntz, M. (1994c). Shin Issei and their adaptation to American society. *Orange Network, 2,* 1–20.

Ishii-Kuntz, M. (1997a). Chinese American families. In M. K. DeGenova (Ed.), *Families in cultural perspective* (pp. 109–130). San Francisco: Mayfield.

Ishii-Kuntz, M. (1997b). Intergenerational relationships among Chinese, Japanese, and Korean Americans. *Family Relations, 46,* 23–32.

Ishii-Kuntz, M. (1997c). Japanese American families. In M. K. DeGenova (Ed.), *Families in cultural perspective* (pp. 131–153). San Francisco: Mayfield.

Jiobu, R. (1988). *Ethnicity and assimilation: Blacks, Chinese, Filipinos, Japanese, Koreans, Mexicans, Vietnamese, and whites.* Albany: State University of New York Press.

Johnson, C. L. (1977). Interdependence, reciprocity and indebtedness: An analysis of Japanese American kinship relations. *Journal of Marriage and the Family, 39,* 351–363.

Jones, J. (1985). *Labor of love, labor of sorrow: Black women, work, and the family from slavery to the present.* New York: Basic Books.

Kamo, Y., & Zhou, M. (1994). Living arrangements of elderly Chinese and Japanese in the United States.

Journal of Marriage and the Family, 56, 544–558.

Kibria, N. (1993). *Family tightrope: The changing lives of Vietnamese Americans.* Princeton, NJ: Princeton University Press.

Kibria, N. (1994). Vietnamese families in the United States. In R. L. Taylor (Ed.), *Minority families in the United States: A multicultural perspective* (pp. 164–176). Englewood Cliffs, NJ: Prentice Hall.

Kim, K., & Hurh, W. M. (1988). The burden of double roles: Korean wives in the U.S.A. *Ethnic and Racial Studies, 11,* 151–167.

Kim, S. (1991). Cultural and other factors in assessing Asian-Americans. *California Psychologist, 24,* 14, 22.

Kitano, H. H. (1994, May). *Recent trends in Japanese American interracial marriage.* Paper presented at the Center for Family Studies Lecture Series. University of California, Riverside.

Kitano, H. H., & Daniels, R. (1988). *Asian Americans: Emerging minorities.* Englewood Cliffs, NJ: Prentice Hall.

Kitano, H. H., & Kikumura, A. (1980). The Japanese American family. In R. Endo, S. Sue, & N. Wagner (Eds.), *Asian-Americans: Social and psychological perspectives* (pp. 3–16). Palo Alto, CA: Science and Behavior Books.

Lebra, T. S. (1982). *Japanese patterns of behavior.* Honolulu: University of Hawaii Press.

Lee, E. (1982). Inpatient psychiatric services for Southeast Asian refugees. In T. Owan (Ed.), *Southeast Asian mental health. Treatment, prevention, services, training, and research* (pp. 307–327). Washington, DC: U.S. Department of Health and Human Services.

Lee, J., & Cynn, V. (1991). Issues in counseling 1.5 generation of Korean Americans. In C. Lee & B. Richardson (Eds.), *Multicultural issues in counseling: New approaches to diversity* (pp. 127–140). Alexandria, VA: American Association for Counseling and Development.

Leonetti, D. (1983). *Nisei aging project report.* Seattle: University of Washington Press.

Luu, V. (1989). The hardships of escape for Vietnamese women. In Asian Women United of California (Ed.), *Making waves: An anthology of writings by and about Asian American women* (pp. 60–72). Boston: Beacon Press.

Marciano, T., & Sussman, M. B. (1991). Wider families: An overview. In T. Marciano & M. B. Sussman (Eds.), *Wider families: New traditional family forms* (pp. 1–8). New York: Haworth Press.

McDermott, J. F., Char, W., Robillard, A., Hsu, J., Tseng, W.-S., & Ashton, G. (1984). Cultural variations in family attitudes and their implications for therapy. In S. Chess & A. Thomas (Eds.), *Annual progress in child psychiatry and child development* (pp. 145–154). New York: Brunner/Mazel.

Min, J., & Min, P. G. (1992, August). *The relationship between Korean immigrant parents and children.* Paper presented at the annual meeting of the American Sociological Association. Pittsburgh, PA.

Morris, T. (1990). Culturally sensitive family assessment. *Family Process, 29,* 105–116.

Nakano, M. (1990). *Japanese American women: Three generations 1890–1990.* Berkeley, CA: Mina Press.

Nee, V., & Wong, H. Y. (1985). Asian American socioeconomic achievement: The strength of the family bond. *Sociological Perspectives, 28,* 281–306.

Nihira, K., Mink, I., & Shapiro, C. (1991). *Home environment of developmentally disabled children: A comparison between Euro-American and Asian-American families.* Paper presented at the biennial meeting of the Society for Research in Child Development, Seattle, WA.

Ong, P., & Hee, S. (1994). Economic diversity. In P. Ong (Ed.), *The state of Asian Pacific America: Economic diversity, issues, and policies* (pp. 31–56). Los Angeles: LEAP Asian Pacific American Public Policy Institute and University of California at Los Angeles, Asian American Studies Center.

Ong, P., & Umemoto, K. (1994). Life and work in the inner-city. In P. Ong (Ed.), *The state of Asian Pacific America: Economic diversity, issues, and policies* (pp. 87–112). Los Angeles: LEAP Asian Pacific American Public Policy Institute and University of California at Los Angeles, Asian American Studies Center.

Osako, M. M. (1976). International relations as an aspect of assimilation: The case of Japanese Americans. *Sociological Inquiry, 46,* 67–72.

Osako, M. M., & Wong, H. Z. (1986). Intergenerational relations and the aged among Japanese Americans. *Research on Aging, 8,* 128–155.

Portes, A., & Rumbaut, R. B. (1990). *Immigrant America: A portrait.* Berkeley: University of California Press.

Risman, B. (1987). Intimate relationships from a micro-structural perspective: Men who mother. *Gender and Society, 2,* 58–81.

Romero, M. (1992). *Maid in the U.S.A.* New York: Routledge.

Santos, R. A. (1983). The social and emotional development of Filipino-American children. In G. Powell (Ed.), *The psychosocial development of minority group children* (pp. 131–146). New York: Brunner/Mazel.

Shon, S., & Ja, D. (1982). Asian families. In M.

McGoldrick, J. Pearce, & J. Giordano (Eds.), *Ethnicity and family therapy* (pp. 208–229). New York: Guilford Press.

Shu, R., & Satele, A. (1977). *The Samoan community in southern California: Conditions and needs.* Chicago: Asian American Mental Health Training Center.

Stanfield, J. H., II. (1993). Epistemological considerations. In J. H. Stanfield, II, & R. M. Dennis (Eds.), *Race and ethnicity in research methods* (pp. 16–36). Newbury Park, CA: Sage.

Sue, D. (1989a). Ethnic identity: The impact of two cultures on the psychological development of Asians in America. In D. Atkinson, G. Morton, & D. W. Sue (Eds.), *Counseling American minorities: A cross-cultural perspective* (pp. 103–115). Dubuque, IA: W. C. Brown.

Sue, D. (1989b). Racial/cultural identity development among Asian Americans: Counseling/therapy implications. *Journal of the Asian American Psychological Association, 13,* 80–86.

Sue, D. W., & Kirk, B. (1973). Differential characteristics of Japanese-American and Chinese-American college students. *Journal of Counseling Psychology, 20,* 142–148.

Sue, S., & Morishima, J. (1982). *The mental health of Asian Americans.* San Francisco: Jossey-Bass.

Sung, B. L. (1990). Chinese American intermarriage. *Journal of Comparative Family Studies, 21,* 337–352.

Takagi, D. Y. (1994). Japanese American families. In R. L. Taylor (Ed.), *Minority families in the United States: A multicultural perspective* (pp. 146–163). Englewood Cliffs, NJ: Prentice Hall.

Takaki, R. (1989). *Strangers from a different shore: A history of Asian Americans.* New York: Penguin.

Taylor, R. L. (1994). Black American families. In R. L. Taylor (Ed.), *Minority families in the United States: A multicultural perspective* (pp. 19–46). Englewood Cliffs, NJ: Prentice Hall.

Thompson, L., & Walker, A. (1989). Gender in families: Women and men in marriage, work, and parenthood. *Journal of Marriage and the Family, 51,* 845–871.

Toji, D. S., & Johnson, J. H. (1992). Asian and Pacific Islander American poverty: The working poor and the jobless poor. *Amerasia, 18,* 83–91.

Tsui, P., & Schultz, G. (1988). Ethnic factors in group process: Cultural dynamics in multi-ethnic therapy groups. *American Journal of Orthopsychiatry, 58,* 136–142.

Uba, L. (1994). *Asian Americans: Personality patterns, identity, and mental health.* New York: Guilford Press.

U.S. Bureau of the Census. (1992). *Statistical abstract of the United States: 1992* (112th ed.). Washington, DC: U.S. Government Printing Office.

U.S. Bureau of the Census. (1993). *We the American Asians.* Washington, DC: U.S. Government Printing Office.

West, C., & Zimmerman, D. (1987). Doing gender. *Gender and Society, 1,* 125–151.

Wilson, W. J. (1987). *The truly disadvantaged.* Chicago: University of Chicago Press.

Wong, M. G., & Hirschman, C. (1983). Labor force participation and socioeconomic attainment of Asian-American women. *Sociological Perspectives, 26,* 423–446.

Wooden, W. S., Kawasaki, H., & Mayeda, R. (1983). Lifestyles and identity maintenance among gay Japanese-American males. *Alternative Lifestyles, 5,* 236–243.

Yamamoto, J., & Kubota, M. (1983). The Japanese-American family. In G. Powell (Ed.), *The psychosocial development of minority group children* (pp. 237–247). New York: Brunner/Mazel.

Yamanaka, K., & McClelland, K. (1994). Earning the model-minority image: Diverse strategies of economic adaptation by Asian-American women. *Ethnic and Racial Studies, 17,* 79–114.

Yanagisako, S. J. (1985). *Transforming the past: Tradition and kinship among Japanese Americans.* Stanford, CA: Stanford University Press.

Yao, E. (1985). A comparison of family characteristics of Asian-American and Anglo-American high achievers. *International Journal of Comparative Sociology, 26,* 198–208.

Yap, S. G. H. (1989). *Gather your strength, sisters: The emerging role of Chinese women community workers.* New York: AMS Press.

Yu, E., Chang, C-F., Liu, W., & Fernandez, M. (1989). Suicide among Asian American youth. In M. Feinleib (Ed.), *Report of the secretary's task force on youth suicide* (pp. 157–176). Washington, DC: U.S. Department of Health and Human Services.

Yu, K., & Kim, L. (1983). The growth and development of Korean-American children. In G. Powell (Ed.), *The psychosocial development of minority group children* (pp. 147–158). New York: Brunner/Mazel.

PART VI
Class Diversities in Families

CHAPTER **15**

Poverty and Economic Hardship in Families

MARK R. RANK

One of the primary goals of this Handbook is to describe and understand the diverse range of family experiences and the family members who make up such experiences. The households discussed in these chapters represent a richness of familial variation. Yet there is an experience that can touch virtually all of the families discussed—poverty. Regardless of a family's race, age, or structure, poverty and economic hardship can penetrate its boundaries. At the same time, poverty is more likely to be experienced by those households falling outside the often referenced category of white, married couple households. In other words, poverty is an experience that is particularly relevant for many of the families and individuals examined in this Handbook.

Poverty is also one of the most far-reaching social issues in the United States. Whether the discussion revolves around the use of welfare, racial inequalities, single-parent families, educational inequities, infant mortality, or a host of other topics, poverty underlies each one. Ultimately, it is one of the great challenges that our society (and all societies) must face. How we confront this challenge depends, to a large extent, upon an accurate assessment of its condition and causes.

Finally, the existence of poverty in an affluent society, such as the United States, is troubling. The fact that a sizable number of American families and individuals are touched by poverty should be disquieting to those concerned about the principles of fairness, equity, and justice. For these reasons, I have developed and sustained my interest in poverty.

The purpose of this chapter is to provide an overview of poverty's terrain as it affects American families. Several questions are examined: (1) How is poverty measured? (2) How has the landscape of poverty changed over time? (3) How long and often are households poor? (4) Who are the poor? (5) How does the United States compare with other countries in regard to poverty? (6) What is the human meaning of poverty? and (7) What impact does poverty have upon family dynamics? To conclude, I provide a brief conceptual framework in which to place the answers to these questions.

HOW IS POVERTY MEASURED?

By its very definition, poverty represents a lack or absence of essential resources. Webster (1996) defines *poverty* in three complementary ways: "1. the state or condition of having little or no money, goods, or means of support; 2. deficiency of necessary or desirable ingredients, qualities, etc.; 3. scantiness; insufficiency."

Assuming we could roughly agree on these definitions, how is such a level determined? Until President Lyndon Johnson's declared War on Poverty in 1964, the United States had no measure of poverty. The task of devising such a standard fell on Molly Orshansky—an economist who was then working for the Social Security Administration—to devise the country's yardstick for measuring poverty (see Fisher, 1992, and Orshansky, 1965, for a descriptive history of her approach; for extended discussions on various ways of measuring poverty, see Haveman, 1993; Mayer & Jencks, 1989; "Measuring Poverty," 1995; National Research Council, 1995; Renwick & Bergmann, 1993; Ruggles, 1990, 1992; Sycheva, 1997; Vaughan, 1993; Walker, 1994).

The tack that Orshansky chose was consistent with Webster's definition. That is, she conceptualized poverty as the failure to have the income necessary to purchase a basic basket of goods and services that allows for a minimally decent level of existence. The way that this level of existence was (and still is) calculated is straightforward. One begins by estimating the household costs of obtaining a minimally adequate diet during the course of the year. Orshansky considered four food plans developed by the U.S. Department of Agriculture (in 1961) to calculate what a minimal diet would cost. The most frugal, entitled the Economy Food Plan, was eventually chosen. The cost of this minimal diet is then multiplied by 3. The result is a figure that represents the official poverty line. The reason for using 3 as a multiplier is that Orshansky relied on a 1955 U.S. Department of Agriculture survey showing that families with three or more persons spent approximately one third of their income on food and the remaining two thirds on other such items as clothing, housing, and heating.

To illustrate this procedure, in 1995 a family of four would need to spend $5,190 to purchase an adequately minimal diet. This figure is then multiplied by three ($5,190 * 3 = $15,569), which constitutes the official poverty line for a family of four. The logic in this example is that if $5,190 will purchase a subsistence diet for a family of four, then

the remaining $10,379 should provide enough income to purchase the other basic necessities needed to maintain a minimal level of existence.

The measuring stick to determine whether individuals fall above or below the poverty threshold is household, not family, income. According to the U.S. Bureau of the Census (1996c, p. A1), members of a household "consist of all persons who occupy a housing unit," whereas the term *family* "refers to a group of two or more persons related by birth, marriage, or adoption who reside together; all such persons are considered as members of one family." Throughout this chapter, both definitions are used in discussing the poverty stricken. In many cases they are one and the same—e.g., a three-person household consisting of a mother and her two children. In other cases, they are not. For example, a single man or woman living alone would constitute a household but not a family, according to the Census Bureau.

Several other points regarding the measurement of poverty are important. Each year the poverty levels are adjusted to take inflation into account. Obviously, it costs more to purchase a basic basket of goods today than it did 30 years ago. Second, when the measure of poverty was devised in 1964, it was backdated to 1959. Consequently, the official measurement of and trends in poverty began in 1959. Third, household income is based on annual income, calculated from pretax dollars, and does not include in-kind program benefits, such as Medicaid or food stamps. Fourth, the actual estimate of how many Americans fall below the poverty line is derived from the annual Current Population Survey of approximately 60,000 households, conducted by the U.S. Bureau of the Census. Fifth, the levels of poverty established each year do not differentiate between differences in the cost of living in various parts of the country. Finally, the monetary amount necessary for a small household's basic needs obviously differs from that required for a larger household; therefore, the poverty levels are adjusted for household size. For example, in 1995 the poverty level for a household of one was $7,763, while that of a household of nine or more was $31,280.

There is considerable debate as to whether these levels are set too low, too high, or just right. Those who argue that they are set too high point to the failure of the official measure to take into account benefits accrued from in-kind programs (such as food stamps and Medicaid). Those who contend that the poverty levels are set too low note that certain costs, such as housing or child care, have escalated dramatically since the poverty lines were established.

However, to illustrate what these numbers mean in a day-to-day sense, consider the 1995 poverty level for a family of four—$15,569. Using the one third/two thirds split, a hypothetical family would have $5,190 available for food during the year, or $99.81 a week, $14.22 a day, or $3.56 a day for each family member. Assuming that family members eat three meals per day, this amount works out to $1.19 per person, per meal, per day. Similarly, the remaining two thirds of the poverty line's threshold—$10,379—provides a family with $199.60 per week for all other expenses, including housing, utilities, transportation, clothing, child care, medical expenses, and the various additional expenditures that a family of four may have. Bringing the poverty line down to this level allows for a more meaningful sense of what these numbers represent in terms of people's lives. As I explain in a later section, to live below the poverty line embodies physical hardship.

Indeed, the Gallup poll has asked the following question over the past 50 years, "What is the smallest amount of money a family of four (husband, wife, and two children) needs each week to get along in this community?" The average amounts given by the respondents have been substantially higher than what the weekly poverty level for a family of four would be. Furthermore, in 1989 the Gallup Organization asked respondents in four monthly samples the following question, "People who have income below a certain level can be considered poor. That level is called the 'poverty line.' What amount of weekly income would you use as a poverty line for a family of four (husband, wife and two children) in this community?" Individuals set the poverty line, on average, 23 percent higher than the official poverty line for a family of four (see O'Hare, Mann, Porter, & Greenstein, 1990, and Vaughn, 1993, for an extensive discussion of this issue). The bottom line is that Americans' subjec-

tive opinions of what constitutes poverty are significantly more generous than the official measurement of poverty.

In addition, it is important to keep in mind that this example captures poverty at its most opulent level. Yet families fall to varying degrees below the poverty line. In 1995, 38.1% of all poor persons were living in households with incomes below half their respective poverty threshold (U.S. Bureau of the Census, 1996c). Taking 50% of the poverty threshold for a family of four works out to $49.91 per week for food and $99.80 per week for all other expenses.

Yet another way of translating the meaning of poverty into one's life can be seen in the following statistic. In 1995, the median income for a family of four in the United States was $59,738 (U.S. Bureau of the Census, 1996b). In the same year, the median income of a family of four below the poverty line was $8,953. The average income of such a family was therefore 15% of the average income for a family of four in the United States.

Some who are reading this chapter may be near the average in terms of household income. A number of you (as I do) may occasionally find it difficult to keep up with various household expenses and needs. Now imagine that instead of the income currently coming in for this month, next month you will be receiving just 15% of your income. The other 85% is suddenly gone. That 85% is the distance between the average standard of living and the standard of living of those below the poverty line. In essence, to survive on 15% of the average family income is roughly what it means to live in poverty.

Finally, in an important respect, today's poverty is harsher than it was 40 years ago. In 1947 the poverty threshold for a family of four would have stood at 69% of the median four-person family income (Fisher, 1992). When the United States began counting the number of poor Americans in 1959, it had dropped to just below 50% of the median. By 1995, the poverty threshold had fallen to 31% (U.S. Bureau of the Census, 1996c). During the 1950s and 1960s, increases in income were well above the overall rates of inflation, whereas the poverty thresholds simply kept up with the levels of inflation. Thus, the gap between the two got wider during these periods of the growth in real wages.

Being categorized today as poor has consequently meant living further afield from the economic midpoint than in the past. Hence, if one were to apply in 1995 the economic distance of families in poverty from the median that was found in 1959, the poverty threshold for a family of four would rise from its current $15,569 to $24,347. In this sense, poverty has become harsher today than it was 40 years ago.

HOW HAS THE FACE OF POVERTY CHANGED OVER TIME?

Over the past four decades, two major changes have significantly altered the face of poverty: (1) the shifting risk of poverty across age groups and (2) the changing composition of poor families. Although other shifts have occurred as well, these two changes capture much of the historical dynamic in American poverty.

Trends in the Risk of Poverty

Figure 15.1 illustrates the changes in the risks of poverty during the past 40 years. It graphs both the key American success (the elderly) and failure (children) with respect to averting poverty over time and compares them to the country's overall rate of poverty. In 1959, the total poverty rate stood at 22.4%. The rate for children (under age 18) was 27.3%, and that for the elderly (aged 65 and over) was 35.2%. Children's poverty rate was 22% above the overall rate, while the elderly's poverty rate was 57% above the overall rate.

From 1959 to 1969, all three groups (but particularly children and the general population) displayed a dramatic reduction in poverty. The rates of poverty for children and the overall population were cut approximately in half during that time. As a result, by 1969 the poverty rate was 12.1% for the general population, 14.0% for children, and 25.3% for the elderly. The child poverty rate was only 16% higher than the general rate, whereas the elderly's poverty rate was 108% higher.

What occurred after 1969 was a dramatic shift in the relative positions of these three groups. From 1969 to 1974, the overall rate of poverty decreased slightly to 11%, while the rate for children began to rise. At the same time, the poverty rate for the elderly dropped dramatically. Consequently, by 1974 the poverty rate for the elderly was, for the first time, below the rate for children.

From 1974 to 1979, the relative positions of these three groups and their distance from one another held steady, but from 1979 to 1984 children's poverty rates rose sharply, the elderly's poverty rates declined even further, and the overall rate of poverty increased moderately. As a result, from 1982 onward, the elderly's poverty rate fell below that of the general population and well below that of children.

The relative positions of these groups thus dramatically reversed over the course of four decades. In 1959, the elderly had some of the highest rates of poverty of any group. Today, they have some of the lowest. In 1969, the poverty rate for children was fairly close to the overall average. Today, children (particularly young children) are the age group most likely to be poor in America. As I mentioned earlier, these changes represent America's greatest success and failure in averting poverty.

There are several reasons why such changes have occurred. In the case of the elderly, the substantial reduction in the risk of poverty is directly attributed to the increasing generosity of the Social Security program, as well as the introduction of Medicare in 1965 and the Supplemental Security Income program in 1971. During the 1960s and 1970s, social security benefits were substantially increased, which helped many of the elderly get above the poverty line. It is estimated that today, without the Social Security program, the poverty rate for the elderly would be close to 50% (Danziger & Weinberg, 1994). Put another way, social security is responsible for getting 75% of the elderly above the poverty line who would be poor in its absence. One reason for this success is that the amount that individuals have been getting back from social security has been well above what they and their employers contributed. For example, the average person who retired in 1980 recouped within four years of retirement what he or she and the employers had paid into social security (Kollman, 1995).

FIGURE 15.1
Poverty Rates for the Overall Population, Children, and the Elderly, 1959–95

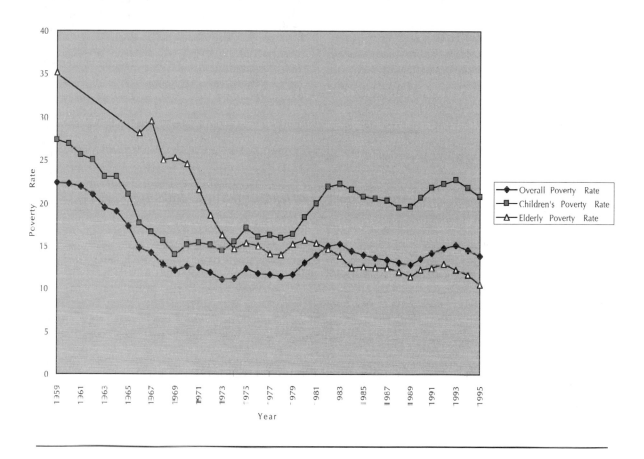

In the case of children, three reasons stand out as to why their risk of poverty has increased from 1969 onward. First, at the same time that the social safety net for the elderly was becoming stronger, that for the nation's children was beginning to unravel (Preston, 1984). From the early 1970s onward, social welfare programs to assist low-income children have lost ground to inflation, resulting in more children falling below the poverty line (U.S. House of Representatives, 1994).

Second, the median annual earnings of young (under age 30) heads of households with children have dropped significantly over the past two decades. They fell an average of 44% from 1973 to 1990, regardless of differences in family structure,

race, and levels of education (Edelman, 1992). As a result, young children have faced an increasing risk of poverty.

Third, there have been dramatic changes in family structure from the mid-1960s onward. As a result of the increasing rates of divorce and out-of-wedlock childbearing, more youngsters have been spending periods of their childhood in female-headed families. In 1959, 9.4% of all families with children under age 18 were headed by women. By 1969, the percentage had grown slightly to 11.3%. However, by 1979 the percentage had jumped to 18.6% and stood at 23.8% in 1995 (U.S. Bureau of the Census, 1996a). That the risk of poverty in female-headed families is substantially greater than that in married-couple families has put children in a more precarious position vis-à-vis poverty and is reflected in the changes in the overall rates of child poverty shown in Figure 15.1.

Family Structural Changes

This family structural change has led to the second important shift in the face of poverty—the living arrangements of poor children have changed significantly. Figure 15.2 plots the percentage of poor families (with children under age 18) that were headed by mothers from 1959 to 1995. What is readily apparent is the dramatic shift in the household living arrangements of children in poverty. In 1959, 1 out of 4 white families and 1 out of 3 black families with incomes below the poverty line were female headed. From 1964 to 1978, the percentage of poor families that were female headed increased rapidly, so that by 1978, 1 out of 2 white families, 4 out of 5 black families, and 3 out of 5 overall families with poor children were headed by women.

FIGURE 15.2
Percentage of Poor Families (with Children under Age 18) Headed by a Mother only, 1959–95

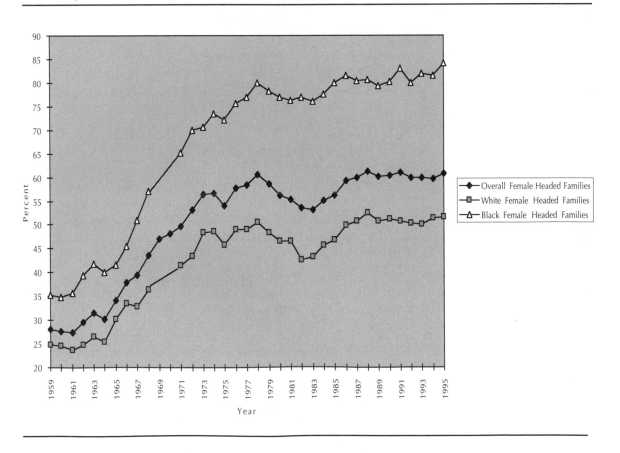

These percentages dipped somewhat during the early 1980s, but have since returned to their previous high levels.

This then constitutes the second major change in the face of poverty that has occurred over the past four decades. Poor children are now more likely to be living in female-headed families than in married-couple families, and black children are substantially more likely to do so. Although this change has occurred in the United States across all income categories, it has been particularly dramatic for families with income below the poverty line.

The poor of today are therefore more likely to be children, particularly children in female-headed families, than the poor of yesteryear. The face of poverty has become younger and more closely associated with one-parent families than it was in the past.

WHAT IS THE DYNAMIC OF POVERTY SPELLS?

Overall Patterns

Until recently, policy makers who saw the type of cross-sectional data plotted in Figure 15.1 often assumed that the same families were poor year in and year out. With the advent of several national panel studies (e.g., the Panel Study of Income Dynamics, National Survey of Youth, Survey of Income and Program Participation), considerable light has been shed on this subject. By following the same households over time, one can observe and track what the dynamics of poverty spells and income mobility actually are (poverty spells refer to the length of time that individuals consecutively fall below the poverty line, often measured in years, whereas poverty dynamics refer to the overall pattern of poverty spells). Several broad conclusions can be drawn from these data.

First, most spells of poverty are of fairly modest length. Households typically are impoverished for several years and then manage to rise above the poverty line (Bane & Ellwood, 1986; Blank, 1997; Duncan, 1984; Stevens, 1994). They may stay there for a period, only to experience an additional fall into poverty at some later point. Because their eco-

nomic distance above the poverty threshold is often narrow, when a detrimental economic event, such as the loss of a job or the breakup of a family occurs, it can easily throw a family back below the poverty line.

In contrast, a much smaller number of households experience chronic poverty for years at a time. These are the cases that one generally thinks of when the term *underclass* is used. Generally, they have characteristics that put them at a severe disadvantage vis-à-vis the labor market (e.g., individuals with serious work disabilities, female-headed families with large numbers of children, racial minorities living in inner-city areas). Their prospects for getting out of poverty for any significant period are severely diminished.

Blank (1997) relied on data from the Panel Study of Income Dynamics (PSID) to calculate the occurrence of poverty over a 13-year period. The PSID has followed a nationally representative sample of approximately 5,000 households each year from 1968 to the present. She found that from 1979 to 1991, one third of Americans experienced a spell of poverty. However, of those who fell below the poverty line, half were poor for three years or less, one third were in poverty between 4 and 9 years, 14.6% fell below the poverty line for 10 of the 13 years, and 4.5% fell below the poverty line for each of the 13 years.

Blank (1997) also found that the likelihood and duration of poverty varied sharply by race. One quarter of white Americans, versus two thirds of black Americans experienced poverty at some point during the 13-year period. Furthermore, 67% of whites who experienced poverty were poor for three years or less, whereas the figure for blacks was only 30%. Consequently, black Americans were more likely to be touched by poverty and more likely to be exposed to poverty for substantially longer periods.

In a similar analysis, Devine and Wright (1993) used the PSID data to examine the dynamics of poverty from 1969 to 1987. They found that 38.1% of the total population experienced a spell of poverty during that period, but that only 1.1% of the sample were poor during all 19 years. However, Devine and Wright also observed that the number of individuals who experienced spells of persistent poverty (measured in various ways) was on the rise during those two decades. Finally, they found that being black and/or female strongly increased the probability of experiencing poverty, particularly long-term poverty.

Research on the dynamics of poverty has also shown that many households will reexperience poverty in the future. Using annual estimates of poverty from the PSID data, Stevens (1994) calculated that of all persons who had managed to get themselves above the poverty line, over half returned to poverty within five years.

A slightly different way of illustrating these patterns is to focus on monthly, rather than annual, rates of poverty. The Survey of Income and Program Participation (SIPP) data set allows for such a focus. The SIPP has been administered by the U.S. Bureau of the Census monthly from 1983 onward, with individuals from approximately 20,000 households interviewed at four-month intervals.

The SIPP's monthly measurement of poverty between 1992 and 1993 revealed that the duration of impoverishment for most households is short (U.S. Bureau of the Census, 1996d). After 4 months, close to half of all poor persons had risen above the poverty line; after 8 months, two thirds; and after one year, three quarters. Only 13.5% of persons fell below the poverty line continuously for each of the 24 months. The median length of time below the poverty threshold was 4.9 months. As with the annual rates, the duration of poverty varies by particular demographic characteristics. Blacks and Hispanics, children and the elderly, female-headed families, inner-city and nonmetropolitan residents, and individuals with less education were all more likely to experience longer spells of poverty. However, even for these households, poverty measured monthly was of short duration. Finally, many of those who work their way above the monthly poverty line will find themselves below that line in the future. The recidivism rates become considerably higher when one deals with monthly, rather than annual, measures of poverty.

Thus, although the typical spell of poverty may not last long, poverty can touch a fairly large per-

centage of the overall population, Devine and Wright (1993, p. 105) indicated:

> While the proportion of families officially designated as poor in any given year is somewhere between 11% and 15% (for the years in question), the proportion who experience at least one year of poverty over a two-decade span is nearly 40 percent—two or three times the annual poverty rate. If one could extend this analysis over the average lifetime of a family, the proportion experiencing at least a year of poverty would have to increase and might easily reach or exceed half. Is it truly possible that half the households in this affluent, postindustrial society are destined to spend at least one of their years beneath the poverty line? Remarkably, the answer appears to be yes.

The picture of poverty that is drawn from both the annual and monthly analyses is thus a more fluid one than what had traditionally been depicted. Individuals tend to weave their way in and out of poverty, depending upon the occurrence or nonoccurrence of particular events. This tendency then leads to the second major conclusion derived from the research on poverty dynamics.

Events Triggering Poverty Spells

Spells of poverty are generally triggered by unfavorable events that occur to households, the loss of employment and earnings being the most important. Using the PSID data, Duncan et al. (1995) found that two thirds of all entries into poverty were associated with either a reduction in work (48%) or the loss of work (18%). In addition, divorce and separation were associated with approximately 10% of all spells of poverty. Employment-related factors were much more likely to trigger spells of poverty in the United States than they were in countries such as France, Germany, or the Netherlands because of the higher wages paid in such countries and their more generous unemployment policies.

Blank (1997) also found that employment and earnings were highly influential in getting people out of poverty. Two thirds of those below the poverty line escaped impoverishment as a result of increases in the individual earnings of family members or increases from other sources of income. The remaining third had their spells of poverty end as a result of changes in family structure (such as marriage or a child leaving the household). In summarizing her findings on poverty dynamics, Blank stated,

> Changes in earnings and work opportunities are very important in many families, driving them into poverty or helping them to escape. To a lesser extent, changes in family composition are also important in "creating" and "dissolving" poor families. But . . . for some substantial minority among the poor—particularly the black poor—poverty is long-term and escape is infrequent. (p. 27)

WHO ARE THE POOR?

Who encounters a spell of poverty? This question can be examined in one of two ways—what characteristics place an individual and his or her family at a greater risk of experiencing poverty, and what are the compositional characteristics of the poor population? These questions lead to slightly different pictures of who the poor are.

Demographic Differences in Poverty Rates

Using data from the U.S. Bureau of the Census (1996c), Table 15.1 focuses on a small number of demographic characteristics. The overall U.S. rate of poverty for 1995 was 13.8%, representing 36.4 million Americans. Multiplying the poverty level by 1.25 (in other words, increasing the poverty level by 25%) results in a rate of 18.5%, or 48.8 million Americans (not shown in Table 15.1). Consequently, 12.4 million Americans were living precariously close to the poverty line.

The official rate of 13.8% in 1995 provides a benchmark to gauge if certain attributes result in higher or lower probabilities of poverty. With regard to race, the poverty rate for whites stood at 11.2%, or 8.5% when those who identified themselves as Hispanic were not included. It should be noted that Hispanic is a category of ethnicity, rather than race. Consequently, Hispanics can be either white or black, although the vast majority classify themselves as white.

In contrast, the rates of poverty for blacks (29.3%) and Hispanics (30.3%) were well over three times that of whites in 1995, and the rate for Asian and Pacific Islanders (14.6%) was slightly above the average. However, the racial group with the highest levels of poverty is Native Americans living on reservations. It is estimated by the Bureau of Indian Affairs that at least half the 1.3 million American Indians who live on reservations are poor, with unemployment rates running at approximately 50 percent.

As Table 15.1 shows, children are the age group most likely to be poor, with 1 out of 5 children falling below the poverty line in 1995. Furthermore, nearly 1 out of 4 children under age 6 (23.7%) were impoverished in that year (not shown). Young adults in their 20s also had a relatively high level of poverty. The level of poverty dropped substantially for individuals in their prime income earning years: 35–54. Finally, there was a slight increase in the level of poverty for older Americans, particularly those over age 75 (13.0%, not shown).

For individuals aged 18 and over, women experience poverty at a rate that is 50% higher than that for men (13.4% versus 9% in 1995). One reason for this discrepancy lies in the next category—household status—in which the risk of poverty varies dramatically. In 1995, the poverty rate for family members in married-couple households was 6.8%, whereas the rate for female-headed households was 36.5%. As Figure 15.2 indicated, the percentage of female-headed families below the poverty line increased substantially from 1959 to 1995, endangering a greater number of women and their children to economic destitution. The poverty rate for persons living without relatives was 20.9% in 1995.

Poverty also varies in terms of where people live. In 1995, central-city areas were marked by poverty rates of 20.6%; followed by rural areas, 15.6%; and metropolitan areas outside central cities, 9.1%.

The last two characteristics in Table 15.1, education and work disability, are strongly associated with the risk of poverty. In 1995, the poverty rate for those with less than a high school education was 25.6%, compared to 10.4% for those with high school diplo-

TABLE 15.1
Poverty Rates and Demographic Composition of the Poor and Overall Populations, 1995

Household Characteristics	Poverty Rate	Percentage of the Poor Population	Percentage of the Overall Population
Total	13.8	100.0	100.0
Race			
White	11.2	67.1	82.7
Not of Hispanic origin	8.5	44.7	74.0
Black	29.3	27.1	12.8
Hispanic	30.3	23.5	10.7
Asian and Pacific Islander	14.6	3.9	3.2
Age			
Under 18	20.8	40.3	26.8
18 to 24	18.3	12.5	9.4
25 to 34	12.7	14.3	15.5
35 to 44	9.4	11.2	16.3
45 to 54	7.8	6.8	12.0
55 to 64	10.2	5.9	8.0
65 and over	10.5	9.1	12.0
Gender (18 and over)			
Women	13.4	61.7	52.0
Men	9.0	38.3	48.0
Household Status			
Married Couple*	6.8	32.4	66.0
Female-headed household*	36.5	39.0	14.8
Unrelated individual	20.9	22.6	15.0
Other	—	6.0	4.2
Residence			
In metropolitan areas	13.4	77.8	80.4
In central cities	20.6	44.7	30.0
Outside central cities	9.1	33.1	50.4
Outside metropolitan areas	15.6	22.2	19.6
Education (25 and over)**			
Less than 12	25.6	46.0	19.8
12	10.4	33.5	35.4
13 to 15	7.0	14.6	23.0
16 or more	3.0	5.9	21.9
Work Disability (16 to 64)**			
No Work Disability	10.1	76.8	90.4
Work Disability	28.9	23.2	9.6
Severe Work Disability	35.8	16.8	5.6

*Includes all married couple and female-headed families with and without children under age 18 in the household.
**Data are for 1992.
Sources: U.S. Bureau of the Census. (1993). *Current Population Reports* (Series P-60, No. 185). Washington, DC: U.S. Government Printing Office; and U.S. Bureau of the Census. (1996). *Current Population Reports* (Series P-60, No. 194). Washington, DC: U.S. Government Printing Office.

mas, 7% for those with some college education, and only 3% for those with college degrees. Likewise, individuals with a work disability (28.9%), particularly one that was severe (35.8%), were much more likely to experience poverty than their counterparts without a work disability (10.1%).

Each of the characteristics in Table 15.1 is strongly associated with the risk of poverty. Rather than being randomly distributed, poverty varies in a systematic way across the demographic characteristics found in the table. Furthermore, as these characteristics overlap with one another, the risk of poverty increases or decreases substantially. For example, the poverty rate for children under age 6, who are black and were living in female-headed families was a stunning 70.6% in 1995 (U.S. Bureau of the Census, 1996c).

What all these characteristics have in common is

that they increase or decrease the vulnerability of individuals vis-à-vis the labor market. As is discussed in the concluding section, the risk of poverty for specific households can be largely understood in terms of the households' economic vulnerability. Households move into poverty largely because of detrimental events, such as the loss of work, a reduction in earnings, or the dissolution of a marriage. Individuals with less advantageous characteristics (for example, a low level of education) are more likely to experience such events and to be more fully exposed to the negative brunt of such events when they occur. Consequently, minorities, children and young adults, women, female heads of household, residents of central cities, and individuals with less education or work disabilities all face greater risks of poverty.

Demographic Composition of the Poverty Population

A slightly different picture emerges if one looks at the overall demographic composition of the poverty population (found in the second column of Table 15.1). While some groups exhibit a low rate of poverty, they may constitute a majority of the poor if their overall proportion within the general population is large. Race is an illustration of this fact. The poverty rate for whites (not of Hispanic origin) is 8.5%, but whites make up 44.7% of the total poor population because their overall percentage of the general population is 74%. Conversely, although the poverty rate for blacks is 3½ times higher than that of whites (29.3%), blacks make up a much lower proportion of the overall poor population (27.1%) than do whites because their overall percentage of the general population is only 12.8%.

What characterizes the demographic composition of the poor as found in Table 15.1?

- Two thirds of the poor are white, or 44.7% if Hispanics are counted separately.
- Blacks make up slightly over one quarter of the poor population, with Hispanics making up an additional quarter.
- Forty percent of the poor are children, and two thirds of the poor are below age 35.

- Women make up three fifths of the poverty population over age 18.
- Just under 40% of those below the poverty line live in female-headed families, one third in married-couple families, and 22.6% on their own without relatives.
- Three quarters of the poor reside in metropolitan areas, with 44.7% living in central cities, 33.1% in other metropolitan areas, and 22.2% in rural areas.
- Close to half the poor (aged 25 and over) do not have high school diplomas.
- One quarter of the poor (aged 16 to 64) are plagued with work disabilities.

Several additional points can be made regarding the demographic composition of the poor. First, as in my study of welfare recipients (Rank, 1994), it is helpful to conceptualize the poor as falling into one of four household-age categories. These mutually exclusive categories constitute 92.4% of the poor. The first three consist of those below age 65: (1) female-headed families with children (36.9% of the poor), (2) married couples with or without children (30.0% of the poor), (3) men or women living without relatives (16.4% of the poor), and (4) the elderly (9.1% of the poor). The remaining 7.6% of the poor fall into various other categories. Individuals in each of these household types have their own unique circumstances associated with why they are below the poverty line, as well as their own unique sets of problems and strengths (Rank, 1994).

Second, although three quarters of the poor reside in metropolitan areas, refining this a bit further gives one a somewhat different image. Through the use of census-tract information from the 1990 census, Jargowsky (1997) found that only 11.8% of the total U.S. poverty population lived in highly impoverished urban ghetto neighborhoods (those with poverty rates in excess of 40%). Even among the black poor, only 25% lived in such neighborhoods. Consequently, most of the poor do not reside in the often-portrayed residential image of urban ghettos. However, Jargowsky also found that the percentage of the poor living in high poverty neighborhoods had been increasing over time. In 1970 the figure was 7.0%; in 1980; 8.7%; and by 1990, 11.8%.

Finally, the picture that emerges from focusing on the demographics of the poverty population is a slightly different one when compared to the rates of poverty. Nevertheless, what is noticeably apparent in either case is that the poor are characterized by less advantageous labor market attributes.

HOW DOES THE UNITED STATES COMPARE WITH OTHER COUNTRIES?

The next question posed in this chapter is how the rates of poverty in the United States compare with those of other countries. Specifically, in what ways is the United States similar or dissimilar to other industrialized nations? This question allows me to place the prevalence of U.S. poverty within a more global context.

Several problems have made such comparisons difficult. First has been the lack of comparable data sets that are large enough to allow for such an analysis. Fortunately, this obstacle has been partially overcome with the Luxembourg Income Study (LIS). Begun in the 1980s, it contains income and demographic information on households in 25 different nations from 1967 to the present. By standardizing variables across 70 data sets, it allows one to conduct cross-national analyses of poverty and income inequality.

Table 15.2 draws on an analysis by Smeeding (1997b) that used the LIS to compare the rates of poverty in 17 developed nations. A relative measure of poverty is used in the first four columns—the percentage of persons living with incomes below half the median income. In the case of the United States, this works out to approximately 125% of the current poverty thresholds discussed earlier.

TABLE 15.2
Extent of Poverty in 17 Developed Countries (various years)

Country	Percentage of the Population Below 50% of the Median Income				Percentage of the Population with Incomes Below $14.40 per Day
	Overall	Children	Adults	Elderly	Overall
United States (1994)	19.1	24.9	16.4	19.6	14.1
United Kingdom (1991)	14.6	18.5	10.7	23.9	13.1
Australia (1989)	12.9	15.4	10.3	21.6	7.8
Japan (1992)	11.8	12.2	10.2	18.4	3.7
Canada (1991)	11.7	15.3	11.2	5.7	5.9
Ireland (1987)	11.1	13.8	9.6	7.6	36.5
Spain (1990)	10.4	12.8	9.2	11.4	21.1
Germany (1989)	7.6	8.6	7.3	7.5	11.5
Denmark (1992)	7.5	5.1	7.3	11.3	7.6
France (1984)	7.5	7.4	8.1	4.8	12.0
Netherlands (1991)	6.7	8.3	6.6	4.1	14.4
Sweden (1992)	6.7	3.0	8.1	6.4	4.6
Norway (1991)	6.6	4.9	5.4	13.5	2.6
Italy (1991)	6.5	10.5	6.1	4.4	—
Finland (1991)	6.2	2.7	5.8	14.4	3.8
Belgium (1992)	5.5	4.4	4.6	11.9	12.0
Luxembourg (1985)	5.4	5.2	4.1	12.9	4.3
Overall average	9.3	10.2	8.3	11.7	10.9

Source: Smeeding, T. M. (1997). America's income inequality in a cross-national perspective: Why are we so different? *Luxembourg Income Study Working Paper Series* (No. 157). Differdange, Luxembourg: CEPS/INSTEAD.

The U.S. rates of poverty are substantially higher than those in any of the other 16 nations. The overall U.S. rate using this measure stands at 19.1%. The next closest country to the United States is the United Kingdom at 14.6%; followed by Australia, Japan, and Canada; with the Scandinavian and Benelux countries falling near the bottom. The average for all 17 nations is 9.3%.

The same patterns are evident in the rates for children and adults. The United States leads all nations in having the highest rates of child poverty at 24.9%, with the nearest countries (again the United Kingdom and Australia) being 6 and 9 percentage points lower, and the overall average standing at 10.2%. Furthermore, the United States remains near the top when this rate is broken down by poverty in one- and two-parent households.

The same pattern can be found among adults. Only in the case of the elderly does the United States not lead the developed world. Here, U.S. poverty rates are third from the top, falling only behind the United Kingdom and Australia. Additional analyses using the LIS looked at the trends in poverty over time, finding that it has increased most rapidly in the United Kingdom and the United States (Smeeding, 1997b).

The final column in Table 15.2 presents a recalculation of the overall poverty rates using an absolute measure. A critique of the rates in columns 1 to 4 is that, although the United States has a high rate of relative poverty, the standard of living that poor Americans experience is potentially greater than the poor or near-poor in many of the comparison countries because the overall levels of income and standards of living are higher. Consequently, column 5 shows the recalculation of the poverty rates as persons who fall below the equivalent of 14.40 U.S. dollars per day (which was the 1985 poverty line for a single person in the United States).

Predictably, the lowest per capita income countries in this sample, Ireland and Spain, also have the highest rates of poverty using this measure (36.5% and 21.1%). Next are the Netherlands and the United States, at 14.4% and 14.1%, followed by the United Kingdom, France, Belgium, and Germany.

Finally, the Scandinavian countries, along with Canada, Luxembourg, and Japan, have the lowest rates. Consequently, even when differences in the standard of living are taken into account, the United States' level of absolute poverty remains among the highest in the industrialized world (for a somewhat different analysis and conclusion, see Mayer, 1995).

To summarize, when poverty is analyzed as the number of persons who fall below 50% of a country's median income, the United States has far and away the highest overall poverty rate in this group of 17 developed nations. It is also near the top in terms of an absolute measure of poverty. Furthermore, as one adopts more stringent measures of relative poverty (33% of the median income) or absolute poverty ($7.20 a day), the United States performs progressively worse vis-à-vis other countries. What is surprising about these findings is that the United States is arguably the wealthiest nation in the world.

This paradox is revealed in additional LIS analyses that have examined how well children and adults from the middle and upper ends of the income scale do. It is not surprising that the United States has the highest standard of living at these points in the income distribution scale. The conclusion to be drawn from these divergent patterns regarding American children was stated succinctly by Rainwater and Smeeding (1995, p. 9).

> In other words, while the United States has a higher real level of income than most of our comparison countries it is the high and middle income children who reap the benefits (and much more the former than the latter). Low income American children suffer in both absolute and relative terms. The average low income child in the other 17 countries is at least one-third better off than is the average low-income American child.

The reasons for such a discrepancy are twofold. First, the social safety net in the United States is much weaker than in virtually every other country in Table 15.2. Second, the United States is plagued by relatively low wages at the bottom of the income distribution scale when compared to other developed countries (Smeeding, 1997a). These factors significantly contribute to both the relative and absolute depths of U.S. poverty in comparison to other industrialized nations.

WHAT IS THE HUMAN MEANING OF POVERTY?

Although many experiences are associated with poverty, there are three that I believe capture the essence of the American experience of poverty in individuals' and families' lives—having to make significant compromises regarding the daily necessities that those not in poverty take for granted, enduring sizeable levels of stress as a result of such insufficiencies, and experiencing one's own and children's development stunted as a result of impoverishment. These are the painful and all-to-human dimensions of what it means to be poor in an American context of plenty. Each is explored in the following sections.

Doing Without

The experience of poverty is epitomized by having to do without. It entails insufficiencies and compromises involving basic resources, such as food, clothing, shelter, health care, and transportation. It also entails not having additional items and services that many of us take for granted. In short, quoting from the earlier Webster definition, poverty embodies a "deficiency of necessary or desirable ingredients" that most Americans have. Several of these deficiencies are discussed next.

Living in poverty often means having to do without a sufficiently balanced diet and adequate intake of calories (Clancy & Bowering, 1992; Poppendieck, 1997; Uvin, 1994). Several large-scale studies have indicated that those in poverty routinely have bouts of hunger, undernutrition, and/or a detrimental altering of the diet at some point during a month (Breglio, 1992; Cook & Brown, 1992; Physician Task Force on Hunger in America, 1985; U.S. Conference of Mayors, 1994; VanAmburg Group, 1994). This risk affects children, working-age adults, and the elderly (Cohen, Burt, & Schulte, 1993; Food Research and Action Center, 1991).

Having enough food on the table is thus a constant battle for families in poverty. As Glickman (1997), the Secretary of Agriculture aptly noted:

> One in three of our kids live in families that do constant battle with hunger—whether it's missed meals the last few days before a paycheck, or skipped medical appointments in favor of putting food on the table. These kids are at [a] constant risk of malnutrition and the lifetime of chronic illness that can accompany it.

Good health is a second area that families in poverty often have to do without. One of the most consistent findings in epidemiology is that the quality of an individual's health is negatively affected by lower socioeconomic status, particularly impoverishment. Poverty is associated with a host of health risks, including elevated rates of heart disease, diabetes, hypertension, cancer, infant mortality, mental illness, undernutrition, lead poisoning, asthma, dental problems, and a variety of other ailments and diseases (Klerman & Parker, 1991; Leidenfrost, 1993; Sherman, 1994; Williams & Collins, 1995). The result is a death rate for the poverty stricken that is approximately three times higher than that for the affluent (Pappas, Queen, Hadden, & Fisher, 1993). As Leidenfrost (1993, p. 1) noted in her review of the literature, "Health disparities between the poor and those with higher incomes are almost universal for all dimensions of health."

Furthermore, poverty often has a negative effect on children's health status, which, in turn, has an impact on their well-being as adults (Korenman & Miller, 1997). According to Schiller (1998, p. 97),

> A child born to a poverty-stricken mother is likely to be undernourished both before and after birth. Furthermore, the child is less likely to receive proper postnatal care, to be immunized against disease, or even to have his or her eyes and teeth examined. As a result, the child is likely to grow up prone to illness and poverty, and in the most insidious of cases, be impaired by organic brain damage.

The connection between poverty and ill health exists for several reasons, including the lack of an adequate diet, less access to medical care, residing in unhealthy and stressful physical and mental environments, and less educational awareness regarding health issues. The result is an increase in pain and suffering by the poor.

Although Medicaid and Medicare have helped to increase the poor's access to health care, when the use of health services is compared to the need for services, low-income households still have the lowest rate (Wolfe, 1994). Furthermore, approximately 40% of the poor and near-poor have no health insurance, and when they do have insurance, it is often restrictive in terms of what is covered.

Just as good health is often compromised as a result of poverty, so is living in a safe and decent neighborhood. Although it is true that most of the poor do not live in neighborhoods that are characterized as impoverished inner-city areas (as was discussed earlier), nevertheless poverty significantly limits the overall quality of life in a neighborhood. In addition, racial discrimination in the housing market further restricts the options available to minorities, particularly blacks (Jargowsky, 1997; Massey & Denton, 1993; Yinger, 1995).

Being confined to a low-income neighborhood, coupled with transportation problems, often results in the poor paying more and spending more time acquiring basic necessities (Caplovitz, 1963; Dunbar, 1988; Edin & Lein, 1997). Doing without adequate transportation also affects the ability to compete for and hold a job (Gureron & Pauly, 1991).

What is perhaps most bitter regarding all these hardships is that they take place within a context of abundance. In other words, most U.S. citizens have plenty to eat and decent clothes to wear, experience good health and safe neighborhoods, and so on. This message of abundance can be seen daily from shopping malls to television programs. The result is that poverty in the United States has an especially bitter taste. It imprints upon the poor a strong sense of relative deprivation and failure (see Tyler, Boeckmann, Smith, & Huo, 1997, for an extended discussion of the literature on relative deprivation).

In short, living in poverty is epitomized by the struggle to acquire and, at times, forgoing the daily necessities and resources that most people in the United States take for granted. It is the paradox and humiliation of having to do without in a land of plenty. It is the bitter taste of being left out of many of the simple pleasures of life.

The Stressful Weight of Poverty

A consequence of the struggles noted earlier is that impoverishment exerts a heavy weight upon the shoulders of most who walk in its ranks. In essence, poverty acts to amplify the daily stress found in everyday life and its relationships.

Consider the situation that female-headed families face. Single mothers often have no partner to turn to to give them a helping hand during the routine crises and struggles outlined earlier. Furthermore, most female heads of households work at two full-time jobs (in the labor force and at home). The result is often stress, frustration, and exhaustion, which, in turn, influence the caring and rearing of children (Berrick, 1995; McLanahan & Sandefur, 1994; Sidel, 1996).

For single men and women in poverty, impoverishment also exerts a stressful weight upon their shoulders. In these cases, particularly among the elderly, this weight can be exasperated by a physical or mental disability. For example, in my study of welfare recipients (Rank, 1994), many of the single men and women who were receiving some form of public assistance also had physical and mental disabilities, which, in combination with poverty, created significant levels of stress in their lives.

Poverty also exerts considerable stress on married couples, as is discussed later. It serves to intensify the areas of friction that couples routinely encounter. The result is an increase in marital dissatisfaction, violence, and divorce.

The daily trials and tribulations of living in poverty place a heavy strain on the poor. The constant battle they wage against the formidable pressures exerted by poverty results in considerable anxieties and tensions. These anxieties affect not only the individual, but spill over into relationships with family members and friends.

Stunted Growth

Having to do without, combined with the stress of living in poverty, often produces a stunting of growth. Sometimes this stunting is visibly apparent, but it often lies beneath the surface. In addition, the longer the duration of poverty and the greater the depth of poverty, the greater the negative effects generally are.

These negative impacts occur in a wide variety of areas, but are perhaps most salient in the stunting of young children's physical and mental growth. Poor infants and young children in the United States are much more likely to have lower levels of physical and mental growth (as measured in a variety of ways) when compared to their nonpoor counterparts (Duncan & Brooks-Gunn, 1997; Korenman & Miller, 1997; Smith, Brooks-Gunn, & Klebanov, 1997).

Furthermore, both the duration and depth of poverty intensify these negative outcomes. For example, in their research on poverty's effects on young children's cognitive and verbal ability and early school achievement, Smith et al. (1997, p. 164) reported:

> Duration of poverty has very negative effects on children's IQ, verbal ability, and achievement scores. Children who lived in persistently poor families scored 6–9 points lower on the various assessments than children who were never poor. In addition, the negative effects of persistent poverty seem to get stronger as the child gets older. . . . The effects of family poverty varied dramatically depending on whether a family was very poor (family income below 50 percent of the poverty level), poor, or near poor. Children in the very poor group had scores 7–12 points lower than did children in the near-poor group.

Likewise, in a study that examined the impact of the duration of poverty upon children's mental health, McLeod and Shanahan (1993) found that the length of time spent in poverty was directly associated with children's feelings of unhappiness, anxiety, and dependence.

As children grow older and if they continue to reside in poverty, the disadvantages of growing up poor multiply. These disadvantages include attending inferior schools (Schiller, 1998), coping with the problems associated with disadvantaged neighborhoods (Brooks-Gunn, Duncan, & Aber, 1997), residing in less educationally stimulating home environments (Mayer, 1997), having health needs left unattended to (Sherman, 1994), among a host of other disadvantages. By the time they reach their early 20s, poor children are often at a significant disadvantage in their ability to compete effectively in the labor market, which, in turn, increases their risk of experiencing poverty as adults (as is discussed in the concluding section).

As adults age, the stunting effects of poverty become less pronounced but are nevertheless still real. These effects include poor physical and mental health, lower productivity as workers, and reduced participation in civic activities and other aspects of life (Rank, 1997).

Compounding the daily experience of living in stress and doing without, a third bitter taste of poverty involves not being able to achieve the full development of one's own and one's children's potential. This is perhaps the most painful pill to swallow, for it represents the undercutting of the capabilities found in all of us.

WHAT IMPACT DOES POVERTY HAVE ON FAMILY DYNAMICS?

Just as poverty affects individual development and growth, it can also influence family dynamics and relationships, particularly for those who experience long-term bouts of poverty. Several of these effects are discussed next.

Extended Kinship

Various anthropological studies (see, for example, Edin & Lein, 1997; Harvey, 1993; Lewis, 1966; Stack, 1974) have indicated that those in poverty are more likely than the nonpoor to use a large network of kin to exchange resources and services. This extended network serves as a coping mechanism for dealing with the uncertainties and hardships of poverty that were discussed earlier.

For example, in her study of a poor, black community called The Flats, Stack (1974) found that it was virtually impossible for families to cover completely their various expenses and needs on their own. Consequently, a system of collective sharing arose within The Flats as an adaptive strategy for surviving the daily uncertainties and depravity of poverty. As Stack wrote:

> In the final months of my life in The Flats, I learned that poverty creates a necessity for this exchange of

goods and services. The needs of families living at bare subsistence are so large compared to their average daily income that it is impossible for families to provide independently for fixed expenses and daily needs. Lacking any surplus of funds, they are forced to use most of their resources for major monthly bills: rent, utilities, and foods. After a family pays these bills they are penniless. (p. 29)

This system of exchange encompassed a wide network of kin and friends in The Flats. Only through such a collective response were families able to get through the daily trials and tribulations of long-term poverty.

Likewise, in Harvey's (1993) ethnographic study of a white, displaced farming population that had located in a community called Potter Addition, a similar process of mutual sharing and obligation developed across a wide network of kin. Family and kin members could be counted on to help in various situations, just as they would receive assistance from others.

Likelihood of Marriage

As with kinship, a long line of ethnographic, sociological, and demographic studies (see, for example, Cheal, 1996; Lewis, 1966; Rank, 1994; Stack, 1974) have indicated that the likelihood of marriage is substantially reduced among the poverty stricken when compared with the nonpoor. The fundamental reason for this relationship is that individuals who contemplate marriage generally seek (or desire to be) economically secure partners (Becker, 1981; Cherlin, 1996). Since poverty undermines the availability of such partners, individuals in these situations are more likely to delay or forgo marriage.

Most recently and well known within this vein of research has been the work of Wilson (1987; 1996). Wilson's analyses have focused on the increasing problems found in the inner city among blacks and the reasons why such problems appear to have worsened over the past three decades. A critical factor in understanding the falling rate of marriage in the inner-city population has been the recent economic restructuring that has resulted in the movement of capital and job opportunities out of central-city areas. As Wilson (1987, p. 145) wrote:

The black delay in marriage and the lower rate of remarriage, each associated with high percentages of out-of-wedlock births and female-headed households, can be directly tied to the employment status of black males. Indeed, black women, especially young black women, are confronting a shrinking pool of "marriageable" (that is economically stable) men.

As a result, Wilson argued, the rate of marriage in poverty-stricken inner cities is considerably lower than that within the general population.

Childbearing

Demographic data indicate that there is an association between lower levels of income and higher rates of fertility. For example, if one examines the total number of births per 1,000 women aged 15 to 44 in 1995, one finds that women residing in families with incomes below $10,000 had a rate of 91.0, those with family incomes between $30,000 and $34,999 had a rate of 60.6, and those with family incomes over $75,000 had a rate of 53.1 (U.S. Bureau of the Census, 1997). Looking at women aged 15 to 29 reveals even more striking rates: 132.7, 89.2, and 28.9, respectively.

In addition, women at lower income and educational levels tend to have children at earlier ages and are more likely to bear children out of wedlock. For example, the fertility rates per 1,000 unmarried women aged 18 to 24 are 300.9 for those with 0 to 8 years of education, 123.5 for women with 12 years of education, and 23.7 for those with 13 to 15 years of education (National Center for Health Statistics, 1997).

Two factors appear critical in understanding why poverty is associated with these patterns. First, research indicates that the poor have less access to information on birth control (Luker, 1996). In addition, the poor are least able to afford contraception (especially abortion). As a result, poor women are more likely than nonpoor women to report that they have experienced unwanted or unintended births (Maynard, 1997). Second, women in dire poverty, particularly teenagers, have high fertility rates because they perceive the lack of future opportunities (Dash, 1989). In a world of negatives, having a child may be seen as one of the few positive actions one can take (Anderson, 1990; Stack, 1974; Wilson, 1996). The Children's Defense Fund (1985, p. 3) expressed this idea aptly: "In many ways, the best contraceptive is a real future."

Marital Dissatisfaction and Dissolution

Research has consistently found that poverty and lower income are associated with a greater risk of separation and divorce, as well as spousal and child violence (Drake & Pandey, 1996; Gelles, 1993; Sedlak & Broadhurst, 1996; U.S. Bureau of the Census, 1992). When unemployment precipitates a fall into poverty (as discussed earlier), it can place a tremendous strain on a marriage. Research has shown that the impact of unemployment on the marital relationship is deleterious (Vosler, 1996), yet when unemployment is blended with poverty, the combination may be particularly destructive (Voydanoff, 1990).

In short, married couples in poverty tend to face significant economic stress, which negatively affects their levels of marital happiness and well-being (Conger, Ge, & Lorenz, 1994). This pattern, in turn, increases the likelihood that couples will attempt to resolve such dissatisfaction through separation or divorce.

A WIDER CONTEXT

This chapter's brief overview of the landscape of U.S. poverty has revealed several prominent features in the terrain. Among these features are that children have become the age group with the highest risk of poverty, that the duration of poverty for many American households is short term but periodic, that those with less advantageous labor market characteristics are much more likely to be poor and for longer periods, that the United States leads the developed world in the extent and severity of its poverty, and that poverty entails significant material and psychological hardships for individuals and families.

To conclude this chapter, I briefly place these findings within a larger conceptual framework. I have argued (Rank, 1994, forthcoming) that an understanding of the patterns and characteristics of poverty is enhanced through a framework I have called structural vulnerability. Three components make up this framework: the tenuous condition of economic vulnerability, the importance of social class, and the lack of opportunities for all Americans. Each is discussed briefly next.

The first factor is the concept of economic vulnerability. Individuals and families who are more likely to experience poverty often have a set of attributes that place them at a disadvantage vis-à-vis their earnings ability in the labor market. As I have discussed in this chapter, these attributes include a variety of characteristics, such as a low level of education, being black or Hispanic, having a disability, being female, living in a single-parent family, and residing in an inner city. For various structural and human capital reasons, such characteristics often limit the earnings potential of individuals.

However, these attributes do not simply cause poverty. What they often do is to place an individual and family in an economically vulnerable position when faced with a crisis like the loss of a job, severe illness, and having a child out of wedlock. Individuals and families who are marginalized in terms of their ability to participate in the free market system will have a more difficult time weathering such crises. When such an event takes place, it can often reduce members of these households to poverty for a period until they are able to get back on their feet. For many households, that period will be short; for others, it may be longer (as I noted earlier).

Think of economic hardship as walking a fine line. If nothing out of the ordinary happens, many of these families are able just to get by. However, if a crisis occurs, it generally propels the household into an economic tailspin. These families are indeed living on the edge.

For example, many of the families who I interviewed for my book, *Living on the Edge* (Rank, 1994), were straddling the borderline between self-sufficiency and dependence. One wrong step, and they were likely to land back in poverty and on welfare. They simply did not have the resources and assets necessary to tide them over for more than several weeks. The phrase "one paycheck away from poverty" is particularly apt. These patterns are consistent with the dynamics and events that precipitate poverty, as I reviewed earlier.

Consequently, the first critical factor in understanding the occurrence of poverty is the concept of economic vulnerability. People who have fewer skills and education, or who live in populations that have traditionally faced greater discrimination and barriers in the labor market (e.g., racial minorities and women) are more likely to be adversely affected when a crisis occurs.

Given that skills and education bear on poverty (by causing various degrees of vulnerability), why are individuals lacking them in the first place? Obviously, there are a number of reasons for this situation, but a major reason that is often ignored in this country is the importance of social class. This is the second component of the structural vulnerability framework.

Analyses of the American system of stratification have shown that although some amount of social mobility does occur, social class as a whole tends to reproduce itself (Beeghley, 1996). Those whose parents are from the working or lower class are likely to remain working- or lower class themselves. Similarly, those whose parents are affluent are likely to remain affluent. Why? Differences in parental class result in significant differences in the resources and opportunities available to children. These differences, in turn, affect children's future life chances and outcomes, including the accumulation of skills and education. While it is possible for someone to rise from rags to riches, doing so tends to be much more the exception than the rule. Likewise, race and sex are inherited qualities that often affect and shape future life chances, including education and skills.

A game analogy illustrates this process of class reproduction. Imagine three players beginning a game of Monopoly. Normally, each player is given $1,500 at the start of the game. Thus, the playing field is level, with each player's outcome determined by the roll of the dice, as well as his or her own skills and judgments.

Now let us imagine a modified game of Monopoly, in which the players start out with different advantages and disadvantages, much as they would in life. Player 1 begins with $5,000 and several Monopoly properties on which houses have already been built. Player 2 starts out with the standard $1,500 and no properties. Finally, player 3 begins the game with only $250.

Who will be the winners and losers in this modified game of Monopoly? Both luck and skill are still involved, but given the different sets of resources and assets that each player begins with, they become much less important in predicting the game's outcome. Certainly, it is possible for player 1, with $5,000, to lose, and for player 3, with $250, to win, but that outcome is unlikely, given the unequal allocation of money at the start of the game. Moreover, while player 3 may win in any individual game, over the course of hundreds of games (with the modified starting conditions just enumerated), the odds are that player 1 will win considerably more often, even if player 3 is much luckier and more skilled.

In a similar fashion, children from lower- or working-class backgrounds simply do not have the range and depth of opportunities that children from middle- or upper-class backgrounds do. The earlier discussion of poverty's impact on children's development and the vast differences in educational quality by residence and income quickly illuminate the magnitude of these differences in opportunity.

Thus, to understand why people lack skills and education in the first place, one important place to look is the impact that growing up in a low-income family versus a well-to-do family has on a child's economic outcome. This impact is often overlooked in political and policy discussions, but unfortunately the class into which a person is born has wide-ranging implications for the person's life course. As Billie Holiday sang 50 years ago, "Them that's got shall get, them that's not shall lose. So the Bible says, and it still is news."

The third critical factor in understanding poverty from a structural vulnerability perspective is the lack of opportunities for all American citizens. Research has repeatedly demonstrated that the reasons underlying poverty have little to do with counterproductive attitudes among the poverty stricken or with a welfare system that is supposedly too generous. Rather, poverty is ultimately due to the inability of the U.S. economic, social, and political systems to provide decent opportunities for all citizens (Rank, 1994).

Another game analogy illustrates this point and the shift in thinking that I believe is needed to confront poverty. From a structural vulnerability perspective, what we are doing in this country is playing a large-scale version of the game of musical chairs. The key to this analogy is whether we choose to analyze the losers of the game or the game itself.

Let us imagine 8 chairs and 10 players. The players begin to circle around the chairs until the music stops. Who fails to find a chair? If we focus on the winners and losers of the game, we will conclude that some combination of luck and skill is involved. In all likelihood, the losers will be those in an unfavorable position when the music stops, somewhat slower, less agile, and so on. In one sense, these are appropriately cited as the reasons for losing the game.

However, if we focus on the game itself, then it is clear that given only eight chairs, two players are bound to lose. Even if every player was suddenly to double his or her speed and agility, there would still be two losers. From this broader context, it really does not matter what the loser's characteristics are, given that two are destined to lose.

I would argue that this musical-chairs analogy can be applied to what has been occurring in the United States economically, socially, and politically. Given that there is unemployment; that the country is producing more and more low-paying jobs without benefits; that countless inner-city and rural communities have been devastated by economic restructuring; that there is a scarcity of decent-quality, affordable child care; and that there are few provisions to care for those who can no longer participate in the economy because of illness, someone is going to lose at this game.

The losers are generally those who lack skills, education, and training and therefore cannot compete as effectively and are more vulnerable than their counterparts who have acquired greater skills and education. In one sense, we can focus on these deficits, such as the lack of education, as the reasons why some individuals are at a greater risk of becoming poor.

Yet, if we focus on the game itself, then the causes of poverty move from the individual's lack of skills or education to the fact that the economy produces unemployment, creates low-paying jobs, bypasses low-income communities, lacks affordable child care, and does not provide for those who can no longer participate economically due to an illness. These, then, become the more fundamental reasons why so many people are poor in this country.

When we focus solely on personal characteristics, such as education, we can shuffle individual people up or down in terms of their being more likely to find a job, but someone will still lose out if there are not enough decent-paying jobs to go around. In short, we are playing a game of musical chairs in this country with 10 players but only 8 chairs.

In summary, to understand the dynamics and characteristics of poverty in the United States, the three components of structural vulnerability are heuristic—the tenuous condition of economic vulnerability, the importance of social class, and the lack of opportunities for all in this country. Much of the earlier patterns of poverty can be understood within the general rubric of this structural vulnerability perspective. Perhaps what is the most salient for this Handbook is that the experience of poverty disproportionately affects many of the families discussed in this volume (e.g., minority families and single-parent families). These families have often been excluded from the social, economic, and political mainstream. Unfortunately, the same can not be said with regard to the experience of poverty.

REFERENCES

Anderson, E. (1990). *StreetWise: Race, class, and change in an urban community.* Chicago: University of Chicago Press.

Bane, M. J., & Ellwood, D. T. (1986). Slipping into and out of poverty: The dynamics of spells. *Journal of Human Resources, 21,* 1–23.

Becker, G. S. (1981). *A treatise on the family.* Cambridge, MA: Harvard University Press.

Beeghley, L. (1996). *The structure of social stratification in the United States.* Boston: Allyn & Bacon.

Berrick, J. D. (1995). *Faces of poverty: Portraits of women and children on welfare.* New York: Oxford University Press.

Blank, R. M. (1997). *It takes a nation: A new agenda for fighting poverty.* Princeton, NJ: Princeton University Press.

Breglio, V. J. (1992). *Hunger in America: The voter's perspective.* Lanham, MD: Research/Strategy/Management.

Brooks-Gunn, J., Duncan, G. J., & Aber, J. L. (1997). *Neighborhood poverty: Context and consequences for children.* New York: Russell Sage Foundation.

Caplovitz, D. (1963). *The poor pay more: Consumer practices of low-income families.* Glencoe, IL: Free Press.

Cheal, D. (1996). *New Poverty: Families in postmodern society.* Westport, CT: Greenwood Press.

Cherlin, A. J. (1996). *Public and private families. An introduction.* New York: McGraw-Hill.

Children' Defense Fund. (1985). *Preventing children having children. A special conference report* (Clearinghouse Paper No. 1). Washington, DC: Author.

Clancy, K. L., & Bowering, J. (1992). The need for emergency food: Poverty problems and policy responses. *Journal of Nutrition Education, 24,* 12S–17S.

Cohen, B. E., Burt, M. R., & Schulte, M. M. (1993). Hunger and food insecurity among the elderly (Project Report). Washington, DC: Urban Institute.

Conger, R. D., Ge, X. J., & Lorenz, F. O. (1994). Economic stress and marital relations. In R. D. Conger & G. H. Elder, Jr., *Families in troubled times: Adapting to change in rural America* (pp. 187–203). New York: Aldine de Gruyter.

Cook, J. T., & Brown, J. L. (1992). Estimating the number of hungry Americans (Working Paper No. HE01-090292). Medford, MA: Center for Hunger, Poverty and Nutrition Policy, Tufts University.

Danziger, S. H., & Weinberg, D. H. (1994). The historical record: Trends in family income, inequality, and poverty. In S. H. Danziger, G. D. Sandefur, & D. H. Weinberg (Eds.), *Confronting poverty: Prescriptions for change* (pp. 18–50). Cambridge, MA: Harvard University Press.

Dash, L. (1989). *When children want children: The urban crisis of teenage childbearing.* New York: Morrow.

Devine, J. A., & Wright, J. D. (1993). *The greatest of evils: Urban poverty and the American underclass.* New York: Aldine de Gruyter.

Drake, B., & Pandey, S. (1996). Understanding the relationship between neighborhood poverty and specific types of child maltreatment. *Child Abuse and Neglect, 20,* 1003–1018.

Dunbar, L. (1988). *The common interest: How our social-welfare policies don't work, and what we can do about them.* New York: Pantheon.

Duncan, G. J. (1984). *Years of poverty, years of plenty: The changing economic fortunes of American workers and families.* Ann Arbor: Institute for Social Research, University of Michigan.

Duncan, G. J., & Brooks-Gunn, J. (1997). *Consequences of growing up poor.* New York: Russell Sage Foundation.

Duncan, G. J., Gustafsson, B., Hauser, R., Schmaus, G., Jenkins, S., Messinger, H., Muffels, R., Nolan, B., Ray, J., & Voges, W. (1995). Poverty and social-assistance dynamics in the United States, Canada, and Europe. In K. McFate, R. Lawson, & W. J. Wilson (Eds.), *Poverty, inequality and the future of social policy: Western states in the new world order* (pp. 67–108). New York: Russell Sage Foundation.

Edelman, M. W. (1992, May–June). Vanishing dreams of America's young families. *Challenge,* pp. 13–19.

Edin, K. & Lein, L. (1997). *Making ends meet: How single mothers survive welfare and low-wage work.* New York: Russell Sage Foundation.

Fisher, G. M. (1992). The development and history of the poverty thresholds. *Social Security Bulletin, 55,* 3–14.

Food Research and Action Center. (1991). *Community childhood hunger identification project: A survey of childhood hunger in the United States.* Washington, D.C.: Food Research and Action Center.

Gelles, R. J. (1993). Poverty and violence towards children. *American Behavioral Scientist, 35,* 258–274.

Glickman, D. (1997, June 17). *Remarks of Secretary Dan Glickman at the FRAC annual dinner.* Washington, DC: Food Research and Action Center.

Gueron, J. M., & Pauly, E. (1991). *From welfare to work.* New York: Russell Sage Foundation.

Harvey, D. L. (1993). *Potter addition: Poverty, family, and kinship in a heartland community.* New York: Aldine de Gruyter.

Haveman, R. (1993). Changing the poverty measure: Pitfalls and potential gains. *Focus, 14,* 24–29.

Jargowsky, P. A. (1997). *Poverty and place: Ghettos, barrios, and the American city.* New York: Russell Sage Foundation.

Klerman, L., & Parker, M. B. (1991). *Alive and well? A research and policy review of health programs for poor young children.* New York: National Center for Children in Poverty, Columbia University School of Public Health.

Kollman, G. (1995, January 9). Social security: The relationship of taxes and benefits for past, present and future retirees. *CRS report for Congress.* Washington, DC: Library of Congress, Congressional Research Service.

Korenman, S., & Miller, J. E. (1997). Effects of long-term poverty on physical health of children in the national longitudinal survey of youth. In G. J. Duncan, & J. Brooks-Gunn (Eds.), *Consequences of growing up poor* (pp. 70–99). New York: Russell Sage Foundation.

Leidenfrost, N. B. (1993). *An examination of the impact of poverty on health* (Report prepared for the Extension Service). Washington, D.C.: U.S. Department of Agriculture.

Lewis, O. (1966). The culture of poverty. *Scientific American, 215,* 19–25.

Luker, K. (1996). *Dubious conceptions: The politics of teenage pregnancy.* Cambridge, MA: Harvard University Press.

Massey, D. S., & Denton, N. A. (1993). *American apartheid: Segregation and the making of the underclass.* Cambridge, MA: Harvard University Press.

Mayer, S. E. (1995). A comparison of poverty and living conditions in the United States, Canada, Sweden, and Germany. In K. McFate, R. Lawson, & W. J. Wilson (Eds.), *Poverty, inequality and the future of social policy: Western states in the new world order* (pp. 109–151). New York: Russell Sage Foundation.

Mayer, S. E. (1997). *What money can't buy: Family income and children's life chances.* Cambridge, MA: Harvard University Press.

Mayer, S. E., & Jencks, C. (1989). Poverty and the distribution of material hardship. *Journal of Human Resources, 24,* 88–113.

Maynard, R. A. (1997). *Kids having kids: Economic costs and social consequences of teen pregnancy.* Washington, DC: Urban Institute Press.

McLanahan S., & Sandefur, G. (1994). *Growing up with a single parent: What hurts, what helps.* Cambridge, MA: Harvard University Press.

McLeod, J. D., & Shanahan, M. J. (1993). Poverty, parenting, and children's mental health. *American Sociological Review, 58,* 351–366.

Measuring poverty: A new approach. (1995). *Focus, 17,* 2–13.

National Center for Health Statistics. (1997). Birth and fertility rates by educational attainment: United States, 1994. *Monthly Vital Statistics Report,* 45 (10S). Washington, DC: U.S. Government Printing Office.

National Research Council. (1995). *Measuring poverty: A new approach.* Washington DC: National Academy Press.

O'Hare, W., Mann, T., Porter, K., & Greenstein, R. (1990). *Real life poverty in America: Where the American public would set the poverty line.* Washington, DC: Center on Budget and Policy Priorities and the Families USA Foundation.

Orshansky, M. (1965). Counting the poor: Another look at the poverty profile. *Social Security Bulletin, 28,* 3–29.

Pappas, G., Queen, S., Hadden, W., & Fisher, G. (1993). The increasing disparity in mortality between socioeconomic groups in the United States, 1960 and 1986. *New England Journal of Medicine, 329,* 103–115.

Physician Task Force on Hunger in America. (1985). *Hunger in America: The growing epidemic.* Middletown, CT: Wesleyan University Press.

Poppendieck J. (1997). The USA: Hunger in the land of plenty. In G. Riches (Ed.), *First World hunger: Food security and welfare politics* (pp. 134–164). New York: St. Martin's Press.

Preston, S. H. (1984). Children and the elderly: Divergent paths for America's dependents. *Demography, 21,* 435–457.

Rainwater, L., & Smeeding, T. M. (1995). Doing poorly: The real income of American children in a comparative perspective. *Luxembourg Income Study Working Paper Series* (No. 127). Differdange, Luxembourg: CEPS/INSTEAD.

Rank, M. R. (1994). *Living on the edge: The realities of welfare in America.* New York: Columbia University Press.

Rank, M. R. (1997, July 5–7). *The ties that bind: Rebuilding our social obligations to the economically vulnerable.* Paper presented at the International Conference on Socio-Economics, Montreal, Canada.

Rank, M. R. (forthcoming). *In the shadows of plenty: Reexamining American poverty.* New York: Oxford University Press.

Renwick, T. J., & Bergmann, B. R. (1993). A budget-based definition of poverty with an application to single-parent families. *Journal of Human Resources, 28,* 1–24.

Ruggles, P. (1990). *Drawing the line: Alternative poverty measures and their implications for public policy.* Washington, DC: Urban Institute Press.

Ruggles, P. (1992). Measuring poverty. *Focus, 14,* 1–9.

Schiller, B. R. (1995). *The economics of poverty and discrimination.* Englewood Cliffs, NJ: Prentice Hall.

Sedlak, A. J., & Broadhurst, D. D. (1996). *Third national incidence study of child abuse and neglect: Final report.* Washington, DC: U.S. Department of Health and Human Services.

Sherman, A. (1994). *Wasting America's future: The Children's Defense Fund report on the costs of child poverty.* Boston: Beacon Press.

Sidel, R. (1996). *Keeping women and children last: America's war on the poor.* New York: Penguin.

Smeeding, T. M. (1997a). America's income inequality in a cross-national perspective: Why are we so different? *Luxembourg Income Study Working Paper Series* (No. 157). Differ dange, Luxembourg: CEPS/INSTEAD.

Smeeding, T. M. (1997b). Financial poverty in developed countries: The evidence from LIS. Final report to the United Nations Development Programme. *Luxembourg Income Study Working Paper Series* (No. 155). Differdange, Luxembourg: CEPS/INSTEAD.

Smith, J. R., Brooks-Gunn, J., & Klebanov, P. K. (1997). Consequences of living in poverty for young children's cognitive and verbal ability and early school achievement. In G. J. Duncan, & J. Brooks-Gunn (Eds.), *Consequences of growing up poor* (pp. 132–189). New York: Russell Sage Foundation.

Stack, C. B. (1974). *All our kin: Strategies for survival in a black community.* New York: Harper & Row.

Stevens, A. H. (1994). The dynamics of poverty spells: Updating Bane and Ellwood. *American Economic Review, 84,* 34–37.

Sycheva, V. S. (1997). Measuring the poverty level: A history of the issue. *Sociological Research, 36,* 45–59.

Tyler, T. R., Boeckmann, R. J., Smith, H. J., & Huo, Y. J. (1997). *Social justice in a diverse society.* Boulder, CO: Westview Press.

U.S. Bureau of the Census. (1992). *Studies in household and family formation: Current Population Reports* (Series P-23, No. 179). Washington, DC: U.S. Government Printing Office.

U.S. Bureau of the Census. (1996a). *Household and family characteristics: March 1996 (update): Current Population Reports* (Series P-20, No. 495). Washington, DC: U.S. Government Printing Office.

U.S. Bureau of the Census. (1996b). *Money income in the United States: 1995: Current Population Reports* (Series P-60, No. 193). Washington, DC: U.S. Government Printing Office.

U.S. Bureau of the Census. (1996c). *Poverty in the United States: 1995: Current Population Reports* (Series P-60, No. 194). Washington, DC: U.S. Government Printing Office.

U.S. Bureau of the Census. (1996d). *Who stays poor? Who doesn't? Current Population Reports* (Series P-70, No. 55.). Washington, DC: U.S. Government Printing Office.

U.S. Bureau of the Census. (1997). *Fertility of American women: June 1995 (update): Current Population Reports* (Series P-20, No. 499). Washington, DC: U.S. Government Printing Office.

U.S. Conference of Mayors. (1994). *A status report on hunger and homelessness in American cities.* Washington, DC: Author.

U.S. House of Representatives. (1994). *1994 green book: Overview of entitlement programs.* Washington, DC: U.S. Government Printing Office.

Uvin, P. (1994). The state of world hunger. *Nutrition Reviews, 52,* 1151–1161.

VanAmburg Group. (1994). *Second harvest. 1993 national research study.* Chicago: Second Harvest.

Vaughan, D. R. (1993). Exploring the use of the public's views to set income poverty thresholds and adjust them over time. *Social Security Bulletin, 56,* 22–46.

Vosler, N. (1996). *New approaches to family practice: Confronting economic stress.* Thousand Oaks, CA: Sage.

Voydanoff, P. (1990). Economic distress and family relations: A review of the eighties. *Journal of Marriage and the Family, 52,* 1099–1115.

Walker, R. (1994). *Poverty dynamics: Issues and examples.* Aldershot, England: Avebury.

Webster. (1996). *Webster's encyclopedic unabridged dictionary of the English language.* New York: Gramercy Books.

Williams, D. R., & Collins, C. (1995). U.S. socioeconomic and racial differences in health: Patterns and explanations. *Annual Review of Sociology, 21,* 349–386.

Wilson, W. J. (1987). *The truly disadvantaged: The inner city, the underclass, and public policy.* Chicago: University of Chicago Press.

Wilson, W. J. (1996). *When work disappears: The world of the new urban poor.* New York: Alfred A. Knopf.

Wolfe, B. L. (1994). Reform of health care for the nonelderly poor. In S. H. Danziger, G. D. Sandefur, & D. H. Weinberg (Eds.), *Confronting poverty: Prescriptions for change* (pp. 253–288). Cambridge, MA: Harvard University Press.

Yinger, J. (1995). *Closed doors, opportunities lost: The continuing costs of housing discrimination.* New York: Russell Sage Foundation.

CHAPTER 16

Diversity in Family Structure: Effects on Schooling*

DORIS R. ENTWISLE AND KARL L. ALEXANDER

PREAMBLE

As sociological researchers, our interests in the institution of family and in family diversity are long standing but secondary to our interest in schools as institutions. Our academic careers have focused mainly on trying to understand the phenomenon of schooling. Students learn in school, of course, but they learn in many other places as well, and schools foster many other kinds of development in addition to academics.

Alexander started research by doing large-scale studies on secondary school students, especially on how curriculum tracking affected them. Entwisle began her research with methodological and linguistic studies of grade-school children. Together they started the Beginning School Study in 1982 and have collaborated ever since, following the schooling of that panel of students up to the present. Almost all their joint research on schooling has concerned how social structure (ethnicity, families' economic standing, and the like) produces advantage for some students and disadvantage for others. With the demographic structure of children's families changing so dramatically over the past two decades, it is becoming clearer and clearer that family structure has more impact on school experience than was true earlier.

Some but not all the variation in children's schooling associated with family diversity can be attributed to the variation in the socioeconomic resources of families with different structures, and at this point it is hard to pinpoint exactly how other family characteristics explain school outcomes. Therefore, this chapter makes only a start at answering questions about the effects of structural diversity on children's schooling. It shows that in addition to the well-documented differences in school achievement favoring young children who live in two-parent families over those in one-parent families, considerable variability exists in children's schooling according to whether a single parent was never married or is divorced or separated and maintains a residence with or without other adults. An important way that family structure may affect schooling—not covered in this chapter—is that schools, teachers, and classmates may regard or treat children from single-parent families differently from how they treat other children. Other issues that are not covered are how schooling is affected by family stability versus structural changes or by the household moves that often accompany structural changes. More research is needed on these important issues.

DIVERSITY IN FAMILY STRUCTURE: EFFECTS ON SCHOOLING

Perspectives and Setting

This chapter attempts to shed light on the ways that family diversity, mainly various family structures, shapes the schooling of U.S. youngsters. The major issue is how family structure may create advantage for some children and disadvantage for others, or put another way, why children from some families seem to derive more benefit from school than do others.

*We are grateful to several governmental agencies and private foundations, without whose support this work could not have been done: National Institute of Child Health and Human Development (HD29343, 23728, 21044 and 16302), National Science Foundation (SES8510535), Spencer Foundation (B1517), and the W. T. Grant Foundation (83079682, 82079600, and 95-164195).

Three main intellectual legacies undergird this chapter. The first, which could be described as "mainstream child development," picks up where research like the National Collaborative Perinatal Study stopped when it concluded that social factors far outweigh biological or medical factors in explaining children's success in school. The second is status attainment, a subfield of sociology that focuses on how the social resources of families support schooling and children's cognitive growth. The third is research on human development that takes a life-course perspective. This latter type of research emphasizes such things as how parents' marital situations affect their children's psychological well-being or how being a teenage mother affects children's school careers. A few words will make clear how each of these legacies contributes to the understanding of family diversity and children's early schooling.

Somewhat belatedly, child developmentalists came to realize that long-term and large-scale research in natural settings is needed to understand children's development. For example, in the mid-1950s, the National Collaborative Perinatal Study began to monitor children born into 50,000 families in 14 sites scattered across the country. Its purpose was to see how specific medical events in the perinatal period affected developmental disorders in children over the long term. The implicit hypothesis was that there would be fairly clear connections between medical events and learning disorders, for instance, that birth trauma or early postnatal difficulty would explain why some children of normal intelligence do poorly in school. Broman, Nichols, and Kennedy (1975) compared about 1,000 children at age 7 who had normal intelligence but poor school performance with 6,000 others in the same study whose school performance was "normal." Sameroff (1985, p. xix) summarized the findings as follows: The "primary causal factors [of poor performance] reside not in the child's biomedical history but in . . . the social context of development; . . . lower socioeconomic status, less maternal education, higher birth order and larger family size related to higher rates of academic failure."

About the same time that mainstream child developmentalists realized how strongly children's social environments could affect their development, sociologists began serious study of status attainment, that is, how one generation confers social status on the next (Blau & Duncan, 1967). This research centered on how individuals sort themselves into occupations of various levels of prestige, particularly how individuals' families helped them obtain the educational credentials that govern this sorting. With few exceptions, students in high school or college, rather than in pre- or elementary school, monopolized sociologists' attention (see for example, Sewell & Hauser, 1976). Even so, performance in the earliest grades sets the stage for all that follows, so, in our opinion, the lack of research on family contexts in the earliest grades severely undercuts understanding of how social inequality is created and maintained. This chapter aims to make clearer why this is so.

A third intellectual legacy, and in some ways the most fundamental, is the growing body of research on human development that takes a life-course approach, beginning with Elder's (1974) *Children of the Great Depression.* These studies assume that development is malleable to a considerable extent, and in this regard they contrast sharply with earlier studies of child development, derived from a Freudian perspective, which saw the quality of adult life as more or less fixed by early childhood events. The life-course approach emphasizes the importance of family for human development at every stage of life and emphasizes change, as well as continuity, in development. For example, in his early work that traced the connections between the loss of family income in the Great Depression and youngsters' life chances, Elder (1974) found that in families that had suffered equally severe economic deprivation, daughters in working-class families were given less chance to attain a higher education than were daughters in middle-class families. More recent studies that have taken similar approaches have examined why parents' marital disruption depresses children's school performance (Morrison, 1992) or how a mother's receipt of welfare affects an adolescent's schooling (Furstenberg, Brooks-Gunn, & Morgan, 1987). A life-course approach asks why family structure is associated with school performance, as found in the National

Collaborative Perinatal Study, or why a father's education matters for educational attainment, as found in status attainment research. All three traditions try to explain human development, but the life-course approach places more emphasis on explaining the effects of family context on children's development than do the other two.

Family Structure and Schooling

Increasingly, national surveys have shown that children who grow up in single-parent families do not do as well in school as their counterparts in two-parent families (Zill, 1996). Still, how or why family structure affects schooling is not clear, and the causes of deficits in schooling of children in single-parent families are a matter of some controversy (Alexander & Entwisle, 1996; McLanahan & Sandefur, 1994; Zill, 1996). The deficits in children's school performance are certainly linked to the dearth of economic resources in single-parent homes, but whether the living arrangements of single mothers also make a difference is not clear. A few early studies suggested that African American children of single mothers who live in extended families adjust better to school (Furstenberg, 1976; Kellam, Ensminger, & Turner, 1977; Thompson, Alexander, Entwisle, & Sundius, 1992) and have higher preschool cognitive scores than do children whose mothers live alone (Furstenberg et al., 1987). But precise comparisons between children whose single mothers share or do not share their residences with other adults are difficult. For one thing, mothers who share residences with other adults are generally younger and have fewer children than are single mothers who live alone, and these confounded factors cloud the picture. Also, evidence concerning various kinds of school outcomes for children who are being raised in various types of families is lacking. For example, children of single parents who are being raised in homes that mothers share with other adults seem to adapt more easily to the classroom than do children of mothers who live alone, but how their achievement trajectories in reading and mathematics compare over the course of elementary school remains to be determined.

This chapter is organized along the lines of two basic questions about family structure and children's schooling: (1) What kinds of differences in school outcomes are associated with different family structures? and (2) What are the mediating factors? To answer these questions, we drew on the relevant literature and the Beginning School Study (BSS) to supplement the findings in the literature. The BSS was not directed only, or even mainly, toward understanding how the structure of children's families affects their school performance, but it gathered longitudinal information from several hundred Baltimore parents and their children that cover children's marks, test scores, and other school-performance measures, plus demographics and information about parents' attitudes and activities related to their children's schooling. In addressing the kinds of differences in school outcomes associated with different family structures, we examine cognitive outcomes of schooling (test scores, marks, retention rates, and the like) *and* noncognitive outcomes (classroom behavior, absences, and so on) for BSS children over the first five years of school and compare youngsters in three kinds of families: (1) children who live with their mother and father, (2) children whose single mothers share residences with other adults (not the children's fathers) (called "mother-other families"), and (3) children whose single mothers maintain residences by themselves (called "mother-alone families"). In addressing the second question, we examine differences in BSS parents' economic and psychological resources—such as parents' expectations for and activities with their children—that could affect schooling. The overall aim is to tally a wide range of school outcomes for children in these three types of families over the elementary years and to see whether differences in outcomes are related to how parental resources vary across the three family arrangements.

BSS Sample

In 1982, a two-stage random sample of children who were beginning the first grade in the Baltimore City Public Schools was chosen to participate in the

BSS. First, a sample of 20 schools, stratified by racial mix (6 predominantly African American, 6 predominantly white, and 8 integrated schools) and by socioeconomic status (14 inner-city or working-class and 6 middle-class schools) was randomly selected. The proportion of African American students averaged 99.5% in the 6 African American schools, 6% in the 6 white schools, and 48% in the 8 integrated schools (range 17% to 87%). Second, within each school, students were randomly sampled from every first-grade classroom. Three percent of the parents refused to have their youngsters participate, so the final sample consisted of 790 students who were beginning the first grade for the first time (nonrepeaters) in the fall of 1982. Although the city school system enrolled about 77% African Americans at that time (U.S. Bureau of the Census, 1983), the BSS oversampled whites to sustain ethnic comparisons (45% of its students are white). The parents' educational levels ranged from less than eighth grade to graduate and professional degrees, averaging just under 12 years (11.9), with a standard deviation of 2.6. School records indicated that 67% of the BSS families qualified for free or reduced-price meals at school, about the average citywide at that time.

The BSS data referred to in this chapter come mostly from the first five school years (1982–88), with a few additional data taken from later years. Beginning in the summer and fall of 1982, data were collected in face-to-face interviews with the students and parents. Teachers responded to questionnaires, and school records were examined for data on marks, test scores, and the like. In later years, most of the parents' questionnaires were answered by mail or telephone, but the students were always interviewed individually.

Over 80% of the youngsters in one-parent homes were eligible for meal subsidies, compared to 53% of those in two-parent homes. The parents' education levels also favored those in two-parent homes (12.3 years), compared with those in mother-other families (11.6 years) or mother-alone families (11.4 years). The mother's age at the child's birth was the lowest in mother-other families (20.9 years), the next lowest in mother-alone families (23.5 years),

and the highest for mother-father families (25.1 years). There are more siblings in the mother-alone (1.4) and mother-father families (1.6) than in the mother-other families (1.0).[1]

Roughly 24% of the African American children and 14% of the white children lived in mother-alone families when they began school. About 28% of the African American and 12% of the white children lived in mother-other households; in 40% of these households, a grandmother was an additional adult. About 44% of the African American and 70% of the white children lived in mother-father households (both mother stepfather and mother-biological father).

Children in One- and Two-Parent Families

Children today have different family experiences from those of their parents. About one third of the births in the United States are now to unmarried mothers (Musick & Bumpass, 1997), and of these children, 1 in 5 spends his or her entire childhood in a single-parent family (Aquilino, 1996). Between 1970 and 1993, for example, the proportion of children living in single parent families jumped from 11% to 23% (U.S. Bureau of the Census, 1994), so that by 1993, more than 19 million children lived in families that did not contain two parents. In fact, single parenting is the mode for African Americans; in 1993, only 36% resided in homes with two parents (U.S. Bureau of the Census, 1994). Also, over the past two decades, an increasing number of single parents are fathers. The number of families in which children lived with never-married fathers increased 15fold (from 22,000 to 345,000) between 1970 and 1990; by 1990, about 14% of single-parent families were father-only families (U.S. Bureau of the Census, 1990).

Family configuration overlaps economic disadvantage. Children in two-parent families fare best. In 1992 the average household income in two-parent families was about 2 1/2 times as great as that in mother-only homes (about $47,000 versus $18,000) (U.S. Bureau of the Census, 1992), while the

---

[1]Further descriptive information about the BSS is available in Entwisle, Alexander, and Olson (1997)

poverty rate of children in two-parent families (10%) was only one fifth the rate of children in female-headed households (53%) (U.S. Bureau of the Census, 1992). One reason why the proportion of mother-only families has swelled is the upswing in nonmarital births. In 1970 less than 6% of white births were nonmarital, but by 1991, this proportion had more than tripled (22%). Parallel proportions for African Americans are over three times those for whites (U.S. Bureau of the Census, 1994): about 38% in 1970 and 68% in 1991. Children of these never-married mothers are the worst off financially. Their poverty rate exceeded 66% in 1992 (U.S. Bureau of the Census, 1992), partly because only 27% of their mothers had child-support awards (U.S. Bureau of the Census, 1996).

At the beginning of the 21st century, it is becoming increasingly clear that children who grow up in single-parent families do not do as well in school as do their counterparts in two-parent families. What is not so clear is why family structure affects schooling or, put another way, exactly what causes the schooling deficits of children in single-parent families. This chapter mainly reconsiders how and why family configuration affects children's elementary schooling. As we said, to do so, it draws extensively on data from the BSS, which began in Baltimore in 1982 by enrolling a random sample of youngsters who were beginning the first grade. It then followed those students until they finished high school or dropped out of school. At this writing, the BSS panel is entering young adulthood—age 23—and is still being followed. The BSS is the only longitudinal study known to us that has tracked the entire elementary, middle, and high school years of a sizable cohort of both African American and white students and that has fine-grained data on children's standardized test scores and school adjustment, as well as on parents' characteristics and other school factors. All the measures of the children's school performance began when the children started the first grade, and additional data were obtained directly from the parents, teachers, and schools about the characteristics of families and classrooms all the way along. In addition to parents' marital histories and their children's school performance, the BSS archive can summon data on family life events (job

loss, illness, and the like), parents' occupations and education, the sizes of families, and living arrangements, as well as on parents' attitudes and activities related to children's schooling. This chapter is concerned mainly with the elementary school period, but occasionally we refer to longer-term outcomes that link back to those early years.

An important caveat is that this chapter primarily considers schooling in the elementary grades, while most other studies of single parenting and schooling have focused on older students. The family-configuration effects described in what follows could differ for younger and older children. For one thing, the dearth of economic resources in single-parent families may affect adolescents more than younger children if only because being older, the adolescents have experienced poverty for a longer time. Also elementary school children are more cloistered—their classmates tend to be much like them, and they play mainly with neighbors and relatives who live nearby. For these reasons, poor elementary school children could feel less relative deprivation than do poor secondary school youngsters whose schools contain classmates from a much wider band of economic backgrounds. The peer pressures that adolescents experience in terms of clothes, cars, and the like and their need for expensive equipment like computers and software could be less of a problem for younger children.

School Outcomes for Children in Different Types of Families

Compared to children in two-parent families, national studies have found that those who are raised in single-parent families have lower IQs and scores on achievement tests (McLanahan & Sandefur, 1994; Zill, 1996), more often repeat a grade (Dawson, 1991) and drop out of school (Coleman, 1988; McLanahan & Bumpass, 1988), and less often go to college (Zill, 1996). In fact, living in a single-parent family substantially increases the likelihood of being a high school dropout and decreases the likelihood of attending college, even when current family income and mother's education are held constant (McLanahan & Bumpass, 1988; Zill, 1996).

Living in a single-parent family is also problematic for students' classroom behavior and adjustment (Garfinkel & McLanahan, 1986; Zill, 1996). Children's academic success depends partly on their social and emotional adjustment, but the overlap between children's cognitive and affective growth has prompted little large-scale research. Still, whether children attend school regularly and are well behaved can matter a great deal for their long-term academic prospects, especially in the first grade, because their adjustment to the student role has large and lasting effects on their test scores and marks. These "adjustment" effects on school outcomes can be as large or larger than effects associated with their initial standardized test scores (Alexander & Entwisle, 1988)

Allowing for differences in families' economic backgrounds and ethnicity, children in single-mother families are over 2.5 times as likely to be suspended or expelled between Grades 6 and 12 as are those in mother-father families, and children of single mothers are more often tardy or truant (Zill, 1996). These children also display more disruptive behavior in class, receive more problem referrals, and rate lower on social skills, "personality," completion of homework, and study habits than do children in two-parent homes (see Epstein, 1984; Garfinkel & McLanahan, 1986; Hetherington, Camara, & Featherman, 1983; McLanahan & Sandefur, 1994; Santrock & Tracy, 1978).

Data about the youngsters in the BSS who were growing up in single-parent families enriches the picture just sketched. At the time the BSS children started the first grade, they showed relatively small but significant deficits in their scores on standardized tests of reading and mathematics compared to those in two-parent families (a little less than one quarter of a standard deviation), and these deficits increased as time passed. After five years in school, the children in one-parent families were behind those in two-parent families by more than one third of a standard deviation in both reading and mathematics (see Table 16.1).

The BSS children from single-parent families also performed less satisfactorily than those in two-parent families in terms of nonacademic criteria. They were absent only a little more often in the first grade (14 versus 12 days), but they were late twice as often (8 versus 4 days). At the end of the first grade, the BSS teachers rated the conduct of 39% of the boys in one-parent homes as needing improvement versus about 19% of the boys in two-parent homes. Differences in the girls' conduct associated with family type were less marked, but also favored those in two-parent homes (20% versus 9% were described as needing improvement). When adjusted for family background characteristics and parental expectations, many of the differences just listed were no longer significant, but even with such controls taken into account, the conduct of children from mother-alone families failed to improve over the first school year, whereas the conduct of all the other children did (Thompson et al., 1992).

The BSS teachers rated the first-grade children's classroom behavior on scales of attention span–restlessness, cooperation-compliance, and interest-participation. On each scale, children from two-parent homes scored significantly above those in one-parent homes by about one quarter of a standard deviation. A one-standard deviation increase in a child's rating for interest-participation or attention span–restlessness in the first grade was associated with improved reading marks (more than one third of a unit in that year and by one fifth of a unit even at the end of Grade 4). Better participation and attention ratings also led to substantial increases in scores on standardized tests: 15–20 points in both reading and mathematics at the end of the first grade, with smaller but significant effects still visible in Grade 4 (Alexander, Entwisle, & Dauber, 1993). In fact, the interest-participation and attention span–restlessness scales each predict children's gains on standardized achievement tests in reading comprehension better than do scores on the same achievement tests obtained when the children began the first grade (Alexander et al., 1993). Teachers' ratings of students' "adjustment" in the first grade thus matter a great deal for children's academic careers.

Differences Among Single Parents

Before we consider what could hamper the school performance of children from single-parent fami-

TABLE 16.1

BSS Students' Characteristics, Early Elementary Performance Measures, and Parental Expectations, by Family Type and Mother's Marital Status

	Family Type[a]			Single Mother's Marital Status[a]		
	Mother Alone	Mother-Other Adults	Mother-Father	Never Married	t-tests[b]	Divorced/ Separated
Proportion African American	.67	.73	.43	.86	*	.49
Proportion female	.45	.53	.52	.53		.50
Mother's age at student's birth	23.53	20.94	25.14	20.82	*	24.84
Number of siblings	1.43	1.04	1.60	1.02	*	1.52
Proportion on meal subsidies	.82	.86	.53	.91	*	.72
Parent's education	11.38	11.57	12.26	11.16		11.66
California Achievement Test: Reading Comprehension						
Fall Year 1	280	277	286	280		286
Spring Year 1	328	338	346	331		342
Spring Year 2	377	381	400	373	*	390
Spring Year 5	462	475	496	463	*	495
California Achievement Test: Mathematics Concepts						
Fall Year 1	289	289	297	287	*	297
Spring Year 1	336	336	346	329	*	344
Spring Year 2	374	378	391	371	*	383
Spring Year 5	458	469	487	460	*	480
Report Card Marks						
Reading: Fall Year 1	1.72	1.84	1.99	1.67	*	2.00
Reading: Spring Year 1	2.06	2.09	2.46	1.97	*	2.37
Reading: Spring Year 2	2.20	2.21	2.50	2.06	*	2.39
Reading: Spring Year 5	2.26	2.21	2.51	2.17		2.29
Mathematics: Fall Year 1	2.09	2.11	2.36	2.03	*	2.33
Mathematics: Spring Year 1	2.37	2.49	2.66	2.32	+	2.58
Mathematics: Spring Year 2	2.37	2.42	2.65	2.29	*	2.54
Mathematics: Spring Year 5	2.17	2.41	2.59	2.29		2.44
Conduct: Fall Year 1	1.67	1.68	1.81	1.70		1.73
Conduct: Spring Year 1	1.68	1.73	1.86	1.73		1.74
Conduct: Spring Year 2	1.70	1.68	1.80	1.69		1.62
Conduct: Spring Year 5	1.61	1.65	1.72	1.61		1.65
Proportion retained in Grade 1	.25	.20	.12	.21		.18
Proportion retained, Grades 1–5	.51	.47	.39	.49		.41
Total days absent, Year 1	14.29	13.62	12.24	16.28	*	10.53
Total days late, Year 1	7.76	7.73	3.85	10.14	*	4.12
Work habits, spring Year 1	8.43	8.71	9.01	8.57		8.87
Parent's expectations for student's marks						
Reading: Fall Year 1	2.54	2.56	2.77	2.55		2.60
Mathematics: Fall Year 1	2.64	2.71	2.75	2.68		2.65

$* p < .05, + p < .10.$
[a] Sample sizes differ because coverage varies for different variables. Ranges in sample size are mother-only, $N = 103$–148; mother-other adults, $N = 102$–156; mother-father, $N = 247$–422; never-married, $N = 100$–135; divorced/separated, $N = 69$–92. Marital status is not available for all single mothers.
[b] Reported significant differences are for t-tests comparing means of never-married and divorced/separated mothers.

lies, a word is needed about differences among single parents. Until fairly recently, most research on single parenting and youngsters' schooling centered on children who lived with separated or divorced single mothers (see Garfinkel & McLanahan, 1986; Kurdek & Sinclair, 1988; McLanahan & Sandefur, 1994). In the past decade, however, it has become clear that school outcomes, such as test scores and dropout, differ not only between children from one- and two-parent families but among children whose single mothers are widowed, never married, divorced, or separated (Moore, 1995).

In 1970, 73% of the children in single-parent families were living with divorced or separated parents, another 20% were living with widowed parents, and only 7% were living with never-married parents. Two decades later, 31% of the children who were living with one parent were in homes with never-married parents. In 1990, over half (52%) the African American children in single-parent homes were living with never-married parents compared to only 14% in 1970 (U.S. Bureau of the Census, 1991).

Children of never-married mothers have much severer schooling deficits than do children of divorced or separated mothers. Almost 20% of the children of never-married mothers versus 16% of the children of other single mothers repeat a grade, and compared to the children in biological two-parent families, twice as many children of never-married mothers have been the focus of a parent-teacher conference (26% versus 13%) (Dawson, 1991). Children of never-married mothers are also by far the poorest. They are spared the trauma of a marital breakup, but far less financial resources are available to them than to children in other single-mother homes; in 1992, for example, the average income for never-married mothers ($14,802) was about two thirds that of divorced mothers ($21,880). Never-married mothers also have distinctly lower levels of education than do other mothers: 59% are high school graduates compared to 82% of divorced mothers (U.S. Bureau of the Census, 1992).

A key distinction between never-married mothers and other single mothers is that they are more likely to have given birth as teenagers, and a mother's age at her child's birth appears to have some effect on the child's scores on standardized tests, retention in grade, and teachers' other evaluations of performance, even after associated factors, such as mother's income, education, and the like, are taken into account (Grissmer, Kirby, Berends, & Williamson, 1994; Hofferth, 1987). Roughly 70% of unmarried parents are teenagers (Elster, Ketterlinus, & Lamb, 1990), and among adolescents aged 15–19 who became mothers in 1975–79 (the same 5-year period in which the BSS children were born), about 32% of the white and 80% of the African American births were nonmarital (O'Connell & Rogers, 1980).

To make the picture even more problematic, the social ties of never-married mothers are limited. These mothers spend more hours at home with their children than do divorced mothers, but they are less likely than divorced mothers to participate in a variety of family activities and to provide an intellectually stimulating home environment for their children (Zill & Rogers, 1988).

The contrasts among the BSS children of never married and other parents are less marked than the contrasts drawn from the census data just summarized because the BSS mothers as a group are more disadvantaged than are the mothers in national samples. Still, the never-married BSS mothers had finished only 11.2 years of school, whereas the divorced or separated BSS mothers had finished 11.7 years of school; also as first graders, 91% of the BSS children of never-married mothers qualified for meal subsidies compared to 72% of the children of divorced or separated mothers. The divorced or separated mothers in the BSS, as well as the BSS mothers in two-parent families, were considerably older than the never-married mothers (25.1 and 24.8 years versus 20.8 years). About 46% of those who became mothers before they were age 20 were not married when their children were born versus 16% of those who became mothers at age 20 or later.

In terms of school outcomes, about 21% of the BSS children of never-married mothers were retained in the first grade versus 18% of the children from other single-mother homes, and by the end of elementary school, retention rates for the children of never-married mothers reached 49% versus 41% for other single mothers (see Table 16.1). Over elementary school, compared to those from other single-parent families, the children of never-married mothers consistently received lower marks in reading and mathematics, earned lower scores on standardized tests, and were more often absent or late. By the end of the fifth year of school, their reading comprehension scores were almost half a standard deviation below those of the children in other single-mother homes. Absences in the early grades are a particular concern because they affect the later school performance mainly of children whose home backgrounds are weak (Douglas & Ross, 1965). The BSS children of never-married mothers were absent 16 days in the first grade compared to 10 days for the children of other single mothers.

POSSIBLE MEDIATORS OF THE EFFECTS OF SINGLE PARENTING

For many reasons single parenting could have negative effects on children's schooling: (1) the relative dearth of economic resources in single-parent families; (2) the greater difficulty that single parents have in socializing children for school; (3) the number of children in the family, which differs between one- and two-parent households; and (4) the family's living arrangements, because many single mothers share residences. In the following sections, each of these reasons is discussed in turn, first in terms of published evidence available in the literature and then in terms of the findings of the BSS.

Economic Resources

Using four national data sets, McLanahan and Sandefur (1994) estimated that about half the "single-parent" decrement in children's schooling stems from economic deprivation. Other researchers have held similar views (see, for example, Bianchi & McArthur, 1991; Schneider & Coleman, 1993). The BSS children's gains on standardized tests over the first two years of school likewise indicated that families' economic standing is a major reason that gains

in achievement differ for children in one-parent and two-parent households (Entwisle & Alexander, 1995, 1996). With family size, mother's age, and other relevant variables held constant but economic resources allowed to vary, the BSS found that the children from two-parent homes gained 26 more points (more than half a standard deviation) on standardized tests in both reading and mathematics over the first two years of school than did the children from single-parent homes. However, when economic resources were controlled, the difference still favored the children in two-parent households but had dropped enough so the differences in performance among the children from the various types of families were no longer significant.

Socialization for School

Another reason that children from one-parent families fare less well than do those in two-parent families is that one-parent families are less effective in socializing children for school (Garfinkel & McLananhan, 1986). Single parents, for instance, are less likely than those in two-parent families to monitor their children's schoolwork (Astone & McLanahan, 1989; 1991) and to supervise them at home (Dornbusch et al., 1985). Parental supervision matters for children's academic performance because well-monitored children get higher grades and better conduct ratings than do other children (Crouter, MacDermid, McHale, & Perry-Jenkins, 1990). The benefits conferred by home supervision are also borne out by the superior performance of children who live in extended families, in which single mothers share residences with grandparents or other adults. These children have higher preschool cognitive scores (Furstenberg et al., 1987) and less difficulty adjusting to school than do children who live with mothers only (Furstenberg, 1976; Kellam et al., 1977).

In the BSS, the conduct of African American children in mother-other homes improved significantly over their first year of school, whereas the conduct of those in mother-alone homes did not, so the socialization effects of extended families seem important (Thompson et al., 1992). Also the children in mother-other homes earned better reading marks in the first grade than did either the children in other single-parent homes *or* those in two-parent homes, when the usual background factors, plus mother's age and sibship size, were controlled (Entwisle & Alexander, 1996). These latter factors, usually not controlled in studies of coresidence, could cloud the picture. Mothers who live with other relatives tend to be considerably younger[2] and have fewer children than do single mothers who live on their own.

Family Size

Children's school performance is negatively correlated with family size both in intact and nonintact families (Blake, 1989; Lloyd & Miner, 1993; Mercy & Steelman, 1982). The number of siblings tends to be larger in two-parent than in one-parent families (Blake, 1981, 1989), but how family size and parental configuration *together* affect young children's school performance remains to be discovered. Single parenting has negative effects, but the relatively smaller size of single-parent families could help compensate for them. Also the negative effects of large family size on school performance are based on study populations that included families with 7 or more children (Mercy & Steelman, 1982). Since both family size and the variance in family size have decreased sharply in recent years, any current effects of family size are probably much smaller.

By the time the BSS children entered school, those in two-parent households had more siblings (1.6) than did those in single-mother households (1.2), but the BSS single mothers who lived alone had more children (1.4) than did those who lived with other adults (1.0). With family type controlled, the teachers rated the BSS children with more siblings as having better conduct when they started the first grade than the children with fewer siblings

(Thompson et al., 1992). However, the benefits of having siblings held only for children with *one* sibling compared to children with no sibling; those with two or more siblings were rated worse. Possible differences favoring children in two-child versus one-child families, like those for the BSS children who were starting school, could have been present all along in other studies but overlooked.

Why would children with no siblings have difficulty settling into school? For one reason, only children receive more help and nurturance from their parents than do other children (Sutton-Smith & Rosenberg, 1970), so they may have trouble adjusting to a classroom group. In addition, only children are more likely to come from families with divorced or separated parents (Blake, 1989), so could have fewer social ties than other children because they belong to fewer organizations, have fewer friends, and visit friends less often (Falbo, 1982).

Living Arrangements of Single Parents

Data on the school performance of children whose single mothers choose various living arrangements are scarce, but the living arrangements for children in single-parent families vary considerably. About the same *percentage* of African American (39%) as white (40%) children of single mothers live in mother-other families (U.S. Bureau of the Census, 1992), but because about 58% of African American families are headed by single mothers compared to about 18% of white families, the likelihood that an African American child will live in an extended family arrangement is much greater (U.S. Bureau of the Census, 1992). The common empirical finding is that the African American single mother lives with other adults because it helps her manage scarce economic resources (Stack, 1974; Staples & Mirande, 1980), but this living arrangement occurs irrespective of financial pressures because even with income controlled, extended family arrangements are twice as likely for African Americans as for whites (Farley & Allen, 1987).

As we noted, research on whether the school performance of children of single mothers who live alone differs from that of children of single mothers who live in extended arrangements is thin, but two

[2]Why a mother's age at her child's birth should affect the child's school performance is unclear because age itself does not seem to affect the quality of parenting. Nevertheless, a whole constellation of other factors covary with the small effects of maternal age on children's schooling (Chase-Lansdale, Brooks-Gunn, & Zamsky, 1994). Teenage mothers are more likely than are other adolescents to have had problems in school—suspension, truancy, drug use, fighting, or even dropout (Elster et al., 1990).

studies cited earlier showed that African American children of single mothers who lived in extended families adjusted better to the first grade than did children of mothers who lived alone (Furstenberg, 1976; Kellam et al., 1977). Even so, national studies have found that although having a grandmother in the household increased parental supervision but having a male partner did not, the average child raised by a mother and a grandmother did about the same in school as did the average child raised only by a single mother (see McLanahan & Sandefur, 1994).

Residential patterns for the BSS mothers are consistent with national trends: 12% of the white mothers and 28% of the African American mothers were living in extended arrangements, and most mothers in both groups who lived in extended arrangements shared residences with "other relatives" (for 40%, these other relatives were the grandmothers). In both groups also, single mothers who lived alone had more children and were about three years older than were those who lived in mother-other adult families.

The BSS children who lived in mother-other homes did consistently better in school than did the children in mother-alone homes. Although the differences were not statistically significant, their test scores and marks over the first five years of school were consistently higher (see Table 16.1). Furthermore, if children's test scores when they began the first grade are taken into account, the gains made by the children in mother-other families were 198 points in reading comprehension by the end of the fifth year compared to 182 points by children in mother-alone families and 210 points by children in mother-father families. Allowing for where the children started, then, the five-year gains from when they started the first grade of those who lived in mother-other families came closer to the gains of those who lived in mother-father families than to the gains of those in other one-parent families. Also the first reading mark and initial work-habits scores of the children who lived in mother-other families were significantly higher than were those of the children in mother-alone *or* mother-father families when family background and other variables were

controlled (Entwisle & Alexander, 1996; 1997; Entwisle et al., 1997).

Mother-Grandmother Families

An important question is whether some subset of the mother-other families has a distinct profile in terms of children's school performance. At the beginning of the first grade, the test scores in reading comprehension of children in the mother-grandmother subset of mother-other families were higher (marginally significant) than the test scores of children in the remainder of that group (284 versus 272). Significant differences were also found in the work-habits scores and first reading marks of the children in mother-grandmother families from those in the rest of the mother-other group when they began first grade (see Table 16.2). The children in mother-grandmother families thus seemed to have an advantage over the children in the rest of the mother-other group in their socialization for school because when they began the first grade, they had better work habits, and their work habits were even a little better than those of the children in mother-father settings. Still, by the fifth year, this difference had faded because all the children in the other families then scored about the same in work habits. Also the children in the mother-grandmother group did *not* gain significantly more over the entire five-year period on standardized tests than did the children in the rest of the mother-other group (see Table 16.2); after the first year, those in the mother-grandmother families and those in different mother-other arrangements did about the same. The work habits and reading-mark advantages of the children in mother-grandmother families were strong assets that gave the children a boost over the first-grade transition, however.

A significant advantage in a child's first reading mark is extremely important because every BSS youngster who failed reading in the first grade was retained. Thus, a big difference in first-year retention status separates children in mother-grandmother families from the remainder of the mother-other group (0% retained versus 28% retained). By the end of the fifth year, only 27% of the children in

TABLE 16.2
Comparison of Mother-Other Families With and Without Grandmothers Present[a]

	Mother-Grandmother		Mother-Other Adult
	Mean	t-tests[b]	Mean
Parent and Family Measures			
Proportion on meal subsidies	.97		.89
Mother's years of schooling	11.5		11.3
Mother's age	20.9		20.7
Proportion of teenage mothers	.55		.51
Parent's expectations for student's reading mark, fall year 1	2.65		2.59
Parent's estimate of child's ability, at the beginning of year 1	3.77		3.65
Parent's expectation for child's education, year 1	3.16		3.10
Parent's depression scale, year 6	12.5	+	13.9
Parent's locus of control (Rotter) year 6	9.78		10.1
Children's School Outcomes			
California Achievement Test: Reading Comprehension			
Beginning of year 1	284		272
End of year 5	487		480
Reading mark, Beginning of year 1	2.13	*	1.67
Proportion retained, end of year 1	.00	*	.28
Proportion retained, end of year 5	.27	*	.50
Noncognitive Outcomes			
Total days absent, year 1	10.1	*	14.7
Total days late, Year 1	5.45	+	10.5
Work habits, Beginning of year 1	8.87	*	7.71
Work habits, end of Year 5	8.52		8.66
Proportion who attended parent-teacher conferences, year 1	.23	*	.47

* $p \le .05$, + $p \le .10$.
[a] The mother-grandmother category contained 31 cases, and the mother–other adult category contained 49 cases.
[b] t-tests compare means of mother-grandmother and mother–other adult families.

mother-grandmother families had been retained compared to 50% of the children in the rest of the mother-other families *because of the advantage in first reading mark*. From the second year on, their retention rates look about the same as the other children in single-mother families. In sum, the children of single mothers in mother-grandmother families did better in the transition to the first grade than did the children of all other single mothers (whether they lived alone or shared a residence with a non-grandmother). What is probably the most important, the children in mother-grandmother families were retained much less often in the first grade.

What could explain the better transition of children in mother-grandmother families to the first grade? Two possible answers are that (1) mothers who share a residence with their own mothers are a select group, compared to mothers who live with other relatives, or (2) grandmothers help socialize children so they are better able to settle into the student role. As to the first hypothesis (selection), the mothers who shared residences with the grandmothers were similar to those who shared residences with other relatives. The mothers who did or did not live with grandmothers were closely matched in age (20.9 versus 20.7 years), years of schooling (11.5 versus 11.3), parental depression (12.5 versus 13.9), parental locus of control (9.8 versus 10.1), and whether or not they were employed (30% versus 33%). Judging from these data, "selection" does not appear to be important. But the mother-grandmother children started school with marginally higher reading scores and an advantage in work habits and reading marks. The evidence in Table 16.2, especially the better work habits, seems to favor the more effective socialization of children for school over maternal selection as an explanation of why children in mother-grandmother families do better in the first grade.

A number of possibilities may explain why grandmothers could be more effective socializers than other relatives. One is that grandmothers are more invested in the children than are other relatives; another is that grandmothers are more willing to help mothers than are other adults, so mothers have more time for parenting. But many other explanations need to be considered. Currently, approximately one tenth of all children of single parents coreside for some time with grandmothers or other relatives (Aquilino, 1996). Considering the likelihood that these family arrangements may mitigate, to some degree, the negative risks of the poor school outcomes of these children, more research is needed on how other relatives may help socialize children for school.

PARENTING RESOURCES THAT SUPPORT SCHOOLING

Children who live with single parents or stepparents receive less encouragement and help with schoolwork than do children from intact families (Astone & McLanahan, 1991). But probably the most important parental resource is the parent's capacity to have "developmentally sensitive interaction with a child . . . that satisfies the child's need to grow socially, psychologically, and cognitively" (Bronfenbrenner, 1991, p. 1). This capacity is not necessarily tied to any of the mediators on the list considered earlier, whether income, living arrangements, or anything else. Parents' reduced capacity to act in ways that support their children's schooling, however, is an

increasingly persuasive reason to explain why children from single-parent families do not do as well in school as do those from two-parent families (Entwisle & Alexander, 1996; McLanahan & Sandefur, 1994; Schneider & Coleman, 1993; Zill, 1996). A cluster of parents' attitudes and behaviors (parental involvement in school, parental supervision, and parents' aspirations) account for over half the difference in the rate of high school dropout between children from single-parent and two-parent families, for example, and for all the difference in boys' idleness (not working or not in school) (McLanahan & Sandefur, 1994, p. 109). Supportive parenting in the prekindergarten period predicts children's school adjustment in Grade 6, when adjustment to kindergarten is controlled, and mitigates the effects of socioeconomic disadvantage and single parenthood (Pettit, Bates, & Dodge, 1997). A key component of parents' psychological resources to support schooling seems to be the level of their expectations and aspirations for their children. In national data sets, two-parent families' aspirations for their children have been consistently higher than have those of one-parent families (McLanahan & Sandefur, 1994, p. 106), for example.

Parents' Expectations

In line with these trends in national data, all through elementary school single parents in the BSS had lower expectations for their children's performance than other parents did.[3] Compared to the mothers in two-parent families, the single mothers expected their children to get lower marks on the first report card. Furthermore, the gradient in parents' expectations by family type maps directly onto the gradient in the BSS first graders' reading marks: The Children of single mothers who lived alone earned an average mark of 1.72 (below a C), the children in mother-extended families were slightly higher (1.84), but the children in two-parent families

---

[3]We did not distinguish here between the expectations of mothers and fathers, although the majority of parent respondents of every age were mothers. Other research on the relative effects of parental variables has found stronger effects for mothers than for fathers (see Musick & Bumpass, 1997).

earned solid Cs (1.99). Thus, parents' expectations, measured in the fall of the first grade before the children's first report cards (*before* the parents had received feedback on their children's school performance), were higher than the marks the children received on those report cards, even though by the spring of the first grade, the BSS children's marks in reading rose by almost half a grade point and were closer to the parents' expectations. The single parents' expectations for how far their children would go in school were also lower than those of the other parents (37% of the single parents expected their children to finish college versus 44% of the parents from two-parent families).

Most large-scale research on single parenting has not explicitly considered parents' expectations for children's school performance, yet parents' opinions and attitudes have extremely powerful and long-lasting effects on young children's school performance (Seginer, 1983). Entwisle and Hayduk (1988), for instance, found that parents' forecasts of their children's ability to do schoolwork in the primary grades had large and significant effects on the children's scores on the California Achievement Test and Iowa Test of Basic Skills four to nine years later, *with later scores on cognitive ability tests controlled*. Stevenson and Newman (1986) likewise found that in Grade 10, youngsters' self-concepts and academic attitudes were predicted by their mothers' ratings of their ability in Grade 5 and earlier (see also Alexander & Entwisle, 1988; Alexander, Entwisle, & Dauber, 1994; Entwisle & Hayduk, 1982; Hess & Holloway, 1984; Parsons, Adler, & Kaczala, 1982; Parsons & Ruble, 1977). The efficacy of parents' involvement in school (Zill, 1996) or of parents' visiting school (Lareau, 1987) may stem largely from the overlap between parents' involvement and expectations: Parents who expect their children to do well in school are more likely to take steps to encourage this outcome, such as attending parent-teacher meetings and providing resources at home to help their children do well in school.[4]

Why would parents' expectations for their children's school performance differ by family structure? Probably because parents are acutely aware of their own life situations and draw on that knowledge when they form expectations for their children's schooling. The realities are that compared to married parents, single parents have fewer financial resources, and financial resources affect psychological resources. The median family income of mother-child families is less than one third that of two-parent families, with about 50% of the children from single-parent families living in poverty (Bianchi, 1995).

The BSS parents of various levels of socioeconomic status did differ in their psychological resources, including their expectations for their children's school performance. Before their children started the first grade, the poorer BSS parents expected their children to get lower marks in both reading and mathematics and aspired to lower-status jobs for their children as adults than did the better-off parents (see Table 16.3). Even though the children on meal subsidies were doing just as well in the first grade as those not on subsidies (both groups gained equal amounts on standardized tests between the beginning and end of the first-grade school year), the poorer parents rated their children as lower in classroom cooperation and higher in aggression at the beginning of the next school year. Also, over the first four years of school, the better-off parents' expectations of their children's marks and estimates of their children's abilities rose a little more than did the parallel estimates of the poorer parents, even though the expectations of the better-off parents were considerably higher to start with.

It is not surprising that the parents' expectations of their children's school performance were related to the quality of the parent-child relationship (data not shown). The BSS parents with higher expectations tended to have warmer feelings for their children than did those with lower expectations. In the second year, the BSS parents rated their children's favorable and unfavorable qualities on three scales that focused on the children's socioemotional status (for instance, whether the children were "enthusias-

[4]Ho and Willms (1996) found that of four factors in parental involvement, home discussion of school-related activities was the most potent in affecting students' academic achievement.

TABLE 16.3
Parent's Psychological Resources, Years 1–4, by Student's Meal-Subsidy Status

	On Meal Subsidy (Mean)	t-tests[a]	Not on Meal Subsidy (Mean)
Parent's Educational Aspirations for Child[b]			
Year 1	2.8	**	3.5
Year 2	3.1	**	3.7
Year 3	2.9	**	3.7
Year 4	2.7	**	3.5
Parent's Job Aspirations for Child[c]			
Year 1	57.0	**	66.0
Year 2	55.0	**	64.0
Year 3	58.3	**	67.7
Parent's Estimate of Child's Ability			
Year 1	3.6		3.7
Year 2	3.6	*	3.8
Year 4	3.6	*	3.8
Parent's Expectation for Child's Mathematics Mark			
Year 1	2.6	**	2.9
Year 2	2.9	**	3.1
Year 3	2.9	**	3.1
Year 4	2.7	**	3.1
Parent's Expectation for Child's Reading Mark			
Year 1	2.6	**	2.9
Year 2	2.9	**	3.2
Year 3	2.9	**	3.2
Year 4	2.7	**	3.1
Parent's Rating of Child's Classroom Behavior			
Year 2: Interest-participation	24.3		24.7
Year 2: Cooperation-compliance	19.0	**	20.0
Year 2: Aggression-restlessness	19.1	**	20.2

* $p \leq .05$
** $p \leq .01$

[a] t-tests compared means of students on meal subsidies with those not on meal subsidies.

[b] Parent's educational aspirations were coded 1–5, with 2 = high school graduate and 3 = 1 or 2 years of college.

[c] Featherman-Stevens occupational status scores (Featherman & Stevens, 1982) based on earnings and educational characteristics of both men and women workers. Typical job scores are clergy = 66.0, dentist = 89.6, librarian = 65.6, social worker = 66.1, elementary school teacher = 70.9, nurse = 46.4, police = 38.0, waiter = 18.9.

tic and liked to do things," "high-strung or fidgety," or "happy and well liked"). Those who had high expectations for their children in reading also rated their children at almost the maximum on these scales, whereas those with low expectations rated their children a full standard deviation lower (data not shown). In essence, the parents who expected their children to get high marks saw them as having appealing *personalities,* while the parents who expected low marks saw their children as considerably less appealing. Whether children with appealing qualities do better in school or whether those

who do well react by being easier to get along with, there is little doubt that a warmer or more positive relationship between parents and children would support children's achievement growth.

Parental Actions

The BSS parents' expectations in the first year also matched the actions they took. For example, 81% of the parents who expected their children to get an "excellent" rating in reading reported that they read to their children more than 10 minutes a day, compared to 54% of the parents who expected an "unsatisfactory" rating; 59% of the parents who expected an "excellent" rating had seen their children's school records during the past year versus 27% of the parents who expected an "unsatisfactory" rating; 63% of the parents who expected their children to get an "excellent" rating reported that their children had borrowed books from the library in the summer, compared to 31% of the children whose parents expected an "unsatisfactory" rating; and the parents who expected an "excellent" rating reported that their children averaged nearly six summer trips, while those who expected an "unsatisfactory" rating reported only three summer trips.

Do these parents' opinions and activities matter? First, for every school outcome, whether marks, test scores, retention in grade, or dropout, BSS research has shown that parents' expectations are among the strongest predictors—stronger by far than children's own expectations (see Alexander & Entwisle, 1988; Alexander, Entwisle, & Bedinger, 1994; Entwisle & Alexander, 1990, 1996; Pallas, Entwisle, Alexander, & Stluka, 1994.) Second, parents' initial expectations when their children started school—before any report cards were issued—predicted a number of students' characteristics that are important for schooling, such as their academic self-images and feelings of competence. The level of these parental expectations also has large *negative* correlations with the academic or other problems that children develop in the first grade and with whether children are held back or placed in special education classes. Thus, children whose parents hold lower expectations have more problems in the first grade than do other children.

The models to explain the BSS children's cumulative gains on standardized tests over the first two years of school point to parents' expectations and families' economic status as the two *major* explanatory variables (Entwisle & Alexander, 1996). These two kinds of resources are roughly of the same importance and largely independent of each other in explaining the BSS children's school achievement. It is essential to note that these resources add up. Although they are correlated, one does not replace the other. Better-off parents have more reading

materials at home and visit more places, but they also tend to have more of the psychological resources that foster children's development, such as higher expectations.

The family's willingness to make large investments in children *relative to the resources available* probably deserves more attention than do particular family activities like taking children to the library or museums (Heyns, 1978). For example, high-income parents may purchase all kinds of educational books and toys but have little day-to-day contact with their children, whereas low-income parents may not be able to buy books but can take their children to the library and read to them. Parents of all economic levels, including those of the most limited circumstances, can supply the psychological supports to help young children do well in elementary school, and these supports have strong positive effects that reinforce the effects of financial supports (Entwisle & Alexander, 1996; Lee, Bryk, & Smith, 1993).

In sum, the expectations of the BSS parents vary by economic status but represent an additional resource that is positively and strongly related to children's school performance. Expectations reflect parents' attitudes *and* behaviors; they index the parents' aspirations for the children and the emotional quality of the parent-child relationship as well as the specific actions parents take to help children learn. Parents who expect children to do well encourage them to have high expectations for themselves (Entwisle & Hayduk, 1982), and when children have high expectations, they are more likely to raise their hands and otherwise participate in class (Entwisle & Webster, 1972).

Parents' early expectations also have profound and long-lasting effects. The BSS parents' expectations for children's first-grade marks correlated with how far they expected the children to go in school ($r = .30$) when they were asked about long-term educational plans in the first year and correlated even more strongly eight years later ($r = .51$). Other evidence of the potency of parents' early expectations is that the first-grade children whose parents expected them to go to college were twice as likely to take algebra as to take a lower-level mathematics course in the eighth grade, with their families' economic status and the children's ability and performance in the first grade controlled. These findings suggest that policies that foster parental involvement in school may be successful mainly because they channel parents' expectations and suggest specific ways for parents to implement their expectations.

SOCIAL TIES

Single-parent families have less income and fewer psychological resources than do two-parent families, but they are also involved in fewer social relationships and organizations (Coleman, 1988). Social support, often critical for dealing with various kinds of crises, is also essential for day-to-day functioning in the parent role. Having more than one parent helps in the communication of family rules and discipline (Kellam, Branch, Agrawal, & Ensminger, 1975; Weiss, 1979), and even though residential fathers do little child care compared to mothers, the presence of another parent in the home can increase the families' psychological resources. For example, two parents often have different interests and skills, so that one parent may follow professional sports and talk about batting averages, game rules, and the like, while the other parent may talk about family history and rituals and share activities related to holidays that center on family care and the preparation of meals (Bryant & Zick, 1996). Having only one parent living with children also automatically leads to fewer social connections outside the family, for example, connections with the absent parent's relatives, coworkers, and friends, and fewer connections between the home and the school (see Booth & Dunn, 1996). One parent has less time to visit the school and take part in school activities than two do. Even if the second parent does not visit, his or her presence in the home can make it easier for the primary parent to visit.

Aside from skills or social connections, two parents who reside in the same home can help each other maintain the psychic stamina required to provide steady and consistent discipline of children. Thomson, McLanahan, and Curlin (1992) found that single parents, whether male or female, have more difficulty exerting control over children and making demands on them when another adult is not present in the home. Perhaps the most challenging aspect of parenting is its unremitting nature: Not just infants, but children of all ages require monitoring 24 hours a day, 7 days a week. Two parents are much better able to meet this challenge than is one. A single parent living alone cannot shop for groceries in the evening or even hunt for a job in the daytime without engaging a baby-sitter.

On the negative side, however, family relationships may carry many kinds of negative valences that can affect schooling negatively. For example, psychological resources contributed by the father could be negative if he is not only physically absent but avoids visiting or supporting the children. Economic hardship reduces both parents' psychological resources. Job loss undercuts fathers' mental and physical well-being and often strains relationships with the children (McLoyd, 1989). Likewise, for single divorced mothers, financial stress predicts increased maternal demands and childrearing restrictions (Colletta, 1983).

OVERVIEW

Norms governing marriage, divorce, and the expectations for gendered behavior evolved in the latter half of the 20th century and led to dramatic changes in children's family contexts. Research over the past decade has filled in some pieces of what has turned out to be a complicated picture. Even so, the full consequences of variations in family structure for elementary children's schooling still need to be spelled out.

One severe hindrance to research on how family diversity affects schooling is that the phenomenon of schooling itself is extremely complex. Cognitive status, as measured by scores on standardized tests, is often used as the exclusive benchmark to evaluate children's schooling, but *gains* on standardized tests are a more suitable indicator of the effects of schooling. Also, children's marks, retention, dropout, social adjustment, psychological well-being, and other outcomes of schooling can respond differently or more strongly to various family characteristics. For example, for the BSS children, the differences in first-year retention rates favoring children in mother-grandmother families were striking. The avoidance of retention in the first grade is extremely important for children's long-term school success, but without data on retention rates, this outcome favoring children in mother-grandmother families would have been missed.

Another severe hindrance is that evidence about the linkages between family structure and children's outcomes is often ambiguous (Seltzer, 1994). It is particularly difficult to isolate the effects of family composition from the effects of age. For example, for reasons mentioned earlier, the lack of economic resources does not have the same impact on preschoolers as on adolescents, nor do developmental outcomes have to be the same for socioemotional and cognitive growth (Furstenberg et al., 1987). A particularly troubling issue is the effects of selection. For example, in the case of grandmothers' coresidence and the first-grade transition, children who are easy to handle may reside (with their mothers) more often in grandmother-present homes than may more difficult children.

The particular historical period in which a study is carried out also makes a difference. The conclusion from earlier studies that children raised in two-parent or one-parent families do about the same on standardized tests (Ferri, 1976; Garfinkel & McLanahan, 1986; Hetherington et al., 1983) can now be called into question. More recent analyses, including those in this chapter, have shown that the test scores of children in single-parent families are consistently lower than those of children in two-parent families (Entwisle & Alexander, 1992; McLanahan & Sandefur, 1994; Zill, 1996). These deficits in test scores are linked to the lower economic status and lower expectations of single parents (Entwisle & Alexander, 1996; McLanahan & Sandefur, 1994), but, as this chapter points out, single parents are not a homogeneous group. More work is needed to distinguish among outcomes for children in different kinds of single-parent families and what mediates those outcomes.

Still another issue is the lack of attention to contextual effects. Teachers have more negative perceptions of children from single-parent homes than of children from two-parent homes (Epstein, 1984), and they rate children from divorced homes more negatively on happiness, adjustment, and the ability to cope with stress (Santrock & Tracy, 1978). If a child is labeled as coming from a divorced family, schoolmates also rate him or her lower in academic, social, and emotional functioning (Guttmann, Geva, & Gefen, 1988). On the one hand, these effects may be fading as the number of divorced parents increases. On the other hand, contextual effects could be even more severe for children of teenage or never-married mothers.

Given the findings now at hand, it seems unlikely that alterations in family structure are the root cause of failure in school (see Zill, 1996). Still, national data for children over a wide age range are consistent with Zill's assertion that divorce and single parenthood have *some* negative effects on children's achievement in school, and the BSS data point to a significant deficit for children of never-married mothers. The BSS data also point to the importance of parents' expectations and their variation across family types—parental resources that appear to be critical for achievement even after test scores are controlled (Entwisle & Hayduk, 1988; Hess & Holloway, 1984; Seginer, 1983; Stevenson & Newman, 1986).

The two basic questions pertaining to family structure and children's schooling asked at the beginning of this chapter are whether differences in school outcomes associated with family structure are large and consistent, and what the mediating factors are. It is not surprising that the answers are not simple. On average, children in two-parent homes do better than those in one-parent homes, but children live in many kinds of "one-parent" homes, including a number not discussed in this chapter. As for mediating factors, to the extent that they can be separated, the dearth of economic and psychological resources in single-parent families is critical, but the effects of contexts, including the living arrangements of single parents, can be dramatic. Much more research is needed on how contextual effects interact with family structure to affect children's schooling.

REFERENCES

Alexander, K. L., & Entwisle, D. R. (1988). Achievement in the first two years of school: Patterns and processes (Serial No. 218). *Monographs of the Society for Research in Child Development, 53*(2).

Alexander, K. L., & Entwisle, D. R. (1996). Schools and children at risk. In A. Booth & J. F. Dunn (Eds.), *Family-school links How do they affect educational outcomes?* (pp. 67–88). Mahwah, NJ: Lawrence Erlbaum.

Alexander, K. L., Entwisle, D. R., & Bedinger, S. D. (1994). When expectations work: Race and socioeconomic differences in school performance. *Social Psychology Quarterly, 57,* 283–299.

Alexander, K. L., Entwisle, D. R., & Dauber, S. L. (1993). First grade classroom behavior: Its short- and long-term consequences for school performance. *Child Development, 64,* 801–814.

Alexander, K. L., Entwisle, D. R., & Dauber, S. L. (1994). *On the success of failure: A reassessment of the effects of retention in the primary grades.* New York: Cambridge University Press.

Aquilino, W. S. (1996). The life course of children born to unmarried mothers. *Journal of Marriage and the Family, 58,* 293–310.

Astone, N. M., & McLanahan, S. S. (1989). *Family structure and success in high school: The role of parental socialization.* Paper presented at the meeting of the Population Association of America. Baltimore, MD.

Astone, N. M., & McLanahan, S. S. (1991). Family structure, parental practices and high school completion. *American Sociological Review, 56,* 309–320.

Bianchi, S. M. (1995). The changing demographic and socioeconomic character. In S. Hanson (Ed.), *Single parent families: Diversity, myths, and realities* (pp. 71–97). New York: Hayworth Press.

Bianchi, S. M., & McArthur, E. (1991). *Family disruption and economic hardship: The short-run picture for children: Current Population Reports* (Series P-70, No. 23). Washington, DC: U.S. Government Printing Office.

Blake, J. (1981). Family size and the quality of children. *Demography, 18,* 421–442.

Blake, J. (1989). *Family size and achievement.* Berkeley: University of California Press.

Blau, P. M., & Duncan, O. D. (1967). *The American occupational structure.* New York: John Wiley.

Booth, A., & Dunn, J. F. (1996). *Family-school links: How do they affect educational outcomes?.* Mahwah, NJ: Lawrence Erlbaum.

Broman, S. H., Nichols, P. L., & Kennedy, W. (1975). *Preschool IQ: Prenatal and early developmental correlates.* Hillsdale, NJ: Lawrence Erlbaum.

Bronfenbrenner, U. (1991). What do families do? *Family Affairs, 4,* 1–6.

Bryant, W. K., & Zick, C. D. (1996). An examination of parent-child shared time. *Journal of Marriage and the Family, 58,* 227–237.

Chase-Lansdale, P. L., Brooks-Gunn, J., & Zamsky, E. S. (1994). Young African American multigenerational families in poverty: Quality of mothering and grandmothering. *Child Development, 65,* 373–393.

Coleman, J. S. (1988). Social capital in the creation of human capital. *American Journal of Sociology, 94*(Suppl.), S95–S120.

Colletta, N. D. (1983). Stressful lives: The situation of divorced mothers and their children. *Journal of Divorce, 6,* 19–31.

Crouter, A. C., MacDermid, S. M., McHale, S. M., & Perry-Jenkins, M. (1990). Parental monitoring and perceptions of children's school performance and conduct in dual- and single-earner families. *Developmental Psychology, 26,* 649–657.

Dawson, D. A. (1991). Family structure and children's health and well-being: Data from the 1988 National Health Interview Survey on child health. *Journal of Marriage and the Family, 53,* 573–584.

Dornbusch, S. M., Carlsmith, J. M., Bushwall, S. J., Ritter, P. L., Leiderman, H., Hastorf, A. H., & Gross, R. T. (1985). Single parents, extended households, and the control of adolescents. *Child Development, 56,* 326–341.

Douglas, J. W. B., & Ross, J. M. (1965). The effects of absence on primary school performance. *British Journal of Educational Psychology, 35,* 28–40.

Elder, G. H., Jr. (1974). *Children of the Great Depression: Social change in life experience.* Chicago: University of Chicago Press.

Elster, A. B., Ketterlinus, R., & Lamb, M. E. (1990). Association between parenthood and problem behavior in a national sample of adolescents. *Pediatrics, 85,* 1044–1050.

Entwisle, D. R., & Alexander, K. L. (1990). Beginning school math competence. *Child Development, 61,* 454–471.

Entwisle, D. R., & Alexander, K. L. (1992). School performance and family configuration. In *New directions in child and family research: Shaping Head Start in the 90's.* New York: National Council of Jewish Women.

Entwisle, D. R., & Alexander, K. L. (1995). A parent's economic shadow: Family structure versus family resources as influences on early school achievement. *Journal of Marriage and the Family, 57,* 399–409.

Entwisle, D. R., & Alexander, K. L. (1996). Family type and children's growth in reading and math over the primary grades. *Journal of Marriage and the Family, 58,* 341–355.

Entwisle, D. R., Alexander, K. L., & Olson, L. S. (1997). *Children, schools and inequality.* Boulder, CO: Westview Press.

Entwisle, D. R., & Hayduk, L. A. (1982). *Early schooling: Cognitive and affective outcomes.* Baltimore, MD: Johns Hopkins University Press.

Entwisle, D. R., & Hayduk, L. A. (1988). Lasting effects of elementary school. *Sociology of Education, 61,* 147–159.

Entwisle, D. R., & Webster, M. J. (1972). Raising children's performance expectations. *Social Science Research, 1,* 147–158.

Epstein, J. L. (1984). *Single parents and the schools: The effect of marital status on parent and teacher evaluations* (Report No. 353). Baltimore, MD: Center for Social Organization of Schools, Johns Hopkins University.

Falbo, T. (1982). Only children in America. In M. E. Lamb & B. Sutton-Smith (Eds.), *Sibling relationships: Their nature and significance across the life span.* Hillsdale, NJ: Lawrence Erlbaum.

Farley, R., & Allen, W. E. (1987). *The color line and quality of life in America.* New York: Russell Sage Foundation.

Featherman, D. L., & Stevens, G. (1982). A revised socioeconomic index of occupational status: Application in analysis of sex differences in attainment. In R. M. Hauser, D. Mechanic, A. O. Haller, & T. S. Hauser (Eds.), *Social structure and behavior: Essays in honor of William Hamilton Sewell* (pp. 141–182). New York: Academic Press.

Ferri, E. (1976). *Growing up in a one-parent family: A long term study of child development.* London: National Foundation for Educational Research.

Furstenberg, F. F., Jr. (1976). *Unplanned parenthood: The social consequences of teenage childbearing.* New York: Free Press.

Furstenberg, F. F., Jr., Brooks-Gunn, J., & Morgan, S. P. (1987). *Adolescent mothers in later life.* New York: Cambridge University Press.

Garfinkel, I., & McLanahan, S. S. (1986). *Single mothers and their children: A new American dilemma.* Washington, DC: Urban Institute Press.

Grissmer, D. W., Kirby, S. N., Berends, M., & Williamson, S. (1994). *Student achievement and the changing American family.* Santa Monica, CA: RAND Corporation.

Guttmann, J., Geva, N., & Gefen, S. (1988, Winter). Teachers' and school children's stereotypic perceptions of the child of divorce. *American Educational Research Journal, 25,* 555–571.

Hess, R. D., & Holloway, S. D. (1984). Family and school as educational institutions. In R. D. Parke (Ed.), *Review of child development research. Vol. 7: The family* (pp. 179–222). Chicago: University of Chicago Press.

Hetherington, E. M., Camara, K. A., & Featherman, D. L. (1983). Achievement and intellectual functioning in one-parent families. In J. Spence (Ed.), *Achievement and achievement motives* (pp. 205–284). San Francisco: W. H. Freeman.

Heyns, B. (1978). *Summer learning and the effects of schooling.* New York: Academic.

Ho, E. S., & Willms, J. D. (1996). Effects of parent involvement on eighth-grade achievement. *Sociology of Education, 69,* 126–141.

Hofferth, S. L. (1987). Social and economic consequences of teen-age childbearing. In S. L. Hofferth & S. D. Hayes (Eds.), *Risking the future* (pp. 123–144). Washington, DC: National Academy Press.

Kellam, S. G., Branch, J., Agrawal, K., & Ensminger, M. E. (1975). *Mental health and going to school: The Woodlawn program of assessment, early intervention, and evaluation.* Chicago: University of Chicago Press.

Kellam, S. G., Ensminger, M. E., & Turner, R. J. (1977). Family structure and the mental health of children: Concurrent and longitudinal community-wide studies. *Archives of General Psychiatry, 34,* 1012–1022.

Kurdek, L. A., & Sinclair, R. J. (1988). Relation of eighth graders' family structure, gender, and family environment with academic performance and school behavior. *Journal of Educational Psychology, 80,* 90–94.

Lareau, A. (1987). Social class differences in family-school relationships: The importance of cultural capital. *Sociology of Education, 60,* 73–85.

Lee, V. E., Bryk, A. S., & Smith, J. B. (1993). The organization of effective secondary schools. In L. Darling-Hammond (Ed.), *Review of Research in Education* (pp. 171–267). Washington, DC: American Educational Research Association.

Lloyd, K. M., & Miner, S. (1993, August). *Sibsize and educational achievement among individuals from non-intact families: The case of whites, blacks and*

Hispanics. Paper presented at the annual meeting of the American Sociological Association, Miami, FL.

McLanahan, S. S., & Bumpass, L. (1988). A note on the effect of family structure on school enrollment. In G. Sandefur & M. Tienda (Eds.), *Divided opportunities* (pp. 195–201). New York: Plenum.

McLanahan, S. S., & Sandefur, G. (1994). *Growing up with a single parent: What hurts, what helps*. Cambridge, MA: Harvard University Press.

McLoyd, V. (1989). Socialization and development in a changing economy: The effects of paternal income and job loss on children. *American Psychologist, 44,* 293–302.

Mercy, J. A., & Steelman, L. C. (1982). Familial influences on the intellectual attainment of children. *American Sociological Review, 47,* 532–542.

Moore, K. A. (1995). Nonmarital childbearing in the United States (Public Health Service No. 95-1257-1). Hyattsville, MD: U.S. Department of Health and Human Services.

Morrison, D. R. (1992). *The divorce process and children's well-being: A longitudinal analysis*. Doctoral dissertation, Johns Hopkins University, Baltimore, MD.

Musick, K., & Bumpass, L. (1997, October 30–31). *How do prior experiences in the family affect transition to adulthood*. Paper presented at the conference, Transitions to Adulthood in a Changing Economy, Pennsylvania State University, University Park.

O'Connell, M., & Rogers, C. C. (1980). The legitimacy status of first births to U.S. women aged 15–24, 1939–1978. *Family Planning Perspectives, 12,* 16–25.

Pallas, A. M., Entwisle, D. R., Alexander, K. L., & Stluka, M. F. (1994). Ability-group effects: Instructional, social or institutional? *Sociology of Education, 67,* 27–46.

Parsons, J. E., Adler, T. F., & Kaczala, C. M. (1982). Socialization of achievement attitudes and beliefs: Parental influences. *Child Development, 53,* 322–339.

Parsons, J. E., & Ruble, D. N. (1977). The development of achievement-related expectancies. *Child Development, 48,* 1075–1079.

Pettit, G. S., Bates, J. E., & Dodge, K. A. (1997). Supportive parenting, ecological context and children's adjustment: A seven year longitudinal study. *Child Development, 68,* 908–923.

Sameroff, A. (1985). Foreword. In S. Broman, E. Bien & P. Shaughnessy (Eds.), *Low achieving children* (pp. vii–xi). Hillsdale, NJ: Lawrence Erlbaum.

Santrock, J. W., & Tracy, R. L. (1978). The effects of children's family structure status on the development of stereotypes by teachers. *Journal of Educational Psychology, 70,* 754–757.

Schneider, B. L., & Coleman, J. S. (1993). *Parents, their children, and schools*. Boulder, CO: Westview Press.

Seginer, R. (1983). Parents' expectations and children's academic achievements: A literature review. *Merrill-Palmer Quarterly, 29,* 1–23.

Seltzer, J. A. (1994). Consequences of marital dissolution for children. *Annual Review of Sociology, 20,* 235–266.

Sewell, W. H., & Hauser, R. M. (1976). Causes and consequences of higher education: Models of the status attainment process. In W. H. Sewell, R. M. Hauser, & D. L. Featherman (Eds.), *Schooling and achievement in American society* (pp. 9–28). New York: Academic Press.

Stack, C. B. (1974). *All our kin*. New York: Harper & Row.

Staples, R. R., & Mirande, A. (1980). Racial and cultural variations among American families: A decennial review of the literature on minority families. *Journal of Marriage and the Family, 42,* 157–173.

Stevenson, H. W., & Newman, R. S. (1986). Long-term prediction of achievement and attitudes in mathematics and reading. *Child Development, 57,* 646–659.

Sutton-Smith, B., & Rosenberg, B. G. (1970). *The sibling*. New York: Holt, Rinehart & Winston.

Thompson, M. S., Alexander, K. L., Entwisle, D. R., & Sundius, M. J. (1992). The influence of family composition on children's conformity to the student role. *American Educational Research Journal, 29,* 405–424.

Thomson, E., McLanahan, S. S., & Curlin, R. B. (1992). Family structure, gender and parental socialization. *Journal of Marriage and the Family, 54,* 368–378.

U.S. Bureau of the Census. (1983). *Census of population: 1980, vol. 1. Characteristics of the population*. Washington, DC: U.S. Government Printing Office.

U.S. Bureau of the Census. (1990). *Household and family characteristics: March 1990 and 1989: Current Population Reports* (Series P-20, No. 447). Washington, DC: U.S. Government Printing Office.

U.S. Bureau of the Census. (1991). *Marital status and living arrangements: March 1990: Current Population Reports* (Series P-20, No. 450). Washington, DC: U.S. Government Printing Office.

U.S. Bureau of the Census. (1992). *Marital status and living arrangements: March 1992: Current Population Reports* (Series P-20, No. 468). Washington, DC: U.S. Government Printing Office.

U.S. Bureau of the Census. (1994). *Statistical abstract of the U.S.: 1994.* Washington, DC: U.S. Government Printing Office.

U.S. Bureau of the Census. (1996). *Statistical abstract of the U.S.: 1995.* Washington, DC: U.S. Government Printing Office.

Weiss, R. S. (1979). *Going it alone: The family life and social situation of the single parent.* New York: Basic Books.

Zill, N. (1996). Family change and student achievement: What we have learned, what it means for schools. In A. Booth & J. F. Dunn (Eds.), *Family-school links: How do they affect educational outcomes?* (pp. 139–174). Mahwah, NJ: Lawrence Erlbaum.

Zill, N., & Rogers, C. C. (1988). Recent trends in the well-being of children in the United States and their implications for public policy. In A. H. Cherlin (Ed.), *The changing American family and public policy* (pp. 26–116). Washington, DC: Urban Institute.

PART VII
Applications for Working With Families

CHAPTER **17**

Culture and Narrative as Metaphors for Clinical Practice With Families*

JOAN LAIRD

Cultural diversity, multiculturalism, culturally sensitive practice, and *cultural competence* are terms that indicate renewed emphases in the 1990s in the mental health professions. But the term *culture* may be understood and interpreted in a vast number of ways. We all use words like *culture, gender, race, ethnicity, social class,* and *sexual orientation* as if they had consistent definitions and there were some agreement on their meanings.

Mental health practitioners are repeatedly exhorted to become culturally competent and to practice in ethnic-sensitive ways. Doing so usually means educating ourselves about the characteristics of the "other" and discovering how others—people from other countries, with other skin colors, with different genitalia, or with same-sex partners—are different from us and what they can tell us about ourselves. To learn about the other, anthropologists have said, is to learn about us. As Bateson (1979, p. 68) put it, "it takes two somethings to create a difference"; thus, I know I am French because someone else is Swedish; I know I am short because you are tall. In Western culture, at least, people have

organized themselves around "difference," particularly around binary oppositions—male-female; black-white; gay-straight, rich-poor. To be culturally competent has meant, then, to know about and to appreciate "difference." But "different from" often means "less than" and keeps the culture of the seeker in the center and unexamined. What are other ways to think about thinking about culture?

Culture is a vast interdisciplinary topic that, in the past decade, has generated floods of literature and research in the social sciences and central discussions in academia and the popular culture and at professional conferences. How do we move beyond the cliché-ridden, often meaningless or undefined ways these notions are tacked on to diagnostic and other clinical languages, receiving little more than honorable mention? How do we surface our own cultural stories and cultural identities? In the world of therapy, how do we locate the cultural stories and meanings of the people with whom we work, so they can reexamine them in ways that open up hope and possibility.

The terms *culture, ethnicity, race, gender,* and so on are defined and used in many different ways. My approach to understanding and using these enormously complex ideas will become clear in the pages that follow. But it is important to say some-

*Portions of this chapter were previously published in M. McGoldrick (Ed.), *Revisioning family therapy: Race, culture, and gender in clinical practice*, and are included here with the permission of Guilford Press.

thing here about how I use the notion of culture. Many writers use the term *culture* synonymously with that of *ethnicity,* and both terms are used in narrow and static ways to refer to the identification of people with a set of traditions, in turn, associated with such variables as national origin, geographic area, values, beliefs, dress, kinship arrangements, social and political patterns, and religion—characteristics of a people that can be studied and tallied. The concept of race, similarly reified, is thought by many to refer to biological origins that result in skin color and other phenotypic characteristics, even though most anthropologists have long since abandoned biological explanations of race. Thus, people speak of Italian culture, black culture, or American Indian culture, identifying themselves and others by national origins or skin color. In this society, these identities are always positioned in contrast to dominant Anglo-American culture, which seems to refer to people of northern European or British origin. Anglo- or white American culture is usually assumed and unmarked; the white American is, it is often assumed, nonethnic; raceless; and, as many have argued, prototypically heterosexual, middle class, and male.

The history of anthropology and cultural study is one of searching for the elusive definition of culture. The field has moved from an early period in which anthropologists believed that culture could be identified and described through a comprehensive mapping of traits and practices. Today, many anthropologists (see, for example, Myerhoff, 1978; Rosaldo, 1989) see culture as a constantly changing phenomenon—"emergent," "written," "performed," always existing in the borderlands and inextricable from the eye of the beholder. It is this latter cadre of ideas that is slowly entering the family field and has captured my own imagination.

In this chapter I offer a number of ideas, or metaphors, that may be useful for thinking about how to think about culture, and, using those ideas, to generate some guidelines for a culturally centered approach to practice. I conclude with brief illustrations of those principles in action. The ideas presented here have, in turn, been inspired by ideas that have come from many directions, among them the interdisciplinary postmodern revolution in the arts, humanities, and sciences; feminist critiques; recent

work on gender and sexuality; and, most of all, the people with whom I have been privileged to dialogue and collaborate over the years—students, people seeking help, colleagues, and friends. Because I believe that our own life experiences provide some of the richest resources for learning, I begin with a brief story about my own travels toward some of the ideas expressed in this chapter, that is, with a narrative that I hope will place some of my thinking and experience in context. In narrative-therapy circles, this act is called "situating oneself," or making oneself "transparent," that is, sharing with clients where one's ideas have come from. These ideas, offered tentatively, are legitimate not because they represent the "truths" of some privileged body of superior professional knowledge, but because they represent the therapist's thinking that is based on his or her professional and personal life experience.

A WANDERING AND MARGINAL SKEPTIC

As with most social workers and other mental health professionals of the time, educated and practicing in the late 1960s and early 1970s, the foundation for my education was located primarily in psychoanalytic theory. In social work, there was always an attempt to include and be sensitive to "the social" and the environment, but we lacked theories for capturing the elusive interfaces between the psychological and the social. Only slightly seduced by psychoanalytic theory, I recognized that much of this body of thought either rendered invisible or "pathologized" my experiences as a woman, a lesbian, and a mother. More profoundly, this body of theory provided little help for me in trying to help poor, overburdened, chaotic families stay together. I could do a crackerjack "psychosocial assessment" on one person, but, when I added up six of them, I did not have a way to understand a family. I, like many others, was immediately drawn to newly emerging theories and models for understanding and working with relational networks of people and quickly became a family therapy groupie. The family therapy pioneers and the models, theories, and training programs that accompanied the family-systems revolution largely abandoned the pathologizing psychological theories and medical metaphors derived from psychoanalytic theory. New theories of helping individuals and families were being built on ecological, systemic, cybernetic, structural, and biological metaphors. We no longer believed in faulty people; we believed in the faulty functioning of family systems. Thus, the family might be out of balance with its environment, and it was that interface, the family's ecology, that needed to be corrected (see Auerswald, 1968). Perhaps the symptom was maintaining the system, and hence, the family's homeostasis-maintaining processes needed to be interrupted (see Selvini-Palozzoli, Boscolo, Cecchin, & Prada, 1978, 1980). Others (Jackson, 1957, 1967, 1968) viewed the family as an information-processing system whose circular processes of communication needed to be challenged. And still others (see, for example, Haley, 1976, 1980; Minuchin, 1974; Minuchin & Fishman, 1981) saw the family as an organization whose proper hierarchical arrangements needed to be restored or various subsystem boundaries appropriately strengthened or altered. The family was like a biological organism and was suffering from fusion or undifferentiation as a result of unresolved conflicts over the generations (Bowen, 1978); therefore, the task was to foster greater differentiation inside the family.

These ideas were enormously exciting for many mental health professionals, who began flocking to family therapy conferences in the 1960s and entering newly emerging training programs, but were seen as a threat by others and resisted by many professional schools and academic departments. During those years, in addition to teaching social workers about families and family therapy, I helped to cofound a family therapy practice, research, and training center that would allow for the application and sharing of family theory. I coauthored a text for social workers that integrated the various major approaches to understanding and helping families and applied them to settings and populations that were common to social work practice (Hartman & Laird, 1983). In that work, Hartman and I discussed at considerable length prevailing ways of defining *family* because how the family is defined profoundly affects the directions of both social policy and family-centered practice and shapes family theory. Searching for a pluralistic perspective, we liked the simple definition promulgated by Richmond, an early social work leader (1930): A family includes

all that share a common table. We adopted a phenomenological stance and an equally simple definition, arguing that

> a family becomes a family when two or more individuals have decided they are a family, that in the intimate, here-and-now environment in which they gather, there is a sharing of emotional needs for closeness, of living space which is deemed "home," and of those roles and tasks necessary for meeting the biological, social, and psychological requirements of the individuals involved. (Hartman & Laird, p. 30)

This open, flexible, and inclusive conception of the family avoided definitions limited by biological relatedness or legal sanction and was broader than those implicit in much of family therapy theory at the time. But it is not inclusive enough for today's widely varied ways of creating families. Some families today, for example, rarely share a common table (which I take as a metaphor for who lives in a household), and there is wide variation in the roles that families assume.

In keeping with a philosophy of therapy based on cultural, constructionist, and narrative metaphors, I am prepared to accept whatever definition of family clients bring to therapy, although many such families are not recognized as families by prevailing social institutions.

In this early period of the family therapy movement, gender, race, ethnicity, social class, and sexual orientation were largely invisible in writing and theorizing. There seemed to be an unwritten and unchallenged assumption that, if we were thinking systemically, our theories were universal—they applied to everyone equally. Family members from young to old and from both sexes were all caught in games without end, creating dysfunctional or unbalanced hierarchies, stuck in family togetherness, and equally contributing to faulty family processes. Power was not something that belonged to persons but must be understood systemically (Bateson, 1979). The notions of inequality or injustice were rarely addressed. One did not find articles on family violence, incest, or child sexual abuse in the family therapy literature of the time. Families of color; lesbian or gay-headed families; and even three-generation, remarried, grandparent-headed, and solo parent families were largely invisible. The family field, greatly influenced by structural-functional social theories of the time, assumed the "traditional" white—to a large extent middle-class—family in which mothers were responsible for the home and children and fathers for responsible for breadwinning.

In the late 1970s, having then taught and practiced family-centered social work for over a decade, I began to search for a doctoral program within commuting range where I could study and research what I had come to call the "culture" of families—the powerful ways of acting and performing and regulating themselves that seemed to develop over generations. In this period, the scientific metaphor was dominant in the social sciences, the professions, and family therapy research, but over the years I had come increasingly to believe that it was not "science"—at least in the ways that science seemed to translate into most family research protocols—that had proved most useful for understanding families or changes in families. One might better read T. S. Eliot or Dostoyevsky to probe the complex depths of family themes. In searching for a site for further study, I found that the psychology department in the local university had one family course and that it was the controlled laboratory experimental design that was considered most accurate and elegant, while in sociology, survey methodology was preferred and the search for a grand theory held sway. Few people seemed interested in the mundane, everyday life experiences of people living in small groups. In social psychology, I discovered, studies of perception and cognition dominated the curriculum. It was difficult for me to make connections between what I learned from the fact that rats preferred Mozart to Wagner to helping the depressed and abused Saudi Arabian student I had seen before class or the overwhelmed, angry, and despairing family I would be talking with after class.

Discovering Anthropology

Although I had never taken a course in anthropology and had little idea what anthropologists did or studied, I had been enthralled with the works of Oscar Lewis, Jules Henry, and Carol Stack, anthropologists who had spent years studying a small number of families and had produced thickly described (Geertz, 1973), arresting portraits of family life, much like the kinds of intensive case studies a talented and scholarly therapist might produce. Some time later, I enrolled in a joint social work–anthropology Ph.D. program, finding myself again the marginal person, in a sense, a stranger in both worlds. In my social work program, a narrow, quantitative positivist science reigned, and questioning that foundation was discouraged. As an older but neophyte anthropology student, it took at least a year of study for me to become acquainted and comfortable enough with the language and cultures of anthropology itself to begin thinking about what the connections might be between the anthropological gaze and its uses for family theorizing. Anthropologists, with rare exceptions, did not seem to talk or write about families. Nor at the time, in my program at the University of Michigan, did they conduct their studies in the United States. One should earn one's ethnography stripes in an exotic setting like New Guinea, not in a counseling center down the street. But they were patient and willing to humor my interests. In this program, there were no courses in statistics or methodology. One was supposed to "observe," "join," and hang out in the field," often for years, to enter and to try to understand the experience of the "other." This experience-near approach, merged with the interpretive lens of the scholar who had underdone years of rigorous study (Geertz, 1974), came closer to what I thought clinicians actually did than any I had encountered. Further, there was a valuing and recognition of "difference" that became exciting and humbling at the same time, as one learned that one's own cultural ways of living and believing were just as peculiar or mundane or exotic as anyone else's.

Perhaps the most valuable piece of wisdom that came from my anthropological experience, or at least I consider it so, was one professor's comment that one could never "compare" societies or cultures and one could not "transfer knowledge" from one field setting to another. Each society (and, I thought, each person, each family) was unique. What the scholar could do, however, was to transfer principles of learning, the ability to ask "good questions" that proved generative and valuable from one study to another. I became increasingly convinced that the categories and approaches that anthropologists used to study small societies were highly relevant for the study of American families—categories like ritual, myth, story, narrative, folklore, social discourse, language, values, beliefs, economics, kinship, gender arrangements, and spirituality. These categories were the windows into culture. Why, then, would they not be windows into family life? I became convinced that our therapeutic languages—psychological, systemic, or other—were more abstract, more distanced, and at least once removed from human experience and the ways people live and describe their lives, themselves, and their worlds. Why could we not simply use more "natural" metaphors than the machinelike and even warlike metaphors of systemic, structural, and communication theories or the elaborate structural mythology of psychoanalytic thought? Why did we need intervening metaphors that seemed removed from the languages and lived experiences of actors in the cultural drama?

In the early days of the family therapy movement, some family theorists (see, for example, Ferreira, 1963; Friedman, 1980; Selvini-Palazzoli et al., 1978) were writing about ritual and myth, but, in general, family theorists seemed to view these universal categories as problematic without fully examining and understanding how they worked in all families and how important they were to family culture and functioning. Families were seen as insufficiently or too rigidly ritualized or caught up in powerful mythologies that were dysfunctional and that needed to be exposed and even shattered. These interventions were often planned without a full appreciation of the meanings and importance of ritual and myth in every society and in the construction of family life everywhere. I began to believe that I could make a small contribution by bringing "cultural" ideas into the social work and family therapy fields and began by studying and writing about ritual, story, and folklore in family life (Allen & Laird, 1990; Laird, 1984, 1989).

Questioning Neutrality: Where Are the Women?

But I was not completely comfortable with the anthropological gaze, nor did I think the stance—or

perhaps the political and social position of the ethnographer—was identical to that of the clinician. For one thing, anthropologists strove for neutrality and, in general, if a cultural custom seemed bizarre or destructive, we learned that it was simply our own cultural lenses and biases that led us to see it that way. We needed to understand the cultural context. Thus, anthropologists studied bride burning in India and clitoridectomy in African tribal cultures, approaching these practices just as they might differences in eating habits or kinship arrangements. Social workers and family therapists, on the other hand, were in the business of helping people change, sometimes in ways that were mandated by larger communities of reference—the courts, schools, and child welfare system.

Feminist theory was just entering anthropology. Except in the work of Margaret Mead and a few others, the culture, history, and everyday lives of women had been largely ignored. I found myself asking, in class after class, What is known about the women in this society? How can we understand culture if we are ignoring half the population? It seemed to me that there were powerful gender and other inequities in many of the societies we studied with such interest, passion, and a presumably neutral countenance. Power, in fact, seemed an abstract idea, something encountered in studies of governing or kinship hierarchies, but irrelevant to gender and family relationships. In the early 1980s, anthropology and family therapy were both about to enter the postmodern era and the beginnings of what was to become a lively, if often discounted, feminist critique. For me, it would be an era in which a number of questions and discontents about much of what I had learned and was doing as a therapist and teacher of therapy would gradually be addressed. A larger culture of therapy I could feel more at home in would gradually take shape.

Ethnic Pride and Sensitivity

In the 1970s and early 1980s, some family therapists, attuned to the growing interest in race and ethnic studies in the social sciences, began to focus their attention on these themes. A debate in family therapy emerged over how to think about these dimensions of human experience in working with people. Although most clinicians believed that race and ethnicity were important issues and should be taken into account, we had little idea about how to understand cultural meanings and experiences, and there was little agreement on how such "knowledge" should be brought into the world of practice. In fact, some theorists questioned the usefulness of the cultural metaphor altogether. Friedman (1980), a rabbi and family therapist, argued that culture is "camouflage," that is, it is used in families in manipulative or controlling ways as a red herring, to preserve the status quo, bind children to their parents, keep family boundaries closed, and so on. Others like Montalvo and Gutierrez (1983, p. 16) saw culture or ethnicity as a potential "mask" that could obscure people's problem-solving modes:

> By using cultural constraints selectively . . . the family can pull the therapist away from reality. The therapist is made to deal instead with a cultural image of the ethnic group. In the process the family—as simply people having difficulties in solving problems—is lost.

These authors believed that if one was simply a good listener or, as in the case of various family therapies, able to surface the family structure, rules, and other patterns, what was important about culture would emerge. One needed no special knowledge about specific cultural groups.

McGoldrick (1993), perhaps the most articulate and dedicated spokesperson in the clinical arena for the importance of the cultural dimension in family life, took a different position:

> Ethnicity patterns our thinking, feeling and behavior in both obvious and subtle ways, playing a major role in determining what we eat, how we work, how we relate, how we celebrate holidays and rituals, and how we feel about life, death, and illness. (p. 335)

In her view, although to learn about ethnic group practices and beliefs is to risk stereotyping, to pretend that there are no patterns is to mystify and disqualify human experience and to "perpetuate negative stereotyping" (McGoldrick, 1993, p. 335).

Until recently, influenced by the principles of modernism, the goal of "learning about the other" has been central in both my fields—family therapy and social work. Numerous publications have been devoted to articulating the experiences of various ethnic and racial groups, training manuals for working with various "minorities" have been prepared and distributed, and courses devoted to countering the "isms" have been developed.

My view both combines and is somewhat different from any of these positions. I agree with McGoldrick (1993) about the power of culture and ethnicity (and gender, sexuality, social class, and so on) in shaping the self and the human story and about how important it is for clinicians to learn how to gain access to these stories. If we are to unpack cultural stories, we need to know enough to ask good questions, to "notice" culture in its many guises. I also believe, unlike Montalvo and Gutierrez (1983) or Friedman (1980), that whatever our therapeutic models, listening and questioning in and of themselves are not quite good enough and that special "knowledges" about specific groups or cultural practices are helpful *as long as we hold them tentatively.* For if we do not learn "about" our cultural selves and the culture of the other, it will be difficult to move beyond our cultural lenses and biases when we encounter practices that we do not understand or find distasteful. We will not be able to ask the questions that help surface subtle ethnic, gender, or sexuality meanings, and we may not see or hear such meanings when they are right in front of us.

Our cultural narratives help us to organize our thinking and anchor our lives, but they also can blind us to the unfamiliar and unrecognizable and can foster injustice. One needs only to think about the gender blindness that dominated the mental health professions for nearly a century to understand how invisible crucial influences on people's lives can be, a blindness that largely continues today in relation to lesbian, gay, bisexual, transgendered, and transsexual people. Learning about cultures can teach us how to ask good questions in a way that not only helps to surface clients' cultural meanings for our inspection, but makes it possible for clients to hear their own cultural stories in a newly reflective way. It is this cultural-questioning process—not cultural characteristics—that has transferability across cultural categories. Although we can never completely shed our experience-distant interpretive stance (Geertz, 1974), we can strive to maintain a critical, tentative, and humble perspective on our own cultural "truths."

On the other hand, we also need to move beyond the curiously static and decontextualized ways that ethnicity is often theorized, taught, and applied in clinical practice. We have leaned on theories and definitions of ethnicity that stress clusters of attributes and experiences, what may be called first-order learning, rather than learning how to learn about culture. We are urged to help people preserve their culture, as if culture was a set of essential and unchanging characteristics, an "it" that is identifiable and can be preserved in unaltered form. These normative ideas, in which we are all embedded, encourage stereotyping, narrow possibilities, and prevent us from recognizing the dynamic complexity and continuously changing nature of ethnic, racial, gender, social class, or sexual identity and experience. We are constrained by our nouns, as if words like *nature, identity,* and *culture* imply "things" that hold fast over time. We also find it enormously difficult either to pivot or shift the center; to divest ourselves of or, at least, hold our canons more tentatively; and both to begin with and enter the experiences and meanings of our informants. Furthermore, as investigators, ethnographers, and therapists, we are "positioned subjects who are prepared to know certain things and not others" (Rosaldo, 1989, p. 8). The challenge, as hooks (1984) framed it, is to move the subjugated experience from the margin to the center.

My stance may be described as "informed notknowing" (Shapiro, 1995). I use not-knowing, here, in the sense that Anderson and Goolishian (1992) used it, to mean that we are never "expert," "right," or have an edge on "the truth." On the other hand, I believe that only if we become as informed as possible—about ourselves and those whom we perceive as different—will we be able to listen in a way that has the potential for surfacing our cultural biases and recognizing the cultural narratives of "the other." Learning "about culture" from one friend, one book, one client, or one trip gives us the possibility of hearing and seeing even more at the next opportunity; it enriches our repertoire of good and important questions.

Before I discuss a number of ideas that I believe have the potential to move us away from more essentialist and fixed notions of culture, it may be useful to take a side trip here and briefly describe what have been the two most influential trends in the family therapy field in the past 15 years or so—feminism and postmodernism. Current ideas about culture and therapy owe much to these two movements, which provide the context for my own thinking and discussion.

FEMINISM AND POSTMODERNISM COME TO FAMILY THERAPY

Two trends in the family therapy field, beginning in the late 1970s and growing in influence throughout the 1980s, unsettled the various crystallizations of theory and method that had taken shape into "schools" of thought and thus were to change the face of the field. The first was the feminist critique, launched in 1978 with an article by Hare-Mustin, "A Feminist Approach to Family Therapy," an incisive discussion that lay somewhat dormant and unnoticed for several years. A second marker was Goldner's 1985 article, "Feminism and Family Therapy." Both women accused family therapy theorists of ignoring the historical and contextual gendered arrangements of hierarchy and power that were being played out in the contemporary family in ways that faulted women. Women were being blamed and "treated" for the very patterns of mothering they had been socialized to perform. Perhaps primary was the criticism that family theorists had ignored the larger social contexts in which families were embedded and that prescribed different positions in families and in the world for men and women. The alleged neutrality of power in families became a prime target for feminist theorizing. With this critique came an expose, in line with what was emerging in the beginning postmodern movement, of how therapists had assumed the traditional family form and the various dominant and biased normative ideas associated with this model. A 1987 article by Goldner challenged the prevailing notion in family therapy that families were organized by age or generation while gender, a vital force in family life the world over, had been ignored.

Two national retreats for leading female family therapists, organized by Monica McGoldrick,

Froma Walsh, and Carol Anderson, were held in 1983 and 1985 (Laird, 1986). These gatherings fostered an extended dialogue and networking among female family therapists, during a period in which women began to question many of the assumptions and practices underlying the major family therapy models. These meetings helped foster a number of important collaborations and a series of feminist family therapy books published in the late 1980s (Braverman, 1987; Goodrich, Rampage, Ellman, & Halstead, 1988; Luepnitz, 1988; McGoldrick, Anderson, & Walsh, 1989; Walters, Carter, Papp, & Silverstein, 1988). Women began to be more visible and to attain positions of influence in the major family therapy organizations and on the editorial boards of professional journal and to leave male-dominated training centers to found their own programs. Although female family therapists were not yet using postmodern language, they were clearly working to deconstruct central family therapy narratives, asking critical questions such as Whose interests do these theories or models serve? Whose voices are being subjugated? How do cultural family values and politics shape prevailing theories?

Although feminism came somewhat late to the family therapy field, clearly feminist family therapists were both responding and contributing to the exciting ideas that were emerging from the second wave of feminism. A period of "gendering" what had previously been ungendered theories and practice models in which male experience had been privileged assumed a shape that I see as parallel to the directions that ethnic theorizing was taking. The works of feminist theorists, such as Chodorow (1978); Gilligan (1982); Belenky, Clinchy, Goldberger, and Tarule (1986); Miller (1976); the scholars at the Stone Center at Wellesley College (see Jordan, 1986; Surrey, 1985); and others sought to articulate women's "different" voices and "different" experiences and to suggest that women's "differences" should be recognized and valued. Following a brief period of deconstruction of gender biases and privilege in family therapy theory and a certain degree of acrimony and disruption in the field, feminist family therapists turned from critique to creation, gradually rethinking and developing feminist

models of family-centered practice that might avoid the shortcomings of the past.

The second and overlapping challenge to family-therapy thinking arrived with the postmodern critique of positivist science, a critique some family theorists embraced and to which they made original contributions beginning in the late 1970s (see Watzlawick, 1976, 1984). Throughout the 1980s, evidence that several family therapists from around the world were pioneering new ways of thinking about family therapy began to seep into the leading journals. Before long, family therapists were flocking to conferences and workshops to hear Andersen (1987, 1991) from Norway, who originated the reflecting team idea; White from Australia and Epston from New Zealand (White & Epston, 1990), who were pioneering the use of ideas of narrative theory in what they called a "therapy of literary merit"; and Anderson and Goolishian (1992) from the United States, who stated that problems existed "in language." Influenced by writings from philosophy, literary criticism, anthropology, and other disciplines, these pioneers shared an emphasis on language, a view that individual and family problems are socially constructed, and a wish to dismantle the hierarchical power arrangements in the therapist-client relationship.

These movements have been followed by a new, greatly changed, emphasis on race, culture, and ethnicity in the journals and in the major family therapy associations. At present culture is at the center of a lively discussion, as the field pays renewed attention to the intersections among race, social class, gender, sexuality, and other cultural categories. One central issue at stake in narrative therapy concerns the role of the political, an issue that mirrors the debate among feminist postmodernists about the place of identity politics (see Butler, 1991; Epstein, 1987). To oversimplify what is a complex matter, some therapists believe, for example, that to interject feminist ideas or to deconstruct gender arrangements in work with a couple or family is to impose one's political or religious-like beliefs, out of keeping with the aims of narrative therapies (see Anderson, 1997; Hoffman, 1992). Others, such as White (1994), have argued that every therapeutic act is a political one and that it is incumbent on therapists to help expose the messages of powerful and perhaps unjust social discourses that pathologize personal narratives and close off hope and possibility (Hare-Mustin, 1994; Laird, 1989, 1995).

THE MANY DIMENSIONS OF THE CULTURAL METAPHOR

In the following pages, I present my ideas about the meanings of culture, in ways I believe have the potential to move us away from more static and essential notions and that are compatible with a narrative stance and emphasis in practice, particularly as developed in the ideas of Freedman and Combs (1996), White and Epston (1990), and Zimmerman and Dickerson (1996). These ideas, in turn, generate some guidelines for practice. Two recent examples from practice illustrate some of the themes.

Culture Is Performative and Improvisational

Culture is performed; its forms and meanings are situated and communicated in various "contexts for action, interpretation, and evaluation" (Bauman, 1986). We "perform" our cultural stories of gender, ethnicity, race, and social class as we move through the days in time and space. Furthermore, each performance, each enacted storying, is both unique and located in the larger social discourses of meaning from which we gather narrative threads, symbols, and ritual possibilities—a combination of tradition and imagination (Laird, 1989). This process can be thought of as improvisational, a term that I first heard Myerhoff (1978) use in reference to culture. Myerhoff suggested that we make culture up and we make ourselves up as we go along, forcing our experiences to fit into particular sets of meanings. She discovered that the aging Jews in Venice, California, who thought they were preserving Yiddishkeit, largely were making it and themselves up through highly improvisational stories and rituals, not so much re-creating the old as creating the new. Drawing on the work of Burke, Myerhoff suggested they were "dancing an attitude." This is what we all do—we dance attitudes.

Culture Is Fluid-Emergent

Culture is contextual, dialogic, and relational; thus, because no two contexts are ever the same, it is always more or less changing and always emerging. Although certain personal narratives are relatively enduring and we all strive to integrate new experiences and new meanings into a sense of a coherent "self" we can present to the world, I believe that the self changes, however minutely, from moment to moment in shifting settings. We are, as Gergen (1991) argued, all multiple cultural selves. I am culturally different when I am in a classroom on the campus of Smith College; vacationing in my Maine cabin in the woods; marching in the Gay, Lesbian, Bisexual March in Washington, DC; driving in heavy traffic by myself; driving in heavy traffic with a casual friend or acquaintance; eating dinner at the college president's house; or visiting my mother in central Florida. What I am aware of is that I change various cultural markers and symbols. I alter my language and topics of conversation, my costumes, my positioning, and how much and what I eat or drink. I become more or less feminine or masculine, more or less gay or straight, more or less middle class, more or less my mother (Protestant, English, and German in heritage) or my father (Catholic, Irish, and French-Canadian). I never wear jeans to the college president's house, I never call anyone an "ass——" when I am performing professionally in public, and I try not to swear in front of my young granddaughter. I do not talk about my career in the same way when I am with my family as when I am with my friends or colleagues. I, like all of us, dance an attitude.

This is not to trivialize, for example, the importance and centrality to our lives of race, gender, or other aspects of cultural identity. As African American family therapist Hardy (1996) pointed out, as a person and a therapist, race is always salient for him, whether he is working with a white family or another black man, in a way that it may not (but would be if we could shift the center) feel salient for a white therapist working with a white family. For Hardy, it is always part of the "discourse in the mirrored room" (Hare-Mustin, 1994). Although some white therapists may have difficulty recognizing or dealing with salient issues of race and racism in therapy situations in which clients identify as people of color, what is more pervasive is the failure of white therapists to recognize the importance and meanings of their own racial identities in therapy with anyone.

Any cultural categorization or identity—gender, race, class, sexuality—seems more salient at the margins, where there is heightened awareness of how one may be defined as "other" and deprivileged. Further, if one lives on the margins, rather than at the center, it is more important to maintain what some have called a dual perspective—one informed eye on the dominant culture and the other on one's own. Nevertheless, other than skin color, which has different meanings in different contexts, and one's anatomically distinct characteristics, which can be altered, little about gender, race, or any other cultural category can be construed as unchanging.

Chicano anthropologist Rosaldo (1989, p. 208) called these shifts in context "cultural borderlands" and suggested that they should be regarded as "sites of creative cultural production." Culture is creative and unpredictable, and because it is creative,

> It has its distinctive tempo, and it permits people to develop timing, coordination, and a knack for responding to contingencies. These qualities constitute social grace, which in turn enables an attentive person to be effective in the interpersonal politics of everyday life. (Rosaldo, p. 112)

Culture Is Intersection

One is never simply a Chicana or a man or gay or working class or an American. In any one moment, the same person may be all these things and much more. None of these categorizations is stable or fixed, and no one is ever one of these stories without being all the others at the same time, although one story, one self, may be more salient in one context and time than in another. For a lesbian with children, being a woman-mother may be far more important at particular times in her life than her sexual orientation, shaping her activities, her friends, and her presentation of self (Lewin, 1993). Like the turn of a kaleidoscope, variously colored and shaped pieces fall into patterned arrangements in which one or the other color or pattern seems to stand out.

Some scholars (such as Anderson & Collins, 1992; Spelman, 1988) have reminded us that neither race, class, nor gender (and, I would add, any other cultural identity) ever stands alone. Carrying the cultural narrative of a middle-aged, heterosexual, Irish, working-class woman from Boston implies different meanings and different experiences from being a middle-aged heterosexual Irish-American, middle-class woman from Boston, or being an Irish working-class woman may have different meanings from being a Navajo working-class woman, and so on. An African American college teacher may use one language in her classroom, another in her church, and a third when she returns to her old neighborhood. She is differently African American in each context, drawing on various parts of her ethnic self-story. All are emergently ethnic, differentially performing their ethnicities in dialogues with others, drawing on traditional ideas and symbols, as well as assimilating and acculturating according to the situation. Gender is raced and classed and shifts in meaning with age, sexual orientation, and other "selves." Similarly, ethnicity is gendered, raced, classed, and so on.

Furthermore, there is tremendous within-group diversity. One can never assume common sets of meanings within any one group—not even all middle-class, middle-aged, white, English-descent, heterosexual, feminist, East Coast men share common meanings about gender or, for that matter, anything else. But the study of this or any other population can help family therapists ask good questions, questions that elicit their cultural meanings. How is *this* person performing culture?

Culture Is Definitional and Constitutive

Culture is not measurable or generalizable; it cannot be defined, except perhaps in a way that is satisfying to positivist social scientists and others who are enamored of statistical portraits that reveal, for example, the number of in-group members who are bar mitzvahed, who intermarry, who attend Sunday school, who march on St. Patrick's Day, or who can speak the native language. Such studies do, indeed, produce useful working "knowledges" and generate new questions to pursue. But in the end, ethnicity, race, or gender cannot be decontextualized and held up for examination and definition because they are not things or objects; they are changing clusters of meanings drawn from the past, present, and future in a never-ending process that is itself definitional and constitutive. Part of one's cultural identity may be strengthened in situations of contrast or difference; as Bateson (1979) implied, these situations provide information. One may feel more "manly" when performing a task that requires physical strength. A woman may develop a heightened consciousness of her Jewish heritage—usually dormant—when she is with her British American in-laws for a holiday.

Ethnic, gender, social class, and other narratives not only mirror or re-create existing meanings, but create new ones as they are being performed and improvised. The larger culture, the ethnic group, and the family offer us symbols, stereotypes, and narratives from which to choose as we, in bricolage fashion, constitute and reconstitute ourselves. The adult lesbian or gay coming-out experience is a clear example of how this process can work.

In a fascinating description of the relationships among race, ethnicity, class, and particularly gender and sexual orientation, Weston (1996), through extended narrative interviews, pivoted around and deconstructed the "tomboy" story as new lesbians draw upon this larger cultural story in a retrospective effort to make sense of their current actions and to construct a lesbian identity:

> You might think that lesbians would want to dismiss the tomboy-grows-into a-dyke narrative for the stereotype it is. But drawing upon the inversion model, a woman can use gender to argue for the "realness" of her gay identity. How? She slips continuity into her descriptions of the ways she has gendered herself over the years. She reminds you that her first words were, "Play ball," but forgets to tell you about the time she tried out for cheerleading or homecoming queen. (p. 44)

"Is gendering," Weston asked, "usually consistent over a lifetime, or is consistency an impression pro-duced by the stories people tell about those formative years?" (p. 45). The tomboy narrative, she argued, is raced and classed—a story told far more by white working-class women to make sense of their emerging lesbian identities.

Culture Is Political

We know that all stories, whether they are about race, gender, or physical ability, are not equal, that is, people do not have an equal voice in shaping their personal narratives, nor do all people have equal opportunities to have their particular stories prevail. Feminist family therapists have demonstrated, for example, how powerfully gendered social discourses and personal gender premises influence how we construct our narratives (Goldner, Penn, Sheinberg, & Walker, 1990; Hare-Mustin, 1994; Laird, 1989). Our personal and family narratives are shaped and constrained by larger cultural narratives that provide the possibilities from which we can choose to make meaning. When these narratives are "problem saturated" (White & Epston, 1990), invisible, unjust, or simply narrow and constraining, they can benignly inhibit the ways individuals can make sense of themselves and their experiences and lethally influence the development of shameful, defeating, and even deadly self-narratives.

In sum, I suggest that culture is an individual and social construction, a constantly evolving and changing set of meanings that can be understood only in the context of a narrativized past, a cointerpreted present, and a wished-for future. It is always contextual; emergent; improvisational; transformational; political; and, above all, a matter of linguistics or of languaging, of discourse. It is meaning defined and definitional and constitutive.

IMPLICATIONS FOR PRACTICE

Growing out of these thoughts on culture and drawing on narrative, constructionist, and other postmodern ideas that are emerging in the family therapy field, the following are suggestions for a practice in which the culture of the client is centered, rather than peripheral or additive. Furthermore, it is an approach to practice in which the client's ideas and experiences, rather than the therapist's theories are privileged as much as possible.

Making culture the Central Metaphor for Therapy

The term *culture*—with a lower-case "c" and meant to include any of the sociocultural categorizations people draw on to constitute and understand themselves and others—should be the central, not a peripheral, metaphor for practice. Ritual, story, narrative, folklore, mythology, kinship patterns, relationships organized by gender and generation, national and community beliefs, values, and practices are just some of the metaphors for understanding the lives of others without superimposing other metaphors that are arbitrarily constructed, reductionistic, and more removed from daily experience. Cultural metaphors, because they are used in every society by ordinary folk, have the potential to provide us with a more experience-near positioning, one that is closer to the ground of everyday life and everyday experience than the more abstract and objectifying metaphors usually invented by professionals to label consumers of mental health services.

Culture is constituted through language, narrative, story, and social discourse, and these narratives are performed, in private, when one of our multiple selves is talking to another, or in public, when we are talking to the "other." Culture is put into action by individuals to constitute and define themselves and others. The cultural metaphor makes room for behavior, internal narrative, thought, emotion, language, fantasy, myth, speech, action, and intersubjectivity. It is, indeed, a metaphor that allows for movement between inner experience and the outer world. Using a cultural metaphor frees therapists to look for strengths, rather than weaknesses.

This does not mean that culture is a metaphor without risk. Cultural categorizations are susceptible to use for stereotyping and power politicking and to rationalize severe forms of oppression, such as the appalling practice of "ethnic cleansing" (otherwise known as genocide), violence against women, or gay bashing. Although *culture* may be misused by some to justify oppression within fami-

lies or in the larger world and to heighten and exploit "difference," rather than to foster the appreciation of diversity, when used intelligently and empathically, it is a way of entering the lives of people using their own voices and everyday experiences.

Taking a Decentering Ethnographic Stance

Borrowing from anthropologists and congruent with the notion of culture as metaphor, several writers in the family field, including me, have argued that the ethnographic metaphor should be used in practice (Anderson & Goolishian, 1992; Falicov, 1995; Laird, 1989, 1994). What this stance is most fundamentally about is figuring out how to enter the experience of another individual or group of individuals as unfettered as possible with one's own cultural luggage, to leave at home one's powerful cultural assumptions, and to create the conversational spaces in which the voices of the "other" can emerge. Dyche and Zayas (1995) suggested that the stances of "cultural naïveté" and "respectful curiosity" are as important as knowledge and skill. Knowledge, or what they call "cultural literacy," they believe, can obscure our views and privilege our own representations over those of clients.

It is important to reiterate that we can never completely leave our own cultural assumptions behind. Even the choices we make about whom to talk to or about where to position the video camera reflect our own cultural visions and thus direct our gaze. We cannot escape culture; we can only try to meet it on its own terms. For this reason it is vital, as so many scholars have cautioned, to keep working on understanding our own "local knowledges" (Geertz, 1983), our own cultural narratives, and to make them as accessible as possible to ourselves and transparent to others.

We must also be highly informed "not-knowers" if we are to ask good questions. Learning about the culture of one society does not produce replicable and transferable knowledge, just as learning about the experiences of one individual or family is not replicable and transferable to another. What *are* replicable and transferable, however, are ideas that emerge from one ethnographic or practice experience and that generate questions to ask of another group or person. We do not know the experiences of our informants; relying on previous understandings or our professional knowledges may well preclude our understanding the meanings of the person or family in view, creating what we expected to see. But as informed not-knowers, we may bring a wealth of expertise in asking good questions, questions that help make more visible—to us and to the "other"—their meanings, as well as the sources of those meanings.

Furthermore, several advocates of a narrative and ethnographic stance (Freedman & Combs, 1996; Laird, 1994, 1995; White & Epston, 1990; Zimmerman & Dickerson, 1996), in their efforts to help clients become the experts on their own lives and as part of the effort to destabilize the hierarchical power arrangements in traditional therapies, may make their own narratives part of the therapeutic conversation. The therapist may make clear the origins of her or his comments, ideas, values, empathic feelings, and so on, locating them in personal or professional experiences.

Decentering one's own culture is extremely difficult—in teaching, practice, and ordinary everyday conversation. Displacing whiteness (Frankenberg, 1993) or heterosexuality (Kitzinger, Wilkinson, & Perkins, 1992), for example, if one is a member of the dominant culture, requires constant vigilance, for categories like whiteness and heterosexuality are unmarked and assumed in this society. Paradoxically, people of marginalized races, genders, social classes, sexuality, and so on, are both marked and highly visible, but their experiences may be rendered invisible in the context of powerful and dominant discourses.

Assuming a Narrative Stance

In the past decade, a number of therapists have pioneered and articulated a narrative stance for therapy (see, for example, Andersen, 1987, 1991; Anderson & Goolishian, 1992; Hoffman, 1992; White & Epston, 1990). The literature on narrative therapy is rapidly expanding as therapists draw on the work of the pioneers, add to and deepen the ideas, and apply the ideas to various kinds of problems and populations. There is not enough space here to review this

work, but I believe that the implied therapeutic stance—a stance that is highly respectful, collaborative, and nonhierarchical—is one that encourages the expression of multiple ideas and possibilities. It avoids blame or pathologizing; searches for strengths, rather than defects; is grounded in a value stance; and fosters transparency by the therapist, that is, the therapist situating ideas in her or his own experience. It is a stance uniquely suited to culturally sensitive practice.

Falicov (1995), in one effort to avoid the risks of stereotyping, advocated what she called a multidimensional, comparative training framework. She used what she termed "basic parameters" that are common to all families—such as ecological niche, migration patterns, degrees of acculturation, and life-cycle events—to think comparatively. I see this effort partly as an attempt to learn about how diverse people approach common human experiences, rather than about ethnic group attributes, one way of shifting the center and avoiding the "different from" stance.

Deconstructing Cultural Self-Narratives

This is a simple idea much lost in translation in many therapies. Many therapists, who hope and plan to practice in a culturally sensitive way, fail to see or hear the cultural, because their own prior texts are so powerful. Most therapies emphasize "listening." But listening usually means listening for something in particular—for example, for therapist-client relational or transferential material, for evidence to make a diagnosis, for material to confirm our impressions of dysfunction or pathology. To deconstruct the cultural self-narrative also means listening and questioning, but not based on assumptions. It means to explore how a client's cultural meanings and cultural premises—whether linked to race, ethnicity, social class, gender, sexuality, work, religion, or spirituality; ideas about health and illness, death and mourning; and so on—are being performed and how they are influencing both the self-story and the problem (Akamatsu, 1995). Furthermore, it means listening "radically," in a way that Weingarten (1995) defined as authenticating; a way that is respectful, accepting, and welcoming;

and a way that searches for the unsaid as well as the said, the invisible as well as the visible.

It is important to recognize that there will be many different cultural narratives in the same family and that those stories are also gendered, raced, classed, aged, and so on and responsive to differences in degrees of acculturation, access to new cultural narratives, generational differences, and many other influences. East Indian parents who are raising their children in the United States may be hurt and bewildered when their daughter chooses to live in a coed dorm at her university or dates a European American man, and a Chinese American husband may be in despair at the freedoms his wife is claiming in this country. Can we listen in ways that are authenticating and socially just and responsible for all concerned?

Locating Cultural Narratives in the Larger Social Discourse

"Local knowledges" (Geertz, 1983) do not spring simply from the local experience, no matter how intersubjective. For example, in this society, a teenage girl's profound contempt for her mother may be connected to society's much more pervasive profound contempt of women. For the young girl to accept, value, and identify with her mother may mean envisioning for herself a future that is filled with both subtle and overt forms of oppression—a future she sees as intolerable. By repudiating her mother, she may be able to venture down another path in her own adult life. An African American man's depression or fury at his wife may have its roots in larger devaluing and invalidating narratives of African American men's experiences.

Our self-narratives are embedded in larger social discourses, negotiated over time within relations of knowledge and power (Foucault, 1980), which gain acceptance as "truth." These narratives can be subjugating; they can cut us off from a fuller range of possibilities for ourselves and our lives. Thus, it is crucial to find a way to bring these larger social discourses into therapy to create the possibility for clients to challenge them; this is one way to create a context in which clients may be empowered to take better charge of their own lives. The good

question searches out the family stories that have prevailed in shaping a particular family's or family member's life narratives. Do these stories fit the individual members' lived experiences? Are they nurturing and empowering stories, or are they self-defeating ones? Do they trivialize or even render invisible some of the member's experiences? Do the self-stories demean the person's worth and ideas and privilege the ideas and interpretations of others? Do the stories contain contradictions or double binds that are invalidating? For example, is a woman of color receiving competing messages about who she is and what she should be choosing from the dominant society and from her own ethnic group? Is a poor woman on public assistance told, on the one hand, that she lacks a work ethic and, on the other hand, blamed, when she locates work, for neglecting her children because there is no affordable day care? Is a man taught to bury his emotions, to be a warrior and to solve problems and handle challenges aggressively, but punished when he uses these same self-narratives to "discipline" his wife and children? Can a transsexual find any stories that affirm his identity narrative, in which he can locate his own isolating and invisible experiences? Are our stories liberating or subjugating?

Resisting Culture or Interrogating the Subjugating Narrative

Family therapists and other mental health and social services professionals have learned and taught others to respect ethnic differences and what are called ethnic or cultural or class or gender or sexuality values, both in families and in and among ethnic groups. Dilemmas arise, however, when those values and cultural practices privilege the position of one group or subgroup of a family and deprivilege or subjugate the experiences of another. For example, strong cultural prescriptions against homosexuality may result in Latino gays (Morales, 1996) or African American lesbians (Greene, 1994) being rejected in their larger ethnic group or family. A Chinese American girl may be devalued in her family and larger ethnic group, while the voice and aspirations of a white, middle-class, European American woman may be deprivileged in relation to the men in her family. Weingarten (1995) described, for example, how mothers in this society are constrained by cultural messages about what constitutes "good" and "bad" mothering, so they try to story their lives in ways that will be acceptable within these definitions, not in ways that more accurately reflect their lived experiences. Women's narratives, I have learned, are often silenced, and even their speech genres are ridiculed (Laird, 1989).

Should professional counselors, who have been taught to respect various ethnic customs and values, take a stand against what they may perceive as oppression in the family? As I mentioned earlier, some narrative therapists think that bringing culture into the therapy room in a way that challenges dominant ethnic practices or cultural discourses as an imposition of personal politics. Others, concerned about subjugation and injustice, take a different stance. White (1994), for example, argued that clients need to be helped to deconstruct not only their self-narratives, but the dominant cultural narratives and discursive practices that constitute their lives, a view that is compatible with mine. Deconstruction means to explore how these dominating discourses are shaped, whose interests they serve and whose they may subjugate, to expose the marginalized possibilities. How have dominant and subjugated narratives influenced the "local" story or the stories at hand in the clinical situation? This does not mean that therapists should deliver their political views as truths, but that they remain sensitive to the spoken stories, as well as to the underlying ones that have not been voiced because of the lack of power or knowledge. Alertness to the privileging of some narratives in unjust and colonizing dominant discourses allows us to open up conversational spaces in which new and more potentiating narratives may emerge.

Beyond the Mirrored Room Toward a Culturally Just Practice

Finally, and most neglected, is the role of the family therapist in moving beyond the therapeutic conversation to a position between the client and the community. Interpersonal family practices reflect injustices in the larger surround, just as family troubles often reflect oppression and the lack of opportunities. Minuchin (1991) wondered whether postmodern theory is rescuing us from having to face the evils and hopelessness in the world around us and reducing our concerns to the individual story, when the plots of these stories are often dictated by powerful forces outside the interviewing room.

Justice is raced, gendered, and classed, a lesson cast into bold relief in recent years with the Rodney King beating, the Anita Hill and Clarence Thomas case (Morrison, 1992), the navy Tailhook incident, and the O. J. Simpson saga. It is our responsibility not only to surface cultural stories of oppression and marginalization in people's lives in our offices, but to go beyond the cases to help our clients tell their stories in new and larger contexts. We must also bear witness to those suppressed stories in the schools, courts, legislatures, and media. In other words, we need to add our voices when those larger cultural discourses do not fairly represent the experiences of our clients and do not allow their stories to be heard.

CASE STUDIES

Practice Situation 1

The following story illustrates some of the facets of a practice that I view as grounded in both cultural and narrative metaphors, one in which the client's voice and language are privileged. It comes from the work of Sallyann Roth, a creative family therapist who is widely known for her clinical and training work at the Family Institute of Cambridge in Massachusetts and for her influence in bringing to the attention of American therapists the contributions of Michael White of Australia, David Epston of New Zealand, and the important cross-cultural work of the Family Centre of Lower Hutt, New Zealand. The illustration is followed by brief reflections from her and from me.

> I [Sallyann Roth] saw a young woman in her 20s who was working here in the U.S., trying to decide whether to stay here or return to her home in Asia. In the weeks prior to her leaving, we tried to consolidate the work she had done and to find ways to discuss what she could "hold" when she was far away. One of the con-

versations we had resulted in her saying that she wanted to hold onto her goal, to remember it across contexts. This goal was to be able to stay connected with those she cared for, even when their views and opinions were different from hers, and—at the same time—to stay connected with what she wanted for herself, even if it was different from what others wanted for her. She stated clearly that this was a commitment she was making to herself—not to diminish her connection with her own wishes and her own voice and not to lose connection with people who had different wishes for her and wished she spoke in a different voice.

Because English was not her first language and it was clear that this was a very important, highly affectively charged commitment, I asked her to speak her commitment in her native language, even though I would not be able to understand her words. She looked horrified and told me that she could not. When I asked why, she told me that she could not because that was the language she used with her family. She would, however, like to say it in her homeland's official language. She then did speak it in her nation's tongue. As she did, her body was animated. She pulled herself tall, she smiled, and she made wide body gestures with her hand to her heart. This was clearly a powerful commitment. She was energized, almost electric. I then asked her if she would like to try speaking it in her native language. She said that she would like to try now that she had said it in her official language. When she spoke in her native tongue, her voice was softer and her gestures were smaller and dramatically restrained. When I asked her about the differences among these three speakings of the same message, she spoke movingly of the degree of acceptance for that statement she experienced in each of the different contexts. We spoke together about the effect on her of making the statement in all three of her languages. She was clear that this was the first time she understood the way in which the language she used and the cultural context within which she spoke affected what she could say and how she could say it. She was amazed and delighted with this discovery. It was truly something she could take home with her and continue to work with. Now she was taking her commitment and some tools to work with it.

Sallyann Roth's reflections.

This vignette is one demonstration of two things that are distinctive about my current work. First, in part I

work with people in their languages of origin. With couples who share another first language, I ask them to speak to each other in highly charged moments in that language and only later to tell me what they want me to know of what they have said. Some people have told me that only certain aspects of their emotional lives are available in each of their languages. I work with them to be sure that the voices, the affect, the ideas, that reside in their different languages, the different parts of their history, can speak with each other, so that they do not feel as fragmented as people often feel in a host culture. I am committed to not letting the fact that I speak only English limit the work that people with other languages can do. Second, I work with people's many different voices, even when they are all found in the same language.

My reflections.   I see this as a stunning and creative slice of practice that illustrates many of the points I hope have been made in this chapter. Most important, one has no sense that the therapist's theories or prior ideas dominate what she sees, hears, and asks. What stands out most for me is how she strives to privilege the voice, the language, the culture of the client, to move the client's culture and language from the margin (the usual experience in a dominant cultural context) to the center. The therapist uses both cultural and narrative metaphors (story, voice, speech, language), that is, metaphors close to the ground of everyday experience. She has the client speak not to her, but to those who are important in her life world—kin, friends, and others who have powerful voices in her real life. The therapist here is an ethnographer in the sense that she tries as much as she is able to, within the limits of her own language and linguistic biases, to listen radically to the woman's cultural and personal voice. This therapist and this client are working with what so often becomes a challenge in cross-cultural experience—how to respect, honor, and hold onto one's cultural origins, prescriptions, and connections while one cocreates a new narrative that contains hope and opportunity. Here that effort, as the client phrased it, is to stay connected with what she wants for herself and to stay connected to those she cares for, even when the messages and goals conflict. The fact that the therapist encouraged the expression of these dilemmas in three languages allowed the client to move across, yet to hold, her various cultural selves.

This process operates no differently in families that have been in this country for many generations. Every young person, in fact, must decide which of the family's and culture's values and practices he or she will hold fast to and what he or she will relinquish in the path to adulthood and in the development of his or her own story.

Practice Situation 2

I am also indebted to Duncan Laird, my son, who is a social worker and program director of a partial hospitalization program, and his colleague Joanna Smith, for sharing the following example of practice in which cultural consciousness and sensitivity to a client's narrative are central.

> Sreng, a 27-year-old Cambodian man, diagnosed with schizophrenia, paranoid type, had had several recent hospitalizations because of hallucinations. He reported hearing persistent and intrusive voices instructing him to kill his mother in order to "save her." At one point, he had put his hands around her neck as if to strangle her, but had not hurt her. When questioned, he explained that he thought killing her was the only way he could help her, since it was his responsibility to look after her and he was failing. He saw killing her as an altruistic act.
>
> Sreng immigrated to this country at age 15, fleeing the genocidal Khmer Rouge regime of Pol Pot. His father had been forced into labor camps, starved and beaten, and sent home to his village to die. Sreng had been severely beaten on numerous occasions for "taking food." He had been hearing voices since about age 9. He has a sister living in a nearby community but it is he on whom his mother depends for driving, cooking, shopping, and so on. His mother is isolated, even from the local Cambodian community. The local hospital psychiatrist felt that Sreng's symptomatology was a result of his mother's dependence on him, which resulted in Sreng's extreme anger at her. Sreng refused to stay on medication, which the hospital personnel blamed on the influence of the local Cambodian community, particularly the members of the Buddhist temple.
>
> Once on the inpatient unit and on medication,

Sreng's voices subsided, and after a month he was discharged to the partial hospitalization program. But Sreng was highly ambivalent about attending the program and felt anxious about returning home to find work, earn money, and take care of his mother. In the past, his contacts with posthospitalization services had been fleeting and sporadic. The next period was characterized by the staff's attempts to convince Sreng that the best way to help his mother was for him to get better. Although he became increasingly angry, he continued to attend. Finally, one staff member asked a question that proved significant: What would it mean for him to break his commitment to coming to the program? Sreng stated that he would never break such a commitment. The fact that he did not feel he was being helped was inconsequential, and he went on to explain how important commitment is in Cambodian culture. This exchange led to an extended conversation about his commitment to his mother. The staff told Sreng that they had not been listening well enough and had not truly heard how important commitment to family was in his culture, particularly how important his commitment to his mother was to him. They had, they felt, been listening to their own cultural voices. Now they could better help him focus on his mission of responsibility to his mother.

This turning point resulted in Sreng brightening and becoming more active in the groups, where he began to talk about his family life. He expressed his anger at his sister, whom he felt had not been helping to care for their mother, and his own shame and helplessness at not being able to take better care of her. He also indicated that he thought that his symptoms were the result of bad karma.

The staff, with his permission, then began to reach out to Sreng's potential community of support. First, a local Cambodian mental health professional agreed to act as an interpreter and attended a meeting with Sreng's mother, sister, several monks from the temple, and the newly assigned family therapist. Each was asked to share his or her thoughts about how the "system" might be more helpful. The Cambodians each voiced a fear that the treatment staff viewed Sreng as "sick" and would take Sreng away from his family and community. This was why, they thought, medication would not be helpful.

The staff listened to and acknowledged these concerns and wondered how they could be addressed. One therapist wondered if an "Eastern/Western" approach might be helpful, that is, one that would combine ideas for helping from everyone concerned. She asked if they might all agree to follow a treatment plan in which Sreng would continue to take medication, while the staff would continue to listen carefully to and be responsive to the concerns of the community of support. The monks, who had heard Sreng's concerns about his mother's loneliness and isolation, encouraged the mother to come to the temple. It was not long before Sreng was free of voices, looking for work, and greatly relieved that his mother was leaving the house daily to participate in family life.

My reflections.   The situation of Sreng, his family and community, and the treatment context seems simple and straightforward enough. But I believe it contains several subtle components that illustrate how a slight decentering of the dominant culture can make all the difference. To begin with, the initial interpretations of the hierarchical mental health system personify not only the diagnostic, "expert" approach, but the strong individualist character of American culture. Sreng's commitment to his mother is framed as unrealistic and a result of mutual overdependence. The answer, as it so frequently is in American mental health culture, is to foster separation and differentiation and to redraw family boundaries to fit American definitions of the well-functioning family. The complex notion of the meanings of commitment and loyalty and respect in the Asian community and family are poorly understood, and there is no understanding of what health or illness, mental health treatment, and medication may mean to a young Cambodian man.

The seemingly simple act of a staff member's ethnographic decentering of her own culture, her acknowledgement of the possibility that the staff had not been able to hear Sreng, led her to listen to him radically, to privilege his own narrative, to render him the expert on his own feelings and experience. When he was able to tell his story in a listening context that, for a moment at least, displaced the dominant European-American perspective, a whole new realm of hope and possibility emerged.

The staff also widened the therapeutic community to include all who are "in language" about the problem and, in the words of Anderson and Goolishian (1992), the problem began to be "dis-solved"

rather than "resolved." One can also see the possibilities of using the insights from this work to foster greater understanding and change in larger contexts. For instance, the staff might, with Sreng's collaboration and participation, present his story in a hospitalwide grand rounds. The hospital might sponsor a conference for the surrounding professional community on how to understand Cambodian ideas about family, community, and health issues and how to be more helpful to Cambodian immigrants. A program might be developed in which the hospital would establish ongoing connections and mutual consultation relationships with Cambodian community leaders and indigenous helpers.

CONCLUSION

In this chapter, I have argued that culture and narrative should become central metaphors in clinical practice with individuals, couples, and families. Integrating these metaphors into practice implies what Bateson (1979) might have called second-order change. In this case, it means that rather than counselors simply learning about how to respect ethnic, gender, class, and other kinds of diversity—group by group—(which has been the direction in much writing and training on ethnicity), culture and narrative actually become the primary metaphors for understanding and change. Culture, in my view, is not a matter of relatively enduring characteristics, customs, and historical traditions; it is emergent, contextual, improvisational, performative, and political. Therapists must learn to be highly conscious of their own cultural narratives and, at the same time, to deprivilege them to hear the narrative of the other. Recent developments in narrative family therapy suggest a path into practice that is not only culturally sensitive, but that can help people resist dominant narratives that are demoralizing or constraining, as well as some of their own cultural practices that may be outworn or oppressive to others. It is suggested that therapists, if they are to participate in a practice that is just, must also resist constraining narratives and practices by moving out of the therapy room and into the wider community with their cultural learning.

REFERENCES

Akamatsu, N. N. (1995). The defiant daughter and compliant mother: Multicultural dialogues on woman's role. *In Session: Psychotherapy in Practice, 1,* 43–55.

Allen, J., & Laird, J. (1990). Men and story: Constructing new narratives in therapy. *Journal of Feminist Family Therapy, 2*(3–4), 75–100.

Andersen, T. (1987). The reflecting team: Dialogue and meta-dialogue in clinical work. *Family Process, 26,* 415–428.

Andersen, T. (1991). *The reflecting team: Dialogues and dialogues about the dialogues.* New York: W. W. Norton.

Anderson, H. (1997). *Conversation, language, and possibilities: A postmodern approach to therapy.* New York: Basic Books.

Anderson, H., & Goolishian, H. (1992). The client is the expert: A not-knowing approach to therapy. In S. McNamee & K. Gergen (Eds), *Therapy as social construction* (pp. 25–39). Newbury Park, CA: Sage.

Anderson, M. L., & Collins, P. H. (Eds.). (1992). *Race, class, and gender: An anthology.* Belmont, CA: Wadsworth.

Auerswald, E. (1968). Interdisciplinary v. ecological approach. *Family Process, 7,* 202–215.

Bateson, G. (1979). *Mind and nature: A necessary unity.* New York: Dutton.

Bauman, R. (1986). *Story, performance, and event: Contextual studies of oral narrative.* New York: Cambridge University Press.

Belenky, M. F., Clinchy, B. M., Goldberger, N. R., & Tarule, J. M. (1986). *Women's ways of knowing: The development of self, voice and mind.* New York: Basic Books.

Bowen, M. (1978). *Family therapy in clinical practice.* New York: Jason Aronson.

Braverman, L. (Ed.) (1987). *Women, feminism, and family therapy.* New York: Haworth Press.

Butler, J. (1991). Imitation and gender insubordination. In D. Fuss (Ed.), *Inside/out: Lesbian theories, gay theories* (pp. 13–31). New York: Routledge.

Chodorow, N. (1978). *The reproduction of mothering: Psychoanalysis and the sociology of gender.* Berkeley: University of California Press.

Dyche, L., & Zayas, L. H. (1995). The value of curiosity and naivete for the cross-cultural therapist. *Family Process, 34,* 389–399.

Epstein, S. (1987). Gay politics, gay identity: The limits of social constructionism. *Socialist Review, 93–94,* 9–54.

Falicov, C. J. (1995). Training to think culturally: A multidimensional framework. *Family Process, 34,* 373–388.

Ferreira, A. J. (1963). Family myth and homeostasis. *Archives of General Psychiatry, 9,* 457–463.

Foucault, M. (1980). *Power/knowledge: Selected interviews and other writings.* New York: Pantheon Press.

Frankenberg, R. (1993). *The social construction of whiteness: White women, race matters.* Minneapolis: University of Minnesota Press.

Freedman, J., & Combs, G. (1996), *Narrative therapy: The social construction of preferred realities.* New York: W. W. Norton.

Friedman, E. (1980). Systems and ceremonies. In E. A. Carter & M. McGoldrick (Eds.), *The family life cycle: A framework for family therapy.* New York: Gardner Press.

Geertz, C. (1973). Thick description: Toward an interpretive theory of culture. In C. Geertz, *The interpretation of cultures* (pp. 3–30). New York: Basic Books.

Geertz, C. (1974). From the native's point of view: On the nature of anthropological understanding. *Bulletin of the American Academy of Arts and Sciences, 28* (1).

Geertz, C. (1983). *Local knowledge: Further essays in interpretive anthropology.* New York: Basic Books.

Gergen, K. J. (1991). *The saturated self: Dilemmas of identity in contemporary life.* New York: Basic Books.

Gilligan, C. (1982). *In a different voice: Psychological theory and women's development.* Cambridge, MA: Harvard University Press.

Goldner, V. (1985). Feminism and family therapy. *Family Process, 24,* 31–47.

Goldner, V. (1987). Generation and gender: Normative and covert hierarchies. *Family Process, 27,* 17–31.

Goldner, V., Penn, P., Sheinberg, M., & Walker, G. (1990). Love and violence: Gender paradoxes in volatile attachments. *Family Process, 29,* 343–364.

Goodrich, T. J., Rampage, C., Ellman, B., & Halstead, K. (1988). *Feminist family therapy: A casebook.* New York: W. W. Norton.

Greene, B. (1994). Lesbian women of color: Triple jeopardy. In L. Comas-Diaz & B. Greene (Eds.), *Women of color: Integrating ethnic and gender identities in psychotherapy* (pp. 389–427). New York: Guilford Press.

Haley, J. (1976). *Problem-solving therapy.* San Francisco: Jossey-Bass.

Haley, J. (1980). *Leaving home.* New York: McGraw-Hill.

Hardy, K. (1996, June). *The ethics of participation: Bringing culture into the room: A narrative therapy approach. (Reflections).* Paper presented at the annual meeting of the American Family Therapy Academy, San Francisco.

Hare-Mustin, R. (1978). A feminist approach to family therapy. *Family Process, 17,* 181–194.

Hare-Mustin, R. (1994). Discourses in the mirrored room: A postmodern analysis of therapy. *Family Process, 33,* 19–35.

Hartman, A., & Laird, J. (1983). *Family-centered social work practice.* New York: Free Press.

Hoffman, L. (1992), A reflexive stance for family therapy. In S. McNamee & K. J. Gergen (Eds.), *Therapy as social construction* (pp. 2–24). Newbury Park, CA: Sage.

hooks, b. (1984). *Feminist theory: From margin to center.* Boston: South End Press.

Jackson, D. (1957). The question of family homeostasis, *Psychiatric Quarterly Supplement, 31,* 79–90.

Jackson, D. (Ed.). (1967). *Communication, marriage, and the family.* Palo Alto, CA: Science and Behavior Books.

Jackson, D. (Ed.). (1968). *Therapy, communication, and change.* Palo Alto, CA: Science and Behavior Books.

Jordan, J. (1986). *The meaning of mutuality* (Work in Progress No. 23). Wellesley, MA: Stone Center, Wellesley College.

Kitzinger, C., Wilkinson, S., & Perkins, R. (1992). Theorizing heterosexuality. Editorial introduction to special issue on heterosexuality. *Feminism & Psychology, 2,* 293–324.

Laird, J. (1984). Sorcerers, shamans, and social workers: The use of ritual in family-centered practice. *Social Work, 29,* 123–129.

Laird, J. (1986, Fall). Women, family therapists, and other mythical beasts. *American Family Therapy Association Newsletter,* No. 25, 32, 35.

Laird, J. (1989). Women and stories: Restorying women's self-constructions. In M. McGoldrick, C. Anderson, & F. Walsh (Eds.), *Women in families: A framework for therapy* (pp. 427–450). New York: W. W. Norton.

Laird, J. (1994). "Thick description" revisited: Family therapist as anthropologist-constructivist. In E. Sherman & W. J. Reid (Eds.), *Qualitative research in social work* (pp. 175–189). New York: Columbia University Press.

Laird, J. (1995). Family-centered practice in the postmodern era. *Families in Society: The Journal of Contemporary Human Services, 76,* 150–162.

Luepnitz, D. (1988). *The family interpreted: Feminist theory in clinical practice.* New York: Basic Books.

Lewin, E. (1993). *Lesbian mothers: Accounts of gender in American culture.* Ithaca, NY: Cornell University Press.

McGoldrick, M. (1993). Ethnicity, cultural diversity, and normality. In F. Walsh (Ed.), *Normal family processes* (2nd ed., pp. 331–360). New York: Guilford Press.

McGoldrick, M., Anderson, C., & Walsh, F. (Eds.). (1989). *Women in families: A framework for family therapy.* New York: W. W. Norton.

Miller, J. B. (1976). *Toward a new psychology of women.* Boston: Beacon Press.

Minuchin, S. (1974). *Families and family therapy.* Cambridge, MA: Harvard University Press.

Minuchin, S. (1991). The seductions of constructivism. *Family Therapy Networker, 15*(5), 47–50.

Minuchin, S., & Fishman, H. C. (1981). *Family therapy techniques.* Cambridge, MA: Harvard University Press.

Montalvo, B. & Gutierrez, M. (1983). A perspective for the use of the cultural dimension in family therapy. In C. Falicov (Ed.), *Cultural perspectives in family therapy* (pp. 15–32) Rockville, MD: Aspen Systems.

Morales, E. (1996). Gender roles among Latino gay and bisexual men: Implications for family and couple relationships. In J. Laird & R. J. Green (Eds.), *Lesbians and gays in couples and families: A handbook for therapists* (pp. 272–297). San Francisco: Jossey-Bass.

Morrison, T. (1992). *Race-ing justice, en-gendering power: Essays on Anita Hill, Clarence Thomas, and the construction of social reality.* New York: Pantheon Books.

Myerhoff, B. (1978). *Number our days.* New York: Simon & Schuster.

Richmond, M. (1930). *The long view.* New York: Russell Sage Foundation.

Rosaldo, R. (1989). *Culture and truth: The remaking of social analysis.* Boston: Beacon Press.

Selvini-Palazzoli, M., Boscolo, L., Cecchin, G., & Prada, J. (1978). *Paradox and counterparadox.* New York: Jason Aronson.

Selvini-Palazzoli, M., Boscolo, L., Cecchin, G., & Prada, J. (1980). Hypothesizing—circularity—neutrality: Three guidelines for the conductor of the session. *Family Process, 19,* 3–12.

Shapiro, V. (1996). Subjugated knowledge and the working alliance: The narratives of Russian Jewish immigrants. *In Session: Psychotherapy in Practice, 1*(4), 9–22.

Spelman, E. (1988). *Inessential woman: Problems of exclusion in feminist thought.* Boston: Beacon Press.

Surrey, J. (1985). *Self-in-relation. A theory of women's development* (Work in Progress, No. 13). Wellesley, MA: Stone Center, Wellesley College.

Walters, M., Carter, B., Papp, P., & Silverstein, O. (1988). *The invisible web: Gender patterns in family relationships.* New York: Guilford Press.

Watzlawick, P. (1976). *How real is real?* New York: Random House.

Watzlawick, P. (1984). *The invented reality: How do we know what we believe we know?* New York: W. W. Norton.

Weingarten, K. (1995). Radical listening: Challenging cultural beliefs for and about mothers. *Journal of Feminist Family Therapy, 7*(1–2), 7–22.

Weston, K. (1996). *Render me, gender me: Lesbians talk sex, class, color, nation, studmuffins . . .* New York: Columbia University Press.

White, M. (1994). *The politics of therapy: Putting to rest the illusion of neutrality.* Adelaide, South Australia: Dulwich Family Centre.

White, M., & Epston, D. (1990). *Narrative means to therapeutic ends.* New York: W. W. Norton.

Zimmerman, J. L., & Dickerson, V. C. (1996). *If problems talked: Narrative therapy in action.* New York: Guilford Press.

CHAPTER 18

Family Diversity and Family Life Education

JUDITH A. MYERS-WALLS

INTRODUCTION

Boiling down the field of family life education (FLE) to its essence, family life educators educate families and educate about families. Although the field is not that simple, such simplicity helps to illuminate several points regarding families and diversity. First, family life educators need to grapple with definitions of "family" and of effective "education." Second, FLE is faced with questions of family diversity from at least three perspectives: (1) What will an educator teach? that is, from which family forms, types, and situations will the content be drawn? (2) Whom will an educator teach? that is, which families or individuals will participate in the program? (3) How will an educator teach? that is, whose teaching-learning style will he or she use, and how will he or she choose the goals that will guide the program?

Concerns about diversity in FLE are the same as the concerns that are discussed in other chapters of this book: gender dynamics; family structure; racial, ethnic, and cultural groups; and class, but FLE also deals with the issue of diversity of learning styles. Thus, diversity becomes a challenge both when dealing with mixed FLE groups and when targeting groups with distinct cultural, class, or family-structure characteristics. In other words, an appreciation of diversity leads an educator to be respectful and inclusive in heterogeneous settings and to target programs appropriately for homogeneous groups. This chapter explores these issues.

People learn many things in life. They learn how to talk and walk and to express anger when family members take something from them, most learn how to add numbers, and some learn how to pro-

gram a VCR. Although many educational processes are similar, some important characteristics of learning about family life differentiate it from other learning activities. First, some family information, skills, and attitudes are learned from birth (if not before), long before skills like the manipulation of numbers and grammar develop. Therefore, consistent with social learning theory, all people who have spent any time in a family have some knowledge about and attitudes toward family, including a concept of what they think "normal" means. As a result, they enter FLE with some established ideas and behaviors that are based on their experiences. Second, unlike discrete skills, such as programming a VCR, family-related subject matter is highly emotional and value laden, making it a volatile topic for education. Third, there are few absolutes or rules, in contrast to domains like mathematics skills. Because of these characteristics, FLE is often controversial, slippery, and/or vague, and may challenge participants to relearn or alter existing patterns of thought or behavior.

Participants are not the only ones who come to FLE with an existing mindset; educators are also influenced by the family settings in which they grew up and in which they currently live. Educators and learners both know a great deal about the family form, culture, religious affiliation, and living situation of the group they call "my family," although they may not have organized that knowledge. They also know a lot, consciously or subconsciously, about how they personally deal with the world and learn about new things. Because "my family" is usually a small group of people and includes a limited number of situations, family background is an immediate limitation to educators as they attempt to develop materials for or about diverse groups. That is, it is often difficult for educators to know when their knowledge is widely applicable to others and when it is specific to their own background. Recognizing diversity in learning styles may be even more difficult than recognizing cultural, ethnic, or family-structure diversity because it is even more idiosyncratic than family background and receives less attention in most academic training.

PERSONAL REFLECTIONS

My background opened some doors to the world of diversity and closed others. I grew up in Pennsylvania and Illinois. I had two parents who married at the end of their college careers and started having children three years later (translation: I had lots of direct experience with two-parent families and educated families, but little experience with adolescent pregnancy or divorce). During most of my childhood, I had one brother and one sister close in age; later, another sister was born (translation: I had experience with sibling relationships and both small and large age differences between siblings, but little experience with only children or multiple births). All my family members, their spouses, and their children are European American (with a strong emphasis on Pennsylvania Dutch) and, so far, heterosexual (translation: I had a great deal of direct experience with the majority culture and some with a specific subculture, but little with minority status or gay or lesbian issues). In spite of my generally mainstream background, I had a sense of being different in some important ways, and my parents focused on teaching me that being different was positive.

The ways in which our family was different from mainstream society and the "typical" family were relatively invisible. We were pacifists and lived a simple lifestyle. We belonged to a small Protestant denomination (Church of the Brethren) that has been known as a "historic peace church." Although the immediate family membership looked traditional in structure, many other people became part of our extended family circle: exchange students, volunteers in the parishes where my father was pastor, foster children—both official and informal—

and a wide variety of pets. These experiences led me to feel comfortable with many different kinds of individuals, lifestyles, and backgrounds (and even species), but did not put me in a position of dealing personally with discrimination or intolerance in most situations. It was not until college that I began to give voice to the sexism I had experienced in my childhood and youth. Most of the time, I could choose when I wanted to contrast myself with others and when I wanted to blend in. In late adolescence, I was an exchange student in Switzerland and had new experiences with diversity and belonging, although in most cases my difference there also was hidden until I opened my mouth.

I developed a certain passion for social justice and equality that was nurtured by my family background. I took a special pride in my father having an official role during the Poor People's Campaign in the 1960s and was excited to know that he had met Martin Luther King, Jr., and others in the Southern Christian Leadership Conference.

As an adult, I am married with two children. I have a doctorate in child development and family studies with an emphasis on child development. I work as a university professor, but my job assignment is with the Cooperative Extension Service. This job assignment means that rather than teach in a college classroom, most of my work is with families and professionals outside academia. I reach over 1,000 people directly each year and many more indirectly through mass media, training programs for trainers, and the distribution of written materials and curricula. My immediate family members are vegetarians, and all share our hyphenated name, factors that consistently set us apart. My job assignment is another characteristic that defines difference for me because I do not quite fit with other community practitioners or other university professors.

My background facilitates my FLE skills by helping me feel comfortable with a varied collection of people and situations. However, as a member of the generally privileged class, I encounter difficulties when I try to create as effective programs as I would like for disenfranchised or oppressed people. I have concentrated on building my awareness of how audiences view me and my position and status and how that perception influences the programs I facilitate.

I have three primary goals in programming for diversity. First, I try to listen to and learn from family members' stories. Second, I attempt to devise multiple methods for including participants and their perspectives in programming. Third, I strive to locate or create inclusive curricula or to find techniques for using curricula that were originally designed for restricted audiences in ways that include diverse audiences.

My understanding of the connections and differences among people is that people are all alike in some ways and all unique in some ways, and all belong to groups that are both like other groups and different from them. The needs, emotions, and sensory experiences shared by human beings connect them as the human family. At the same time, each person has unique fingerprints and retinal patterns and an entirely individual history and idiosyncratic beliefs and dreams. These similarities and differences exist in a social setting that creates groups and subgroups on the bases of appearance, history, beliefs, proximity, and many other characteristics. Furthermore, these groups are located in a social structure that assigns them levels of status, power, and prestige and considers them either mainstream or "other." As time has gone on, I have realized that the position I take regarding that diversity in my programming is a political statement—one that changes with changes in my consciousness and goals. A lasting goal, however, is for the participants in my family life education programs to learn to recognize the qualities that they share with others and those that are unique, to understand their group identities, and to value themselves as individuals and group members.

WHAT IS FAMILY LIFE EDUCATION?

Definitions of family life education have been explored by a number of groups and individuals, at least since the 1960s (Arcus, Schvaneveldt, & Moss, 1993). The National Commission on Family Life Education (1968, p. 211), organized by the National Council on Family Relations (NCFR), grounded primarily in the fields of sociology and home economics, described the purpose of FLE as "to help individuals and families learn what is known about human growth, development, and behavior throughout the life cycle . . . The central concept is that of relationships through which personality develops, about which individuals make decisions, to which they are committed, and in which they develop self esteem." Speaking from a public health perspective, Herold, Kopf, and deCarlo (1974, p. 365) later defined FLE as "the study of individual roles and interpersonal relationships, family patterns and alternative life styles, emotional needs of individuals at all ages, and the physiological, psychological, and sociological aspects of sexuality." The Family Service Association, grounded primarily in the field of social work, defined FLE this way "Basically, family life education is a service of planned intervention that applies the dynamic process of group learning to improving the quality of individual and family living" (Apgar, et al., 1982, p. xi). A more recent definition by Tennant (1989, p. 127) noted that FLE "is devoted to enabling adults to increase the effectiveness of their skills in daily living, that is, in relating to others, in coping with life events, and in realizing personal potential." Yet other groups have used the broad term *family life education* but have meant only a specific portion of the concept. This usage is illustrated by the multidisciplinary publication *Family Life Educator* (Family Life Education Network, 1982, p. 2), which defined FLE as "courses designed cooperatively with parents, educators, community professionals and youth; which provide individuals with adequate and accurate knowledge of family life in its physical, psychological, social and moral dimensions; which help clarify and strengthen values and attitudes as they relate to the family and to sexuality; which enhance feelings of self-worth and self-esteem; and which increase family values and the values of others and encourage communication between parents and their children." The journal was devoted almost exclusively to sexuality education.

Although many of these definitions are vague, they provide one source of input for family life educators as they define their roles. One metaphorical way to conceptualize the implications of these definitions for family life educators' roles is to think of educators as the directors of art museums. Sometimes they teach art classes, guiding students through activities that build skills and result in new creations, illustrated by definitions of FLE that refer to "planned intervention" and "enabling adults to increase the effectiveness of their skills." At other times, they organize exhibits of artwork, publish critiques, and provide lectures on art history—tasks that are similar to the focus of definitions of FLE that include such phrases as "help individuals and families learn what is known," "the study of individual roles and interpersonal relationships," and "provide individuals with adequate and accurate knowledge."

Some of the definitions of FLE address programming topics, some describe goals, and some discuss process. To understand such a complex term as FLE, however, it is important to understand all its components. All the definitions located so far leave two critical questions unanswered: Just what is *family life,* and how does it operate most effectively? and What is the nature of effective *education?* In both areas, diversity is a critical component.

THE "FAMILY" IN FAMILY LIFE EDUCATION

Defining *family* deals with the question of "what" educators will teach and "who" they will teach. Many FLE materials and programs, however, neglect to address the definition of families or family life, either in delineating subject matter or in targeting audiences. Regarding the former, most programs appear to have avoided the broad debate surrounding the definition of the family. Regarding the latter, Arcus and Thomas (1993, p. 23) stated that, "there has been little consideration of the specific characteristics of the audiences for which such programs are planned." The target audiences of most broad-based FLE programs are described simply as "families" or "parents" or as "family life educators" or "family studies students." In spite of the absence of a definition, however, the presumed definition becomes clear from the underlying assumptions, artwork, and examples in many broad, general curricula.

The assumption, consistent with the empirical literature on family studies (see Allen & Demo, 1995; Thompson & Walker, 1995), is that both the subject matter and the target audiences of the programs are heterosexual, European American, two-parent families—usually with two or three children of both genders. This assumption is consistent with Macklin's (1981, p. 567) observation that "our dominant culture has assumed that its adult members would select a mate of the opposite sex, marry, have children, be sexually exclusive, live together till death did them part, and acknowledge the male as primary provider and ultimate authority. . . . Given such a world, it was appropriate for FLE to focus primarily on such topics as mate selection, parenting, home management skills, and the developmental phases of the nuclear family." There is a growing trend toward including photographs and illustrations of families of various races, but this is mostly a cosmetic change. The situations and examples remain primarily white, middle class, and marriage centered. They also assume that families are literate and do not equally represent all members of these families. Carter and Kahn (1996) reported that 80%–85% of parent education providers served mostly women. It is clear that the majority of participants in FLE have been and are expected to be women and mothers (MacDermid, Jurich, Myers-Walls, & Pelo, 1992), and therefore most curricula are aimed at a female audience.

Nationality is another assumption. FLE, as defined in most of the literature I found, has been primarily a U.S. and Canadian phenomenon and represents North American culture. Its developmental course is consistent with a history of socializing immigrants and filling in for the extended families that the immigrants left behind. Although the United States and Canada are not the only countries that try to educate families, their approach is unique. A study by the UNESCO Institute of Education (Stern, 1960) reported that the U.S. approach to the FLE subfield of parent education was to treat it as a distinct activity that was the focus of numerous organizations. UNESCO saw the U.S. activities as self-consciously and actively promoted and closely related to research. In contrast, the movements in other countries were more restricted in sponsorship and scope.

These historical contrasts among countries appear to have continued. Almost any bookstore in the United States and Canada has shelves overflowing with parenting and family life self-help books, and parenting classes and marriage enrichment opportunities are offered in almost every community by many different organizations. In contrast, family education center schools in China are a recent phenomenon; most family education is expected to occur in the family setting with little or no outside intervention (Dai, in press). In Russia, there is a trend toward the formation of localized family organizations, but these organizations appear to serve a support, rather than an educational, function (Achildieva, 1988). The United States seems to export many curricula to other countries, however. For example, a recent catalog from Parenting Press in Bowling Green, Kentucky, advertised that the *SOS for Parents* curriculum (by L. Clark) was available in Turkish, Taiwan Chinese, Beijing Chinese, Korean, and English, and instructions were included for international orders. Another thrust in the United States is to provide family life information to new immigrants. Most of the emphasis of these international programs is on language translations, rather than cultural ones, and on using U.S. techniques and teaching U.S. concepts to groups in or from other nations. This emphasis can lead to some severe violations of cultural norms and expectations. For example, a graduate student from Taiwan with whom I worked expressed concern about the fit between Taiwanese society and the Systematic Training in Effective Parenting (STEP) program that was being promoted extensively in her country. An exploration and comparison of the cultural expectations of the program and of her society uncovered that some recommendations were inappropriate for the Taiwanese culture.

The dangers of not defining families explicitly in FLE programs are primarily twofold. First, implied definitions place some categories of families at the center of programs, while other families become invisible to the educator and to other participants, either as an audience or as subject matter. Second, some types of families may become the standard of comparison by which other families are judged (Allen, 1978; Scanzoni, Polonko, Teachman, & Thompson, 1989; Wilson, 1986).

The tendency to define audiences vaguely or not at all also reflects the failure to recognize a basic tenet of adult education—"discovering your audience" (Draves, 1988)—even though many FLE audiences consist of adults. "Quite simply, by knowing who your participants are, you can gauge what they might most like to learn. Then you can better prepare your presentation to fit those needs" (Draves, p. 3). As some colleagues and I (MacDermid et al., 1992) stated, feminist pedagogy asserts that there is a critical connection among the knower, the known, and the educator. By not encountering the audience personally, educators risk missing the target and then losing that connection and thereby losing the audience, violating some of their basic values or beliefs, and/or being insensitive to their diversity.

The failure to define *family* also represents the failure in the FLE field to recognize the biases in the literature. Because most practitioners use the information provided by researchers and theoreticians as the basis for their programming, family life educators inherit the biases and weaknesses that taint that literature. As Dilworth-Anderson and McAdoo (1988, p. 267) argued, "if researchers continue to create a knowledge base that is not culturally sensitive at all levels of the research process, inappropriate policies and interventions may be designed for ethnic minority families based on information researchers provide." Feminists have also identified research biases related to gender and have attempted to reorient the literature (Allen, 1988; Ferree, 1990; Thorne, 1982). I believe that the same principle applies to other areas of diversity in addition to culture, ethnicity, and gender.

When audiences are not defined, a default norm is developed representing the majority group or the group in power in the educational setting. Anyone who does not fit in that default audience becomes "other." "Being the *other* is feeling different; it is awareness of being distinct; it is consciousness of being dissimilar. Otherness results in feeling excluded, closed out, precluded, even disdained and scorned" (Madrid, 1988, p. 10). For example, programs or literature that constantly refer to "mothers and fathers" state over and over to single parents, grandparents acting as parents, and same-sex couples that they do not belong. Another result of otherness is invisibility or the lack of validity or voice, which Madrid called being "missing persons." This invisibility occurs when certain groups (e.g., minorities, teenage parents, or stepfamilies) are not allowed to assume a leadership or expert role.

Defining Families by Life Stage

When the audiences and subject matter for FLE programs are more explicitly defined, the most common approach is to use family developmental stages. The Family Service Association (Apgar et al., 1982), which concentrated on dealing with life transitions in FLE, listed the following life stages (based on Prochaska & Fallon, 1979): engagement, marriage, considering parenthood, families with young children, families with adolescents, last child leaving home, retirement, and death of a spouse. As an addendum to that list they included divorce, single parenthood, and remarriage. This chronology includes many individuals and families, but excludes others, such as single adults, childless couples, gay and lesbian couples, people who adopt older children, teenage parents, and grandparents who raise their grandchildren. These exclusions may be especially insensitive to some cultures in which intergenerational households are common and multigenerational child rearing is the norm (Wilson, 1986) or in which courtship, marriage, and childbearing follow "atypical" time sequences. As Arcus et al. (1993, pp. 21–22) pointed out, "recent work in the study of families suggests that the concept of 'proceeding through developmental stages' may no longer adequately describe the diversity of families and of family experience over time."

A similar age-based approach is the framework for life-span FLE described by Arcus (1987) and distributed by the NCFR (1997). This framework outlines curricular guidelines based on individual developmental stages, specifically childhood, adolescence, adulthood, and older adulthood, and characterizes both the subject matter and the audiences in programs. Although family life stages stem from sociology while individual developmental stages are more closely tied to psychology, both the NCFR's and the Family Service Association's approaches are based on similar assumptions: that individuals will experience similar life events and will share similar needs and goals and that most family life concerns will derive from those life stages. This approach masks a number of important family life issues for some families. Many of these developmental materials also assume that adults who attend programs are heterosexual, will marry, and will be parents and that other students-participants will be interested in studying primarily those families. In addition, the NCFR outline is easiest to use if families have children in just one of the age groups, even though new and unique issues and patterns arise with combinations of children from different age groups.

Defining Families by Targeting Subgroups

In contrast to these broad, general approaches that either do not define families or define them by life stage, many FLE programs are directed at specific subgroups, often defined by family composition. Single-parent families, stepfamilies, families with disabled children, black parents, adolescent parents, and families with incarcerated members are a few examples of the specific family types for whom programs have been created. These materials are usually respectful and inclusive of the targeted groups, but sometimes make further assumptions regarding family form and situation that ignore multiple forms of diversity. This limited approach to inclusiveness may reflect a general tendency in society to relegate individuals to only one non-mainstream category; many people fail to recognize multiple and intersecting dimensions of diversity. This tendency was stated clearly by a member on a parenting panel that I organized: "Many people don't know my partner and I are lesbians. Because I am in a wheelchair, people assume that my partner is just my caregiver. They don't think you can be both disabled and lesbian." In other cases, people may assume that certain categories are inexorably linked, such as assuming that all black single mothers are poor, ignoring the fact that it is possible to be black, single, a mother, and middle class.

Defining Families in Context

Most of the attempts to define families for FLE focus on age or family composition as the defining features. These definitions overlook some of the equally (if not more) important dimensions related to the context of families. Using the ecological approach of Bronfenbrenner (1977) moves definitions of families away from a listing of members or categorization by age to the contextual placement of families in a social reality. Taylor, Chatters, Tucker, and Lewis (1990) applied this approach to the study of families. They stated: "As with all social science, research and writing on black families transpires within a larger social and political context that influences the nature and direction of inquiry, as well as the interpretation and application of findings" (p. 993). Their assertions can be transferred easily to FLE.

Unfortunately, few FLE programs have used a contextual approach, even when specific subcultures or family forms have been targeted. Some of the best-known programs, such as STEP (Dinkmayer & McKay, 1976) project the belief that their recommendations will work in any family and in any situation if they are simply used correctly, ignoring the outer rings of Bronfenbrenner's model. Dinkmeyer and McKay stated that "you must be patient and willing to study and practice the philosophy presented in STEP. . . . Through diligent study and commitment, you will 'graduate' as a more effective parent" (p. 4). In the fields of sociology and anthropology, however, studies of cultural context have been numerous, and they have highlighted characteristics on which cultures and therefore families may differ. These cultural frameworks suggest some of the domains of family life that may need to be considered when devising FLE programs that are sensitive to diversity. They also allow educators to explore the characteristics of diverse families in a dynamic way without resorting to static descriptions of stereotyped groups.

I reviewed several of these cultural variation outlines (e.g. Hofstede, 1980; Kluckholm & Strodtbeck, 1961) along with the literature on parenting characteristics to develop a framework for the cultural variability of families (Myers-Walls, 1993). I applied this summary to providing FLE programs in the areas of parenting and child guidance. My listing appears in Table 18.1.

I made this chart into a worksheet and recommended that family life educators use it to explore the populations with which they work, building a broad picture of each group's macrosystem. Programs may then be structured to be sensitive to the identified characteristics.

Defining Families in a Way That Recognizes and Responds to Diversity

I admit that I have fallen into some of the same traps as many other professionals when I have addressed the issue of defining families. I have tried to avoid offering definitions of families because of the issue's ability to divide people and take the focus away from the important unifying issues related to family strengths. At the base, I feel the important defining features that make a group of people into a family are intensive interactions—either symbolic or actual—and a long-term commitment to each other based on a feeling of intimacy, obligation, and/or attachment. Most important, if individuals consider themselves to be a family, I will try to respect their identity as such. I have taken seriously the recommendation from colleagues of avoiding referring to "the family" and instead refer to "families," believing that there is a multiplicity of family forms, styles, and functions. That base is not useful for planning and delivering educational programs, however, so I try to move quickly from it to a more detailed exploration of the characteristics and needs of specific audiences or populations. Age-stage, composition, and cultural characteristics are some of the factors I try to incorporate into the picture of the families of interest, but none of those characteristics is seen as either uni- or bidimensional.

Returning to the analogy of art museum directors illustrates some of the implications of definitions of family. It is important for museum directors

TABLE 18.1
The Cultural Context of Families

Dimension	Possible Values
Population-Environmental Context	
Population mix	Homogeneous versus heterogeneous
Geography and climate	Uniting or separating families and individuals
Socioeconomic status	Mix of have's and have-not's
Religious orientation	Homogeneous versus heterogeneous, along with specific religious values and practices
Age/maturity of the community	Long history versus recent establishment or change
Community resources	Many versus few resources and services available
Levels of racism and discrimination	High versus low
Views of Children	
Child-rearing responsibility	Individual parents, extended family members, the community, tribe, or other
Investment in child rearing	Demanding of time and energy versus easy and requiring little effort
Children's contributions	Children as producers of goods and services versus as consumers who receive more than they return
Children's role	Blessing versus burden
Interpersonal Relationships	
Means of dealing with conflict	Physical versus social techniques
Whose needs predominate?	Children, adults, or the group
Sharing problems with others	Seen as a request for help, a sign of weakness, or entertainment
Means of working together	Cooperation versus competition; communalism versus individualism
Views on gender	Men dominant, women dominant, or shared roles; sons or daughters more highly valued or both valued equally

to do market research and to program appropriately. If they are trying to provide exhibits that will appeal to a broad or mixed audience, assuming that everyone wants only Picasso paintings is likely to result in low traffic through the museum. Either one specific group will like the exhibits and respond enthusiastically while the others go elsewhere or perhaps no one will like them. A varied and eclectic exhibit will function better. In the same way, a family life educator who uses narrow definitions of family may create programs or lessons that resonate with a few but leave others feeling left out, unreached, or invisible, or the programs may represent no one's reality. Another outcome of narrow programming is that the institution or sponsor will acquire a reputation for being oriented to only one group of people (e.g., white, middle-class women). Therefore, educators would benefit from being aware of the family definitions that are guiding them and making sure that those definitions include as many families in the desired audience and in the content as is reasonable.

On the other hand, using the art museum analogy again, a director may want to target specific groups, rather than to reach a broad audience. There may be classes for beginners through experts, and he or she

may target people who want to learn drawing, pottery, or weaving. There could be exhibits of children's art, photography, and impressionist painters for specific groups, even though they exclude or turn off some others. In the same way, targeted FLE programs can do things that other programs cannot. To target programs (or exhibits) effectively, however, a good understanding of particular audiences is crucial. It should be clear to the planners who is being invited into the program and who is being left outside the door.

THE "EDUCATION" IN FAMILY LIFE EDUCATION

The nature of effective education is the second fundamental question left unanswered by most definitions of FLE. Avery and Lee (1964, p. 32) identified the ultimate goal of FLE as "the development of stable families contributing constructively to the society in which they live." In addition to the fact that such a goal again leads to the questions, "Just what is meant by stable families?" and "What is the society like in which they live?" it also suggests the next question: "*How* can an educator facilitate healthy development in families?" There are numerous hints in FLE materials regarding how the field has answered these questions, but there does not appear to be consensus on the desired outcomes or processes.

The goals that have been listed in FLE fall into several categories: increasing knowledge-understanding, changing attitudes, building skills, changing behavior, and "exploring new ways of behaving" (National Commission on Family Life Education, 1968, p. 211). At the heart of the issue is a debate about whether effective education is based on knowing more information, behaving differently, discovering one's own wisdom within, or effecting social change. This question is relevant to issues of diversity in at least three areas: (1) Are the goals and objectives of the program appropriate for the individuals and groups in the audience? (2) Are the content of the program and sources of information or knowledge base applicable to the audience? and (3) Are the teaching methods and styles respectful of and effective with the audience?

The *Webster's Ninth Collegiate Dictionary* (1987) defines *educate* using phrases such as *rear, provide schooling for, persuade,* and *develop mentally.* Mace (1981) pointed out that *education* comes from the Latin verb *duco,* which means *to lead, conduct, draw,* or *bring,* and the prefix *ex,* which means *out of* or *from.* He concluded that the original meaning of the word therefore suggests that an educator's job is to help students locate and bring out the knowledge and wisdom that are already in them, not to inject them with information they do not have. Mace challenged family life educators to move from "learning for knowing" to "learning for doing."

On the other hand, Thomas, Schvaneveldt, and Young (1993) argued that the predominance of behavioral change models of education in the FLE field has underemphasized cognitive growth and knowledge development. They also stated that many FLE programs are training, not education, because education requires that one not simply "know how," but also "know what." This dichotomy between the two educational approaches has been challenged in the feminist literature, however. As some colleagues and I noted (MacDermid et al., 1992, p. 31), "Rejecting the notion of discontinuity between learning to know and learning to live, feminist perspectives help learners to do both."

A Continuum of Educator Roles

The first diversity issue related to educational process grows out of this discussion. The philosophical argument regarding educational goals translates into a continuum representing a range of roles for family life educators that are closely related to the location of power. At one end of the continuum, the curriculum and knowledge base take precedence, and the educator wields the power. At the other end, the participants, their experiences and needs, social change, and flexibility are the most important. The former approach has been labeled the "expert" or "traditional" approach (Hoopes, Fisher, & Barlow, 1984; Wright & L'Abate, 1977). The latter has been called the "facilitator approach" or "liberation pedagogy" (Shor, 1987; Shor & Freire, 1987) and is consistent with feminist pedagogy (Allen, 1988; Belenky, Clinchy, Goldberger, & Tarule, 1986). In the middle of the continuum is a collaborator approach in which educators and participants share power (Hiemstra & Sisco, 1990).

In the traditional or expert mode, presenters base their programs on the belief that they have information and skills that the participants do not have and would benefit from learning. Adherents to this philosophy believe that education should be structured and that an agenda should be prepared and followed closely. Answers lie with informed experts. The lives of the participants will be improved if they learn the material and follow instructions. By definition, most packaged curricula fall toward this end of the continuum, directing participants to specific information and behaviors.

The facilitator approach makes different assumptions. The participants need to decide what is important to them and direct the learning experience based on their needs and desires. The educator participates by facilitating group discussion at times, locating information when requested, and reflecting on the discussion of the group. The participants already have a large amount of knowledge; the role of the facilitator is to help them gain access to it. There is no agenda; the program flows as the participants direct it. The goal is to empower the participants, which leads to social activism and the overcoming of oppression. Few, if any, packaged curricula entirely fit this category because of the open and flexible quality that is necessary.

In between the expert and facilitator approaches lies the collaborator style. In this mode, the participants and educator share responsibility for directing the program and choosing focus topics. Both have important information and perspectives to contribute. There is usually an agenda, but it may have been created jointly by the participants and the educator, and the content of each session is negotiable. The participants are encouraged to contribute ideas and reflections, but the educator maintains some control of the schedule and the content of the discussions. Using a self-assessment questionnaire (Myers-Walls, 1992), I have found that the vast majority of family life educators identify themselves as collaborators, and most curricula are probably delivered in a style that is consistent with this approach.

Educators who want to be sensitive and responsive to diversity may have difficulty with an approach that is rooted too firmly in the first style—the expert approach. In that style, the participants become consumers of, rather than creative contributors to, the educational process. Because it does not allow for any substantial input from participants, the expert approach could overlook variations in family forms or needs and, in its extreme, does not provide any mechanism for feedback by participants who believe their perspectives are being disregarded. It is especially likely that members of oppressed groups will feel disregarded and marginalized in programs conducted in that way, which remind them of their powerlessness. This approach also relies heavily on the literature, and, to the extent that the literature is limited and biased, it may perpetuate stereotypes or majority-culture domination. Liberation pedagogy and feminist pedagogy, on the other hand, were developed for use with disenfranchised and oppressed groups. They provide a strong sense of inclusion by placing participants in leadership and program-development positions, which makes it highly probable that diversity will be respected. This does not mean that all programs can or should become liberationist, however. If the participants want or need specific

information, this style will not serve them well, or liberation or feminist pedagogy may or may not fit the culture of the audience. In addition, liberation pedagogy requires a significant period for building groups and forming a direction. Such a period is not always available.

Each educational style may fit particular situations, subject matter, and audiences. The key issue in addressing diversity seems to be that educators must include in their conceptualization of the educator role a mechanism for the participants to take some responsibility in directing the program and responding to materials and activities. Another key is to understand the target audience, the participants' preferred educational setting, and how the participants interpret educators' styles.

To return to the analogy of the art museum directors, one director (the expert) could be a strong leader who displays only the types of exhibits being shown in the top galleries of New York and Paris. Formal critiques are likely to be part of the exhibits. Classes may provide finished examples for students to emulate. Criteria for excellence would be clear. A second director (the collaborator) could come to the museum with ideas for exhibits, but would consult with patrons and museum personnel before decisions are made. Interactive displays that allow the patrons to touch appropriate artworks and react to exhibits would be common. As a teacher, this person would always provide some choices of projects for students to complete. Finally, a third director (the liberation facilitator) may set up a gallery for art displays, but would expect the patrons to contribute art objects for displays. Anyone who enters the museum would be encouraged to react to the displays, but there would be no predetermined criteria of excellence. Art supplies would be plentiful for those who wanted to create something of their own. The director would be available, as needed, to consult about the properties of particular media or the characteristics of various styles but would expect the projects to be self-directed.

Applying the model to FLE, the expert would work from a structured curriculum, have lots of handouts and homework, and expect the participants to learn specific information and adopt particular behaviors. There would be little or no opportunity for the participants to share their own ideas and experiences. Collaborators would bring a planned agenda and materials, but would give the participants an opportunity to review and revise those plans. There would be regular opportunities to reassess the group's direction and focus. Educators using a liberation pedagogy approach would come to a session with a few comprehensive resources, but would sit to the side and let the participants control the flow of the discussion. The facilitator would occasionally provide feedback to the group about the concepts that could be gleaned from their discussions but would not guide the discussion. It would be up to the participants to determine the goals and desired outcome.

Learning Styles and Diversity

A second diversity issue related to educational process is learning style. Each person in a learning setting has a preferred and comfortable learning style, but many settings do not recognize or adapt to this diversity. McCarthy (1996) suggested dealing with this challenge in a way that values diversity and encourages growth and balance.

McCarthy (1996) identified four primary learning styles. Type 1 learners focus on connecting learning to other aspects of their lives and ask the question "Why?" They look for patterns and context and are concerned about their fellow participants in the learning experience. Type 2 learners spend a good deal of time looking for facts and information. They want answers from the experts and ask the question "What?" Type 3 learners want instructions and to get to the business at hand; they forge ahead and act on the knowledge that is provided. They ask the question "How?" Finally, Type 4 learners adapt and alter information as it has been given to them. They find new combinations of ideas and fresh applications of knowledge, asking "What if?"

Returning to the art museum again, Type 1 learners want to learn about the personal backgrounds of the artists and to have opportunities to interact with other patrons. They are also interested in how the different styles developed and relate to each other. If they participate in classes, they want to know what art does to enhance development and the emotional impact of various colors and techniques. They would enjoy creating joint projects with others. Type 2 learners want to know how to recognize particular artists and are interested in critiques by art experts. They want an analysis of the works from various perspectives and to know how valuable each artwork is. If they participate in classes, they want to know exactly what they are expected to do and how, but they would really rather watch. Type 3 learners, on the other hand, do not have much interest in the exhibits, but would enjoy the classes as long as the instructions are clear. They want to know how to create certain effects, what the final product should look like, how much time they will have, and how many projects they need to finish. Then just give them the materials and get out of the way and let them do it. Finally, Type 4 learners want to be able to go back and forth among exhibits to get ideas. Then they will suggest improvements for the artwork on display. In the classes, they would like to create their own projects starting from raw materials and may work on several projects at once. They also have lots of ideas for new projects, ways to redesign the museum, new classes to be offered, new techniques for using media, and so forth.

When educators have explored learning styles, they often have attempted to "type" people and put them in learning groups and settings that match particular styles. An important aspect of the approach recommended by McCarthy (1996) is to view the four learning styles as a progression and part of a whole. Each person must first connect learning to personal experiences and put them in context, then organize those experiences by overlaying theories and facts. Next the person must apply that knowledge in a directed way through action and with coaching before finally moving to a personalization process of designing new approaches and adapting the actions to his or her own life, completing the learning cycle. Rather than remaining fixed in one's preferred learning style, McCarthy suggested, the goal of building on that preference and learning how to enhance one's less-preferred styles results in a more balanced learner. In the same way, a learning environment or classroom is enriched when it is composed of individuals representing all learning styles.

This approach moves beyond *accepting* diversity to *needing* it to make a learning experience complete and effective. Logically, this belief leads to an appreciation of other types of diversity. The skills involved in "teaching around the wheel" (teaching to all learning styles in a progressive manner) are similar to skills that help educators reach out to and include many participants in diverse groups. Effective teachers start by exploring and identifying their own learning styles and then work to understand the other styles and to integrate all styles in a single educational setting. The same process of understanding self and then others could apply to other types of diversity.

As I have dealt personally with the question of defining "effective" education, I have been faced with the heritage of graduation from the public school system, which relies heavily on both an expert approach and an instructional style consistent with McCarthy's Type 2. As I have built a larger experience base as an educator and have been exposed to a variety of theories and approaches, I have gravitated toward the facilitator-feminist end of the educational style continuum. Because of the assigned and chosen objectives for many of the programs I lead, however, I also lean heavily toward the collaborator style in many of the settings in which I take a leadership role. I have found McCarthy's outline of learning styles to be energizing and empowering to me as an educator and have discovered that sessions are easier to create and result in more favorable outcomes when I try to teach participants with all the styles in an integrated way. I am sure that I am not yet "done" as an educator, though, and hope to continue to develop in response to professional development experiences and interactions with participants.

PROGRAMMING FOR DIVERSITY

Although the roots of FLE lie in home economics and social work and with white, middle-class, heterosexual American women, that is not where the future of the field is likely to be. In most locations and settings, FLE audiences are becoming increasingly diverse and the environments in which the participants live, work, and travel include people from an increasing variety of backgrounds. There are steps an educator can take, however, to respond to this diversity in respectful and growth-producing

ways. Educators can prepare themselves, assess the needs of the participants, examine background materials, develop and deliver programs respectfully, and evaluate the impact of programs appropriately.

PREPARE YOURSELF AS AN EDUCATOR

Get to Know Yourself

As Dilworth-Anderson and McAdoo (1988) pointed out, the study of diversity begins with oneself. Butler (1987) stated that family researchers (and, presumably, family life educators) carry with them the "baggage" of their experiences and contexts, including social factors, culture, and history. Arms, Davidson, and Moore (1992) placed special emphasis on family of origin: "The particular family into which we are born or adopted emphasizes what is considered important and unimportant. . . . In fact, anyone or anything different from our family is often considered suspect" (p. 1). Therefore, to understand others and their situations, to educate a diverse range of families, and to teach about diversity, educators must get to know themselves and their origins. Doing so includes knowing *who* they are and to which groups they belong, knowing what they *know,* and knowing how they *feel* about themselves and others.

Learn Who You Are. The first step, then, is to identify one's personal characteristics and the groups to which one belongs. Because the educator is an integral component in the educational process and is connected to both the content and the participants (MacDermid et al., 1992), self-awareness is critical. London and Devore (1988) maintained that acquiring "insights into one's own ethnicity and an understanding of how this may affect professional practice" (p. 176) is an essential step in building "layers of understanding" of ethnic minority families. This step may be especially important for European Americans and other dominant majority groups because of their tendency to be considered the "default" population. Those who are outside the mainstream are constantly faced with challenges to their identity and self-definition. On the other hand, those who think they are similar to most other people have few opportunities to explore such domains. In fact, I think that there is a crisis of ethnic identity among white Americans; they are not aware of their culture. The same lack of conscious identity could apply to men, the middle class, heterosexuals, North Americans, and other dominant groups.

Devore and Schlesinger (1987) proposed some questions that may spur the process of self-awareness, beginning with the obvious inquiry, "Who am I?" To construct an answer, educators could simply list all the groups and classifications to which they belong. This list may start with obvious categories, such as race, gender, age, and religious affiliation, but could continue with their and their family members' job statuses, physical characteristics, marital statuses, sexual orientations, political affiliations, and learning styles. Because people have difficulty seeing themselves clearly, however, it may be important for educators to enlist the help of others to mirror their identities. People who see us most clearly are often those who are different from us. The next step is to consider how these characteristics place one in groups and then list the characteristics and trends associated with the groups. Finally, it is helpful to explore how these characteristics and group memberships create bridges or barriers among oneself, others, and educational content.

Discover What You Know.   The second step is to explore what one knows. This type of self-assessment could be accomplished by questionnaires covering such areas as cultural, religious, ethnic, and gender information. The results of such questionnaires indicate areas of expertise and ignorance. Alternative ways to assess knowledge are by reading materials that describe groups and again asking for feedback from others about one's behavior and attitudes. In some cases, educators may discover that some areas of ignorance include not only other cultures, but their own.

Discover How You Feel.   Finally, educators would benefit from assessing their attitudes and values. "Practitioners should have a knowledge of themselves which enables them to be aware of and to take responsibility for their own emotions and attitudes. Awareness is an essential area of knowledge" (London & Devore, 1988, p. 311). Devore and

Schlesinger's (1987) self-assessment includes questions, such as, "Who am I in relation to my feelings about myself and others? Who am I in the ethnic sense? What does that mean to me? How does it shape my perceptions of persons who are my clients?" A central question with which to begin a self-assessment is whether one views diversity as a problem to be solved or an opportunity to be realized. That basic attitude will guide and color anything an educator does regarding diversity.

I have taken a similar approach to personal attitudes and parent education. In addition to the educational-style questionnaire mentioned earlier, I have also created a questionnaire with which parent educators may assess their philosophical approach to parenting, thereby identifying the major parent education packages, if any, that are compatible with that approach (Myers-Walls, 1992). This questionnaire assumes that although educators may be able to teach approaches that they may not use themselves, they will be most effective when they are at least aware of what they believe.

In addressing diversity, it is also important to assess one's willingness to take risks and confront the existing power structure and social order. If an educator wants to reach out to oppressed and marginalized families or to challenge the default assumptions of society, he or she needs to be prepared to face struggles and criticism. There is no way to reach out to the marginalized and not be rejected (Ariarajah, 1997). To paraphrase Buddha, one must *be* the change to bring about change. Such conscious living means that activities that were simple and automatic before one committed to social change become complex and sometimes agonizing afterward. Therefore, before beginning such efforts, educators would benefit from making conscious decisions to enter the fray. Those who choose to include people who have been excluded should bring an honest concern and caring for the groups they wish to bring into the circle.

Explore Your Limits

To program effectively for diversity, family life educators are encouraged to be flexible, rather than rigid. They are challenged to think in varied ways and examine their assumptions about ideals, goals, and values. By expanding their view in that way, they may be able to sidestep the biases and pitfalls of programming for and about a default population. But such an unbiased approach also carries risks and dangers. Professionals who are so accepting and flexible that they are willing to support anyone and anything may stand for nothing at all (Cherlin, 1982). Therefore, educators must explore their ethical, empirical, and personal limits. To do so effectively, they must first get to know themselves and then take additional steps.

There are at least three methods of establishing limits. The first is to identify ethical standards and professional guidelines, the second is to define basic behavioral guidelines for healthy families, and the third is to pinpoint personal standards and boundaries.

Ethical Standards and Professional Guidelines. The goal of most codes of ethics is to help professionals "make personal and social choices about critical questions and dilemmas in human experience" (Czaplewski & Jorgensen, 1993, p. 68). According to London and Devore (1988), "layers of understanding" begin with "adherence to a set of personal and professional practice values that affirm the qualities of uniqueness" (p. 314), and they summarize several codes of ethics that are relevant to family intervention. There is not one universally accepted code of ethics that is followed by family life educators, however. Leigh, Loewen, and Lester (1986) and Brock (1993) proposed ethical guidelines, but these guidelines have not been universally recognized or adopted. Leigh et al.'s recommendations do not deal directly with family diversity, but they do include "Show respect for individual rights," "Demonstrate responsibility in dealing with their own and others' values," and "Demonstrate concern and a responsibility of how interventions impact participants and their families," all of which are related to respect for diversity. Brock's guidelines list a nondiscrimination policy as a traditional principle, but, like others, Brock did not address family diversity directly. The contributions of Leigh et al. and Brock are rooted in the therapy tradition, but they do not address all my concerns as an educator.

Some additional issues that could be included in a code of ethics for family life educators are suggested by other sets of FLE guidelines, such as "Criteria for the Evaluation of Family Life Education Materials" (Griggs, 1981). Griggs focused heavily on bias issues in materials, encouraging educators to examine materials for biased or stereotyped information on age, gender, race-ethnicity-culture, family composition, and socioeconomic background. At the same time, she suggested that family life educators review materials to see that all have a strong research base, balance, authority, and integrity. In other words, although materials should be inclusive and unbiased, some criteria for quality should be met for all audiences. By establishing such ethical standards and professional guidelines that are based on these or other criteria, educators who want to honor diversity can chart a path using a compass of respect for and inclusion of families and individuals from diverse backgrounds while maintaining a clear sense of their overall direction.

Behavioral Guidelines for Healthy Families. The second approach to establishing limits is to construct behavioral guidelines for families to identify a subject-matter foundation that is relevant to all families. The rationale for this activity is that some family behaviors are healthier than others, regardless of context. That is, sometimes it may be more responsible professionally to challenge a group's norms and practices than to affirm them.

Garbarino (1991) reflected this philosophy when he said that there are three ways that cultures can be "wrong." First, a culture may maintain beliefs about itself that are simply inaccurate; for example, members of a group may believe that domestic violence is rare for them, when it is actually common. Second, a culture's beliefs and practices may be inconsistent with each other, for example, when individuals claim to support individual rights and freedoms but then advocate against legislation to affirm those freedoms for a particular group. Third, practices, norms, and beliefs may be anachronistic. Parents may believe that kindergarten needs to be a half-day program to accommodate children's needs, but actually half-day programs may have been scheduled because, in the past, children were not accustomed to group settings and many mothers were home to care for their children during the day. Those situations are generally no longer the case.

Using behavioral guidelines and definitions of healthy families, educators may be able to discern a reference point in FLE and support appropriate aspects of diversity while building healthy families. This is a delicate task, however, because conservative forces apply pressure to support the status quo and uphold assumptions about normality and desirability that are based on the existing power structure, rather than on empirical and unbiased information. At the same time, more liberal forces may tout the virtues of acceptance with a latitude so broad that standards are undetectable. Wong (1991) encouraged educators to "avoid separatist anarchy" by establishing high and consistent standards of quality. He said it is possible to establish standards, but that "standards, like truth, should be inclusive rather than exclusive" (p. 52) and that the standards must move beyond the abstract to the specific to be inclusive. Garbarino speaking as a panel member with colleagues (Hyman et al., 1997) also commented on this issue, saying that cultural context may influence a person's experience of family life, but that some practices are "toxic," even when accepted in the culture. Specifically, Garbarino stated that spanking is always toxic for a child, but that it may not always be traumatic because of societal expectations and norms.

I have been a part of an attempt to define inclusive behavioral guidelines in one area of FLE. The National Extension Parent Education Model (see Table 18.2) is a list of 23 critical parenting practices in six categories (Smith, Cudaback, Goddard, & Myers-Walls, 1994). The model is based on empirical research and was reviewed by professionals from a variety of backgrounds across the United States. As Wong (1991) recommended, the practices are specific, not abstract. The model attempts to balance the need for universality with the need to respect diversity. It does so by concentrating on *what* a parent should do, rather than *how* the parent should do it. For example, a critical parenting practice is to "teach kindness," a behavior that can be carried out in a myriad of ways in different settings, yet the basic recommendation remains the same.

One family may teach kindness through the use of aphorisms and traditional stories, while another may use close parent-child contact and modeling, while a third chooses to have a pet so the child can learn the skills of kindness and caring.

Personal Standards and Boundaries. Determining one's limits should also involve considering personal values, abilities, and experiences. This task goes beyond the intellectual or theoretical exercise of listing "shoulds" and moves to a reality based self-examination. For example, one educator may believe that domestic violence is a critical topic and include the issue in programs for general audiences, but may not feel capable of providing respectful programs for convicted abusive male partners. In such cases, the critical point is to identify the nonnegotiable issues early and continually. Educators may then avoid the "hot buttons" in programming or may need to explain their personal stance to students and program sponsors. For example, my feelings about the military establishment make it necessary for me to avoid any joint programs between the Cooperative Extension Service and the military. I also have strong feelings about parents' responsibility to teach their children about sexuality at an early age, but I handle those feelings by stating my bias, sometimes explaining that my daughter was present at my son's birth before she was 4 years old. I hope that each educator will have only a limited number of nonnegotiables, but knowing what they are is critical. As educators grow and learn new information, those limits may move or disappear or new limits may be identified, but that growth process will be facilitated by awareness that the limits exist.

Assess Needs

After educators explore their own attitudes and abilities, they need to explore their audience's attitudes, situation, and needs using a needs-assessment process. During this process, educators figure out what they want to know, what the current situation is, which goals are reasonable and appropriate for the audience and their situation, and how to proceed to reach those goals. Needs assessment is a type of

TABLE 18.2
National Extension Parent Education Model of Critical Parenting Practices

Critical Care for Self Practices

- Manage personal stress
- Manage family resources
- Offer support to other parents
- Ask for and accept support from others when needed
- Recognize one's own personal and parenting strengths
- Have a sense of purpose in setting child-rearing goals
- Cooperate with one's child-rearing partners

Critical Understand Practices

- Observe and understand one's children and their development
- Recognize how children influence and respond to what happens around them

The Critical Guide Practices

- Model appropriate desired behavior
- Establish and maintain reasonable limits
- Provide children with developmentally appropriate opportunities to learn responsibility
- Convey fundamental values underlying basic human decency
- Teach problem-solving skills
- Monitor children's activities and facilitate their contact with peers and adults

Critical Nurture Practices

- Express affection and compassion
- Foster children's self-respect and hope
- Listen and attend to children's feelings and ideas
- Teach kindness
- Provide for the nutrition, shelter, clothing, health, and safety needs of one's children
- Celebrate life with one's children
- Help children feel connected to family history and cultural heritage

The Critical Motivate Practices

- Teach children about themselves, others, and the world around them
- Stimulate curiosity, imagination, and the search for knowledge
- Create beneficial learning conditions
- Help children process and manage information

Critical Advocate Practices

- Find, use, and create community resources when needed to benefit one's children and the community of children
- Stimulate social change to create supportive environments for children and families
- Build relationships with family, neighborhood, and community groups

Developed by Charles A. Smith, Dorothea Cudaback, H. Wallace Goddard, and Judith A. Myers-Walls in collaboration with extension professionals throughout the United States. This project was supported by the Extension Service, U.S. Department of Agriculture, and the Cooperative Extension Service, Kansas State University, under special project number 92-EXCA-2-0182.

target practice; educators figure out where the target is, where it should be, how close to the target their aim is now, and how to improve their aim.

In honoring diversity, educators should consider whether the target is placed appropriately for the participants in the program. That is, are the goals and objectives inclusive and appropriate? Are they realistic considering the participants' current status? Do they mesh with the participants' values and life goals? One way to improve the goal-setting process is by including representatives of the target population on the needs-assessment team. It is essential to avoid taking goals and objectives for granted, especially when funding sources or program administrators assign the targets.

If placement of the target is based on an analysis of each target audience and its characteristics, the methods of hitting the target are likely to be effective with that audience. London and Devore (1988) noted that professionals should build an understanding of individual and family development in the context of the target culture and should nurture their sensitivity to the life experiences of ethnic-minority persons in this country. They should then modify and adapt their intervention techniques to fit the needs and characteristics of the audience. These recommendations can be extrapolated to fit all types of diversity.

There are two pitfalls to avoid in this process, however. One pitfall is overgeneralization. Educators may assume that population trends for African Americans, urban families, or single fathers describe all individuals who fall into those categories or ask one person to present his or her view and then assume that the person speaks for the groups he or she represents (MacDermid et al., 1992). Another pitfall is to ignore the multiple categories into which individuals and families fall. Although most people in an audience may be Vietnamese immigrants, that is not the only characteristic that applies to them. Single-parent families, families caring for dependent elderly parents, and families dealing with unemployment may also be in the population.

Examine a Program's Content and Sources of Information

The content of FLE programs may come from a variety of sources. Some programs are based on a specific literature base, others use a broad literature base, and some use the personal experiences and beliefs of their creators. Those that use a liberation pedagogy or feminist approach combine the knowledge and beliefs of the participants with literature that the audience may wish to consult. The diversity of the FLE field itself complicates this issue, because background information comes from biology, psychology, and education (Gaylin, 1981) along with sociology, history, and other disciplines.

It is clear that materials based on an individual's thoughts and opinions will carry the same biases or preferences as their creator. As I mentioned earlier, programs based on empirical literature may also carry biases and preferences. As Dilworth-Anderson and McAdoo (1988) stated, the backgrounds and value systems of the researchers help to determine which research questions are asked, which research subjects are included, and how the results are interpreted.

No matter what its basis, a program can be only as good as the foundation from which it is derived. Therefore, a program based on personal experience and preferences, whether of the facilitator or the participants, will be limited by the extent of those experiences and preferences. Thus, diversity may be best honored in programs that either avoid a personal opinion-experience base or consciously combine a variety of opinions and experiences, perhaps using the natural diversity of the group. In the same way, a program based on empirical research will be limited by the quality and inclusiveness of the research. This is a constant difficulty in FLE programs for and about diverse groups. Until a broad base of data is available on a wide variety of families, FLE programs will be challenged to address effectively all the families that may participate in or be the subjects of those programs.

Educators would benefit from examining the sources of information for their programs and looking for two things: breadth-inclusiveness and applicability to the participants. Breadth and inclusiveness of sources increase the likelihood that diversity will be honored in the program. Educators can accomplish this goal by presenting several different bodies of research, by exposing participants to different cultures or lifestyles as models for the group to examine, or by facilitating the sharing of diverse opinions and backgrounds among the participants. Ensuring that more than one picture is presented is perhaps the best way to maintain a sense of openness in programs. This approach suggests that the participants are not taught how things are or should be, but are exposed to possibilities. The entire group can then learn about those options while identifying choices and learning to understand others.

In programs targeted toward specific groups, it is important to look for literature and materials that apply to them, but also to identify sources that can broaden their view. Literature that lists the characteristics of healthy families but is based on research with only European Americans should not be assumed to be appropriate for Japanese immigrants, and models of intimate relationships that grew out of research with first-time heterosexual partnerships may not apply to stepfamilies. Again, when the literature does not include the audience of interest, it could be used as a discussion starter or as a description of possibilities, but it should not be presented as the "truth."

Develop and Deliver Programming

Diversity becomes a part of FLE programs when educators either design inclusive programs and deliver them in inclusive ways or target their programs responsively for particular groups. Diversity may also become a topic in itself. Three "epigrams" from Wong (1991, p. 54) remind educators that diversity is meaningful only in the context of social relationships with others: "First, diversity without community becomes anarchy. Second, community without diversity becomes fantasy, if not anachronism. Third, community with diversity is an act of creation rather than an act of tradition; perhaps it is an act of recreating tradition." To restate, diversity is unifying and meaningful only in the context of building social relationships. A goal for inclusive programming is to foster a sense of community among all the participants in an FLE program. Finally, one cannot simply depend on traditional means of achieving FLE goals regarding diversity.

Educators may want to keep in mind that there are multiple dimensions to diversity. Diverse characteristics may be visible or invisible, chosen or inherent, shared by many people or only a few, and associated with rejection or acceptance by others. Educators may be aware of these characteristics or not, and it may or may not be appropriate to ask the participants to disclose their diversity. In any case, they can create an atmosphere that reduces the likelihood that the participants will feel they are "other" or invisible by facilitating acceptance and respect—qualities that allow the community to understand and value the diversity that characterizes it.

Keys to creating an accepting and respectful atmosphere include using inclusive language, setting guidelines for the group that increase feelings of safety, providing opportunities for participants to give feedback, using activities and homework assignments that are respectful of differences in resources, and allowing for multiple methods of communication and self-expression. If an educator steps into a learner role rather than an expert role, the participants can share responsibility for making the environment inclusive.

Just as educators benefit from learning to know themselves first, participants in FLE programs may benefit from exploring who they are and what they know before they can build a sense of community. Educators may provide the same experiences to their participants that they themselves engaged in. Macklin (1981) recommended the use of family genograms, observations of one's family, and interviews with family members as self-assessment activities. These assignments grow in depth and meaningfulness when the participants share their findings and insights with each other.

Helping people get to know and understand themselves when the educator is not a member of the group or groups to which the participants belong is a particular challenge. Again, it is critical to consider sources of information. In this case, the participants may offer the best foundation for programming. Although they may not have processed and organized their self-knowledge, the educator may be able to facilitate the emergence of such insight by teaching general principles regarding gender, race, family structure, power, or oppression. In this way, every group may have the raw materials needed to create a rich and inspiring educational experience on the topic of diversity.

When teaching or learning about any diverse group, a danger is the disembodiment of people or the decontextualization of practices. This concern was addressed by Gannon (1994), who observed that many attempts at cultural education resulted in people learning isolated practices and facts about groups without understanding how those practices and facts fit together or build meaning. As a result, many people who have been trained in cultural awareness still make many mistakes. For example, I have heard professionals working in a youth-exchange program between the United States and Japan explain in detail some Japanese customs but also say that the Japanese youth who come to this country are immature because they are not independent. This statement indicates the lack of understanding of the communal culture in which these youth are developing. Gannon encouraged the use of cultural metaphors or larger, holistic pictures of a people to understand not only isolated pieces of a culture, but a culture as a whole. The participants can be asked to create their own metaphors for themselves or a group that they are studying.

When possible, the best pictures of a group are presented by members of the group itself. Rather than talk *about* people, it is best to talk *with* them. The participants who listen to members of diverse families will be able to experience the humanity and shared life events and, by doing so, make the new group less "other." Beyond the diversity inherent in the participants, it may be helpful to invite representatives of various groups to discuss their lives and backgrounds with the participants. Opportunities should be provided to allow any outside guests to become "real" and to identify connections between them and the audience. I helped to arrange such a program when the topic was parenting in nontraditional situations. Instead of talking hypothetically about parents who had young children late in life, grandparents who were raising their grandchildren, and gay and lesbian parents, the participants were able to interact with several individuals in each category.

Finally, educators must be sensitive to tensions that exist among subgroups within the educational setting. In some cases, it may be most appropriate to avoid bringing certain people together, but in many cases, a safe and inclusive environment could contribute to the creation of at least a partial sense of community.

Evaluate a Program's Impact

When the program session, series, or course is over and the educator heads home, how will he or she feel about it? How will the participants feel? Evaluation loops back to the needs-assessment process and the need to place the program in a context that fits the setting. Wong (1991) challenged educators not to define diversity as the end in and of itself. Instead, he quoted John Slaughter as saying, "Diversity is the point at which equity and excellence meet" (p. 52). Whether or not excellence has met equity in an FLE setting depends on a balance of flexibility and groundedness, and measures of success should be diverse and inclusive. At the end of the day, however, the assessment takes place in the hearts of people, whose needs, dreams, and families are as diverse as their fingerprints yet as connected as their shared love of family.

REFERENCES

Achildieva, E. F. (1988). *Peculiarities of interfamily informal associations in the USSR.* Unpublished manuscript. Moscow: Russian Academy of Science, Institute of Sociology.

Allen, K. R. (1988). Integrating a feminist perspective into family studies courses. *Family Relations, 37,* 29–35.

Allen, K. R., & Demo, D. H. (1995). The families of lesbians and gay men: A new frontier in family research. *Journal of Marriage and the Family, 57,* 111–127.

Allen, W. (1978). The search for applicable theories of black family life. *Journal of Marriage and the Family, 40,* 117–131.

Apgar, K., Callahan, B. N., Coplon, J., Eaton, J. T., Fallon, B. C., Gall, D., Kalafus, L., Lilly, E., & Riley, D. P. (1982). *Workshop models for family life education: Training leaders for family life education.* New York: Family Service Association of America.

Arcus, M. E. (1987). A framework for life-span family life education. *Family Relations, 36,* 5–10.

Arcus, M. E., Schvaneveldt, J. D., & Moss, J. J. (1993). The nature of family life education. In M. E. Arcus, J. D. Schvaneveldt, & J. J. Moss (Eds.), *Handbook of family life education: Vol. 1. Foundations of family life education* (pp. 1–25). Newbury Park, CA: Sage.

Arcus, M. E., & Thomas, J. (1993). The nature and practice of family life education. In M. E. Arcus, J. D. Schvaneveldt, & J. J. Moss (Eds.), *Handbook of family life education: Vol. 2. The practice of family life education* (pp. 1–32). Newbury Park, CA: Sage.

Ariarajah, S. W. (1997, August). *Called to serve in the context of marginalization.* Address presented at Caring Ministries 2000: Challenges and Opportunities as the Church Cares for a Hurting World in the Next Century, Manchester College, North Manchester, IN.

Arms, K. G., Davidson, J. K., & Moore, N. B. (1992).

Cultural diversity and families. Dubuque, IA: Brown & Benchmark.

Avery, C. E., & Lee, M. R. (1964). Family life education: Its philosophy and purpose. *Family Coordinator, 13*(2), 27–37.

Belenky, M. F., Clinchy, B. M., Goldberger, H. R., & Tarule, J. M. (1986). *Women's ways of knowing: The development of self, voice, and mind.* New York: Basic Books.

Brock, G. W. (1993). Ethical guidelines for the practice of family life education. *Family Relations, 42,* 124–127.

Bronfenbrenner, U. (1977). Toward an experimental ecology of human development. *American Psychologist, 32,* 513–531.

Butler, J. S. (1984). Social research and scholarly interpretation. *Society, 24*(2), 13–18.

Carter, N., & Kahn, L. (1996). *See how we grow: A report on the status of parenting education in the U.S.* Philadelphia: Pew Charitable Trusts.

Cherlin, A. (1982, October). *The conservative challenge and the progressive response.* Address presented at the annual meeting of the National Council on Family Relations, Washington, DC.

Czaplewski, M. J., & Jorgensen, S. R. (1993). The professionalization of family life education. In M. E. Arcus, J. D. Schvaneveldt, & J. J. Moss (Eds.), *Handbook of family life education: Foundations of family life education* (Vol. 1, pp. 51–76). Newbury Park, CA: Sage.

Dai Keijing (in press). The tradition and change of family education in Mainland China. In J. A. Myers-Walls, P. Somlai, & R. N. Rapoport (Eds.), *Families as educators for global citizenship.* London: Ashgate.

Devore, W., & Schlesinger, E. G. (1987). *Ethnic sensitive social work practice* (2nd ed.). Columbus, OH: Merrill.

Dilworth-Anderson, P., & McAdoo, H. P. (1988). The study of ethnic minority families: Implications for practitioners and policymakers. *Family Relations, 37,* 265–267.

Dinkmeyer, D., & McKay, G. D. (1976). *Parent's handbook: Systematic training for effective parenting.* Circle Pines, MN: American Guidance Service.

Draves, W. A. (1988). *How to teach adults in one hour.* Manhattan, KS: Learning Resources Network.

Family Life Education Network. (1982). *Family Life Educator, 1*(1), 2.

Ferree, M. M. (1990). Beyond separate spheres: Feminism and family research. *Journal of Marriage and the Family, 52,* 866–884.

Gannon, M. J. (1994). *Understanding global cultures: Metaphorical journeys through 17 countries.* Thousand Oaks, CA: Sage.

Garbarino, J. (1991, June). Dinner address. Address delivered at Empowering Educators to Empower Families at Risk, sponsored by Parent Education Advisory Committee, University of Minnesota, St. Paul.

Gaylin, N. L. (1981). Family life education: Behavioral science Wonderbread? *Family Relations, 30,* 511–516.

Griggs, M. B. (1981). Criteria for the evaluation of family life education materials. *Family Relations, 30,* 549–555.

Herold, E. S., Kopf, K. E., & deCarlo, M. (1974). Family life education: Student perspectives. *Canadian Journal of Public Health, 65,* 365–368.

Hiemstra, R., & Sisco, B. (1990). *Individualizing instruction: Making learning personal, empowering, and successful.* San Francisco: Jossey-Bass.

Hoopes, M. H., Fisher, B. L., & Barlow, S. H. (1984). *Structured family facilitation programs: Enrichment, education, and treatment.* Rockville, MD: Aspen Systems.

Hyman, I. A., Graziano, A., Straus, M., Cohen, P., Garbarino, J., Eron, L, & Farley, F. (1997, August). *Should APA take a position on spanking? A child advocacy perspective.* Symposium conducted at the annual convention of the American Psychological Association, Chicago.

Kluckholn, F., & Strodtbeck, F. (1961). *Variations in value orientations.* Evanston, IL: Row, Peterson.

Leigh, G. K., Loewen, I. R., & Lester, M. E. (1986). Caveat emptor: Values and ethics in family life education and enrichment. *Family Relations, 35,* 573–580.

London, H., & Devore, W. (1988). Layers of understanding: Counseling ethnic minority families. *Family Relations, 37,* 310–314.

MacDermid, S. M., Jurich, J. A., Myers-Walls, J. A., & Pelo, A. (1992). Feminist teaching: Effective education. *Family Relations, 41,* 31–38.

Mace, D. (1981). The long, long trail from information giving to behavioral change *Family Relations, 30,* 599–606.

Macklin, E. D. (1981). Education for choice: Implications of alternatives in lifestyles for family life education. *Family Relations, 30,* 567–577.

Madrid, A. (1988). Diversity and its discontents. *Black Issues in Higher Education, 5,* 10–11, 16.

McCarthy, B. (1996). *About learning.* Schaumburg, LL: Excel.

Myers-Walls, J. A. (1992, May). *Why are you doing that and why should I believe you? Developing individual philosophy and credibility in parent education.* Paper presented at the Fourth National Conference of the Family Resource Coalition, Chicago.

Myers-Walls, J. A. (1993). *Part II: Examination of the cultural context of families as a guide to designing culturally appropriate programs.* In K. C. Morgan (Ed.), *Parents, children, and discipline: An extension guidebook for programming: Module I. Parenting and family programs for culturally diverse audiences* (pp. 21–36). Washington, DC: U.S. Department of Agriculture.

National Commission on Family Life Education. (1963). Family life education programs: Principles, plans, procedures: A framework for family life educators. *Family Coordinator, 17,* 211–214.

National Council on Family Relations. (1997). *Standards and criteria for the certification of family life educators, college/university curriculum guidelines, and content guidelines for family life education: A framework for planning programs over the life span* (rev. ed.). Minneapolis, MN: Author.

Prochaska, J., & Fallon, B. (1979). Preparing a community for family life education *Child Welfare, 58,* 665–672.

Scanzoni, J., Polonko, K., Teachman, J., & Thompson, L. (1989). *The sexual bond.* Newbury Park, CA: Sage.

Shor, I., (1987). *Freire for the classroom: A sourcebook for liberatory teaching.* Portsmouth, NH: Boynton/Cook.

Shor, I., & Freire, P. (1987). *A pedagogy for liberation.* New York: Bergin & Garvey.

Smith, C. A., Cudaback, D., Goddard, H. W., & Myers-Walls, J. A. (1994). *The national extension parent education model final report.* Manhattan, KS: Kansas State Cooperative Extension.

Stern, H. H. (1960). *Parent education: An international survey.* Hamburg: University of Hull and UNESCO Institute for Education.

Taylor, R. J., Chatters, L. M., Tucker, M. B., & Lewis, E. (1990). Developments in research on black families: A decade review. *Journal of Marriage and the Family, 52,* 993–1014.

Tennant, J. (1989). Family life education: Identity, objectives, and future directions. *McGill Journal of Education, 24,* 127–142.

Thomas. J., Schvaneveldt, J. D., & Young, M. H. (1993). Programs in family life education: Development, implementation, and evaluation. In M. E. Arcus, J. D. Schvaneveldt, & J. J. Moss (Eds.), *Handbook of family life education: Foundations of family life education* (Vol. 1, pp. 106–130). Newbury Park, CA: Sage.

Thompson, L., & Walker, A. J. (1995). The place of feminism in family studies. *Journal of Marriage and the Family, 57,* 847–865.

Thorne, B. (1982). Feminist rethinking of the family: An overview. In B. Thorne & M. Yalom (Eds.), *Rethinking the family. Some feminist questions* (pp. 1–24). New York: Longman.

Websters Ninth Collegiate Dictionary (1987). Springfield, MA: Merriam-Webster.

Wilson, M. N. (1986). The black extended family: An analytical consideration. *Developmental Psychology, 22,* 246–256.

Wong, F. F. (1991). Diversity and community: Right objectives & wrong arguments. *Change, 23*(4), 50–54.

Wright, L., & L'Abate, L. (1977). Four approaches to family facilitation: Some issues and implications. *Family Coordinator, 26,* 176–181.

CHAPTER 19

Family Diversity and Family Policy

RICHARD M. LERNER, ELIZABETH E. SPARKS, AND LAURIE D. MCCUBBIN

Our lives and personal experiences reflect the key focus of this chapter: the relationship between family diversity and family policy. Each of us is of a different racial background and a different religion. Two of us are female and one is male, and among us there are age differences of more than a generation. Furthermore, although we three all have immediate and extended families that span multiple generations, our locations in these generational groups vary. For instance, one of us is a member of the youngest generation in her family constellation, another is the parent of several teenagers and contributes to the support of an aged mother. Add to this diversity the fact that in our respective lives, we have had experiences with immediate and extended families that pertained to both normative life events, such as births, deaths, marriages and divorces, and to nonnormative life events like unexpected illnesses, changes in family structure, financial calamities, and severe accidents.

Together, these lifetimes of personal and experiential diversity have resulted in our seeking and receiving emotional, physical, and even financial support or assistance from immediate and extended family members, neighbors and friends, and community institutions (e.g., religious institutions, civic societies, or governmental bodies). At times, this support was just what was needed to match the particular circumstances faced by one of us; at other times, however, the programs that were available to help us cope with life events (e.g., the death of a father, no life insurance policy, a mother too ill to work, a brother in junior high school, and the desire of one of us to stay in college) did not match the uniqueness of our situations. Thus, we have learned, through both our scholarship and our personal lives, that if the programs that are available to support families and the rules or principles from

which these programs are derived, that is, the policies pertinent to families, are to be maximally useful, they need to be developed to fit the characteristics of the diversity of the families they are intended to help.

To link family diversity and family policy adequately, we need to ask two questions: What sorts of families does one find in the contemporary United States? How are these families comparable to those in previous decades?

These questions capture the two temporal (historical) perspectives that may be applied to the study of family diversity. The former question is predicated on a point-in-time, or cross-sectional, perspective, and the latter is derived from an interest in cross-time, longitudinal analysis. Both temporal perspectives are needed to appreciate the plasticity of structure that characterizes the family and to make inferences about the potential range of structural variation that may exist. The presence of potential variation—not only in structure but in function—is vital if policies are to be realistic guides for actions that can produce desired changes (Lerner, 1984).

Public policies represent standards, or rules, for the conduct of individuals, organizations, and institutions. The policies that are formulated and followed structure behavior and enunciate to others how they may expect people to function with regard to the substantive issues to which the policies pertain. Moreover, they reflect what we, as members of society, value, what we believe, and what we think is in our best interests; they indicate the things in which we are invested and about which we care. Policies that are aimed at enhancing the family are, implicitly, temporal initiatives. They are social actions designed to change family structure or function from a "status" at one point in time to a "status" at another. Inherently, then, policies also have to be seen in the context of the same two temporal parameters within which the study of family diversity is embedded. The cross-sectional and longitudinal diversity of family structures may provide practical boundaries that frame the changes that policies seek to create. In turn, the temporal parameters of family diversity give some empirical justification that there is plasticity in family structure (and, it may be argued, in family function) sufficient to enable public policies to create theoretically inferred, new forms of the family. In short, historical change—temporality—is a key parameter of both family diversity and family policy. It is useful, then, to discuss the point-in-time and cross-time components of family.

THE FAMILY: HISTORICAL AND CONTEMPORARY PERSPECTIVES

The first author of this chapter grew up at a time when the stereotypical American family was European American, intact, and nuclear; it had two biological parents and two or three children (named either David and Ricky or Bud, Kitten, and Princess,

respectively). Yet, today, only 1 in 5 married couples with children fits this still-popular stereotype of living in what has been termed the "Ozzie and Harriet" family—the intact, never-divorced, two-parent–two-child family (Ahlburg & De Vita, 1992; Hernandez, 1993). Even a smaller proportion of African American and Latino children live in two-parent families in which the fathers are the breadwinners and the mothers are homemakers. As Table 19.1 illustrates, children and parents live in several different family contexts (see Allison, 1993; Lerner, Castellino, Terry, Villarruel, & McKinney, 1995).

This diversity of family structures or, at the least, of contexts serving the socialization functions of families (Lerner & Spanier, 1980) requires a definition of family that is broader than the intact, nuclear family in which parents raise their biological children. We see a family as not merely a household, but an institution in which individuals, related through biology or enduring social commitments and representing similar or different generations and genders engage in roles involving mutual socialization, nurturance, and emotional exchange.

The number of children living in many of the types of family contexts shown in Table 19.1 has

TABLE 19.1
Some Contemporary "Family" Contexts of Children and Youth[a]

Intact nuclear (biological)
Single parent (biological)
Intact nuclear (adoptive)
Single parent (adoptive)
Intact (blended)
Single parent (step)
Intergenerational
Extended, without parent
  {e.g., child-aunt}
In loco parentis families or institutions
  Foster care homes
  Group homes
  Psychiatric hospitals
  Residential treatment facilities
  Juvenile detention facilities
Runaways
Street children or youth
  {e.g., adolescent prostitutes}
Homeless children

[a]The family contexts listed can be heterosexual, gay, or lesbian. *Source:* Lerner, R. M., Castellino, D. R., Terry, P. A., Villarruel, F. A., & McKinney, M. H. (1995). A developmental contextual perspective on parenting. In M. H. Bornstein (ed.), *Handbook of parenting: Vol. 2. Biology and ecology of parenting* (pp. 285–309). Hillsdale, NJ: Lawrence Erlbaum.

increased dramatically in recent years. For example, between 1987 and 1991, the number of children in foster care increased by more than 50%, from 300,000 to 460,000. Infants under age 12 months are among the age groups of children who are most likely to be placed in such care (Carnegie Corporation, 1994). As with many of the other statistics on children who live in poverty and in nontraditional family arrangements, the percentage of children of color living in such settings is disproportionately higher than the percentage of European American children.

In addition, the cross-sectional location of people in one of the family contexts noted in Table 19.1 is complicated by the fact that such settings may change longitudinally over the course of the lives of children and parents and thus across generations (i.e., across history). This observation raises the need for a historically embedded "developmental demographics" of child-parent relationships (Allison, 1993), a point underscored by the research of Featherman, Spenner, and Tsunematsu (1988) and, Hernandez (1993). For instance, Featherman et al. demonstrated that, even with a contextual variable as seemingly general (and presumably stable) as social class, only about 46% of American children remain at age 6 in the social class in which they were born. Indeed, approximately 22% of all children born in the United States change from their initial social class during their first year of life. Given that social class structures the large majority of the resources and cultural values that influence families, these magnitudes of change underscore the need to appraise the diversity of child-family relationships longitudinally (historically), as well as cross-sectionally.

This viewpoint was brought to the fore by the scholarship of Hernandez (1993). Using census and survey data, Hernandez described several profound changes that have characterized the life courses of U.S. children and their families over the past 50 to 150 years. Hernandez argued that a person's life trajectory is constituted by, and differentiated from, those of others on the basis of the specific order, duration, and timing of the particular events and resources experienced and by the number, characteristics, and activities of the family members with

whom the person lives. Using this viewpoint, Hernandez describes what he labeled eight *revolutions* in the lives of U.S. children across this century.

Eight Revolutions in U.S. Children's Lives

1. The Disappearance of the Two-Parent Farm Family and the Growth in the One-Parent Family. Hernandez (1993) noted that from the late 18th century to almost the end of the 19th century, the majority of U.S. children from birth to age 17 lived in two-parent farm families. At the beginning of the 20th century, about 40% of all children in this age range still lived in such families; slightly more than 40% lived in nonfarm, two-parent families with breadwinner fathers and homemaker mothers; and the remainder lived in either dual-earner nonfarm families, one-parent families, or no-parent situations. A larger percentage of African American children were in this last category because the normative family arrangement in the African American community at that time was for both parents to be wage earners, and there were many mother-only families.

In 1990, however, fewer than 5% of U.S. children lived in two-parent farm families during the first 17 years of their lives, and fewer than 30% of the children in this age range lived in intact nonfarm families. About 70% of all U.S. children in this age range lived either in dual-earner nonfarm families or in one-parent families. Indeed, approximately 25% lived in one-parent families. With regard to non-European U.S. children, about 38.2% of African American and 34.2% of Puerto Rican children lived in mother-only households.

2. The Decrease in the Number of Siblings in Families. In 1890, 46% of American children lived in families with 8 or more siblings, 30% lived in families with 5 to 7 siblings, and 16% lived in families with 3 or 4 siblings; only 7% lived in families with 1 or 2 siblings. In 1990, however, only 1% of U.S. children lived in families with 8 or more siblings, 5% lived in families with 5 to 7 siblings, and about 38% lived in families with either 3 or 4 siblings. However, about 57% lived in families with either 1 or 2 siblings (Hernandez, 1993).

3. The Increase in Parents' Education. In the 1920s, about 60% of U.S. children had fathers with at least 8 years of schooling, whereas about 15% had fathers with at least 4 years of high school; the corresponding rates for mothers were a few percentage points higher than those for fathers. In the 1950s, parental educational attainment had markedly increased. Approximately 90% of mothers and about 87% of fathers had 8 or more years of schooling, and 60% of mothers and about 55% of fathers had at least 4 years of high school. Through the end of the 1980s, these trends in increasing parental education continued. By that time, about 96% of mothers and fathers had 8 or more years of schooling, and about 80% of mothers and about 85% of fathers had at least 4 years of high school (Hernandez, 1993).

These statistics reflect trends for all children, regardless of race. However, the trends for specific ethnic minority families are different. Despite a substantial narrowing of the racial gap in parents' education, African American children continue to lag substantially behind European American children in their chances of having parents who completed at least four years of high school or college. By the 1970s, Latino children (of any race) and non-Hispanic blacks had about equal chances of being disadvantaged with respect to parental education, and first-generation Latino children (of any race) were somewhat more disadvantaged. By 1988, Latino children (of any race) born to parents in the U.S. continued to be fairly similar to non-Hispanic blacks in their chances of being disadvantaged by lower levels of parents' education (Hernandez, 1993).

4. The Increase in Mothers in the Labor Force. As Hernandez (1993) and Lerner (1994) documented, the percentage of children with mothers in the labor force increased dramatically between 1940 and 1990. In 1940, only 10% of U.S. children had mothers in the labor force, and, in 1950, only 16% did. However, in 1960, 26% of U.S. children had employed mothers, and, in 1970, this proportion had grown to 36%. In 1980, 49% of U.S. children had mothers in the labor force, and by 1990 this figure had risen to 59% (Hernandez, 1993).

In the African American community, these percentages have been higher since the 1920s, when African American women entered the labor force in large numbers to help support their families. In 1980, 53.1% of all African American women were in the labor force, and by 1995, 59.5% were. In 1995, the percentages of African American women with children who were in the labor force and were living with their spouses were even higher: 76.3% with children under age 3 and 77.3% with children under age 6.

5. Changes in Fathers' Full-Time Employment. The marked growth in maternal employment since 1940 has been coupled with the fact that from the 1940s to the 1980s, many U.S. children lived with fathers who were not employed full time year-round (Hernandez, 1993): 40% in 1940, 32% in 1950, and 24% in 1980. However, between 1950 and 1980, the 8% decrease in children living with fathers who were not employed full time was offset by an 8% increase in children who did not have fathers at home (Hernandez, 1993). Given the percentage of U.S. children who lived in such father-absent homes during this period, from the 1950s to the 1980s, only about 60% of U.S. children lived with fathers who worked full time all year (Hernandez, 1993).

6. The Growth of Single-Parent, Female-Headed Families. As we noted earlier, from 1940 to 1990, there was a dramatic increase in the percentage of U.S. children living in mother-headed households (Hernandez, 1993). In 1940, 1950, and 1960, the proportion of children living in these families remained relatively steady, at 6.7%, 6.4%, and 7.7%, respectively. However, between 1960 and 1990, the percentage of children in such families rose from 7.7% in 1960 to 11.8% in 1970, to 16.2% in 1980, and to 20% in 1990 (Hernandez, 1993). These percentages were higher in non-European American families.

In addition to out-of-wedlock births, a major reason for the growth of female-headed families is the rising rates of divorce in the United States. In 1906, less than 1% of children per year experienced the divorce of their parents, but, by 1993, almost

50% of all children did, and, for non-European American children, these figures were even higher (Carnegie Corporation, 1994). On average, European American children live five years in single-parent families, and for African American children this period tends to be longer.

Two new family patterns that are often related in a family's history to single-headed households are cohabitation and stepparent families (Bumpass & Sweet, 1989; Bumpass, Raley, & Sweet, 1994). Families formed by cohabitation (by living together without marriage) have increased while marriage rates have fallen (Bumpass & Sweet, 1989). Marriages preceded by cohabitation can be short-lived and are more likely to end in a divorce (Bumpass & Sweet, 1989). Thus, cohabitation is a factor that is reshaping the range of diversity of family structures in the United States. Indeed, one fourth of unwed mothers are cohabiting with the children's fathers at the time of birth (Bumpass et al., 1994).

The substitution of cohabitation for marriage and remarriage means that many children gain stepparents through their parents' cohabitation rather than marriage. One third of women are likely to live in stepfamilies caused by marriage-remarriage, and one fourth of children have lived in families with stepparents (Bumpass et al., 1994). However, when cohabiting is included in the definition of a stepparent family, 40% of women and 30% of all children spend time in such a family unit. A higher proportion of African American mothers (50%) and African American children (40%) live in this type of stepfamily, despite the lower rates of marriage and remarriage among African Americans. Indeed, one third of the children who enter stepfamilies do so after birth to unwed mothers, rather than after a divorce or separation, and about two thirds enter through cohabitation. Two thirds of African American families and 55% of European American families create stepparent families by cohabitation.

About 25% of the couples in cohabiting stepfamilies marry within one year, and 50% marry within five years. Nearly half (40%) the children in stepfamilies created by cohabitation experience family disruption in five years. Stated differently, 60% of such families are still intact after five years (Bumpass et al., 1994).

7. The Disappearance of the "Ozzie and Harriet" Family. As we noted earlier, over the course of the 20th century, the stereotypically predominant intact, two-parent family, in which the father is the breadwinner, the mother is the homemaker, and two to three children spend their lives in socioeconomic and personal security or are faced with problems that require only about 30 minutes (the time of the typical American television situation comedy) to resolve, has disappeared in the United States. Hernandez (1993) demonstrated that not only are such stereotypical family milieus largely absent in this country, but, since the 1940s, a decreasing minority of children have been born into such families. Hamburg (1992) noted that until the beginning of the 1960s, most people in the United States believed that much of this stereotype was true.

In 1940, 1950, 1960, and 1970, the percentages of children born into "Ozzie and Harriet"-type European American families were 40.8%, 44.5%, 43.1%, and 37.3%, respectively. However, by 1980, this percentage fell to 27.4% (Hernandez, 1993). Moreover, few Americans spend their entire childhoods and adolescent years in such families. In 1920, only 31% of children and youth lived their first 17 years in these types of families, compared to 16.3% in 1960 and less than 10% in succeeding decades (Hernandez, 1993).

8. The Reappearance of Widespread Child Poverty. The final revolution described by Hernandez (1993) pertains to the changing distribution of children across relative income levels and, as such, to the growth of child poverty, especially during the 1980s (see Chapter 15, this volume). After the Great Depression, the relative poverty rate among children dropped from 38% in 1939 to 27% in 1949 to 24% in 1950, and to 23% in 1969 (Hernandez, 1993). However, between 1969 and 1988, this trend reversed, and, by 1988, relative poverty among children had grown by 4%. In other words, during the 1980s, the percentage of children living in poor families returned to the comparatively high level of 1949. Moreover, the percentage of children living in "middle-class comfort" decreased between 1969 and 1988, from 43% to 37% (Hernandez, 1993). Although most children in poverty are

European American, a disproportionate number are African American and Latino. The poverty rates for these non-European American groups have tended to follow a similar pattern through the years (*Child Welfare Stat Book*, 1993).

Comtemporary Issues Associated With Poverty

Hernandez (1993) embedded the child-parent relationship within a historically changing matrix of variables involving family structure and function and other key institutions of society (e.g., the educational system and the economy). The import of Hernandez's scholarship for this discussion is that the American family is a product of multidimensional historical changes in the contexts of family life. As such, historical variation provides both a basis for the diversity of the family at any point in time and suggests the parameters of changes that may influence the future course of this diversity. Indeed, the importance of focusing on an historically embedded analysis of diversity in U.S. families is further illustrated by an appraisal of the contemporary differences in family relations among poor and nonpoor families and different racial-ethnic groups.

The diversity in American families is dramatic when one examines the effects of poverty on children. In essence, a rich array of individual and contextual protective factors promote resilience and successful, healthy development among poor and minority children and their families. The presence and strength of these "adaptive modes" (Spencer, 1990) underscore McLoyd's (1990, p. 263) view that "it is myopic, costly, and perilous to ignore the cultural, ecological, and structural forces that enhance" the development of poor and minority youth and families.

Yet, despite the impressive capacity for resilience, adaptation, and success among diverse, particularly minority, families, the presence of multiple risk factors, especially when they are associated with poverty, makes family stress and problematic child development much more likely (Huston, 1991; Schorr, 1988). In light of McAdoo's (1995) belief that poverty is the greatest challenge to resilience for African American families, it is appropriate to discuss child poverty in America because of the "rotten outcomes" (Schorr, 1988) linked to poverty in regard to family life and child development.

CHILD POVERTY WITHIN THE ECOLOGY OF AMERICA'S FAMILIES

By the end of the 1980s, approximately 20% of American children were poor, an increase of 17% during that decade. Moreover, Phillips and Bridgman (1995, p. 1) noted that in 1993 "poverty among American children reached its highest level in 30 years." Indeed, 22.7% (or 15.7 million) American children were poor in 1993 (U.S. Bureau of the Census, 1994).

Poverty exists in different proportions among different racial-ethnic groups. In 1989, 44% of African American children were poor, a rate four times greater than the corresponding rate for European American children, and, among Latino children, the rate was 38%, an increase of 25% across the 1980s—the greatest increase for any racial-ethnic group in the United States (Center for the Study of Social Policy, 1993). In terms of absolute numbers, data from the 1990 census (cited in Children's Defense Fund, 1992) indicated that 5.9 million European American children lived in poverty, compared to 3.7 million African American children, 346,000 Asian American children, 260,000 Native American children, and 2.4 million Latino children.

As Huston (1991) noted, race is the most striking and disturbing distinction between children for whom poverty is chronic and those for whom it is transitory. For instance, Duncan (1991) reported that the average African American child in the Panel Study on Income Dynamics spent 5.5 years in poverty, compared to 0.9 years for the average non-African American child. Furthermore, as with race and ethnicity, poverty is not equally distributed across age groups. In 1989, about 20% of children younger than age 6 were poor versus about 17% of 6- to 17-year olds; the rates for Americans aged 18 to 64 years and those aged 65 or older were about 11% and 13%, respectively (Children's Defense Fund, 1992).

During the 1980s, the percentage of children living in single-parent families increased 13%. From 1987 to 1991, 18.1%, 30% and 56.7% of European American, Latino, and African American children, respectively, lived in single-parent households (Center for the Study of Social Policy, 1992). Most of these single-parent households were female headed, and the poverty rates in them were, by the beginning of the 1990s, 29.8% for European American families, 50.6% for African American families, and 53% for Latino families (U.S. Department of Commerce, 1991). Similarly, in 1989, 34.2% of the households of 25 of the largest Native American tribes were single-parent families, and of these families, 27.2% were living in poverty. Because the average income of female-headed families is often three or more times lower than that of two-parent families and lower than that of single parent, male-headed families, the fact that an increasing proportion of children live in these families means that financial resources to support parenting are less likely to be available (Center for the Study of Social Policy, 1993).

As the poverty rates of U.S. children worsen, exceeding those of all other major industrialized nations (Huston, 1991), the structure of the family is also changing in ways that have placed poor children and parents at a greater risk of problems in family life and individual development. To illustrate, in 1990, 90.3% of children lived with their parents, 7.3% lived with other relatives, and 2.3% lived outside their families (Center for the Study of Social Policy, 1992). However, only 41.9% of African American children aged 10–14 lived with both their parents, compared to 67.7% of Latino children and 78.5% of European American children, and of those aged 15–17, only 41%, 63%, and 76% of African American, Latino, and European American children, respectively, lived in two-parent families (Simons, Finlay, & Yang, 1991). According to Reddy (1993), only about half the Native American families were traditional "two-parent biological" families.

These trends in child poverty and the family structure and parenting resources to which poor children have access are associated with problems in family life and child development. For instance, there is substantial information to suggest that families' economic adversity is likely to have a strong and negative influence on children (see, for example, Huston, 1991). To illustrate, Moore, Morrison, Zaslow, and Glei (1994), in an analysis of data from the National Longitudinal Study of Youth involving an overrepresentation of African American and Latino youth, found that youth whose families were on welfare continuously from 1986 to 1991 and those whose families had moved off welfare but did not move out of poverty were more likely to have high levels of behavioral problems than were youth whose families were never on welfare and never poor. In addition, youth whose families were not poor in 1986 but were both poor and on welfare in 1990 had the highest likelihood of behavioral problems. Poor children are also at a high risk of dying from violence. According to the Center for the Study of Social Policy (1993), between 1985 and 1992 the rate of violent deaths to 15–19 year olds increased 13%; for European American youths this rate increased 10%, whereas for African American youth, it increased 78%. The third leading cause of death among Native American youth aged 15–24 was homicide, almost twice the rate for European American youth (*Indian Health Service Trends*, 1995).

If poor children do not die, their life chances are often squandered by school failure, underachievement, and dropout; by crime; teenage pregnancy and parenthood; the lack of job preparedness; prolonged dependence on welfare; and the feelings of despair and hopelessness that pervade the lives of children in poverty and who see themselves as having little opportunity to do better, that is, to have a life marked by societal respect, achievement, and opportunity (Dryfoos, 1990; Lerner, 1995; Schorr, 1988). Compared to their nonpoor age-mates, poor youth are 50% more likely to have physical or mental disabilities; almost twice as likely not to have visited a doctor or dentist in the most recent two years of their lives; 300% more likely to be high school dropouts; and, as was noted earlier, significantly more likely to be victims of violence (Simons et al., 1991). Furthermore, poor children are at a high risk of low self-confidence, conduct problems, depression, peer conflict, and severe health problems (Klerman, 1991; McLoyd & Wilson, 1991).

In summary, the societal and cultural conditions that have created and maintained poverty in the United States and "distributed" it nonrandomly among families represent a formidable challenge for research—and for interventions that, ideally, should be informed by, if not derived from, research sensitive to the diverse conditions of poverty. Poor children live in diverse families or family-type settings, including foster care homes, institutions, shelters, other types of placements, and no fixed settings (are homeless) (Allison, 1993; Huston, 1991). The lack of attention to this contextual variation may lead to an inadequate appreciation of the diverse role of "the family" in poor children's development. It may also lead to insufficiently differentiated policies and programs that are pertinent to the family lives of poor children. For example, in the current welfare reform legislation, there is little acknowledgment of the heterogeneity of the welfare population and their diverse needs and few provisions for welfare recipients who need intensive, longer-term assistance to move toward becoming self-sufficient. This refusal to recognize the diversity among the poor has resulted in policies that have the potential to increase the adversity for poor children and their families.

Some may think it impolite or impolitic to note that a shortcoming of scientific inquiry is the failure to pay sufficient attention to the diversity of American families or to the diversity of the people in them. However, the lack of sensitivity to human individual and contextual diversity cannot continue. It is, clearly, morally repugnant to many people *and,* at least equally important in this context, is simply bad science (Lerner, 1991, 1998).

The basis of this assertion is the emphasis on the importance of a focus on diversity in developmental contextual theory—a key conceptual perspective involved in the systemic understanding of human individual and social structure, function, and change (Lerner, 1998; Thelen & Smith, 1998; Wapner & Demick, 1998). It is useful to review the key features of developmental contextualism to under-

stand the implications of the study of diversity for the conduct of science and for the derivation of policies and programs from such scholarship.

DEVELOPMENTAL CONTEXTUALISM: AN OVERVIEW

Developmental contextualism (Lerner, 1986, 1991, 1995, 1998) is an instance of a theoretical orientation to human development termed developmental systems theory (Ford & Lerner, 1992; Thelen & Smith, 1998). Developmental contextualism has its roots in the multidisciplinary and multiprofessional field of home economics (Lerner & Miller, 1993), now called family and consumer sciences. In addition, developmental systems theory, in general, and developmental contextualism, in particular, are important theoretical orientations within the field of human development because of their coevolution with the life-span view of human development (Baltes, 1987), the life-course study of human development (Elder, 1974), and the ecological view of human development (Bronfenbrenner, 1979).

The life-span developmental perspective extends the study of development throughout the life course by conceptualizing the basic process of development as *relational,* that is, as involving associations between the developing individual and his or her complex and changing social and physical contexts, or ecology. The broadest level of this ecology is history. As we noted earlier, embedding change within a historical context provides a temporal perspective to the study of a phenomenon. Linking the changes that characterize individual life-span development with an ecology that includes temporality focuses scholarship on the degree of *plasticity* (of the potential for systematic change) (Lerner, 1984) that may exist throughout life. In addition, there is a concern with the characteristics of the person and his or her context that may foster continuity or discontinuity in development.

The life-course and human ecological perspectives on human development also consider developmental processes to be relational in character. The life-course perspective significantly extends the analysis of the developmental process beyond the individual by considering the contributions of institutional structure, function, and change to the person-context relation and the experiences of individuals and groups of individuals (cohorts) developing within specific historical periods. For example, people who were children during the economically difficult period of the Great Depression developed differently across their lives than did people who grew up in more economically favorable historical periods (Elder, 1974).

The human ecological perspective provides developmentalists with an understanding of the dynamics of person-context relations in a specific setting (e.g., the family or household) in which a person develops (a microsystem); the interconnected set of specific systems (e.g., the household, the school, and the neighborhood) in which the person develops (the mesosystem); the settings (the exosystem) in which the person does not interact (e.g., the workplace of a young child's parent) but which developments occur (e.g., the parent's experience of job-related stress) that influence behavior in the micro- or mesosystem; and the broad social institutional context (the macrosystem) that, by virtue of its cultural and public policy components, textures social commerce and influences all other systems embedded within it. For instance, as a result of public policies related to the eligibility of adults to receive public assistance for their children (e.g., Aid to Families with Dependent Children, AFDC) and cultural attitudes about people who receive welfare, specific communities may place time limits on an adult's eligibility for welfare and require the person to enter either job training or an educational program. The challenges and stressors may influence the emotional character of interactions with the welfare recipient's child, who may carry the "residue" of his or her interaction with the parent into interactions with peers in the classroom.

This example of the applicability of the human ecology perspective can be extended by reference to the life-course perspective. Here we might consider the effects on cohorts of poor children growing up in a context in which major changes in their families' lives occur as a consequence of a historically significant change in public policy regarding welfare. In turn, the life-span perspective would

extend this example still further by asking whether and how the course of personal development was altered as a consequence of the specific changes that occurred in individual-context relations as a consequence of the historically nonnormative change in public policy.

Clearly, then, there are important interconnections between the life-span, life-course, and human ecology perspectives. Each viewpoint focuses on the linkages between changes in a person over the course of his or her life and the changing structure and function of his or her family, peer group, school, workplace, and community setting, which, in turn, are embedded within policy, cultural, and historical contexts. Each perspective is concerned with the way in which the pattern or system of these relations shapes human development over the course of life. Simply, each perspective is concerned with the developmental system and, specifically, with development-in-relation-to-context. By providing a theoretical frame for these viewpoints, developmental contextualism offers a means of integrating and further understanding the dynamic (that is, bidirectional or reciprocal) relations between people and the settings within which they live their lives.

Accordingly, developmental contextualism takes an integrative approach to the multiple levels of organization that are presumed to make up the nature of human life, that is, *"fused"* (Tobach & Greenberg, 1984) and *changing relations* among biological, psychological, and social and physical contextual levels constitute the process of developmental change. Rather than approach variables from these levels in either a reductionistic or parallel-processing way, the developmental contextual view rests on the idea that variables from these levels of analysis are dynamically interactive—they are reciprocally influential over the course of human ontogeny.

Thus, within developmental contextualism, levels are conceived of as integrated organizations. If the course of human development is the product of the processes involved in the "fusions," or "dynamic interactions," (Lerner, 1978, 1979, 1984) among integrated levels, then the processes of development are more plastic than was previously believed (cf. Brim & Kagan, 1980). In this perspective, the context for development is seen not merely as a simple stimulus environment, but as an "ecological environment . . . conceived topologically as a nested arrangement of concentric structures, each contained within the next" (Bronfenbrenner, 1979, p. 22) and including variables from biological, psychological, physical, and sociocultural levels, all changing interdependently throughout history (Riegel, 1975, 1976a, 1976b).

Given this conception, it is clear why the central idea in developmental contextualism is that changing, reciprocal relations (or dynamic interactions) between individuals and the multiple contexts within which they live are the essential process of human development (Lerner, 1986; Lerner & Kauffman, 1985). Moreover, because time—history—cuts through all the levels of this developmental system, all portions of the system of person-context relations envisioned in developmental contextualism change over time. Diversity (variation) is created as change across time (across history) introduces variation into all the levels of organization involved in the human development system. Accordingly, in developmental contextualism, diversity is a topic of central importance, particularly changes in a person over time (intraindividual change) and differences among people's patterns of intraindividual change.

THE SUBSTANTIVE IMPORTANCE OF A FOCUS ON DIVERSITY

Theoretical ideas represented in developmental contextualism provide clear reasons why diversity should be of substantive concern to scholars who are interested in families, children, and society. In addition, and legitimated, in part, by these theoretical ideas, there are several empirical reasons why diversity should be a key focus of concern in the study of human development (Lerner, 1991, 1992, 1998).

As McLoyd (1994) noted, by 1990, about 25% of all Americans had African, Asian, Hispanic, or Native American ancestry. Moreover, the proportion of Americans from other than European backgrounds will continue to grow, because more than 80% of legal immigrants to the United States con-

tinue to be from non-European backgrounds (Barringer, 1991). McLoyd (1994) notes that higher fertility rates among minority groups continue to contribute to the increasing proportion of the American population that is comprised of groups that are now considered minorities. However, by the year 2000, the Latino population will have increased by about 21%; the Asian American population, by about 22%; and the African American population, by about 12%; but the European American population, only by about 2% (Barringer, 1991; McLoyd, 1994; Wetzel, 1987). The Native American and Alaskan Native populations are growing at an estimated rate of more than 2% per year; between 1980 and 1990, the Native American population grew 54% (Office of Special Education, 1995).

Accordingly, by the year 2000, approximately 33% of all children in the United States will be from "minority" groups, and, in some states (e.g., California, Texas, and New Mexico), the majority of youth are from minority groups (Dryfoos, 1990; Henry, 1990; McLoyd, 1994). Given these demographic trends, it is not appropriate—and may be disastrous for the future health and welfare of the United States—for scientific research or outreach to ignore the diversity of children in this country.

Given the insensitivity of research in child development to the general environment, or context, within which children develop (Bronfenbrenner, 1977, 1979; Hagen, Paul, Gibb, & Wolters, 1990), it is not surprising that little attention has been paid to the variation *within* any given setting. After all, if the context in general has not been of particular concern to child development researchers, then it is understandable that even less interest has been shown in the potential importance of variation among or within contexts for development (Elder, Modell, & Parke, 1993).

One example is the lack of attention to important contextual diversity in poor or low-income communities (Kretzmann & McKnight, 1993; McKnight & Kretzmann, 1993). Often these communities are characterized exclusively by needs and deficits. Although such communities often have considerable needs, a sole focus on such problems will result in a significant underestimation of the communities' capacity to marshal the human, and even fiscal, resources necessary to design and implement programs that promote positive features of human development. McKnight and Kretzmann (1993) reported that poor neighborhoods have numerous assets, such as cultural and religious organizations, public schools, and citizen associations.

In sum, because of the diversity among people and their settings, one cannot assume that general rules of development exist for, or apply in the same way to, all children and families. Moreover, one cannot assume, even if only small portions of the total variance in human behavior and development reflect variance that is unique to an individual or group, that this nonshared variance is not the most salient information we have for understanding or enhancing the quality of the lives of a person or a group. Accordingly, we advocate a new research agenda, which would focus on diversity and context and attend to individual development, contextual changes, and the mutual influences between the two. Simply, the study of diversity and context should be moved to the fore of scholarly concern. Such scholarship would have important implications for policies and programs that are pertinent to the lives of individuals and families.

DIVERSITY, POLICIES, AND PROGRAMS

If the diversity- and context-sensitive developmental scholarship promoted by developmental contextualism is to have a positive impact on policies and the programs derived from them, then such interventions must be designed to fit the diverse characteristics of the people served by, or involved in, these actions. Such diversity may pertain to variation in family structure and function and/or developmental differences in the members of the generations of a family.

As Table 19.1 and our discussion of the scholarship of Hernandez (1993) illustrates, there is great historical and contemporary diversity in families and in the characteristics of the people in them. People differ in age, generational group, race (membership in a culturally defined group that is purported to share biological-reproductive characteristics), ethnicity (membership in a culturally defined group that is purported to share historical

and cultural characteristics, including, in some cases, geographic areas of group origin), physical attributes (e.g., gender and the possession of physical disabilities); health status (e.g., the presence of an acute or chronic disease), sexual orientations (heterosexual, gay, lesbian, or bisexual), religions, and numerous psychological characteristics (e.g., political affiliations, attitudes and values, and gender-role and lifestyle preferences).

The families within which such diverse people live are even more varied, because two or more people whose individual diversity *across* domains of characteristics, such as those just noted, constitute a family unit. For instance, an intact family with children comprised of a Latino and an Asian American adult and a biological child with a chronic illness differs from a single-parent family headed by a European American mother with two healthy children or a family consisting of a gay or lesbian couple and their biological or adopted children. Similarly, a family with a Latino parent of Puerto Rican ethnic background is different from one with a parent of Mexican or Chilean ethnicity. Each dimension of diversity complicates issues for policy development.

Listing the literally thousands, if not millions, of instances of family diversity that assuredly exist in our nation is certainly beyond the scope (and point) of this chapter. Indeed, the presence of such vast differences in the constitution of the family underscores the importance of the need to develop policies that recognize and address family diversity. At times, such policy innovations can involve nothing more than the relatively simple decision to allow people who identify themselves on governmental forms (e.g., in the census) to specify in their own terms the racial and/or ethnic group with which they associate themselves.

At other times, however, the issues for policy development are much more complex—a point that should be obvious, given the different domains of diversity we have just discussed. For instance, can we appropriately frame a "family" policy in the United States without recognizing that families with children differ from those without them? And does not this issue get more complicated when we consider that a family with young children is different from one with adolescent or grown children, and still different from one in which the parents are adult children with the responsibility of caring for their own aged parents? Should accommodations in family policy be made to recognize the great frequency in the United States of family dissolution and reconstitution? Should policies be developed that treat single-parent families formed when teenage girls become unmarried mothers as different from single-parent families that are formed when middle-aged women with growing children are divorced or widowed? Should policies be developed that provide the same loan and health benefits to families with gay and lesbian partners as to families with heterosexual partners? And, in recognition of the trends in maternal employment, and thus of changing gender roles in America, should policies be developed to support specifically what is now the majority of women who seek to have families *and* careers outside their homes?

It is not possible to address all these questions and the numerous other similar ones we might pose within the confines of one chapter or even one book. What we can do, however, is provide an example of how the theoretical frame we bring to the study of such questions can help address the complexities of aligning policy with the diversity of individuals in U.S. families. Thus, to enhance the development of children in this country, we apply developmental contextual thinking to policy by arguing for a national policy on youth (Lerner, 1995).

TOWARD THE DEVELOPMENT OF A NATIONAL YOUTH POLICY

Children constitute 100% of the future human and social capital on which our nation must depend. The healthy rearing of children has often been identified as the essential function of the family (Lerner & Spanier, 1980). Thus, although family policy is not isomorphic with child or youth policy (e.g., family policies may involve aged adults living in retirement and without children or grandchildren), it is arguably the case that there are no policy issues of greater concern to U.S. families than those that pertain to the health and welfare of their children.

Nevertheless, today, all too many Americans do not see the need for a comprehensive and integrated national policy applicable to all our nation's children. To the contrary, many Americans consider youth problems to be associated with other people's children. Their stereotyped image of the "at-risk" or poor child is of a minority youth living in the inner city. Yet, the probability that an American child or adolescent will be poor—and thus experience the several "rotten outcomes" (Schorr, 1988) of poverty—does not differ, whether that youth lives in an urban or rural setting (Huston, 1991). Moreover, the high incidence of risk behaviors among our nation's youth (Dryfoos, 1990; 1994) extends the problems of U.S. children and adolescents far beyond the bounds associated with the number of poor or minority children.

These reasons alone should be sufficient for developing a national youth policy that is pertinent to all U.S. children and adolescents. However, there are additional reasons. Just as we may be concerned with developing better policies for sustaining or enhancing American agricultural, industrial, manufacturing, and business interests, it would seem clear that we must not lose sight of the need to sustain the communities—and the people—that are involved in the production, distribution, and consumption of the products of our economy.

Still, we often neglect the fact that problems of rural and urban youth—problems that are similarly structured, similarly debilitating, and similarly destructive of U.S. human capital—significantly diminish our nation's present and future ability to sustain and enhance its economic productivity. Clearly, then, from the standpoints both of the problems of children and adolescents and of enlightened self-interest in our industrial, agricultural, business, and consumer communities, policies need to be directed toward enhancing the development of and preventing the loss of human capital associated with the breadth and depth of the problems confronting our children and youth.

Problems Resulting From the Absence of a National Youth Policy

Despite the historically unprecedented growth in the magnitude of the problems facing children and youth in the United States (Dryfoos, 1990; Hamburg, 1992; Lerner, 1995) and of the contextual conditions that exacerbate these problems (e.g., changes in family structure and function and in child and adolescent poverty rates), few major policy initiatives have been taken to address these increasingly dire circumstances. As a result, the United States has no national youth policy per se (Hahn, 1994). Rather, policies and the programs associated with them tend to focus only on the family (e.g., AFDC) and not on youth per se (Huston, 1991). Hence, although these policies may influence the financial status of the family, they may not readily affect, and certainly fail to emphasize, the development of children and adolescents, that is, the enhancement of their capacities and potential. For instance, a welfare reform policy or program that provides a job for an unemployed single mother, but results in the placement of her child in an inadequate day care environment for an extended period may enhance the financial resources of the family—but at the cost of placing the child in an unstimulating and, possibly, detrimental environment.

Accordingly, if we are to reduce substantially the current waste of human life and potential caused by the problems confronting contemporary American youth, new policy options must be pursued— ones that focus on children and adolescents and that emphasize the positive development of youth, not only the amelioration, remediation, and/or deterrence of problems. That is, arguing that the prevention (of problems) is not the same as the promotion (of healthy development), Pittman and Zeldin (1994, p. 53) stated:

> The reduction of problem behaviors among young people is a necessary policy goal. But it is not enough. We must be equally committed to articulating and nurturing those attributes that we wish adolescents to develop and demonstrate.

What is required for the promotion of positive development is the application of "assets," that is, the strengths of a person (e.g., a commitment to learning, a healthy sense of identity), a family (e.g., caring attitudes toward children, child-rearing styles that both empower youth and set boundaries

and provide expectations for positive growth), and a community (e.g., social support, programs that provide access to the resources for education, safety, and mentorship available in a community) (Benson, 1997). Consistent with Benson's perspective, Pittman and Zeldin (1994) presented several policy recommendations that provide a frame for us to discuss the development of a national youth policy that would support the positive development of children and adolescents.

Potential Dimensions of a National Youth Policy

Benson (1997) and Pittman and Zeldin (1994) emphasized that such a policy must focus on the development of children and adolescents, not on the deterrence of problems. As Benson noted, assets must be marshaled to promote the competencies and potential of youth, and programs designed to promote these positive attributes need to be developed and evaluated. Accordingly, policy must go beyond two necessary but not sufficient goals: (1) "meeting basic human needs [through ensuring] economic security, food, shelter, good and useful work, and safety" (Benson, p. xiii) for youth and the members of their families and (2) targeting and reducing or even eliminating "the risks and deficits that diminish or thwart the healthy development of children and adolescents. Guns, unsafe streets, predatory adults, abuse, family violence, exclusion, alcohol and other drugs, racism, and sexism are among the threats" (Benson, pp. xiii–xiv). Policy must add the third component that is crucial for building a strong young person supported by positive relationships with his or her family and community—assets.

This is a vision of a new direction in U.S. public policy, one that has been brought to the fore by such recent events as the April 1997 Presidents' Summit in Philadelphia. (America's Promise, 1997) At the summit, all the living presidents forwarded a vision for the development of policy that would provide every child in the United States with nurturance from at least one adult who was committed unconditionally to the child's welfare and positive development; a healthy life start for all children; a safe environment within which to live; the opportunity to have an education that will result in the attainment of marketable skills; and the inculcation of values for and opportunities to "give back" to others, that is, to volunteer to serve the community.

To deliver these assets, it is important to capitalize on the important role played by youth-serving organizations in enhancing the life chances of children and adolescents (cf. Carnegie Corporation, 1992; Dryfoos, 1990; National Research Council, 1993; Schorr, 1988). That is, policies must promote the financial support, and broad acceptance, of community-based youth organizations (Pittman & Zeldin, 1994) through the support of the socialization experiences and youth services provided by these organizations. However, to promote the acceptance of community programs, the "policy goal of facilitating youth development must be translated and incorporated into the public institutions of education, employment and training, juvenile justice, and health services" (Pittman & Zeldin, 1994, p. 53).

The translation involved in this policy step is predicated on the view, emphasized by Dryfoos (1990), Schorr (1988), and Hamburg (1992), that the promotion of youth development is not the exclusive province of any single organization or agency. Therefore, an integrated, communitywide effort is necessary to foster the positive development of youth (Dryfoos, 1990; Hamburg, 1992; Schorr, 1988) and to evaluate the success of such efforts (Weiss & Greene, 1992). Hamburg (1992) made a similar point, suggesting three policy initiatives that, together, would enhance the capacity of communities to (1) provide comprehensive and integrated services that (2) promote positive youth development through (3) the provision of effective programs delivered by well-trained staff. Thus, Hamburg (p. 166) noted that he would

> [f]irst, use federal and state mechanisms to provide funding to local communities in ways that encourage the provision of coherent, comprehensive services. State and federal funding should provide incentives to encourage collaboration and should be adaptable to local circumstances. Second, provide training programs to equip professional staff and managers with the necessary skills. Such programs would include training for collaboration among professionals in

health, mental health, education, and social services, and would instill a respectful, sensitive attitude toward working with clients, patients, parents, and students from different backgrounds. Third, use widespread evaluation to determine what intervention is useful for whom, how funds are being spent, and whether the services are altogether useful.

Thus, policy must move from a focus on just building effective programs to building cohesive and effective communities (National Research Council, 1993; Pittman & Zeldin, 1994). Indeed, a report by the National Research Council (1993, p. 239) noted that building supportive communities for youth faced with the destruction of their life chances

> will require a major commitment from federal and state governments and the private sector, including support for housing, transportation, economic development, and the social services required by poor and low income residents.

Finally, Pittman and Zeldin (1994) emphasized that for youth development programs to attain sustained successes—across the span of individual lives and multiple generations—issues of individual and economic diversity must be clearly and directly confronted. Specifically, an awareness of issues pertinent to poverty and racism must be a continuing, core focus of social policy. We must continue to be vigilant about the pernicious sequelae of poverty among children and adolescents, the vast overrepresentation of minority youth among the ranks of our nation's poor, and the greater probability that minority youth will be involved in the several problem behaviors besetting their generation.

In sum, then, the policy recommendations forwarded by Pittman and Zeldin (1994), Benson (1997), Hamburg (1992), the National Research Council (1993), and the 1997 Presidents' Summit (America's Promise, 1997) stress the importance of asset-based, comprehensive, and integrative actions, involving both proximal community participation and the contributions of broader segments of the public and private sectors; community-based evaluations; diversity; and promoting positive development across the life span. These ideas are consistent with those brought to the fore by a developmental contextual perspective.

IMPLICATIONS OF DEVELOPMENTAL CONTEXTUALISM FOR THE DESIGN, DELIVERY, AND EVALUATION OF POLICIES FOR FAMILIES AND YOUTH

From the perspective of developmental contextualism, policies—and the programs that do (or should) derive from them—synthesize basic and applied research. That is, policies and programs represent the means through which ecologically valid interventions may be enacted; the evaluation of these interventions provides information, then, both about the adequacy of these "applied" endeavors *and* about "basic" theoretical issues of human development—about the bases for enhancing the life courses of individuals, families, and communities (Lerner et al., 1994; Lerner & Miller, 1993).

Thus, policies and the evaluation of their influences allow scholars to contribute to the understanding of, and to serve the diverse children, adolescents, and families of our nation. However, developmental contextualism provides more than a structure for the integration of basic and applied scholarship and a frame for viewing policy engagement and programming as the "methods" for this integration (Fisher & Lerner, 1994). It also promotes at least six substantive directions for the development of policies for children and families in the United States.

The first direction for policy is associated with the fact that developmental contextualism promotes an emphasis on the developmental system (Ford & Lerner, 1992). Within this system, development involves changes in *relations* between the growing person and his or her context (Lerner, 1991). Accordingly, to enhance the positive development of youth and families, we must focus on this system, not on either the individual (cf. Dryfoos, 1990; Schorr, 1988) or the context per se. Therefore, policies should be aimed at building programs that enhance *relationships* for youths and families across the breadth of the system, that is, among peers, schools, and institutions of the proximal community and the more distal society.

Second, we must recognize that the system within which youth, families, and the programs aimed at them are embedded is also the system that contains the institutions that do (or could) provide resources for the promotion of positive youth and family development. Accordingly, we should use the multiple connections within the developmental system to create innovative approaches to generating resources to design, deliver, evaluate, and sustain effective family- and youth-serving programs.

Little (1993) presented an example of the potential of such an innovation, noting that programs that may be viable are all too often not implemented or sustained, primarily because the procedure used to obtain funding for the programs is not effective. That is, whereas a person with ideas starts a program, often at the grassroots level, he or she typically has to go to a person with institutional power (e.g., a supervisor or a director of an organization) to find a potential advocate for the program. If this person with institutional power is persuaded to be an advocate for the program, he or she would be in a position to approach yet another person, someone with authority over resources (e.g., a program officer of a community foundation), to obtain resources for the program. This procedure is, at best, only intermittently successful, and Little stated, represents a weak link in the system through which program funding occurs. Accordingly, Little recommended that new linkages be formed in the system, ones between people of influence (those with control over resources) and people of ideas.

For instance, the International Youth Foundation promotes the direct involvement of program officers from indigenous, grant-making, community foundations with the communities and programs that they fund. This "systems change" represents an important paradigm shift in the nature of the process involved in funding community-based youth programs.

Along with new linkages, there is also a need for a "meeting of the minds" between community-based programs and the institutions that fund their work. Sparks (1996) discussed the theoretical and ideological mismatch that can occur between these two groups. The staff of community-based programs have an understanding of the problem that is derived from daily interactions with the children and families they serve. They develop perspectives that tend to be culture specific and reflective of lived experiences, which often differ with the definition of problems that result from academic research. Funders are more likely to endorse the research-based perspectives because of the position of the academy in the power hierarchy and to support proposals for funding that reflect this orientation.

Third, a system that is open to change for the better is also open to change for the worse. Accordingly, to produce sustained enhancement of the lives of youth and the functioning of families, we need policies that promote long-term interventions. A one-shot intervention will not "inoculate" a youth and his or her family for life against the potentially risk-actualizing perturbations of the developmental system within which they live. Thus, we need to build (and fund) long-term—that is, life span-oriented—"convoys" of social support (Kahn & Antonucci, 1980) to reinforce the positive developments that may accrue from effective youth and family programs.

The life-span nature of the developmental system within which youth and families are embedded is associated with the fourth direction for the development of policy. Transitions occur across the life span (Lerner & Spanier, 1980) and are often qualitative in nature. For example, the transitions involved in the period between childhood and early adolescence involve qualitative alterations in thinking abilities (the emergence of "formal operational" ability; Piaget, 1950, 1972); emotions and personality (e.g., involving the psychosocial crisis of identity versus role confusions; Erikson, 1959); social relationships (e.g., a shift in the primary social group—from parents to peers; Guerney & Arthur, 1984); and physiology (the emergence of a new sexual drive and new hormones; Freud, 1969; Katchadourian, 1977).

Given such qualitative changes, a program that provides a "goodness of fit" (Lerner & Lerner, 1989; Thomas & Chess, 1977) with the characteristics of the person during childhood may not continue to fit during adolescence. Similarly, a family that is at the beginning stage of the family life cycle differs qualitatively from one with adolescent children or one in which the children have left the "nest" and established families of their own (Duvall, 1971). Accordingly, to be sure that the features of programs remain valid across the life span of individuals and families, we must monitor and calibrate our programs to attend to developmental changes and contextual transitions, such as the shift from elementary school to middle or junior high school (see Simmons & Blyth, 1987) or from a family with children to an empty nest situation (see Duvall, 1971).

The fifth policy direction, which is closely related to the idea of transitions throughout life, pertains to the issues of individual or interfamilial differences (diversity) and transformations of individuals, families, and their broader contexts. Developmental contextualism stresses that diversity—of individuals, families, contexts (including cultural ones), and individual-context relations—is the "rule" of human behavior and development. "One size," that is, one type of intervention, does not "fit all." As we have emphasized repeatedly in this chapter, policies and programs that are fit and effective for a family of one social, racial, ethnic, community, or cultural group may be irrelevant, poorly suited, or even damaging to families with other characteristics of diversity. As such, policies and programs must be sensitive to, and organized to provide a goodness of fit with, the instances of human diversity that are relevant to the individual, family, or community to which they are directed.

However, it will not be sufficient just to have policies that promote the development of diversity-sensitive programs. Such policies must also promote a continuing awareness that individual differences *increase* as people and families develop across the courses of their life cycles (Baltes, 1987; Duvall, 1971; Lerner & Spanier, 1978; Schaie, 1979). Therefore, we must enable programs to be adjusted to fit the transformations in individuals and families that emerge throughout their lives.

For instance, as each person develops across life, he or she becomes increasingly different from other people as a consequence of his or her individual history of experiences, roles, and relationships (Lerner, 1988; Lerner & Tubman, 1989). Thus, the initial characteristics of individuality are continually transformed over the course of life into different instances of individuality. As a result, we must develop programs that are attentive to both initial and emergent characteristics of individuality—of the person; the family; and, especially, person-family relations.

The stress on individuality in developmental contextualism leads to the final direction for policy. Developmental contextualism conceives of evaluation as providing information about the efficacy of policies and programs and about how the course of human development can be enhanced through policies and programs. Indeed, because the approach to evaluation that is often associated with developmental contextualism involves the active participation of the individuals served by the program (Lerner, 1995; Lerner, Ostrom, & Freel, 1995; Ostrom, Lerner, & Freel, 1995; Weiss & Greene, 1992), evaluation is also a means of empowering program participants and enhancing their capacities to engage in actions that promote their own and their families' positive development. In this way, evaluation serves many of the same empowerment ends as does action research (Whyte, 1991).

Accordingly, policies should promote the use of participatory-normative evaluation procedures (Weiss & Greene, 1992). Such evaluations will increase understanding of the lives that are developing within the context of the policies and programs being implemented and, simultaneously, will inculcate greater capacities of, and thus further empower, the youth, families, and communities involved in the programs that are being evaluated.

The important role that participatory evaluation procedures can play within a developmental contextual approach to youth and family policy raises the issue of the potential contributions of academe and academicians to addressing the problems besetting America's children, families, and communities. If our nation's universities are to be part of effective community coalitions that enact and foster the continued development of integrative and comprehensive national youth and family policies, social policy innovations must be coupled with alterations in academic policies and practices. Without such changes in academe, universities will not be able to be integral participants in addressing the needs of our country's children and families. It is important, then, to discuss some of the changes in the approach to scholarship that may need to be introduced for such participation to occur.

CONCLUSION: TOWARD A REVISED SCHOLARLY AGENDA

To be complete, the integrative research promoted by a developmental contextual view of human development must be synthesized with two other foci. Research in human development that is concerned with one or even a few instances of individual, family, and broader contextual diversity cannot be assumed to be useful for understanding the life course of all people and families. Similarly, policies and programs that are derived from such research or are associated with it in the context of a researcher's tests of ideas pertinent to human plasticity cannot be assumed to be applicable to, or equally appropriate and useful for, all families or all individuals. Accordingly, the development of developmental and individual differences-oriented policy and the design and delivery of programs (interventions) would need to be integrated fully with the new research base for which we are calling (Lerner & Miller, 1993; Lerner et al., 1994).

As is emphasized in developmental contextualism, the variation in settings within which people live means that studying development in a standard (e.g., a "controlled") environment does not provide information pertinent to the actual (ecologically valid) developing relations between individually distinct people and their specific contexts (e.g., their particular families, schools, or communities). This point underscores the need to conduct research in real-world settings and highlights the ideas that (1) policies and programs constitute natural experiments and (2) the evaluation of such activities becomes a central focus in the developmental contextual scholarly agenda we have described.

In this view, then, policy and program endeavors do *not* constitute secondary work or derivative applications, conducted after research evidence has been compiled. To the contrary, the development and implementation of policy and the design and delivery of programs become integral components of this vision for research; the evaluation component of such policy and intervention work provides critical feedback on the adequacy of the conceptual frame from which this research agenda should derive. This conception of the integration of multidisciplinary research endeavors with policies, programs, and evaluations is illustrated in Figure 19.1.

A vision of the integration of developmental research and policies and programs was articulated more than two decades ago by Bronfenbrenner (1974). Bronfenbrenner argued that engagement with social policy not only enhances developmental research, but, as is consistent with the developmental contextual perspective, augments understanding of key theoretical issues pertinent to the nature of person-context relations. He argued that

> [i] discussions of the relation between science and social policy, the first axiom, at least among social scientists, is that social policy should be based on science. The proposition not only has logic on its side, but what is more important, it recognizes our proper and primary importance in the scheme of things. The policymakers should look to us, not only for truth, but for wisdom as well. In short, social policy needs science.
>
> My thesis in this paper is the converse proposition, that, particularly in our field, science needs social policy—needs it not to guide our organizational activities, but to provide us with two elements essential for any scientific endeavor—vitality and validity (p. 1). . . . I contend that the pursuit of [social policy] questions is essential for the further development of knowledge and theory on the process of human development (p. 2).

To be successful, Bronfenbrenner's vision about the critical linkage between policy engagement and the enhancement of the theory, method, and substance of developmental science requires scholars to continue to educate themselves about the best means available to promote enhanced life chances among *all* American youth and families, but especially among those whose potentials for positive contributions to our nation are most in danger of being wasted (Lerner, 1993a; 1993b). The collaborative expertise of the research and program-deliv-

FIGURE 19.1

A Developmental Contextual Model of the Integration of Multilevel, Multidisciplinary Research, Aimed at Diversity and Context, With Policies, Programs, and Evaluations

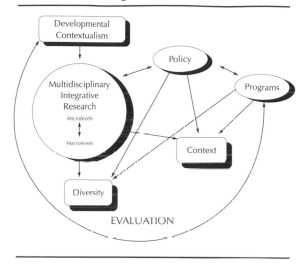

ery communities can provide much of this information, especially if it is obtained in partnership with strong, empowered communities. Policies that promote such coalitions will be an integral component of a national youth and family development policy aimed at creating caring communities with the capacity to nurture the healthy development of children and families.

Given the enormous—indeed historically unprecedented—challenges that American families face, especially as they strive to raise healthy and successful children who will be capable of leading our nation productively, responsibly, and morally in the 21st century (Benson, 1997; Damon, 1997; Lerner, 1995), there is no time to lose in the development of such policies. Our society as we know it—and, even more, as we believe it can be—may be severely compromised unless we act now. All the strengths and assets of our universities, our institutions, and our people must be marshaled for this effort.

REFERENCES

Ahlburg, D. A., & De Vita, C. J. (1992). New realities of the American family. *Population Bulletin, 47,* (2), 1–44.

Allison, K. W. (1993). Adolescents living in "non-family" and alternative settings. In R. M. Lerner (Ed.), *Early adolescence: Perspectives on research, policy, and intervention* (pp. 37–50). Hillsdale, NJ: Lawrence Erlbaum.

America's Promise (1997, April). Alliance for Youth Presidential Summit. Philadelphia, PA.

Baltes, P. B. (1987). Theoretical propositions of life-span developmental psychology: On the dynamics between growth and decline. *Developmental Psychology, 23,* 611–626.

Barringer, F. (1991, March 11). Census shows profound change in racial makeup of the nation. *New York Times,* pp. 1, A12.

Benson, P. (1997). *All kids are our kids: What communities must do to raise caring and responsible children and adolescents.* San Francisco: Jossey-Bass.

Brim, O. G., Jr., & Kagan, J. (Ed.). (1980). *Constancy and change in human development.* Cambridge, MA: Harvard University Press.

Bronfenbrenner, U. (1974). Developmental research, public policy, and the ecology of childhood. *Child Development, 45,* 1–5.

Bronfenbrenner, U. (1977). Toward an experimental ecology of human development. *American Psychologist, 32,* 513–531.

Bronfenbrenner, U. (1979). *The ecology of human development.* Cambridge, MA: Harvard University Press.

Bumpass, L., & Sweet, J. (1989). National estimates of cohabitation, *Demography, 26,* 615–625.

Bumpass, L., & Raley, R., & Sweet, J. (1994, January 20–21). *The changing character of stepfamilies: Implications of cohabitation and nonmarital childbearing* (NSFH Working Paper No. 63). Paper presented at the RAND Conference, Santa Monica, CA.

Carnegie Corporation of New York. (1992). *A matter of time: Risk and opportunity in the nonschool hours.* (Available from Carnegie Council on Adolescent Development, P.O. Box 753, Waldorf, MD 20604).

Carnegie Corporation of New York. (1994, April). *Starting points: Meeting the needs of our youngest children* (Available from Carnegie Corporation of New York, P.O. Box 753, Waldorf, MD 20604).

Center for the Study of Social Policy. (1992). *1992 KIDS COUNT data book: State profiles of child well-being* (Available from the Center for the Study of Social Policy, Suite 503, 1250 Eye Street, NW, Washington, DC 20005).

Center for the Study of Social Policy. (1993). *1993 KIDS COUNT data book: State profiles of child well-being* (Available from the Center for the Study of Social Policy, Suite 503, 1250 Eye Street, NW, Washington DC 20005).

Child Welfare Stat Book 1993. Washington, DC: Child Welfare League of America.

Children's Defense Fund. (1992). *Child poverty up nationally and in 33 states.* Washington, DC: Author.

Damon, W. (1997). *The youth charter: How communities can work together to raise standards for all our children.* New York: The Free Press.

Dryfoos, J. G. (1990). *Adolescents at risk: Prevalence and prevention.* New York: Oxford University Press.

Dryfoos, J. G. (1994). *Full service schools: A revolution in health and social services of children, youth and families.* San Fransico: Jossey-Bass.

Duncan, G. J. (1991). The economic environment of childhood. In A. C. Huston (Ed.), *Children in poverty: Child development and public policy* (pp. 23–50). Cambridge, England: Cambridge University Press.

Duvall, E. M. (1971). *Family development* (4th ed.). Philadelphia: J. P. Lippincott.

Elder, G. H., Jr. (1974). *Children of the Great Depression: Social change in life experiences.* Chicago: University of Chicago Press.

Elder, G. H., Jr., Modell, J., & Parke, R. D. (Eds.). (1993). *Children in time and place: Developmental and historical insights.* New York: Cambridge University Press.

Erikson, E. H. (1959). Identity and the life-cycle. *Psychological Issues, 1,* 18–164.

Featherman, D. L., Spenner, K. I., & Tsunematsu, N. (1988). Class and the socialization of children: Constancy, change, or irrelevance? In R. M. Lerner, E. M. Hetherington, & M. Perlmutter (Eds.), *Child development in life-span perspective* (pp. 67–90). Hillsdale, NJ: Lawrence Erlbaum.

Fisher, C. B., & Lerner, R. M. (Eds.). (1994). *Applied developmental psychology.* New York: McGraw-Hill.

Ford, D. L., & Lerner, R. M. (1992). *Developmental systems theory: An integrative approach.* Newbury Park, CA: Sage.

Freud, A. (1969). Adolescence as a developmental disturbance. In G. Caplan & S. Lebovier (Eds.), *Adolescence* (pp. 5–10). New York: Basic Books.

Guerney, L., & Arthur, J. (1984). Adolescent social relationships. In R. M. Lerner & N. L. Galambos (Eds.), *Experiencing adolescents: A sourcebook for parents, teachers, and teens.* New York: Garland.

Hagen, J. W., Paul, B., Gibb, S., & Wolters, C. (1990, March). Trends in research as reflected by publications in *Child Development:* 1930–1989. In *Biennial Meeting of the Society for Research on Adolescence.* Atlanta, GA: Society for Research on Adolescence.

Hahn, A. B. (1994). Towards a national youth development policy for young African-American males: The choices policymakers face. In R. B. Mincy (Ed.), *Nurturing young black males: Challenges to agencies, programs, and social policy* (pp. 165–186). Washington, DC: Urban Institute Press

Hamburg, D. A. (1992). *Today's children: Creating a future for a generation in crisis.* New York: Time Books.

Henry, W. (1990, April 9). Beyond the melting pot. *Time,* pp. 28–31.

Hernandez, D. J. (1993). *America's children.* New York: Russell Sage Foundation.

Huston, A. C. (Ed.). (1991). *Children in poverty: Child development and public policy.* Cambridge, England: Cambridge University Press.

Indian Health Service trends in Indian health—1995 tables. (1995). Rockville, MD: Division of Program Statistics, Office of Planning, Evaluation, and Legislation, Public Health Service, Department of Health and Human Services.

Kahn, R. L., & Antonucci, T. C. (1980). Convoys over the life course: Attachment, roles, and social support. In P. B. Baltes & O. G. Brim (Eds.), *Life-span development and behavior, 3* (pp. 253–286). Hillsdale, NJ: Lawrence Erlbaum.

Katchadourian, H. (1977). *The biology of adolescence.* San Francisco: W. H. Freeman.

Klerman, L. V. (1991). The health of poor children: Problems and programs. In A. C. Huston (Ed.), *Children in poverty: Child development and public policy* (pp. 1–22). Cambridge, England: Cambridge University Press.

Kretzmann, J. P., & McKnight, J. L. (1993). *Building communities from the inside out: A path toward finding and mobilizing a community's assets* (Available from Center for Urban Affairs and Policy research, Northwestern University, 2040 Sheridan Road, Evanston, IL 60208).

Lerner, J. V. (1994). *Working women and their families.* Thousand Oaks, CA: Sage.

Lerner, R. M. (1978). Nature, nurture, and dynamic interactionism. *Human Development, 21,* 1–20.

Lerner, R. M. (1979). A dynamic interactional concept of individual and social relationship development. In R. L. Burgess & T. L. Huston (Eds.), *Social exchange in developing relationships* (pp. 271–305). New York: Academic Press.

Lerner, R. M. (1984). *On the nature of human plasticity.* New York: Cambridge University Press.

Lerner, R. M. (1986). *Concepts and theories of human development* (2nd ed.) New York: Random House.

Lerner, R. M. (1988). Personality development: A life-span perspective. In E. M. Hetherington, R. M. Lerner, & M. Perlmutter (Eds.), *Child development in life-span perspective* (pp. 21–46). Hillsdale, NJ: Lawrence Erlbaum.

Lerner, R. M. (1991). Changing organism-context relations as the basic process of development: A developmental contextual perspective. *Developmental Psychology, 27,* 27–32.

Lerner, R. M. (1992). Diversity. *SRCD Newsletter,* pp. 2, 12.

Lerner, R. M. (1993a). Early adolescence: Toward an agenda for the integration of research policy, and intervention. In R. M. Lerner (Ed.), Early adolescence: Perspectives on research, policy, and intervention (pp. 1–13). Hillsdale, NJ: Lawrence Erlbaum.

Lerner, R. M. (1993b). Investment in youth: The role of home economics in enhancing the life chances of America's children. *AHEA Monograph Series, 1,* 5–34.

Lerner, R. M. (1995). *America's youth in crisis: Challenges and options for programs and policies.* Thousand Oaks, CA: Sage.

Lerner, R. M. (1998). Theories of human development: Contemporary perspectives. In W. Damon (Series Ed.) & R. M. Lerner (Vol. Ed.), *Handbook of Child Psychology: Vol. 1. Theoretical models of human development* (5th ed., pp. 1–24). New York: John Wiley.

Lerner, R. M., Castellino, D. R., Terry, P. A., Villarruel, F. A., & McKinney, M. H. (1995). A developmental contextual perspective on parenting. In M. H. Bornstein (Ed.), *Handbook of parenting: Vol. 2. Biology and ecology of parenting* (pp. 285–309). Hillsdale, NJ: Lawrence Erlbaum.

Lerner, R. M., & Kauffman, M. B. (1985). The concept of development in contextualism. *Developmental Review, 5,* 309–333.

Lerner, R. M., & Lerner, J. V. (1989). Organismic and social contextual bases of development: The sample case of early adolescence. In W. Damon (Ed.), *Child development today and tomorrow* (pp. 69–85). San Francisco: Jossey-Bass.

Lerner, R. M., & Miller, J. R. (1993). Integrating human development research and intervention for America's children: The Michigan State University model. *Journal of Applied Developmental Psychology, 14,* 347–364.

Lerner, R. M., Miller, J. R., Knott, J. H., Corey, K. E., Bynum, T. S., Hoopfer, L. C., McKinney, M. H., Abrams, L. A., Hula, R. C., & Terry, P. A. (1994). Integrating scholarship and outreach in human development research, policy, and service: A developmental contextual perspective. In D. L. Featherman, R. M. Lerner, & M. Perlmutter (Eds.), *Life-span development and behavior, 12* (pp. 249–273). Hillsdale, NJ: Lawrence Erlbaum.

Lerner, R. M., Ostrom, C. W., & Freel, M. A. (1995). Promoting positive youth and community developmen through outreach scholarship: Comments on Zeldin and Peterson. *Journal of Adolescent Research, 10,* 486–502.

Lerner, R. M., & Spanier, G. B. (1980). *Adolescent development: A life-span perspective.* New York: McGraw-Hill.

Lerner, R. M., & Tubman, J. (1989). Conceptual issues in studying continuity and discontinuity in personality development across life. *Journal of Personality, 57,* 343–373.

Little, R. R. (1993, March). *What's working for today's youth: The issues, the programs, and the learnings.* Paper presented at an ICYF Fellows Colloquium, Michigan State University, East Lansing.

McAdoo, H. P. (1995). African-American families: Strengths and realities. In H. I. McCubbin, E. A. Thompson, A. I. Thompson, & J. E. Futrell (Eds.), *Resiliency in ethnic minority families: African-American families* (Vol. 2, pp. 17–30). Madison: University of Wisconsin System, Center for Excellence in Family Studies.

McKnight, J. L., & Kretzmann, J. P. (1993). Mapping community capacity. *Michigan State University Community and Economic Development Program Community News* (pp. 1–4).

McLoyd, V. C. (1990). Minority children: Introduction to the special issue. *Child Development, 61,* 263–266.

McLoyd, V. C. (1994). Research in the service of poor and ethnic/racial minority children: A moral imperative. *Family and Consumer Sciences Research Journal, 23,* 56–66.

McLoyd, V. C., & Wilson, L. (1991). The strain of living poor: Parenting, social support, and child mental health. In A. C. Huston (Ed.), *Children in poverty: Child development and public policy* (pp. 105–135). Cambridge, England: Cambridge University Press.

Moore, K., Morrison, D. R., Zaslow, M., & Glei, D. A. (1994, December 5–6). *Ebbing and flowing, learning and growing: Family economic resources and children's development.* Paper presented at the research briefing of the Board on Children and Families or Child Trends, Washington DC.

National Research Council. (1993). *Losing generations: Adolescents in high-risk settings.* Washington, DC: National Academy Press.

Office of Special Education, Department of Education. (1995). *16th annual report to Congress: Study of special populations of Native American students with disabilities.* Washington, DC: Author.

Ostrom, C. W., Lerner., R. M., & Freel, M. A. (1995). Building the capacity of youth and families through university-community collaborations: The development-in-context evaluation (DICE) model. *Journal of Adolescent Research, 10,* 427–448.

Phillips, D. A., & Bridgman, A. (Eds.). (1995). *New findings on children, families, and economic self-sufficiency: summary of a research briefing.* Washington, DC: National Academy Press.

Piaget, J. (1950). *The psychology of intelligence.* London: Routledge & Kegan Paul.

Piaget, J. (1972). Intellectual evolution from adolescence to adulthood. *Human Development, 15,* 1–12.

Pittman, K. J., & Zeldin, S. (1994). From deterrence to development: Shifting the focus of youth programs for African-American males. In R. B. Mincy (Ed.), *Nurturing young black males: Challenges to agencies, programs, and social policy* (pp. 45–55). Washington, DC: Urban Institute Press.

Reddy, M. (1993). *Statistical records of Native North Americans.* Detroit: Gale Research.

Riegel, K. F. (1975). Toward a dialectical theory of development. *Human Development, 18,* 50–64.

Riegel, K. F. (1976a). The dialectics of human development. *American Psychologist, 31,* 689–700.

Riegel, K. F. (1976b). From traits and equilibrium toward developmental dialectics. In W. J. Arnold & J. K. Cole (Eds.), *Nebraska symposium on motivation* (pp. 348–408). Lincoln: University of Nebraska Press.

Schaie, K. W. (1979). The primary mental abilities in adulthood: An exploration in the development of psychometric intelligence. In P. B. Baltes & O. G. Brim Jr. (Eds.), *Life-span development and behavior, 2* (pp. 67–115). New York: Academic Press.

Schorr, L. B. (1988). *Within our reach: Breaking the cycle of disadvantage.* New York: Doubleday.

Simmons, R. G., & Blyth, D. A. (1987). *Moving into adolescence: The impact of pubertal change and school context.* Hawthorne, NJ: Aldine.

Simons, J. M., Finlay, B., & Yang, A. (1991). *The adolescent and young adult fact book.* Washington, DC: Children's Defense Fund.

Sparks, E. (1996). The challenges facing community health centers in the 1990s: A voice from the inner city. In M. B. Lykes, A. Banuazizi, R. Liem, & M. Morris (Eds.), *Myths about the powerless: Contesting social inequalities* (pp. 237–257). Philadelphia: Temple University Press.

Spencer, M. B. (1990). Development of minority children: An introduction. *Child Development, 61,* 267–269.

Thelen, E., & Smith, L. B. (1998). Dynamic systems theories. In W. Damon (Series Ed.) & R. M. Lerner (Vol. Ed.), *Handbook of Child Psychology: Vol. 1. Theoretical models of human development* (5th ed., pp. 563–634). New York: John Wiley.

Thomas, A., & Chess, S. (1977). *Temperament and development.* New York: Brunner/Mazel.

Tobach, E., & Greenberg, G. (1984). The significance of T. C. Schneirla's contribution to the concept of levels of integration. In G. Greenberg & E. Tobach (Eds.), *Behavioral evolution and integrative levels* (pp. 1–7). Hillsdale, NJ: Lawrence Erlbaum.

U.S. Bureau of the Census. (1994). *Supplemental tables, historical income, historical poverty, and valuing noncash benefits. Washington, DC: U.S. Department of Commerce.*

U.S. Department of Commerce. (1991, August). *Poverty in the United States: 1990: Current Population Reports* (Series P-60, No. 175). Washington, DC: U.S. Government Printing Office.

Wapner, S., & Demick, J. (1998). Developmental analysis: A holistic, developmental, systems-oriented perspective. In W. Damon (Series Ed.) & R. M. Lerner (Ed.), *Handbook of Child Psychology: Vol. 1. Theoretical models of human development:* (5th ed., pp. 761 805). New York: John Wiley.

Weiss, H. B., & Greene, J. C. (1992). An empowerment partnership for family support and education programs and evaluations. *Family Science Review, 5,* 131–148.

Wetzel, J. (1987). *American youth: A statistical snapshot.* New York: William T. Grant Foundation.

Whyte, W. F. (1991). *Participatory action research.* Newbury Park, CA: Sage.

PART VIII
Conclusion

CHAPTER **20**

Family Diversity and Intersecting Categories: Toward a Richer Approach to Multiple Roles

STEPHEN R. MARKS AND LEIGH A. LESLIE

At the beginning of this new millennium, it is timely to consider how slowly things seem to change. Women are still victimized by rape, domestic terror, and "milder" forms of everyday harassment. The U.S. government remains unwilling to ensure every full-time worker a living wage or to proclaim that minimal health care should be a right, not a social-class privilege. On prime-time television, in anticipation of a central sitcom character coming out as a lesbian, the prebroadcast hoopla turned the evening into a national media event.

Meanwhile, the gains of the civil rights movement have been woefully thin, and Martin Luther King Jr.'s dream of people not being judged by the color of their skin has remained unrealized. A few African American newscasters appear on television, and commercials feature a quick mix of skin colors enjoying this or that consumer bounty, but the numbers about race and income tell a different story: For a disproportionate number of African American, Latino, and Native American families, this is not a land of opportunity. In 1995, the average household income of white families was $35,766; of African American families, $22,393;

and of Latino families, $22,860—a handicap for both of the latter cases of more than 30%. Furthermore, although almost 1 out of every 6 white households had incomes of $75,000 or greater, only about 1 of every 17 African American or Latino households reached such levels of affluence (U.S. Bureau of the Census, 1995).

Accepting diversity and addressing systematic inequality do not come easy to us as a nation, but we are slowly learning. It is no longer much of a surprise, as it was back in the 1960s or 1970s, to see a woman driving a forklift, piloting a plane, or doctoring a patient. The problems of rape, domestic terror, and sexual harassment have come squarely out on the table, and there is an increasing national determination to address them. The U.S. government is slowly raising the minimum wage, and cities, such as Baltimore, Boston, Denver, and Portland, Oregon, now require private employers with large city contracts to pay their workers a living wage (Benner & Rosner, 1998). Recognizing the legacy of troubled race relations in this country, President Clinton initiated a national dialogue on race in an effort to generate, at all levels of society, the often-avoided discussions of the significance of race in our lives. And the right of lesbians and gay men to enjoy the same legal protections and conveniences as other categories of people is also more on the public agenda than ever before, notwithstanding the persistence of heterosexist ignorance and intolerance.

FOCUS OF THE CHAPTER

Few topics generate more emotional and political intensity than issues of race, class, gender, age, sexual orientation, and that "illimitable *et cetera*" of other categories that people invent to mark the lines of difference between one person and another (Butler, 1990). Perhaps no topic is more thorny to grasp or more difficult to analyze than is the multiple intersections *among* categories. In this chapter we begin with some personal reflections about the origins of our interest in this topic and proceed to a general orientation to social categories and their intersection. We then survey some of the history of this area of study, starting with a few of the pioneering statements and then moving quickly through some of the more contemporary landmarks of analysis. Next, we explore what we see as some of the more pivotal theoretical issues and challenges facing students of intersecting categories and attempt to locate this kind of analysis within some overall currents of modern social science.

In the second half of the chapter, we attempt to apply to one area—the study of multiple roles and work-family research—an alertness to structural categories and their intersections. In this half, we begin with an illustrative review of this content area, followed by a more elaborated discussion of how a research program may become more attuned to issues of intersection. Though we focus on just one broad area, we model this kind of alertness in a way that will help other social scientists become sensitized to these issues as they design and carry out their work.

Before we proceed to our specific substantive focus, we briefly address two questions that the editors posed formally to us: What do *we* mean by "family"? What is the link between our personal histories and the issues we discuss in this chapter?

Defining Family

Our struggles with the "what is family?" question somewhat mirror the uncertainty of both the discipline and the society at large. As soon as we offer any defining set of parameters, we exclude some group of people who experience themselves as family. And exclusions wrought by academic definitions are compounded by political exclusions, such as the difficulties that lesbian and gay couples have in sharing health insurance policies because they are not "really" family.

We each searched for a nonreducible aspect of family—one element that, if absent, would signal for each of us a nonfamily status. For Stephen, wariness about problems of exclusion leads him almost to skirt the issue by reframing family simply as people who share a household. For Leigh, the emotional bonds are the nonreducible element—if you *affectively experience* yourselves as a family, then you are one. These are differences merely of emphasis, in that Leigh recognizes the significance of household and Stephen recognizes the significance of affective bonds. Perhaps our different professional training—Stephen in sociology and Leigh in marriage and family therapy—has contributed to our different foci as well. Above all, we fully agree that disciplines that deal with "families" must have an inclusive reach and remain ever alert to the question of who gets left out by how we see and define social reality.

Personal Histories

We both come from ethnically and religiously homogeneous backgrounds marked by traditionally gendered patterns of family interaction. We both experienced tensions of living in families that were ideologically progressive for their respective communities, yet were often unaware of the sexism and racism that governed their own behavior, as well as that of the dominant culture. It is a history shared with many of our white colleagues of the baby-boom generation. Yet, within that similarity are different trajectories that have brought us to an appreciation of the significance of intersecting social categories in social science research.

Stephen's History. While growing up in Miami Beach in the 1940s and 50s, my family taught me of insiders and outsiders. There were Jews like us, and there were gentiles, referred to anonymously as "the *goyim.*" Concerning race, the official belief system of my family was that public racial segregation was an unmitigated evil and that skin color should make no difference in the way people are treated. In everyday informal talk, however, the racial divide was as big as the Grand Canyon. There were white people and there were *Schvartzas*— African American people, whom I encountered only in their apparent function of working for people like us. To be sure, whether African American or white, whoever worked for us in our household, waited on us in restaurants, or worked in my father's physician's practice (including my mother) was not my father's equal. I knew this both from the way he talked to these people about whatever service he wanted and from the more contemptuous way he sometimes spoke about them when he found their services or appreciation to be wanting. Hierarchy abounded—in matters of race, social class, and my parents' gender relations. In the community, the world seemed to exist only for us Jewish, well-heeled, heterosexual white folks; everyone else was either an outsider, an employee, or invisible. No one I knew had an inkling of how colonizing this attitude was—not my parents, not my friends, and certainly not me.

In retrospect, the legacy of my youth was a clear and present entitlement complex, and, like all children, I innocently internalized much of the world presented to me. But I also knew fully what it was like to be an outsider, for I was born with a cleft palate, which caused me to have a speech defect. In school and on playgrounds, my nasal speech was a constant source of unwanted attention. Throughout my youth, I was called "snot-nose;" I was frequently asked (often innocently enough) if I had a cold, and I was mocked unceasingly by peers who held their noses while they spoke in an attempt to imitate the sound of my voice. Perhaps this experience of outsiderhood helped me become more curious about the process of stigmatization and about differences in general. Also important was leaving Miami Beach to attend a New England prep school, where I first encountered African Americans as classmates and peers; my driving curiosity about people and what they are about (myself included); my unwanted distance from my father (his naked prejudices were thereby easier to identify and to hold at arm's length); my coming face to face with diverse students in my classrooms; and the incredible capacity of social science to find and appreciate diversity. These are some elements of my awakening. I see this as a lifelong process, of which I believe I am still at the beginning.

Leigh's History. Growing up female in a fundamentalist religion in West Texas, I knew few people who were different from me; there were no ethnic minorities (except one African American baseball star who transferred to our all-white high school to be on our state-championship team), no one whom *I thought* might be gay or lesbian, and only a handful of non-Christians. Yet, it seems I have always been aware of the notion of category. I knew from an early age that because girls had to wear dresses to school, we never got to play the really fun games and had to sit in contorted positions so the boys would not laugh at seeing our underwear. And I knew that women never stood before the congregation to lead in worship.

Yet, mine was an upbringing of gender contradictions. My father was the liberal in our fundamentalist community, oxymoronic though that sounds. He encouraged me to be athletic and took me to play baseball with my brother long before it was common—although I spent more time shagging balls and my brother spent more time hitting. While I was being taught to accept a supportive role to a husband's leadership, I was expected to achieve all I was capable of. Although I could not articulate my frustration at the gender inequities or understand the confusion that came from trying to meet the standards of two different views of women's roles, the tension this confusion created in my life was one of the dominant themes of my early adolescence.

Fueled by my loosely formed awareness of inequity and my dawning recognition of the great racial divide in our community, I was drawn to issues of racial inequality and injustice in later adolescence. At 17, the power, pain, and anger of

Eldridge Cleaver's *Soul on Ice* (1967) grabbed me and, in some ways, has never let go. I began to grasp the notion of oppression and see that my community's strategy of ignoring difference ("We're all the same in God's eyes") served to maintain the status quo by attributing variations in lifestyle, achievement, education, and so forth to issues of personal character instead of social opportunities. I became drawn to hearing a person's story, to truly learning about the differences among us.

It would take my leaving West Texas and going to graduate school to begin to *know* people who were different from me. The process I have tried to engage in of giving voice to the differences in our lives has sometimes been clumsy, awkward, and even painful; on occasion, it has dominated the fabric of a relationship when it should have been a thread. But I have come to understand that whatever disadvantages I encounter as a woman are typically offset by the privileges I accrue as white, heterosexual, and educated. Teaching students how to listen to others' stories and to see how both disadvantages and privilege are organizing principles of people's lives is now one of the most exciting things I do.

WHAT ARE SOCIAL CATEGORIES? WHAT ARE INTERSECTIONS?

We begin with many more questions than answers, since the problems of understanding even a single social category can become monumental. Does gender, for example, refer to something that someone physically is or to something purely discursive—that is created in social interaction? Is it merely something that gets imposed on someone? When an organized application of a category acquires a history, under what conditions does the categorization turn into an identity, perhaps glorified, perhaps stigmatized? And does the taking up of an identity, even a glorified one, enhance the world of the taker or narrow it? Put differently, when people attempt to build communities based on membership in a category, does their commonality rest mainly on the foundation of excluding nonmembers, as postmodernists like Young (1990) have suggested is true of any such project?

When we speak of "intersections" between such categories as race, class, gender, and sexual orientation, what do we mean phenomenologically (experientially)? What is *felt* to be intersecting with what? What *is* that point of convergence where race meets class meets gender meets sexual orientation meets age meets physical ability meets religion? What is the phenomenology of being Hispanic *and* poor *and* male *and* elderly? Of being African American *and* poor *and* female *and* 15 years old? Or of being white *and* lesbian *and* wealthy *and* physically disabled *and* 60 years old? As objective assemblages of categories, perhaps each of these three examples will evoke images of persons living at particular intersections for some readers. And for each example, there are real people at the center of that particular intersection, pulling the categories together into some sort of embodiment, however fluid or ephemeral that embodiment may be (see Butler, 1990, 1993). That said, the fact remains that we have no complex phenomenology of intersection, nothing that goes beyond the experience of just two or, at most, three of the many categories that each of us intersects (see West & Fenstermaker, 1995b, p. 508, for another discussion of the fit, or lack of fit, between objective intersections and subjective awareness).

THE STUDY OF INTERSECTING CATEGORIES: A BRIEF HISTORY

The study of intersecting categories is a latecomer to Western academic social science, and two reasons for this tardiness stand out. First, the acknowledged founders in the late 19th and early 20th centuries, as well as the next several generations of social scientists, were almost exclusively white men. The gates of the academy in Europe and the United States had long been closed to everyone else (Bordo, 1990), and the fledgling social sciences continued the tradition: These men did not often train their sensibilities on issues that ran counter to the interests of other white men. Second, Marxism emerged as the dominant conflict theory of society, replete with a well-articulated theoretical structure and an extensive body of historical documentation to support it. Marxism's economic determinism, its insistence that class struggles over the means of production are the "real" drivers of history and that everything else is a mere "echo" of these economic forces, precluded any consideration of race, gender, or other categories as independent organizing bases of micro- and macro-social structures. And "twentieth-century Marxism [continues] to delegitimize demands of women, black people, gays, lesbians, and others whose oppression cannot be reduced to economics" (Nicholson, 1990, p. 11; see also Bonilla-Silva, 1997).

A notable exception to white male hegemony in the academy was the great African American historian and sociologist W. E. B. DuBois whose *The Souls of Black Folk* (1903/1961) gave clear expression to issues of intersecting categories, often anticipating contemporary thinking nearly 100 years later. "One ever feels his twoness," BuBois wrote:

> An American, a Negro; two souls, two thoughts, two unreconciled strivings; two warring ideals in one dark body, whose dogged strength alone keeps it from being torn asunder.... [The African American] wishes neither of the older selves to be lost.... He simply wishes to make it possible for a man to be both a Negro and an American, without being cursed and spit upon by his fellows, without having the doors of Opportunity closed roughly in his face. (p. 17)

Along with his focus on race and citizenship, DuBois was keenly alert to issues of class: "To be a poor man is hard, but to be a poor race in a land of dollars is the very bottom of hardships" (p. 20).

Outside the academy, African American women took the lead in recognizing intersecting categories of oppression. In her survey of some notable early contributions, C. W. White (1995, p. 531) cited Sojourner Truth's 1867 declaration, just after the Civil War: "If colored men get their [voting] rights, and not colored women theirs, you see the colored men will be masters over the women, and it will be just as bad as it was before." One hundred years later, when a wave of feminist resurgence joined forces with the civil rights movement and other forms of minority protest and advocacy, African American women were again the leaders in calling attention to multiple and intersecting forms of oppression. Beale's (1969) essay offered a clear

recognition of class differences between European American and African American women and chided African American men for their backward views about gender: "Let me state here and now that the black woman in America can justly be described as a 'slave of a slave'" (pp. 342–343).

Beale's interest in intersecting oppressions was further elaborated in 1977 by the Combahee River Collective (1982), a group of African American lesbian feminists who had been meeting since 1974: "We do not have racial, sexual, heterosexual, or class privilege to rely upon, nor do we have even the minimal access to resources and power that groups who possess any one of these types of privilege have" (p. 18).

Some three years later at Amherst College in 1980, Lorde (1984) delivered her paper on intersections between age, race, class, gender, and sexual orientation—perhaps the clearest statement to that point about multiple and intersecting hierarchies and an equally clear call to open ourselves to the enriching potential of diversity. By then, white feminists had also begun to write about intersections. That same year, Rich (1980) published an essay that unmasked the intersection between gender and sexual orientation. She challenged heterosexually identified women to consider how their "natural" heterosexual inclinations are "a means of assuring male right of physical, economic, and emotional access" (p. 647) to females. Women thereby participate in some benefits that historically have accrued to male power, but they often sacrifice their self-determination, and their relationships with other women may also be curtailed. Frye (1983) added that in choosing white men as partners, white women gain not only their partners' social-class benefits but their racial bonuses.

Emerging within Lorde's and Rich's work was a focus on both the adversities and the joys accompanying any point of intersection. The story of intersecting oppressions is not simply about multiple disadvantage and impoverishment; intersecting privileges are not merely matters of multiple advantage and global well-being. As DuBois (1903/1961) observed, the oppression side may be mixed with uncommon strength, resolve, dignity, and deep connection with others. And the privilege side may be fraught with colossal ignorance, insularity, arrogance, narcissistic self-absorption, and a myriad of other liabilities, as McIntosh (1988) and Lugones (1990) showed more recently.

In the 1980s and 1990s, the recognition that no single point of intersection is accompanied by any inevitable consequence added richness and complexity to our understanding. There is greater clarity now that oppression in one category may be accompanied by either oppression or privilege in some other category. A generation earlier, Goffman (1963, pp. 137–138) made this point incisively, and his analysis of stigma deserves to be revisited:

> May I repeat that stigma involves not so much a set of concrete individuals who can be separated into two piles, the stigmatized and the normal, as a pervasive two-role social process in which every individual participates in both roles, at least in some connections and in some phases of life. The normal and the stigmatized are not persons but rather perspectives. . . . And since interaction roles are involved, not concrete individuals, it should come as no surprise that in many cases, he who is stigmatized in one regard nicely exhibits all the normal prejudices held toward those who are stigmatized in another regard.

There are "few pure victims or oppressors," Collins (1990) wrote more recently. "Each individual derives varying amounts of penalty and privilege from the multiple systems of oppression which frame everyone's lives" (p. 229).

Absent here is the simplistic idea that any social category is of such signal importance that it binds together all the members of it, regardless of whatever else they are. The particular "whatever elses" may just as easily erode the connection as strengthen it. Racial identities and alliances may get overshadowed by gender or social-class differences, as African American writers have pointed out again and again (hooks, 1996; West, 1994). Feminists have likewise exposed the vulnerability of feminism to the competing identities that may easily overshadow the sense of a common identity as women. Whereas white lesbian writers may focus on the connective force of women loving women, African American lesbians may be more alert to the blindness that white lesbians have to

white advantage. In *Zami,* Lorde (1982) wrote of "gay-girls" in the 1950s and of her white lover Muriel's blindness to racialized experience:

> Even Muriel seemed to believe that as lesbians, we were all outsiders and all equal in our outsiderhood. "We're all niggers," she used to say, and I hated to hear her say it. It was wishful thinking based on little fact; the ways in which it was true languished in the shadow of those many ways in which it would always be false. . . . I was Black and she was not, and that was a difference between us that had nothing to do with better or worse, or the outside world's craziness. Over time I came to realize that it colored our perceptions and made a difference in the ways I saw pieces of the worlds we shared. (pp. 203–204; see also Jordan [1998b] for a vivid personal account of the instability and unpredictability of people's categorical connections)

Plainly, Lorde did not want her own awareness of two interlocking oppressions—race and sexual orientation—to be sacrificed to some singular notion of lesbian community. Of course, the complexity may quickly multiply. Phelan (1989) noted the split that emerged historically between "bar dykes," whose community was limited to gay bars, and academic feminist lesbians. Phelan saw this split as falling largely along social-class lines, the bar dykes dwelling principally in a working-class world and the academic lesbians dwelling in a middle-class world (see also Faderman, 1991). The focus shifts here from the intersection of race with sexual orientation to the intersection of social class, lesbian style, and feminism. Feinberg's (1993) gripping novelistic account of a person who was unable to fit comfortably into the bipolar world of *either* female *or* male adds further documentation, including a glimpse of the era when academic feminist lesbians were so adept at stigmatizing the butch-femme pattern of bar dykes that the latter felt bereft of the only community they knew (see also Nestle, 1987). Put race back in this picture, and note how the identity complexities multiply: straight-gay, white-colored, feminist-nonfeminist, middle class-working class—we are already up to 16 combinations. These are not merely logical possibilities. Real people are to be found in each cell of the resulting 4 × 4 table, and it is impossible to predict which category, if any, will emerge as *the* cardinal identity for particular persons or whether coalition building will be effective in bridging a variety of identities. (The classic work on coalition building among diversely identified people is by Reagon, 1983; for a subtle analysis of how thinking openly about butches and femmes reveals how unstable any identity category may become, see Martin, 1994).

In the 1990s, developments within postmodernism and its unruly child "queer theory" added new complexity to thinking about categories, identities, agency, community, and feminism. Butler's (1990, 1993) postmodernist focus on gender and implicit challenge to contemporary feminism have been particularly provocative. As Butler (1990, p. 4) wrote, "the premature insistence on a stable subject of feminism, understood as a seamless category of women, inevitably generates multiple refusals to accept the category." Put simply, there is no monolithic category of "woman" for whom emancipatory projects can be launched. "Woman" is unstable precisely because it keeps on changing its identifying contours in accordance with other historical factors (e.g., race, class, and sexual orientation) within which particular women are always embedded, and to the extent that analysts try to hold on to "woman" per se, they wind up obliterating these other dimensions. As we discuss later, Butler's view complicates any theorizing about intersection, at times "troubling" the work of both the theorist and the political activist through demonstrations of how no stable center of intersection can exist.

The emergence of queer theory has added still more complexity to issues of intersection. Starting as a reclamation of the term *queer* from its earlier stigmatizing usage, it has both a political ("We're here, we're queer, get used to it") and a theoretical component. The theoretical aspect is an extension of the postmodernist suspicion of bipolar categories and the identities that result from them—e.g., gay-lesbian, man-woman, feminist-nonfeminist (Lorber, 1996; Walters, 1996). Queer theorists have attempted to normalize all outcast positions, especially marginal sexualities, through the concept of "performativity." That is, both gender and sexual style become repetitive display, or performance. For example, if one looks closely at the hard work of drag queens preparing for their performances, one can also see the work of "normal heterosexuals" going about *their* performances. Drag queen and heterosexual identities hence become equalized: *Any* gender or sexual identity is hard work! Above all, queer theory challenges rigid, bipolar choices by flooding the visual marketplace with images in which gender and sexuality become too fluid or too outlandish to freeze into anything permanent. Gender becomes nothing more than whatever we stage. "Sexual orientation" becomes not something we are, but something we put on or act out. As we turn to a closer look at issues of theory building, we will consider whether queer theory has potential as a theory of intersection.

THEORIES OF INTERSECTION

The development of theoretical approaches to intersecting categories has proceeded haphazardly. There are some important descriptive statistics. We know, for example, that in 1994 African American women were more likely to be victims of a rape or sexual assault than were white women. African Americans at every level of family income were more likely than whites to be victimized by robberies, but the gap between the highest- and lowest-income African Americans was much smaller than the corresponding gap for whites (Bureau of Justice Statistics, 1997). In other words, the racial disadvantage in a racialized society almost canceled out any class advantage that wealthier African Americans may have otherwise enjoyed. The 1996 General Social Survey (Barkan, 1998) provided data on the percentage of people who say they would be afraid to walk in their neighborhoods alone at night. The results showed that African American women are the most afraid, followed by white women, African American men, and white men. Data such as these are useful because they demonstrate unmistakably that there are real consequences for people at particular intersections. Making sense of these data through careful social theory, however, has not proceeded apace with the descriptive knowledge.

One reason, noted earlier, is the lack of clear-cut phenomenological underpinnings to anchor theoretical work within concrete *experiences* of intersection. The kind of vivid, personal accounts that have done so much to propel our thinking and theorizing about race *or* poverty *or* homophobia *or* misogyny have not been forthcoming for the intersectionality of these or other categories. Consider Gomez's account (in Gomez & Smith, 1990, p. 515) of her experience of going with her African American female partner to find a rental in a two-family home:

> I remember we called this one place, and I was in stark terror. In my mind, I was thinking about a white couple looking at us and seeing two Black people that they were going to potentially bring into their home. It terrified me because I could see them insulting us or even possibly slamming the door in our face. And then just as we were about to get out of the car, it occurred to me that this white couple would also look at us and see two lesbians.

Gomez added that, at that time, she was not yet "out" as a lesbian, and her own homophobia may have obscured the potential for homophonic hostility from others. The thought of these potential landlords seeing two lesbians hence came only as an afterthought. But if the categories African American and lesbian had been fully interlocked in her mind, would the terror she experienced have been formed in such a way as to encompass both categories, not simply one at a time or in an additive way, but in full cognizance of their intersection? And could the landlords, looking from the other side of the front door, likewise invoke the intersectionality of both categories and their *own* racial and sexual orientation categories?

Perhaps there is (or can be) an irreducible *feeling* of intersection. An African American lesbian couple, a white heterosexual couple—all four people *could* feel some of the fullness of their assemblages of categories. The two African American lesbians might be more likely to do so than the white heterosexual couple, simply because they were more likely to encounter penalties that accrue to their stigmatized categories, while the white heterosexual couple, having less experience of such penalties, were less likely to become aware that they *had* categories (Frye, 1983). But even for those who intersect several oppressed categories, the awareness of intersection per se may remain elusive, nothing more than a vague and inchoate feeling, perhaps a generalized sense of defeat, anger, anguish. What is needed is progress in moving from inchoate feeling to more articulated feeling and from there to conceptualization and analysis. Wellman's (1996) description of growing up in the only white household in an African American neighborhood in Detroit and learning that "melanin didn't matter if one was cool" (p. 35), arriving at graduate school in Berkeley and feeling that the white middle-class world around him was totally alien, and finally identifying himself as a "border person" gives vivid expression to this process of moving from vague feeling to conceptualization.

The recent focus on metaphors of intersection (such as border person) is perhaps a search for imagery to name and identify better this "feeling" component. West and Fenstermaker (1995a) claimed that additive or "multiplicative metaphors" (such as interlocking categories or distinct axes) cannot precisely convey the effects of intersectionality (a term that is itself a spatial metaphor). They suggested that the temporal metaphor—"simultaneity"—is a better way of expressing how multiple categories are experienced, and their notion of *doing* difference adds, through the word *doing,* the metaphor of work in the sense of something getting actively "produced" whenever people invoke categories. Thorne (1995, p. 499) noted that although "doing difference" inadequately captures the complexities of multiple intersecting categories, "we [do] need a range of metaphors and theories honed in many sites of analysis."

It may be that the phenomenological developments must await linguistic changes in the culture at large or, at least, in linguistic communities. Perhaps a single word for black-elderly-lesbian or young-white-heterosexual-male would render these intersections more vivid, much as the category lesbian surely helped to render the intersection of the categories of woman and homosexual more irreducibly vivid for the generation of women who attempted to build communities on that foundation (Stein, 1997). Experiences, words, and analysis are intertwined.

Queer Theory as Intersectionality

Postmodernists argue that the creation of any category may throw people together coercively and foster yet another binary opposition between members and nonmembers of the category, much like women-men or straights-gays." We see merit in this postmodernist caution, especially about categories that are most fueled by the logic of binary opposition. But people will continue to create categories, and some of them will be useful tools for discovering interconnections (Bordo, 1990) without necessarily erasing the differences that lie outside the particular commonalities. The resurrection of the category queer has sometimes been heralded as precisely this kind of linguistic tool. Unfortunately, when this category is used in a way that retains any specificity, it focuses on types of sexual identity or expression, and when it expands to embrace any standpoint that is vaguely beyond the pale of conventional propriety, its openness then loses all meaningful concreteness. Walters (1996, p. 842) was less than fully sanguine about the "opening up of queerness to articulations of 'otherness' beyond the gender divide.":

> If queer can be seen to challenge successfully gender hegemony, then it can make both theoretical and political space for more substantive notions of multiplicity and intersectionality. However, queer can "de-race" the homosexual of color in much the same way "old-time" gay studies often did, effectively erasing the specificity of "raced" gay existence under a queer rubric in which whiteness is not problematized.

Is queer a category that, in its contemporary usage, expresses (or might express) any sense of intersectionality? And what are the "more substantive notions of multiplicity and intersectionality" to which Walters appealed? If there is a growing edge of queer theory that might move attention beyond the intersection of sexuality and gender, it remains to be developed. In her writings, Butler (1990,

1993) often takes a dim view of the prospect that *any* identity category (or "subject position") could adequately capture the intersectionality of race, class, gender, and sexuality, which means, of course, that we have no choice but to remain fragmented in our multiplicity of selves and categories. It is not surprising, then, that Butler (1993) equivocates: She sees identity categories as "necessary errors" for the sake of affiliation, but she holds them to be inadequate "totalizations" (p. 230) at the same time, given that they inevitably lead to failures of representation of the people on behalf of whom they are made.

Our concern with Butler's position is simply one of a different emphasis. History is both the great creator and the great destroyer of categorical identity umbrellas. If any such category (including queer) is a "necessary error" on behalf of affiliation, not all umbrella categories are equal. Some may be less prone to "error" (better suited to represent contemporary complexities, however temporary and historically contingent these categories may be) than others. Butler's suspicions about the "regulatory" aspects of *all* categories deserve scrutiny, but we think she is premature in declaring an end to identity, and end to the "subject." History will continue to create categories. Let us see how much multiplicity subjects embolden themselves to hold and allow for the categories they create (such as articulations of queer) to hold it.

Oppression Theory

Outside postmodernism and queer theory, Collins (1990, p. 222) offered what is arguably the most concerted attempt to theorize about intersectionality, calling for "reconceptualizing race, class, and gender as interlocking systems of oppression," thereby enabling us to focus on how "each [of these systems] needs the others in order to function." She added that although these three systems have been historically the most consequential ones for African American women, they are not necessarily the most fundamental oppressions for other subordinated groups. It is up to particular empirical assessments to uncover the particular "matrix of domination" that is operative, the assumption being that such a matrix is there to be exposed, challenged, and opposed. Collins's appeal to the variability of what are the most relevant categories was echoed by Bordo (1990, p. 139), who cautioned that there is often a "coercive, mechanical requirement that *all* enlightened feminist projects attend to 'the intersection of race, class and gender.' What happened to ethnicity? Age? Sexual Orientation?" But Bordo also counseled that we cannot attend to everything:

> No matter how local and circumscribed the object or how attentive the scholar is to the axes that constitute social identity, some of these axes will be ignored and others selected. . . . This selectivity, moreover, is never innocent. We always "see" from points of view that are invested with our social, political, and personal interests, inescapably "centric" in one way or another, even in the desire to do justice to heterogeneity. (p. 140)

Andersen and Collins's (1998) focus on the "matrix of domination" is an example of this kind of selective interest, an invitation to become "centric" about issues of domination and subordination. Whatever the particular matrix, they argued that it is best seen as a "*societal* [italics added] configuration" (p. 3). Here, the authors signaled a form of analysis that starts at the macro (societal) level and then hones in on more microlevel outcomes. In their words, the matrix of domination is a "structural pattern [that] affects individual consciousness, group interaction, and group access to institutional power and privileges" (p. 3). In the remainder of this chapter, we attempt to link issues of intersection with an area that has always been a prominent interest for both of us—multiple roles and the particular branch of this topic known as the work-family interface. As part of this analysis, we reexamine the macro to micro procedural strategy to see if it is fully adequate for the exploration of this particular content area.

SOCIAL CATEGORIES, MULTIPLE ROLES, AND WORK-FAMILY RESEARCH

The empirical study of multiple roles in family studies was spawned by the influx of middle-class white women into the labor force beginning in the late 1960s and early 1970s. Seeing this group of women, and to a lesser extent their male partners, move away from the traditional role division generated a century earlier by the "cult of domesticity" (Welter, 1966), researchers began to study the impact on individuals and families of men and women occupying several demanding roles simultaneously. The initial assumptions were based largely on a deficit model: The taking on of multiple roles would generate role overload and role conflict (Goode, 1960), and perhaps there would be deleterious effects on other aspects of health and well-being as well. This model was then challenged by an "enhancement" perspective (Marks, 1977; Sieber, 1974), which suggested that multiple roles may have a salutary impact on people's lives, rather than a negative one. As research developed to explore these competing perspectives, one key finding that emerged was that it is the nature of the role or role configuration, not the mere accumulation of roles, that is associated with psychological and physical health, as well as family functioning (e.g., Barnett & Baruch, 1985; Barnett, Brennan, Raudenbush, & Marshall, 1994; Gove & Zeiss, 1987; House, Landis, & Umberson, 1988). Research in this area, along with the companion research focus on the division of household labor, has flourished in recent decades. Researchers, mental health providers, and policy makers have all sought to understand this momentous shift from a gender-stratified division of work and family roles in marriage to an arrangement that, although still gender linked, could allow both wives and husbands to participate in multiple domains.

Ironically, this empirical focus on multiple roles was born of both a recognition and a denial of diversity. While potential gender differences in the impact of multiple role experience were acknowledged, scant attention was given to possible racial or social class differences. The focus was on changes in white middle-class marriages, with little recognition that women and men of color had been participating in family and employment domains for generations, as had white couples with modest annual incomes. This bias that was evident in the original research on multiple roles is still apparent some 30 years later. Studies still overwhelmingly focus on white heterosexual middle-class dual-income couples. Much less attention is given to variations as a function of race, social class, or household structure, and almost no attention given to sexual orientation. Understanding the impact of *intersecting* social categories (e.g., heterosexual, female, divorced, African American) on one's functioning in multiple roles has remained deferred.

An illustrative review of this literature is useful for identifying some issues that have been considered and for indicating how social categories and their intersections typically have or have not been addressed. This review serves as an introduction to the final section of the chapter, in which we deal more with how the research might change if we were to incorporate a keener alertness to issues of intersectionality.

The Focus on Gender

Most of the empirical literature on multiple roles has been concerned with the association between multiple roles and the well-being of individuals and couples. How does being a spouse, parent, and employee affect one's quality of life, marital satisfaction, physical and mental health, division of household labor, and a host of other personal and family variables? Concerning social categories, gender has been the central focus in this work. For example, how do spouses' work characteristics, such as hours employed and the demands of jobs, affect one another's evaluations of their marriage? Working from an assumption that men's core roles revolve around work and women's core roles revolve around family (Barnett & Baruch, 1987), researchers seemed surprised to discover the importance of family roles for men's well-being and the parallel value of paid work roles for women's, particularly in mediating the stress associated with the role of mother (Barnett & Baruch, 1987; Coleman, Antonucci, Adelmann, & Crohan, 1987). They found that although work demands were marginally more likely to contribute to work-family conflict among men and family demands were more likely to contribute to conflict for women, this gender difference was slight and weaker (Voydanoff, 1988) than they had expected it to be.

Concerning parenting and other household work, the hope that wives' increased career involvement would be matched by husbands' increased household labor was soon dashed. Husbands' participation in these roles remained limited, and it increased only marginally, if at all, as women moved into the labor force (Berardo, Shehan, & Leslie, 1987; Leslie & Anderson, 1988; Pleck, 1985). LaRossa (1988) demonstrated that a more responsive *culture* of fatherhood has not been accompanied by changes in fathers' actual conduct, and Hochschild (1989) popularized the notion of wives having a "second shift" when they get home from work, noting that the average woman in her sample had a month less total leisure time per year than her husband.

Conspicuously absent from the empirical work was the kind of diversity-oriented macroperspective advanced by Collins (1990). Changes in the labor force have had an uneven impact on families, varying considerably by social class and by race. Again, work-family research was responsive principally to the emerging career opportunities of white, middle-class women and was fueled, in part, by the partial success of the liberal white feminist agenda: to compete with men for exciting careers, to enlist support from husbands or potential husbands for a dual-career couple pattern, and to press for the kind of changes in the division of child and domestic work that would enable these married women to ease into this pattern without undue stress and strain.

This agenda did not resonate with poor women, women of color, or lesbians, nor did it tap into the typical concerns of poor men, men of color, or gay men. A more inclusive understanding of the work-family interface would recognize a five-dimensional space of social class, gender, race, household structure (e.g., married-single), and sexual orientation, even if it did not attend to all these dimensions in every study. Instead, most of the research has focused on the one-dimensional social space of gender variation, with a second dimension—social-class variation, as measured by income—occasionally added to the research design. When whiteness, married status, and heterosexuality become *the* frames of reference, then the resulting social science can mirror only these particular interests, while contributing unwittingly to the marginalization of nondominant statuses by rendering them invisible (a partial exception is Blumstein & Schwartz, 1983).

Steps Toward a Recognition of Intersection

We look more closely at some contributions to the work-family literature about African Americans because these studies have often attended to the intersection of race and gender, unlike samples of white families in which race remains invisible. Although this is only a small segment of the work-family literature, several authors take as a starting point the recognition of African American men's and women's unique history of involvement in the labor force as a result of racism. With many such families needing two incomes to survive and women often providing a substantial portion of the financial support of their families, gendered patterns of participation in family roles have historically been more flexible in African American families; that is, African American men have participated in child care to a greater extent than have their white counterparts (Billingsley, 1992; see also Chapter 12, this volume). Working from this historical context, several authors have examined the impact of work and family roles for African Americans' mental and physical well-being and satisfaction with family life.

Studies that have focused exclusively on African American families have broadened the lens beyond white families alone, but they have often failed to clarify how being African American rather than white may be influencing the findings. Moreover, the findings themselves are not clear. Coleman et al., (1987) and Waldron and Jacobs (1989) found that the role of employee had beneficial health effects for African American women, particularly mothers, and Rushing, Ritter, and Burton (1992) found that it had positive health effects for African American men. However, Broman's (1991) study of married people found that marriage, not employment, was associated with the well-being of both African American men and women. Broman indicated that employment was associated with women's lower satisfaction with family life. It may

be that being employed enhances African American women's psychological and physical health, as is largely the case for white women, but makes them more frustrated with family life (particularly when household demands are factored in, as Broman, 1993, noted), even though African American men have higher levels of involvement in family roles than do men in other racial groups. As Hossain and Roopnarine (1993) pointed out, although African American fathers may be more involved in child care and housework, the majority of the household roles in middle-class dual-income African American families still fall to the women and, like their white counterparts, these men's household labor does not vary in response to their wives' work demands.

This research may suggest that few race differences exist in the work and family interface, but it is important to assess what race means in the context of one's life. An examination of a particular study is illustrative of how research, even when it attends to the intersection of race and gender, may fail to specify how race actually mediates the work and family connection. Frone, Russell, and Cooper (1992) found no variations between African Americans and whites in the fit of their model of the work-family interface. Specifically, one portion of the model found no racial differences in three types of work stress (work pressure, lack of autonomy, role ambiguity) or in the impact of these work stressors on work and family conflict or depression. It may be premature to conclude that racial differences do not exist in the effect of work stress on work and family conflict. Perhaps racial differences exist in the *sources* of work stress, and by ignoring such differences, Frone and his colleagues may have unintentionally neutralized the significance of race. For example, white employees seldom deal with the stress of having coworkers attribute a normal problem at work to their race or assume they got the job only because of their race. This unique source of "racialized work stress" may cause African American employees to respond in numerous ways, such as working longer hours, distancing themselves from colleagues, or not sharing their workdays with their spouses, any of which could lead to increased family conflict.

Research on marital satisfaction has indirectly supported the notion that racialized work stress may be an unrecognized factor in family life. Several researchers have found that African Americans report less satisfaction with their marriages than do white Americans (Broman, 1993; Oggins, Veroff, & Leber, 1993). This main effect for race cannot be fully explained by demographic variables, such as education, income, or parental status (Oggins et al., 1993) or by marital interaction patterns, such as spousal support or the division of housework (Broman, 1993). Yet, the suggestion (Hacker, 1992; Oggins et al., 1993) that this racial difference may result from the experience of racism in the lives of African Americans and the stress and anger that can be transferred to the home has not been explored empirically.

Franklin (1993) showed how this process can unfold. On the basis of his clinical work with African American families and his own experience as an African American man, Franklin poignantly described how African American men, regardless of their educational and professional accomplishments and status, can "within a single hour . . . be viewed as a potential rapist—hugely frightening—and as a doorman—absolutely insignificant" (p. 34). The daily insults in the work environment, such as having a waiter place the bill in front of the white client you have taken out for a business lunch, can take an enormous emotional toll on African American men. Franklin found that many African American men, who want to present themselves as successful and strong in their roles as husband and father (roles that generations of African American men have been denied the opportunity to fill successfully), do not share these experiences with family members, thereby distancing themselves emotionally from their families. Note, however, that these kinds of invaluable clinical insights have not found their way into work-family research with nonclinical samples. Even though our models of the work-family interface may show few statistical differences between African American and white racial groups, this may be simply because we are not yet adequately oriented to the differences in racialized experience.

Orbuch and Custer's (1995) quantitative study of middle-class couples merits extended consideration

here because it considered multiple role experience in a way that was alert to racialized history, and in using a sampling design that included both African Americans and whites, it enables us to see some impacts that result from racial differences. Acknowledging cultural differences and family patterns that have resulted, in part, from racism in the job market, Orbuch and Custer examined husbands' participation in housework, gender-role attitudes, and household incomes as moderators of the relationship between wives' employment and husbands' well-being. The results indicated that income was a significant moderator for African American men: When wives worked out of economic necessity, their employment had no effect on their husbands' level of depression; if wives worked outside the home when their husbands' income was sufficient to support the family, African American husbands had higher rates of depression. No such pattern was found for white husbands, who had *lower* rates of depression when their wives had careers. Given that African American men have historically had fewer viable opportunities to support their families, it makes sense that the sufficiency of a husband's income would have different meanings for these two races.

Consistent with earlier research, Orbuch and Custer's results also indicated that employed white women's husbands who did more housework had higher levels of anxiety. In contrast, African American men's participation in housework did not significantly moderate the association between their wives' work status and their own well-being. Again, a recognition of the historical and social context of African American men being more highly involved in family labor and a wider acceptance of such participation in the African American community led the researchers to build a research design in such a way as to highlight meaningful racial differences.

MULTIPLE-ROLES RESEARCH: HOW CAN WE ADDRESS INTERSECTING SOCIAL CATEGORIES?

In the work-family literature, few studies have gone as far as Orbuch and Custer's (1995) in exploring the link between roles and well-being while remaining alert to the impact of racial and other categorical differences. In the remainder of this chapter, we scrutinize more closely some of this literature. Our strategy is not to attack this work, but to ask how it might be improved by a greater attention to issues of diversity and intersectionality. Along the way, we consider conceptual as well as methodological issues.

We begin with a general question arising from the legacy of role theory: Given multiple roles (e.g., work, parenthood, intimate partnership, friendship, and leisure), is some form of overload inevitable, or do some people manage to create a busy life pattern without undue stress, perhaps even with some levity and joyfulness? Some time ago, Marks (1977) issued a challenge to the idea that complex, multiple roles are inherently overdemanding (Goode, 1960), and, more recently, Marks and MacDermid (1996) demonstrated that people who score higher on a role-balance scale also score higher on role "ease" and lower on role "overload" than do those with lower scores on role balance. They also found that this "balancing" tendency is associated with higher self-esteem and enhanced functioning in aspects of daily activity. Perhaps the most important implication was that it is not so much the particular things that people *do* that generate strain or ease as the underlying identity work, the consequences either of identifying oneself evenhandedly across one's different activities or privileging some parts of oneself more than others.

This theory of the salutary consequences of role balance and the implicit notion of *self* balance that underlies it, bears a remarkable kinship to words from Lorde (1984, p. 120), who posed the issue of self-balance in terms of the social categories of race, gender, sexual orientation, and feminism:

> As a Black lesbian feminist comfortable with the many different ingredients of my identity, and a woman committed to racial and sexual freedom from oppression, I find I am constantly being encouraged to pluck out some one aspect of myself and present this as the meaningful whole, eclipsing or denying the other parts of self. But this is a destructive and fragmenting way to live. My fullest concentration of energy is available to me only when I integrate all the parts of who I am, openly, allowing power from particular sources of my living to flow back and forth freely through all my different selves, without the

restrictions of externally imposed definition. Only then can I bring myself and my energies as a whole to the service of those struggles which I embrace as part of my living. (for another compelling statement, reframed as "multiple-subjectivity," see Green, 1996, p. 262)

Lorde's elegant expression of her commitment to wholeness offers a clear signal that refining the integrity among our multiple *selves* will also expand the "energies" available for the different things that we *do*. At the same time, however, Lorde added an important structural element that social research has left unexplored: The work of self-balance may be encumbered, repeating Lorde's words, by "the restrictions of externally imposed definition." Lorde reminded us here that our self-integrity and the energies that flow out of it do not exist in a social vacuum. Social structures are real—as outer structures of opportunity or constraint and as inner structures of self-definition. The reality of these structures may crystallize in many forms. Systematic violence is one form, and terms of derogation are another: People who are deemed "faggots," "bitches," and "niggers" are not given good jobs, nor can they easily withstand the assault on their identities. Can an African American lesbian balance her skin color, sexual orientation, and gender with the rest of herself if her embodiment of these social categories is unacceptable to the more dominant white, male, heterosexual majority around her? "The quest for black identity involves self-respect and self-regard," Cornel West (1993) wrote, "realms inseparable from, yet not identical to, political power and economic status" (p. 97). Self and social structure are linked, and our theoretical and empirical work needs to attend more closely to that linkage.

A Research Vision

If we were to incorporate race, class, gender, sexual orientation, and other categories of difference into studies of multiple roles and selves or of the work-family interface, what would our work look like? How would it change? What conceptual and theoretical obstacles stand in our way?

Consider research that has explored the impact of people's self-reported marital-role quality, parental-role quality, and job-role quality on their reports of anxiety and depression. In one of the most methodologically refined studies to date, Barnett, Marshall, and Pleck (1992) found that the qualities of men's marital roles are no less predictive of their psychological distress than are the qualities of their job roles, thus calling into question the popular belief that men are more driven by work than by family concerns. Perhaps even more important is Barnett's (1994) finding that among full-time dual-earner couples who are parents, both spouses experience the work-home interface similarly: "When marital or parental experiences are positive, there is little relationship between job experiences and distress. When marital or parental experiences are negative, there is a stronger relationship between job experiences and distress" (p. 655).

Although it is tempting to accept at face value Barnett's (1994) and Barnett et al.'s (1992) conclusion that gender is not very predictive of whether job quality will lead to distress, we believe this conclusion to be premature for two reasons. First, it neglects the myriad ways in which the positiveness of marital and parental experiences may itself be differentially gendered. Komter (1989) documented the "hidden power" in marriage—a set of gendered privileges and entitlements. When husbands' preferences are given greater weight because they have "stronger feelings" about an outcome than wives do and/or wives are striving harder to obtain consensus and minimize contention, this is hidden power (for elaborated examples of these processes, see Johnson & Huston, 1998; Zvonkovic, Greaves, Schmiege, & Hall, 1996; for an argument on behalf of exploring the differentially gendered *meanings* of roles, see Simon, 1995). Could a process of hidden power likewise be gendering husbands' and wives' assessments of the "rewards" and "concerns" that Barnett was scoring? If a wife's balance of marital rewards and concerns is positive because she is protecting the marriage by giving her husband what he wants and the husband's is positive because he is *getting* what he wants and if their high marital-quality scores are protecting both of them from the distress that might otherwise result when job-role quality is low, what

does this mean about the impact of gender? For us, it would mean, paradoxically, that gender is accounting for little or no variance in distress only *because of* or *through* unrecognized gendered processes of constructing the rewards and concerns within marriage.

The second reason why the finding of no gender difference needs to be qualified is that Barnett and her colleagues (1992) drew a random sample that was overwhelmingly white, predominantly middle class, and exclusively heterosexual. We need to be especially wary of universalizing white, heterosexual experience because it may reflect a legacy of privileges and entitlements that are not enjoyed by people in nondominant social categories.

Consider some alternatives. Suppose the design had been more ambitious, more funding had been available, and the sample had included sufficient numbers not only of African American and Latino men and women but of gay and lesbian couples and of dual-worker couples with more traditionally working-class jobs. Surely, this expanded design would be an improvement, and we think Barnett and her colleagues (1992) would heartily agree. At the least, we could then know if having nondominant racial statuses or sexual orientations results in different effects on psychological distress than having dominant statuses within these categories. Furthermore, we could know if nondominant status in some way moderates the relationship between the quality of experience in one role and the quality of experience in another.

Suppose we found that controlling for job quality, parental quality, and marital quality, African American men suffer from higher levels of psychological distress than do white men or that for African American women with high parental-role quality and high marital-role quality, lower job-role quality is accompanied by an increase in psychological distress, unlike the situation for the white women. Although we would have learned something important, we would still be left at the starting point of a good analysis because we could only conjecture about the sources of the racial differences. Perhaps the explanation of the hypothetical finding about African American women is that prejudice and discrimination toward African Americans in the workplace are felt strongly enough to override the salutary psychological impacts of positive marital and parental experiences. To find out if this is so, however, we would need additions to the job-concern and job-reward scales—in this case, perhaps some items tapping the conviction that one's coworkers believe that the source of one's job was affirmative action requirements, not one's bona fide qualifications, or the conviction that no matter how competently an African American woman performs her job, her performance is going to be under much greater scrutiny than it would be if she were white.

Surely, if we are exploring a full array of rewards and concerns within the interweave of worker, parent, and partner roles, our picture will be incomplete unless the impact of racial, patriarchal, and social-class oppressions (or the impact of their absence) are part of it. *Racism or sexism on the job may create enormous role strain and psychological distress! Freedom from racism and sexism may reduce the role strain that may otherwise be present and elevate one's psychological health.* Oppression, when present, must be researched as a potential "concern"; freedom from oppression must be counted as a "reward" insofar as distress would be greater without it. We arrive, then, at the following procedural imperative: *If we want to discourse about the impact of structural categories, such as race, class, and gender, we must not simply include them in our research as dummy variables but also gather direct data about how these categories make their impact. And because this impact may be different for groups lower on the hierarchy than for groups higher on it, it follows that the data collected (e.g., the nature of the items in survey studies) will need to reflect the full range of typical experiences that may predictably occur not simply at one point on a hierarchy of privilege, but at any number of different points across the full spectrum of the hierarchy.*

The complexities of including structural categories in our work do not end here, however. Bowen and Pittman (1995) noted that people are not always aware, subjectively, of the full array of the "contextual effects" that are impinging on them; indeed,

behavior, health, and psychological distress may be affected by elements of the social context that are perceived dimly, if at all, by those who enjoy them or suffer from them. Researchers should have a good idea of what some of these contextual elements are, as obtained from qualitative, quantitative, and historical studies. In the example given earlier, one could survey the white workers to find out, for example, if *they* think they know an African American coworker who got his or her job because of affirmative action. Then we could see if there is some relationship between the prevalence of such attitudes among white workers and the variations of psychological distress reported by African American workers.

In this contextual-effects perspective, we are invited to include measures of macrolevel effects derived from units of analysis that are at a different level of abstraction from either the immediate work or family contexts themselves. Examples offered by Bowen and Pittman (1995) include community rates of poverty and unemployment, business failures, and ratios of minority-to-majority employment. To return to a previous example, suppose we found that among dual-earner couples, African American men have higher levels of psychological distress than do African American women, when marital-role quality and parental-role quality were controlled. If we had community-level data, we could then test the hypothesis that African American male workers are more prone to psychological distress than are African American female workers only when the rates of African American men's employment in the community are lower than those of African American women's employment.

The Problem of Context

We believe that research designs with inventive strategies for getting at the "contextual effects" of categories, such as race, class, and sexual orientation, on roles like intimate partner, parent, and worker would be considerable refinements of current research practice. At the same time, however, we have some misgivings about the theoretical assumptions (and the resulting conceptual lenses) that would confine structural categories, such as race, to the language of "context," while always keeping roles, such as parent or worker, as the main event of the analysis. What does it mean to theorize race as "context" in family studies? What would we be trying to accomplish analytically? What procedural, practical, political, methodological, theoretical, or value-driven problems would we be trying to attend to?

To explore these questions, we revisit the issue of context represented in an article on a symposium (Collins, 1995) that appeared soon after the publication of West and Fenstermaker's "Doing Difference" (1995a). Two issues strike us as pivotal. The first is the macro-micro problem: At what level of social structure should analyses of race, class, and gender be pitched? The second issue has to do with the connection between theory and praxis or, put differently, with the focus of human agency in confronting oppression. Both issues are closely related.

Although West and Fenstermaker (1995a) claimed that the macro-micro distinction is a false one, they seem to see the microlevel as fundamental, through their call to focus on the production of racial, class, and gender categories "as ongoing, methodical, and situated accomplishments" (p. 30). Any person may be held "accountable" for their actions through appeals to his or her presumed racial, class, and/or gender characteristics, and because these appeals are generated in everyday interactions, analysis must begin here, at the microlevel. In contrast, Collins (1995) was impatient with "theories stressing representations over institutional structures and social policies" (p. 494) because they omit any direct consideration of the history of power relations and the oppressions that flow out of that history. The starting point of analysis is "the macro level connections linking systems of oppression such as race, class, and gender." Collins did add "micro-level processes" to the picture—"how each individual and group occupies a social position within interlocking structures of oppression" (p. 492). Note, however, that the flow of causality is from the macro- to the microlevel: "The interlocking systems of oppression of race, class, and gender . . . *produce* [italics added] positions characterized by intersectionality" (p. 493). Collins

was not suggesting that oppressed groups are merely passive victims of the agency of those with more power, since she stressed oppositional strategies that actively *confront* the powerful. But she wanted confrontations that are born of people linking their microlevel experiences to oppressions that are held to flow downward from the macrolevel. (For similar views in this debate, see Ebert, 1996; Maldonado, 1995; Weber, 1995; Winant, 1995).

In summary, if particular intersections are seen as the contexts or environments or climates within which people act in families and elsewhere, then our attention will be drawn to macrolevel influences on people's lives—perhaps to the racial and gender composition of the different sectors of the workforce or of the U.S. Congress; to the impact of social policies, such as affirmative action, on people of color; to the history of relationships between the police and African American men in public spaces; or to the way that popular media images insinuate their way into people's consciousness and implicitly stigmatize those who do not fit the images. In contrast, if race, class, and gender are seen as ongoing accomplishments, if social categories can persist only insofar as people do the interactional work that maintains them as active identities—as in *doing* gender or *doing* difference—then attention will be drawn to all the trivial (as well as the "important") episodes of interaction in which categorical differences are invoked, restored, challenged, or resisted. In this case, what was seen from a macroperspective as the surrounding *context* of action is now seen more as the action itself.

We favor an ecumenical spirit in response to this debate, notwithstanding Andersen and Collins's (1998, p. 221) point that whereas "identities have an enormous impact on individual experience, . . . seeing race, class, and gender from an individualist viewpoint overlooks how profoundly embedded these identities are in the structure of American institutions." We see ample room for both micro- and macroapproaches to race, class, gender, and other social categories, and we do not think that either approach is a more authentic site for radical analysis or radical politics. We have shown that in work-family studies, the contextual-effects approach laid out by Bowen and Pittman (1995) is a useful strategy for bringing macrolevel variables into quantitative research. At the same time, we question why contextual considerations should be restricted to macrolevel variables. Although employment rates and other community or societal-level data may be important, various microlevel influences should also qualify as part of the environment or "context" within which the individual acts and experiences. Again, structural categories, such as race, class, and gender, may be studied as macrostructures that are conceived as external to the individual on whom they make their impact. They may also be studied as microstructures, and in the latter case, it is arbitrary to "contextualize" them theoretically as *apart* from parenthood, work, or partnership.

How, then, might we integrate a sharp focus on people's role experiences as workers, parents, and partners with a microfocus on their structural categories, such as race, class, and gender? We appeal to some emerging attempts to bridge the specificity of roles with the greater fluidity of social categories.

Identity Theory, Roles, and Social Categories

Structural symbolic interactionists provide a useful theoretical bridge between roles and their categories. Their current analytic practice is to speak of "role identities"—conceptions of self that are linked to role relationships, such as friend, student, parent, worker, spouse or partner, and so on (Thoits, 1992). The difference between a role and a role identity is that the latter is both more fluid and less transitory than a role; identities spill over the boundaries of particular situations, whereas roles are more rooted to one or another social location. One conceptual advantage of theorizing roles as identities is that the sharp divide between roles (e.g., worker, parent) and social categories (e.g., gender, race) tends to disappear when both are seen as identities. Consider the following identity statement from Jordan (1998a, p. 438):

> I can voice my ideas without hesitation or fear because I am speaking, finally, about myself. I am Black and I am female and I am a mother and I am bisexual and I am a nationalist and I am an antinationalist. And I mean to be fully and freely all that I am!

Jordan combined some *role* identities (mother, nationalist) with *categorical* identities (African American, female) without trumpeting them all within a singular self-affirmation and without any postmodernist dread of losing herself within a single social category (see White & Burke's, 1987, case for expanding identity analyses to include social categories).

The potential here is that once social categories are conceived as identity variables, we then have another way of treating race, class, gender, and sexual orientation as metric variables instead of merely as dummy variables in multiple-roles research. We agree with Bowen and Pittman's (1995) claim that using dummy codes for "male" and "female" forfeits a deeper understanding of "gendering" and that similar omissions occur when one uses dummy codes for race, family structure, and so on. But although Bowen and Pittman developed the case for converting such dummy variables into metrically operationalized macrovariables, we argue for a parallel strategy of creating microvariables and for striving to include both classes of variables (macro and micro) within the same quantitative studies of multiple roles.

Treating social categories, such as race, class, gender, and sexual orientation, as identity variables is a way to accomplish the micropiece of this strategy. Here are some identity-relevant accounts: Green (1996, p. 258) wrote of his mother's stories teaching him that as an African American, he could depend on the pride, strength, and hope of people in the African American community he did not even know, as well as his own family members, but he also wrote of learning early on to hide his gayness because "one of the worst things I could ever do was to bring disgrace to my race by expressing the wrong sexual feelings and desires." In Stein's (1997) sample, many of the younger lesbians did not connect with the notion of a lesbian identity (much less a lesbian community) and did not go through an intense "coming out" ritual, yet they felt fully comfortable with their sexuality. Wellman (1996) wrote of growing up in the only white family in an African American neighborhood, learning to fear the white police while fully trusting his African American neighbors, and finding himself to be totally out of synch with the white world in his Berkeley graduate program. Lugones (1990) feels such love for her Latino heritage that she interspersed her English writing with some Spanish, so as not to betray something so central to who she is. Stoltenberg (1990) wrote of internalizing the radical feminist critique of patriarchy so thoroughly that he sees nothing in "manhood" to which he would lay claim for the purpose of consolidating a healthy identity. Together, these cases give evidence of a continuum of the relevance that structural categories may have for people's identities and well-being.

Building on these and other suggestive personal accounts, researchers might use a variety of strategies to explore how categorical identities affect the work-family interface. In qualitative studies, respondents might be asked how particular combinations of identities affect their functioning at work and at home. Sample questions could be, "How has being a Latina [Latino] affected your expectations of yourself as an employee?" or "How does being a gay [lesbian] African American affect what you share about your work with your partner?" For quantitative researchers, perhaps a first step is to construct identity statements that are specified in terms of work and family variables and scored on 5-point or 7-point Likert-type scales, with responses ranging from "strongly agree" to "strongly disagree" or from "very much" to "very little" and so on. In this case, sample questions could be, "My race gives me comfort and strength to cope with the stresses at work that come from coworkers," "I take pride in being a gay [lesbian] professional," and "I would bring fewer stresses home from work if my race and gender were different."

CONCLUDING THOUGHTS

The fact that most of our methodological suggestions have been quantitatively focused does not mean that we are arguing for an exclusively quantitative approach to the exploration of social categories. We do think, however, that when quantitative researchers become more serious about the inclusion of such categories in their studies, our knowledge of families will take a great leap forward. Still, the best leads concerning *how* to include these categories will probably come from qualitative researchers. Narrative phenomenological accounts, open-ended interviews, novels and films, autobiographical statements, focus groups, and case studies from clinicians are all examples of sources on which quantitative researchers might draw (Dilworth-Anderson, Burton, & Johnson, 1993). The best research has always been an imaginative reconstruction of how the world works. The links we draw between work and home, the items we create to measure the strength of a racial, sexual, gender, feminist, or social-class identity, the way we operationalize the stresses at work or at home that spring in some way from our social categories, the way we see if a particular identity is either exacerbating or attenuating stress from work, the strategies we devise for including both the macro- and microcontext as variables that enhance or hinder the bridging of work and home are creative analytical challenges. They will best be addressed through drawing on the diversity of perspectives that make up our disciplines, our passions, and our politics.

Earlier, we considered theories of intersectionality that emphasize the simultaneous impact of multiple social categories. We also appealed to the need for greater clarity in identifying intersectionality as something recognizably *lived*. Later, in thinking about how to include social categories in quantitative studies, we sometimes reverted more to an additive model—how do we explore important variations in well-being that are due to race, *and* class, *and* gender, *and* other elements of that "illimitable et cetera" of categories? (Butler, 1990, p. 143). The casualty of this second approach, of course, is that we lose the *meeting points* of categories, their intersectionality. For now, we must live with the contradiction. Conceptualization and theory always run ahead of quantitative research practice, and we do not yet know how to build concepts of intersectionality into quantitative studies. In the meantime, the best we can do is to urge theorists to continue to think about how social categories intersect and researchers to pay much closer attention to the multiple hierarchies that shape people's experiences in families.

REFERENCES

Andersen, M., & Collins, P. H. (Eds.). (1998). *Race, class, and gender: An anthology* (3rd ed.). Belmont, CA: Wadsworth.

Barkan, S. (1998). *Discovering sociology: An introduction using Explorit.* Bellevue, WA: MicroCase.

Barnett, R. C. (1994). Home-to-work spillover revisited: A study of full-time employed women in dual-earner couples. *Journal of Marriage and the Family, 56,* 647–656.

Barnett, R. C., & Baruch, G. K. (1985). Women's involvement in multiple roles and psychological distress. *Journal of Personality and Social Psychology, 49,* 135–145.

Barnett, R. C., & Baruch, G. K. (1987). Social roles, gender, and psychological distress. In R. C. Barnett, L. Biener, & G. K. Baruch (Eds.), *Gender and stress* (pp. 122–143). New York: Free Press.

Barnett, R. C., Brennan, R. T., Raudenbush, S. W., & Marshall, N. L. (1994). Gender and the relationship between marital-role quality and psychological distress. *Psychology of Women Quarterly, 18,* 105–127.

Barnett, R. C., Marshall N. L., & Pleck, J. H. (1992). Men's multiple roles and their relationship to men's psychological distress. *Journal of Marriage and the Family, 54,* 358–367.

Beale, F. (1969). Double jeopardy: To be black and female. In R. Morgan (Ed.), *Sisterhood is powerful* (pp. 340–353). New York: Vintage Books.

Benner, C., & Rosner, R. (1998). Living wage: An opportunity for San Jose. Working Partnerships USA: www.atwork.org/wp/lw/

Berardo, D. H., Shehan, C. L., & Leslie, G. R. (1987). A residue of tradition: Jobs, careers, and spouses' time in housework. *Journal of Marriage and the Family, 49,* 381–390.

Billingsley, A. (1992). *Climbing Jacob's ladder: The enduring legacy of African-American families.* New York: Simon & Schuster.

Blumstein, P., & Schwartz, P. (1983). *American couples.* New York: Morrow.

Bonilla-Silva, E. (1997). Rethinking racism: Toward a structural interpretation. *American Sociological Review, 62,* 465–480.

Bordo, S. (1990). Feminism, postmodernism, and gender-scepticism. In L. J. Nicholson (Ed.), *Feminism/ postmodernism* (pp. 133–156). New York: Routledge.

Bowen, G. L., & Pittman, J. F. (Eds.). (1995). *The work and family interface: Toward a contextual effects per-spective.* Minneapolis, MN: National Council on Family Relations.

Broman, C. L. (1991). Gender, work-family roles, and psychological well-being of blacks. *Journal of Marriage and the Family, 53,* 509–520.

Broman, C. L. (1993). Race difference in marital well-being. *Journal of Marriage and the Family, 55,* 724–732.

Bureau of Justice Statistics. (1997). *Criminal victimization in the United States, 1994: A national crime victimization survey report.* Washington, DC: U. S. Department of Justice.

Butler, J. (1990). *Gender trouble: Feminism and the subversion of identity.* New York: Routledge.

Butler, J. (1993). *Bodies that matter: On the discursive limits of "sex."* New York: Routledge.

Cleaver, E. (1967). *Soul on ice.* New York: McGraw-Hill.

Collins, P. H. (1990). *Black feminist thought: Knowledge, consciousness, and the politics of empowerment.* New York: Routledge.

Collins, P. H. (1995). Symposium on West and Fenstermaker's "Doing Difference." *Gender & Society, 9,* 491–494.

Coleman, L. M., Antonucci, T. C., Adelmann, P. K., & Crohan, S. E. (1987). Social roles in the lives of middle-aged and older black women. *Journal of Marriage and the Family, 49,* 761–771.

Combahee River Collective. (1982). A black feminist statement. In G. T. Hull, P. B. Scott, & Smith (Eds.), *All the women are white, all the blacks are men, but some of us are brave* (pp. 13–22). New York: Feminist Press.

Dilworth-Anderson, P., Burton, L. M., & Johnson, L. B. (1993). Reframing theories for understanding race, ethnicity, and families. In P. G. Boss, W. J. Doherty, R. LaRossa, W. R. Schumm, & S. K. Steinmetz (Eds.), *Sourcebook of family theories and methods* (pp. 627–646). New York: Plenum.

DuBois, W. E. B. (1961). *The souls of black folk.* New York: Crest. (Original work published 1903)

Ebert, T. L. (1996). *Ludic feminism and after: Postmodernism, desire, and labor in late capital.* Ann Arbor: University of Michigan Press.

Faderman, L. (1991). *Odd girls and twilight lovers: A history of lesbian life in twentieth-century America.* New York: Penguin.

Feinberg, L. (1993). *Stone butch blues.* Ithaca, NY: Firebrand.

Franklin, A. J. (1993, July–August). The invisibility syndrome. *Family Therapy Networker,* pp. 33–39.

Frone, M. R., Russell, M., & Cooper, M. L. (1992). Antecedents and outcomes of work-family conflict: Testing a model of work-family interface. *Journal of Applied Psychology, 77,* 65–78.

Frye, M. (1983). *The politics of reality: Essays in feminist theory.* Freedom, CA: Crossing Press.

Goffman, E. (1963). *Stigma: Notes on the management of a spoiled identity.* Englewood Cliffs, NJ: Prentice Hall.

Gomez, J. L., & Smith, B. (1990). Taking the home *out of* homophobia. In L. Richardson & V. Taylor (Eds.), *Feminist frontiers III* (pp. 513–519). New York: McGraw-Hill.

Goode, W. J. (1960). A theory of role strain. *American Sociological Review, 25,* 483–496.

Gove, W. R., & Zeiss, C. (1987). Multiple roles and happiness. In F. J. Crosby (Ed.), *Spouse, parent, worker: On gender and multiple roles* (pp. 126–137). New Haven, CT: Yale University Press.

Green, H. (1996). Turning the myths of black masculinity inside/out. In B. Thompson & S. Tyagi (Eds.), *Names we call home: Autobiography on racial identity* (pp. 253–263). New York: Routledge.

Hacker, A. (1992). *Two nations: Black and white, separate, hostile, unequal.* New York: Ballantine.

Hochschild, A. (1989). *The second shift: Working parents and the revolution at home.* New York: Viking Press.

hooks, b. (1995). *Killing rage.* New York: Henry Holt.

Hossain, Z., & Roopnarine, J. L. (1993). Division of household labor and child care in dual-earner African-American families with infants. *Sex Roles, 29,* 571–583.

House, J. S., Landis, K. R., & Umberson, D. (1988). Social relationships and health. *Science, 241,* 540–545.

Johnson, E. M., & Huston, T. L. (1998). The perils of love, or why wives adapt to husbands during the transition to parenthood. *Journal of Marriage and the Family, 60,* 195–204.

Jordan, J. (1998a). A new politics of sexuality. In M. L. Andersen & P. H. Collins (Eds.), *Race, class, and gender: An anthology* (3rd ed., pp. 437–441). Belmont, CA: Wadsworth.

Jordan, J. (1998b). Report from the Bahamas. In M. L. Andersen & P. H. Collins (Eds.), *Race, class, and gender: An anthology* (3rd ed., pp. 34–43). Belmont, CA: Wadsworth.

Komter, A. (1989). Hidden power in marriage. *Gender & Society, 3,* 187–216.

LaRossa, R. (1988). Fatherhood and social change. *Family Relations, 37,* 451–457.

Leslie, L. A., & Anderson, E. A. (1988). Men's and women's participation in domestic roles: Impact on quality of life and marital adjustment. *Journal of Family Psychology, 2,* 212–226.

Lorber, J. (1996). Beyond the binaries: Depolarizing the categories of sex, sexuality, and gender. *Sociological Inquiry, 66,* 143–159.

Lorde, A. (1982) *Zami: A new spelling of my name.* Freedom, CA: Crossing Press.

Lorde, A. (1984). Age, race, class and sex: Women redefining difference. In *Sister outsider* (pp. 114–123). Freedom, CA: Crossing Press.

Lugones, M. (1990). Hablando cara a cara/Speaking face to face: An exploration of ethnocentric racism. In L. Richardson & V. Taylor (Eds.), *Feminist frontiers III* (pp. 51–56). New York: McGraw-Hill.

Maldonado, L. A. (1995). Symposium on West and Fenstermaker's "doing difference." *Gender & Society, 9,* 494–496.

Marks, S. R. (1977). Multiple roles and role strain: Some notes on human energy, time, and commitment. *American Sociological Review, 42,* 921–936.

Marks, S. R., & MacDermid, S. M. (1996). Multiple roles and the self: A theory of role balance. *Journal of Marriage and the Family, 58,* 417–432.

Martin, B. (1994). Sexualities without genders and other queer utopias. *Diacritics, 24,* 104–121.

McIntosh, P. (1998). White privilege and male privilege: A personal account of coming to see correspondences through work in women's studies. In M. L. Andersen & P. H. Collins (Eds.), *Race, class, and gender: An anthology* (3rd ed., pp. 94–105). Belmont, CA: Wadsworth.

Nestle, J. (1987). *A restricted country.* Ithaca, NY: Firebrand.

Nicholson, L. J. (Ed.). (1990). *Feminism/postmodernism.* New York: Routledge.

Oggins, J., Veroff, J., & Leber, D. (1993). Perceptions of marital interaction among black and white newlyweds. *Journal of Personality and Social Psychology, 65,* 494–511.

Orbuch, T., & Custer, L. (1995). The social context of married women's work and its impact on black husbands and white husbands. *Journal of Marriage and the Family, 57,* 333–345.

Phelan, S. (1989). *Identity politics: Lesbian feminism and the limits of community.* Philadelphia: Temple University Press.

Pleck, J. H. (1985). *Working wives/Working husbands.* Beverly Hills, CA: Sage.

Reagon, B. J. (1983). Coalition politics: Turning the century. In B. Smith (Ed.), *Home girls: A black feminist anthology* (pp. 356–358). New York: Kitchen Table Press.

Rich, A. (1980). Compulsory heterosexuality and lesbian existence. *Signs, 5,* 631–660.

Rushing, B., Ritter, C., & Burton, R. P. (1992). Race differences in the effects of multiple roles on health: Longitudinal evidence from a national sample of older men. *Journal of Health and Social Behavior, 33,* 126–139.

Sieber, S. (1974). Toward a theory of role accumulation. *American Sociological Review, 39,* 567–578.

Simon, R. (1995). Gender, multiple roles, role meaning, and mental health. *Journal of Health and Social Behavior, 36,* 182–194.

Stein, A. (1997). *Sex and sensibility: Stories of a lesbian generation.* Berkeley: University of California Press.

Stoltenberg, J. (1990). *Refusing to be a man.* New York: Meridian.

Thoits, P. A. (1992). Identity structures and psychological well-being: Gender and marital status comparisons. *Social Psychology Quarterly, 55,* 236–256.

Thorne, B. (1995). Symposium on West and Fenstermaker's "doing difference." *Gender & Society, 9,* 497–499.

U.S. Bureau of the Census. (1995). *Statistical abstracts of the U.S.: The national data book.* Washington, DC: U.S. Department of Commerce, Economics and Statistics Administration.

Voydanoff, P. (1988). Work role characteristics, family structure demands, and work/family conflict. *Journal of Marriage and the Family, 50,* 749–761.

Waldron, I., & Jacobs, J. A. (1989). Effects of multiple roles on women's health—Evidence from a national longitudinal study. *Women & Health, 15,* 3–19.

Walters, S. D. (1996). From here to queer: Radical feminism, postmodernism, and the lesbian menace (Or, why can't a woman be more like a fag?). *Signs, 21,* 830–869.

Weber, L. (1995). Symposium on West and Fenstermaker's "doing difference." *Gender & Society, 9,* 499–503.

Wellman, D. (1996). Red and white in black America: Discovering cross-border identities and other subversive activities. In B. Thompson & S. Tyagi (Eds.), *Names we call home: Autobiography on racial identity* (pp. 29–41). New York: Routledge.

Welter, B. (1966). The cult of true womanhood. *American Quarterly, 18,* 151–174.

West, C., & Fenstermaker, S. (1995a). Doing difference. *Gender & Society, 9,* 8–37.

West, C., & Fenstermaker, S. (1995b). Reply: (Re)doing difference. *Gender & Society, 9,* 506–513.

West, C. (1994). *Race matters.* New York: Vintage Books.

White, C. L., & Burke, P. J. (1987). Ethnic role identity among black and white college students. *Sociological Perspectives, 30,* 310–331.

White, C. W. (1995). Toward an Afra-American feminism. In J. Freeman (Ed.), *Women: A feminist perspective* (5th ed., pp. 529–546). Mountain View, CA: Mayfield.

Winant, H. (1995). Symposium on West and Fenstermaker's "doing difference." *Gender & Society, 9,* 503–506.

Young, I. M. (1990). The ideal of community and the politics of difference. In L. J. Nicholson (Ed.), *Feminism/postmodernism* (pp. 300–323). New York: Routledge.

Zvonkovic, A. M., Greaves, K. M., Schmiege, C. J., & Hall, L. D. (1996). The marital construction of gender through work and family decisions: A qualitative analysis. *Journal of Marriage and the Family, 58,* 91–100.

CHAPTER 21

The Handbook's Tail: Toward Revels or a Requiem for Family Diversity?

JUDITH STACEY

On a spring afternoon half a century from today, the Joneses are gathering to sing "Happy Birthday" to Junior.

There's Dad and his third wife, Mom and her second husband, Junior's two half brothers from his father's first marriage, his six stepsisters from his mother's spouse's previous unions, 100-year-old Great-Grandpa, all eight of Junior's current "grandparents," assorted aunts, uncles-in-law and stepcousins.

While one robot scoops up the gift wrappings and another blows out the candles, Junior makes a wish—that he didn't have so many relatives.

The family tree by the year 2033 will be rooted as deeply as ever in America's social landscape, but it will be sprouting some odd branches.

—*U.S. NEWS & WORLD REPORT*, 1983

Seventeen years ago, *U.S. News & World Report* (When "family" will have a new definition, 1983) posed the same impossible challenge to an assortment of social scientists that the editors of this volume assigned me—to project the future trajectory of family change into the next half century. I open with the magazine's synthesis of that earlier collective crystal-ball exercise to simplify my present, more solitary, one. Our world today has traveled one third of the distance to the year 2033. Perhaps by assessing the ways in which contemporary family patterns and meanings compare with the kind of kinship formation those 1983 forecasters predicted would have become normative by then, I can prepare a more prophetic one.

However bold and visionary those social scientists may have felt, the presumptions governing the contours of Junior's imaginary kindred that they projected should strike their counterparts today as almost quaintly traditionalist. Indeed, what now seems odd about their portrait of a modal 21st century family is how innocently conventional, parochial, and ethnocentric it already appears. The trajectory they predicted seems to presume a linear progression from the practices of serial marriage, divorce, and remarriage that have become increasingly normative among primarily white, Euro-American, middle-class, heterosexuals. The kindred they chose to conjure are the presumptively white, Anglo Saxon, protestant Joneses, after all, who gather to celebrate the birth of one of their patronymically christened "Junior" heirs in a technologically well-equipped abode. Apparently all Junior's relatives either live within easy reach or enjoy sufficient affluence to afford long-distance travel to attend birthday celebrations for even a stepcousin. Curiously, too, all the assembled guests are related by birth, marriage, or divorce. Junior appears to have no chosen kin or friend that he or the party's hosts take to be as intimate or valued as even distant relatives. The social forecasters gave no indication that any of Junior's relatives might be lesbian, gay, or in any way "queer." He has neither adoptive nor foster kin. None of his adult relatives seems to be a single parent or to cohabit.

Indeed, the social scientists seem to have presumed that well into the 21st century "dad" and "mom" would remain singular and unproblematic concepts. They felt no cause to specify whether the "dad" would be a sperm dad or a social father, or whether "mom" would be a birth mom, a gestational mom, a custodial mom, or a co-mom. They mentioned no surrogates, paraparents, godparents, or guardians. They made no reference to progeny conceived with the assistance of reproductive technology or alluded to the specter of cloning. No workplace demands prevented a relative from attending, nor did ill health, death, custody disputes, or incarceration threaten to diminish the number or joy of Junior's assembled kin. In short, as the other chapters of this Handbook make clear, even though we have not yet traversed half the distance to the family future that prominent social scientists envisioned in 1983, the branches that our families are sprouting now are already much "odder" and far more diverse than they then dared to imagine.

Equally quaint today appears the social scientists' confidence that "the family tree" will remain so "firmly rooted," not to speak of so harmoniously extended. Few of those scholars' contemporary counterparts seem as sanguine about the character or security of family ties. Note how many anxious titles adorn books about U.S. family life that were published in the 1990s—*Brave New Families* (Stacey, 1990), *Embattled Paradise* (Skolnick, 1991), *Fatherless America* (Blankenhorn, 1995), *No Man's Land* (Gerson, 1993), *Families on the Fault Line* (Rubin, 1994), *Declining Fortunes* (Newman, 1993), *Promises to Keep* (Popenoe, Elshtain, & Blankenhorn, 1996), *Life Without Father* (Popenoe, 1996), *Balancing Act* (Spain & Bianchi, 1996), *Divorce Culture* (Whitehead, 1997), *The Abolition of Marriage* (Gallagher, 1996), *Divided Families* (Furstenberg & Cherlin, 1991), *The Way We Really Are* (Coontz, 1997), *The Minimal Family* (Dizard & Gadlin 1991), and *The Neutered Mother, the Sexual Family and Other Twentieth Century Tragedies* (Fineman, 1995). Note, too, the incessant outpouring of jeremiads about family crisis, instability, and decline that flourished in the media and the political arena as the 20th century expired. Despite the fact that the right-wing "profamily" movement had already played a prominent part in the Reagan "revolution," the social scientists queried in 1983 seem

to have believed that the movement's impact on future family forms would be inconsequential. Clearly, they did not anticipate how rapidly campaigns for "family values" would proliferate across the ideological spectrum, let alone that within a decade, some social scientists themselves would be spearheading a secular "cultural crusade" for family values with vast influence on public discourse and politics.[1]

It seems unlikely, therefore, that those social scientists would have predicted the character of the four items that one family meteorologist would be adding to her clippings files on a day in June 1997 when she first sat down to speculate in family futures:

1. A *New York Times* article announcing, "Louisiana Approves Measure to Tighten Marriage Bonds" (Sack, 1997)

2. An E-mail message from a Norwegian colleague alerting me that "the Danes are just about to put up a ban for buying sperm for women who are not in a stable heterosexual relationship with a man (We Norwegians already have a ban, because sperm is only available at public clinics, and there they accept only heterosexual couples)" (personal communication from Hanne Haavind, June 23, 1997)

3. A *San Francisco Chronicle* journalist's report on a three-day conference held at Georgetown University, entitled "Conservatives Brand Homosexuality a 'Tragic Affliction'" (Lochhead, 1997)

4. A *San Francisco Chronicle* wire service story on militant antiabortion leader Randall Terry, entitled "Operation Rescue Head to Run for Congress" (1997)

Can a contemporary family scholar fare any better predicting how historians in the year 2033 will be inclined to interpret these four shards of contemporary family politics than the 1983 *U.S. News & World Report* summary seems to have done in anticipating these events? That is, of course, for readers and ultimately for history to judge. It may

[1] I discuss the use and abuse of social science by secular family-values crusaders at length in Stacey (1996).

help the former to understand some of the personal and professional stakes I bring to the task. (Or so, at least, the editors of this volume believe, since they asked the contributors to account for our interest in family diversity in such terms.) It is quite a challenge to do so briefly without resorting to the use of politicized labels and concepts that can mislead and estrange many readers.

ROOTS OF RESISTANCE

If I begin, for example, by identifying some of my interest in family diversity as rooted in feminist theory and politics, many readers will take it as an admission of a compromising "bias" and fear it will lead me to violate scholarly conventions of "objectivity" and "balance." Some are likely to presume that I harbor hostility to men or perhaps even to "the family" itself. Indeed, there is a misleading kernel of truth in the latter of these worries. Like many feminists, I find the concept of "the family" to be unwittingly pernicious, as well as intellectually misguided, because it fuels the illusion that there is a timeless, uniform, "natural" character to appropriate gender and kinship relationships. All my personal experience and research indicate the reverse, however—that gender and kinship forms assume dramatically different forms and meanings across historical time and cultural space. To modify a wise Marxist axiom, men *and women* make *families and* history, but not under conditions of our own choosing.

The natal family conditions that I did not choose were part of the underbelly of the 1950s "Leave It to Beaver" male breadwinner family. In fact, there is a private double-entendre to the subtitle, "Stories of Domestic Upheaval in Late Twentieth Century America" that I gave to one of my books about family change (Stacey, 1990). My own family history is marked by upheavals that intersect with many of those I narrated in the ethnographic portions of that book, as with the broader social trends the book interpreted. Indeed, I could readily produce a reductionist, but not false, narrative about how my long intellectual preoccupation with family transformations, as well as the best-honed undergradu-

ate course I teach on the making and unmaking of the modern family, were propelled by the painful discrepancy between the sentimentalized 1950s family ideology that was culturally dominant during my teenage years and the grittier texture of life in my troubled natal family.

I grew up in New Jersey during the 1940s and 1950s suffering the underside of Ozzie and Harriet-land in an "intact," lower-middle-class, nuclear family. Until both her children had begun their own first marriages, my mother—a frustrated, socially ambitious, intermittently full-time homemaker—sustained an overtly hostile, incompatible marriage to my father—a distant, depressed, working-class breadwinner—for fear of the severe social stigma and economic risks of divorce. My quotidien, experiential curriculum documented the hollowness of the modern family ideal, but, like most children, I fancied my own family's pain no critique of the institution, but an anomalous and disgraceful instance of its failure. In consequence, it was a family pattern I felt compelled to replicate until I was liberated by the "domestic upheavals" of the 1960s.

A true product of the 1950s gender culture, I had no educational or career goals of my own, but devoted my undergraduate years in the early 1960s to seeking a husband. Immediately after I graduated from college, I married a medical student and moved with him to Chicago, where I spent the next three years teaching social studies in secondary schools, earning what we young working wives of student doctors in that period called our Ph.T. (putting hubby through) degrees. Synergistic effects of Sputnik, Vietnam, civil rights, marijuana, and later feminism gradually rescued me from this ill-suited, feminine life course.

Thus, I had already divorced my first spouse, as had my parents by then, and had begun to develop a political consciousness, when feminism entered and redirected my life in 1970. "Feminism provided an analysis and rhetoric for their discontent, and it helped each woman develop the self-esteem she needed to exit or reform her unhappy modern marriage" (Stacey, 1991, p. 23) and to pursue educational and occupational interests of her own, I would write 20 years later about Pam and Dotty, the central subjects of *Brave New Families* (Stacey, 1990). However, I neglected to indicate the autobiographical roots of this insight. So profoundly did feminism alter my consciousness and commitments that it has inspired my vocation ever since. In this sense, whatever hostility motivates my research on family diversity is directed not to men, but to social injustice. I know with head and heart that an idealized family structure can be far from ideal in practice and that the very practice of idealizing one form can cause harm, not only to those it excludes, but to those who appear to inhabit it. Thus, I commit a good deal of my intellectual resources and pedagogical efforts to promoting social support for family diversity. Recently I have joined other family researchers and clinicians in organizing the Council on Contemporary Families to foster better public understanding of the causes and consequences of our changing patterns of family life.

BACK TO THE FUTURE AGAIN

Will the society that future historians inhabit share my commitment to family diversity? Will it have achieved the kind of harmonious equanimity regarding divorce-extended kin ties that the 1983 social scientists envisioned? Two years after the *U.S. News & World Report* story, novelist Atwood (1985) imagined a future convention of historians meeting some time after their society had been liberated from a repressive patriarchal regime that she named Gilead. The epilogue to Atwood's dystopia, *The Handmaid's Tale,* parodies the discourse of scholars who, during a session of the 12th Symposium on Gileadean Studies at the International Historical Association Convention held in June of 2195, struggle to interpret a harrowing captivity diary written by a woman who had been conscripted into service as a gestational surrogate under the, by-then extinct, totalitarian, patriarchal family regime of Gilead.

It is easy to imagine such scholars reading my June 1997 file clippings as archival evidence that our society is in the midst of a historical prelude to the world in which the novel's protagonist, the handmaid Offred, recorded her ordeal. For on the

surface, all four items recorded overtly reactionary efforts to repudiate family diversity and to return to a singular model of family life composed of heterosexual married couples and their biological children. Future family historians could read these documents as evidence that as the 20th century drew to close, a backlash against family diversity was progressing on a global scale. They might read in these events the rise of a Gilead. Indeed, one can readily make a case that prospects for the emergence of the kind of repressive patriarchy that Atwood's dystopia projected have gained, rather than lost, credibility since *The Handmaid's Tale* was published in 1985.

At the same time, however, my four file clippings also offer evidence of the strength (and, I will argue, irreversibility) of the very postmodern family condition—a condition of fluidity, diversity, patchwork, ambiguity, and contest—that they quixotically try to oppose. There are three definitive features of postmodern kinship, and they show few signs of waning. First, postmodern kinship refers to the global reorganization of the gender division of labor and identity in families and work that long characterized the "modern industrial system." Whereas the male breadwinner–female homemaker nuclear family model dominated that epoch, postindustrial labor conditions have disrupted that system and have generated family fluidity and diversity. Second, and perhaps most definitively postmodern, the once seemingly natural character of "the family" has dissolved as formerly integrated domains of intimacy have become discrete and discretionary. Whereas marriage, heterosexuality, procreation (even conception and gestation), parenthood, child rearing, and kinship status once involved relatively uniform, integral, and orderly relationships and practices, now each is separable, contingent, and unpredictible. It is possible, for example, for one woman to "donate" an ovum that can be fertilized by anonymous sperm in a laboratory setting, implanted in the uterus of another woman to gestate, until it becomes a baby, who, in turn, can be adopted and reared by yet another woman, a man, a couple, or a group of individuals of any genders. Who is the "mother" or "father" of such a child?

And what is the child's "family?" Precisely because the answers to questions like these, which once seemed self-evident, are no longer obvious, a third feature of the postmodern family condition is now endemic. Contests over the underlying meanings of gender and sexuality and of the "family values" they encode have become ever more visible, divisive, politicized, and consequential. No single model of family enjoys the kind of undisputed statistical or cultural hegemony that the modern family system once had.

Consider, for example, a cartoon about contemporary family life that appeared in 1994—the year mandated by the United Nations as the International Year of the Family—in the *New Yorker,* a magazine popular among many members of the intelligentsia in the United States. The cartoon depicts a Caucasian mother in a middle-class home, who, angry with her child, chastizes him with this threat: "Just wait until your *other* mother gets home, young man!" To understand the humor in this cartoon, one needs a specific kind of local cultural knowledge. First, you have to recognize the commonplace threat, "Just wait til your father gets home, young man [or young lady]!" which exasperated mothers of one vanishing type of family in the United States—the male breadwinner–full-time female homemaker nuclear family—used to level at their disobedient offspring. Next you must recognize the new and controversial kind of family pattern spoofed in the cartoon—a nuclear family composed of two lesbians and children who were conceived through alternative insemination. The "other mother" is a lesbian coparent, of course.

Yet further reflection on this cartoon helps to underscore the historical and cultural specificity of family meaning, change, and politics. Even in the contemporary United States, many respondents may supply various different and plausible spontaneous answers to the question "who is the other mother?" Feminist sociologist Collins (1990), for example, used the term "other mothers" to signify a pattern of diffused and shared responsibility for child rearing practiced among networks of low-income African American female kin and friends. The "other mother" could also refer to a stepmother

in a "blended" family formed through remarriage after the divorce of one or both of the spouses. Alternatively, the cartoon figure could be a nanny working for a working mother (like the television-sitcom heroine, Murphy Brown, who became a symbolic figure during the 1992 U.S. presidential election) or a "surrogate" mother with visitation rights to her biological child or an adoptive mother waiting for the child's birth mother to arrive. The possibilities are numerous, almost as numerous as the types of family life practiced in the United States today, and they would expand greatly if the cartoon was circulated beyond the nation's borders. The cartoon figure could refer to polygynous cowives, for example, or matrilineal sisters. For "mother," as feminists have demonstrated, is not a biological, but a social, category, one that changes meaning across cultural and historical terrain.

The social character of the concept is even more true of "the family." Although all the cultures and historical eras that I know of have applied some category like mother to a woman who bears and nurtures the young, not nearly so many have used the category "the family." Nor have those that did, used it to mean what people in much earlier times and other places connoted with that term. The concept is a peculiarly Western and modern one, and it has a particular history that has brought the concept, along with the kinship system it came to index, into a period of intense political contest and acrimony.

Thus, the four additions to my family files, despite their reactionary thrust, all signal postmodern processes that denaturalize and politicize reproduction and kinship. Moreover, each of the events they documented is likely to produce unanticipated effects on future families. Indeed, they promise not to resolve, but to deepen the contradictions and paradoxes of postmodern kinship and thereby to foster *more,* rather than less, family diversity. For example, in its wish to "slow down the hemorrhaging of the American family through the no-fault divorce system" (Sack, 1997, p. A14), the Louisiana legislature voted, with near-unanimity, to give heterosexual couples the option of voluntarily entering a "covenant marriage" that would be far more binding than ordinary marriage contracts. The legislators believed, as the bill's sponsor explained, that this option "will prevent potentially weak marriages in some cases" (quoted in Sack, 1997, p. A14) by forcing couples to reflect more seriously on their level of commitment and compatibility: "When a man says he wants a no-fault marriage," the sponsor elaborated, "and a woman says she wants a covenant marriage, that's going to raise some red flags. She's going to say, 'What? You're not willing to have a lifelong commitment to me?'" (Sack, 1997, p. A14). Whether or not the covenant-marriage option will ultimately serve to strengthen marriage as an institution—an outcome I think is unlikely—in adopting a two-tier system of marriage and divorce, the Louisiana legislature has unwittingly proliferated family diversity. Compelling couples to choose between "no-fault" and "covenant" marriage expands the range of legitimate family structures and fosters greater self-consciousness about our culture's pluralist family values. Moreover, the addition of covenant marriage is likely to further diminish the social status and perhaps the seriousness of noncovenant marriage vows. Such a development may even open a back door to institutionalizing cohabitation and, paradoxically, may ultimately lower political barriers to same-sex marriage. For example, a two-tier marriage system may raise questions about the applicability of the antigay federal Defense of Marriage Act, such as these: To which kind of marriage would or should it apply? Should the state defend the marriages of heterosexuals who are unwilling to enter a covenant? If not, why not extend noncovenant marriage rights to same-sex couples?

The new Danish proposal to restrict access to sperm in clinics to heterosexual couples is equally paradoxical, as well as surprising in light of Denmark's global leadership in providing all the legal rights of marriage except adoption and custody to same-sex "registered partnerships." Although restricting access to sperm may seem consistent with this policy, it, too, further institutionalizes family diversity by distinguishing between procreative and nonprocreative family structures, as well as between public and private family planning strategies. Also ripe with paradox was the 1997 confer-

ence that the conservative American Public Philosophy Institute organized at Georgetown University to portray homosexuality "as a tragic affliction, with harmful consequences for both individuals and society" (quoted in Lochhead, 1997, p. A4). Reversing the conventional political polarities of the age-old nature-nurture debate, the conference speakers dismissed biological explanations for homosexuality. Historically, progressives have vigorously opposed biologically determinist social theories, rejecting them as politically reactionary. Indeed, in the current period, postmodernist and queer theorists have criticized "essentialism" so dogmatically that even Ehrenreich (1997), a feminist leftist, has challenged this stance as the "new creationism." Paradoxically, the conservatives at Georgetown ridiculed the search for a "gay gene" as a ploy by gay activists to gain public sympathy for gay rights (Lochhead, 1997).

Finally, Randall Terry, head of Operation Rescue, announced his candidacy for Congress on an antiabortion, antigay platform. Yet when he promised to fight for "legal protection for preborn babies" and against "militant homosexuals who are trying to destroy the institution of marriage and seduce our sons and daughters" ("Operation Rescue Head," 1997, p. A3), he also escalated contemporary political contests over reproduction and sexuality by inciting a countermobilization to defend the very rights to abortion and sexual expression that his campaign threatened.

Although one cannot possibly predict how future historians will interpret these archival shards of our contemporary family culture, I feel safe predicting the futility of efforts to reverse family diversity. For better and worse, we cannot go "home" again to the comparative regularities and certitudes of the modern gender and family regime. Modernization theorists once predicted that all societies in the world would converge toward the modern Western conjugal family system (see Goode, 1963). Instead, we are witnessing global convergence toward the postmodern condition of family diversity, flux, instability, and ideological struggle. As I indicate later, instead of *raising* "the family" as a standard around the world, the development of a "global village" has *razed* "the family" system in postindustrial societies and disrupted traditional family and kinships systems elsewhere.

RAZING "THE FAMILY"

The global character of these upheavals is readily documented. Not only throughout postindustrial societies, but increasingly in Third World societies, demographers have recorded rising rates of divorce and unwed motherhood, declining birth rates, the feminization of poverty, and the increasing economic contributions and burdens of women who are struggling to sustain their families while increasing numbers of men join the ranks of what U.S. politicians call "deadbeat dads" or what historian Gillis (1996) more aptly termed "family-less fathers." In short, kinship forms are feminizing and diversifying internationally.

"Divorce culture," as some alarmists have termed it, is a prominent feature of global family life. A recent U.S. cartoon captured some of the cultural impact of the normalization of divorce: A minister performing a wedding ceremony addresses the assembled guests: "If there is anyone present who for even one minute believes this union will last forever, speak now so the rest of us can have a good laugh" (Pisaro, 1996). The humor intended here is becoming ever more comprehensible across national borders. Between the 1970s and the 1990s, according to the Population Council in the United States, the divorce rate doubled in most postindustrial nations. For example, in France, it rose from 12% in 1970 to 31.5% in 1990, and in Denmark, it rose from 25% to 44% (Bruce, Lloyd, Leonard, Engle, & Duffy, 1995, p. 20). Demographers (see Bumpass & Sweet, 1987) have estimated that between 45% and 60% of contemporary marriages in the United States will end in divorce. Even in most of the "less developed" nations surveyed by the Population Council, at least 25% of first marriages dissolve by the time women are in their 40s (Bruce et al., 1995, p. 15).

Similarly, births to unwed mothers have risen sharply throughout postindustrial societies and in many underdeveloped societies. More than one third of all births in northern Europe occur outside marriage, with Sweden, where unwed childbearing is now more commonplace than marital births, in the "lead" (Bruce et al., 1995, p. 20). Approximately one third of contemporary births in the United States take place outside marriage, and the rates among African American women are more than twice as high as the national average. Although the rates of unwed childbearing in Western Europe are somewhat lower, around 20%, they are almost exactly what they were among African American women in the 1960s, when Moynihan (1965) issued his alarmist report on the "tangle of pathology" in such families. Again, this is not exclusively a postindustrial phenomenon because similar rates of unwed childbearing have also become widespread throughout many impoverished regions of sub-Saharan Africa and the Caribbean.[2]

Declining birth rates are equally dramatic throughout postindustrial societies and in numerous industrializing nations. Particularly startling is the fact that Italy and Spain—two European nations with predominantly Catholic populations, both of which have less developed postindustrial economies than others—have birth rates that are among the lowest in the world. Likewise, since the fall of communism, many Eastern European nations of the former Soviet Union have been confronting population crises because their birth rates have fallen well below replacement rates (Kinzer, 1994). At the same time, China's aggressive one-child family policy, designed to address the reverse crisis of overpopulation, has dramatically reduced Chinese birth rates.

The normalization of paid employment for women, particularly married mothers of even young children, is one of the definitive features of postindustrial societies and the postmodern family condition. In the United States, nearly 50% of married women in the paid labor force are earning at least half their families' income (Bruce et al., 1995), and 29% of employed wives now earn more than their husbands do (Clark, 1996). However, because men have displayed much less willingness to per-

[2]For example, more than 20% of the births in Botswana, Cameroon, Kenya, Liberia, Madagascar, Namibia, and Tanzania are out of wedlock. Even several Latin American countries, like Bolivia, Columbia, and Paraguay, have reported rates of out-of-wedlock births greater than 10% (Bruce et al., 1995, p. 19).

form women's traditional unpaid work of caretaking, child rearing, and household maintenance, the double burden that women bear is also increasingly international. Time-budget studies have indicated that employed women's actual work hours exceed those of employed men by 20% in 12 industrialized nations. The situation is even worse in studies of "less developed nations" summarized in Bruce et al. (1995, pp. 29–33): Women work an average of 30% to 40% more hours than do the men in their societies. In Ghana, half the households with children are supported primarily or exclusively by women. In the Philippines, women earn one third of their families' cash resources, but the value of their unpaid productive labor (such as growing food and gathering wood) boosts their contribution to the support of their households to 55%. Moreover, throughout the world, even when men earn more than do the women in their families, women typically contribute a much higher proportion of their earnings than do men to the collective familial pot.

Finally, the problem of collecting child support from divorced men is also increasingly international. In the United States, where two fifths of divorced fathers pay no child support to their children and many others fail to pay the full amount demanded by the courts, "deadbeat dads" now preoccupy state and federal governments that are eager to reduce welfare subsidies to divorced and other single mothers. Even in Japan, the postindustrial society with the lowest divorce rate, three fourths of divorced men provide no support to their children. Again, this situation is not restricted to postindustrial societies. In Argentina, almost two thirds of divorced men fail to support the children of their former marriages, as do half of such men in Malaysia (Bruce et al., 1995, pp. 57–58).

Even this cursory sampling of international data makes it easy to perceive the grounds for transnational interest in the politics of family change, the sort of concern that prompted the United Nations to proclaim 1994 the International Year of the Family. There has indeed been an international convergence toward the postmodern family condition of diversity, pastiche, instability, and contest. In fact, the sort of aggregate national data I just reported grossly understate the extent and impact of family

diversity because they ignore how profoundly different are the family cultures that coexist so uneasily within individual nations—differences between contiguous geographic regions, races and ethnic groups, social classes, and religions. In Italy, for example, although the aggregate national proportion of marriages that end in divorce is still below 20%, divorce rates in the central and northern regions approach the far-steeper rates of the Nordic countries. Likewise, rates of marriage, fertility, unwed childbearing, and even maternal employment vary sharply among different racial, ethnic, and income groups in postindustrial countries like the United States and the United Kingdom (Blossfeld, DeRose, Hoem, & Rohwer, 1995). There is little reason to expect such differences to disappear any time soon.

IT'S A SMALL WORLD, AFTER ALL

Indeed, the transnational character of the postmodern family condition should not surprise us because it stems from increasingly global social, economic, and political forces. Most prominent, of course, is the globalization of capitalist production and markets, of which the fall of communism is both a product and further impetus. Second, demographic imbalances of under- and overpopulation, such as in Italy and India, have intersected with the worldwide spread of reproductive technologies, strategies, and conferences. Third, feminism has become an increasingly international movement, for which global conferences on the status of women that the United Nations has sponsored during the past two decades have served as significant arenas and opportunities. Finally, grassroots and national struggles for gay liberation and rights have begun to coalesce into a significant, visible international force. The combined and synergistic effects of these factors, which have operated unevenly and differently in diverse local sociopolitical and cultural contexts, have spread the postmodern family condition around the world.

I see no reason to expect that these sources of family diversity will experience a "reversal of fortune" in the 21st century. The spread of a transnational capitalist economy produced the shift in postindustrial societies from the modern industrial gender division of labor, which underwrote the modern family system, to the more contested, uneven, and unresolved gender division of labor of the postmodern condition. In postindustrial societies, this shift entailed a change in occupational structure from one that provided reasonably secure, high-wage jobs—that is, a "family wage"—to relatively uneducated, white, male industrial workers, to one whose working conditions, rewards, and risks are increasingly segmented by race, education, and cultural capital. On the one hand, the bulk of the workforce in postindustrial economies performs service, sales, and clerical work under conditions of relatively insecure and intermittent employment and for lower wages than trade unions once obtained for modern industrial workers. Men from subordinate racial and ethnic groups and women of all races are now overrepresented in these sectors. On the other hand, less-educated men, including members of the former "labor aristocracy" of modern industrial employment, face a shrinking labor market characterized by rising rates of unemployment and underemployment and severe declines in real earnings. The "outsourcing" of manufacturing from First- to Third World countries weakened the power of labor unions in the former and disrupted local economies and kinship systems in the latter. As one consequence, waves of primarily male "guest workers" have migrated from their peasant families in the south of the global village to perform the least desirable and least compensated labor in the north. Meanwhile, many of their wives, sisters, and daughters remain to manage and support the families left behind, sometimes by working in those very outsourced manufacturing jobs from which First World workers have been displaced.

The intersection between international concerns over population imbalances and the development and dissemination of reproductive technologies has produced some of the more contradictory and paradoxical aspects of postmodern family life. Most significantly, technological interventions in fertility, conception, genetic screening, gestation, and childbirth have contributed greatly to denaturalizing maternity and definitions of family, in ways like

the one spoofed in the *New Yorker* cartoon I described earlier. We inhabit a brave new world of reproduction—replete with drugs to prevent, facilitate, or even multiply ovulation; with sperm banks and donor insemination, ovum extraction, in vitro fertilization, and surrogate pregnancies; tests to determine fetal abnormalities and fetal gender; surgical procedures performed in utero; fetal monitors and labor-inducing or labor-inhibiting pharmaceuticals; and, recently, even the prospect of cloning. It is not surprising that this reproductive order is pregnant with paradoxes. For example, while definitions of maternity have become more uncertain and multiple—with genetic mothers, gestational mothers, and social mothers of various configurations competing for official maternal status and rights—technology has nearly conquered the classical problem of the "uncertainty of paternity," at least of biological paternity. Indeed, this is one of the factors that contributed to the campaign to require unmarried women to identify the paternity of the potentially future "deadbeat daddies" of their babies in the United States. Because this Orwellian tapestry renders undeniable the social and political character of familial relationships, it also unleashes enormous levels of social and political angst.

Although advances in contraception, abortion, and reproductive technology have enhanced the options and reduced the risks and burdens of reproduction for many comparatively privileged women, they have reduced the options and increased the burdens for others. For example, lesbians and unmarried women in many postindustrial societies can now choose motherhood outside heterosexual relationships. Ironically, some vanguard lesbian couples in the United States have begun to use reproductive technologies to make biological, and thereby legal, claims to maternity. In a few pioneering legal test cases, lesbian couples have engaged in ovum extraction, in vitro fertilization, and implantation techniques to impregnate one woman with her lover's fertilized ovum. The National Center for Lesbian Rights in the United States, a legal rights organization, reported that one California court found that both the genetic and gestational mothers met the legal standard for natural motherhood set by the Uniform Parentage Act, and a second case is pending in Boulder, Colorado (Kendell, 1997). At the same time, however, reproductive technologies have also made it possible for patrilocal societies, like China and India, to encourage or coerce women into practicing selective abortion and even female infanticide for sex-selection purposes. As a result, females have become an "endangered sex" in many villages and regions of these societies (Miller, 1981). Less exotic, but equally significant, the widespread use of effective contraception, abortion, and sterilization techniques in postindustrial societies has yielded the "graying" of these populations, which is distorting demographic age balances in our societies. Aging populations exacerbate economic and political conditions that fuel contemporary crises in postindustrial welfare systems.

International feminism has also become an undeniable, irreversible historical force that is actively engaged in reorganizing gender and family relationships. Facilitated by global modes of communication, by international conferences sponsored by the United Nations, by nongovernmental organizations, and other international cultural and educational exchanges, feminists have joined to challenge common and distinct forms of male domination—from such global patterns like women's unequal access to income, education, health care, employment, and political rights in our own societies to more regionally specific forms of oppression, including dowry deaths in India, genital mutilation in many African and Middle Eastern cultures, and sexual slavery and the international sex trade in women and young girls that flourishes most visibly in many parts of Asia. International feminist struggles have begun to convince human rights bodies to include the abuse of women's bodies, minds, and rights in their definitions of human rights violations. In several highly publicized instances, postindustrial societies have granted political asylum to women from Third World societies who refused to subject themselves or their daughters to such practices, thereby further challenging traditional patriarchal authority and kinship patterns.

Fourth and finally, an emergent international gay rights movement has also linked its struggle with the broader global arena of human rights. Increasingly, this movement is making a bid to obtain family rights, such as access to legal marriage, child custody, and adoption, for gays and lesbians. Although no postindustrial nation has yet granted full and equal marital or parental rights to same-sex partners, these are issues whose time has clearly come. In 1989, as I indicated earlier, Denmark became the first nation to legalize "registered partnerships," which grant all the rights of marriage except parental custody to same-sex couples, and the other Nordic nations soon followed suit. In a highly visible, politicized judicial struggle in the United States, the state supreme court of Hawaii was on the verge of fully legalizing same-sex marriages in 1998 until backlash forces succeeded in amending the state constitution to prohibit them. In exchange, however, the state is moving to expand domestic partnerships and civil rights protections to lesbians and gays. Even more remarkable is the situation in postapartheid South Africa, where the new Constitution includes sexual orientation in its roster of forbidden grounds for discrimination.

Together, these features of the global village have razed "the family" in postindustrial, First World societies by eroding its material foundations and challenging the ideological assumptions of the modern gender regime that the family encoded. In the former Second World, paradoxically, the fall of communism appears to have raised aspirations for access to the male breadwinner, female homemaker division of labor of the modern gender regime that the Soviet industrial regime neither legitimated nor supported. Full-time homemaker-wives, engaging in what many would consider to be obscene levels of conspicuous consumption have come to symbolize elite status for the new capitalist breed of Russian robber barons, and such wives are beginning to suffer acute cases of "the problem that has no name" (Stanley, 1997). However, whether the majority of women in the former Second World truly covet such "modern" family status, most have been forced to contend with conditions so severe—economic crisis, social dislocation, ethnic warfare and pillage, and the erosion of many former state protections and rights—that mere familial survival can seem a major achievement. Likewise, the staggering human toll claimed by massive economic and political crises, migrations, and ethnic wars in much of the Third World has irreversibly disrupted prevailing peasant kinship systems worldwide, enabling backlash movements for extremist, often exaggerated, forms of fundamentalism and patriarchal kinship to represent themselves as resisting the familial and social depredations of Western cultural imperialism. The victorious Taliban movement in Afghanistan, which has banned education for girls and employment for women and has instituted the penalty of death by stoning for adulterers, is but the most recent and extreme example of the triumph of a patriarchal system that bears a terrifying resemblance to Gilead.

AT THE HEAD OF THE CLASS

One third of the distance to the year 2033, the path ahead for family diversity seems more volatile, contradictory, and unpredictable than it did to the social scientists who recorded their forecast in *US News & World Report* in 1983. In the name of the family, (also the title of my latest book; Stacey, 1996), it is possible to mask the pursuit of a host of other political agendas. Such displacements, particularly those that involve the politics of gender, sexuality, race, and class, have become most advanced and politicized in the United States during the past couple of decades. They congealed in the backlash against the welfare state that achieved its most pronounced victory in the misnamed "welfare reform" or Personal Responsibility and Work Opportunity Reconciliation Act (104th Congress, 1996)—perhaps more accurately called "welfare repeal" and the "Social Irresponsibility" act) that the U.S. Congress passed and President Clinton signed in 1996. The preamble to the act actually identifies family breakdown as one of the consequences of "welfare dependency" that it seeks to redress. Opening with the assertion that "marriage is the foundation of a successful society," the bill declares, for example, that "the negative consequences of an out-of-wedlock birth on the mother, the child, the family, and society are *well documented*" [italics added]. This

claim to the mantle of social science is no accident; rather it is evidence that social scientists who are active in the secular campaign for family values have successfully convinced U.S. policy makers and many of their constituents that the decline of "the family," rather than postindustrial restructuring and inequalities, is the root cause of nearly all forms of social malaise (Stacey, 1996, chap. 3).

Politicized contests over "family values" have begun to spread to other postindustrial nations, primarily because all such societies now confront similar demographic and economic dislocations that threaten their welfare states, but also because they are the products of a direct U.S. export industry. During the 1980s, the Conservative regime led by Margaret Thatcher in Great Britain—emulating Reaganism in the United States—played the "family values" chord in a minor key. Whereas family values was then an explicitly conservative doctrine, during the 1990s centrist politicians in the U.S. Democratic Party and in the British Labour Party began to embrace it as well. At the party conference in 1995, Tony Blair, the British Labour Party leader and now prime minister, (quoted in Mandelson & Liddle, 1996, p. 124): proclaimed: "Strengthening the family has to be a number-one social priority." This transatlantic passage of the politics of family values is no coincident. Some of the very social scientists who have spearheaded the centrist campaign in the United States, including Amitai Etzioni, former president of the American Sociological Association, directly influenced Blair, his Labour Party colleagues, and some journals in the British media (Harding, 1999; Reinhold, 1994).

It seems likely that as the "global village" continues to erode the division of labor and the wages of the male breadwinner that underwrote "the family" in industrial societies and as welfare state protections diminish throughout the postindustrial world, backlash campaigns for family values will spread as well. However, it does not seem likely that they will become as politically influential or divisive elsewhere as they have been in the United States. There are at least three distinctive features of U.S. society that underwrite the exceptional appeal of the discourse on and politics of family values.

First, because "free-market" values and institutions enjoy such undisputed hegemony in the United States, the U.S. welfare system of benefits has never been as extensive, universal, or broadly legitimated as in other advanced industrial nations. The campaign for family values serves, in part, as a proxy for privatization—pitting big government against "the family." Paradoxically enough, however, "the family" also serves as the most sacred of the legitimated collectivities that U.S. citizens seem willing to invoke when they rail against the evils of rampant materialism and individualism. Thus, instead of adopting public measures to ease postmodern conflicts between work and family responsibilities—a route that most European societies favor—the trajectory of tax cuts and domestic reductions in spending serves to heighten them. There are many historical reasons for the limited national capacity for a more broadly inclusive collectivity, not the least of which is the history of racial inequality and hostility that has severely weakened the recognition of class solidarities. Finally, and perhaps less obvious, the decentralized system of family law in the United States has allowed an array of anomalies, contradictions, and paradoxes to emerge in family policies and practices that keep controversies over postmodern kinship issues perpetually newsworthy and provocative.

Here, I mention just two of the many striking contrasts that these factors seem to produce in the family practices and policies in the United States compared with those in other postindustrial societies. First, although unwed childbearing has increased throughout postindustrial societies and is even more common in northern Europe than in the United States, a dramatically higher percentage of unwed teenage girls become single mothers in the United States than elsewhere. Moreover, despite national affluence, the poverty rate for single-mother families in the United States is vastly higher than in other Western postindustrial societies. It is higher because most postindustrial societies have been more willing and able than the United States to address conflicts between family needs and maternal employment and to take measures to mitigate some of the injurious effects of family diver-

sity on children and their caretakers (Kamerman & Kahn, 1988; Millar, 1994).

Second, at the same time that the backlash against family change is most heated and politically central in the United States, lesbian and gay families, as well as their struggles for legitimacy, are also far more visible, diverse, and avant garde than in even those postindustrial societies, like the Scandinavian, that officially endorse greater tolerance for sexual diversity and have pioneered a form of legal gay marriage rights. For example, lesbians and other unmarried women in the United States with sufficient financial resources enjoy much greater access to sperm banks and fertility services than do unmarried women almost anywhere else. As the E-mail message I received about the Danish proposal to restrict such access indicated, most European nations, including those in Scandinavia, restrict public fertility services to heterosexual married women. Similarly, several states in the United States now grant custody and adoption rights to lesbians and gay men, whereas the Scandinavian nations explicitly excluded such rights when they legalized same-sex "registered partnerships." If the Hawaii Supreme Court had legalized same-sex marriages in that state, no such exclusions would have been possible. That the U.S. Constitution provides for interstate recognition of legal marriages helps to explain how gay marriage has come to play a significant, controversial role in contemporary U.S. electoral politics. Hoping to exploit popular homophobia during the 1996 presidential election, the Republican Party introduced the Defense of Marriage Act (DOMA) (the "offensive marriage act" would be more accurate, in my view), which defines marriage in exclusively heterosexual terms and exempts same-sex marriages from protection under the "full faith and credit" clause of the Constitution. Similarly, during the 1996 campaign, the Republican governor of California—a state in which lesbian and gay families and the struggle for gay rights are particularly visible—proposed state legislation to reverse recent gay parental gains by again restricting adoption and child custody rights to married couples. However, the proposal's prospects plummeted when the Republicans lost control of the California legislature in that election ("Capital matters; California; a roundup of important bills, regulatory news, upcoming legislative issues and recent appointments," 1996). Similarly, on the day that a commanding bipartisan majority in the U.S. Congress passed the DOMA, a compensatory bill, the Employment Non-Discrimination Act to protect gays and lesbians from employment discrimination, failed by only one vote (Baker, 1996; Lochhead, 1996).

BEST- AND WORST-CASE FUTURES FOR FAMILY DIVERSITY

As the 21st century begins, are we on the road to repressive Gilead or to a family diversity jubilee? Will the backlash against pluralist family patterns and values triumph, or will birthday celebrations in the year 2033 draw a multiracial, gender-bending, rainbow blend of "natural," social, adoptive, legal, fictive, para- and "queer" kin? Will our society adapt to postmodern family conditions by taking measures to realize more of the democratic potential of the forms of family diversity they generate and to mitigate the disruptive harms they inflict? Or will we continue to pursue the politics of nostalgic denial and displacement that fuel our retreat from collective responsibility for family welfare, exacerbate postindustrial conflicts between family and work, and inflict harm on the majority of actual families?

Present indicators are decidedly contradictory. On the one hand, the climate of political reaction and the triumph of the global market furnish abundant road signs of a route to Gilead. Campaigns for family values continue to achieve victories, like DOMA and the advent of "covenant marriage." Moreover, assaults on welfare; tax cuts that continue to widen the gap between rich and poor families; the erosion of secure, living-wage jobs for undereducated men; and escalating rates of incarceration for men of color are turning marriage into a form of class and race privilege, just as it was in Atwood's (1985) imaginary Gilead. Conditions like these guarantee that marital instability will continue, regardless of family values. Even if the current move to curb divorces gains force, as seems possible, it is unlikely to increase dramatically the

proportion of marriages that remain intact physically and emotionally, as well as legally. Couples can be prevented from obtaining legal divorces, but only a blatantly coercive regime like Gilead or the Taliban in Afghanistan can do much to prevent desertion, flight, or "no-fault" separations. Consequently, the rate of de facto marital dissolution is likely to remain high, fluctuating, I would conjecture, around the current range of 45% to 60%. Indeed, the fact that marrying couples now face even odds on achieving conjugal endurance until death do them part is perhaps about as much as one should expect within a marriage system that is based on the principles of romantic love, monogamy, companionship, and the free choice of individuals. After all, few cultures have ever expected the conjugal relationship to meet as many needs for intimacy and gratification as ours does, let alone to do so under such contradictory conditions and with such poor social support.

Clearly, the present climate gives scant cause to expect a turn to the kind of humane realism and economic democracy that would nurture the more democratic implications of the postmodern family condition. Nonetheless, the prospects for placing those disruptive genies—particularly the global economy and reproductive technology—back in their lamps strike me as even dimmer. Many of the same economic exigencies that fuel the reaction will also ensure that maternal employment is here to stay, and the backlash against welfare mothers actively promotes this situation. Likewise, reproductive technology is not going to disappear, and whereas donor insemination, as my Norwegian colleague pointed out, is actually a low-tech, readily available, process, the state cannot readily regulate women's access to voluntary sperm donors. Indeed, even the current political outcry to curb research that might achieve human cloning is apt to prove no more effective than spitting in wind. Test tube babies themselves no longer seem to belong to the realm of science fiction.

Similarly, despite the backlash, struggles for gender equity and gay rights are unlikely to cease. For one thing, most women "can't go home again" (Stacey, 1986) even if they wanted to, and substantial numbers do not want to, not even if they had husbands who could afford to support them. Most postindustrial women want to combine parenting with paid work and want men to pull their load in both domains (Hochschild 1989; Presser, 1995). Hence, we can confidently anticipate that women will continue to struggle for relief from the gymnastic "balancing act" between family and work demands and from the "stalled revolution" of shared domestic labor (Hochschild 1989; Spain & Bianchi, 1996). Demands for affordable, acceptable child care; paid family leaves; flextime; and paternal involvement in child rearing are more likely to increase than to disappear.

Moreover, there are millions of lesbian and gay parents and families. I find it difficult to imagine that they or their successors will acquiesce in a return to the closet or to family purgatory. On the contrary, one of the few progressive arenas of family reform that I feel comfortable predicting during this reactionary era will be the gradual legalization of same-sex marriage and of gay and lesbian custody rights. Although the majority of citizens—58% in a 1996 *Newsweek* poll (Support for Clinton's stand on gay marriage, 1996)—still oppose same-sex marriage, the trend in public opinion surveys has been moving rapidly in the progressive direction. To gain some perspective on contemporary public-disapproval ratings for gay marriage, it is instructive to remember the history of the legalization of interracial marriage. It was not until 1967 that the U.S. Supreme Court ruled that state bans on interracial marriages were unconstitutional. Nonetheless, five years later, when the Gallup Organization began to survey white attitudes toward such marriages, only 25% of the whites who were polled expressed their approval,

and even 30 years after the *Loving v. Virginia* decision, the white approval rating was only 61% (Holmes, 1997). In contrast, a higher percentage of heterosexuals already claim to support same-sex marriage than the proportion of whites who supported interracial marriage five years after it became the law of the land.

TOMORROWLAND

Is the glass that holds the fate of postmodern family fortunes half empty or half full? The very week of the antigay conference at Georgetown, the Southern Baptists voted to boycott the Walt Disney Company the corporation that was once thought to be synonymous with mainstream family values. The denomination took this action to protest the corporation's recent "gay-friendly" policies, such as its provision of domestic-partner benefits to employees and sponsorship of *Ellen*, the first television sitcom to feature a lesbian lead character. The Southern Baptists' action represents a paradigmatic instance of the contentious contemporary politics of family values. If the future of family diversity were to hinge on the fate of the denomination's contest with Disney's "tomorrowland," I would readily lay odds that new branches will continue to sprout on the nation's family trees. How comfortably these branches will be embraced or how widely scorned is much more difficult to guess.

Which branches will enjoy a place at the table when our Juniors gather to celebrate their birthdays in the year 2033? The future of family diversity depends on how we pursue the politics of family values today.

REFERENCES

Atwood, M. (1985). *The handmaid's tale.* New York: Ballantine Books.

Baker, P. (1996, September 22). President quietly signs law aimed at gay marriages. *The Washington Post,* p. A21.

Blankenhorn, D. (1995). *Fatherless America: Confronting our most urgent social problem.* New York: Basic Books.

Blossfeld, H.-P., Dehose, A., Hoem, J. M., & Rohwer, G.

(1995). In K. Oppenheim Mason & A.-M. Jensen (Eds.), *Gender and family change in industrialized countries* (pp. 200–222). Oxford, England: Clarendon Press.

Bruce, J., Lloyd, C. B., & Leonard, A., with Engle, P. A., & Duffy, N. (1995). *Families in focus: New perspectives on mothers, fathers, and children.* New York: Population Council.

Bumpass, L., & Sweet, J. (1987). *Recent trends and dif-*

ferentials in marital disruption. (Working Paper 87-20). Madison: Center for Demography and Ecology, University of Wisconsin.

Capital matters; California; A roundup of important bills, regulatory news, upcoming legislative issues and recent appointments. (1996, November 8). *Los Angeles Times,* p. D2.

Clark, K. (1996, August 5). Women, men and money. *Fortune, 134,* pp. 60–61.

Collins, P. H. (1990). *Black feminist thought.* London: Unwin Hyman.

Coontz, S. (1997). *The way we really are.* New York: Basic Books.

Dizard, J. E., & Gadlin, H. (1991). *The minimal family.* Amherst, MA: University of Massachusetts Press.

Ehrenreich, B. (1997, June 9). The new creationism. *The Nation,* pp. 11–16.

Fineman, M. (1995). *The neutered mother, the sexual family and other twentieth century tragedies.* New York: Routledge.

Furstenberg, F. F., Jr., & Cherlin, A. (1991). *Divided families.* Cambridge, MA: Harvard University Press.

Gallagher, M. (1996). *The abolition of marriage: How we destroy lasting love.* Washington, DC: Regenery.

Gerson, K. (1993). *No man's land: Men's changing commitments to family and work.* New York: Basic Books.

Gillis, J. (1996). *A world of their own making: Myth, ritual and the quest for family values.* New York: Basic Books.

Goode, W. J. (1963). *World revolution and family patterns.* New York: Free Press.

Harding, L. (1999). Family values and conservative government policy: 1979–the mid-1990s. In C. Wright & G. Jagger (Eds.), *Changing family values: Difference, diversity and the decline of male order.* London: Routledge.

Hochschild, A., with Machung, A. (1989). *The second shift: Working parents and the revolution at home.* New York: Viking Press.

Holmes, S. A. (1997, June 15). A rose-colored view of race. *New York Times,* p. E4.

Kamerman, S. B., & Kahn, A. J. (1988). What Europe does for single-parent families. *Public Interest, 93,* 70–86.

Kendell, K. (Ed.). (1997). *Lesbians choosing motherhood: Legal implications of alternative insemination and reproductive technologies* (3rd ed.). San Francisco: National Center for Lesbian Rights.

Kinzer, Stephen. (1994, November 25). $650 a baby. *New York Times,* p. A1.

Lochhead, C. (1996, September 11). Senate OKs gay marriage restrictions; Job discrimination bill fails by one vote. *San Francisco Chronicle,* p. A1.

Lochhead, C. (1997, June 20). Conservatives brand homosexuality a "tragic affliction." *San Francisco Chronicle,* p. A4.

Mandelson, P., & Liddle, R. (1996). *The Blair revolution: Can new labour deliver?* London: Faber & Faber.

Millar, J. (1994). State, family and personal responsibility: The changing balance for lone mothers in the United Kingdom. *Feminist Review, 48,* 24–39.

Miller, B. (1981). *The endangered sex: Neglect of female children in rural north India.* Ithaca, NY: Cornell University Press.

Moynihan, D. P. (1965). *The Negro family: The case for national action.* Washington, DC: U.S. Department of Labor.

Newman, K. (1993). *Declining fortunes: The withering of the American dream.* New York: Basic Books.

Operation rescue head to run for Congress. (1997, June 23). *San Francisco Chronicle,* p. A3.

104th Congress. (1996). *Personal Responsibility and Work Opportunity Reconciliation Act of 1996.* (P. L. 104–193). Washington, DC: U.S. Government Printing Office.

Pisaro. (1996). "Bizarro" cartoon, *San Francisco Chronicle.*

Popenoe, D. (1996). *Life without father.* New York: Free Press.

Popenoe, D., Elshtain, J. B., & Blankenhorn, D. (Eds.). (1996). *Promises to keep: Decline and renewal of marriage in America.* Lanham, MD: Rowman & Littlefield.

Presser, H. B. (1995). Are the interests of women inherently at odds with the interests of children or the family? A Viewpoint. In K. Oppenheim Mason & A.-M. Jensen (Eds.), *Gender and family change in industrialized countries* (pp. 297–319). Oxford, England: Clarendon Press.

Reinhold, S. (1994). Through the parliamentary looking glass: "Real" and "pretend" families in contemporary British politics. *Feminist Review, 48,* 61–79.

Rubin, L. (1994). *Families on the fault line: America's working class speaks about the family, the economy, race, and ethnicity.* New York: HarperCollins.

Sack, K. (1997, June 24). Louisiana approves measure to tighten marriage bonds. *New York Times,* pp. A1, A14.

Skolnick, A. (1991). *Embattled paradise: The American family in an age of uncertainty.* New York: Basic Books.

Spain, D., & Bianchi, S. (1996). *Balancing act: Marriage, motherhood, and employment among American women.* New York: Russell Sage Foundation.

Stacey, J. (1990). *Brave new families: Stories of domestic upheaval in late twentieth century America.* New York: Basic Books.

Stacey, J. (1991). Backward to the postmodern family: Reflections on gender, kinship and class in the Silicon Valley. In A. Wolfe (Ed.), *America at century's end* (pp. 17–34). Berkeley: University of California Press.

Stacey, J. (1996). *In the name of the family: Rethinking family values in the postmodern age.* Boston: Beacon Press.

Stanley, A. (1997, March 11). Russian wives learn what money can't buy. *New York Times,* p. A1.

Support for Clinton's stand on gay marriage. (1997, May 25). *San Francisco Chronicle,* p. A6.

When "family" will have a new definition. (1983, May 9). *U.S. News and World Report,* p. A3.

Whitehead, B. D. (1997). *The divorce culture.* New York: Alfred A. Knopf.

CHAPTER 22

Family Diversity in the 21st Century: Implications for Research, Theory, and Practice

MARK A. FINE, DAVID H. DEMO, AND KATHERINE R. ALLEN

Taken together, the chapters in this book demonstrate that family diversity has characterized our past and present and will continue to shape our future. We have assembled the empirically informed opinions of a wide variety of scholars with different views of the concept of family diversity. As editors, we shaped the organization of the book by asking each author to address specific issues, such as structure and process in diverse families, and to pay particular attention to social stratifications of race, social class, gender, family structure, sexual orientation, and age. One result is that we have collected multiple viewpoints on a central question: What is the extent of our knowledge on family variations in structure and process? As described in Chapter 1, we encountered a number of dilemmas and controversies about how to present the ideas for this collection. We came to understand that there was no perfect solution and that each direction we pursued provided only a partial view of the multifaceted and complex concept of family diversity.

If diversity is so common, why do we call attention to "old" stratifications, such as race and socioeconomic status, that many researchers have worked to relinquish? Our authors have shown us that it is still necessary to attend to these dimensions of stratification within families. Without the explicit recognition that all families are marked by variations in race, class, gender, sexual orientation, and age, it is easy to forget diversity and focus exclusively on an image of the family that is more ideal than real (Coontz, 1992). Individually, the chapters in this handbook make unique contributions to our understanding of family diversity. Collectively, they do not form some perfect or shared whole, but fan out into multiple shades, variations, and meanings. The combination of chapters provides evidence of the opportunities and the challenges families face because of structural limitations and conditions imposed by social stratification. Families have always been charged with the task of caring and providing for dependent members, and although the particulars of time and geography vary, the chapters in this book attest to the lasting importance and indispensability of families in society.

The chapters also differ in terms of the extent to which the authors acknowledged the political climate in which families live. Some authors explicitly dealt with the social contexts of the families they described, others concentrated on the extant research, and still others divided their attention between social contexts and the research literature. These discrepancies in how authors approached their chapters may appear contradictory, as if we, the editors, were not sure what we wanted. Yet, we have come to realize that the multiple scholarly styles used to present information in this book reflect the complex and ambiguous findings that appear in the literature. First-person accounts, survey data, and historical analyses are just some of the methodologies the authors relied on to illustrate family diversity on their particular topics. These strategies inform each other and together provide complex descriptions of phenomena that are constantly changing. The chapters give witness to the reality that there are multiple ways of living in and studying families and that not all families are treated the same. The study of family diversity is, by necessity, a dynamic pursuit, in which the very issues under investigation are also the issues we experience in daily life. The acknowledgment of family complexity that the authors demonstrated in their compelling depictions of family diversity at the beginning of the 21st century is perhaps the one common thread running through this book. We hope these contributions provide an authoritative reference to enlighten students of family diversity and enrich our understanding of the ways in which families evolve and change over time.

WHAT HAVE WE LEARNED ABOUT FAMILY DIVERSITY?

The contributors to this volume have documented an impressive and provocative set of lessons about family diversity. These teachings provide a broad and comprehensive view of the manifestations of diverse family experiences. We hope it will be helpful for readers to integrate and reflect on these lessons in this concluding chapter.

Diversity Is Broader than How It Is Typically Presented

Diversity is often presented as narrowly applying only to structural and demographic dimensions, such as race, ethnicity, family structure, social class, and sexual orientation. However, we have seen that diversity in families reflects far more than is conveyed by these "social-address" labels. For example, families vary considerably in the nature of their interaction patterns, behaviors, and processes. They are diverse in the involvement of extended and chosen kin, parenting styles, gender dynamics, communication patterns, partner relations, parent-child relations, values of desirable ways for families to function, worldviews, and so forth. From an applied perspective, these "process" forms of diversity may be even more salient than the social-address forms. We say this because interaction patterns and behaviors can be changed in growth-producing ways, whereas social addresses are either generally immutable (e.g., sex, race) or remain fairly stable over time (e.g., social class).

Furthermore, it is important to recognize that structural and processual forms of family diversity are interrelated and should be examined simultaneously and longitudinally. For example, we cannot simply assume that father-absent residential arrangements, increasingly common in U.S. families and the modal household type for African American children, translate into fathers' infrequent (or nonexistent) contact with children. Many nonresidential fathers, particularly African American fathers (see Chapter 12, by Taylor, this volume), maintain regular and routine interactions with their children (Mott, 1990), and when families are observed over several years, we notice that many children move from one household to another to live with a different parent (Maccoby & Mnookin, 1992). Similarly, as is pointed out by Hetherington and Stanley-Hagan in Chapter 9, parenting and stepparenting styles have an important influence on children's development in stepfamilies.

Diversity is reflected not only in family structure and family processes, but in the dimensions of family well-being that we choose to examine. In this volume, some contributions, such as Entwisle and Alexander's discussion of academic outcomes among children in different family structures in Chapter 16, have considered primarily socioeconomic dimensions of family adjustment; some, such as Savin-Williams and Esterberg in Chapter 10) have considered primarily socioemotional dimensions; and still others have examined a combination of socioeconomic and socioemotional indices of family well-being.

Attention to family diversity and sensitivity to differences in family structure, family relationships, and family well-being should also not blind us to similarities in family experiences across social groupings. For example, Kurdek (1995) documented that although gay or lesbian couples, in comparison to heterosexual couples, tend to adhere more closely to an ethic of equality in their partnerships and more often view their partners as their best friends, the four types of relationships (heterosexual married couples, heterosexual cohabiting couples, and gay and lesbian couples) are similar in their satisfaction with and the stability of their relationships. Awareness of and sensitivity to family diversity are essential ingredients in the design and conceptualization of research, but an obsession with differences can obscure and distort similarities in family experience across diverse groups.

Diversity Is Inextricably Intertwined with Social Context

Families and the diversity within and among them cannot be understood or appreciated without considering the contexts in which families live. Several chapters contributors have illustrated how the family lives of Latino American (Chapter 13, by Baca Zinn and Wells), Asian American (Chapter 14, by Ishii-Kuntz), and African American families (Chapter 12, by Taylor), as well as many families in poverty (Chapter 15, by Rank), are influenced by racism and discrimination. Similarly, we have seen that other types of families, such as those with gay, lesbian, or bisexual members (Chapter 10, by Savin-Williams and Esterberg), are perceived negatively and victimized by heterosexism and discrimination. Furthermore, ageism is prevalent, because older adults are stigmatized, marginzalized, and neglected (see Chapter 11, Bedford and Blieszner). Another consistent theme throughout this volume—particularly in Chapters 4, by Rutter and Schwartz; 5, by Peterson, Bodman, Bush, and Madden-Derdich; 6, by Umberson and Slaten; and 7, by Johnson—has been that gender has a strong influence on family experiences for women, men, and children, at least partly through the effects of sexism.

Not to appreciate this lesson is to fall victim to what Ryan (1976) called "blaming the victim." One blames the victim when one concludes that behaviors and life conditions are due primarily to the characteristics of individuals and families, rather than to the social circumstances in which the individuals and families are embedded. Certainly, the behavioral styles and interactions of particular families are not due solely to their social circumstances; family functioning is determined by a balance of intra- and extra-familial forces.

Diversity Is Not Just an Academic or Cognitive Exercise

We edited this volume because we believe that family diversity has, does, and will play an essential role in the lives of family members throughout the country (and, of course, the world, although we address international issues only occasionally in this volume). The chapters in this book underscore the extensive influence that matters of diversity have for families, not just for family scholars. As Lerner, Sparks, and McCubbin argued in Chapter 19, this pervasive influence means that family diversity is, by necessity, at least implicitly involved in social policy, but there are compelling reasons for this connection to be explicit. Similarly, in Chapter 18, on family life education, Mayers-Walls contends that diversity issues, as well as an examination of both the instructor's and the participants' values, need to be at the forefront of educational efforts with and for families.

Recognizing the important effect of social policies on families and acknowledging that the consequences of legislation for families should be a part of the public debate, Wisconsin has instituted a series of successful Family Impact Seminars that are designed to influence the public discourse on the family effects of proposed legislation and to build bridges among state policymakers, agency officials, researchers, and practitioners (Bogenschneider, 1995). Policymakers and researchers should institutionalize this type of discourse so that policymakers can make thoughtful and conscious policy decisions based on an appreciation and understanding of diversity, incorporating extensive input and collaboration from the diverse families affected by social policies.

Current examples of how views on diversity influence policy discussions and family functioning include debates over the meaning and utility of affirmative action, welfare reform, universal health care coverage, and immigration policies. Discussions of the advantages and disadvantages of particular policy preferences in these areas necessarily reflect individuals' views and values regarding particular types of families, desirable ways for families to function, and social goals. Unfortunately, the discourse pertaining to many of these important policy areas is conducted without a thorough and explicit statement and discussion of underlying values and beliefs, other than a falsely dichotomous division of individuals into "liberal" and "conservative" camps. Placing core values and beliefs directly in the middle of the discussion can only help policymakers formulate more effective policies. However, as we explicitly examine and discuss these core values, we need to recognize not only that values affect social institutions, but that the social institutions in which we live influence our values and how they are expressed. As Coontz (1992, p. 22) noted:

> Our values may make a difference in the way we respond to the challenges posed by economic and political institutions, but those institutions also reinforce certain values and extinguish others. The problem is not to berate people for abandoning past family values, nor to exhort them to adopt better values in the future—the problem is to build the institutions and social support networks that allow people to act on their best values rather than on their worst ones.

Diversity Is Socially Constructed

Just as there is clearly no one definition of *family*, there is also no clear consensus on the meaning of *diversity*. In this volume, we have seen a wide array of views of diversity, as evidenced by both the contributors' personal reflections on their interests in diversity and by the discussions of the diverse family living arrangements and relationships that characterize U.S. families. It is clear to us that diversity is a social construction that takes numerous forms. However, the social constructionist nature of diversity should not be considered evidence of its weakness as a concept or as an indication that it is so subjective as to render social discourse meaningless. To the contrary, by showing that there are a variety of structures and processes that can facilitate effective family functioning, the authors in this volume have shown that diversity is a strength. Perhaps above all, diversity is best reflected in attitudes—an openness and acceptance of difference and a critical stance toward social mores of what is "normal" family life. How this attitude is expressed varies considerably among individuals, and this variability is itself a manifestation of family diversity.

Existing Family Theories Need to Be Extended

We believe that existing theories of family life are useful in understanding diversity, but considerably more work is necessary to extend, refine, and apply them. We have seen in this volume that a variety of theoretical and conceptual perspectives underlie contemporary family research, including feminist, critical, life-course, ecological, and symbolic interactionist perspectives. However, many extant theories overemphasize the normative appropriateness of certain types of families (such as white, heterosexual, middle-class, married couples with children) and have not been extended to advance our understanding of diverse types and forms of families. Yet family theorists have reason to embrace diversity. As Demo and Allen (1996) noted with respect to gay and lesbian families, studying diverse families provides an exciting opportunity to test, revise, expand, and enhance theories so that they provide better explanations of the divergent life trajectories, household arrangements, and relationship dynamics of postmodern families. Rather than merely critiquing the contributions of existing theories of family life, these theories should be nurtured with evidence from conceptual and empirical advances so that they provide richer and more accurate accounts of families and how they function.

Diversity Is Necessarily Multidimensional

A meaningful understanding of diversity requires an attention to multiple dimensions and how they intersect with one another. As Marks and Leslie argued in Chapter 20, our view of families should approximate as closely as possible the multiple and intersecting realities—such as race, financial hardship, and sexual orientation—that family members experience in their lives. Clearly, members of an African American family are affected and characterized by more than their racial grouping; they have a socioeconomic position, a family structure, a routine mode of functioning, values regarding family life, and a variety of other unique (and shared) qualities. Yet, too often, race becomes a code for an intractable set of assumptions that are applied to anyone occupying that racial category. Similarly, a woman is presumed to have feminine characteristics by virtue of her being female.

Of course, our call for attention to intersections among the dimensions of diversity is not novel; a number of scholars have encouraged researchers and practitioners to avoid monolithic views of particular groups of families. For example, as Amato noted in Chapter 8, single-parent families vary considerably in social class, race, ethnicity, sexual orientation, extent of social support, parenting styles, and many others dimensions. Although we suspect that few would quarrel with our emphasis on attending to these intersections, the complexity required by this attention to intersecting dimensions poses a severe challenge that restricts progress in this endeavor. It is much easier to refer to a particular category of families, such as Latino families, and to attempt to describe their typical characteristics than it is to grapple with the complexity inherent in describing how groups of families vary along countless dimensions. For example, from a pragmatic methodological perspective, attempting to define groups of families along intersecting dimensions presents formidable obstacles in terms of recruiting a sufficient number of families to conduct meaningful between-group and within-group analyses. Identifying a sufficient number of Asian American, stepparent, lesbian, lower-income families for a survey (but not necessarily for a qualitative study) can be exceedingly difficult. To some extent, the large number of dimensions of diversity wards off efforts to make progress in understanding intersections. However, in line with the discussion in Chapter 20, by Marks and Leslie, we believe that such efforts are still justified, partly because social scientists have been somewhat successful in identifying a few of the most salient and influential dimensions (e.g., social class, gender, race, family structure, and sexual orientation) along which families vary. Furthermore, as Laird noted in Chapter 17, family scholars and practitioners need to learn to ask new questions and to suspend the imposition of their own cultural beliefs about families as they study and work with others.

A Purely Relativistic View of Diversity Is Undesirable

Views of the effectiveness of family functioning vary along a continuum, ranging from completely relativistic (all forms of family functioning are equally adaptive) to completely absolute (there is only one successful way to function as a family). Our call for an increased sensitivity to and understanding of diversity should not be confused with a call for a purely relativistic view. We do not believe that all behaviors and processes in families are equally effective; we believe that some types of family interactions (e.g., supportive nurturance when a family member is burdened with an interpersonal concern) are inherently adaptive and that others (e.g., domestic violence) are inherently undesirable, regardless of the context. Proponents of diversity are often misrepresented as advocating the extreme relativistic end of the spectrum, when, in most cases, they are merely promoting a move away from the extreme absolute end of the continuum. This misrepresentation provides ammunition for those who question and challenge efforts to enhance sensitivity to diversity.

Our perspective is based on the assumption that one cannot view differences among families in isolation from values of the "good." As human beings, we all have notions of better and worse ways of living and functioning and cannot separate ourselves from these values. Instead of trying to present our views as value-free, we believe that it is more accurate and honest to acknowledge these values explicitly. In this context, our attention to family diversity reflects our belief that there are numerous, although not unlimited, ways for families to function effectively in the contexts in which they live. Furthermore, the modes of family functioning that we identify as effective reflect our values of desirable goals for family members, the family as a unit, and the society in which they exist. We have seen in this handbook a variety of values regarding appropriate ways of behaving in families, and these values are reflected in the authors' evaluations of the functional effectiveness of the families they study.

FUTURE DIRECTIONS IN THE STUDY OF FAMILY DIVERSITY

The chapters in this volume suggest numerous directions for future research on family diversity. In this section, we review several of these directions.

Need for Sensitivity to the Intersections Among Dimensions of Diversity

As is noted in several ways throughout this volume, we argue that it is important to move beyond an approach that examines single dimensions of diversity (e.g., race or socioeconomic status) at a time. Although some valuable information has been gained from studies that focused on one dimension, such an approach can result in misleading conclusions regarding the experiences of families and their members.

At the same time, we realize that studying multiple and intersecting dimensions of diversity is methodologically challenging and time consuming. It is difficult to control conditions in "real family life." Funding agencies may be wary of supporting research proposals that are designed to investigate aspects of diversity using methods that appear to lack experimental precision. Yet, it is our responsibility as scholars and practitioners to devise new and creative methods that are sensitive to the complexity of family life. In this endeavor, we believe that there are places for both quantitative and qualitative approaches, used separately and in combination. To devise such new and creative methods, researchers and practitioners should routinely and consciously interrogate themselves about their motivations and agenda in raising the kinds of questions they investigate, the ways they gather information, and the strategies they use to analyze and determine the meaningfulness of results. It is also important for researchers to consider the ends to which their research is or could be used. That is, they need to take responsibility for the potential political ends of their research.

Need for Multiple Methodological Approaches

We suggest that our inquiry into family diversity will be best served by using a variety of methodological approaches that incorporate observational methods, in-depth interviews, large-scale surveys, detailed life histories, ethnographies, case studies, narrative accounts, content analyses, and other methods. We echo other researchers' calls for methodological triangulation, highlight the artificial and somewhat arbitrary distinction between quantitative and qualitative methods, and argue for the development of approaches that integrate aspects of both sets of methods. Of course, the choice of the most suitable approaches to be used in a particular line of inquiry ultimately depends on the nature of the research questions of interest, but methodological pluralism is necessary to ask new questions that allow us to gain a better understanding of family diversity.

Need for Interdisciplinary, Not Just Multidisciplinary, Efforts

As Acitelli (1995) noted, most work conducted in the social sciences is unidisciplinary. When researchers from more than one discipline are involved in a particular field (multidisciplinary), they tend to conduct their work separately from one another, naturally and understandably using the methods in which they were trained and with which they feel comfortable. The resulting products, although helpful, are often limited in breadth and depth by the disciplinary roots and boundaries of the investigators' disciplines. In a field as broad and fragmented as family diversity, we see a need for researchers to engage in truly interdisciplinary work in which there is a critical and collaborative dialogue among researchers from different disciplines, yielding scholarly products that are greater than the sum of their individual disciplinary parts.

To accomplish this work, professionals need to spend time with each other, learning to listen to and reflect on multiple viewpoints. Often, conversations about family diversity devolve into debates and attacks, with polarized views (e.g., conservative versus liberal) substituting for complex, meaningful dialogue. Many scholars argue for a middle ground, in which the changes and uncertainty in American family lives can be recognized, explored, understood, and addressed. To steer this middle course (Cherlin, 1996), we must progress beyond both nostalgia about the way we wish families were and moral panic about the loss of "family values" (Skolnick, 1991) to deal with families as they really were and are (see Coontz, 1997, and Chapter 2, this volume). In addition, we need to melt down the boundaries and walls among disciplines and begin to identify ourselves as social scientists with particular strengths, interests, and skills that we can bring to interdisciplinary projects.

Realistically, for this to happen, greater incentives need to be provided for researchers to work with other scholars outside their root disciplines. Current departmental standards in academia present a range of barriers to interdisciplinary work. For example, in some disciplines in some universities, scholars are given considerably more "credit" for publishing in disciplinary journals than in multi- or interdisciplinary ones. Frequently, interdisciplinary work is done above and beyond the work of one's home department. Involvement in women's studies, for example, is often an overload for feminist scholars. At the same time, interdisciplinary work can rejuvenate and educate those who participate in it. The cross-fertilization of ideas and methods is a path toward a richer understanding of diversity.

Need for Further Exploration of Definitions of Family

Readers of this volume have seen experts in specific domains of family studies define the term *family* in different ways, emphasizing different concepts and reflecting different values and preferences. These definitions have ranged from the census operationalization that families consist of people with blood or legal ties living in the same household (Chapter 3, by Teachman) to operationalizations emphasizing ongoing and mutual commitment and caring among a particular group of people (Chapter 10, by Savin-Williams and Esterberg) to units in which both living and deceased kin are included as family (Chapter 11, by Bedford and Blieszner). Again, defining *family* is not merely an academic exercise because the manner in which a family is defined has important implications for daily living. We have already discussed the financial and policy implications of the way in which a family is defined, but there are socioemotional implications as well. The term *family* has strong symbolic meaning for individuals, who tend to rely on their families during times of need, celebrate with them in good times, and live on a day-to-day basis with them. Thus, how individuals define their families

has considerable influence on how well they function in their lives. Researchers need to devote more energy to understanding how individuals define *family*, including how these definitions vary even among members of the same family, and we need to explore the various implications that different definitions have.

Need for Reflexivity

Inspired by approaches, such as those of Thompson and Tyagi (1996), who asked their contributors to reflect on their development of a racial self-identity; Bochner, Ellis, and Tillmann-Healy (1997, 1998), who integrated personal narratives as an essential component of their scholarly work; and Sollie and Leslie (1994), who invited authors to reflect on how feminism has intersected with their research careers, we thought that including a reflective element would not only enrich the material in this book, but would illustrate to our audience how these scholars became interested in and have studied family diversity. Accordingly, we asked the contributors to share some personal reflections on their interests, motivations, inclinations, experiences, values, and attitudes related to family diversity, and we provided some of our own reflections in the opening chapter. This is a difficult task for most social scientists, including us, because it is a process and activity that, for the most part, is frowned upon or lacking in our training. Our contributors provided personal reflections in diverse and interesting ways, and we hope they enriched the readers' understanding of the material presented in this book. Reflections on subjective perspectives qualitatively shift the way in which information is imparted and received. Integrating personal reflections into social science is an important step in creating more genuine and responsible knowledge about families (Fine, Weis, Powell, & Wong, 1997; Game & Metcalfe, 1996; Krieger, 1991).

Need for Both Insiders' and Outsiders' Perspectives

A common debate in family studies (and other fields) is whether we should strive to understand families primarily by the ways that their members do (the "insider's" perspective) or by the ways that experts do (the "outsider's" perspective). Contributors to this volume have taken different positions on this issue, although most have only implicitly stated their views. Clearly, those who study families as the U.S. Bureau of the Census defines them are at least implicitly supporting the value of the outsider's perspective, whereas those who study families according to individuals' own definitions are at least implicitly supporting the value of the insider's perspective. Like the distinctions between qualitative and quantitative research methods and between healthy and unhealthy family functioning, we find this to be a somewhat arbitrary distinction. Furthermore, depending on what one is attempting to learn about families, both the insider's and outsider's perspectives have value in family studies. The outsider's perspective has the merit of allowing for some generalizable inferences about families that are defined in a systematic and consistent way (the nomothetic perspective), but has the disadvantage of defining some groups as families (or as not being families) in a manner that is inconsistent with individuals' own definitions. The insider's perspective has the merit of accurately reflecting the symbolic meaning attached to families by allowing individuals to define who is and who is not in their families (the idiographic perspective). However, it also has the disadvantages of making it difficult to compare family experiences across dissimilarly defined groups or to draw conclusions about families in general.

Need for the Study of Family Process Variables

One major reason we undertook this project was our belief that discussions of diversity often focus solely on structural, or "social address," variables, such as race, socioeconomic status, and family structure. Stated another way, we know much more about family demographics than we do about family processes. Thus, we encouraged our contributors to attend to diversity in processes, interactions, and behaviors in families, as well as *within* various types of families, to the extent that the literature permitted them to do so. Again, partly because of

the lack of scholarly attention to family processes, this was a challenging task, but we believe that our contributors were successful in this endeavor and encourage continued movement in this direction.

Need for a Postpositivist Approach

It will be no surprise to the readers of this volume that we find, as did Stacey in her engaging look at families in the future in Chapter 21, considerable value in postpositivist conceptual and methodological approaches. We believe that a genuine commitment to diversity requires that one accept that there are a multitude of healthy, adaptive, and successful ways for families to function. We resist the notion that there is only one "truth" regarding how children, parents, and families should function and believe that successful family functioning depends on a variety of contextual factors, such as one's value system, environment, historical context, and economic circumstances. We do not intend for this statement to be interpreted as a criticism of quantitative approaches, for we are certain that quantitative approaches can (and do) yield valuable insights if they are interpreted in the appropriate context. Our position is that an eclectic array of approaches, ideally involving triangulation, should be used to advance the understanding of family diversity.

CONCLUSION

In closing, we hope the chapters in this book will enlighten readers as much as they have enlightened us. Embarking on a project as comprehensive as this handbook has brought some surprises. We are pleased by the multiple versions of family diversity the authors provided. The interdisciplinary study of families is alive and well, empirical and personal, passionate and somber. This handbook covers serious issues that Americans face today, which reflect our country's past and reach into the future. We find value and inspiration in the variety of viewpoints represented here and are grateful to the contributors for bringing their unique perspectives to life throughout this book.

REFERENCES

Acitelli, L. K. (1995). Disciplines at parallel play. *Journal of Social and Personal Relationships, 12,* 589–595.

Bochner, A. P., Ellis, C., & Tillmann-Healy, L. M. (1997). Relationships as stories. In S. W. Duck (Ed.), *Handbook of personal relationships* (2nd ed., pp. 307–324). New York: John Wiley.

Bochner, A. P., Ellis, C., & Tillman-Healy, L. M. (1998). Mucking around looking for truth. In B. M. Montgomery & L. A. Baxter (Eds.), *Dialectical approaches to studying personal relationships* (pp. 41–62). Mahwah, NJ: Lawrence Erlbaum.

Bogenschneider, K. (1995). Roles for professionals in building family policy: A case study of state family impact seminars. *Family Relations, 44,* 5–12.

Cherlin, A. J. (1996). *Public and private families.* New York: McGraw-Hill.

Coontz, S. (1992). *The way we never were: American families and the nostalgia trap.* New York: Basic Books.

Coontz, S. (1997). *The way we really are: Coming to terms with America's changing families.* New York: Basic Books.

Demo, D. H., & Allen, K. R. (1996). Diversity within lesbian and gay families: Challenges and implications for family theory and research. *Journal of Social and Personal Relationships, 13,* 415–434.

Fine, M., Weis, L., Powell, L. C., & Wong, L. M. (Eds.). (1997). *Off white: Readings on race, power, and society.* New York: Routledge.

Game, A., & Metcalfe, A. (1996). *Passionate sociology.* London: Sage.

Krieger, S. (1991). *Social science and the self: Personal essays on an art form.* New Brunswick, NJ: Rutgers University Press.

Kurdek, L. A. (1995). Lesbian and gay couples. In A. R. D'Augelli & C. J. Patterson (Eds.), *Lesbian and gay identities over the lifespan: Psychological perspectives on personal, relational, and community processes* (pp. 243–261). New York: Oxford University Press.

Maccoby, E. E., & Mnookin, R. H. (1992). *Dividing the child: Social and legal dilemmas of custody.* Cambridge, MA: Harvard University Press.

Mott, F. L. (1990). When is a father really gone? Paternal-child contact in father-absent homes. *Demography, 27,* 499–517.

Ryan, W. (1976). *Blaming the victim* (2nd ed.) New York: Random House.

Skolnick, A. S. (1991). *Embattled paradise: The American family in an age of uncertainty.* New York: Basic Books.

Sollie, D. L., & Leslie, L. A. (Eds.). (1994). *Gender, families, and close relationships: Feminist research journeys.* Thousand Oaks, CA: Sage.

Thompson, B., & Tyagi, S. (Eds.) (1996). *Names we call home: Autobiography on racial identity.* New York: Routledge.

INDEX